Fodor's 6th Edition

Portugal

D0111813

The Guide
for All Budgets

Completely
Updated

Where to Stay, Eat,
and Explore

On and Off
the Beaten Path

When to Go,
What to Pack

Maps, Travel Tips,
and Web Sites

Fodor's Travel Publications • New York, Toronto, London, Sydney, Auckland
www.fodors.com

Fodor's Portugal

EDITOR: Laura M. Kidder

Editorial Contributors: Emmy de la Cal, Justine de la Cal, Martha de la Cal, Peter Collis, Satu Hummasti, Paul Murphy, Josephine Quintero
Editorial Production: Tom Holton
Maps: David Lindroth, *cartographer*; Robert Blake and Rebecca Baer, *map editors*
Design: Fabrizio La Rocca, *creative director*; Guido Caroti, *art director*; Jolie Novak, *senior picture editor*; Melanie Marin, *photo editor*
Cover Design: Pentagram
Production/Manufacturing: Colleen Ziemba
Cover Photograph (Alfama, Lisbon): Yvan Travert/DIAF

Copyright

Sixth Edition

ISBN 1–4000–1116–7

ISSN 0071–6510

Important Tip

Although all prices, opening times, and other details in this book are based on information supplied to us at press time, changes occur all the time in the travel world, and Fodor's cannot accept responsibility for facts that become outdated or for inadvertent errors or omissions. So **always confirm information when it matters,** especially if you're making a detour to visit a specific place.

Dedication

In memory of Peter Collis, whose knowledge of Portugal and dedication as a writer have enriched this book beyond measure.

Special Sales

PRINTED IN THE UNITED STATES OF AMERICA

10 9 8 7 6 5 4 3 2 1

CONTENTS

Maps

ON THE ROAD WITH FODOR'S

A trip takes you out of yourself. Concerns of life at home completely disappear, driven away by more immediate thoughts—about, say, what marvels will beguile the next day, or where you'll have dinner. That's where Fodor's comes in. We make sure that you know all your options, so that you don't miss something that's around the next bend just because you didn't know it was there. Mindful that the best memories of your trip might have nothing to do with what you came to Portugal to see, we guide you to sights large and small all over the island. You might set out to just tour a Lisbon area museum or palace and lounge on an Algarve beach, but back at home you'll find yourself unable to forget sampling port at an *adega* or sighing during a fado performance.

About Our Writers

Our success in showing you every corner of Portugal is a credit to our extraordinary writers. Although there's no substitute for travel advice from a good friend who knows your style, our contributors are the next best thing—the kind of people you would poll for travel advice if you knew them.

Martha de la Cal, a freelance writer based in Lisbon, covered the north and central regions of Portugal—a lot of ground, indeed. Martha, a correspondent for *Time* magazine, has lived the best part of the past 40 years on the Iberian Peninsula.

Paul Murphy, who updated Lisbon and its environs as well as the Algarve and Madeira, has been travel writing for a dozen years or so, during which time he has authored 35 guidebooks and contributed to as many again. He specializes in the Mediterranean (and near neighbors) and is especially fond of the Algarve, covering it regularly over the last decade. He also writes for British magazines.

Smart Travel Tips updater **Josephine Quintero** worked as a journalist for several magazines and newspapers during her 14 years living in California. Further travels took her to Kuwait, where she edited the *Kuwaiti Digest* and was briefly held hostage during the Iraqi invasion. She moved to the relaxed shores of Andalucía shortly after

and has subsequently worked on more than 15 travel guides, many covering destinations on the Iberian Peninsula. Josephine has also served as a contributing editor for *Go Airways One-Line-Guide* (British Airways) and has written extensively for other in-flight magazines.

You can rest assured that you're in good hands—and that no property mentioned in the book has paid to be included. Each has been selected strictly on its merits, as the best of its type in its price range.

How to Use This Book

Up front is Smart Travel Tips A to Z, arranged alphabetically by topic and loaded with tips, Web sites, and contact information. Destination: Portugal helps get you in the mood for your trip. Subsequent chapters in the guide are arranged regionally. The Lisbon chapter begins with exploring information, with a section for each neighborhood (each recommending a good tour and listing sights alphabetically). The regional chapters are divided geographically; within each area, towns are covered in logical geographical order, and attractive stretches of road between them are indicated by the designation En Route. To help you decide what you'll have time to visit, all chapters begin with our writers' favorite itineraries. (Mix itineraries from several chapters, and you can put together a really exceptional trip.) The A to Z section that ends every chapter lists additional resources. At the end of the book you'll find Background and Essentials, including a brief overview of the Portugal's art, architecture, and *azulejos* (tiles) as well as a primer on the country's wines, followed by a Portuguese vocabulary section.

Icons and Symbols

★ Our special recommendations
✕ Restaurant
🏨 Lodging establishment
✕🏨 Lodging establishment whose restaurant warrants a special trip
🐥 Good for kids (rubber duck)
☞ Sends you to another section of the guide for more information
✉ Address

☎   Telephone number

☉   Opening and closing times

✉   Admission prices (those we give apply to adults; substantially reduced fees are almost always available for children, students, and senior citizens)

Numbers in white and black circles ③ ❸ that appear on the maps, in the margins, and within the tours correspond to one another.

For hotels, you can assume that all rooms have private baths, phones, TVs, and air-conditioning unless otherwise noted and that all hotels operate on the European Plan (with no meals) if we don't specify another meal plan. We always list a property's facilities but not whether you'll be charged extra to use them, so when pricing accommodations, do ask what's included. For restaurants, it's always a good idea to book ahead; we mention reservations only when they're essential or are not accepted.

All restaurants we list are open daily for lunch and dinner unless stated otherwise; dress is mentioned only when men are required to wear a jacket or a jacket and tie. Look for an overview of local dining-out habits in Smart Travel Tips A to Z and in the Pleasures and Pastimes section that follows each chapter introduction.

Don't Forget to Write

Your experiences—positive and negative—matter to us. If we have missed or misstated something, we want to hear about it. We follow up on all suggestions. Contact the Portugal editor at editors@fodors.com or c/o Fodor's at 1745 Broadway, New York, New York 10019. And have a fabulous trip!

Karen Cure

Karen Cure
Editorial Director

Portugal

0 ——— 50 miles
0 ——— 50 km

N

ATLANTIC OCEAN

SPAIN

ALGARVE

Minho

Valença

Viana do Castelo
Lima
Serra do Gerês N103
Braga
Barcelos
Guimarães
Póvoa de Varzim
Vila do Conde
A3/IP1
Oporto
Amarante
Penafiel
Douro
Espinho
Oliveira dos Azeméis
Albergaria-a-Velha
Vouga
Aveiro
Mealhada
Mira
Cantanhede
Coimbra
Figueira da Foz
Arganil
Pombal
Leiria
Nazaré
Batalha
Ourém
Alcobaça
Sra. do Aire
Fátima
Tomar
Caldas da Rainha
Obidos
IP6
Abrantes
Aveiras de Cima
Tejo
Torres Novas
Torres Vedras
Mafra
Santarém
Sintra
Vila Franca de Xira
Sorraia
Cascais
Estoril
Lisbon
N10
Seixal
A2/IP
Setúbal
Cabo Espichel
Sado
A2
Alcácer do Sal
Montemor-o-Novo
N2
Évora
TO THE AZORES
Sines
Cabo de Sines
Santiago do Cacem
IP1/E1
Ferreira do Alentejo
TO MADEIRA ISLAND
Odemira
Mira
N120
Ourique
Castro Verde
Monchique
Almodovar
Portimão
EN125
E1/IP1
Vila do Bispo
Lagos
Albufeira
Cabo de S. Vicente
Sagres
Faro
Olhão
Tavira
IP1
S. Brás de Alportel
Vila Real de S. António
Chança
Guadiana
N122
Serpa
Vilaverde de Ficalho
Moura
Beja
Mértola
Reguengos
Vila Viçosa
Sra. de Ossa
A6/IP1
Arraiolos
Estremoz
Elvas
Badajoz
A6
Avis
Ponte de Sor
Portalegre
IP2
Nisa
N118
Tagus
Proença-a-Nova
IP2
Castelo Branco
Serra da Gardunha
N233
Penamacor
Zêzere
Fundão
Covilhã
Serra da Estrêla
Guarda
Pinhel
Mondego
Sta. Comba Dão
Viseu
IP5
S. Pedro do Sul
Moimenta da Beira
Lamego
Douro
Duoro
Mogadouro
Sabor
N102/IP2
Mirandela
A4/IP4
Vila Real
Chaves
Bragança
N110
Tâmega
N1

N8

ESSENTIAL INFORMATION

AIR TRAVEL

For much of the year, TAP Air Portugal has daily nonstop flights from New York (Newark Liberty International Airport) to Lisbon. Mid-December to mid-January and mid-June to mid-September, the number of TAP flights increases to 10 each week.

Continental's daily nonstop flights between Newark Liberty International Airport and Lisbon are scheduled to provide convenient connections from destinations elsewhere in the eastern and southern United States. The carrier also has a second daily flight from New York (Newark) to Lisbon via Amsterdam, with the connecting flight on KLM, Continental's code-share partner.

British Airways and TAP have regular nonstop flights from the United Kingdom to several destinations in Portugal, and Aer Lingus has service from Dublin to Faro. There are no direct flights from Australia or New Zealand, but the national Australian airline, Qantas, has a code-sharing agreement with British Airways for flights via the United Kingdom.

BOOKING

When you book **look for nonstop flights** and **remember that "direct" flights stop at least once.** Try to avoid connecting flights, which require a change of plane. Two airlines may operate a connecting flight jointly, so ask if your airline operates every segment of the trip; you may find that the carrier you prefer flies you only part of the way. To find more booking tips and to check prices and make on-line flight reservations, log on to www.fodors.com.

CARRIERS

Domestic air travel options are limited and expensive, given the distances involved. You're better off renting a car or taking the train or bus, unless time is an issue. TAP Air Portugal and PGA (Portugália Airlines) fly between Lisbon, Oporto, and Faro, and Aerocondo and Omni have some intercity flights. TAP also has daily flights from Lisbon to Funchal, Madeira.

➤ MAJOR CARRIERS: **Aer Lingus** (☎ 0818/365000 in Ireland, WEB www. aerlingus.com). **British Airways** (☎ 800/247–9297 in the U.S.; 0845/ 773–3377 in the U.K.; WEB www. british-airways.com). **Continental** (☎ 800/231–0856, WEB www.continental. com). **Qantas** (☎ 13–13–13 in Australia; 800/808767 in New Zealand; 845/774–7767 in the U.K.; WEB www. qantas.com). **TAP Air Portugal** (☎ 800/221–7370 in the U.S.; 0845/601–0932 in the U.K.; 205700 in Portugal; WEB www.tap-airportugal.pt).

➤ SMALLER CARRIERS: **Aerocondor** (☎ 21/846–4964 in Portugal, WEB www.aerocondor.com). **Omni** (☎ 21/445–8600 in Portugal, WEB www.omni.pt). **PGA** (☎ 21/842–5559 in Portugal, WEB www.pga.pt).

CHECK-IN AND BOARDING

Always **ask your carrier about its check-in policy.** Plan to arrive at the airport about two hours before your scheduled departure time for domestic flights and 2½ to 3 hours before international flights. Assuming that not everyone with a ticket will show up, airlines routinely overbook planes. When everyone does, airlines ask for volunteers to give up their seats. In return, these volunteers usually get a certificate for a free flight and are rebooked on the next flight out. If there are not enough volunteers, the airline must choose who will be denied boarding. The first to get bumped are passengers who checked in late and those flying on discounted tickets, so **get to the gate and check in as early as possible,** especially during peak periods.

Always **bring a government-issued photo I.D. to the airport;** even when it's not required, a passport is best.

CUTTING COSTS

The least expensive airfares to Portugal are priced for round-trip travel. Book early: the lowest fares have limited availability, so prices may well be more expensive if you book closer to your intended departure date. Airlines generally allow you to change your return date for a fee; most low-fare tickets, however, are nonrefundable. It's smart to **call a number of airlines,** and when you are quoted a good price, **book it on the spot**—the same fare may not be available the next day. Always **check different routings** and look into using alternate airports. Also, price off-peak flights, which may be significantly less expensive than others. Travel agents, especially low-fare specialists (☞ Discounts and Deals, *below*), are helpful.

Consolidators are another good source. They buy tickets for scheduled international flights at reduced rates from the airlines, then sell them at prices that beat the best fare available directly from the airlines. Sometimes you can even get your money back if you need to return the ticket. Carefully read the fine print detailing penalties for changes and cancellations, purchase the ticket with a credit card, and **confirm your consolidator reservation with the airline.**

Consider flying to London first and picking up an onward charter flight: you might save money *and* have a wider choice of destinations in Portugal. There are often good deals to Faro, in particular, as the Algarve is popular with British vacationers. In summer, last-minute, round-trip flights have cost as little as $150. From Australia or New Zealand, look for a cheap charter to London or Amsterdam and then a second direct charter to Portugal.

➤ CHARTER FLIGHTS: **EasyJet** (WEB www.easyjet.com). **Last Minute** (WEB www.lastminute.com).

➤ CONSOLIDATORS: **Cheap Tickets** (☎ 800/377–1000 or 888/922–8849, WEB www.cheaptickets.com). **Discount**

Airline Ticket Service (☎ 800/576–1600). **Unitravel** (☎ 800/325–2222, WEB www.unitravel.com). **Up & Away Travel** (☎ 212/889–2345, WEB www.upandaway.com). **World Travel Network** (☎ 800/409–6753).

ENJOYING THE FLIGHT

State your seat preference when purchasing your ticket, and then repeat it when you confirm and when you check in. For more legroom, you can request one of the few emergency-aisle seats at check-in, if you're capable of lifting at least 50 pounds—a Federal Aviation Administration requirement of passengers in these seats. Seats behind a bulkhead also offer more legroom, but they don't have under-seat storage. Don't sit in the row in front of the emergency aisle or in front of a bulkhead, where seats may not recline.

Ask the airline whether a snack or meal is served on the flight. If you have dietary concerns, **request special meals when booking.** These can be vegetarian, low-cholesterol, or kosher, for example. Note that some charter companies, such as EasyJet, don't serve meals but do sell sandwiches and other items. If you're on a special diet, pack appropriate snacks in your carry-on bag. Regardless of your dietary concerns, it's always good to bring a small (plastic) bottle of water. On long flights, try to maintain a normal routine, to help fight jet lag. At night, **get some sleep.** By day, **eat light meals, drink water** (not alcohol), and **move around the cabin** to stretch your legs. For additional jet-lag tips consult *Fodor's FYI: Travel Fit & Healthy* (available at bookstores everywhere).

FLYING TIMES

The flying time to Lisbon is 6½ hours from New York, 9 hours from Chicago, and 15 hours from Los Angeles. The flight from London to Lisbon is about 2½ hours.

HOW TO COMPLAIN

If your baggage goes astray or your flight goes awry, complain right away. Most carriers require that you **file a claim immediately.** The Aviation Consumer Protection Division of the

Department of Transportation publishes *Fly-Rights,* which discusses airlines and consumer issues and is available on-line. At PassengerRights.com, a Web site, you can compose a letter of complaint and distribute it electronically.

➤ AIRLINE COMPLAINTS: **Aviation Consumer Protection Division** (✉ U.S. Department of Transportation, Room 4107, C-75, Washington, DC 20590, ☎ 202/366–2220, WEB www.dot.gov/airconsumer). **Federal Aviation Administration Consumer Hotline** (☎ 800/322–7873).

RECONFIRMING

Check the status of your flight before you leave for the airport. You can do this on your carrier's Web site, by linking to a flight-status checker (many Web booking services offer these), or by calling your carrier or travel agent. Always confirm international flights at least 72 hours ahead of the scheduled departure time.

AIRPORTS

The major gateway to Portugal is Lisbon's Aeroporto Portela, approximately 8 km (5 mi) north of the center of the city. Oporto's Aeroporto Francisco Sá Carneiro also handles international flights, as does the Aeroporto de Faro, which has the largest number of charter flights given its location in the popular tourist destination of the Algarve. The organization that oversees Portugal's airports, Aeroportos de Portugal (ANA), has a handy Web site with information in English.

➤ AIRPORT INFORMATION: **Aeroporto de Faro** (☎ 289/800801). **Aeroporto Francisco Sá Carneiro** (☎ 229/412–141). **Aeroporto Portela** (☎ 218/413–700). **ANA** (WEB www.ana-aeroportos.pt).

BIKE TRAVEL

Portugal is one of Europe's more mountainous countries. Although country roads can be crowded with speeding trucks, bicycle trips can take you along some unforgettably scenic routes, and there are great mountain bike opportunities in the country's rugged hills.

➤ LOCAL RESOURCES: **Federação Portuguesa de Cicloturismo** (✉ Rua Campolide 170, Benfica, Lisbon, ☎ 21/381–3040).

BIKES IN FLIGHT

Most airlines accommodate bikes as luggage, provided they are dismantled and boxed; check with individual airlines about packing requirements. Airlines sell bike boxes, which are often free at bike shops, for about $15 (bike bags start at $100). International travelers often can substitute a bike for a piece of checked luggage at no charge; otherwise, the cost is about $100. Domestic and Canadian airlines charge $40–$80 each way.

BUS TRAVEL

The Eurolines/National Express consortium runs regular bus service from the United Kingdom (out of London's Victoria Coach Station) to Lisbon, Oporto, Coimbra, Fátima, Faro, Lagos, and other destinations. The company also has service from Paris, its other major hub. In Lisbon Intercentro Eurolines handles inquiries about Eurolines transportation. There are many companies that offer service between Spain and Portugal and to Portugal from other parts of Europe, so it's best to make arrangements with a travel agent.

Bus service within Portugal is fairly comprehensive, and in some places, such as the Algarve, buses are the main form of public transportation. Some luxury coaches even have TVs and food service—a comfortable way to travel. Three of the largest bus companies are Rede Expressos, which serves much of the country; Rodo Norte, which serves the north; and Eva Transportes, which covers the Algarve.

Note that bus travel can be slow; it can also be difficult to arrange on your own. For schedules within Portugal it's best to inquire at tourist information offices, since routes and companies change frequently, and bus company personnel rarely speak English. If you buy from a specific bus company's ticket office, give yourself plenty of time to purchase before you depart. Most travel agents can sell you a bus ticket in advance; it's always wise to reserve a ticket at least a day ahead, particularly in summer for destinations in the Algarve.

➤ Bus Companies: **Eva Transportes** (WEB www.eva-bus.com). **Rede Expressos** (WEB www.rede-expressos.pt). **Rodo Norte** (WEB www.rodonorte.pt).

➤ From the U.K.: **Eurolines/National Express** (☎ 0990/808080; 0990/143219 for information; or 01582/488970 for ticket cancellation). **Intercentro Eurolines** (✉ Rua Actor Taborda 55, Estefânia, Lisbon, ☎ 21/330–1500).

PAYING

You can pay by credit card or travelers checks if you book your bus journey through a travel agent. If you plan to buy tickets directly from the bus station in Portugal, you must pay cash.

BUSINESS HOURS

Lunchtime is taken very seriously throughout Portugal with many businesses, particularly outside of urban areas, closing between 1 and 3 and opening again until 6 or 7. Government offices typically open from 9 to noon and 2 to 5. It's worth noting religious and public holidays, as most businesses grind to a halt, and even the local transport service may be reduced.

BANKS AND OFFICES

Banks are open weekdays 8:30–3. Money exchange booths at airports and train stations are usually open all day (24 hours at Portela Airport in Lisbon).

GAS STATIONS

Most gas stations on main highways are open 24 hours. In more rural areas, stations will be open 7 AM to 10 PM.

MUSEUMS AND SIGHTS

Museums and palaces generally open at 10, close for lunch from 12:30 to 2, and then reopen until 5; a few, however, remain open at midday. Many museums are closed on Monday, though some close on Tuesday or Wednesday.

PHARMACIES

Pharmacies are usually open weekdays 9 to 1 and 3 to 7 and Saturday 9 to 1. When they're closed, pharmacies display a card on their doors indicating where to find a nearby pharmacy that's open all night or on Sunday.

SHOPS

Although the number of *hipermercados* (giant supermarkets), *supermercados* (regular supermarkets), and shopping centers has mushroomed in recent years—and they're typically open seven days a week 10 AM–midnight—most shops are open weekdays 9–1 and 3–7, Saturday 9–1. In December, Saturday hours are the same as weekdays. Shops often close on Sunday.

CAMERAS AND PHOTOGRAPHY

The *Kodak Guide to Shooting Great Travel Pictures* (available at bookstores everywhere) is loaded with tips.

➤ Photo Help: **Kodak Information Center** (☎ 800/242–2424, WEB www.kodak.com).

EQUIPMENT PRECAUTIONS

Don't pack film and equipment in checked luggage, where it's much more susceptible to damage. X-ray machines used to view checked luggage are becoming much more powerful and therefore are much more likely to ruin your film. Try to **ask for hand inspection of film,** which becomes clouded after repeated exposure to airport X-ray machines, and **keep videotapes and computer disks away from metal detectors.** Always **keep film, tape, and computer disks out of the sun.** Carry an extra supply of batteries, and **be prepared to turn on your camera, camcorder, or laptop** to prove to airport security personnel that the device is real.

VIDEOS

Videos are in PAL format, not the NTSC format used in the United States. A four-hour blank tape costs around €3.

CAR RENTAL

Rates in Lisbon begin at around $45 a day, though there are three-day rates starting at $105 and weeklong rates starting at $160 for a standard economy car with unlimited mileage. The VAT tax on car rentals is 17%.

Automatic cars are more expensive and harder to find. The good news is that most rental cars have air-conditioning. Among the most common car makes are Citroën, Opel, Nissan, Fiat, and Ford.

➤ MAJOR AGENCIES: **Alamo** (☎ 800/522–9696, WEB www.alamo.com). **Avis** (☎ 800/331–1084; 800/879–2847 in Canada; 02/9353–9000 in Australia; 09/526–2847 in New Zealand; 0870/606–0100 in the U.K.; WEB www.avis.com). **Budget** (☎ 800/527–0700; 0870/156–5656 in the U.K.; WEB www.budget.com). **Dollar** (☎ 800/800–6000; 0124/622–0111 in the U.K., where it's affiliated with Sixt; 02/9223–1444 in Australia; WEB www.dollar.com). **Hertz** (☎ 800/654–3001; 800/263–0600 in Canada; 020/8897–2072 in the U.K.; 02/9669–2444 in Australia; 09/256–8690 in New Zealand; WEB www.hertz.com). **National Car Rental** (☎ 800/227–7368; 020/8680–4800 in the U.K.; WEB www.nationalcar.com).

CUTTING COSTS

Local car-rental agencies generally offer the same service and conditions as the international giants, and their rates are often lower, too. One leading national agency is Auto Jardim, which has offices at the airports in Lisbon and Faro. Rentauto is another reliable company. For a good deal, **book through a travel agent who will shop around.**

➤ LOCAL AGENCIES: **Auto Jardim** (☎ 21/846–3187 in Lisbon). **Rentauto** (☎ 21/846–2294 in Lisbon).

INSURANCE

When driving a rented car you are generally responsible for any damage to or loss of the vehicle. Collision policies that car-rental companies sell for European rentals typically don't cover stolen vehicles. Before you rent—and purchase collision or theft coverage—see what coverage you already have under the terms of your personal auto-insurance policy and credit cards.

REQUIREMENTS AND RESTRICTIONS

Most agencies won't rent to you if you're under the age of 21 or over 69, unless you make special arrangements.

In Portugal your own driver's license is acceptable.

SURCHARGES

Before you pick up a car in one city and leave it in another, **ask about drop-off charges or one-way service fees,** which can be substantial. Note, too, that some rental agencies charge extra if you return the car before the time specified in your contract. To avoid a hefty refueling fee, **fill the tank just before you turn in the car,** but be aware that gas stations near the rental outlet may overcharge. It's almost never a deal to buy the tank of gas in the car when you rent it; the understanding is that you'll return it empty, but some fuel usually remains. There's generally no surcharge for additional drivers, though some agencies do charge extra for children's car seats.

CAR TRAVEL

Although your driver's license from home is recognized in Portugal, an international driving permit (IDP) is a good idea. You can acquire one through the American and Canadian automobile associations and, in the United Kingdom, from the Automobile Association and Royal Automobile Club. These international permits, valid only in conjunction with your regular driver's license, are universally recognized; having one may save you a problem with local authorities.

AUTO CLUBS

➤ IN AUSTRALIA: **Australian Automobile Association** (☎ 06/247–7311).

➤ IN CANADA: **Canadian Automobile Association** (CAA; ☎ 613/247–0117).

➤ IN NEW ZEALAND: **New Zealand Automobile Association** (☎ 09/377–4660).

➤ IN PORTUGAL: **Automóvel Clube de Portugal** (✉ Rua Rosa Araújo 24/26, Marquês de Pombal, Lisbon 1200, ☎ 21/318–0100 for general information).

➤ IN THE U.K.: **Automobile Association** (AA, ☎ 0990/500600). **Royal Automobile Club** (RAC, ☎ 0990/722722 for membership; 0345/121–345 for insurance).

➤ IN THE U.S.: **American Automobile Association** (☎ 800/564–6222).

EMERGENCY SERVICES

All large garages in and around towns have breakdown services, and you'll see orange emergency (SOS) phones along turnpikes and highways. The national automobile organization, Automóvel Clube de Portugal, provides reciprocal membership with AAA and other European automobile associations.

➤ EMERGENCY CONTACT: **Automóvel Clube de Portugal** (☎ 21/942–9103 for breakdowns south of Pombal; 22/ 834–0001 for breakdowns north of Pombal).

GASOLINE

Gas stations are plentiful. Prices are controlled by the government and are the same everywhere. At research time gasoline cost €0.99 a liter (approximately ¼ gallon) for 98 and 95 octane *sem chumbo* (unleaded) and €0.69 for diesel. Credit cards are frequently accepted at gas stations.

ROAD CONDITIONS

Major EU-funded work has been done on Portugal's highway system; commercially operated *autoestradas* (toll roads with four or more lanes identified with an "A" and a number) link the principal cities, including Oporto, with Lisbon, circumventing congested urban centers. The long-awaited autoestrada from Lisbon to Faro was completed in July 2002, and a toll road now links Lisbon with Portugal's eastern border with Spain and the highway to Madrid. Many main national highways (labeled with "N" and a number) have been upgraded to toll-free, two-lane roads identified with "IP" (Itinerario Principal) and a number. Highways of mainly regional importance have been upgraded to IC (Itinerario Complementar). Roads labeled with "E" and a number are routes that connect with the Spanish network. Because road construction is still underway, you may find that one road has several designations—A, N, IP, E, etc.—on maps and signs.

Tolls seem steep in Portugal, but time saved by traveling the autoestradas usually makes them worthwhile. Minor roads are often poor and winding with unpredictable surfaces. The local driving may be faster and less forgiving than you're used to, and other visitors in rental cars on unfamiliar roads can cause problems: drive carefully.

In the north the IP5 shortens the drive from Aveiro to the border with Spain, near Guarda. Take extra care on this route, however. It's popular with trucks (you may find yourself stuck behind a convoy), *and* it has many curves and hills. The IP4 connects Oporto through Vila Real to once-remote Bragança. You can pick up the IP2 just southwest of Bragança and continue to Ourique in the Alentejo, where it connects to the IP1 straight down to Albufeira on the southern coast. This same IP1 is an autoestrada from Albufeira and runs east across the Algarve to the Spanish border near Ayamonte, 1½ hours east of Seville.

Heading out of Lisbon, there's good, fast access to Setúbal and to Évora and other Alentejo towns, although rush-hour traffic on the Ponte 25 de Abril (25 de Abril Bridge) across the Rio Tejo (Tagus River) can be frustrating. An alternative is taking the 17-km-long (11-mi-long) Ponte Vasco da Gama (Europe's second-longest water crossing after the Chunnel) across the Tejo estuary to Montijo; you can then link up with southbound and eastbound roads. Signposting on these fast roads isn't always adequate, so keep your eyes peeled for exits and turnoffs.

ROAD MAPS

Contact the national automobile association, Automóvel Clube de Portugal for a first-rate road map of the country.

➤ CONTACT: **Automóvel Clube de Portugal** (✉ Rua Rosa Araújo 24/26, Marquês de Pombal, Lisbon 1200, ☎ 21/318–0100).

RULES OF THE ROAD

Driving is on the right. At the junction of two roads of equal size, traffic coming from the right has priority. Vehicles already in a traffic circle have priority over those entering it from any point. The use of seat belts is obligatory. Horns shouldn't be used in built-up areas, and you should always carry a reflective red warning triangle, for use in a breakdown, your drivers license, and proof of car insurance. The speed limit on turnpikes is 120 kph (74 mph); on other roads it's 90 kph (56 mph), and in built-up areas, 50 kph–60 kph (30 mph–36 mph).

Billboards warning you not to drink and drive dot the countryside, and punishable alcohol levels are low. Portuguese drivers are notoriously rash, and the country has one of the highest traffic fatality rates in Europe—**drive defensively.**

CHILDREN IN PORTUGAL

When traveling in Portugal you'll see children of all ages accompanying their parents everywhere, including bars and restaurants. Shopkeepers may well smile and offer your child a *bombom* (candy), and even the coldest waiters tend to be friendlier when you have a child with you. Museum admissions, buses, and mêtro rides are generally free for children under 5 and half price for children under 12.

Be sure to plan ahead and **involve your youngsters** as you outline your trip. When packing, include things to keep them busy en route. On sightseeing days try to schedule activities of special interest to your children. If you are renting a car, don't forget to **arrange for a car seat** when you reserve. For general advice about traveling with children, consult *Fodor's FYI: Travel with Your Baby* (available in bookstores everywhere).

FLYING

If your children are two or older, **ask about children's airfares.** As a rule, infants under two not occupying a seat fly at greatly reduced fares or even for free. When booking, **confirm carry-on allowances** if you're traveling with infants. In general, for babies charged 10% of the adult fare you're allowed one carry-on bag and a collapsible stroller; if the flight is full, the stroller may have to be checked or you may be limited to less.

Experts agree that it's a good idea to use safety seats aloft for children weighing less than 40 pounds. Airlines set their own policies: U.S. carriers usually require that the child be ticketed, even if he or she is young enough to ride free, since the seats must be strapped into regular seats. Do **check your airline's policy about using safety seats during takeoff and landing.** Safety seats are not allowed everywhere in the plane, so get your seat assignments as early as possible.

When reserving, **request children's meals or a freestanding bassinet** (not available at all airlines) if you need them. But note that bulkhead seats, where you must sit to use the bassinet, may lack an overhead bin or storage space on the floor.

FOOD

Children are made welcome in virtually all restaurants. Throughout Portugal, the number of fast-food chains with dishes that appeal to kids is increasing. Many such establishments are in shopping malls, which often have U.S.-style food courts. Although you won't find children's menus outside of these chains and the international-style restaurants, most kitchens will fix something special for children. Even the smallest *tasca* (town restaurant-bar) can make a *sandes de queijo* (cheese sandwich), and straightforward dishes such as roast chicken (*frango assado*) are on most menus.

LODGING

Most hotels in Portugal allow children under five or so to stay in their parents' room at no extra charge, but others charge for them as extra adults; be sure to check first.

SIGHTS AND ATTRACTIONS

Places that are especially appealing to children are indicated by a rubber-duckie icon (🐤) in the margin.

SUPPLIES AND EQUIPMENT

Disposal diapers are widely available. The local *fralda* (diaper) equivalent to Pampers is Dodo, and you can also find Huggies. Local brands, however, are cheaper. Powdered and premixed baby formulas are available, as are soy-based formulas for babies allergic to dairy products.

CONSUMER PROTECTION

Whether you're shopping for gifts or purchasing travel services, **pay with a major credit card** whenever possible, so you can cancel payment or get reimbursed if there's a problem (and you can provide documentation). If you're doing business with a particular company for the first time, **contact your local Better Business Bureau and the attorney general's offices** in your state and (for U.S. businesses) the company's home state as well. Have any complaints been filed? Finally, if you're buying a package or tour, always **consider travel insurance** that includes default coverage (☞ Insurance, *below*).

➤ BBBs: **Council of Better Business Bureaus** (✉ 4200 Wilson Blvd., Suite 800, Arlington, VA 22203, ☎ 703/276–0100, FAX 703/525–8277, WEB www.bbb.org).

CUSTOMS AND DUTIES

When shopping abroad, **keep receipts** for all purchases. Upon reentering the country, **be ready to show customs officials what you've bought.** If you feel a duty is incorrect, appeal the assessment. If you object to the way your clearance was handled, note the inspector's badge number. In either case, first ask to see a supervisor. If the problem isn't resolved, write to the appropriate authorities, beginning with the port director at your point of entry.

IN AUSTRALIA

Australian residents who are 18 or older may bring home A$400 worth of souvenirs and gifts (including jewelry), 250 cigarettes or 250 grams of tobacco, and 1,125 ml of alcohol (including wine, beer, and spirits). Residents under 18 may bring back A$200 worth of goods. Prohibited items include meat products. Seeds, plants, and fruits need to be declared upon arrival.

➤ INFORMATION: **Australian Customs Service** (Regional Director, ✉ Box 8, Sydney, NSW 2001, ☎ 02/9213–2000; 1300/363263; or 1800/020504 quarantine-inquiry line; FAX 02/9213–4043, WEB www.customs.gov.au).

IN CANADA

Canadian residents who have been out of Canada for at least seven days may bring in C$750 worth of goods duty-free. If you've been away fewer than seven days but more than 48 hours, the duty-free allowance drops to C$200; if your trip lasts 24 to 48 hours, the allowance is C$50. You may not pool allowances with family members. Goods claimed under the C$750 exemption may follow you by mail; those claimed under the lesser exemptions must accompany you. Alcohol and tobacco products may be included in the seven-day and 48-hour exemptions but not in the 24-hour exemption. If you meet the age requirements of the province or territory through which you reenter Canada, you may bring in, duty-free, 1.5 liters of wine *or* 1.14 liters (40 imperial ounces) of liquor *or* 24 12-ounce cans or bottles of beer or ale. If you are 19 or older you may bring in, duty-free, 200 cigarettes and 50 cigars. Check ahead of time with the Canada Customs and Revenue Agency or the Department of Agriculture for policies regarding meat products, seeds, plants, and fruits.

You may send an unlimited number of gifts (only one gift per recipient, however) worth up to C$60 each duty-free to Canada. Label the package UNSOLICITED GIFT—VALUE UNDER $60. Alcohol and tobacco are excluded.

➤ INFORMATION: **Canada Customs and Revenue Agency** (✉ 2265 St. Laurent Blvd. S, Ottawa, Ontario K1G 4K3, ☎ 204/983–3500, 506/636–5064, or 800/461–9999, WEB www.ccra-adrc.gc.ca/).

IN NEW ZEALAND

All homeward-bound residents may bring back NZ$700 worth of souvenirs and gifts; passengers may not pool their allowances, and children can claim only the concession on goods intended for their own use. For those 17 or older, the duty-free allowance also includes 4.5 liters of wine or beer; one 1,125-ml bottle of spirits; and either 200 cigarettes, 250 grams of tobacco, 50 cigars, *or* a combination of the three up to 250 grams. Meat products, seeds, plants, and fruits must be declared upon arrival to the Agricultural Services Department.

➤ INFORMATION: **New Zealand Customs** (Head office: ✉ The Customhouse, 17–21 Whitmore St., Box 2218, Wellington, ☎ 09/300–5399 or 0800/428786, WEB www.customs. govt.nz).

IN PORTUGAL

Visitors age 15 and over are permitted to bring in 200 cigarettes, or 100 cigarillos, or 50 cigars, or 250 grams of loose tobacco. Those 17 years of age and older may bring in 1 liter of liquor over 22 proof and 2 liters of wine. Perfume is limited to 50 grams, eau de cologne to ¼ liter. It's a good idea to **carry sales receipts for expensive personal items to avoid paying export duties when you leave.**

➤ INFORMATION: **Direção Geral das Alfândegas** (✉ Rua da Alfândega 5, Alfama, Lisbon, ☎ 21/881–3700).

IN THE U.K.

If you're a U.K. resident and your journey was wholly within the European Union, you probably won't have to pass through customs when you return to the United Kingdom. If you plan to bring back large quantities of alcohol or tobacco, check EU limits beforehand. In most cases, if you bring back more than 200 cigars, 800 cigarettes, 10 liters of spirits, and/or 90 liters of wine, you have to declare the goods upon return.

➤ INFORMATION: **HM Customs and Excise** (✉ Portcullis House, 21 Cowbridge Rd. E, Cardiff CF11 9SS, ☎ 029/2038–6423 or 0845/010–9000, WEB www.hmce.gov.uk).

IN THE U.S.

U.S. residents who have been out of the country for at least 48 hours may bring home, for personal use, $800 worth of foreign goods duty-free, as long as they haven't used the $800 allowance or any part of it in the past 30 days. This exemption may include 1 liter of alcohol (for travelers 21 and older), 200 cigarettes, and 100 non-Cuban cigars. Family members from the same household who are traveling together may pool their $800 personal exemptions. For fewer than 48 hours, the duty-free allowance drops to $200, which may include 50 cigarettes, 10 non-Cuban cigars, and 150 milliliters of alcohol (or perfume containing alcohol). The $200 allowance cannot be combined with other individuals' exemptions, and if you exceed it, the full value of all the goods will be taxed. Antiques, which the U.S. Customs Service defines as objects more than 100 years old, enter duty-free, as do original works of art done entirely by hand, including paintings, drawings, and sculptures.

You may also send packages home duty-free, with a limit of one parcel per addressee per day (except alcohol or tobacco products or perfume worth more than $5). You can mail up to $200 worth of goods for personal use; label the package PERSONAL USE and attach a list of its contents and their retail value. If the package contains your used personal belongings, mark it PERSONAL GOODS RETURNED to avoid paying duties. You may send up to $100 worth of goods as a gift; mark the package UNSOLICITED GIFT. Mailed items do not affect your duty-free allowance on your return.

➤ INFORMATION: **U.S. Customs Service** (for inquiries, ✉ 1300 Pennsylvania Ave. NW, Washington, DC 20229, ☎ 202/354–1000, WEB www.customs. gov; for complaints, ✉ Customer Satisfaction Unit, 1300 Pennsylvania Ave. NW, Room 5.5A, Washington, DC 20229; for registration of equipment, ✉ Office of Passenger Programs, 1300 Pennsylvania Ave. NW, Room 5.4D, Washington, DC 20229, ☎ 202/927–0530).

DINING

The explosion of fast-food restaurants in recent years hasn't dented the Portuguese affection for old-fashioned, white-tablecloth dining—even though the tablecloth and napkins may now be made of paper. Hamburger places do a roaring lunchtime trade in towns all over the country, but so do the traditional little restaurants that offer office workers home cooking at a modest price. Don't expect much in the line of decor, and if you have trouble squeezing in, remember the rule of thumb: if it's packed it's probably good.

Although Portugal's plush, luxury restaurants can be good, they seldom measure up to their counterparts in other European countries. The best food by far tends be found in the moderately priced and less expensive spots. Restaurants featuring charcoal-grilled meats and fish, called *churasqueiras*, are also popular (and often economical) options, and the Brazilian *rodízio*-type restaurant, where you are regaled with an endless offering of spit-roasted meats, is entrenched in Lisbon, Oporto, and the Algarve. Shellfish restaurants, called *marisqueiras*, are numerous along the coast; note that lobsters, mollusks, and the like are fresh and good but pricey. Restaurant prices fall appreciably when you leave the Lisbon, Oporto, and Algarve areas, and portion sizes increase the farther north you go.

While you ponder the menu, you may be served an impressive array of appetizers. If you eat any of these, you'll probably be charged a small fee called a *couberto* or *couvert*. If you don't want these appetizers, you're perfectly within your rights to send them back. As in many European countries, Portuguese restaurants serve an *ementa* (or *prato*) *do dia*, or set menu. This can be a real bargain—usually 80% of the cost of three courses ordered separately.

The restaurants we list in this book, each indicated by a knife-and-fork icon, ✕, are the cream of the crop in each price category. Establishments marked with ✕⊞ stand out equally for their restaurants and their rooms.

SPECIALTIES

Portugal has a rich, varied gastronomy. The Portuguese introduced coriander, pepper, ginger, curry, saffron, and paprika to Europe as a result of their explorations and establishment of trade routes. They brought back tea from the Orient—it was the 11th-century Portuguese princess Catherine of Bragança, wife of England's King Charles II, who popularized the aromatic beverage in England—coffee and peanuts from Africa, and pineapples, tomatoes, and potatoes from the New World.

The country's many rivers and its proximity to the sea mean that there's an abundance of seafood dishes: Be sure to try the *caldeirada* (seafood stew) and fresh *sardinhas assadas* (grilled sardines). *Lulas recheadas*, squid stuffed with sausage and rice, is a unique combination of texture and flavor. Chicken and pork are good everywhere, and the mention of golden and crunchy *leitão da bairrada* (roast suckling pig) in the north is enough to give anyone an appetite. Sautéed or grilled *bife á português* (steak), often cooked in a port-wine sauce, is served throughout the country. *Bacalhau* (codfish) can be served 365 different ways (or so legend has it). Soups of all kinds are popular, and most restaurants serve *caldo verde*, a filling blend of shredded cabbage and potatoes. The famous pork-and-clam dish called *porco á Alentejana* is made with diced marinated pork and clams and served with potatoes or rice. Desserts tend to be sweet and egg-based, with *pudim flan*, a caramel custard, almost a national passion.

MEALTIMES

Breakfast is the lightest meal; lunch, the main meal of the day, is served between noon and 2:30, although nowadays, office workers in cities often grab a quick sandwich in a bar instead of stopping for a big meal. At about 5 there's a break for coffee or tea and a pastry; dinner is eaten at around 8. Unless otherwise noted, the restaurants listed in this guide are open daily for lunch and dinner.

PAYING

A surprising number of restaurants in Portugal still don't accept credit cards. Always check first, or you may end the evening washing dishes.

RESERVATIONS AND DRESS

Reservations are always a good idea; we mention them only when they're essential or not accepted. Book as far ahead as you can, and reconfirm as soon as you arrive. (Large parties should always call ahead to check the reservations policy.) We mention dress only when men are required to wear a jacket or a jacket and tie.

WINE, BEER, AND SPIRITS

Portuguese wines are inexpensive and, in general, good. Even the *vinho da casa* (house wine) is perfectly drinkable in most restaurants. Among the most popular are Bairrada from the Coimbra/Aveiro region, Ribatejo and Liziria from the Ribatejo region, and the reds from the Dão region. The light, sparkling *vinhos verdes* (green wines, named not for their color but for the fact they're drunk early and don't improve with age) are also popular. Both the Instituto de Vinho de Porto (Port Wine Institute) and the Comissão de Viticultura da Região dos Vinhos Verdes (Vinho Verde Region Viticulture Commission) have fascinating Web sites—with information in several languages, including English—that will help you learn more about Portuguese wines.

The leading brands of Portuguese beer—including Super Bock, Crystal, Sagres, and Imperial—are available on tap and in bottles or cans. They're made with fewer chemicals than the average American beers, and are on the strong side with a good, clean flavor. Local brandy—namely Macieira and Constantino—is cheap, as is domestic gin, although it's marginally weaker than its international counterparts.

Portugal has the world's highest alcohol consumption after Russia, so licensing laws are lax. As long as you're over 16 (the legal drinking age), you can buy alcohol at shops, supermarkets, bars, and restaurants. And having brandy with your morning coffee will mark you as a local.

➤ WINE INFORMATION: **Comissão de Viticultura da Região dos Vinhos Verdes** (WEB www.vinhoverde.pt). **Instituto de Vinho de Porto** (WEB www.ivp.pt).

DISABILITIES AND ACCESSIBILITY

Portugal isn't one of the easiest countries for travelers with disabilities: many smaller towns and hilltop castles have difficult terrain. Things are beginning to change, however, and buildings constructed here within the last few years should be accessible, as are some of the larger museums and

other sites. It's best to check either with the tourist office, your hotel, or your travel agent before booking a reservation or heading off to an attraction.

Portugal's major airports—and their rest rooms—are wheelchair-accessible. For more information about facilities and transport access for travelers with disabilities, contact the Secratariado Nacional de Reabilitiação.

➤ LOCAL RESOURCE: **Secratariado Nacional de Reabilitiação** (⊠ Av. Conde de Valbom 63, Saldanha, Lisbon 1000, ☎ 21/793–6517).

RESERVATIONS

When discussing accessibility with an operator or reservations agent, **ask hard questions.** Are there any stairs, inside *or* out? Are there grab bars next to the toilet *and* in the shower/tub? How wide is the doorway to the room? To the bathroom? For the most extensive facilities meeting the latest legal specifications, **opt for newer accommodations.** If you reserve through a toll-free number, consider also calling the hotel's local number to confirm the information from the central reservations office. Get confirmation in writing when you can.

➤ COMPLAINTS: **Aviation Consumer Protection Division** (☞ Air Travel, *above*) for airline-related problems. **Departmental Office of Civil Rights** (for general inquiries, ⊠ U.S. Department of Transportation, S-30, 400 7th St. SW, Room 10215, Washington, DC 20590, ☎ 202/366–4648, FAX 202/366–3571, WEB www.dot.gov/ost/docr/index.htm). **Disability Rights Section** (⊠ NYAV, U.S. Department of Justice, Civil Rights Division, 950 Pennsylvania Ave. NW, Washington, DC 20530; ☎ 800/514–0301; 202/514–0301 ADA information line; 202/514–0383 TTY; 800/514–0383 TTY; WEB www.usdoj.gov/crt/ada/adahom1.htm).

TRAVEL AGENCIES

In the United States, the Americans with Disabilities Act requires that travel firms serve the needs of all travelers. Some agencies specialize in working with people with disabilities.

➤ TRAVELERS WITH MOBILITY PROBLEMS: **Access Adventures** (⊠ 206

Chestnut Ridge Rd., Scottsville, NY 14624, ☎ 716/889–9096, dltravel@ prodigy.net), run by a former physical-rehabilitation counselor. **Flying Wheels Travel** (✉ 143 W. Bridge St., Box 382, Owatonna, MN 55060, ☎ 507/451–5005, FAX 507/451–1685, WEB www.flyingwheelstravel.com).

DISCOUNTS AND DEALS

If you're undeterred by potentially wet weather, consider traveling November to March, when many hotels discount their rates by up to 20%. In Lisbon and Oporto, **check with the tourist office about discount cards offering travel deals** on public transport, reduced or free entrance to certain museums, and discounts in some shops and restaurants.

Be a smart shopper and **compare all your options** before making decisions. A plane ticket bought with a promotional coupon from travel clubs, coupon books, and direct-mail offers or purchased on the Internet may not be cheaper than the least expensive fare from a discount ticket agency. And always keep in mind that what you get is just as important as what you save.

DISCOUNT RESERVATIONS

To save money, **look into discount reservations services** with Web sites and toll-free numbers, which use their buying power to get a better price on hotels, airline tickets, even car rentals. When booking a room, always **call the hotel's local toll-free number** (if one is available) rather than the central reservations number—you'll often get a better price. Always ask about special packages or corporate rates.

When shopping for the best deal on hotels and car rentals, **look for guaranteed exchange rates,** which protect you against a falling dollar. With your rate locked in, you won't pay more, even if the price goes up in the local currency.

➤ AIRLINE TICKETS: ☎ 800/AIR–4LESS.

➤ HOTEL ROOMS: **Hotel Reservations Network** (☎ 800/964–6835, WEB www.hoteldiscount.com). International Marketing & Travel Concepts (☎ 800/790–4682, WEB www.imtc-travel.com). **Steigenberger Reservation Service** (☎ 800/223–5652, WEB www.srs-worldhotels.com). **Travel Interlink** (☎ 800/888–5898, WEB www.travelinterlink.com). **Turbotrip.com** (☎ 800/473–7829, WEB www.turbotrip.com).

PACKAGE DEALS

Don't confuse packages and guided tours. When you buy a package, you travel on your own, just as though you had planned the trip yourself. Fly/drive packages, which combine airfare and car rental, are often a good deal. If you **buy a rail/drive pass,** you may save on train tickets and car rentals. All Eurail- and Europass holders get a discount on Eurostar fares through the Channel Tunnel.

ELECTRICITY

The electrical current in Portugal is 220 volts, 50 cycles alternating current (AC); wall outlets take plugs with two round prongs. To use your U.S.-purchased electric-powered equipment, **bring a converter and adapter.** If your appliances are dual-voltage, you'll need only an adapter. Most laptops operate equally well on 110 and 220 volts and so require only an adapter. Don't use 110-volt outlets marked FOR SHAVERS ONLY for high-wattage appliances such as blow-dryers.

EMBASSIES AND CONSULATES

➤ AUSTRALIA: **Australian Consular Section** (✉ Av. da Liberdade 200, 2nd floor, Centro, Lisbon, ☎ 21/310–1500).

➤ CANADA: **Canadian Embassy** (✉ Av. da Liberdade 144–156, Centro, Lisbon, ☎ 21/316–4600).

➤ UNITED KINGDOM: **U.K Embassy** (✉ Rua de São Bernardo 33, Estrela, Lisbon, ☎ 21/396–1191).

➤ UNITED STATES: **U.S. Embassy** (✉ Av. das Forças Armadas, Seterios, Lisbon, ☎ 21/727–3300).

EMERGENCIES

The national number for emergencies is 112, which is the universal EU emergency number.

ETIQUETTE AND BEHAVIOR

Portugal has a strong Catholic influence. If you're visiting a church or place of worship, wear conservative clothing.

If you're invited to dinner by a Portuguese family, a bottle of good wine is a thoughtful gift. Shake hands with everyone, including youngsters, on arriving and leaving. If you're more closely acquainted, a kiss on both cheeks is normal (right cheek always first), except between men. Address men as *senhor*, women as *senhora*, and highly respected or older women as *dona* followed by the Christian name.

In cities, most restaurant patrons are sophisticated and well mannered. In the countryside, however, things might be different: try not to show dismay at locals who eat with their fingers or talk with their mouths full.

BUSINESS ETIQUETTE

It's prudent to use a title, such as senhor and senhora during introductions. Shake hands with every man and his dog, and have business cards at the ready. Dress is casual (slacks and nice shirts, with jackets optional) to formal (suits and ties) in Lisbon and Oporto, and casual elsewhere.

Don't expect things to start on time: everybody in Portugal runs late—period. During meetings, avoid direct criticism or confrontation; strive instead for win-win situations. For a lunch or dinner meeting, it's generally understood that the person who issued the invitation will be the one to pay.

GAY AND LESBIAN TRAVEL

The Portuguese are generally very liberal in their attitudes, and gay and lesbian travelers should have no particular difficulties. The rules are those of discretion and good taste—the same ones that apply to heterosexual couples.

➤ GAY- AND LESBIAN-FRIENDLY TRAVEL AGENCIES IN PORTUGAL: ILGA Portugal (✉ Rua de São Lazaro 88, Martim Moniz, Lisbon, ☎ 21/887–3918). Opusgay (✉ Rua da Ilha Terceira 34, Estefânia, Lisbon, ☎ 21/315–1396).

➤ GAY- AND LESBIAN-FRIENDLY TRAVEL AGENCIES IN THE U.S.: Different Roads Travel (✉ 8383 Wilshire Blvd., Suite 902, Beverly Hills, CA 90211, ☎ 323/651–5557 or 800/429–8747, FAX 323/651–3678, lgernert@tzell.com). Kennedy Travel (✉ 314 Jericho Turnpike, Floral Park, NY 11001, ☎ 516/352–4888 or 800/237–7433, FAX 516/354–8849, WEB www.kennedytravel.com). Now, Voyager (✉ 4406 18th St., San Francisco, CA 94114, ☎ 415/626–1169 or 800/255–6951, FAX 415/626–8626, WEB www.nowvoyager.com). Skylink Travel and Tour (✉ 1006 Mendocino Ave., Santa Rosa, CA 95401, ☎ 707/546–9888 or 800/225–5759, FAX 707/546–9891, WEB www.skylinktravel.com), serving lesbian travelers.

HEALTH

Sunburn and sunstroke are common problems in summer in mainland Portugal and virtually year-round on Madeira. On a hot, sunny day, even people not normally bothered by a strong rays should cover up. Carry sunscreen for nose, ears, and other sensitive areas; be sure to drink enough liquids; and above all, limit your sun exposure for the first few days until you become accustomed to the heat. No special shots are required before visiting Portugal (except for yellow-fever shots if you want to visit Madeira and have come from an infected area).

OVER-THE-COUNTER REMEDIES

If your system is sensitive to new and different foods, note that mild cases of diarrhea may respond to Imodium, Lomotil (known generically as loperamide), or Pepto-Bismol (not as strong), all of which can be purchased over the counter. Drink plenty of purified water or *chá* (tea)—*camomila* (chamomile) is a good folk remedy. In severe cases, rehydrate yourself with a salt-sugar solution: ½ teaspoon *sal* (salt) and 4 tablespoons *açúcar* (sugar) per quart of *agua* (water). The word for aspirin is *aspirinha*; Tylenol is pronounced *tee-luh-nawl*.

HOLIDAYS

New Year's Day (January 1); Mardi Gras (better known as Carnaval; the day before Ash Wednesday); Good Friday; Easter Sunday; Liberty Day (April 25); Labor Day (May 1); Corpo de Deus (May 30); Camões Day (June 10); Assumption (August 15); Republic Day (October 5); All Saints' Day (November 1); Independence Day (December 1); Immaculate Conception (December 8); Christmas Day (December 25).

If a national holiday falls on a Tuesday or Thursday, many businesses also close on the Monday or Friday in between, for a long weekend called a *ponte* (bridge). There are also local holidays when entire towns, cities, and regions grind to a standstill. Check the nearest tourist office for dates.

INSURANCE

The most useful travel-insurance plan is a comprehensive policy that includes coverage for trip cancellation and interruption, default, trip delay, and medical expenses (with a waiver for preexisting conditions).

Without insurance you will lose all or most of your money if you cancel your trip, regardless of the reason. Default insurance covers you if your tour operator, airline, or cruise line goes out of business. Trip-delay covers expenses that arise because of bad weather or mechanical delays. Study the fine print when comparing policies.

If you're traveling internationally, a key component of travel insurance is coverage for medical bills incurred if you get sick on the road. Such expenses aren't generally covered by Medicare or private policies. U.K. residents can buy a travel-insurance policy valid for most vacations taken during the year in which it's purchased (but check preexisting-condition coverage). British and Australian citizens need extra medical coverage when traveling overseas. Always **buy travel policies directly from the insurance company**; if you buy them from a cruise line, airline, or tour operator that goes out of business you probably will not be covered for the agency or operator's default, a major risk. Before making any purchase, **review your existing health and home-owner's**

policies to find what they cover away from home.

➤ TRAVEL INSURERS: In the United States: **Access America** (⊠ 6600 W. Broad St., Richmond, VA 23230, ☎ 800/284–8300, FAX 804/673–1491 or 800/346–9265, WEB www.accessamerica.com). **Travel Guard International** (⊠ 1145 Clark St., Stevens Point, WI 54481, ☎ 715/345–0505 or 800/826–1300, FAX 800/955–8785, WEB www.travelguard.com).

➤ INSURANCE INFORMATION: In Australia: **Insurance Council of Australia** (⊠ Level 3, 56 Pitt St., Sydney, NSW 2000, ☎ 02/9253–5100, FAX 02/9253–5111, WEB www.ica.com.au). In Canada: **RBC Travel Insurance** (⊠ 6880 Financial Dr., Mississauga, Ontario L5N 7Y5, ☎ 905/791–8700 or 800/668–4342, FAX 905/813–4704, WEB www.rbcinsurance.com). In New Zealand: **Insurance Council of New Zealand** (⊠ Level 7, 111–115 Customhouse Quay, Box 474, Wellington, ☎ 04/472–5230, FAX 04/473–3011, WEB www.icnz.org.nz). In the United Kingdom: **Association of British Insurers** (⊠ 51 Gresham St., London EC2V 7HQ, ☎ 020/7600–3333, FAX 020/7696–8999, WEB www.abi.org.uk).

LANGUAGE

Portuguese is the seventh most spoken language in the world. It can be difficult to pronounce and understand (most people speak quickly and elliptically). If, however, you have a fair knowledge of a Latin language, you may be able to read a little Portuguese. Just be aware that, with some cognates, appearances can be deceptive—it's best to double-check terms in a pocket Portuguese-English dictionary. Any attempt you make to speak Portuguese will be well received. In large cities and major resorts many people speak English and, occasionally, Spanish or French.

LODGING

Many visitors design their itineraries around *pousadas* (inns). Luxurious resorts provide self-contained surroundings that can tempt guests not to leave. There are new high-rise hotels in cities as well as *residências* (in what were once private homes—the term *residencial* is also often used) and apartment-style accommodations (with suites or one-bedroom units and kitchenettes) in the smallest of towns.

The lodgings we list are the cream of the crop in each price category. We always list the facilities that are available—but we don't specify whether they cost extra: when pricing accommodations, always ask what's included and what costs extra.

Assume that hotels operate on the **European Plan** (EP, with no meals) unless we specify that they're **all-inclusive** (including all meals and most activities) or use the **Breakfast Plan** (BP, with a full breakfast), **Continental Plan** (CP, with a Continental breakfast), **Modified American Plan** (MAP, with breakfast and dinner), or the **Full American Plan** (FAP, with all meals).

APARTMENT AND VILLA RENTALS

If you want a home base that's roomy enough for a family and comes with cooking facilities, **consider a furnished rental**. These can save you money, especially if you're traveling with a group. Home-exchange directories sometimes list rentals as well as exchanges.

The Algarve has the most rental properties in Portugal, but it also the highest occupancy rate. Most apartments and villas are privately owned, with a local management company overseeing the advertising, maintenance, and rent collection. Two reliable Algarve-based agencies are Villas & Vacations and Jordan & Nunn. For lists of rental properties and reputable agents elsewhere in Portugal, contact tourist offices. **Avoid time-share touts** on the street; they'll try to lure you in to view a property with the promise of free holidays and cash. These are often sophisticated (and costly) scams.

➤ INTERNATIONAL AGENTS: **At Home Abroad** (✉ 405 E. 56th St., Suite 6H, New York, NY 10022, ☎ 212/421–9165, FAX 212/752–1591, WEB www.athomeabroadinc.com). **Interhome** (✉ 1990 N.E. 163rd St., Suite 110,

North Miami Beach, FL 33162, ☎ 305/940–2299 or 800/882–6864, FAX 305/940–2911, WEB www.interhome.com). **Villanet** (✉ 11556 1st Ave. NW, Seattle, WA 98177, ☎ 206/417–3444 or 800/964–1891, FAX 206/417–1832, WEB www.rentavilla.com). **Villas and Apartments Abroad** (✉ 1270 Ave. of the Americas, 15th floor, New York, NY 10020, ☎ 212/897–5045 or 800/433–3020, FAX 212/897–5039, WEB www.ideal-villas.com). **Villas International** (✉ 4340 Redwood Hwy., Suite D309, San Rafael, CA 94903, ☎ 415/499–9490 or 800/221–2260, FAX 415/499–9491, WEB www.villasintl.com).

➤ LOCAL AGENTS: **Jordan & Nunn** (✉ Av. Duarte Pacheco 226, Almancil 8135, ☎ 289/399943). **Villas & Vacations** (✉ Apartado 3498, Almancil 8135-906, ☎ 289/390501).

CAMPING

There are more than 100 good campgrounds in Portugal. One of the largest and best equipped is Lisboa Camping, near Estoril. It has tennis courts, a swimming pool, a bank, a restaurant, cafés, fully furnished four- to six-bed cabins, a chapel, a library, a games room, and a minimarket. Another very pleasant site is five minutes from Guincho Beach in Cascais; it's operated by Orbitur, which also has several other well-equipped camps, some with four-person chalets. For more information about camping, contact Orbitur's head office in Lisbon or pick up *Roteiro Campista*, a guide to campsites that's sold in most large bookshops. You'll also find the Roteiro Campista Web site helpful.

➤ INFORMATION: **Orbitur** (☎ 218/117–000). **Roteiro Campista** (WEB www.roteiro-campista.pt).

COUNTRY HOUSES

Throughout the country, though particularly in the north, many *solares* (manors) and *casas de campo* (farm or country houses) have been remodeled to receive small numbers of guests in a venture called Turismo de Habitação (TURIHAB; Country House Tourism). These guest houses are in bucolic settings, near parks or monuments or in historic *aldeias* (villages). Breakfast is always included in the price. The Central Nacional de Turismo no Espaço Rural (National Center for Rural Tourism) serves as a clearinghouse for information from several organizations involved in this endeavor.

➤ INFORMATION: **ANTER** (✉ Rua 24 de Julho 1, Chiado, Évora 7000, ☎ 266/749420). **Central Nacional de Turismo no Espaço Rural** (✉ Praça da República, Ponte de Lima 4990, ☎ 258/741672, 258/742827, or 258/742829, WEB www.center.pt). **Quinta do Campo** (✉ Rua Carlos O'Neill 20, Nazaré 2450–344, ☎ 262/577135) for central and southern Portugal. **TURIHAB** (WEB www.turihab.pt).

HOSTELS

No matter what your age, you can **save on lodging costs by staying at hostels.** In some 4,500 locations in more than 70 countries around the world, Hostelling International (HI), the umbrella group for a number of national youth-hostel associations, offers single-sex, dorm-style beds and, at many hostels, rooms for couples and family accommodations. Membership in any HI national hostel association, open to travelers of all ages, allows you to stay in HI-affiliated hostels at member rates; one-year membership is about $25 for adults (C$35 for a two-year minimum membership in Canada, £13 in the United Kingdom, A$52 in Australia, and NZ$40 in New Zealand); hostels run about $10–$30 per night. Members have priority if the hostel is full; they're also eligible for discounts around the world, even on rail and bus travel in some countries.

➤ ORGANIZATIONS: **Hostelling International—American Youth Hostels** (✉ 733 15th St. NW, Suite 840, Washington, DC 20005, ☎ 202/783–6161, FAX 202/783–6171, WEB www.hiayh.org). **Hostelling International—Canada** (✉ 400–205 Catherine St., Ottawa, Ontario·K2P 1C3, ☎ 613/237–7884 or 800/663–5777, FAX 613/237–7868, WEB www.hihostels.ca). **Youth Hostel Association Australia** (✉ 10 Mallett St., Camperdown, NSW 2050, ☎ 02/9565–1699, FAX 02/9565–1325, WEB www.yha.com.au). **Youth Hostel Association of England**

and **Wales** (✉ Trevelyan House, Dimple Rd., Matlock, Derbyshire DE4 3YH, U.K., ☎ 0870/870–8808, FAX 0169/592–702, WEB www.yha.org.uk). **Youth Hostels Association of New Zealand** (✉ Level 3, 193 Cashel St., Box 436, Christchurch, ☎ 03/379–9970, FAX 03/365–4476, WEB www.yha.org.nz).

HOTELS

Portugal has many excellent and reasonably priced hotels, though good properties can be hard to come by in remote inland areas. The government officially grades accommodations with one to five stars or with a category rating. Ratings, which are assigned based on the level of comfort and the number of facilities offered, can be misleading as quality is difficult to grade. In general, though, the system works.

Most hotel rooms have such basic amenities as a private bathroom and a telephone; those with two or more stars may also have air-conditioning, cable or satellite TV, a minibar, and room service. (Note that all hotels listed in this guide have private bath unless otherwise indicated.) Contact the Portuguese National Tourist Office for a country-wide lodging directory.

High season means not only the summer months, but also the Christmas and New Year's holiday period on Madeira, Easter week throughout the country, and anytime a town is holding a festival. In the off-season (generally November through March), however, many hotels reduce their rates by as much as 20%.

➤ INFORMATION: **Mais Turismo** (WEB www.hotelguide.pt). **Portuguese National Tourist Office** (✉ 590 5th Ave., New York, NY 10036, ☎ 212/354–4403 or 212/354–4404, WEB www.portugalinsite.pt).

➤ TOLL-FREE NUMBERS: **Best Western** (☎ 800/528–1234, WEB www.bestwestern.com). **Choice** (☎ 800/424–6423, WEB www.choicehotels.com). **Four Seasons** (☎ 800/332–3442, WEB www.fourseasons.com). **Holiday Inn** (☎ 800/465–4329, WEB www.sixcontinentshotels.com). **Marriott** (☎ 800/228–9290,

WEB www.marriott.com). **Le Meridien** (☎ 800/543–4300, WEB www. lemeridien-hotels.com). **Sheraton** (☎ 800/325–3535, WEB www. starwood.com/sheraton).

POUSADAS

The term "pousada" is derived from the Portuguese verb *pousar* (to rest). Portugal has a network of more than 40 of these state-run hotels, which are in restored castles, palaces, monasteries, convents, and other charming buildings. Each pousada is in a particularly scenic and tranquil part of the country and is tastefully furnished with regional crafts, antiques, and artwork. All have restaurants that serve local specialties; you can stop for a meal or a drink without spending the night. Rates are reasonable, considering that most pousadas are four- or five-star hotels and a stay in one can be the highlight of a visit. They're extremely popular with foreigners and Portuguese alike, and some have 10 or fewer rooms; make reservations in well advance, especially for stays in summer. Also check for seasonal and senior-citizen discounts, which can be as high at 40%.

➤ INFORMATION: **Keytel International** (✉ 402 Edgeware Rd., London W2 1ED, ☎ 020/7402–8182). **Marketing Ahead** (✉ 433 5th Ave., New York, NY 10016, ☎ 212/686–9213 or 800/ 223–1356). **Pousadas de Portugal** (✉ Av. Santa Joana Princesa 10, Alvalade, Lisbon 1749-090, ☎ 21/ 844–2001, WEB www.pousadas.pt).

SPAS

Portugal has a profusion of *termas* (thermal springs), whose waters reputedly can cure whatever ails you. In the smaller spas, hotels are rather simple; in the more famous ones, they're first-class. Most are open from May through October.

➤ INFORMATION: **Associação das Termas de Portugal** (✉ Av. Miguel Bombarda 110–2, Saldanha, Lisbon 1050, ☎ 21/794–0574, WEB www. termasdeportugal.pt).

MAIL AND SHIPPING

You can expect a letter to take 7–10 days to reach the United States, Australia, or New Zealand and 4–5 days to the United Kingdom or elsewhere in the European Union. All post is sent airmail unless otherwise specified.

The Portuguese postal service—the CTT—has a Web site with some information in English. If you're looking for post office locations and hours, however, you'll need to know a few Portuguese terms: click on the tab labeled *"pesquisa de estações"* ("search for stations or offices"), then click on the words *"estações de correios"* ("mail stations/offices"), and type the name of town or city in the *localidade* (location) field.

➤ INFORMATION: **CTT** (WEB www. ctt.pt).

OVERNIGHT SERVICES

The largest national courier company is Correia Azul, which has branches in cities, large towns, and major resorts. Expect to pay slightly over three times as much as normal postage, and delivery time is generally between two and three days. Other companies include DHL, TNT, and Federal Express. Overnight courier service is only available within Europe.

➤ MAJOR SERVICES: **Correia Azul** (☎ 800/206868). **DHL** (☎ 21/810– 0099). **Federal Express** (☎ 800/ 244144). **TNT** (☎ 21/854–5050).

POSTAL RATES

Airmail letters to the United States and Canada cost €0.54 for up to 15 grams. Letters to the United Kingdom and other EU countries €0.43 for up to 20 grams. Letters within Portugal are €0.28. Postcards cost the same as letters. You can buy *selos* (stamps) at *correios* (post offices) or at kiosks and shops displaying a red CORREIOS–SELOS sign. There are stamp-vending machines scattered about Lisbon.

RECEIVING MAIL

If you're on the move it's best to have your mail sent to American Express; call for lists of offices in Portugal. An alternative is to have mail held at a Portuguese post office; have it addressed to *poste restante* or *lista de correios* (general delivery) in a town you'll be visiting. Postal addresses should include the name of the province and district—for example, Figueira da Foz (Coimbra).

➤ INFORMATION: **American Express** (☎ 800/543–4080).

SHIPPING PARCELS

Although you can send packages by registered air mail, it's best to ship them through the more reliable courier services. In short, don't send anything from a Portuguese post office that you can't afford to lose.

MONEY MATTERS

Lisbon isn't as expensive as most other international capitals, but it's not the extraordinary bargain it used to be. The coastal resort areas from Cascais and Estoril down to the Algarve can be expensive, though there are lower-price hotels and restaurants catering mainly to the package-tour trade. If you head off the beaten track you'll find substantially cheaper food and lodging.

Transportation is still cheap in Portugal when compared with the rest of Europe. Gas prices are controlled by the government, and train and bus travel are inexpensive. Highway tolls are steep but may be worth the cost if you want to bypass the small towns and villages. Flights within the country are costly.

Here are some sample prices. Coffee in a bar: €0.50 (standing), €0.70 (seated). Draft beer in a bar: €0.50 (standing), €0.65 (seated). Bottle of beer: €0.70. Port: €1.50–€10, depending on brand and vintage. Table wine: €5.50 (bottle), €3 (half bottle), €0.60 (small glass). Coca-Cola: €1. Ham-and-cheese sandwich: €1.50. One-kilometer taxi ride: €2.50. Local bus ride: €1. Subway ride: €0.60. Ferry ride in Lisbon: €1–€2, one-way depending on destination. Opera or theater seat: €25—€50, depending on show and location. Nightclub cover charge: €10–€25. Fado performance: €15 for just a show or €25–€40 for dinner and a show. Movie ticket: €4.25–€4.50 (most cinemas offer cheaper tickets on Monday). Foreign newspaper: €1.50–€2.50.

Prices throughout this guide are given for adults. Substantially reduced fees are almost always available for children, students, and senior citizens. For information on taxes, *see* Taxes, *below*.

ATMS

ATMs are ubiquitous, and the Portuguese use them for banking as well as for paying bills and taxes. The Multibanco, or MB, system, is state-of-the-art and reliable. The cards most frequently accepted are Visa, MasterCard, American Express, Eurocheque, Eurocard, and Electron. You need a four-digit PIN to use ATMs in Portugal.

Call Cirrus for locations in the United States and Canada or check out the Web site for locations worldwide. You can also call Plus for locations in North America or use the ATM locator at the Web site. Your local bank can also help you find locations.

➤ ATM LOCATIONS: **Cirrus** (☎ 800/424–7787, WEB www.mastercard.com). **Plus** (☎ 800/843–7587, WEB www.visa.com).

CREDIT CARDS

Throughout this guide, the following abbreviations are used: **AE,** American Express; **DC,** Diners Club; **MC,** MasterCard; and **V,** Visa.

➤ REPORTING LOST CARDS: **American Express** ☎ (21/392–5727); call collect to report loss or theft. **Master-Card** ☎ (800/811272). **Visa** (☎ 800/811107).

CURRENCY

Portugal is one of the European Union countries to use a single currency—the euro (€). Euro notes and coins, issued on 1 January 2002, replaced the escudo, formerly the unit of currency. Coins are issued in denominations of 1, 2, 5, 10, 20, and 50 euro cents. Notes are issued in denominations of €5, 10, 20, 50, 100, 200, and 500.

CURRENCY EXCHANGE

For the most favorable rates, **change money through banks.** Although ATM transaction fees may be higher abroad than at home, ATM rates are excellent because they're based on wholesale rates offered only by major banks. You won't do as well at exchange booths in airports or rail and bus stations, in hotels, in restaurants, or in stores. To avoid lines at airport exchange booths, **pick up some euros before you leave home.**

➤ EXCHANGE SERVICES: **International Currency Express** (☎ 888/278–6628 orders). **Thomas Cook Currency Services** (☎ 800/287–7362 orders and retail locations, WEB www.us. thomascook.com).

TRAVELER'S CHECKS

Do you need traveler's checks? It depends on where you're headed. If you're going to rural areas and small towns, go with cash; traveler's checks are best used in cities. Lost or stolen checks can usually be replaced within 24 hours. To ensure a speedy refund, buy your own traveler's checks— don't let someone else pay for them: irregularities like this can cause delays. The person who bought the checks should make the call to request a refund.

OUTDOORS AND SPORTS

FISHING

Contact the tourist board for a booklet about fishing throughout the country. For information on fishing in the Lisbon area, try the Clube dos Amadores de Pesca de Lisboa (Lisbon Amateur Fishing Club) and the Clube dos Amadores de Pesca da Costa do Sol (Costa do Sol Amateur Fishing Club).

➤ FISHING INFORMATION: **Clube dos Amadores de Pesca da Costa do Sol** (✉ Rua dos Fontainhos 16, Cascais 2750, ☎ 21/484–1691). **Clube dos Amadores de Pesca de Lisboa** (✉ Travessa do Adro 12–1, Vadarande, Lisbon 1100, ☎ 21/885–3385).

GOLF

The Costa Azul, Estremadura, and Beira Alta regions have some of the country's finest championship golf courses; the Algarve alone has more than 23 courses, several of them outstanding. Tourist offices have detailed descriptions of courses and a list of greens fees. You can also get information from the Federação Portuguesa de Golf (Portuguese Golf Federation).

➤ GOLF INFORMATION: **Federação Portuguesa de Golf** (✉ Av. da Túlipas 6, Edificio Miraflores 17, Algés 1495–161, ☎ 21/412–3780). **Golf Web Site** (WEB www.portugalgolf.pt).

HORSEBACK RIDING

Horseback riding is very popular in Portugal, and there are many equestrian centers—particularly in the Algarve—where you can arrange lessons and treks. For information contact the Federação Equestre Portuguesa (Portuguese Equestrian Federation).

➤ HORSEBACK RIDING INFORMATION: **Federação Equestre Portuguesa** (✉ Av. Manuel Maia 24, Chile, Lisbon 1000, ☎ 21/847–8773).

TENNIS

Tennis pros offer classes almost all year long in the resorts; contact tourist offices for a list of courts in the resort areas. For further information, contact the Federação Portuguesa de Tenis (Portuguese Tennis Federation).

➤ TENNIS INFORMATION: **Federação Portuguesa de Tenis** (✉ Box 210, Linda-a-Velha 2795, ☎ 21/419–8472).

WATER SPORTS

Portugal has more than 40 great surfing beaches, including Ericeira and Peniche in Estremadura, Costa Nova in Aveiro, Nazaré, and Esposende in Barcelos. There are also lots of great places for scuba diving. For wind- or kite-surfing, head to Carcavelhos, along the coast toward Cascais; rent a board there and continue on to the awesome beach at Guincho, where shooting a curl is possible even in the winter. Waterskiing is popular in the Algarve and at Lagoa de Óbidos in the Estremadura.

For water-sports information, get in touch with the Federação Portuguesa de Vela (Portuguese Sailing Federation), the Associação Naval de Lisboa (Lisbon Naval Association), the Federação Portuguesa de Atividades Subaquáticas (Portuguese Underwater Sports Federation), and the Federação Portuguesa de Canoagem (Portuguese Canoeing Federation). Water-skiers should contact the Clube Naval de Cascais (Cascais Naval Club).

➤ WATER SPORTS INFORMATION:
Associação Naval de Lisboa (✉ Doca de Belém, Rio Tejo, Lisbon 1300, ☎ 21/661–9480). **Clube Naval de Cascais** (✉ Esplanada Principe D. Luis Filipe, Cascais 2750, ☎ 21/483–0125). **Federação Portuguesa de Atividades Subaquáticas** (✉ Rua José Falcão, Chile, Lisbon 1170, ☎ 21/816–6547). **Federação Portuguesa de Canoagem** (✉ Rua António Pinto Machado 60, Oporto 4100, ☎ 22/543–2237). **Federação Portuguesa de Vela** (✉ Doca de Belém, Rio Tejo, Lisbon 1300, ☎ 21/364–7324 or 21/364–1152).

PACKING

Older generations of Portuguese citizens tend to dress up more than their counterparts in America or the United Kingdom. That said, attitudes toward clothes have become more relaxed in recent years among the younger generations. Jeans, however, are generally still paired with a collared shirt and, if necessary, a sweater or jacket. Dressier outfits are needed for more expensive restaurants, nightclubs, and fado houses, though, and people still frown on shorts in churches. Away from the beaches, bathing suits on the street or in restaurants and shops are not considered good taste. Sightseeing calls for casual, comfortable clothing (well-broken-in low-heel shoes, for example). Summer can be brutally hot; spring and fall, mild to chilly; and winter, cold and rainy. Sunscreen and sunglasses are a good idea any time of the year, since the sun in Portugal is very bright.

In your carry-on luggage, **pack an extra pair of eyeglasses or contact lenses and enough of any medication** you take to last a few days longer than the entire trip. You may also ask your doctor to write a spare prescription using the drug's generic name, since brand names may vary from country to country. In luggage to be checked, **never pack prescription drugs or valuables.** And don't forget to carry with you the addresses of offices that handle refunds of lost traveler's checks. Check *Fodor's How to Pack* (available in bookstores everywhere) for more tips.

To avoid customs and security delays, carry medications in their original packaging. Don't pack any sharp objects in your carry-on luggage, including knives of any size or material, scissors, manicure tools, and corkscrews, or anything else that might arouse suspicion.

CHECKING LUGGAGE

You're allowed one carry-on bag and one personal article, such as a purse or a laptop computer. Make sure that everything you carry aboard will fit under your seat or in the overhead bin. Get to the gate early, so you can board as soon as possible, before the overhead bins fill up.

If you are flying internationally, note that baggage allowances may be determined not by piece but by weight—generally 88 pounds (40 kilograms) in first class, 66 pounds (30 kilograms) in business class, and 44 pounds (20 kilograms) in economy.

Airline liability for baggage is limited to $2,500 per person on flights within the United States. On international flights it amounts to $9.07 per pound or $20 per kilogram for checked baggage (roughly $640 per 70-pound bag) and $400 per passenger for unchecked baggage. You can buy additional coverage at check-in for about $10 per $1,000 of coverage, but it excludes a rather extensive list of items, shown on your airline ticket.

Before departure, **itemize your bags' contents** and their worth, and label the bags with your name, address, and phone number. (If you use your home address, cover it so potential thieves can't see it readily.) Inside each bag, **pack a copy of your itinerary.** At check-in, **make sure that each bag is correctly tagged** with the destination airport's three-letter code. If your bags arrive damaged or fail to arrive at all, file a written report with the airline before leaving the airport.

PASSPORTS AND VISAS

When traveling internationally, **carry your passport** even if you don't need one (it's always the best form of I.D.) and **make two photocopies of the data page** (one for someone at home and another for you, carried separately from your passport). If you lose your passport, promptly call the nearest embassy or consulate and the local police.

U.S. passport applications for children under age 14 require consent from both parents or legal guardians; both parents must appear together to sign the application. If only one parent appears, he or she must submit a written statement from the other parent authorizing passport issuance for the child. A parent with sole authority must present evidence of it when applying; acceptable documentation includes the child's certified birth certificate listing only the applying parent, a court order specifically permitting this parent's travel with the child, or a death certificate for the nonapplying parent. Application forms and instructions are available on the Web site of the U.S. State Department's Bureau of Consular Affairs (www.travel.state.gov).

ENTERING PORTUGAL

Citizens of Australia, Canada, New Zealand, and the United States need a valid passport to enter Portugal for stays of up to 60 days. Visas are required for longer stays and, in some instances, for visits to other countries in addition to Portugal. Citizens of the European Union need a valid passport but can stay indefinitely.

PASSPORT OFFICES

The best time to apply for a passport or to renew is in fall and winter. Before any trip, check your passport's expiration date, and, if necessary, renew it as soon as possible.

➤ AUSTRALIAN CITIZENS: **Australian State Passport Office** (☎ 131–232, WEB www.passports.gov.au).

➤ CANADIAN CITIZENS: **Passport Office** (to mail in applications: ✉ Department of Foreign Affairs and International Trade, Ottawa, Ontario K1A 0G3, ☎ 819/994–3500 or 800/567–6868, WEB www.dfait-maeci.gc.ca/passport).

➤ NEW ZEALAND CITIZENS: **New Zealand Passport Office** (☎ 04/474–8100 or 0800/225050, WEB www.passports.govt.nz).

➤ U.K. CITIZENS: **London Passport Office** (☎ 0870/521–0410, WEB www.passport.gov.uk).

➤ U.S. CITIZENS: **National Passport Information Center** (☎ 900/225–5674, 35¢ per minute for automated service or $1.05 per minute for operator service, WEB www.travel.state.gov).

REST ROOMS

In Portugal restaurants, cinemas, theaters, libraries, and service stations are required to have public toilets, though train stations are likely to have pay toilets. Rest rooms can range from marble-clad opulence to little better than primitive, but in most cases they're reasonably clean. Few are adapted for travelers with disabilities. Women's rest rooms are often looked after by an attendant who customarily receives a tip of €0.50.

SAFETY

Your biggest threat is likely to be petty theft (i.e., pickpocketing and bag snatching). **Don't wear a money belt or a waist pack,** both of which peg you as a tourist. If you carry a purse, choose one with a zipper and a thick strap that you can drape across your body; adjust the length so that the purse sits in front of you at or above hip level. Store only enough money in the purse to cover casual spending. Distribute the rest of your cash and any valuables (including credit cards and your passport) between a deep front pocket, an inside jacket or vest pocket, and a hidden money pouch. Do not reach for the money pouch in public.

Be particularly cautious in crowded areas and in the poorer areas of large cities. Be wary of anyone stopping you on the street to ask for directions, the time, or where you're from—particularly if there's more than one person and if you have recently visited the bank or an ATM.

LOCAL SCAMS

Shopkeepers, restaurateurs, and other business owners are generally honest, and credit card receipts are rarely subject to copying. There have been occasional incidents of highway robbery, where the thief slashes the victim's tires during a stop at a gas station and then follows the victim, offering to "help" when the tire goes completely flat. In other cases, the thief takes advantage of an unwary traveler who has left car keys in the ignition or money or a handbag on the seat while stopped at a gas station.

WOMEN IN PORTUGAL

There's enough of a police presence in Portugal that women traveling solo are relatively safe. Take normal precautions, though. Ask your hotel staff to recommend a reliable cab company, and whenever possible, **call for a taxi instead of hailing one on the street,** especially at night. **Avoid eye contact** with unsavory individuals. If such a person approaches you, discourage him by politely but firmly by saying, "*Por favor, me dê licença*" ("Excuse me, please") and then walk away with resolve. Don't draw attention to yourself by wearing form-fitting clothing, particularly away from the coastal resorts.

SENIOR-CITIZEN TRAVEL

In Portugal, senior citizens usually qualify for museum admission discounts—sometimes of as much as 50% off the cost of an adult ticket. To qualify for age-related discounts, **mention your senior-citizen status up front** when booking hotel reservations (not when checking out) and before you're seated in restaurants (not when paying the bill). Be sure to have identification on hand. When renting a car, ask about promotional car-rental discounts, which can be cheaper than senior-citizen rates.

➤ EDUCATIONAL PROGRAMS: **Elderhostel** (✉ 11 Ave. de Lafayette, Boston, MA 02111-1746, ☎ 877/426–8056, ℻ 877/426–2166, 🌐 www.elderhostel.org). **Interhostel** (✉ University of New Hampshire, 6 Garrison Ave., Durham, NH 03824, ☎ 603/862–1147 or 800/733–9753, ℻ 603/862–1113, 🌐 www.learn.unh.edu).

SHOPPING

The superbly woven baskets sold in markets and gift shops make lightweight and practical gifts. Beautifully hand-embroidered table linens don't weigh much, nor do the embroidered organdy blouses or initialed handkerchiefs that are the specialty of Madeira. Traditional embroidered silk bedspreads are still made in Castelo Branco, and you'll encounter exquisite handmade lace in Vila do Conde near Oporto.

You can find glazed tiles in either single patterns or pictorial panels that you can ship home by freight. Porcelain and pottery are irresistible; Vista Alegre is the oldest and most famous porcelain, with works near Aveiro. The brightly colored roosters (a symbol of Portugal) are made in Barcelos, black pottery in Vila Real, polychrome in Aveiro, and blue and white in Coimbra and Alcobaça. Caldas da Rainha is famous for green glazed plates and dishes made in the form of leaves, vegetables, fruit, and animals. In the Alentejo, particularly in Estremoz, you'll find early Etruscan and Roman shapes reproduced in unglazed red clay pots and jars. There's also a large range of glazed cooking pots in all shapes and sizes, and colored figurines. Marinha Grande is the center for glassware of every kind; Atlantis Crystal is particularly worth seeking out.

The Alentejo is the home of natural cork, and you'll find picture frames, *tarros* (lidded buckets) in which food can be kept hot or cold, and other lightweight gifts. Carved wooden spoons and boxes and lambskin and goatskin slippers are also from this part of the country. Attractive lanterns, fire screens, and outdoor furniture are made from tin, brass, copper, and other metals in the Algarve and Trás-os-Montes. Primitive as well as sophisticated musical instruments (such as guitars, horns, flutes, and bells) are crafted in the Minho, Trás-os-Montes, and the Beiras. Coimbra is famous for its guitars, Estremoz for its clay whistles.

You can buy fine leather shoes, handbags, belts, and gloves all over the country; the same is true of textiles such as cotton and colorful wool blankets. Fine-leather bookbinding is another specialty. Needlepoint and embroidered carpets and rugs are the hallmarks of Arraiolas in the Alentejo, and Portalegre has the nation's finest tapestry shops. Portuguese jewelry is also lovely: The gold is 19.25 karat here, and you can find modern brooches and earrings, as well as many exquisite pieces based on ancient designs.

WATCH OUT

If you buy valuable items, such as antiques, contact agents at the local *alfândega* (customs office). They'll provide you with the necessary forms. Taxes are paid by the receiver, and there are different forms required depending on whether the goods are to be exported within the European Union or outside of it.

STUDENTS IN PORTUGAL

International Student Identity Cards aren't always accepted in Portugal. If you're under 26 years of age, you should also buy a Cartâc Joven (Youth Card) at a post office or a bank. It will definitely get you discounts on admission to many sights and museums.

➤ I.D.s AND SERVICES: **STA Travel** (☎ 212/627–3111 or 800/781–4040, FAX 212/627–3387, WEB www.sta.com). **Travel Cuts** (✉ 187 College St., Toronto, Ontario M5T 1P7, Canada, ☎ 416/979–2406 or 888/838–2887, FAX 416/979–8167, WEB www.travelcuts.com).

TAXES

VALUE-ADDED TAX

Value-added tax (IVA, pronounced *ee-vah*, in Portuguese) is 12% for hotels. By law prices must be posted at the reception desk and should indicate whether tax is included. Restaurants are also required to charge 12% IVA. Menus generally state at the bottom whether tax is included (*IVA incluido*) or not (*mas 12% IVA*). When in doubt about whether tax is included in a price, ask: *Está incluido o IVA?*

When making a purchase, **ask for a V.A.T. refund form.** Have the form stamped like any customs form by customs officials when you leave the country or, if you're visiting several European Union countries, when you leave the EU. Be ready to show customs officials what you've bought (pack purchases together, in your carry-on luggage); budget extra time for this. After you're through passport control, take the form to a refund-service counter for an on-the-spot refund, or mail it back to the store or a refund service after you arrive home.

A refund service can save you some hassle, for a fee. Global Refund is a Europe-wide service with 130,000 affiliated stores and more than 700 refund counters—located at every major airport and border crossing. Its refund form is called a Shopping Cheque. The service issues refunds in the form of cash, check, or credit-card adjustment, minus a processing fee. If you don't have time to wait at the refund counter, you can mail in the form instead.

A number of Portuguese stores, particularly large ones and those in resorts, offer a refund of the 19% IVA on single items worth more than €80. Be sure to ask for your tax-free check; you show your passport, fill out a form, and the store mails you the refund at home.

➤ V.A.T. REFUNDS: **Global Refund** (✉ 99 Main St., Suite 307, Nyack, NY 10960, ☎ 800/566–9828, FAX 845/348–1549, WEB www.globalrefund.com).

TELEPHONES

All phone numbers have nine digits, the first two being the area code in or around Lisbon and Oporto, the first three anywhere else in the country. All fixed-phone area codes begin with 2; mobile numbers, which also have nine digits, begin with 9.

AREA AND COUNTRY CODES

The country code for Portugal is 351. When dialing a Portuguese number from abroad, dial the nine-digit number after the country code.

DIRECTORY AND OPERATOR ASSISTANCE

For general information, dial 118 (operators often speak English). The international information and assistance numbers are 171 for operator-assisted calls, 172 for collect calls, and 177 for information (the operators speak English).

INTERNATIONAL CALLS

Calling abroad is expensive from hotels, which often add a considerable surcharge. The best way to make an international call is to go to the local telephone office and have someone place it for you. Every town has such an establishment, and big cities have several. When the call is connected, you'll be directed to a quiet cubicle and charged according to the meter. If the price is €10 or more, you can pay with Visa or MasterCard. Lisbon's main phone office is in the Praça dos Restauradores, right off the Rossío.

To make an international call yourself, dial 00 followed directly by the country code (1 for the United States, 44 for the United Kingdom, 61 for Australia, and 64 for New Zealand) and the area code and number. The Portuguese telephone directory contains a list of all of the principal world country codes and the codes for principal cities.

LONG-DISTANCE CALLS

To make calls to other areas within Portugal, precede the provincial code with 0 (most phone booths have a chart inside listing the various province codes). The 0 is unnecessary when dialing from outside Portugal.

LONG-DISTANCE SERVICES

AT&T, MCI, and Sprint access codes make calling long distance relatively convenient, but you may find the local access number blocked in many hotel rooms. First ask the hotel operator to connect you. If the hotel operator balks, ask for an international operator, or dial the international operator yourself. One way to improve your odds of getting connected to your long-distance carrier is to travel with more than one company's calling card (a hotel may block Sprint, for example, but not MCI). If all else fails, call from a pay phone.

➤ ACCESS CODES: **AT&T Direct** (☎ 800/800128 in Portugal; 800/222-0300 for other areas). **MCI World-Phone** (☎ 800/800123 in Portugal; 800/444-4141 for other areas). **Sprint International Access** (☎ 800/800187 in Portugal; 800/877-4646 for other areas).

PUBLIC PHONES

You can ask to use the phone in cafés or bars, where they're often metered. The waiter or bartender will charge you after you've finished, though expect to pay a higher rate than the one you would pay in a public phone booth.

The easiest way to call from a public booth is to use a Portugal Telecom *cartão telefônico* (calling card), which you can buy at post offices, newspaper shops, and tobacconists for either €5 or €10. The phones that accept them have digital readouts, so you can see your time ticking away. Instructions in several languages, including English, are posted in the booths. With coin-operated phones you insert coins and wait for a dial tone. The minimum cost for a local call is €0.20; it's €0.50 to call another area, for which you must dial the area code.

➤ INFORMATION: **Portugal Telecom** (WEB www.telecom.pt/uk/).

TIME

Portugal sets its clocks according to Greenwich Mean Time, five hours ahead of the U.S. East Coast. Portuguese summer time (GMT plus one hour) requires an additional adjustment from late March to late October.

TIPPING

Service is included in café, restaurant, and hotel bills, but waiters and other service people are poorly paid, and you can be sure your contribution will be appreciated. If, however, you received bad service, never feel obligated (or intimidated) to leave a tip. An acceptable tip is 10%-15% of the total bill, and if you have a sandwich or *petiscos* (appetizers) at a bar, leave less, just enough to round out the bill to the nearest €0.50. Cocktail waiters get €0.30-€0.50 a drink, depending on the bar.

Taxi drivers get about 10% of the meter; more for long rides or extra help with luggage (note that there's also an official surcharge for airport runs and baggage). Hotel porters should receive €1 a bag; a doorman who calls you a taxi, €0.50. Tip €1 for room service and €1–€2 per night for maid service. Tip a concierge for any additional help he or she gives you.

Tip tour guides €2–€5, depending on how knowledgeable they are and on the length of the tour. Ushers in theaters or bullfights get €0.50; barbers and hairdressers (for a wash and a set) at least €1. Washroom attendants are tipped €0.50.

TOURS AND PACKAGES

Because everything is prearranged on a prepackaged tour or independent vacation, you spend less time planning—and often get it all at a good price.

BOOKING WITH AN AGENT

Travel agents are excellent resources. But it's a good idea to collect brochures from several agencies, as some agents' suggestions may be influenced by relationships with tour and package firms that reward them for volume sales. If you have a special interest, **find an agent with expertise in that area**; the American Society of Travel Agents (ASTA; ☞ Travel Agencies, *below*) has a database of specialists worldwide.

Make sure your travel agent knows the accommodations and other services of the place being recommended. Ask about the hotel's location, room size, beds, and whether it has a pool, room service, or programs for children, if you care about these. Has your agent been there in person or sent others whom you can contact?

Do some homework on your own, too: local tourism boards can provide information about lesser-known and small-niche operators, some of which may sell only direct.

BUYER BEWARE

Each year consumers are stranded or lose their money when tour operators—even large ones with excellent reputations—go out of business. So **check out the operator.** Ask several travel agents about its reputation, and try to **book with a company that has a consumer-protection program.** (Look for information in the company's brochure.) In the United States, members of the National Tour Association and the United States Tour Operators Association are required to set aside funds to cover your payments and travel arrangements in the event that the company defaults. It's also a good idea to choose a company that participates in the American Society of Travel Agents' Tour Operator Program (TOP); ASTA will act as mediator in any disputes between you and your tour operator.

Remember that the more your package or tour includes the better you can predict the ultimate cost of your vacation. Make sure you know exactly what is covered, and **beware of hidden costs.** Are taxes, tips, and transfers included? Entertainment and excursions? These can add up.

➤ TOUR-OPERATOR RECOMMENDATIONS: **American Society of Travel Agents** (☞ Travel Agencies, *below*). **National Tour Association** (NTA; ✉ 546 E. Main St., Lexington, KY 40508, ☎ 859/226–4444 or 800/682–8886, WEB www.ntaonline.com). **United States Tour Operators Association** (USTOA; ✉ 275 Madison Ave., Suite 2014, New York, NY 10016, ☎ 212/599–6599 or 800/468–7862, FAX 212/599–6744, WEB www.ustoa.com).

TRAIN TRAVEL

The country is served by a direct, nightly train between Spain and Portugal. The train departs from Madrid's Chamartin station at 10:45 PM and arrives at Lisbon's Santa Apolónia station at 8:15 the following morning; for the reverse trip, the train leaves Lisbon at 10 PM, arriving in Madrid at 8:25 AM the next day. There's also train service between Lisbon's Santa Apolónia station and Paris (Montparnasse and Austerlitz stations). On some trips, you change onto a French TGV (high-speed train) at the Spain–France border to go on to Paris; note that you may need special reservations for this leg of the journey.

Portugal's train network covers most of the country, though it's thin in the Alentejo region. The cities of Lisbon, Coimbra, Aveiro, and Oporto are linked by the fast, extremely comfortable Alfa and Alfa Pendular (tilt train) services. Most other major towns and cities are connected by InterCidade trains, which are reliable, though slower and less luxurious than the Alfa trains. The regional services that connect smaller towns and villages tend to be infrequent and slow, with stops at every station along the line.

The standards of comfort vary from Alfa train luxury—with air-conditioning, food service, and airline-type seats—to the often spartan conditions on regional lines. Most InterCidade trains have bar and restaurant facilities, but the food is famously unappealing. A first-class ticket will cost you 40% more than a second-class one and will buy you extra leg and elbow room but not a great deal more on the Alfa and InterCidade trains. The extra cost is definitely worth it on most regional services, however. Smoking is restricted to special carriages on all Portuguese trains.

CUTTING COSTS

To save money, **look into rail passes.** But be aware that if you don't plan to cover many miles you may come out ahead by buying individual tickets. Portugal is one of the countries in which you can **use Eurail-passes,** which provide unlimited first-class rail travel, in all of the participating countries, for the duration of the pass. If you plan to rack up the miles, get a standard pass. These are available for 15 days, 21 days, one month, two months, and three months.

In addition to standard Eurailpasses, **ask about special rail-pass plans.** Among these are the Eurail Youth-pass (in second class for those under age 26), the Eurail Saverpass (which gives a discount for two or more people traveling together), a Eurail Flexipass (which allows 10 or 15 travel days within a two-month period), the Euraildrive Pass and the Europass Drive (which combines travel by train and rental car). It's best to **purchase your pass before you leave** for Europe.

Many travelers assume that rail passes guarantee them seats on the trains they wish to ride. Not so. You need to **book seats ahead even if you are using a rail pass;** seat reservations are required on some European trains, particularly high-speed trains, and are a good idea on trains that may be crowded—particularly in summer on popular routes. You will also need a reservation if you purchase sleeping accommodations.

➤ INFORMATION AND PASSES: **Rail Europe** (☎ 800/942–4866 or 800/274–8724; 0870/584–8848 U.K. credit-card bookings; WEB www.raileurope.com).

PAYING

Major credit cards (Visa, Master-Card, American Express) or cash are the best forms of payment. Traveler's checks may or may not be accepted, depending on the size of the station.

RESERVATIONS

Advance booking isn't required on Portuguese trains but is definitely recommended in the case of popular services like the Alfa trains. Reservations are also advisable for other trains if you want to avoid long lines in front of the ticket window on the day the train leaves. You can avoid a trip out to the station to make the reservation by asking a travel agent to take care of it for you.

SCHEDULES

If you speak Portuguese, you can call the general information number of the Caminhos de Ferro Portugueses (CP) for schedule and other information. Otherwise check the Web site, or head to a train station information desk for a printed timetable.

➤ TRAIN INFORMATION: **CP** (☎ 21/888–4025, 800/200904, or 808/208208, WEB www.cp.pt).

TRAVEL AGENCIES

A good travel agent puts your needs first. Look for an agency that has been in business at least five years, emphasizes customer service, and has someone on staff who specializes in your destination. In addition, **make sure the agency belongs to a professional trade organization.** The American Society of Travel Agents (ASTA)—the largest and most influential in the field with more than 24,000 members in some 140 countries—maintains and enforces a strict code of ethics and will step in to help mediate any agent-client disputes involving ASTA members if necessary. ASTA (whose motto is "Without a travel agent, you're on your own") also maintains a Web site that includes a directory of agents. (If a travel agency is also acting as your tour operator, *see* Buyer Beware *in* Tours and Packages, *above*.)

➤ LOCAL AGENT REFERRALS: **American Society of Travel Agents** (ASTA; ⊠ 1101 King St., Suite 200, Alexandria, VA 22314, ☎ 800/965–2782 24-hr hot line, FAX 703/739–3268, WEB www.astanet.com). **Association of British Travel Agents** (⊠ 68–71 Newman St., London W1T 3AH, ☎ 020/7637–2444, FAX 020/7637–0713, WEB www.abtanet.com). **Association of Canadian Travel Agents** (⊠ 130 Albert St., Suite 1705, Ottawa, Ontario K1P 5G4, ☎ 613/237–3657, FAX 613/237–7052, WEB www.acta.ca). **Australian Federation of Travel Agents** (⊠ Level 3, 309 Pitt St., Sydney, NSW 2000, ☎ 02/9264–3299, FAX 02/9264–1085, WEB www.afta.com.au). **Travel Agents' Association of New Zealand** (⊠ Level 5, Tourism and Travel House, 79 Boulcott St., Box 1888, Wellington 6001, ☎ 04/499–0104, FAX 04/499–0827, WEB www.taanz.org.nz).

VISITOR INFORMATION

➤ PORTUGUESE NATIONAL TOURIST OFFICE: In the United Kingdom: ⊠ 22–25A Sackville St., London W1X 1DE, ☎ 020/7494–1441. In the United States: ⊠ 590 5th Ave., 4th floor, New York, NY 10036, ☎ 212/354–4403. In Canada: ⊠ 60 Bloor St. W, Suite 1005, Toronto, Ontario M4W 3BS, ☎ 416/921–7376.

➤ U.S. GOVERNMENT ADVISORIES: **U.S. Department of State** (⊠ Overseas Citizens Services Office, Room 4811, 2201 C St. NW, Washington, DC 20520, ☎ 888/407–4747 or 202/647–5225 interactive hot line, WEB www.travel.state.gov); enclose a business-size SASE.

WEB SITES

Do check out the World Wide Web when planning your trip. You'll find everything from weather forecasts to virtual tours of famous cities. Be sure to **visit Fodors.com** (www.fodors.com), a complete travel-planning site. You can research prices and book plane tickets, hotel rooms, rental cars, vacation packages, and more. In addition, you can post your pressing questions in the Travel Talk section. Other planning tools include a currency converter and weather reports, and there are loads of links to travel resources.

TAP Air Portugal's site, at **www.tap-airportugal.pt/**, has flight schedules and booking information. You'll find general and business information at **www.portugal.net,** which has a link to the slow-to-load but rich-in-wisdom **www.portugalinsite.com**—the official tourism site. You can order tourist-board brochures with information on a variety of travel-related topics and activities through **www.orderportugal.com.**

The Portuguese National Trust has a beautiful site (**www.ippar.pt**) with information on the many historic buildings and monuments that it oversees. The sites **www.portugal-info.net, www.portugaltravelguide.com,** and **www.portugalvirtual.com** provide quick access to a variety of information, including many links.

For details about each of Portugal's state-owned inns, visit **www.pousadas.com.** For information on hotels, try **www.hotelguide.pt.** For wine information, visit **www.vinhoverde.pt** and **www.ivp.pt.** If golf is your game, head to **www.portugalgolf.pt.**

WHEN TO GO

Peak season begins in spring and lasts through the autumn. In midsummer it's never unbearably hot (except in parts of the Algarve and on the mainland plains); along the coast, cool breezes often spring up in the evening. In the Algarve, springtime begins in February with a marvelous range of wildflowers. Late September and early October herald Indian summer, which ensures warm sunshine through November. Winter is mild and frequently rainy, except in Madeira, where it feels like spring every day.

CLIMATE

➤ FORECASTS: **Weather Channel Connection** (☎ 900/932–8437), 95¢ per minute from a Touch-Tone phone.

The following are average daily maximum and minimum temperatures for major cities in Portugal.

FARO

Jan.	59F	15C	May	72F	22C	Sept.	79F	26C
	48	9		57	14		66	19
Feb.	61F	16C	June	77F	25C	Oct.	72F	22C
	50	10		64	18		61	16
Mar.	64F	18C	July	82F	28C	Nov.	66F	19C
	52	11		68	20		55	13
Apr.	68F	20C	Aug.	82F	28C	Dec.	61F	16C
	55	13		68	20		60	10

LISBON

Jan.	57F	14C	May	71F	21C	Sept.	79F	26C
	46	8		55	13		62	17
Feb.	59F	15C	June	77F	25C	Oct.	72F	22C
	47	8		60	15		58	14
Mar.	63F	17C	July	81F	27C	Nov.	63F	17C
	50	10		63	17		52	11
Apr.	67F	20C	Aug.	82F	28C	Dec.	58F	15C
	53	12		63	17		47	9

OPORTO

Jan.	55F	13C	May	68F	20C	Sept.	75F	24C
	41	5		52	11		57	14
Feb.	57F	14C	June	73F	23C	Oct.	70F	21C
	41	5		55	13		52	11
Mar.	61F	16C	July	77F	25C	Nov.	63F	17C
	46	8		59	15		46	8
Apr.	64F	18C	Aug.	77F	25C	Dec.	57F	14C
	48	9		59	15		41	5

FESTIVALS AND SEASONAL EVENTS

Religious celebrations, called *festas* (feasts or festivals), *feiras* (fairs), and *romarias* (pilgrimages or processions), are held throughout the year. Some of the leading annual events are listed below. Verify the dates with the people at the Portuguese tourism office, who can also send you a complete list of events.

➤ FEB.–MAR.: **Carnaval** (Carnival), the final festival before Lent, is held throughout the country, with processions of masked participants, parades of decorated vehicles, and displays of flowers.

➤ MAR.–APR.: Aveiro's large, colorful **Feira do Março** (March Fair) has been celebrated for more than 500 years. It features folk music and dancing on weekends. **Semana Santa**

(Holy Week) festivities are held in Braga, Ovar, Póvoa de Varzim, and other cities and major towns, with the most important events taking place on Monday, Thursday, and Good Friday. On the second Sunday after Easter, Loulé hosts the **Romaria da Senhora da Piedade** (Our Lady of Mercy), a procession to the local shrine of Monte da Piedade. The **Festival de Flores** in the last week of April, brightens downtown Funchal with a carpet of *flores* (flowers), a parade, and a lot of music.

➤ MAY: Legend has it that, in the early 16th century, a peasant who insisted on working on the Day of the Holy Cross saw a perfumed, luminous cross appear on the ground where he was digging. Ever since, Barcelos has held the colorful **Festas das Cruzes** (of the Crosses), with a large fair, concerts, an affecting procession, and a fireworks display on the Rio Cavado. Celebrations enlivened by performances of traditional song and dance take place on **May 1** in Loulé. During the **Romaria de Fátima,** thousands make the pilgrimage to the town from all over the world to commemorate the first apparition of the Virgin to the shepherd children on May 13, 1917. In Coimbra, the **Queima das Fitas** (Burning of the Ribbons) celebrated by the university students is quite a party.

➤ MAY–JULY: The Algarve's **Festival International da Música Clássica**—a series of classical music performances by leading Portuguese and foreign artists—is held in Faro, Tavira, Albufeira, Portimão, and Lagos.

➤ JUNE: Monção celebrates the **Festa do Corpo de Deus** (Corpus Christi), which includes a symbolic battle between good and evil. Amarante hosts the **Festa de São Gonçalo,** when St. Gonçalo is commemorated by the baking of phallus-shape cakes, which are then exchanged between unmarried men and women. Events also include a fair, folk dancing, and traditional singing. The **Feira Nacional** (National Fair) in Santarém has bullfighting, folk songs and dancing, and fair amusements.

Each June 29, São Pedro de Sintra hosts the large **Festa de São Pedro** (St. Peter) with riotous hullabaloo. Lisbon's **Santos Popularos** (Saints' Days) honors Santo António, the city's patron saint, on June 13 and São João (St. John) on June 23 and 24. The **Festa de São João** is especially colorful in Oporto, where the whole city erupts with bonfires and barbecues and every corner has its own *cascatas* (arrangements with religious motifs). Locals roam the streets, hitting passersby on the head with, among other things, leeks and plastic hammers.

➤ JUNE–SEPT.: For four weeks the **Noites de Queluz** (Queluz Nights) festival is staged in the gardens of the Palácio Nacional. Complete with costumed cast and orchestra, this event mimics the concerts, fireworks displays, and other activities held in the gardens to amuse Queen Maria I, who lived in the palace throughout her long reign (1777–1816) and whose eccentric behavior earned her the name "Mad" Queen Maria. The **Festival de Sintra** runs from June through September and features piano recitals, operas, and ballet in the town's palaces, churches, and parks. Performances in the gardens of the Palácio de Seteais are especially popular.

➤ JULY: Silves hosts a **Festival de Cerveja** (Beer Festival), where you can sample all the different kinds of Portuguese beer, watch folk dances, and listen to music. July sees the **Cascais Festival de Jazz.** The **Festa do Colete Encarnado** (Red Waistcoat) in Vila Franca de Xira honors the *campinos* (cowboys) who guard the brave bulls in the pastures of the Ribatejo. Streets are cordoned off, and bulls are let loose as would-be bullfighters try their luck at dodging the beasts.

Held in even-numbered years, Coimbra's **Festas da Rainha Santa** (Queen Saint) is marked by processions and fireworks along the Rio Mondego. In Guimarães the **Festas de São Torcato** (St. Torcato) consists of a fair and a procession to the nearby village of São Torcato. The **Feira de Santiago**

(St. James) in Setúbal includes various folkloric events, rides, food stalls, and other entertainment. Faro's **Festa e Feira da Senhora do Carmo** (Our Lady of Carmen) consists of a religious procession and an agricultural fair.

➤ JULY–AUG.: The **Festival da Música de Estoril** sees concerts by leading Portuguese and foreign artists in several towns along the Estoril Coast.

➤ AUG.: Guimarães's hosts **Festas Gualterianas** (St. Walter) on the first Sunday of the month. It's a boisterous evening that dates from the 15th century. Mirandela's **Festa de Nossa Senhora do Amparo** (Our Lady of Aid), on the first Sunday, includes dancing, games, and fireworks. On the second Sunday, auto drivers celebrating the **Festa de São Cristovão** converge on the church in Penha, near Guimarães, to commemorate their patron St. Christopher. Gouveia's **Festa do Senhor do Calvario** (Our Lord of Calvary) features a colorful procession, a handicrafts fair, games, and a sheepdog competition.

The **Festa de Nossa Senhora do Monte** (Our Lady of the Mountain) attracts pilgrims from all corners of Madeira. Ofir and Esposende celebrate the **Festas do São Bartolomeu do Mar** (St. Bartholomew of the Sea), when rowdy revelries can be enjoyed at the water's edge. Machico celebrates the **Santissimo Sacramento** (Sacred Sacrament) festival with a sunset bonfire of pine-tree logs, branches, and cones in the center of town under a ceremonial arch. Viana do Castelo's three-day **Romaria de Nossa Senhora da Agonia** (Our Lady of Sorrows), on the weekend closest to August 20, includes a procession in which a statue of the lady is carried over carpets of flowers to a chapel. There are also two parades: one of fishermen who head to the sea to be blessed by a bishop, and another of local beauties wearing colorful hand-embroidered costumes.

➤ AUG.–SEPT.: Viseu's **Feira de São Mateus** (St. Matthew), an important agricultural event with folk dancing and singing, has been held since the Middle Ages. During the **Festas de Nossa Senhora dos Remédios** (Our Lady of Remedies), the annual pilgrimage to the shrine, many penitents climb the steps on their knees. The main procession is September 8, but the festivities start at the end of August and include concerts, dancing, parades, a fair, and torchlit processions. The *moliceiros* (kelp boats) are given a fresh coat of paint and can be seen racing against each other during the **Festa da Ria** (of the Ria) held throughout August and September in the Ria de Aveiro.

➤ SEPT.: The **Romaria de São Gens** (St. Gens) brings ceramic vendors from all over the country to Freixo de Cima, west of Amarante. The **Festas de Nossa Senhora de Nazaré** (Our Lady of Nazaré) includes bullfights, folk dancing and singing, and processions of fishermen. The **Festa das Vindimas** (Grape Harvest) in Palmela has a symbolic treading of the grapes and a blessing of the harvest, accompanied by a parade of harvesters, wine tastings, the election of the Queen of the Wine, and fireworks.

In Ponte de Lima the **Feiras Novas** (New Fairs)—which, despite its name, has been held since the 12th century—includes a fair, a procession, fireworks, and music. During the **Festas de Nossa Sehnora de Boa Viagem** (Our Lady of the Good Voyage) in the ancient town of Moita (near Setúbal), the focus is on blessing the fishing boats. In the annual **Festival da Musica e Dança Folclórica** the singing and dancing in all the Algarve's larger towns culminates at Praia da Rocha, with performances by folk groups from all over the country. A **Festival da Colheita do Vinho** (Wine Harvest)—which sees plenty of singing, dancing, and wine tasting—is celebrated in Funchal and nearby Estreito da Câmara de Lobos.

➤ OCT.: Faro's **Feira de Santa Iria** (St. Iria) is another happy excuse to hold traditional celebrations for several days. The **Romaria de Fátima** brings thousands of pilgrims to Fátima to honor the last apparition of the Virgin on October 12, 1917. **Feira de Outubro** (October Fair) in Vila

Franca de Xira, a short distance from Lisbon, has farming and agricultural activities, handicraft displays, bull-fights, and a running of the bulls in the streets. The Algarve's **Feira de Outubro** gathers together crafts, goods, and produce from villages throughout the Serra de Monchique.

➤ LATE OCT.–EARLY NOV.: The **Festival Nacional de Gastronomia** (National Gastronomy Festival) in Santarém consists of traditional regional dishes, cooking contests, and lectures. At Chaves's **Feira dos Santos** (Saints' Fair) you can buy anything from livestock and farm equipment to wool capes, regional black pottery, rugs, baskets, and gold jewelry. The **Feira Nacional do Cavalo** (National Horse Fair) in Golegã coincides with a festival honoring St. Martin, combining parades of saddle and bull-fighting horses with riding competitions, handicrafts exhibitions, and wine tastings.

➤ DEC.: **Festa de São Sylvester** (St. Sylvester), on New Year's Eve, transforms Funchal into a vast fairground, with bands of strolling dancers and singers, thousands of lights, and breathtaking fireworks.

1 DESTINATION: PORTUGAL

Where Europe and the Atlantic Meet

What's Where

Pleasures and Pastimes

Fodor's Choice

Great Itineraries

WHERE EUROPE AND THE ATLANTIC MEET

PORTUGAL DEFIES EXPECTATIONS. West across the Iberian Peninsula from Spain's arid plains and burning sun, it provides many of the same things as Spain, including fine food and wine, spectacular castles, medieval hill towns, and excellent beaches. But the Portuguese language is a world apart from Spanish, and although the two countries share a Mediterranean air, Portugal firmly faces the Atlantic. The contrasts are just as dramatic within the country. The people look markedly Celtic in the north and rather Moorish in the south. The weather along the coast is mild, but bracing Atlantic waters temper the warmth of the beaches. And the coastal towns crowded with sun seekers differ greatly from the verdant valleys and rugged mountains where visitors are few and centuries-old traditions are cherished. Even in Lisbon the differences are apparent—from the Alfama's twisting streets, a remnant of the Moorish occupation, to the austere Romanesque cathedral. The challenge of planning a trip to here is deciding which enchanting aspects to explore.

The Ancients, the Romans, and the Moors

Blessed with a salubrious climate and abundant game and fish, this part of the Iberian Peninsula once supported a flourishing prehistoric population. Many traces of ancient culture remain: the sculpted-stone boar fertility symbols in Trás-os-Montes; the huge Colossus of Pedralva, a mysterious seated granite figure on display in the Museu Martins Sarmento in Guimarães; the fascinating megalithic structures throughout the Alentejo; and the Paleolithic rock engravings in northern Portugal. The later arrival of Celtic peoples in northern Portugal (700 BC–600 BC) is recorded in a series of *citânias* (fortified hill settlements) throughout the Minho; the most impressive example is at Briteiros, between Braga and Guimarães. Phoenicians traded at the site of present-day Lisbon, and the Carthaginians and Greeks set up trading posts on Portugal's southern shore. But it wasn't until the Roman annexation of the peninsula after the Second Punic War

(218 BC–202 BC) that the region came under any kind of unified control.

There was resistance to the Roman advance, particularly in central Portugal, where the heroic chieftain Viriatus of the Lusitani tribe held the legions at bay for several decades, until his defeat in 139 BC. Much from the Roman period survives in modern Portugal. Roads, aqueducts, and bridges (such as those at Chaves and Ponte de Lima) were built, and cities founded. The most substantial remains are near Coimbra, where there are well-preserved ruins of a Roman town called Conímbriga, and at Santiago do Cacém, where remnants of another Roman town, Miróbriga, have been excavated. Évora has one of the best preserved Roman temples on the Iberian Peninsula. A less obvious Roman relic is the system of vast agricultural *latifundia* (estates) established in the Alentejo. Here the Romans introduced the crops that are now mainstays of the Portuguese economy: wheat, barley, olives, and grapes.

The Moorish invasion of the Iberian Peninsula in 711 had a lasting effect on the country, particularly in the south, where place-names and people's features still reflect those times. The Moors established a capital at Silves in the Algarve (derived from the Moorish, *al-Gharb,* meaning "west of the land beyond"), planted great orchards on irrigated land, and spread a Moorish Arab culture of great significance, although they allowed freedom of worship.

Arab rule stood firm until the 12th century, when Christian forces under Dom Afonso Henriques moved south from their stronghold at Guimarães in the Minho to take Moorish towns and castles at Leiria, Santarém, and Sintra. The ramparts and battlements of these fortresses are visible today, a reminder of both the Moorish genius for siting defenses and of the Christian effort in overcoming them. The most significant victory was at Lisbon in 1147, with the storming of the Moorish fortress on the site of the present-day Castelo de São Jorge. A Burgundian by descent,

Afonso Henriques was by then being called the first king of all Portugal, and he ordered the building of Lisbon's proud *Sé* (Cathedral) to celebrate the victory. Many other churches in Portugal mark the path of the reconquest (as the Moors were pushed south), particularly the numerous Romanesque chapels that cover the landscape between the Rios Minho and Douro (Minho and Douro rivers).

Southern Alentejo and the Algarve remained in Arab hands until the mid-13th century, by which time the fledgling kingdom of Portugal extended to its current borders. The country reached its final shape in 1260, when Afonso III—who retook Faro and the western Algarve from the Moors—moved the capital from Coimbra to Lisbon.

An Empire on the Atlantic

The early kings of Portugal, from the dynastic House of Burgundy, quickly established their independent country. Although the nation was recognized by the neighboring Castilian rulers, fortresses were built along the Spanish frontier as a precaution. Those at Beja and Estremoz are evocative examples. A Cortes (Parliament) was assembled, and a university founded, initially in Lisbon in 1290 but transferred to Coimbra in 1308. (The grand university buildings that you see in Coimbra today date from the 16th century, when the scholastic foundation was declared permanent; it remained the only university in Portugal until the last century.)

The House of Burgundy was succeeded by the House of Aviz, whose first king, Dom João I, roundly defeated the Castilian army at the Battle of Aljubarrota (1385) to end any lingering Castilian thoughts of dominion over Portugal. This significant victory secured Portugal's independence for nearly two centuries and allowed the country's kings to turn their attention to the maritime ventures that were to guarantee them fabulous colonial wealth. João I marked the victory by building the extraordinary abbey of Santa Maria da Vitória at Batalha in Estremadura, not far from the battlefield. Triumphant in tone, the abbey celebrates not only the Portuguese release from Castilian interference, but also an important historic link with England. The Treaty of Windsor, signed a year after the battle, confirmed the Anglo-Portuguese alliance, and in 1387 João I married Philippa of Lancaster, daughter of John of Gaunt. Philippa and João are buried side by side in the abbey's chapel, as are their children, one of whom was Prince Henry the Navigator, the man who did the most to influence Portugal's rapid 15th-century expansion.

Based at Sagres, on the Algarve's western tip, Prince Henry surrounded himself with sailors, mapmakers, and astrologers. These men were the first to establish the principles of navigation on the high seas. The caravel, a ship capable of navigating in a crosswind, was developed, and famous maritime discoveries were soon under way: Madeira and the Azores were discovered in 1419 and 1427, respectively, and by 1460 (when Henry died) the west coast of Africa was known to Portuguese seamen. There were no limits to the inquisitiveness or to the bravery of the sailors. Bartolomeu Dias rounded the southern tip of Africa in 1487, naming it the Cape of Good Hope; just 10 years later, Vasco da Gama reached India; and in 1500 Pedro Álvares Cabral sailed to Brazil. By the mid-16th century, the Portuguese empire had spread over four continents, with trading posts in the Far East and a monopoly in force throughout the Indian Ocean.

The wealth gained from this aggressive expansion knew no bounds. Portugal was at the height of its influence, with Lisbon the richest city in Europe, and under Dom Manuel I (1495–1521) the Portuguese crown intervened to take a fifth of the maritime trading profits. Manuel began to adorn the country with buildings and monuments worthy of an imperial power, and the late-Gothic architecture that evolved has since come to be called the Manueline style. If there's any doubt about the brimming confidence of that era, one look at the Manueline buildings will dispel it immediately.

The interior decoration of the Igreja de Jesus (Church of Jesus), begun in 1494 in Setúbal, near Lisbon, is considered the earliest example of the Manueline style. It was soon overshadowed by exuberant works in the capital itself, at Belém's Mosteiro dos Jerónimos (Jerónimos Monastery) and Torre de Belém (Belém Tower). The abbey of Batalha was transformed by its Manueline renovations; in particular the portal of the Capelas Imperfeitas (Unfinished Chapels), which is among the most impressive of all Manueline works. A tour of any of these buildings is a requisite to understanding the untrammeled power and influence of 16th-century Portugal as well as the country's strong national identity. The pride in these buildings, which goes beyond mere architectural prowess, is most evident in Tomar's Convento de Cristo, whose supreme Manueline ornamentation stands as the most eloquent reminder of the Portuguese age of *os descobrimentos* (the discoveries).

The buildings have survived, but the glories of the Portuguese empire were relatively short-lived. Arts and literature flourished for a while with the emergence of the 16th-century dramatist Gil Vicente and the publication in 1572 of the great poet Luís de Camões's epic *Lusiads,* which told of the proud era of discovery. But the disastrous crusade in Morocco by the young Dom Sebastião in 1578, during which the king perished alongside most of the country's nobility, allowed Phillip II of Spain to renew a claim on Portugal. Camões died in the same year Portugal fell to Spain, and it's said his last words were, "I am dying at the same time as my country."

Portugal's Dark Ages
Spanish rule lasted 60 years (1580–1640), during which time many of Portugal's overseas possessions were lost. In 1640 the Portuguese took back their throne when a nobleman from the powerful Portuguese House of Bragança was installed as Dom João IV: the Bragança dynasty would last until the first years of the 20th century. Fueled by the gold and diamonds extracted from Brazil, the Bragança rulers spent extravagantly on the massive monastery at Mafra (which employed 50,000 workmen), the university library at Coimbra, and the decoration of the Capela de São João Baptista (Chapel of St. John the Baptist) in Lisbon. While such irrationally grand projects progressed, the country's domestic economy weakened and its society remained feudal.

It took the appalling devastation of the 1755 earthquake, which destroyed Lisbon, to breathe new life into commerce and industry. The king's chief minister at the time, the Marquês de Pombal, ordered that the capital's dead be buried and the living fed. He then created a new, planned Lisbon that employed the most advanced architectural and social ideas of the age and resulted in an elegant but restrained style of building known as Pombaline. To walk through downtown Lisbon today is to walk through shades of the 18th century, starting in the colonnaded riverside square, the Praça do Comércio, and through the gridded Baixa (Lower) District, expressly designed by Pombal to house the commercial concerns he was keen to promote. Lisbon's glory is its 18th-century buildings and its sense of measured space. Such town planning is repeated elsewhere in Portugal, most notably in the gridded streets of Vila Real de Santo António, the Algarve's easternmost town.

These developments proved to be mere diversions from the economic, social, and moral poverty of the Portuguese crown. In 1808, when Napoléon's armies invaded during the Peninsular War, the royal family fled to Brazil, ruling from Rio de Janeiro rather than Lisbon. With the fall of Napoléon, Dom João VI returned to Portugal, leaving his young son, Pedro I, behind to govern. But Pedro had ideas of his own: he proclaimed Brazil's independence on September 7, 1822, and established the Brazilian Empire.

Napoléon's invasions and the schism with Brazil left the country devastated, and the monarchy was finally overthrown in 1910. A republic was proclaimed, but the rot of instability had set in, and during the next 16 years 44 governments attempted to rescue Portugal from its malaise. A coup d'état followed in 1926, and from 1928 onward the country was governed by the right-wing dictatorship of António Salazar, who—first as minister of finance, then as prime minister—was strongly influenced by the contemporary Italian and Spanish fascist movements led by Mussolini and Franco, respectively. The dictatorship lasted until 1974.

Contemporary Politics, Culture, and Economy
In the 20th century, industrialization bypassed Portugal; the economy remained agricultural, the political system was unreformed, and the lot of the people didn't improve. The country preserved its age-old traditions and customs within an almost feudal social structure, causing it

to fall behind developing nations. Portugal was ready for change. In 1968 its government appointed Dr. Marcelo Caetano to replace then-dictator António de Oliveira Salazar, who had just suffered a severe stroke. Long-brewing discontent among young career army officers in the African colonies of Angola and Mozambique led to the revolution that occurred six years later, on April 25, 1974, in which Caetano was ousted in a virtually bloodless coup (six people were killed). Huge demonstrations in support of the left-wing, officer-led Movimento das Forças Armadas (Armed Forces Movement) left no doubt that Portugal had entered a new era. The remaining colonies were granted independence. Initially it was a relatively peaceful operation in Mozambique and Guinea-Bissau, but in Angola and East Timor (which became part of Indonesia and is now independent) it was fraught with conflict. Land on the huge estates of the Alentejo was redistributed, and in the name of democracy, free elections produced a popular Socialist government.

Today Portugal is a stable country, its people keen to share in the prosperity offered by the developments within the European Union (EU), of which it held the presidency in 1992. In 1994 Lisbon was selected as European City of Culture, and the capital saw massive redevelopment prior to its hosting of the 1998 World Expo. You may find the stability surprising, given the relatively short time since the revolution, and indeed it speaks well for the inherent qualities of the Portuguese. Moreover, since 1975 hundreds of thousands of refugees from former Portuguese colonies in Africa and Asia have been absorbed into the country. The newcomers have inspired welcome change; in Lisbon, for example, African music and dance is popular, and dozens of places serve authentic Brazilian, Mozambican, Angolan, and Goan food. Further, the country agreed to take in as many citizens of Macao as wished to leave before the handover of that territory to China in 1999. Since then more Chinese and Macanese restaurants have opened.

There's a buoyancy in other cultural matters, too, with Lisbon, Oporto, Coimbra, and other major towns offering the best in contemporary Portuguese art, music, and dance. The painter Maria-Helena Vieira da Silva is one of Portugal's most famous names, although others have also been influential, including pioneer modernist Almada Negreiros and Amadeo de Souza-Cardoso. Contemporary writers whose works are translated into English include José Cardoso Pires, António Lobo Antunes, and José Saramago (winner of the 1998 Nobel Prize for literature). Architects strive to re-create that imperial Portuguese sense of confidence in their buildings—Lisbon's vast, colorful Amoreiras shopping and residential complex, the Centro Cultural in Belém, and the Parque das Nações development are as bold as such projects come.

Political stability and artistic confidence couldn't have been maintained without improvements in the economy, and there have been great strides forward since 1974. Membership in the EU has undoubtedly helped, with grants and subsidies paying for the modernization of agriculture; massive aid and loans from the United States have also played a part. Many people are employed in the tourism industry. Accordingly, the resort areas and cities are now anything but undiscovered: the Algarve coast, for example, is one of Europe's most visited regions.

Lisbon, too, has rapidly acquired the trappings of a forward-looking commercial capital. Many of its turn-of-the-last-century buildings are being replaced by skyscrapers, and renovation and modernization have touched every part of the capital. Much of the architecture and culture that once made Portugal unique now stand side by side with contemporary styles and lifestyles. Away from Lisbon and the busy Algarve, however, there are country villages, isolated beaches, crumbling historic towns, and hidden valleys that have barely changed over the past few hundred years.

The government still faces challenges, not the least of which is a marked disparity in economic development between the north and south of the country. But there are few countries in Europe better equipped to deal with them—a young democracy often has an uncommon will to succeed. There's a challenge to visitors, too. Take time to get off the beaten track, and you'll be rewarded with glimpses of a traditional life and culture that have been shaped by the memories of empire and tempered by the experience of revolution.

WHAT'S WHERE

An enormous variety of landscapes can be found in this relatively small nation. A long rectangle slightly larger than the state of Indiana, it's just 560 km (347 mi) from north to south and 220 km (136 mi) at its widest east–west point. It's bordered on the north and east by Spain and on the south and west by the Atlantic Ocean and is temperate year-round, especially along the coasts.

Lisbon

Lisbon is one of Europe's smallest capitals, and to many visitors, it immediately becomes one of the most likeable. In parts of the city, the centuries seem to collide: Out of 17th-century buildings trip designer-clad youths; the fish market at Cais do Sodré resonates with traditional sights and smells; and a short walk from the 18th-century aqueduct sits the modernistic Amoreiras shopping center.

Lisbon's Environs

The palaces, gardens, and luxury *quintas* (manor houses) of Sintra are justly celebrated. At Cascais and Estoril life revolves around the sea, and you can take part in time-honored pastimes: a stroll along the shore, a seafood meal, a game of tennis, a flutter at the casino. To the north, around Guincho's rocky promontory and the Praia das Maças coast, the Atlantic is often windswept and rough, but there's good sailboarding and surfing, as well as excellent coastal drives.

The best beaches lie to the south of the Rio Tejo (River Tagus), on the Setúbal Peninsula, a scenic area known for its traditions, festivals, and agriculture. You can laze on the beach at Sesimbra, sample some of the county's best wines, explore the dramatic mountain scenery of the Serra da Arrábida, and indulge yourself by lodging in one of two old castles that have been converted into *pousadas* (luxury inns).

The Estremadura and Ribatejo

The regions of Estremadura and Ribatejo extend north and east of Lisbon, following a line drawn by the wide valley of the Rio Tejo. The populous Estremadura's rolling hills and glorious coastline contain some of the country's most famous towns and monuments. Summers are long, hot, and bright, particularly in the seaside resorts, which stretch south as far as the Estoril Coast, west of Lisbon. The unique microclimate at work here ensures that the winters are milder than in the capital; in summer, the resorts of Estoril and Cascais enjoy a permanent breeze that offsets the high temperatures. Out of the capital, and across the Tejo, you're soon in Ribatejo (literally translated as the "banks of the River Tagus"), famous as a bull-breeding district, whose mainly flat lands fade into the vast plains of the southern Alentejo region.

Évora and the Alentejo

Once known as the granary of Portugal, the Alentejo is a thinly populated, largely agricultural region of grain fields and cork and olive trees. It is as remote in its way as Trás-os-Montes in the north, though with none of the compensating grandeur. That said, there are some impressive Atlantic beaches (whipped year-round by a strong wind), and a striking eastern section, where the Rio Guadiana forms the frontier with Spain. Alentejo summers start early (March), and there's little shade from the sun. There's also very little rainfall.

The Algarve

Dividing the Alentejo from Portugal's southernmost coastal province is a continuous range of mountains—the Serra de Monchique and the Serra de Caldeirão. The Algarve has some 3,000 hours of sunshine annually, and its low-lying plains, rocky coastline (in the west), sand-bar islands (in the east), and sweeping beaches make up Portugal's busiest tourist region. In August, the midday heat here is almost unbearable, though it's easy to cool off in a pool or in the sea. The Algarve is also the only real year-round destination in Portugal, despite the general clemency of the climate elsewhere. The region feels semitropical: Coastal winter days are warm and bright, the wildflowers strung across the low hills start to bloom early in February, and temperatures stay high until late October.

Coimbra and the Beiras

The central Beiras region contains Portugal's highest mountain range, the Serra da Estrela, which reaches a height of 6,530 ft and offers the country's best hiking and only skiing. In the Beira Alta (Upper Beira)—between Viseu, Guarda, and Covilha—the winter frost is fierce, and the wind whistles through a string of hill towns that, while little known to foreigners, are at the heart of Portugal's history. There's a distinct geographical and climatic shift as you move west toward the coast, leaving the mountains behind for the fertile expanses of the Beira Litoral (Coastal Beira) plain. It's a temperate, low-lying country, threatened by flooding from the mountains, though at Aveiro in the north of the region the water has been tamed by an extensive network of canals and drainage channels. The coast itself, the pine-forested Costa da Prata (Silver Coast), is one of the finest sandy stretches in the country, and inland from the main resort of Figuera da Foz, the university town of Coimbra stands on the banks of the Rio Mondego.

Oporto and the North

In the mountainous northeast you'll find the seldom-visited region with the Shangri-la name of Trás-os-Montes (Beyond the Mountains)—an unspoiled area of rugged beauty, with tumbling rivers, expansive forests, hilltop castles, and quiet villages. Extremes of temperature dictate custom and the local economy: The region's northern part often has long, harsh, winters, but June, July, and August are dry and hot, turning the land tawny. In the milder, more fertile southern part lie the vineyards of the Douro Valley, whose grapes are used to make the famous export, port wine. The vineyards, like all the land of Trás-os-Montes, depend upon the Rio Douro, whose tributaries (the Tamega, Corgo, and Tua) lace the area.

To the west, beyond Vila Real, lies the region known as the Minho. Touching the Atlantic and stretching from the northern border south to Oporto (the country's second-largest city), the Minho displays a gentler character. It contains the lush hinterland of the rivers Minho, Lima, and Douro. In this mass of predominantly green landscape are the Costa Verde (Green Coast), the beautiful pine-tree-lined coast north of Oporto, and the inland hills and valleys where the slightly sparkling *vinho verde* (green wine) is produced. Winters are mild here, with plenty of rain, and the Minho is heavily cultivated. Summers are short and temperate.

Madeira

Off the coast of Morocco, about 600 km (372 mi) due west of Casablanca, lies the Madeiran archipelago, an autonomous possession of Portugal. It consists of Madeira (the largest island of the group), nearby Porto Santo, and the uninhabited islets of Ilhas Desertas and Ilhas Selvagens. (The Azores, whose remote location and relative poverty keep them somewhat unvisited, are Portugal's other autonomous possession; they aren't covered in this book.) A mountain range, volcanic in origin, dominates Madeira's center, creating spectacular summits. Pico Ruivo, the highest peak, reaches an altitude of 6,104 ft. On the lush northern coast, cliffs pierce the sea, and to the west is the arid Paúl da Serra plateau. South along the coast, the landscape becomes gentler—and much more populated. Funchal, the capital, is near the southeastern corner of the island. About 50 km (31 mi) northeast, of Madeira, the 10½-km-long (6½-mi-long) island of Porto Santo has no mountains or ravines, but lots of sandy beaches and a desertlike climate.

PLEASURES AND PASTIMES

Beaches

Despite the tourist boom that has almost completely developed large stretches of the Algarve and the Costa da Prata, you can commune with the sea and the sky in relative solitude along the Costa Azul and the beaches of the Minho and Costa Verde. Decide whether you want the excitement and glamour of a world-class resort, complete with casino and 24-hour nightlife, or whether your spirit would be more refreshed by amber cliffs and yellow sand leading into an indigo sea down south in the Algarve, or lush green mountains and oyster sand meeting the blue-gray ocean, as in the north.

Fado Music

There's one perennial art form that is the essence of Portugal and the Portuguese. In bars and clubs, especially in Lisbon and Coimbra, you can hear fado—"fate" music—a mournful, soulful singing tradition thought to have originated in African slave songs and imported from the colonies by way of the slave trade. There are two distinct strands of fado: In Lisbon, emotive feeling is the dominant force in the lyrics, while Coimbra's fado has an intellectual edge. But both are timeless—the lament of the past, the acceptance of the future.

Nature Reserves

Portugal's varied geography and climate draws nature lovers, and many regions have been turned into reserves. The oldest is Peneda-Gerês, in the extreme north, reaching up to the Spanish border, where wild boar and horses roam the mountains. Lesser northern reserves are those of Alvão, near Vila Real, and the Serra da Malcata on the Spanish frontier, east of the peaks of the Serra da Estrela. Interesting wildlife areas farther south include the mountainous regions around Sintra, near Lisbon, and the Serra da Arrábida, near Setúbal; water-based reserves include the estuary of the Rio Sado, south of Lisbon, and the Algarve coast, from Faro east to Vila Real de Santo António. This last region is a stopover for waders and seabirds on their migration south.

Shopping

The variety of Portuguese crafts is astonishing. Throughout the country, you'll find superb jewelry, basketry, embroidered linens, tapestries and other textiles, glazed tiles or tile panels, porcelain and pottery, and exceptional leather goods. In the Alentejo, look for lightweight gifts made of cork, carved wooden items, and the hallmark carpets of Arraiolos. Metalwork items are specialties of the Algarve and Trás-os-Montes regions, and Coimbra is known for its guitars.

FODOR'S CHOICE

No two people will agree on what makes a perfect vacation, but it can be fun to know what others think. We hope you'll have a chance to experience some of Fodor's choices while visiting Portugal.

Castles and Forts

Castelo de São Jorge, Lisbon. Imposing St. George's Castle, on one of the highest hills in the city's Moorish Alfama District, is a grand place to get your bearings.

Cidadela, Bragança. This grand castle and walled village in the remote Trás-os-Montes region shows you how really good it must have been to be king.

Fortaleza de Sagres, Sagres. Enormous walls high above the sea encircle the buildings—including a captivating chapel—of this Algarve fortress.

Palácio Nacional de Pena, Sintra. A splendid park surrounds this drawbridged palace, whose turrets, ramparts, and domes comprise styles from Arabian to Victorian; interior furnishings are equally eclectic.

Palácio Nacional de Queluz, Queluz. Inspired in part by Versailles, this salmon-pink rococo edifice took 40 years to complete. The formal grounds have ponds, a canal, fountains, and statues.

Palácio Nacional de Sintra, Sintra. The former summer residence of Portuguese royalty, the 14th-century Sintra Palace displays an impressive combination of Moorish, Gothic, and Manueline architecture.

Dining

Restaurante de Cozinha Velha, Queluz. Formerly the kitchen of the Queluz Palace, this restaurant—part of the Pousada de Dona Maria I—takes advantage of its heritage: certain dishes are inspired by 18th-century recipes. $$$–$$$$

Tavares Rico, Lisbon. Superb French-inspired food, an excellent wine list, and a splendid Edwardian dining room have made this restaurant—founded as a café in the 18th century—one of the city's most famous. $$$–$$$$

Redondel, Vila Franca de Xira. You can feast on hearty regional fare at this restaurant inside the walls of a famous bullring. $$–$$$$

O Celeiro, Funchal. The traditional Portuguese cooking —including the Algarve-style seafood stews served in copper-lidded pots—attracts locals and tourists alike. $$–$$$

Palace Hotel Buçaco, Buçaco. The extravagant restaurant at this hotel in the western Beiras region has a carved-wood ceiling, massive Manueline windows, and cuisine worthy of the elegant surroundings. $$–$$$

A Ruina, Albufeira. For charcoal-grilled seafood—especially sardines or a tuna steak—you'll find few places in the Algarve that top this rustic beachside restaurant. $$–$$$

Bonjardim, Lisbon. Nicknamed "Rei dos Frangos" ("King of Chickens"), Bonjardim specializes in superbly spit-roasted chicken; the frenzied waiters are entertaining. $$

Pedro dos Letões, Curia. Between Coimbra and Oporto you'll find several restaurants that specialize in suckling pig. A meal at one such establishment—the ever-popular "Suckling Pig Pete"—is a must. $$

Lodging

Four Seasons Hotel The Ritz, Lisbon. Tapestries and fine paintings decorate the public areas, and guest rooms have luxurious baths, private terraces, and elegant furnishings. $$$$

Hotel Palácio, Estoril. During World War II, exiled European courts stayed at this 1930s hotel in Lisbon's outskirts. It can be your home away from home, too—that is, when you're not on the championship golf course or dining poolside. $$$–$$$$

Pousada dos Lóios, Évora. In the historic 15th-century monastery opposite the Templo Romano, this pousada is among Portugal's most opulent. $$$

Reid's Palace, Funchal. Wonderfully old-fashioned and long popular with aristocrats and tycoons, Reid's is one of Madeira's—if not the country's—most gracious hotels. $$$

Pousada de Santa Marinha, Guimarães. Tiled walls depicting 18th-century Portuguese life decorate this mountaintop structure in the Minho region. It began life as a monastery in the 12th century; today you can spend a comfortable night in what used to be a monk's cell. $$–$$$

Pousada de São Filipe, Setúbal. The location in a 16th-century hilltop castle in Lisbon's environs, the views from the rooms and ramparts, and the interior awash with *azulejo* tiles are no less than splendid. $$–$$$

Albergaria Senhora do Monte, Lisbon. Views from this small, unpretentious hotel in the oldest part of town are some of the best in Lisbon. $$

Grande Hotel do Porto, Oporto. This turn-of-the-19th-century beauty has wonderfully ornate public rooms and cheerful guest quarters that combine chandeliers with satellite-cable TV. $$

Meliá Confort Grão Vasco, Viseu. The hotel's location in a wooded park just a few steps from the main square is ideal, offering the convenience of the city and the quiet of the western Beiras countryside. $$

Pousada do Pico do Arieiro, Madeira. At this cozy hotel in the mountains, at an altitude of 5,963 ft, you'll feel as if you're in heaven when you step out on your terrace and look *down* onto the clouds. $$

Quinta das Sequóias, Sintra. This 19th-century manor house, on 40 acres of wooded grounds outside of Lisbon, has a half dozen guest rooms with period touches. $$

Pousada de São Pedro, Castelo de Bode. Built in 1946 to house engineers constructing the dam on the Rio Zêzere, this pousada sits on a hill above a man-made lake. $$

Memorable Museums

Museu de Arte Antiga, Lisbon. A 17th-century palace is home to Portuguese art (mainly from the 15th through 19th centuries), pieces by Flemish painters, and collections of French silver, Portuguese furniture and tapestries, and Asian ceramics.

Museu Calouste Gulbenkian, Lisbon. The quality of the pieces is magnificent, from the Egyptian artifacts and Greek and Roman coins and statuary to the Chinese porcelain, Japanese prints, and Persian tapestries. The European art collection has pieces representing all the major schools from the 15th through the 20th centuries.

Museu Machado de Castro, Coimbra. The museum, in a wonderful 12th-century palace, contains one of Portugal's finest collections of sculpture.

Ruins and Museum, Conímbriga. In a bucolic setting southwest of Coimbra, these ruins and museum constitute one of the Iberian Peninsula's most important archaeological sites.

Spiritual Structures

Igreja de São Roque, Lisbon. Don't be fooled by the plain facade: Inside, the side chapels of this Renaissance church are decorated with rare stones and mosaics that resemble oil paintings.

Mosteiro de Alcobaça, Alcobaça. Grateful for a decisive battle won, a king built this impressive church and monastery in the 12th century.

Mosteiro dos Jerónimos, Lisbon. Belém's famous monastery is a supreme example of the Manueline style, with elaborate sculptural details.

Mosteiro-Palácio Nacional, Mafra. An enormous 18th-century complex containing a Franciscan monastery, an imposing basilica, and a grandiose royal palace, this was built to celebrate a royal birth.

Sé Velha, Coimbra. Constructed in the 12th century, the Old Cathedral is made of massive granite blocks and crowned by a ring of battlements that makes it look more like a fortress than a house of worship.

Templo Romano, Évora. This temple is one of the finest Roman ruins on the Iberian Peninsula.

Spots for a Stroll

Parque Nacional de Peneda-Gerês. Nearly 173,000 acres were set aside in 1970 to protect the diverse flora and fauna of this wild Minho region of lakes, woods, and hilltop villages.

Praça de Dom Duarte, Viseu. The rough stone pavement, splendid old houses, wrought-iron balconies, and views of an ancient cathedral have a magical effect.

Praça do Giraldo, Évora. This bustling, arcade-lined square was once a Roman forum.

Rossio, Lisbon. The capital's main square since the Middle Ages is a grand space with ornate French fountains and renowned cafés.

GREAT ITINERARIES

Highlights of Portugal

13 to 15 days.

From the Algarve—Portugal's southernmost region of gorgeous beaches, vibrant resorts, and secluded hill villages—the route strikes north through the country's major towns. Landscapes along the way include the picturesque coast and arid plains of the south; vibrant Lisbon and its lush environs; and the rivers, valleys, forests, and mountains of the north. Begin with two days in Faro, the Algarve's historic capital, making side trips to towns such as riverside Tavira.

Évora (*2 days*). Évora's Roman, Moorish, and Renaissance heritage provides a compelling architectural feast. Study the temple ruins, graceful squares, royal palaces, and striking churches. Then stay overnight in the Pousada dos Lóios, a converted monastery, or another historic lodging. ☞ *Chapter 5.*

Lisbon (*3 days*). Don your walking shoes and range across the seven hills of the Portuguese capital. Explore the intricate alleyways of the Moorish Alfama; the checkerboard grid of the Baixa (Lower Town); the cobbled contours of the Bairro Alto (Upper Town); and the superb architectural details of Belém. Don't miss Portugal's finest museum collections—the Museu Calouste Gulbenkian and the Museu de Arte Antiga. ☞ *Chapter 2.*

Óbidos to Leiria (*1 or 2 days*). A slow drive from Lisbon through the fertile Estremadura region rewards you with a glimpse of the celebrated monumental architecture that dominates Óbidos, Alcobaça, and Batalha. At journey's end, the medieval castle at the former royal residence of Leiria is one of Portugal's unsung gems. ☞ *Chapter 4.*

Coimbra (*1 or 2 days*). The country's most prestigious university town is home to timeworn buildings, romantic squares and gardens, and colorful traditions, including the singing of the mournful fado, that most characteristic Portuguese folk music. ☞ *Chapter 7.*

Oporto (*2 days*). Gateway to the north and center of the country's port wine industry, Oporto repays careful investigation. Look beyond the solid commercial nature of Portugal's second-largest city and you'll uncover staunch Gothic mansions, an impressive cathedral, and a vibrant riverside pier, the Cais da Ribeira, where you can tuck into fresh fish at an authentic *tasca* (tavern). ☞ *Chapter 8.*

Braga (*1 day*). Its Romanesque cathedral, Museu de Arte Sacra, and Paço dos Arcebispos announce Braga's credentials as Portugal's religious nerve center. The Easter processions are justly famous, and year-round pilgrims climb the steep steps of the sanctuary-church of nearby Bom Jesus do Monte. ☞ *Chapter 8.*

Viana do Castelo (*1 day*). A low-key Portuguese resort, Viana makes a refreshing change from the international Algarve beach towns. Chug across the Rio Lima by ferry to the local beach, stroll the well-kept streets of the late-medieval center, visit the bustling Friday market, or enjoy the views from the Santa Luzia basilica. ☞ *Chapter 8.*

By Public Transportation

Trains and buses serve all the towns on this itinerary, but connections in the deep south and far north can be time-consuming. The Algarve railway line between Lagos and Vila Real is a useful means of nipping along the south coast—the entire route takes three to four hours. From Faro, it's less than three hours to Évora or around four hours to Lisbon by car or express bus. Fast, frequent trains and buses run from Lisbon to Leiria (one hour), Coimbra (two hours), and Oporto (three or four hours). The journey by car, train, or bus from Oporto to either Braga or Viana do Castelo is around an hour.

Monumental Portugal

10 or 11 days.

Portugal has the eye-catching monuments befitting a land of conquest, discovery, and glory. A stunning range of castles, palaces, monasteries, churches, and ancient ruins lies scattered across the heart of the country, beginning near the border with Spain.

Marvão (*1 day*). The nation was forged and defended in its fortified border towns, of which Marvão is a classic example. A strategic site since Roman times, the cliff-top castle has views worth every tiring step of the walk up through town. ☞ *Chapter 5.*

Vila Viçosa (*1 day*). Heartland of the royal Bragança family since the 15th century, Vila Viçosa once held sway over much of Portugal. Time (and the eventual declaration of the republic) reduced the town's influence, but the marble Ducal Palace still has the capacity to thrill. Its rich interior apartments, armory, and treasury detail

the golden lives of Portugal's last royal family. ☞ *Chapter 5.*

Setúbal (*1 day*). If the 15th-century Igreja de Jesus—a church that is the country's earliest example of Manueline architecture—wasn't enough reason to visit, you'll find all the excuses you need in the mighty shape of the Castelo de São Filipe, which lords over the town. The dramatically situated castle is now a stylish pousada. ☞ *Chapter 3.*

Sintra (*2 or 3 days*). To fully appreciate aristocratic Sintra, retreat of the royals, you need to stay a night or two. Visits to the Palácio Nacional de Sintra, the extraordinarily decorated Palácio Nacional de Pena, and the Castelo dos Mouros are mandatory. Less exalted attractions round out the experience: crafts shopping, a visit to edge-of-the-world Cabo da Roca, and tours of the gardens of Monserrate. ☞ *Chapter 3.*

Estremadura (*2 days*). In the region of Estremadura, whose lands were bitterly contested by the Moors and the Spanish, stand three of the country's most alluring sights. Start in Óbidos, part of whose medieval castle is a lovingly adapted pousada. Nearby, the spectacular church and monastery of Alcobaça was built following a 12th-century victory over the Moors. More than 200 years later, the church and monastery at Batalha was erected, a majestic commemoration of the Portuguese victory at the Battle of Aljubarrota. ☞ *Chapter 4.*

Tomar (*1 day*). The medieval Knights Templar made their headquarters in the graceful town of Tomar. Investigate the gardens, cloisters, and church of their Convento de Cristo before turning your attention to the preserved Jewish Quarter, whose synagogue is Portugal's oldest. ☞ *Chapter 4.*

Conímbriga (*1 day*). No Roman ruins in Portugal are more impressive than those of Conímbriga, once a flourishing town on the route between Lisbon and Braga. Step back in time as you view the mosaic floors, original Roman road (still rutted by cart wheels), and aqueduct. ☞ *Chapter 7.*

Viseu (*1 day*). Holding a commanding position in the western Beiras region, the provincial capital of Viseu has a trio of visually rich old squares. The prosperous mix of imposing public buildings, spacious boulevards, and shady parks is a real treat. ☞ *Chapter 7.*

By Public Transportation

You'll need a car to make the most of this tour or you'll spend much of your time waiting for connections. That said, if you base yourself in Lisbon you can easily see Setúbal (45 minutes), Sintra (40 minutes), and the Estremadura sights (one or two hours) by public transport from there. Coimbra gives you direct access to Conímbriga (25 minutes) and Viseu (two hours). Only Marvão and Vila Viçosa remain resistant to day-trip sightseeing—you'll need a car for these.

Byways and Backwaters

9 to 11 days.

This meandering tour of the northern rivers, valleys, and mountains steers clear of the crowds and highlights local life and culture—Portugal's mellow pleasures.

Monção (*1 or 2 days*). Now a peaceful border town on a serene stretch of the Rio Minho, Monção is home to a castle that's the only reminder of more hectic times. The local wine—the sprightly vinho verde—encourages long lunches, or cut lunch short and follow the river downstream as far as Caminha, with its fortified town hall. ☞ *Chapter 8.*

Ponte de Lima (*1 or 2 days*). A charming Roman bridge is the "ponte" in question, spanning the Rio Lima, known as the River of Oblivion to the Romans, who were sorely taken with its ethereal beauty. Riverside promenades, mansions, elegant manor-house accommodations, and a twice-monthly market are the town's gentle attractions. ☞ *Chapter 8.*

Barcelos (*1 day*). Plan your trip so your arrival here coincides with the Thursday market, one of Portugal's greatest participatory experiences. Organized by locals for locals—that's the key here—it's chockablock with ceramics, baskets, toys, foodstuffs, agricultural supplies,

clothes, shoes, and household equipment. ☞ *Chapter 8.*

Amarante (*1 day*). If you're looking for love, touching the saintly effigy in the Convento de São Gonçalo is recommended by the locals. The rest of the day, stroll across the pretty bridge, wander along the riverbanks, or rent a rowboat. These are the kind of lazy activities that might provide your best memories of Portugal. ☞ *Chapter 8.*

Chaves (*1 day*). Just a few miles from the Spanish border, Chaves once bore the brunt of any attack. Its sturdy fortress is its most prominent feature, but the engaging late-medieval streets, tiled churches, a local museum, and thermal springs provide more pacific pastimes. ☞ *Chapter 8.*

Bragança (*1 day*). Within the walls of the Cidadela is a superbly preserved medieval village. Soak it up, then descend to the modern town where the people of Bragança go about their business in the shops and sidewalk cafés of a typical country town. ☞ *Chapter 8.*

The Eastern Beiras (*2 days*). The rocky highlands of the Eastern Beiras region are for anyone with an interest in rugged, off-the-beaten-track adventure. In out-of-the-way towns like Trancoso, Castelo Rodrigo, and Almeida—each deeply affected through the years by emigration—every castle wall tells a story, while every abandoned house or tower harbors a ghost or two. ☞ *Chapter 7.*

Sortelha (*1 day*). It's not quite the land that time forgot, but Sortelha comes as close as anywhere in Portugal. Ancient walls, crumbling houses, cobbled streets, and simple back-to-basics accommodations all contribute to the age-old atmosphere. ☞ *Chapter 7.*

By Public Transportation

A car is essential to follow the route outlined above, but be prepared for some tortuous cross-country rides in the mountainous Trás-os-Montes and eastern Beiras.

2 LISBON

No longer the sleepy outpost that the country's haunting fado music celebrates, Lisbon is now a beguiling 21st-century European capital. Its people move forward with confidence yet work hard to preserve their proud history. They're true descendants of their *descobrador* (discoverer) ancestors.

By Jules Brown

Updated by
Paul Murphy

L ISBON BEARS THE MARK OF AN INCREDIBLE HERITAGE with laid-back pride. Spread over a string of seven hills north of the Rio Tejo (Tagus River) estuary, the city also presents an intriguing variety of faces to those who negotiate its switchback streets. In the oldest neighborhoods, stepped alleys are lined with pastel-color houses and crossed by laundry hung out to dry; here and there *miradouros* (vantage points) afford spectacular river or city views. In the grand 18th-century center, black-and-white mosaic cobblestone sidewalks border wide boulevards. *Elétricos* (trams) clank through the streets, and blue-and-white *azulejos* (painted and glazed ceramic tiles) adorn churches, restaurants, and fountains.

The city was probably founded by the Phoenicians, who traded from its port. It wasn't until 205 BC, however, when the Romans linked it by road to the great Spanish cities of the Iberian Peninsula, that Lisbon prospered. The Visigoths followed in the 5th century and built the earliest fortifications on the site of the Castelo de São Jorge, but it was with the arrival of the Moors in the 8th century that Lisbon came into its own. The city flourished as a trading center during the 300 years of Moorish rule, and the Alfama—Lisbon's oldest district—retains its intricate Arab-influenced layout. In 1147 the Christian army led by Dom Afonso Henriques took the city after a ruthless siege that lasted 17 weeks. To give thanks for the end of Moorish rule, Dom Afonso planned a great cathedral, and the building was dedicated three years later. A little more than a century after that, the rise of Lisbon was complete when the royal seat of power was transferred here from Coimbra, and Lisbon was declared capital of Portugal.

The next great period—that of *os descobrimentos* (the discoveries)—began with the 15th-century voyages led by the great Portuguese navigators to India, Africa, and Brazil. The wealth realized by these expeditions was phenomenal: gold, jewels, ivory, porcelain, and spices helped finance grand buildings and impressive commercial activity. Late-Portuguese Gothic architecture—called Manueline (after the king Dom Manuel I)—assumed a rich, individualistic style, characterized by elaborate sculptural details, often with a maritime motif. Torre de Belém and the Mosteiro dos Jerónimos (Belém's tower and monastery) are supreme examples of this period.

With independence from Spain in 1640 and assumption of the throne by successive dukes of the house of Bragança, Lisbon became ever more prosperous, only to suffer calamity on November 1, 1755, when it was hit by the last of a series of earthquakes. Two-thirds of Lisbon was destroyed, and tremors were felt as far north as Scotland; 40,000 people in Lisbon died, and entire sections of the city were swept away by a tidal wave.

Under the direction of the prime minister, the Marquês de Pombal, Lisbon was rebuilt quickly and ruthlessly. The medieval quarters were leveled and replaced with broad boulevards; the commercial center, the Baixa, was laid out in a grid; and the great Praça do Comércio, the riverfront square, was planned. Essentially downtown Lisbon has an elegant 18th-century layout that remains as pleasing today as it was intended to be 250 years ago.

Of course, there are parts of Lisbon—particularly several suburbs beyond the city center—that lack charm. Even some of the handsome downtown areas have lost their classic Portuguese appearance as the city and its residents have become more cosmopolitan: shiny office blocks have replaced some 19th- and 20th-century art nouveau buildings and sit alongside others. And older, much-loved trams now share the streets with "fast trams" as well as with belching buses and automobiles.

Some of the modernization—particularly the infrastructure upgrades—has improved the city, though. To prepare for its role as host of the World Exposition in 1998, Lisbon spruced up its public buildings, overhauled its metro (subway) system, and completed an impressive bridge across the Rio Tejo. Today the expo site is an expansive riverfront development known as Parque das Nações, and the city is now a popular port of call for European cruise ships, whose passengers disembark onto a lively, revitalized waterfront.

But Lisbon's intrinsic, slightly disorganized, one-of-a-kind charm hasn't vanished in the contemporary mix. Lisboetas are at ease pulling up café chairs and perusing newspapers against any backdrop, whether it reflects the progress and commerce of today or the riches that once poured in from Asia, South America, and Africa. And quiet courtyards and sweeping viewpoints are never far away.

Pleasures and Pastimes

Dining

There's no doubt that Lisbon takes its food seriously; many businesses have *cut* their lunch break to an hour and a half. In the morning, the smell of coffee issues from a thousand pastry-filled cafés. By lunchtime even the humblest backstreet restaurant has chalked up its specials—thick vegetable soup, grilled fresh fish, clams sprinkled with seasonal herbs, and rotisserie chicken. And where you eat is half the experience: closeted in the dining room of an old mansion, looking out over the river from a designer warehouse-restaurant, or soaking up the street scenes at an outdoor table.

With the exception of some very expensive restaurants with French-influenced menus, most places serve home-style Portuguese cuisine—grilled sardines and squid; simple steaks and cutlets drenched in olive oil and garlic, fresh seafood (always ask the price before ordering); spit-roast chicken; lamb chops; and casseroles. Local specialties include *açorda* (a thick bread-and-shellfish stew sprinkled with cilantro), *ameijoas á bulhão pato* (clams in garlic sauce), and different varieties of *bacalhau* (dried salt cod) or *bife* (steak). *Caldeirada* is a simple fish stew that varies from restaurant to restaurant, and once a week any local place worth its salt dishes up a *cozido*—a boiled meat stew.

In addition, the capital serves the best of the country's regional foods, including *porco à alentejana* (pork and clams) from the Alentejo, lampreys from the Minho region of the north, and many seasonal items. If you want still more variety, try restaurants that specialize in colonial Portuguese food: Brazilian, Mozambican, and Goan (Indian). Vegetarians can enjoy wonderful Portuguese breads, and most chefs are adept at choosing delectable vegetables at the market and then cooking them pleasingly al dente.

Wine is good and reasonably priced, with the *vinho da casa* (house wine) usually more than drinkable. It's a custom to finish your meal with a glass of port. If you stop by the renowned Instituto do Vinho do Porto during your visit, you can taste different varieties and pick your favorite. Locals set more store by a glass of Moscatel de Setúbal, a rich dessert wine from across the river that's available everywhere.

Almost all Lisbon restaurants permit smoking throughout. If you're averse to smoke, choose a large, high-ceilinged room such as those along the trendy riverfront, avoiding seats in any upper levels; dine alfresco;

or plan to eat at top restaurants, including some at the best hotels, which often have powerful filtration systems. You can also try dining early, when the number of nonsmokers tends to be greater.

Lodging

In Lisbon you're spoiled for choice when it comes to finding a room—classy accommodations overlooking the park, modern business hotels on central avenues or in historic houses with gardens, or family-run guest houses in the old city. The only snag is that accommodations aren't the bargains restaurants are, although top-rated hotel prices are a tad lower than in some other European capitals.

You can still find reasonably priced rooms among the city's dozens of modest *pensões* (guest houses), some of which cost less than €40 a night. Be warned, however, that the decor may leave something to be desired, the toilet may be down the hall, and you may have to share a shower. Quality varies greatly from one guest house to another, but the best are spotless and friendly, and many are downtown, around the Rossío and the Praça dos Restauradores, as well as in the Bairro Alto. In summer it's often difficult to find a pensão with vacancies, so you may have to go door to door looking for a suitable place. The tourist office can provide an up-to-date list of reliable places (note, though, that their staffers won't reserve rooms for you).

Museums

Lisbon has some splendid museums, and all of them are reasonably priced. Standouts include the Museu Calouste Gulbenkian and the Museu de Arte Antiga, which have the finest collections of art and artifacts in the country. The singular Museu Nacional do Azulejo concentrates on the art of the country's famous ceramic tiles.

EXPLORING LISBON

The center city is small enough to cover on foot, but because of Lisbon's hills, don't underestimate the distances or the time it takes to cover them. Places may appear close to one another on a map when they're actually on different levels, and the walk can be fearsomely steep. Public transportation is excellent, entertaining, and a bargain to boot. Marvelous old trams, buses, the metro, and turn-of-the-20th-century funicular railways and elevators can transport you up the hills. If time is short or energy lags, taxis are a genuine bargain and can be summoned with a phone call. And, wherever you are, the Rio Tejo is never far away.

The center of Lisbon stretches north from the spacious Praça do Comércio—one of Europe's largest riverside squares—to the Rossío, a smaller square lined with shops and cafés. The district in between is known as the Baixa (Lower Town), an attractive grid of parallel streets built after the 1755 earthquake and tidal wave. The Alfama, the old Moorish quarter that survived the earthquake, lies east of the Baixa. In this part of town are the Sé (the city's cathedral) and, on the hill above, the Castelo de São Jorge (St. George's Castle).

West of the Baixa, sprawled across another of Lisbon's hills, is the Bairro Alto (Upper Town), an area of intricate 17th-century streets, peeling houses, and churches. Five kilometers (3 miles) farther west is Belém, site of the famous Mosteiro dos Jerónimos, as well as a royal palace and several museums. A similar distance to the northeast, Lisbon's Parque das Nações pivots around the spectacular Oceanário de Lisboa.

The modern city begins at Praça dos Restauradores, adjacent to the Rossío. From here the main Avenida da Liberdade stretches northwest to the landmark Praça Marquês de Pombal, bordered by the green expanse of the Parque Eduardo VII beyond.

Numbers in the text correspond to numbers in the margin and on the Exploring Lisbon and Exploring Belém maps.

Great Itineraries

You could easily spend a week exploring the city, visiting its museums, and passing time in its agreeable café-bars. But it's easy to get a feel for Lisbon in a couple of days. By using taxis and public transportation, you can combine multiple neighborhoods in a single day of sightseeing—the Alfama and the Baixa fit together particularly well, and the Chiado and the Bairro Alto make a good unit. Four days, then, is a reasonable compromise, allowing you time to see the major sights and quite a few of the minor ones, too.

IF YOU HAVE 2 DAYS

To view all the major attractions in two days, you'll have to get up early. Start at the Rossío, the main downtown square, and stroll through the Baixa, pausing to window-shop or take a coffee in a café. Wander into the Alfama quarter by way of the Sé, following the winding streets past lookout points and churches as far as the hilltop Castelo de São Jorge. The views here are magnificent, and you can grab lunch at one of the many nearby cafés and restaurants. A tram ride takes you back down to the Baixa, where, in the riverside Praça do Comércio, you pick up another tram for the rattling ride west to Belém and the magnificent Mosteiro dos Jerónimos, the acclaimed Torre de Belém, and the grand *Monumento dos Descobrimentos*. On the way back to the city center, stop off at the Museu de Arte Antiga.

Your second day can be less hectic. Head up to the Bairro Alto and the Chiado shopping area and spend the morning browsing in galleries and stores, visiting the Igreja de São Roque and its small museum, and popping into the Instituto do Vinho do Porto for a glass of port. Have lunch in one of the small taverns or smart restaurants, and then return to the Baixa via the Elevador da Glória. Take the metro uptown to the Fundação Calouste Gulbenkian, where you can spend three or four hours viewing the collections in the Museu Calouste Gulbenkian and the adjacent Centro de Arte Moderna. Alternatively, take the metro to Parque das Nações to visit the Oceanário de Lisboa.

IF YOU HAVE 4 DAYS

Spend the first morning in the Baixa, where the shops and cafés are inviting. At the riverside Praça do Comércio, take a ferry across the river and back for fine city views. Have lunch in the suburb of Cacilhas, where the ferry docks, or return to Praça dos Restauradores, just north of the Rossío, where a side street just off the square—Rua das Portas de Santo Antão—is lined with well-known fish restaurants. Spend the afternoon in the Alfama, taking in the Sé, the Castelo de São Jorge, and the Museu-Escola de Artes Decorativas.

On your second day, catch a tram out to Belém. Spend half the day exploring the monastery and monuments; you'll also have time for at least one of the specialty museums—Museu da Marinha, Museu Nacional de Coches, or Museu de Arte Popular. On your way to or from Belém, stop at the Museu de Arte Antiga.

Split your two remaining days between old and modern Lisbon. One full day should involve seeing the Chiado shopping area and exploring the Bairro Alto. Be sure to pop into the Convento do Carmo's archaeological museum and make a side trip to the Jardim da Estrêla, or you can spend more time at the Oceanário de Lisboa.

On the final day, walk the length of the boulevard-like Avenida da Liberdade to the city's main park, Parque Eduardo VII, where the greenhouses are a treat. From here, it's a simple metro ride to the Museu Calouste Gulbenkian and the Centro de Arte Moderna. Some people spend a full day just in these two galleries, or you could take the metro farther north toward the Jardim Zoológico and the Palácio dos Marqueses da Fronteira.

When to Tour Lisbon

It's best not to visit at the height of summer, when the city positively steams and lodgings are expensive and crowded. Winters are generally mild and usually accompanied by bright blue skies, but for optimum Lisbon weather, visit on either side of summer, in May or late September through October. The city's major festivals are in June; the so-called *santos populares* (popular saints) see days of riotous celebration dedicated to saints Anthony, John, and Peter.

The Alfama

The Moors, who imposed their rule on most of the southern Iberian Peninsula during the 8th century, left their mark on much of Lisbon but nowhere so evidently as in the Alfama district. Here narrow, twisting streets and soaring flights of steps wind up to an imposing castle on one of the city's highest hills. This is a grand place to get your bearings and take in supreme views. Because its foundation is dense bedrock, the district—a jumble of whitewashed houses with flower-laden balconies and red-tile roofs—has survived the wear and tear of the ages, including the great 1755 earthquake.

The timeless alleys and squares have a notoriously confusing layout, but the Alfama is relatively compact, and you'll keep circling back to the same buildings and streets. In the Moorish period this area thrived, and in the 15th century—as evidenced by the ancient synagogue on Beco das Barrelas—it was an important Jewish quarter. Although now a somewhat run-down neighborhood, it has a down-to-earth charm—particularly during the June festivals of the santos populares—and smart bars and restaurants are slowly moving in.

The Alfama's streets and alleys are very steep, and its levels are connected by flights of stone steps, which means it's easier to tour the area from the top down. Take a taxi up to the castle or approach it by Tram 28 from Rua Conceição in the Baixa or Bus 37 from Praça da Figueira.

A Good Walk

Follow the walls of the Moorish **Castelo de São Jorge** ① around into the Largo Rodrigues de Freitas. From here, it's a 10-minute walk down Rua de Santa Marinha and Rua São Vicente to the **Mosteiro de São Vicente** ②, where you can examine the tombs of the Bragança dynasty and climb to the roof-terrace for amazing city views. From outside the church, a short ride on Tram 28 (or a 10-minute walk) takes you to the Alfama's prettiest square, Largo das Portas do Sol, whose terrace offers more glorious vistas of the streets below. Just off the square is the **Museu-Escola de Artes Decorativas** ③, with its splendid decorative arts collections; down the hill about 300 ft is the view-laden **Miradouro Santa Luzia** ④. Head southwest from the miradouro along Rua do Limoeiro—which eventually becomes Rua Augusto Rosa—to the **Sé** ⑤. Below the cathedral is the **Casa dos Bicos** ⑥, a mansion that survived the 1755 earthquake. From here it's an easy walk to the adjacent Baixa district, or you can retrace your steps to the cathedral, outside which Tram 28 stops before heading to the Baixa. Buses from the waterfront Avenida Infante D. Henrique run from the Baixa up toward

Exploring Lisbon (Lisboa)

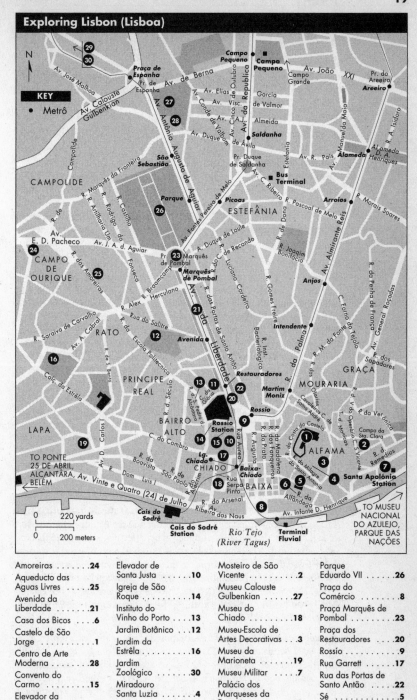

Santa Apolónia station, nearby which is the **Museu Militar** ⑦. To the
northwest of this museum is the **Museu Nacional do Azulejo**; it's a little out of the way, but it's definitely worth the trip.

TIMING

Allow two to three hours to walk the route, perhaps more on a hot
day, when you'll want to rest on the castle grounds or stop for drinks
in a café. A visit to the Museu-Escola de Artes Decorativas will occupy
at least an hour or two. Note that museums are closed on Monday,
and that churches generally close for a couple of hours in the middle
of the day.

Sights to See

⑥ **Casa dos Bicos.** The House of Pointed Stones, an Italianate dwelling
that survived the 1755 earthquake, was built in 1523 for the wealthy
Albuquerque family. It has a striking facade studded with pointed
white stones in diamond shapes. The interior is similarly impressive.
✉ *Rua dos Bacalhoeiros, Alfama,* ☎ *21/888–4827.* 🎫 *Free.* 🕐 *Weekdays 9:30–5:30*

★ ❶ **Castelo de São Jorge.** Although St. George's Castle was constructed
by the Moors, it's on the site of a 5th-century Visigoth fort. At the main
entrance is a statue of Dom Afonso Henriques, who in 1147 besieged
the castle and ultimately drove the Moors from Lisbon. Within the walls
are ramparts, towers, and remnants of a palace that was a residence
of the kings of Portugal until the 16th century. From the Câmara Es-
cura in the Torre de São Lourenço you can spy on visitors going about
their business below. Named after Roman Lisbon, "Olisipónia" is a
multimedia exhibit on the city's history of the city: images projected
onto a large wall convey the drama of such episodes as the Great Earthquake of 1755. The rest of the well-kept castle grounds are home to
swans, turkeys, ducks, ravens, and other birds, and the outer walls encompass the medieval church of Santa Cruz, a few simple houses, and
some restaurants and souvenir shops. Panoramic views of Lisbon can
be seen from the walls; watch the uneven footing. ✉ *Entrances at Largo
do Chão da Feira and Largo do Menino de Deus, Alfama,* ☎ *21/887–
7244 to Olisipónia.* 🎫 *Castle: free. Olisipónia: €3.50.* 🕐 *Apr.–Sept.,
daily 9–7; Oct.–Mar., daily 9–6.*

❹ **Miradouro Santa Luzia.** Hop off Tram 28 at the Miradouro Santa
Luzia, a terrace-garden viewpoint that takes in the Alfama and the river.
It catches the sun all day, and a nearby café serves welcome drinks.
The adjacent Igreja de Santa Luzia (Church of Santa Luzia) is a sorry
sight these days. Its exterior was once adorned with fine azulejos depicting the siege of the castle. They've been replaced by heartfelt graf-
fiti—AQUI HAVIA HISTORIA-CULTURA. AGORA—0 ("Here there once existed
history and culture. Now—nothing")—that makes its point. ✉ *Largo
da Santa Luzia, Alfama.*

❷ **Mosteiro de São Vicente.** The Italianate facade of the twin-towered St.
Vincent's Monastery heralds an airy church with a barrel-vault ceiling, the work of accomplished Italian architect Filippo Terzi (1520–
97). Finally completed in 1704, the church has a superbly tiled cloister depicting the fall of Lisbon to the Moors. The former refectory is
the pantheon of the Bragança dynasty, who were the first rulers of an
independent Portugal. Here, among the solid tombs and weighty in-
scriptions, lies Catherine of Bragança, who married Charles II of England in 1661. There's little to see—save a medieval cistern and a richly
decorated entrance hall—but it's worth the admission fee to climb up
to the towers and terrace for a look over the Alfama, city, and river.
From here you can see the huge white dome of Santa Engraça—the

church immediately behind and below São Vicente in Campo de Santa Clara—which doubles as the country's Panteão Nacional (National Pantheon), housing the tombs of Portugal's former presidents as well as cenotaphs dedicated to its most famous explorers and writers. ✉ *Largo de São Vicente, Alfama,* ☎ *21/882–4400.* ▣ *Monastery: €2. Church: free. Pantheon: €1.50.* ◷ *Monastery: Tues.–Sun. 10–6. Church: Tues.–Fri. 9–6, Sat. 9–7, Sun. 9–12:30 and 3–5. Pantheon: Tues.–Fri. 10–6, Sat. 10–7, Sun. 10–5.*

❸ Museu-Escola de Artes Decorativas. The Museum-School of Decorative Arts, in the 17th-century Azurara Palace, has objects that date from the 15th through 19th centuries. Look for brightly colored Arraiolos, traditional, hand-embroidered Portuguese carpets based on imported Arabic designs as well as silver work, ceramics, paintings, and jewelry. With so many rich items to preserve, the museum has become a major center for restoration. Crafts such as bookbinding, carving, and cabinetmaking are all undertaken here by highly trained staff; you can view the restoration work by appointment. ✉ *Largo das Portas do Sol 2, Alfama,* ☎ *21/881–4600.* ▣ *€4.* ◷ *Tues.–Sun. 10–5.*

NEED A BREAK?	At Largo das Portas do Sol there are a number of small café-bars with outside seats from which you can watch ships on the Rio Tejo. **Cerca Moura** (✉ Largo das Portas do Sol 4, Alfama, ☎ 21/887–4859)—named after the Moorish walls that surround the district—is one of the best.

❼ Museu Militar. The spirit of derring-do is palpable in the huge Corinthian-style barracks and arsenal complex of the Military Museum. As you clatter through endless, echoing rooms of weapons, uniforms, and armor you may be lucky enough to be followed—at a respectful distance—by a guide who, without speaking a word of English, can convey exactly how that bayonet was jabbed or that gruesome flail swung. The museum is on the eastern edge of the Alfama, at the foot of the hill and opposite the Santa Apolónia station. It's easy to get here by Bus 9 or Bus 39. ✉ *Largo de Santa Apolónia, Alfama,* ☎ *21/888–2300.* ▣ *€2.* ◷ *Tues.–Sun. 10–5.*

OFF THE BEATEN PATH	**MUSEU NACIONAL DO AZULEJO** – To fully understand the craftsmanship that goes into making the ubiquitous azulejos, visit this magnificent museum at the 16th-century Madre de Deus convent and cloister. Some of the ceramics exhibited here date from the 1700s. Displays range from individual glazed tiles to elaborate pictorial panels. The 118-ft *Panorama of Lisbon* (1730) is a detailed study of the city and waterfront and is reputedly the country's longest azulejo piece. The richly furnished convent church contains some sights of its own: of note are the gilt baroque decoration and lively azulejo works depicting the life of St. Anthony. There's also a little café-bar and a gift shop that sells tile reproductions. ✉ Rua da Madre de Deus 4 (Bus 104 or 105 from Santa Apolónia station), Madre de Deus, ☎ 21/814–7747. ▣ €2.25. ◷ Tues. 2–6, Wed.–Sun. 10–6.

❺ Sé. Lisbon's austere Romanesque cathedral was founded in 1150 to commemorate the defeat of the Moors; to rub salt in the wound, the conquerors built the sanctuary on the spot where Moorish Lisbon's main mosque once stood. Note the fine rose window, and be sure to visit the 13th-century cloister and the treasure-filled sacristy, which, among other things, contains the relics of the martyr St. Vincent. According to legend, the relics were carried from the Algarve to Lisbon in a ship piloted by ravens. ✉ *Largo da Sé, Alfama,* ☎ *21/886–6752.*

🕮 *Cathedral: free. Cloister: €1. Sacristy €1.50.* ☉ *Cathedral: Tues.–Sat. 9–7, Sun.–Mon. 9–5. Cloister and sacristy: daily 10–1 and 2–6.*

The Baixa

The earthquake of 1755, a massive tidal wave, and subsequent fires killed thousands of people and reduced proud 18th-century Lisbon to rubble. But within 10 years, frantic rebuilding under the direction of the king's minister, the Marquês de Pombal, had given the city a new look: a neoclassical grid design. You can still see this perfectly today in the impressive Baixa, a shopping and banking district that stretches from the riverfront to the square known as the Rossío. Pombal intended the various streets to house workshops for certain trades and crafts, something that's still reflected in street names such as Rua dos Sapateiros (Cobblers' Street) and Rua da Prata (Silversmiths' Street). Near the neoclassical arch at the bottom of Rua Augusta, street stalls selling jewelry and ethnic items sometimes appear on weekends. You may have seen the arch before in the movie *Gulliver's Travels,* in which the Lilliputians wheeled Ted Danson, as Gulliver, through it.

A Good Walk

Begin your exploration at the neoclassical arch, Arco da Vitória, and the **Praça do Comércio** ⑧; a marketplace in the 16th-century, it's now lined with 18th-century buildings. Head up Rua Augusta to Lisbon's main meeting place and crossroads, the Praça Dom Pedro IV. Its popular name, **Rossío** ⑨, matches the names of the metro station opening onto it and the train station just to the north. Note Dom Pedro's statue here; astride his horse, he sits on a pedestal flanked by fountains and wave-patterned paving stones. King for a year, he gave the people a popular charter, then abdicated in favor of his daughter Maria.

Take a moment to admire Rossío's Teatro Nacional de Dona Maria II, named for Dom Pedro's daughter-successor (at night the 1846 neoclassical facade is dramatically illuminated). Its left side fronts the Largo de São Domingos, a square with the Palácio da Independência, where restoration leaders met before overthrowing Portugal's Spanish occupiers in 1640. Straight across the Largo de São Domingos, notice (or step inside) the church of the same name; Inquisition sentences were once determined on its site. Just steps south toward Rua dos Correeiros, Largo de São Domingos turns into the Praça da Figueira, with its statue of Prince Henry the Navigator's father, King João I. Take time to explore the shops and cafés that surround the pigeon-filled square.

Now you are in the heart of Baixa, and it's almost impossible to get lost in its gridded, compact core. Rua Augusta is straight ahead; use it as your point of reference, while exploring the surrounding streets, which run parallel or at right angles and in many cases are for pedestrians only. Take half an hour or half a day; you're never far from a café in which to regroup. Besides offering the chance to shop and people-watch, Rua Augusta also has Roman tunnels underneath No. 62–74, open on some summer Thursday afternoons. From Rua Augusta, a short walk along Rua de Santa Justa will take you to the **Elevador de Santa Justa** ⑩, one of the neighborhood's more remarkable landmarks.

You could hike the Baixa in half an hour, but multiply that by four to allow time to explore the sights and poke into shops. Then add an hour or more for people-watching or lingering in a café, enjoying the Rossío's satisfying chaos.

Sights to See

★ ⑩ **Elevador de Santa Justa.** Built in 1902 by Raul Mésnier, the Santa Justa Elevator, inside a Gothic-style tower, is one of Lisbon's more extraordinary structures. After stepping outside the elevator compartment at the upper level, climb the staircase to the very top of the structure for views of the Baixa district and beyond. There's a windswept café up here, though its prices, like its location, are sky high. There is a walkway at the top of the elevator leading to the Largo do Carmo; however, it was closed for renovations at this writing. ⊠ *Rua Aurea and Rua de Santa Justa, Baixa,* ☎ *21/361–3054.* 🎟 *€0.90 one-way.* ☉ *Daily 7 AM–11:45 PM.*

❽ Praça do Comércio. When the Marquês de Pombal completed his plan for Lisbon, he offset the gridded streets you now see in the Baixa district with the enormous riverfront Praça do Comércio. Known also as the Terreiro do Paço, after the royal palace (the Paço) that once stood here, it's lined with yellow, arcaded, 18th-century buildings. Steps— once used by occupants of the royal barges that docked here—lead up from the water onto the square. The equestrian statue is of Dom José I, king at the time of the earthquake and subsequent rebuilding. In 1908, amid unrest that led to the declaration of a republic, King Carlos and his eldest son, Luís Filipe, were assassinated as they rode through the square in a carriage. Later, during the 1974 revolution, the Praça do Comércio and its surrounding government buildings were among the first places to be occupied by rebel troops. The square itself is a hub for public transportation (trams to Belém leave from here, and ferries cross the Tagus at this point), and it's also worth coming here on Sunday morning, when a market of old coins and banknotes takes place under the arches of the arcade. To the west of the square (your right if you're facing the waterfront) and along Rua do Arsenal is the smart **Lisboa Welcome Centre** (☎ 21/031–2700) with its information desk, modern art gallery, auditorium, tobacco shop, café, deli, and restaurant. It's open daily 9 AM to 8 PM.

NEED A BREAK?
One of the original buildings on Praça do Comércio houses the **Café Martinho da Arcada** (⊠ Praça do Comércio 3, Baixa, ☎ 21/887– 9259), a literary haunt since 1782. The main rooms contain an expensive restaurant; adjacent to it is a more modest café-bar.

★ ❾ Rossío. Lisbon's main square since the Middle Ages is popularly known as the Rossío, although its official name is Praça Dom Pedro IV (whom the central statue commemorates). Although rather overwhelmed by the traffic that circles it, the Rossío is a grand space, with ornate French fountains. Public executions were once carried out here; slightly less dramatic performances these days are on show in the mid-19th-century Teatro Nacional (National Theater). It's at the square's northern edge and was built on the site of the Palace of the Inquisition. You'll probably do what the locals do when they come to the Rossío, though: pick up a newspaper, sit at one of the cafés that line the square's east and west sides, and, perhaps, have one of the roaming shoe shiners give your boots a polish—just be sure to agree on a price first.

Chiado and the Bairro Alto

West of the Baixa is the fashionable shopping district of Chiado. Although a calamitous 1988 fire destroyed much of the area, an ambitious rebuilding program has restored some of the fin-de-siècle facades. And a chic retail complex, hotel, and metro station on the site of the old Armazéns do Chiado—once Lisbon's largest department store— has given the district a modern focus. Along Rua Garrett and Rua do Carmo are some of Europe's best shoe stores as well as glittering jewelry shops, hip boutiques, and a host of cafés and delis. Chiado's narrow, often-cobbled streets lead to the Bairro Alto and often follow contours of the hills, which can make getting around confusing. Although the settlement of the Bairro Alto dates from the 17th century, most of the buildings are from the 18th and 19th centuries and are an appealing mixture of small churches, warehouses, antiques and art galleries, artisans' shops, and town houses with wrought-iron balconies.

Bairro Alto's streets are filled with the sounds of daily life: children scuffle amid the drying laundry, women carry huge bundles from shop to shop, and old men clog the doorways of barrooms. The neighborhood has always had a reputation as being rather rough-and-ready, and there's still a thriving red-light district and back alleys where it would be unwise to venture after dark. On the whole, however, it's safe to walk around; indeed, the Bairro Alto has more bars, restaurants, fado clubs, and discos than any other district.

A Good Walk

As the focus in Chiado is on shopping, it's best to explore the Bairro Alto first, so that you need not lug your purchases around. The least taxing way to tour this hilly district is from the top down. From Praça dos Restauradores, catch the **Elevador da Glória** ⑪. If natural history and flowers are your passions, it's a 20-minute walk north from this creaking funicular railway to the **Jardim Botânico** ⑫. If you prefer wine to roses, though, note that the funicular deposits you immediately across the street from the **Instituto do Vinho do Porto** ⑬, where you can sample some port if it's not too early in the day.

From the institute, turn right and walk down Rua São Pedro de Alcântara. At Largo Trindade Coelho, on your left, is the **Igreja de São Roque** ⑭ and its museum. From the southeast corner of Largo Trindade Coelho, follow Rua Nova da Trindade downhill and take a left at the second corner, Rua da Trindade. This small street leads to Largo do Carmo and the **Convento do Carmo** ⑮, a charming ruin housing an interesting archaeological museum. Along a narrow alley behind the Convento do Carmo is the Elevador de Santa Justa. From here you can either make the lengthy trip west across the quarter (by tram if you prefer) to the **Jardim da Estrêla** ⑯ or you can head down to Chiado for some shopping.

Chiado's main street, **Rua Garrett** ⑰, is full of cafés and shops. Just off it is the Grandes Armazéns do Chiado, whose tony boutiques are ensconced behind the restored facade of what was once Lisbon's largest department store. From Rua Garrett, head down Rua Serpa Pinto see what's on display at the **Museu do Chiado** ⑱, the district's major art gallery. From here, you might want head west to the Madragoa neighborhood and the **Museu da Marioneta** ⑲. Tram 25 or Bus 27 will drop you nearby.

TIMING

The Bairro Alto is remarkably compact, and it takes very little time to walk from one end to the other; an hour would cover it. But once you start diving off into the side streets and lingering in the shops, galleries, and bars, you'll find you can happily spend a morning or afternoon here. Neither the Igreja de São Roque nor the Convento do Carmo will occupy you for more than half an hour. Note that the Instituto do Vinho do Porto doesn't open until 2 PM. If you don't like crowds, avoid the Bairro Alto late at night, especially on weekends, when seemingly the whole of Lisbon comes here to eat, drink, and party.

Sights to See

⑮ **Convento do Carmo.** The partially ruined Carmelite Convent—once Lisbon's largest—was severely damaged in the 1755 earthquake. Today open-air summer orchestral concerts are held beneath its majestic archways. Its sacristy houses the **Museu Arqueológico do Carmo** (Archaeological Museum), a small but worthy collection of ceramic tiles, medieval tombs, ancient coins, and other city finds. The convent is unlikely to delay you long, but the lovely square outside is a great place to pull up a café seat. ⊠ *Largo do Carmo, Chiado,* ☎ *21/346–0473.* ⬛ €2.50. ⊙ *Apr.–Sept., daily 10–6; Oct.–Mar., daily 10–5.*

⑪ Elevador da Glória. One of the finest approaches to the Bairro Alto is via this funicular railway on the western side of Avenida da Liberdade, near Praça dos Restauradores. It runs up the steep hill and takes only about a minute to reach the São Pedro de Alcântara Miradouro, a viewpoint that looks out over the castle and the Alfama. ⊠ *Calçada da Glória, Bairro Alto,* ☎ *21/363–2044.* ⬛ €0.90 one-way. ⊙ *Daily 7 AM–midnight.*

★ **⑭ Igreja de São Roque.** Filippo Terzi, the architect who designed São Vicente on the outskirts of the Alfama, was also responsible for this Renaissance church. Curb your impatience with its plain facade and venture inside. Its eight side chapels have statuary and art dating from the early 17th century. The last chapel on the left before the altar is the extraordinary 18th-century Capela de São João Baptista (Chapel of St. John the Baptist): designed and built in Rome, with rare stones and mosaics that resemble oil paintings, the chapel was taken apart, shipped to Lisbon, and reassembled here in 1747. You may find a guide who will escort you around the church and switch on the appropriate lights so the beauty of the chapel is revealed. Adjoining the church, the **Museu de Arte Sacra** (Museum of Sacred Art) displays a surprisingly engaging collection of clerical vestments and liturgical objects: the capes and drapes are delicately embroidered in gold, and the jewel-encrusted crosses and goblets glitter in their cases. ⊠ *Largo Trindade Coelho, Bairro Alto,* ☎ *21/323–5381.* ⬛ *Church: free. Museum:* €0.75 *Mon.–Sat., free Sun.* ⊙ *Church: daily 8:30–5. Museum: daily 10–5. Metro: Baixa-Chiado.*

★ **⑬ Instituto do Vinho do Porto.** In the cozy, clublike lounge, you can taste some of the Port Wine Institute's more than 300 types and vintages of port—from extra-dry white varieties to red vintages. Service can be slow, but eventually someone will bring you a wine list, and you can order by the glass or bottle. ⊠ *Rua de São Pedro de Alcântara 45, Bairro Alto,* ☎ *21/347–5707,* ⬛Ⱳⱸⱱ *www.ivp.pt.* ⬛ *Free; prices of tastings vary, starting at* €1. ⊙ *Mon.–Sat. 2 PM–midnight. Metro: Restauradores (then take Elevador de Glória).*

⑫ Jardim Botânico. Lisbon's main botanical garden was first laid out in 1874. Hidden between backstreets about 2 km (1 mi) north of the Bairro Alto, it makes a restful stop, with 10 acres of paths, benches, and nearly 15,000 species of subtropical plants; there's also a 19th-century meteorological observatory. The gardens form part of the **Museu de História Natural** (Natural History Museum), whose buildings contain geological, zoological, and anthropological displays. ⊠ *Rua da Escola Politécnica 58; weekday entrance also at Rua do Alegria, near Av. da Liberdade, Principe Real,* ☎ *21/396–1521.* ⬛ *Gardens:* €1. *Museum: free.* ⊙ *Gardens: May–Oct., weekdays 9–8, weekends 10–8; Nov.–Apr., weekdays 9–6, weekends 10–6; guided tours (reservations required) year-round Sat. at 11. Museum: weekdays 10–5.*

⑯ Jardim da Estrêla. Inside the attractively laid out Estrêla Garden, old men sit at tables playing card games. Watch them a while, stroll the shaded paths, and then pull up a chair in the café for a drink or a snack. Towering over the southwestern side is the 18th-century **Basilica da Estrêla**, which is open daily 7:30–1 and 3–7. This spacious baroque basilica has an unusually restrained interior and offers views of the city from its *zimborio* (dome). The gardens lie on the western edge of the Bairro Alto. You can walk here, although it's more pleasant to catch Tram 28, which runs from Rua do Loreto, near Praça Luís de Camões, just west of Largo do Carmo.

❽ Museu do Chiado. The Chiado's prime art gallery—built on the site of a monastery—specializes in Portuguese art from 1850 to the present day, covering various movements: romanticism, naturalism, surrealism, modernism. The museum also hosts international films and temporary exhibitions of paintings and sculpture. ⊠ *Rua Serpa Pinto 6, Chiado,* ☎ *21/343–2148,* ▱ *€3, free Sun. until 2 PM.* ☉ *Tues. 2–6, Wed.–Sun. 10–6.*

☝ ❾ Museu da Marioneta. The intricate workmanship that went into the creation of the puppets on display at this museum is remarkable, and it's not just kids' stuff either: during the Salazar regime, puppet shows were used to mock the pretensions and corruption of the politicians. The collection encompasses both Portuguese and foreign puppets. Those from Santo Aleixo in the Alentejo region (just south of Lisbon) are particularly notable, measuring just over 6 inches high. ⊠ *Convento das Bernardas, Rua da Esperança 146, Madragoa,* ☎ *21/394–2810.* ▱ *€2.50.* ☉ *Tues.–Sun. 10–1 and 2–6.*

❼ Rua Garrett. The Chiado's principal street is lined with old stores and turn-of-the-20th-century, wood-paneled coffee shops. The most famous of the cafés is **Café A Brasileira** (⊠ Rua Garrett 120, Chiado, ☎ 21/346–9541), which has a life-size statue of Portugal's national poet, Fernando Pessoa, seated at an outside table.

The Modern City

The attractions of 19th- to 20th-century Lisbon are as diverse as they are far-flung. Near the large square Praça dos Restauradores, north of Rossío, the southern reaches of the modern city echo some of the Baixa. With its 10 parallel rows of trees, Avenida da Liberdade is an enchanting place in which to linger and an easy-to-find reference point if you get lost in the surrounding backstreets. North of the city's main park, Parque Eduardo VII, the modern city stretches into residential suburbs with only the occasional attraction. You can reach all of them by public transportation or, if time is short, by taxi.

A Good Tour

Start at the plaza where downtown meets uptown, **Praça dos Restauradores** ⑳. If you arrive via metro, note the enamel-on-ceramic painting and decorative tiles in the Restauradores station. A good first stop on the plaza is Palácio Foz, which houses a tourist office. Glance at some of its walls and ceilings painted by early 20th-century artists. At the top of the square, start up the gently sloping **Avenida da Liberdade** ㉑ where, on a mild morning, you can stop for a late breakfast at a garden café. Along the way you might want to detour to **Rua das Portas de Santo Antão** ㉒, a pedestrian-only street full of seafood restaurants that runs parallel to Avenida da Liberdade one block to the east. Avenida da Liberdade's leafy mile is a favorite for stress-free strolls evocative of a lazier Lisbon. When you leave at its northern end, you pass through the **Praça Marquês de Pombal** ㉓. If shopping is your bag you could head left down Avenida J. A. de Aguiar to the **Amoreiras** ㉔ shopping center. Or, if you've called ahead for a group tour, you can turn left on Rua das Amoreiras from Avenida J. A. de Aguiar to see the impressively engineered inner reservoir of Lisbon's **Aqueduto das Aguas Livres** ㉕.

To continue on your tour of the modern city, walk around the Praça Marquês de Pombal to the right—**Parque Eduardo VII** ㉖ will be on your left—and veer right one block onto Avenida Fontes. Turn left up Avenida António Augusto de Aguiar to the **Museu Calouste Gulbenkian** ㉗, home to European, Egyptian, Greek, Roman, and Asian art. (To avoid the half-hour walk, hop onto the metro from the Rotunda station at Praça Marquês de Pombal and ride it for two stops to São Sebastião or three stops to Praça de Espanha.) Adjoining the Museu Calouste Gulbenkian is the **Centro de Arte Moderna** ㉘, with a fine collection of Portuguese art. Be sure to roam the gardens on the two museums' grounds. Hail a taxi or ask the reception desk of the museum to call one. (You can also catch the metro at Praça de Espanha to Sete Rios, then walk 10 to 20 minutes west along Rua São Domingos de Benfica.) The next stop is the **Palácio dos Marqueses da Fronteira** ㉙, an exquisite 17th-century mansion. It's near the **Jardim Zoológico** ㉚ and on the border of Parque Florestal de Monsanto.

TIMING

In expansive, modern Lisbon, choosing sights according to your mood and the weather isn't out of line. You really will have to make choices about what to visit if you have just one day—to see everything, allow two or three days. It could take three hours to do justice to the Gulbenkian alone—especially if you have lunch on the premises. The palace and its gardens justify another hour easily; add another for walking (or two if you eschew any travel by taxis or metro), and perhaps another hour for shopping and a coffee break on the Avenida da Liberdade.

Sights to See

㉔ **Amoreiras.** Before the Parque das Nações site was developed, Lisbon could count its postmodern architectural triumphs on one finger—namely the gigantic pink-and-blue Amoreiras, a striking commercial-and-residential complex west of Parque Eduardo VII. Designed by Tomás Taveira in 1985 and visible from just about everywhere in town, the gleaming complex still turns heads; inside, there's a huge shopping center, a 10-screen movie theater, a food court—even a chapel. On weekends it seems all of Lisbon turns out to roam the corridors. ⊠ *Av. Eng. Duarte Pacheco, Amoreiras,* ☎ *21/381–0200.* ⊘ *Shops and restaurants daily 10 AM–midnight. Metro: Marquês de Pombal.*

㉕ **Aqueduto das Aguas Livres.** Lisbon was formerly provided with clean drinking water by means of the Aqueduct of Free Waters (1729–48), built by Manuel da Maia and stretching for more than 18 km (11 mi) from the water source on the outskirts of the city. It survived the 1755 earthquake, and today its most graceful section consists of 14 arches that soar 200 ft over the pretty neighborhood square of Largo das Amoreiras. The aqueduct itself is off-limits unless you book a group tour, but the square is also the site of the associated Mãe d'Agua, an internal reservoir capable of holding more than a million gallons of water. This extraordinary structure is used for art exhibitions and other cultural displays, giving you the chance to view the vast holding tank, the lavish internal waterfall, and the associated machinery. ⊠ *Largo das Amoreiras, Campolide,* ☎ *21/813–5522 (for tours of aqueduct).*

㉑ **Avenida da Liberdade.** In the Restauradores neighborhood, Liberty Avenue—downtown's spine—was laid out in 1879. What started as an elegant rival to the Champs Élysées has lost some of its allure: many of the late-19th-century mansions and art deco buildings that once graced it have been demolished; others have been turned into soulless office blocks. Vehicles roar down both sides. It's still worth a leisurely stroll up the 1½-km (1-mi) length of the avenue, from Praça dos Restauradores to the Parque Eduardo VII, at least once—if only to cool off with a drink in one of the *esplanadas* (garden cafés). There are two amid the plane trees in the middle of the avenue. Halfway up and on the avenue's western side, the few theaters that make up Lisbon's surviving downtown theater district congregate in Parque Mayer.

OFF THE
BEATEN PATH

CAMPO PEQUENO – Nothing grabs your attention quite so suddenly as the city's circular, redbrick, Moorish-style bullring, an over-the-top structure built in 1892 with small cupolas atop its four main towers. The ring holds about 9,000 people who crowd in to watch weekly bullfights, held every Thursday at 10 PM from June through September; at other times it's used as the venue for circuses and similar events. ⊠ *Praça de Touros do Campo Pequeno, Av. da República, Campo Pequeno,* ☎ *21/ 793–2093. Metro: Campo Pequeno.*

㉘ Centro de Arte Moderna. In the gardens outside the Fundação Calouste Gulbenkian, sculptures hide in every recess. You may want to spend a little time here before following signs to the Modern Art Center, with its two floors of contemporary and modern works—the finest collection of its sort in Portugal. Naturally, Portuguese artists are best represented: look for pieces by Amadeo de Sousa Cardoso, whose painting style varied greatly in his short life; abstract works by Viera da Silva; and the childhood themes explored in the paintings of Paula Rego. There's also a special section set aside for drawings and prints. ⊠ *Rua Dr. N. Bettencourt, São Sebastião,* ☎ *21/782–3000.* 🔳 *€2.50, free Sun.* ☉ *Tues. 2–6, Wed.–Sun. 10–6. Metro: São Sebastião.*

㉚ Jardim Zoológico. With a menagerie of 2,000 animals from more than 370 species, the Zoological Garden is always a popular spot. Admission is pricey, but in addition to the usual habitats and enclosures there's a gorilla house; free range–style areas for larger animals; a children's zoo with miniature houses and small animals; a cable-car ride; and twice-daily animal shows (you have your pick of those that feature parrots, dolphins, or reptiles). You can pack a picnic lunch or eat at one of the on-site snack bars and restaurants. ⊠ *Estrada de Benfica 158, Sete Rios,* ☎ *21/723–2900,* 𝗪𝗘𝗕 *www.zoolisboa.pt.* 🔳 *€11.* ☉ *Apr.–mid-Oct., daily 10–8; mid-Oct.–Mar., daily 10–6. Metro: Jardim Zoológico or Sete Rios.*

★ ㉗ Museu Calouste Gulbenkian. On its own lush grounds, the museum of the celebrated Fundação Calouste Gulbenkian (Calouste Gulbenkian Foundation), a cultural trust, houses treasures collected by Armenian oil magnate Calouste Gulbenkian (1869–1955) and donated to the people of Portugal in return for tax concessions. The collection is split in two: one part is devoted to Egyptian, Greek, Roman, Islamic, and Asian art and the other to European acquisitions. Both holdings are relatively small, but the quality of the pieces on display is magnificent, and you should aim to spend at least two hours here or even the better part of a day. English-language notes are available throughout the museum.

One of the highlights in the astounding Egyptian Room is a haunting gold mummy mask. Greek and Roman coins and statuary, Chinese porcelain, Japanese prints, and a set of rich 16th- and 17th-century Persian tapestries follow. The European art section has pieces from all the major schools from the 15th through the 20th centuries. A room of vivid 18th-century Venetian scenes by Francesco Guardi and paintings by Rembrandt, Peter Paul Rubens, Claude Monet, and Pierre-Auguste Renoir stimulate the senses, as do the Italian and Spanish ceramics, gleaming French furniture, textiles, and art nouveau jewelry.

If it's all too much to take in at one time, break up your visit with a stop in the basement's pleasant café-restaurant. There's an exhibition room here, too, with temporary displays. As you leave the museum, you can buy posters and postcards at the main desk. Free concerts are given some Sundays in the library atrium, and the foundation also has two concert halls, where music and ballet festivals are held in winter and spring. Modestly priced tickets are available at the box office. ⊠ *Av. de Berna 45, São Sebastião,* ☎ *21/782–3000,* WEB *www.museu. gulbenkian.pt.* ☎ *€3.* ☉ *Tues.–Sun. 10–5:45. Metro: São Sebastião or Praça de Espanha.*

㉙ Palácio dos Marqueses da Fronteira. Built in the late 17th century, the Palace of the Marquises, often called the Palácio Fronteira, remains one of the capital's most beautiful houses, containing splendid reception rooms with 17th- and 18th-century tiles, contemporary furniture, and paintings. Note that visits may be limited to guided tours; phone ahead for information. The grounds harbor a terraced walk, a topiary garden, and statuary and fountains. Some of the city's finest azulejos adorn the fountains and terraces and depict hunting scenes, battles, and religious themes. ⊠ *Largo de São Domingo de Benfica 1, São Domingo de Benfica,* ☎ *21/778–2023.* ☎ *Palace and gardens: weekdays €5, Sat. €7.50. Gardens: weekdays €1.50, Sat. €2.50.* ☉ *July–Sept., Mon.– Sat. for guided tours (must be booked in advance) at 10:30, 11, 11:30, and noon; Oct.–May, Mon.–Sat. 11 AM and noon. Metro: Sete Rios.*

㉖ Parque Eduardo VII. Established at the beginning of the 20th century in the São Sebastião district, the city's main park was named to honor the British monarch's 1903 visit here during his brief reign. The sloping, formal gardens are used by surprisingly few of Lisbon's residents. There are, however, magnificent views from the avenue at the top of the park, where modernistic towers topped by concrete wheat sheaves stand like sentinels. The park also has Lisbon's best-kept horticultural secrets: the *estufa fria* (cold greenhouse) and *estufa quente* (hot greenhouse), which contain rare flowers, trees, and shrubs from tropical and subtropical climes. These are gorgeous grottoes in which to stroll, and concerts and exhibitions are held in the estufa fria from time to time. ☎ *21/388–2278 for information on greenhouses.* ☎ *Greenhouses: €1.07.* ☉ *Park: daily dawn–dusk. Greenhouses: Apr.–Sept., daily 9– 6; Oct.–Mar., daily 9–5. Metro: Parque or Marquês de Pombal.*

㉓ Praça Marquês de Pombal. Dominating the center of Marquês de Pombal Square is a statue of the marquês himself, the man responsible for the design of the "new" Lisbon that emerged from the ruins of the 1755 earthquake. On the statue's base are representations of both the earthquake and the tidal wave that engulfed the city; a female figure with outstretched arms signifies the joy at the emergence of the re-fashioned city. The square is effectively a large roundabout—known informally as the Rotunda—and a useful orientation point, since it stands at the northern end of Avenida da Liberdade (in the Baixa district) with Parque Eduardo VII (in the São Sebastião quarter) just behind. New buildings with classic facades are rising along the square's rim, and there are impressive entrances to the Marquês de Pombal metro station.

㉟ Praça dos Restauradores. Although this square, which is adjacent to Rossío train station, marks the beginning of modern Lisbon, it's technically part of the Baixa district. Here the broad, tree-lined Avenida da Liberdade starts its northwesterly ascent. *"Restauradores"* means "restoration," and the square commemorates the 1640 uprising against Spanish rule that restored Portuguese independence. An obelisk (raised in 1886) commemorates the event. Note the elegant 18th-century Palácio Foz, on the square's west side. Prior to World War I, it contained a casino; today it houses a tourist office. The only building to rival the palace is the restored Eden building, just to the south. The art deco masterpiece of Portuguese architect Cassiano Branco now contains the VIP Eden apartment-hotel and a Virgin Megastore.

㉒ Rua das Portas de Santo Antão. Everyone knows that if you want to eat seafood in the center of Lisbon, you come to the Baixa district's Rua das Portas de Santo Antão. Waiters lurk in the doorways of the many fish eateries that line this pedestrian-only street a block east of Praça dos Restauradores. Most establishments display fish on ice slabs and great tanks of lobsters; choose your meal and then sit at a table outside on the cobblestones to enjoy it. Later, if you're daring, pop into one of the street's few surviving *ginginha* bars—cubbyholes where un-shaven gents and local characters stand around throwing down shots of eye-wateringly strong cherry brandy.

Belém

Some of Lisbon's grandest monuments and museums are in the dis-trict of Belém (the Portuguese word for Bethlehem), at the city's south-western edge. It was from here that the country's great explorers set out during the period of the discoveries. The wealth brought back from the New World helped to pay for many of the neighborhood's struc-tures, some of which are the best examples of the uniquely Portuguese late-Gothic architecture known as Manueline.

Although several buses and Tram 18 will get here from Lisbon's center, the 30-minute ride on Tram 15 from the Baixa district's Praça do Comércio in is very scenic. Tram 15 also passes close by or stops right at several of the important sights.

A Good Tour

Heading west from Lisbon by taxi or Tram 15, you'll pass through the wealthy district of Lapa, with its **Museu de Arte Antiga** ㉛. A little far-ther on—at about the halfway point to Belém—you'll pass under the magnificent **Ponte 25 de Abril** ㉜, which spans the Rio Tejo and is one of the city's great landmarks. This bridge is in Lisbon's **Alcântara** ㉝ district, whose dockside—particularly the Doca de Santo Amaro—is important to the city's nightlife scene.

If you planned to make the **Museu Nacional dos Coches** ㉞ your first stop in Belém, you won't be alone—it's collection of baroque carriages is one of Lisbon's biggest draws. Get off Tram 15 near the Praça Afonso de Albuquerque. From the coach museum you can either make the 20-minute walk north along Calçada da Ajuda to the **Jardim Botânico da Ajuda** ㉟ and, just up from it, the **Palácio da Ajuda** ㊱ or continue along the Tram 15 route directly to the **Mosteiro dos Jeróni-mos** ㊲. In a complex of buildings adjoining this famous monastery are the **Planetário Calouste Gulbenkian** ㊳, with its starry displays, and the **Museu de Marinha** ㊴, with its seafaring exhibits. On a short walk south toward the Rio Tejo, you'll pass the **Centro Cultural de Belém** ㊵, an arts venue that contains the Museu do Design, on your way to the riverfront **Museu de Arte Popular** ㊶. East of this museum and its folk-art collection is the **Padrão dos Descobrimentos** ㊷; west of the museum is the **Torre de Belém** ㊸—both stony sentinels look out over the Rio Tejo.

TIMING

Set aside two or three hours for the Museu de Arte Antiga and another hour or two for the Mosteiro dos Jerónimos. This leaves an hour or two for one of the other museums and monuments—after that, you'll probably want to just flop into a chair at an Alcântara district bar or

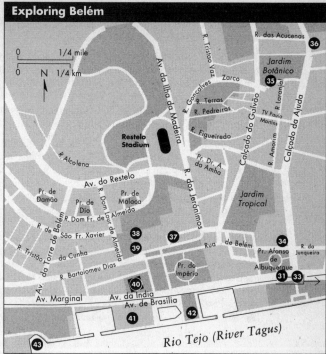

Exploring Belém

restaurant. Note that most of Belém's sights are closed Monday, and Sunday sees free or reduced admission at many attractions.

Sights to See

33 **Alcântara.** The docks are alive with music in Alcântara, where late-night bars attract Lisbon's in crowd. Here, in the lee of the huge Ponte 25 de Abril, the old wharves have been made over, and you can walk along the landscaped riverfront all the way to Belém (a 30-minute stroll). At Doca de Santo Amaro, under the bridge on its east side, a line of fashionable restaurants and clubs has emerged from the shells of former warehouses. On the terrace in front of the marina, the party goes on until late into the night. During the day, the easiest way to get here is by train from Cais do Sodré station or on Tram 15; at night, take a taxi.

40 **Centro Cultural de Belém.** Built of pink granite and marble, the modern Belém Cultural Center won few friends when it was constructed in 1991, although all of Lisbon appreciates its cultural offerings. The main attraction is the **Museu do Design,** which showcases international design from the last 65 years in three main galleries: Luxury, Pop, and Cool. Objects on display include furniture, jewelry, and household items. The center also has a restaurant, a café, and a concert hall. Its roof gardens and terrace bar have fine views of the Mosteiro dos Jerónimos and the Rio Tejo. ⊠ *Praça do Império, Belém,* ☎ *21/361–1444,* WEB *www.ccb.pt.* ☜ *Cultural center: free. Museum: €2.50.* ☉ *Cultural center: daily 8 AM–9:30 PM. Museum: daily 11–8.*

35 **Jardim Botânico da Ajuda.** Portugal's oldest botanical garden—laid out in 1768 by the Italian botanist Vandelli—is an enjoyable place to spend an hour or so. You can stroll up here from the river at Belém, or take Tram 18 from downtown, which terminates near here. The many species of flora, labeled in Latin, are in several greenhouses covering

10 acres; if you call in advance you may be able to arrange a guided tour. ⊠ *Calçada da Ajuda, Alto de Ajuda,* ☎ *21/362–2503.* ☑ *€1.50.* ☉ *Thurs.–Tues. 10–5.*

★ ㉛ **Mosteiro dos Jerónimos.** Conceived and commissioned by Dom Manuel I, Belém's famous Jerónimos Monastery was financed largely by treasures brought back from Africa, Asia, and South America. Construction began in 1502 under the supervision of Diogo de Boitaca (architect of the pioneering Igreja de Jesus at Setúbal) and his successor, João de Castilho, a Spaniard.

The monastery is a supreme example of the Manueline style of building (named after king Dom Manuel I), which represented a marked departure from the prevailing Gothic. Much of it is characterized by elaborate sculptural details, often with a maritime motif. João de Castilho was responsible for the southern portal, which forms the main entrance to the church: the figure on the central pillar is Henry the Navigator, and the canopy shows a hierarchy of statues contained within niches. Inside, the remarkably spacious interior contrasts with the riot of decoration on the six nave columns, which disappear into a complex latticework ceiling. The Gothic- and Renaissance-style double cloister on the lower level was also designed to stunning effect by Castilho. The arches and pillars are heavily sculpted with marine motifs. ⊠ *Praça do Império, Belém,* ☎ *21/362–0034.* ☑ *Cloister: €3, free Sun.* ☉ *May–Sept., Tues.–Sun. 10–6:30; Oct.–Apr., Tues.–Sun. 10–5.*

NEED A
BREAK?
For a real taste of Lisbon, stop at the **Antiga Confeitaria de Belém** (⊠ Rua de Belém 86–88, Belém, ☎ 21/363–7423), a bake shop–café that serves delicious, hot custard pastries sprinkled with cinnamon and powdered sugar. Although you can buy these treats throughout Lisbon, those made here are reputed to be the best.

★ ㉛ **Museu de Arte Antiga.** The only museum in Lisbon to approach the status of the Gulbenkian is the Ancient Art Museum. In a 17th-century palace, it has a beautifully displayed collection of Portuguese art—mainly from the 15th through 19th centuries—that superbly complements the Gulbenkian's general collection. Indeed, Gulbenkian himself donated several pieces to this museum, which opened in 1883.

Of all the holdings, the religious works of the Portuguese school of artists (characterized by fine portraiture with a distinct Flemish influence) stand out, especially the acknowledged masterpiece of Nuno Gonçalves, the *St. Vincent Altarpiece.* Painted between 1467 and 1470 for St. Vincent Chapel in Lisbon's cathedral, the altarpiece has six panels showing the patron saint of Lisbon receiving the homage of king, court, and citizens. Sixty figures can be identified, including Henry the Navigator; the archbishop of Lisbon; and sundry dukes, monks, fishermen, knights, and religious figures. In the top left corner of the two central panels is a figure purported to be Gonçalves himself.

Besides the Portuguese works, there are pieces by early Flemish painters who influenced the Portuguese. Other European artists are well represented, too, and although few of the works are really first rate, there are interesting examples by artists as diverse as Hieronymous Bosch, Hans Holbein, Brueghel the Younger, and painter to the Spanish court Diego Velázquez. There are also extensive collections of French silver, Portuguese furniture and tapestries, Asian ceramics, and items fashioned from Goan ivory.

Tram 15 from Praça do Comércio drops you at the foot of a steep flight of steps below the museum. Otherwise, Buses 27 and 49 from Praça

Marquês de Pombal run straight to Rua das Janelas Verdes. Coming from Belém, Buses 27 and 49 run from Rua de Belém across from the monastery and stop near the museum on their way back to downtown Lisbon. ⊠ *Rua das Janelas Verdes, Lapa,* ☎ *21/396–2825 or 21/396–4151.* ⊡ *€3.* ⊙ *Tues. 2–6, Wed.–Sun. 10–6.*

㊶ Museu de Arte Popular. The Popular Art Museum has examples of the country's folk art, principally a fascinating collection of ceramics, costumes, furniture, domestic and farm implements, and other ethnographic pieces. Displays are organized according to the province from which the objects came. ⊠ *Av. de Brasília, Belém,* ☎ *21/301–1282.* ⊡ *€2.25.* ⊙ *Tues.–Sun. 10–12:30 and 2–5.*

㊴ Museu de Marinha. In a complex of buildings adjoining the Mosteiro dos Jerónimos is the large, inviting Maritime Museum. Here you get a real grasp of the importance of the seafaring tradition in Portugal through maps and maritime codes, navigational equipment, full-size and model ships, uniforms, and weapons. ⊠ *Praça do Império, Belém,* ☎ *21/362–0019.* ⊡ *€2.50, free Sun. 10–1.* ⊙ *June–Sept., Tues.–Sun. 10–6; Oct–May, Tues.–Sun. 10–5.*

㉞ Museu Nacional dos Coches. The National Coach Museum houses one of the world's largest collections of carriages in buildings that once accommodated a riding school. The oldest coach on display was made for Philip II of Spain in the late 16th century, and among the most stunning exhibits are three gold conveyances created in Rome for King John V in 1716. This dazzling collection of gloriously painted and/or gilded baroque vehicles is one of Lisbon's most popular sights. ⊠ *Praça Afonso de Albuquerque, Belém,* ☎ *21/361–0850.* ⊡ *€3, free Sun. 10–1.* ⊙ *Tues.–Sun. 10–6.*

㊷ Padrão dos Descobrimentos. The white, monolithic Monument of the Discoveries was erected in 1960 to commemorate the 500th anniversary of the death of Prince Henry the Navigator. It was built on what was the departure point for many voyages of discovery, including those of Vasco da Gama for India and—during Spain's occupation of Portugal—of the Spanish Armada for England in 1588. Henry is at the prow of the monument, facing the water; lined up behind him are the Portuguese explorers of Brazil and Asia, as well as other national heroes, including Luís de Camões the poet, who can be recognized by the book in his hand. On the ground adjacent to the monument, an inlaid map shows the extent of the explorations undertaken by the 15th- and 16th-century Portuguese sailors. Walk inside and take the elevator to the top for river views. ⊠ *Av. de Brasília, Belém,* ☎ *21/303–1950.* ⊡ *€2.* ⊙ *Tues.–Sun. 9–5.*

㊱ Palácio da Ajuda. In 1802 construction began on the Ajuda Palace, which was intended as a royal residence; its last regal occupant (Queen Maria) died here in 1911. Today the fussy building is home to a museum of 18th- and 19th-century paintings, furniture, and tapestries—hardly unique in Lisbon and, frankly, hardly an essential sight, although temporary exhibitions keep things interesting. It's a 20-minute walk north along Calçada da Ajuda from the Museu Nacional dos Coches, but Bus 14 and Tram 18 run this way, too. ⊠ *Largo da Ajuda, Alto da Ajuda,* ☎ *21/363–7095.* ⊡ *€2.50, free Sun. 10–2.* ⊙ *Thurs.–Tues. 10–4:30.*

☝ ㊳ Planetário Calouste Gulbenkian. Behind the Museu de Marinha, the Calouste Gulbenkian Planetarium presents interesting astronomical shows and displays several times a week. A bulletin posted in the window announces the current program, or you can get updates from the tourist office. ⊠ *Praça do Império, Belém,* ☎ *21/362–0002.* ⊡ *€2.25.*

PRINCE HENRY THE NAVIGATOR

The linkage of England and Portugal and the beginning of Portugal's Age of Discovery can be traced back to the 14th century, when England's John of Gaunt gave his daughter, Philippa of Lancaster, in marriage to King João I. The couple's third son, Infante Dom Henrique, is known widely today as Prince Henry the Navigator. By the end of his lifetime (1394–1460), this multidimensional soldier-scientist had conceptualized, funded, and inspired discoveries beyond the borders of the world that Europe knew. Scholars today, however they assess later misuses of exploration and conquest, generally agree that the prince paved the way for explorers such as Vasco da Gama and Ferdinand Magellan.

Strangely for a royal family in those (or any) times, João and Philippa raised six intelligent, apparently happy children. Alternately contemplative and restlessly athletic, Henry persuaded his father to let the four boys earn their knighthoods in an invasion of Morocco and the capture of its fortress at Ceuta. If the prince had not led his 70 soldier-filled ships to a victory worthy of Spielberg replay, Portugal's Age of Discovery might have been very different. As it is, visitors to Lisbon can stop at breezy Belém on the Rio Tejo, where, at the prow of the ship-shaped *Monumento dos Descobrimentos* (Monument to the Discoveries), Prince Henry stands, leading other Portuguese explorers and even King Afonso V.

At least three achievements secured Henry this place in the vanguard of explorers. In the Algarve, where he was governor, he founded a nearly legendary marine navigation school, which applied scientific principles to what was previously a haphazard endeavor. He also sent ships where none had gone before—especially around Cape Bojador, the "impassable wall" jutting out from West Africa at the end of the European-known ocean. And he required that expeditions chart the seas as they sailed. Charts that these expeditions made of Cape Bojador later led Vasco da Gama to sail around it, then past the Cape of Good Hope and on to India.

Seen through the prism of history, Prince Henry seems a royal contradiction. He earned his knighthood defeating infidels and was eventually named Grand Master of the Order of Christ, the successor to the Knights Templar. But since he lived before the Inquisition began, he may have met some of the Latin-, Greek-, and Hebrew-speaking scholars who came to the royal court. Further, his ships engaged in Africa's lucrative slave trade, but he himself lived simply and, having given away his profits to fund further expeditions, died broke. The navigator-prince was not technically a navigator, and he rarely boarded a ship, but he pointed the way for generations of future explorers.

㉜ **Ponte 25 de Abril.** Completed in 1966 and originally dedicated to Dr. António de Oliveira Salazar, Lisbon's first suspension bridge across the Rio Tejo, linking the Alcântara and Alamada districts, earned a name change after the 1974 revolution, which lurched into action on April 25 of that year. Standing 230 ft above the water and stretching almost 2½ km (1½ mi), it's a spectacular sight from any direction, although most gasps are reserved for the view from the top downward. Crossing by car, bus, or train is a thrill every time—except, perhaps, during rush hours.

★ ㊸ **Torre de Belém.** The openwork balconies and domed turrets of the fanciful Belém Tower make it perhaps the country's purest Manueline structure. Although it was built in the early 16th century on an island in the middle of the Rio Tejo, today the chalk-white tower stands near what has become the north bank—evidence of the river's changing course. It was originally constructed to defend the port entrance, but it also served as a prison from the late 16th through the 19th centuries. Cross the wood gangway and walk inside, not necessarily to see the rather plain interior but rather to clamber up the steep stone steps to the very top. From here you have a bird's-eye view of the river and central Lisbon. ⊠ *Av. de Brasília, Belém,* ☎ *21/362–0034.* ☑ *€2.25.* ⊙ *Tues.–Sun. 10–5.*

Parque das Nações

To prepare for the World Exposition in 1998, Lisbon's officials wisely kept in mind not only the immediate needs of the event, but also the future needs of the city. The result is Parque das Nações, a revitalized district on the banks of the Rio Tejo, 5 km (3 mi) northeast of Lisbon's center. Before it became the expo site, empty warehouses and refuse filled the district, which was once a landing area for seaplanes. Today it has apartment buildings, office complexes, hotels, restaurants, bars, and stores surrounded by landscaped parkland. It's also home to a marina; the Pavilhão Atlântico, a venue for major cultural and sporting events; the Bowling Internacional de Lisboa (BIL), Portugal's largest bowling alley; and the Feira Internacional Lisboa (FIL) convention center.

The centerpiece of the Parque das Nações is the popular Oceanário de Lisboa, an aquarium built for the expo. Nearby it are two museums: the Pavilhão do Conhecimento and the Pavilhão de Realidade Virtual. On Sundays in summer, open-air markets take place from 10 to 7 beside the river. Standing above it all is the Torre Vasco da Gama—from this tower, and from the Teleférico de Lisboa cable car that runs through the area, the views are fine.

If you plan to visit several of the park's attractions, consider buying (€14) a Cartão Parque das Nações. This card—sold at tourist offices, the Parque das Nações information desk, and at the area's various sights—gets you free admission to the aquarium and the tower; allows you to ride the excursion train and the cable car (one-way only) for free; and gives you discounts at the two pavilion attractions, the bowling center, and several restaurants.

A Good Tour

From Lisbon's center, take the metro to the Estação do Oriente. Designed by Spanish architect Santiago Calatrava, the station is distinguished by its handsome vaulted ceilings, white metal columns, and inner atriums. When you exit, you're not far from the information desk—on Alameda dos Oceanos—or the Pavilhão Atlântico, from which you can catch the excursion train. Or head east toward the river; there's a Teleférico de Lisboa stop at the other side of the Pavilhão Atlântico.

You can either take this cable car (11–7 weekdays, 10–8 weekends; €2.50 one-way) or wander along one of the two parallel esplanades to the **Torre Vasco da Gama.**

After taking in the views from the top of the tower, follow one of the esplanades back in the direction from which you came. Along the way, you'll pass musicians, souvenir shops, and restaurants. Off the esplanades, is the **Oceanário de Lisboa,** Europe's largest aquarium. Nearby it are the **Pavilhão de Realidade Virtual,** with virtual reality extravaganzas, and the **Pavilhão do Conhecimento,** with exhibits on science and technology. There's also a series of small water gardens whose themes focus, in turn, on glaciers, streams, waterfalls, and waves. Stepping stones over pools allow you to pass between the waterfalls. If you're ready for some serious shopping, head to the Vasco da Gama mall, just across and a short way down Avenida D. João II.

TIMING

You can spend anywhere from a couple of hours to all day (and all night) sightseeing, shopping, eating, and drinking here. Allot an hour or two for the Torre Vasco da Gama and about two hours for the Oceanário de Lisboa. On summer Sundays, set aside time to explore the markets at the north end of the park. Although some of the public transportation back to Lisbon's center stops running at midnight, taxis wait at the Estação de Oriente until all hours.

Sights to See

★ ℭ **Oceanário de Lisboa.** You cross a footbridge to reach this glass-and-stone complex, which rises from the river. With 25,000 fish, seabirds, and mammals, it's Europe's largest aquarium and the first ever to incorporate several ocean habitats (North Atlantic, Pacific, Antarctic, and Indian) in one place. You view the connected tanks and display areas from above and then from underwater; clever use of acrylic walls means that tropical fish and penguins look as if they inhabit the same space. Displays tell you more about the environments you're experiencing, and at the end you can sink onto a bench in one of the "contemplation" areas and just watch the fish swim by. ⊠ *Esplanada D. Carlos I (Doca dos Olivais), Parque das Nações,* ☎ *21/891–7002 or 21/891–7006,* WEB *www.oceanario.pt.* ☒ *€9.* ☉ *Apr.–Oct., daily 10–8 (last admission at 7); Nov.–Mar., daily 10–7 (last admission at 6).*

NEED A
BREAK?

For pure nectar on a hot day, find one of the many stands or cafés displaying huge bowls of oranges. They have juice machines on which, for about €2, they'll squeeze what seems like a dozen of them for you.

Pavilhão do Conhecimento. The white, angular, structure designed by architect Carrilho de Graça for the expo seems the perfect place to house the Knowledge Pavilion, or Living Science Centre, as it's also known. All of the permanent and temporary exhibits here are related to math, science, and technology; most are also labeled in English (a manual is available for the few that aren't) and all are interactive. A cybercafé with free Internet access, a media library, a gift shop, and a bookstore round out the offerings. ⊠ *Parque das Nações,* ☎ *21/891–7002.* ☒ *€5.* ☉ *Tues.–Fri. 10–6, weekends 11–7.*

Pavilhão de Realidade Virtual. Architect Manuel Vincent's whimsical, virtually surreal structure actually contains the virtually real. The multimedia shows here change every few months, and the drama transcends any language barriers. Performances incorporate a simulator ride that's not recommended for small children or visitors with certain medical conditions. ⊠ *Parque das Nações.* ☎ *21/891–7002.* ☒ *€7.50.* ☉ *Tues.–Sun. noon–6.*

Torre Vasco da Gama. At the park's easternmost edge and rising 480 ft above it, the graceful, white Vasco da Gama Tower is Portugal's tallest structure. Three glass elevators whisk you up 345-ft to the observation deck. In addition to taking in vistas across Lisbon and the Atlantic Ocean, you'll feel as if you're eye-to-eye with the 18-km (11-mi) Ponte Vasco da Gama (Vasco da Gama Bridge). You could lunch up here in the restaurant, but its menu is on the pricey side. ⊠ *Av. Pinto Ribeiro, Parque das Nações,* ☎ *21/896–9869.* ⊡ *€2.49.* ⊙ *Sept.–May, daily 10–8; June–Aug., Sun.–Thurs. 10–8, Fri.–Sat. 10–10.*

DINING

Meals generally include three courses, a drink, and coffee. Many restaurants have an *ementa turistica* (tourist menu), a set-price meal, most often served at lunchtime. Note that you'll be charged a couple of euros if you eat any of the *couvert* (or *couberto*) items—typically appetizers such as bread and butter, olives, and the like—that are brought to your table without being ordered.

Lisbon's restaurants usually serve lunch from noon or 12:30 until 3 and dinner from 7:30 until 11; many establishments are closed on Sunday or Monday. Inexpensive restaurants typically don't accept reservations. In the traditional *cervejarias* (beer hall–restaurants), which frequently have huge dining rooms, you'll probably have to wait for a table, but usually not more than 10 minutes. In the Bairro Alto, many of the reasonably priced *tascas* (taverns) are on the small side: if you can't grab a table you're probably better off moving on to the next place. Throughout Lisbon, dress for meals is usually casual, but exceptions are noted below.

CATEGORY	COST*
$$$$	over €21
$$$	€14–€21
$$	€7–€14
$	under €7

*per person for a main course at dinner

Alcântara, Belém, and Cais do Sodré

$$–$$$$ ✕ **Doca Peixe.** The icy display of the day's catch at the entrance and the small aquarium clue you in to what's served here. In the center of the restaurant a staffer slices well-aged ham or weighs the fish that customers have chosen. You might start with a tomato and mozzarella salad or with oysters on the half shell. Sea bass or bream cooked in garlic, tomato, and onion and cod with turnip leaves are recommended main courses. *Bifinhas com molho de madeira* (small steaks in Madeira wine) is a meaty alternative. ⊠ *Esplanada at Doca de Santo Amaro, Armazém 14, Alcântara,* ☎ *21/397–3565. AE, MC, V. Closed Tues.*

$$$ ✕ **Alcântara Café.** Locals bring visitors here to impress them—it rarely fails. The café's mix of wood, leather, velvet, and steel elements combine to evoke a Lisbon of the 1920s. Portuguese dishes dominate the menu; try the prawns in lemon sauce. There's a large wine list, too, and a splendid bar if you want to sip an aperitif or stay on after dinner—drinks are served until 2 AM. The restaurant is near the Ponte 25 de Abril and close to the nightlife of the Doca de Santa Amaro; the kitchen is open until 1 AM. ⊠ *Rua Maria Luísa Holstein 15, Alcântara,* ☎ *21/363–7176. AE, DC, MC, V. No lunch.*

$$–$$$ ✕ **Espaço Lisboa.** Don't worry if you can't get a table with a view of the Ponte 25 de Abril; there's plenty of space inside this former warehouse. Menu choices include chicken sausage invented—it's said—to

Lisbon Dining

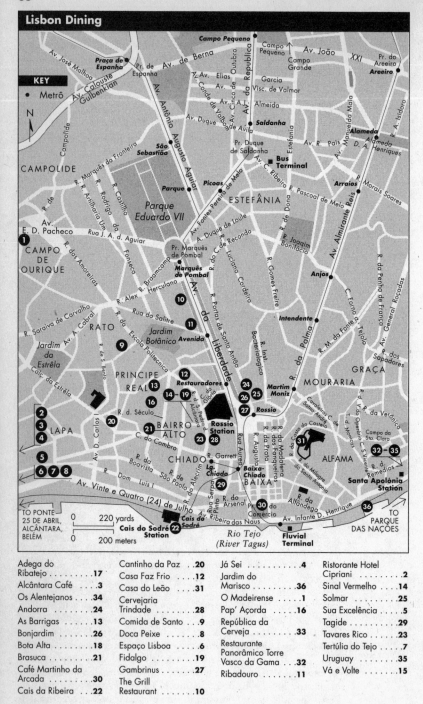

KEY

• Metrô

N

Campolide

CAMPOLIDE

CAMPO DE OURIQUE

Parque Eduardo VII

RATO

Jardim da Estrêla

PRINCIPE REAL

LAPA

BAIRRO ALTO

CHIADO

Restauradores

Rossio Station

BAIXA

Lg. Chiada

Baixa-Chiado

Cais do Sodré Station

Cais da Sodré

Praça de Espanha

São Sebastião

Parque

Picoas

Saldanha

Marquês de Pombal

Avenida

Rossio

Martim Moniz

Jardim Botânico

ESTEFÂNIA

Anjos

Intendente

MOURARIA

GRAÇA

ALFAMA

Santa Apolónia Station

Campo Pequeno

Areeiro

Alameda

Arraios

Bus Terminal

Campo Pequeno
Campo Grande

Rio Tejo (River Tagus)

Fluvial Terminal

TO PONTE 25 DE ABRIL, ALCÂNTARA, BELÉM

TO PARQUE DAS NAÇÕES

0   220 yards
0   200 meters

help Jews who had supposedly converted to Christianity during the Inquisition avoid eating pork; *leitão assado* (suckling pig roasted in a wood-burning oven); and *encharcada do ovos,* a delicious concoction of eggs and sugar. After your meal, sink into a leather armchair in the candelabra-lit bar. Find an excuse to check out the kiosk with old newspapers, the vintage grocery store, or the café museum. ⊠ *Rua da Cozinha Econômica 16, Doca de Santo Amaro, Alcântara,* ☎ 21/361-0212. *AE, MC, V. Closed Tues.*

$$–$$$ ✕ **Já Sei.** Beside the Rio Tejo, this is a fine lunchtime stop, especially in summer when you can sit on the attractive outdoor terrace. The service is smooth service, and the meals are impressive meals. The *arroz de marisco* (seafood rice) for two is particularly memorable. ⊠ *Av. de Brasília 202, Belém,* ☎ 21/321-5969. *Reservations essential. AE, DC, MC, V. Closed Mon. No dinner Sun.*

$$ ✕ **Cais da Ribeira.** An old fisherman's warehouse was converted into this small split-level restaurant. It specializes in fish grilled over charcoal, as well as a filling caldeirada. Whatever you order, the views over the river will complement your meal nicely. ⊠ *Cais do Sodré, behind railway station, Cais do Sodré,* ☎ 21/342-3611. *AE, DC, MC, V. Closed Sun. and Mon. No lunch Sat. and Tues.*

$$ ✕ **Tertúlia do Tejo.** Nothing is pretentious at this dockside restaurant. Large, red umbrellas shade the esplanade tables. Plank floors set the tone in the downstairs dining room, and there's an agreeable madhouse of long tables and camaraderie upstairs. The *pratos do dia* (daily specials) are predictable, but if you try melon with smoked ham or *caldho verde* (green soup) as a starter, and then follow it with something grilled, you can't go wrong. Dinner reservations are advised. ⊠ *Doca de Santo Amaro, Alcântara,* ☎ 21/395-5552. *AE, DC, MC, V.*

Alfama

$$–$$$ ✕ **Casa do Leão.** The location—on the grounds of the Castelo de São Jorge—couldn't be better. In summer, terrace-garden seating grants spectacular views of the center of Lisbon. The food is a high-quality mix of Portuguese and international dishes. Squid comes on a skewer with shrimp, bacon, and peppers; the lamb chops are a standout entrée. You may want to finish with a plate of Portuguese cheeses. ⊠ *Entrances to castle at Largo do Chão da Feira and Largo do Menino de Deus, Alfama,* ☎ 21/887-5962. *AE, MC, V.*

$$–$$$ ✕ **Jardim do Marisco.** A white ceiling tops metal rafters high above the cool grays and warm woods of this restaurant overlooking the esplanade near Lisbon's major cruise ship area. For a starter, consider traditional vegetable sopa or Portuguese oysters on ice, perhaps followed by a lavish portion of bean-based stew with meat or seafood or *espetadas de gambas piri piri* (spicy shrimp brochette). ⊠ *Doca Jardim do Tabaco, Pavilion A/B, Av. D. Henrique 21, Alfama,* ☎ 21/882-4242. *AE, MC, V.*

Avenida da Liberdade

$$–$$$ ✕ **The Grill Restaurant.** As they're on the top floor of the Tivoli Lisboa hotel, the Grill and its O Terraço bar could let the vistas be the draw and not worry too much about the food. All praise, then, that the kitchen turns out high-quality prime rib and lamb cutlets. Here traditional salt cod is baked with potatoes and baby onions; for something different, try the mixed-fish curry. The restrained elegance makes this one of the few hotel-restaurants worth the splurge; in summer there's no nicer place to sit than out on the terrace. ⊠ *Av. da Liberdade 185, Liberdade,* ☎ 21/353-2181. *Reservations essential. AE, DC, MC, V.*

Bairro Alto

$$–$$$$ **✕ Pap' Açorda.** What was once a bakery is now one of Lisbon's most
★ happening restaurants. Art and media types scramble for the closely
packed tables in the minimalist interior. The menu lists cutting-edge
versions of Portuguese classics—grilled sea bass; breaded veal cutlets;
and *açorda* itself, that bread-based stew, rich in seafood and flavored
with cilantro. There's a good wine list (all Portuguese) and a long bar
by the door where those unwise enough not to have made a reserva-
tion wait for a table. ⊠ *Rua da Atalaia 57, Bairro Alto,* ☏ *21/346–
4811. Reservations essential. AE, DC, MC, V.*

$$$ **✕ Brasuca.** The food is Brazilian, and the welcome is warm. With its
open fire, its alcove, and its intimate dining rooms, this converted man-
sion makes you feel as if you're eating in someone's home. Dishes such
as *picadinho á mineira* (minced beef with onions, peppers, and bananas)
or *moqueca* (fish or shrimp in coconut milk) are always reliable. The
beer is Brazilian, too, or you may prefer to sip a more potent *caipir-
inha* (cocktail made with *cachaça,* a rumlike Brazilian liquor, sugar, and
lime). ⊠ *Rua João Pereira da Rosa 7, Bairro Alto,* ☏ *21/342–8542.
AE, DC, MC, V. Closed Mon.*

$$–$$$ **✕ Cantinho da Paz.** The trick is finding this place (take a taxi), but
once you're through the unassuming entrance you'll be glad you made
the effort. It's a joyful mom-and-pop establishment that specializes in
the cuisine of Goa—so spicy curries abound. The shrimp curry is rich
in coconut and cream. The English-speaking owner is happy to guide
you through the menu. ⊠ *Rua da Paz 4, off Rua dos Poiais de São
Bento, Bairro Alto,* ☏ *21/396–9698. Reservations essential. V. Closed
Mon.*

$$–$$$ **✕ Sinal Vermelho.** At this update of a traditional *adega* (tavern), the
split-level dining room is traditionally tiled, and the food is thoroughly
Portuguese, but the prints on the wall are modern, the clientele firmly
professional, and the wine list wide-ranging. Consider starting with a
plate of clams drenched in oil and garlic and follow it with a fresh seafood
dish; the meat dishes are less inspiring, although if you feel daring, you
might try the tripe or the kidneys. ⊠ *Rua das Gáveas 89, Bairro Alto,*
☏ *21/346–1252. Reservations essential. AE, MC, V. Closed Sun.*

$$ **✕ Adega do Ribatejo.** There are fado clubs aplenty in the Bairro Alto,
but none so accessible as this tiled adega. The food is reasonably good;
dishes such as steaks, bacalhau, veal, and fried fish are often on the
changing menu. At the nightly singing sessions, professional musi-
cians serenade you with ear-splitting renditions of traditional songs.
The manager works the tables and sings himself on occasion; even the
cooks sometimes get in on the act. Note that there's a minimum charge
of €10, and unless you book ahead or arrive before 8 PM, you'll prob-
ably have to wait in line. ⊠ *Rua Diário de Notícias 23, Bairro Alto,*
☏ *21/346–8343. MC, V. Closed Sun.*

$$ **✕ As Barrigas.** The clientele are a well-traveled lot judging by the postcards that line the walls of this cozy, wood-paneled adega, but the cook-
ing stays firmly in Portugal. The specialty is a rich arroz *de polvo* (with
octopus), and there are steaks, a fish of the day, and other tavern standards. And the restaurant's name? It means "the stomachs," which you'll
appreciate once you've waded through their large portions. ⊠ *Travessa da Queimada 31, Bairro Alto,* ☏ *21/347–1220. V.*

$$ **✕ Bota Alta.** This wood-paneled tavern is one of the Bairro Alto's old-
est and most favored eateries: lines form outside by 8 PM. There's lit-
tle space between the tables, but this only enhances the buzz. Once you've
secured a seat, choose from a menu strong on traditional Portuguese
dishes—perhaps bacalhau cooked in cream, homemade sausages, steaks
in wine sauce, or grilled fish. The house wine comes in ceramic jugs

and is very good. ⊠ *Travessa da Queimada 37, Bairro Alto,* ☎ *21/342-7959. AE, DC, MC, V. Closed Sun. No lunch Sat.*

$$ ✕ **Casa Faz Frio.** This convivial adega—complete with wood beams, stone floors, paneled booths, blue tiling, and bunches of garlic suspended from the ceiling—is of a type that's fast disappearing. The list of Portuguese dishes on the prix-fixe menu changes daily, and although there's not a large choice, you'll usually find steak, rice dishes, bacalhau, grilled pork, and quail. ⊠ *Rua de Dom Pedro V 96–98, Bairro Alto,* ☎ *21/346–1860. No credit cards.*

$$ ✕ **Fidalgo.** The local intelligentsia have made this low-key, comfortable restaurant their refuge, though friendly owner Eugenio Fidalgo welcomes every sort of patron. He'll gladly help you with the Portuguese menu and the excellent wine list. Specialties include grouper with tomatoes and shrimp as well as several bacalhau dishes. If you've never had *medalhões de javali* (wild boar cutlets), try them here—they're incredibly succulent. ⊠ *Rua da Barroca 27, Bairro Alto,* ☎ *21/342–2900. AE, MC, V. Closed Sun.*

$$ ✕ **Ribadouro.** One of Lisbon's oldest beer halls is also a seafood joint, with a counter full of fresh shellfish priced by weight—go easy, since this can be a costly way to eat. If you stick to the regular fish and meat dishes, you can't go wrong. When crowds spill out of the nearby theaters, you may have to wait for a table; try to arrive before 8 PM on weekends. ⊠ *Av. da Liberdade 155, Bairro Alto,* ☎ *21/354–9411. AE, DC, MC, V.*

$–$$ ✕ **Cervejaria Trindade.** The Trindade is a classic 19th-century cerve-
★ jaria, with colorful tiles, vaulted ceilings, and frenetic service. You can pop in for a beer and a snack or eat a full meal. Hearty dishes such as açorda and steaks form the mainstay; if you opt for the grilled seafood, the tab will jump dramatically. The terrace is an enjoyable spot for dining in summer. ⊠ *Rua Nova da Trindade 20, Bairro Alto,* ☎ *21/342–3506. AE, DC, MC, V.*

$–$$ ✕ **Vá e Volte.** In what's little more than a bar with a couple of small dining rooms, the owner, his wife, the cook, and a small staff keep the meals coming with speed and good humor. Fried or grilled fish or meat dishes are served with enough salad, potatoes, and vegetables to keep the wolf from the door, and the *arroz doce* (rice pudding) is homemade. The house wine is fine, but even if you choose a regional specialty, the price won't break the bank. ⊠ *Rua do Diário de Notícias 100, Bairro Alto,* ☎ *21/342–7888. AE, MC, V. Closed Mon.*

Baixa

$$$–$$$$ ✕ **Gambrinus.** On a busy street that's full of fish restaurants, Gambrinus stands alone, with more than 70 years of experience in serving the finest fish and shellfish. In a series of somber, dark-paneled dining rooms, you're led through the intricacies of the day's seafood specials by waiters who know their stuff. Prawns, lobster, and crab are always available; seasonal choices such as sea bream, sole, and sea bass are offered grilled or garnished with clam sauce. There are meat dishes, too, but they're rather beside the point here. ⊠ *Rua Portas de S. Antão 23–25, Baixa,* ☎ *21/346–8974 or 21/342–1466. AE, DC, MC, V.*

$$$ ✕ **Solmar.** Items from the sea figure prominently on the menu and in the restaurant itself: there's a huge mosaic of an underwater scene. Some have complained that Solmar is resting on its laurels, but the cooking is more hit than miss. In winter the restaurant entices diners with wild boar or venison. There are also cheaper snacks available in the adjacent café, where locals pop in throughout the day for coffee and cakes. ⊠ *Rua Portas de S. Antão 108, Baixa,* ☎ *21/342–3371. AE, DC, MC, V.*

$$–$$$ ✕ **Andorra.** On the renowned Baixa street of fish restaurants, the Andorra is a perfect place for a simple lunch; from the terrace you can people-watch and smell the charcoal-grilled sardines. The friendly staff serves plates of well-cooked Portuguese favorites, and you can choose from a short wine list that caters to most tastes. ⊠ *Rua Portas de Santo Antão 82, Baixa,* ☎ *21/342–6047. MC, V. Closed Sun.*

$$–$$$ ✕ **Café Martinho da Arcada.** This famous café-restaurant, founded in 1782 beneath the arcades of Praça do Comércio, was once frequented by the Portuguese poet Fernando Pessoa and other literary stars. These days the lunchtime crowd in its wood-paneled dining room is mainly businesspeople. The menu lists regional Portuguese cuisine; sometimes there's a colonial splash with the occasional Brazilian dish. Try a *cataplana* (clam stew) from the Algarve, especially if you won't be heading south on this trip. ⊠ *Praça do Comércio 3, Baixa,* ☎ *21/887–9259. MC, V. Closed Sun.*

$$ ★ ✕ **Bonjardim.** In an alley between Praça dos Restauradores and Rua Portas de Santo Antão and known locally as "Rei dos Frangos" ("King of Chickens"), Bonjardim specializes in superbly cooked spit-roasted chicken, best eaten with fries and a salad. The restaurant is crowded at peak times (8 PM–10 PM), but you shouldn't have to wait long, and watching the frenzied waiters is entertaining. An overflow dining room on the opposite side of the alley serves the same menu and has the same good deals. ⊠ *Travessa de S. Antão 11, Baixa,* ☎ *21/342–4389. AE, DC, MC, V.*

Chiado

$$$–$$$$ ✕ **Tagide.** In a fine old house that looks out over the Baixa and the Rio Tejo (reserve a table by the window), you can have one of Lisbon's great food experiences. The dining room lined with 17th-century tiles is a lovely backdrop for sampling regional Portuguese fare. Try the famous *presunto* (smoked ham) from Chaves, stuffed squid from the Algarve, or the classic porco à alentejana (Alentejo-style pork). ⊠ *Largo Academia das Belas Artes 18–20, at bottom of Rua Ivens, Chiado,* ☎ *21/342–0720. Reservations essential. AE, DC, MC, V. Closed Sun. No lunch Sat.*

$$$–$$$$ ★ ✕ **Tavares Rico.** Established as a café in the 18th century, today Tavares Rico pleases its customers with a handsome Edwardian dining room; outstanding service; superb, French-inspired fare; and an excellent wine list. Caviar pushes the price of a meal right up, but there's nothing wrong with lowering your sights—the sole cooked in champagne sauce is a classic, and there are game birds available in season, served roasted in a rich wine sauce. Portuguese tastes can be assuaged by the bacalhau or the *sopa alentejana* (Alentejo-style soup that's a concoction of garlic, bread, and egg). ⊠ *Rua Misericórdia 35–37, Chiado,* ☎ *21/342–1112. Reservations essential. Jacket and tie. AE, DC, MC, V. Closed Sat. No lunch Sun.*

Lapa

$$$$ ✕ **Ristorante Hotel Cipriani.** Why choose northern Italian cuisine when you have *ristorantes* and pizzerias everywhere back home? Because Cipriani's food is exceptional. So is its service, whether you're a solo traveler scanning a book or a part of a designer-clad quartet celebrating a milestone. Waiters whip off domed silver lids in time to the music of a 12-string Portuguese guitar that approaches concert quality. You could start with cannelloni stuffed with ricotta and zucchini or shrimp and spinach–stuffed puff pastry with oyster sauce. Sautéed monkfish on a bed of ratatouille or citrus-glazed duck might follow. Wine prices range from modest to monumental. ⊠ *Lapa Palace hotel, Rua Pau de Bandeira 2, Lapa,* ☎ *21/394–9434. Reservations essential. AE, MC, V.*

$$-$$$ ✕ **Sua Excelência.** In this cozy little town house restaurant, put your-
★ self in the hands of the English-speaking owner, Mr. Queiroz, who will
talk you through the outstanding Portuguese menu. Specialties include
smoked swordfish (an Algarve favorite), baked bacalhau, and Angolan-
style chicken. A meal here is an intimate experience—particularly refreshing after a hectic day of sightseeing. ✉ *Rua do Conde 34, Lapa,*
☎ *21/390–3614. MC, V. Closed Wed. and Sept. No lunch weekends.*

Parque das Nações

$$$-$$$$ ✕ **Restaurante Panorâmico Torre Vasco da Gama.** There's always a view
from atop this Parque das Nações landmark. On one side it's of the
city and the hills beyond; on the other it's of the Ponte Vasco da Gama
floating above the Rio Tejo. To start you might have the salmon carpac-
cio or the fish soup with cheese. Stellar entrées include grouper fillet
with oyster sauce on spinach and leeks or the char-grilled vegetable plate.
Coffee comes with a small, dark chocolate—an incentive, albeit a
small one, to resist the fluffy cheesecake and other tempting desserts.
✉ *Av. Pinto Ribeiro, Parque das Nações,* ☎ *21/893–9550. Reserva-*
tions essential. AE, MC, V. Closed Mon.

$$-$$$ ✕ **Os Alentejanos.** Fans hang down from the ceiling, cooling you as
you feast at at picnic-style or red-, white-, and green-checkered tables.
Wine is served in earthenware jugs that decorate a small bar. To cap-
ture the flavor of the Alentejo, a region south of Lisbon, start with a
fragrant soup made mainly from herbs and bread, then move on to
pork sautéed with fresh clams or a traditional lamb stew. Vegetarians
can ask for the region's typical chickpeas or green beans. Reservations
are advised at dinner and for peak-season lunches. ✉ *Esplanada D.*
Carlos I, facing Oceanário de Lisboa, Parque das Nações, ☎ *21/895–*
6116. AE, MC, V.

$$-$$$ ✕ **República da Cerveja.** This large eating and drinking—or maybe drink-
ing and eating—spot pulses with energy. It's not easy to categorize, with
its German chef and Portuguese manager who arrived via Missouri,
but it's appealing even if you're not tempted by the wide array of beers.
Steak—perhaps flavored with oysters—is always on the blackboard of
ever-changing specials. Pizzas and burgers dominate the late-night
menu; food is served until 1 AM Sunday through Wednesday nights and
until 4 AM Thursday through Saturday nights, when there's often live
music or a show. ✉ *Passeio das Tagides 2, Parque das Nações,* ☎ *21/*
892–2590. AE, MC, V.

$-$$ ✕ **Uruguay.** Soft music and the smell of grilled meat welcome you into
the compact, glass-walled interior, where the rafters are draped with
white canvas panels. Portions are generous, but if you want a starter,
a good choice is warm salad with goat's milk cheese accompanied by
home-baked raisin bread. Few diners resist the grilled brochettes, but
you could opt instead for roast chicken. The fruit tarts and brownies
are tempting. ✉ *Cais dos Argonautas F3, by the water gardens, Par-*
que das Nações, ☎ *21/895–5445. AE, V.*

Rato

$$-$$$ ✕ **O Madeirense.** Although it's in the Amoreiras shopping complex, this
restaurant makes you feel as if you're in Madeira: rural scenes adorn the
walls; staffers wear traditional costumes; and the place is filled with wood,
rattan, and plants. The service is good, and the cooking is assured. Try
the tuna, the swordfish, or the *espetada* (a skewer of steak fillet, rubbed
with salt and spices and hung above the table from a stand so you can
serve yourself). ✉ *Loja 3027, Amoreiras, Av. Eng. Duarte Pacheco, Rato,*
☎ *21/381–3147. Reservations essential. AE, DC, MC, V.*

$$ ✕ **Comida de Santo.** Excellent Brazilian food served in a funky, brightly painted dining room and accompanied by lively Brazilian music keeps this place packed until closing time, at 1 AM. Come and enjoy classic dishes, such as *feijoada* (meat-and-bean stew) or *vatapá* (a spicy shrimp dish). Order a caipirinha while you're waiting. The restaurant is down a side street off Rua Escola Politécnica—easy to miss if you're not on the ball. You have to ring the bell for entrance. ✉ *Calçada Engenheiro Miguel Pais 39, Rato,* ☎ *21/396–3339. Reservations essential. AE, DC, MC, V.*

LODGING

If you've arrived without accommodations, stop by the airport tourist information desk or the downtown tourist office. The staff at either location can provide you with a list of hotels and pensões. Though it's not a complete list, it will get you started in your search.

Even in the city's hotels, consider inspecting a room before taking it: street noise can be a problem and, conversely, quieter rooms at the back don't always have great views (or, indeed, any views). Also, some hotels charge the same rate for each of their rooms, so by checking out a couple you might be able to get a better room for the same price. This is especially true of the older hotels and inns, where no two rooms are exactly alike. And, if rooms for nonsmokers are unavailable, stale smoke can permeate one room, yet be totally absent in its clone down the hall.

Lisbon hosts trade fairs and conventions and is busy year-round, so it's best to secure a room in advance of your trip. Peak periods are Easter–June and September–November; budget pensões are particularly busy in summer. Despite the high year-round occupancy, substantial discounts—sometimes 30%–40%—abound from November through February.

CATEGORY	COST*
$$$$	over €275
$$$	€175–€275
$$	€75–€175
$	under €75

For a standard double room, including tax, in high season (off-season rates may be lower).

Alfama

$$ 🏨 **Albergaria Senhora do Monte.** The views from this small, unpre-
★   tentious hotel in the oldest part of town are fine, especially at night, when the nearby Castelo de São Jorge is softly illuminated. To make the most of the location, opt for one of the junior suites, which have terraces. The top-floor bar–breakfast room has a picture window (making breakfast a real pleasure), and the neighborhood is quiet. It's a steep walk every time you return here, but Tram 28 runs nearby. ✉ *Calçada do Monte 39, Alfama, 1100-250,* ☎ *21/886–6002,* 𝖥𝖠𝖷 *21/887–7783,* 𝖶𝖤𝖡 *www.maisturismo.pt.sramonte. 24 rooms, 4 suites. Bar, in-room safes, cable TV, baby-sitting. AE, DC, MC, V. BP.*

Amoreiras

$$$$ 🏨 **Hotel Dom Pedro Lisboa.** The slightly exotic lobby here hums with comings, goings, and clusters of conversation. Although it's in the Amoreiras business center, facing the shopping complex, the hotel has its own gallery of luxury boutiques as well. Rooms and suites have rich

Lisbon Lodging

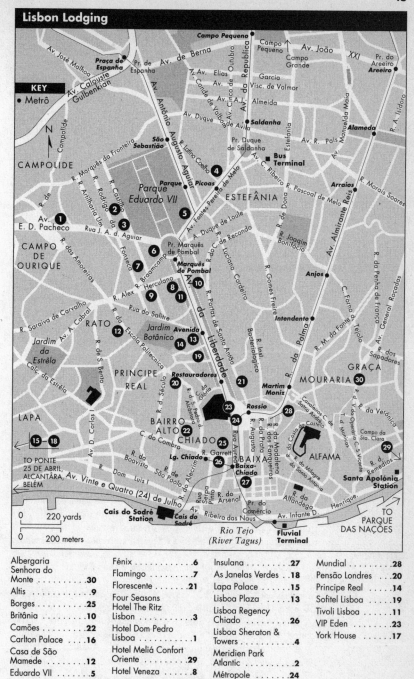

fabrics and polished wood furniture, including executive desks and other amenities for the prosperous business travelers who favor the hotel. Vacationers who love to shop also opt to stay here, owing to its location and its weekend rate reductions. ⊠ *Av. Eng. Duarte Pacheco 24, Amoreiras, 1070-109,* ☎ *21/389–6606,* FAX *21/389–6601,* WEB *www. dompedro-hotels.com. 254 rooms, 9 suites. 2 restaurants, 3 bars, in-room safes, cable TV, minibars, no-smoking floors, room service, Internet, laundry service, meeting rooms. AE, DC, MC, V. EP.*

$$ ⊞ **Fénix.** As the Praça Marquês de Pombal has emerged a better, brighter place, so has this hotel. Guest quarters are done in shades of pastel pink and have large closets, comfortable armchairs, and gleaming bathrooms. Rooms in front overlook the square; those in back face the park. The basement restaurant, O Bodegon, serves good Spanish and Portuguese food in rustic surroundings. ⊠ *Praça Marquês de Pombal 8, Amoreiras, 1269-133,* ☎ *21/386–2121,* FAX *21/386–0131,* WEB *www.hotelfenix.pt. 119 rooms, 4 suites. Restaurant, 2 bars, in-room data ports, in-room safes, cable TV, minibars, room service, laundry service, meeting rooms. AE, DC, MC, V. BP. Metro: Rotunda.*

Avenida da Liberdade and Environs

$$$–$$$$ ⊞ **Tivoli Lisboa.** There's enough marble in the public areas to make
★   you fear for the future supply of the stone, but grandness gives way to comfort in the rooms, where there are fresh decor, well-equipped bathrooms, and a moderate amount of space. In warmer months the outdoor pool and garden offer respite from the bustling city; the grill on the top floor presents wonderful river and city views. A filling morning buffet is served in a restaurant off the lobby. ⊠ *Av. da Liberdade 185, Liberdade, 1269-050,* ☎ *21/353–2181,* FAX *21/357–9461,* WEB *www. tivolihotels.com. 297 rooms, 30 suites. Restaurant, 2 bars, coffee shop, grill, in-room safes, cable TV, minibars, room service, pool, 2 tennis courts, shops, baby-sitting, laundry service. AE, DC, MC, V. BP. Metro: Avenida.*

$$$ ⊞ **Britânia.** The Britânia is in one of the few 1940s buildings near Avenida da Liberdade to have survived progress unscathed. The onetime town house was the work of architect Cassiano Branco, and it originally housed studio apartments, hence the larger than usual rooms. But it's the art deco touches throughout that really impress—from the original marble panels in the baths to the "porthole" windows in the facade, the columns and candelabra in the lobby, and the murals in the bar. Staff members are really friendly. ⊠ *Rua Rodrigues Sampaio 17, Liberdade, 1150-278,* ☎ *21/315–5016,* FAX *21/315–5021,* WEB *www.heritage.pt. 30 rooms. Bar, dining room, in-room safes, cable TV. AE, DC, MC, V. EP. Metro: Marquês de Pombal.*

$$$ ⊞ **Sofitel Lisboa.** Right in the middle of the Avenida da Liberdade, the handsome Sofitel has a high-tech edge to its design. Rooms are pleasingly contemporary—decorated in attractive colors and comfortably appointed. The intimate piano bar makes a good stop after a day's touring, and you can sit by a window in the Cais da Avenida restaurant for sidewalk views of the central artery. ⊠ *Av. da Liberdade 123–125, Liberdade, 1269-038,* ☎ *21/342–9202,* FAX *21/342–9222,* WEB *www. sofitel.com. 166 rooms, 4 suites. Restaurant, bar, room service, laundry service, business services. AE, DC, MC, V. BP, MAP. Metro: Avenida.*

$$ ⊞ **Flamingo.** If you're seeking reliable, good-value lodgings in the city center—and you don't need the creature comforts of a high-end hotel— then the Flamingo is worth a try. The staff is friendly, and the small, simply furnished rooms are pleasant enough for the price; despite double-glazed windows, though, those in front tend to be noisy. As stay

here gets you discounts at the neighboring parking lot, a bonus in this busy area. ⊠ *Rua Castilho 41, Liberdade, 1250–068, ☎ 21/386–2191, FAX 21/386–1216, WEB www.bestwestern.com/pt/hotelflamingo. 39 rooms. Restaurant, bar, in-room data ports, in-room safes, cable TV, minibars, laundry service. AE, DC, MC, V. BP. Metro: Marquês de Pombal.*

$$ ▥ **Hotel Veneza.** Although you might be startled by the contrast of this 1886 hotel's elaborate 19th-century staircase with its modern murals, you'll no doubt enjoy the superb central location and the welcoming service. There's no on-site restaurant, but there are plenty of cafés— as well as an elegant wood-paneled bar—nearby. ⊠ *Av. da Liberdade 189, Liberdade, 1250-141, ☎ 21/352–2618, FAX 21/352–6678, WEB www.3khoteis.com. 38 rooms. Minibars, cable TV. AE, DC, MC, V. CP. Metro: Marquês de Pombal.*

$$ ▥ **Lisboa Plaza.** This welcoming, family-owned hotel behind Avenida
★ da Liberdade has been in business for almost half a century, and the experience shines through. The staff is friendly and helpful, and pastel colors, prints on the walls, attractive ornaments, dried-flower arrangements, and well-stocked marble baths lend character and a sense of comfort. The best rooms are at the back, looking up to the botanical gardens; those in front are closer to the main road and don't have the views, but double-glazed windows keep things quiet. Although it's not included in the room rate, the buffet breakfast is excellent. ⊠ *Travessa do Salitre 7, Liberdade, 1269-066, ☎ 21/321–8218, FAX 21/347–1630, WEB www.heritage.pt. 94 rooms, 12 suites. Restaurant, bar, cable TV, no-smoking rooms, room service, Internet, laundry service, business services, meeting rooms. AE, DC, MC, V. EP. Metro: Avenida.*

Bairro Alto

$ ▥ **Camões.** Typical of Bairro Alto guest houses, the Camões has simple rooms on a couple of floors of an apartment building and is overseen by a bustling matron. For the price, don't expect great comfort; do expect clean, bright rooms with beds that don't sag. Rooms facing the street have little balconies—which make for noisy nights but give you a window onto Bairro Alto life. There's a small breakfast room, or you can step out into the neighborhood for coffee and pastries. ⊠ *Travessa do Poço da Cidade 38, Bairro Alto, 1200, ☎ 21/346–7510, FAX 21/346–4048. 13 rooms, 7 with bath. Breakfast room. No credit cards. CP. Metro: Baixa-Chiado.*

$ ▥ **Pensão Londres.** This modest bed-and-breakfast is a surprisingly agreeable choice in the "you-get-what-you-pay-for" category. Expect a modest but indisputably clean room, with or without bath, starting on the third floor of a former residence in the Bairro Alto section. ⊠ *Rua Dom Pedro III 53, Bairro Alto, 1250-092, ☎ 21/346–2203, FAX 21/346–5682, WEB www.pensaolondres.com.pt. 40 rooms, 13 with bath. Breakfast room, cable TV; no air-conditioning. DC, MC, V. CP. Metro: Avenida.*

Baixa

$$ ▥ **Métropole.** From its balconied late-19th-century facade to its '20s-style bar and lounge, the Métropole has been known to put a grin on the face of many a guest. Its light- and antiques-filled rooms are inviting. Those in front overlook the Rossío—with its flower sellers and cascading fountain—the Alfama, and the Castelo de São Jorge; other quarters have views of the Baixa's constantly changing tableaux. ⊠ *Rossío 30, Baixa, 1100-200, ☎ 21/321–9030, FAX 21/346–9166, WEB www.almeidahotels.com. 36 rooms. Bar, breakfast room, in-room safes, cable TV. AE, DC, MC, V. EP. Metro: Rossío.*

$$ ⊞ **Mundial.** Steps from the Rossío and Restauradores squares, this large property looks uncompromisingly modern, but inside there's lots of good, old-fashioned charm. One wing overlooks the landscaping and fountains of Praça Martim Moniz. Rooms here have elegant light-wood furniture, firm mattresses, and well-equipped bathrooms; at this writing, plans were on the table to give rooms in the original building similar features. Breakfast is served in the rooftop restaurant, Varanda de Lisboa, which has views of the Baixa on one side and the Alfama on the other—no wonder the hotel dubs itself "Lisbon's eighth hill." ⊠ *Rua Dom Duarte 4, Baixa, 1100-198,* ☎ *21/884–2000,* 𝔽𝔸𝕏 *21/884– 2110,* 𝕎𝔼𝔹 *www.hotel-mundial.pt. 245 rooms, 10 suites. Restaurant, bar, coffee shop, cable TV with movies, minibars, room service, meeting rooms. AE, DC, MC, V. BP, MAP. Metro: Rossío.*

$$ ⊞ **VIP Eden.** One of downtown's most exciting art deco buildings— the former Eden theater and movie house—has been converted into an aparthotel. The understated lobby gives little hint at the comfort of the upstairs, studios and one-bedroom apartments. Each unit overlooks a garden and the city and has modern furniture, a tiled bath, and a well-equipped kitchenette. But the biggest thrill is on the top floor, where a breakfast bar opens onto a terrace with castle views; the small pool here gets the sun all day. ⊠ *Praça dos Restauradores, Baixa, 1250- 187,* ☎ *21/321–6600,* 𝔽𝔸𝕏 *21/321–6666,* 𝕎𝔼𝔹 *www.viphotels.com. 75 studios, 59 one-bedroom apartments. Bar, breakfast room, cable TV, kitchenettes, microwaves, refrigerators, pool, Internet, business services, meeting rooms. AE, MC, V. EP. Metro: Restauradores.*

$ ⊞ **Florescente.** Rooms at this inn are on five azulejo-lined floors and vary in size; all are bright and cheerful, with gleaming white-marble baths. Suites with a sleeping alcove are a good choice for budget-conscious families. Only breakfast is served, but you're one block from Praça dos Restauradores and on a street well known for its many seafood restaurants. ⊠ *Rua Portas de Santo Antão 99, Baixa, 1150- 266,* ☎ *21/342–6609,* 𝔽𝔸𝕏 *21/342–7733,* 𝕎𝔼𝔹 *www.residencialflorescente. com. 64 rooms, 8 suites. Breakfast room, cable TV. AE, MC, V. BP. Metro: Restauradores.*

$ ⊞ **Insulana.** One of a series of long-standing, modest hotels in Baixa's shopping area, the Insulana has the edge over most and generally has space even when others are full—possibly because it's a little hidden away, up two flights of stairs through a clothes shop. Rooms are dark and dated, but they're clean and hospitable places to rest your head; ask for a room at the rear to minimize disturbance from street noise. ⊠ *Rua da Assunção 52, Baixa, 1100-044,* ☎ *21/342–3131,* 𝔽𝔸𝕏 *21/ 342–8924,* 𝕎𝔼𝔹 *www.insulana.cjb.net. 32 rooms. Bar, breakfast room, cable TV. AE, MC, V. CP. Metro: Baixa-Chiado.*

Chiado

$$ ⊞ **Lisboa Regency Chiado.** Arriving at the entrance, you may assume the taxi—or Jaguar limo that's available on request—has dropped you at an office. Never assume. This boutique hotel is a showcase of style on the sixth to eighth floors of the Grandes Armazéns do Chiado shopping complex. From the public areas, you look through a three-story window at tile rooftops, the Sé, and the Castelo de São Jorge. Designer Pedro Espírito Santo has blended elements of 16th-century Portugal with those from former colonies, and guest rooms are a mix of antiques and 21st-century amenities. ⊠ *Rua Nova de Almada 114, Chiado, 1200- 290,* ☎ *21/325–6100 or 21/325–6200,* 𝔽𝔸𝕏 *21/325–6161,* 𝕎𝔼𝔹 *www. regency-hotels-resorts.com. 40 rooms, 1 suite. Bar, breakfast room, lounge, in-room data ports, in-room safes, cable TV, room service, shops, laundry service. AE, DC, MC, V. BP. Metro: Baixa-Chiado.*

$ ⊡ **Borges.** The Borges is as old-fashioned as the glove shops and shoe-shine stands that dot the district surrounding it. The hotel is favored by European tour groups as well as those who love to shop. Rooms and bathrooms are fresh and tidy, and you'll have no trouble finding an English-speaking staff member. Although the rate includes a Continental breakfast, you're better off having coffee and a pastry at the famous Café A Brasileira, which is just steps away. ⊠ *Rua Garrett 108–110, Chiado, 1200-503,* ☎ *21/346–1951,* FAX *21/342–6617. 99 rooms. Bar, breakfast room, cable TV. MC, V. CP. Metro: Baixa-Chiado.*

Lapa

$$$$ ⊡ **Carlton Palace.** You'll feel like nobility during a stay at this hotel
★ in the restored Palácio Valle Flôr. The yellow-and-white confection—all arched windows and graceful wrought-ironwork—is a national monument overlooking gardens in a primarily residential area. In the lounges, the Valle-Flôr restaurant, and the suites, white walls sharply contrast with marble mantles, inlaid wooden floors, and gilt plasterwork. Rooms are just as white, though cozier in scale and warmed by light-blue carpeting here or a mint-green upholstered chair there. Throughout, 21st-century amenities have been artfully blended with all the 19th-century elegance. ⊠ *Rua Jau 54, Lapa, 1300-314,* ☎ *21/361–5600,* FAX *21/361–5601,* WEB *www.pestana.com. 176 rooms, 18 suites. 2 restaurants, bar, in-room data ports, in-room safes, cable TV with movies, minibars, no-smoking rooms, room service, 2 pools (1 indoor), hot tub, sauna, Turkish bath, golf privileges, health club, Internet, concierge, laundry service, business services, convention center, meeting rooms. AE, DC, MC, V. EP.*

$$$$ ⊡ **Lapa Palace.** A 19th-century town house in the leafy Lapa district contains one of Portugal's most elegant and welcoming hotels. Marble, antique furnishings, and fresh flowers are ubiquitous. So are such room amenities as a Jacuzzi tub or a stereo with a CD collection. From your guest quarters you might see terraced lawns, a waterfall, the heated pool, or the city and river. Whatever the vista from your room, you can enjoy a 180-degree city view from the terrace of the Rio Tejo Bar, where comfortable chairs and sofas invite you to truly savor your drink or tea. ⊠ *Rua Pau de Bandeira 4, Lapa, 1249-021,* ☎ *21/394–9494,* FAX *21/395–0665,* WEB *www.orient-expresshotels.com. 101 rooms, 7 suites. 3 restaurants, bar, in-room safes, cable TV, some in-room hot tubs, minibars, room service, indoor lap pool, pool, health club, shops, baby-sitting, Internet, laundry service, business services, meeting rooms. AE, DC, MC, V. BP.*

$$$ ⊡ **York House.** Although it was a convent in the 17th-century, this inn
★ is far from austere. Vine-covered staircases climb to the garden from the street, and a shady courtyard invites you to relax over a meal or a drink. Each guest room is unique, though all have good-quality reproduction furniture—including four-poster beds—and beautiful rugs, which also adorn the tiled corridors. Although it's a good way west of the center, York House is on tram and bus routes from downtown and near the Museu de Arte Antiga. It has a loyal, predominately British clientele; book well in advance. ⊠ *Rua das Janelas Verdes 32, Lapa, 1200-692,* ☎ *21/396–2435,* FAX *21/397–2793,* WEB *www.yorkhouselisboa.com. 34 rooms. Restaurant, bar. AE, DC, MC, V. BP.*

$$ ⊡ **As Janelas Verdes.** On the same street as the Museu de Arte Antiga,
★ this late-18th-century mansion was once the home of Portuguese novelist Eça de Queirós. Fittings, furnishings, paintings, and tile work throughout are in keeping with the building's historic character. Its guest rooms are individually furnished and tasteful; some have access to the

garden via an exterior staircase. On the ivy-covered patio, you can eat breakfast and imagine yourself in a different age. Reservations are vital for stays here. ⊠ *Rua das Janelas Verdes 47, Lapa, 1269–066,* ☎ *21/396–8143,* FAX *21/396–8144,* WEB *www.heritage.pt. 17 rooms. Bar, dining room, in-room safes, cable TV. AE, DC, MC, V. EP. Metro: Cais do Sodré.*

Parque das Nações

$$ ⊞ **Hotel Meliá Confort Oriente.** The riverfront, restaurants, and aquarium of Parque das Nações are just steps from the Meliá's door, and the Vasco da Gama mall is just down the street. Rooms are comfortable and functional, if somewhat bland. Excellent train and metro transportation puts you downtown in about 15 minutes. The hotel fills up when there's a convention at FIL. ⊠ *Av. D. João II, Parque das Nações, 1990-083,* ☎ *21/893–0000,* FAX *21/893–0099,* WEB *www.solmelia.es. 90 rooms, 26 suites. Restaurant, bar, in-room safes, cable TV, no-smoking rooms, Internet, laundry service, convention center. AE, MC, V. EP. Metro: Oriente.*

Principe Real

$$ ⊞ **Principe Real.** This small, friendly hotel close to the botanical gardens has charm and old-fashioned warmth. Rooms have antiques and harmonious blue and green color schemes. Each day starts with glorious views accompanying the buffet breakfast in the top-floor restaurant, where terrace dining is encouraged in fine weather. ⊠ *Rua da Alegria 53, Principe Real, 1250–006,* ☎ *21/346–0116,* FAX *21/342–2104. 23 rooms. Restaurant, bar, in-room safes, cable TV with movies, babysitting. AE, DC, MC, V. BP, MAP. Metro: Avenida.*

Rato

$$$$ ⊞ **Altis.** This large, boxy, modern lodging has a broad range of facilities, including an art gallery and a heated indoor lap pool. Its virtue is reliability, which is why it hosts a lot of business travelers. The mezzanine bar-lounge above the lobby is a relaxing spot, and rooms are comfortable, if unexceptional; those on higher floors have fine views of Parque Eduardo VII, as does the top-floor restaurant. ⊠ *Rua Castilho 11, Rato, 1269-072,* ☎ *21/314–2496,* FAX *21/354–8696,* WEB *www.hotel-altis.pt. 290 rooms, 13 suites. 2 restaurants, 3 bars, in-room safes, cable TV, minibars, room service, indoor pool, sauna, gym, shops, Internet, laundry service, business services, meeting rooms. AE, DC, MC, V. BP. Metro: Rotunda.*

$$$$ ⊞ **Four Seasons Hotel The Ritz Lisbon.** The luxury starts the minute you
★   step into the marble reception area and the lounge-bar, whose terrace overlooks the park. Public areas are filled with tapestries, fine paintings, and antique reproductions. Large, airy guest rooms have elegant furnishings and bathrooms as well as private terraces. Rooms in the back with park views are the best choice; on a clear day you can see Castelo de São Jorge and the Rio Tejo from the upper floors. A superb buffet breakfast—as well as lunch and dinner—is served at the Varanda restaurant, which also has a terrace. ⊠ *Rua Rodrigo da Fonseca 88, Rato, 1099-039,* ☎ *21/381–1471,* FAX *21/383–1688,* WEB *www.fourseasons. com. 264 rooms, 20 suites. Restaurant, bar, snack bar, in-room safes, cable TV, minibars, no-smoking floors, room service, gym, shops, Internet, baby-sitting, laundry service, meeting rooms. AE, DC, MC, V. EP. Metro: Marquês de Pombal.*

$$$$ ⊞ **Meridien Park Atlantic.** Business travelers like the distinctive Park Atlantic for its location—right by Parque Eduardo VII—and facilities.

There's plenty for vacationers to admire, too, including the split-level atrium with its cozy brasserie and separate conservatory-style bar. All the sleek rooms have smart bathrooms and soundproofing; more to the point, they all have fantastic views over the city and park. ⊠ *Rua Castilho 149, Rato, 1099-034,* ☎ *21/381–8705.* FAX *21/389–0500,* WEB *www.lemeridien.pt. 313 rooms, 17 suites. Restaurant, bar, cable TV, no-smoking floors, hair salon, sauna, shops, Internet, baby-sitting, laundry service, business services, meeting rooms. AE, DC, MC, V. EP. Metro: Marquês de Pombal.*

$$ 🏨 **Casa de São Mamede.** The Casa de São Mamede is a real survivor. One of the first private houses to be built in Lisbon after the 18th-century earthquake has been transformed into a relaxed guest house endowed with antique, country-style furniture; a tiled dining room; a grand staircase; and stained-glass windows. You're just a 10-minute walk from the Bairro Alto or a long, steep hike from the metro. ⊠ *Rua da Escola Politécnica 159, Rato, 1250-100,* ☎ *21/396–3166,* FAX *21/395–1896. 28 rooms. Dining room; no room phones, no room TVs. No credit cards. CP. Metro: Avenida.*

Saldanha

$$–$$$ 🏨 **Lisboa Sheraton & Towers.** Even those who eschew chain hotels appreciate this Sheraton overlooking modern Lisbon. Its many advantages include a huge reception area with a comfortable bar, a helpful staff, an agreeable restaurant, and modestly sized guest rooms with many amenities. Tower rooms have parquet floors, coffeemakers, a club lounge, and private check-in and checkout. Executive rooms have large desks and fax-modem outlets. The top-floor Panoramic Bar is the perfect place for an aperitif. Although the hotel is near Parque Eduardo VII and the Gulbenkian museum's gardens, most of your sightseeing days will start and end with a bus or taxi ride. ⊠ *Rua Latino Coelho 1, Saldanha, 1069-025,* ☎ *21/357–5757,* FAX *21/354–7164,* WEB *www.sheraton.com. 377 rooms, 7 suites. Restaurant, 2 bars, grill, some in-room data ports, in-room safes, cable TV, room service, pool, massage, sauna, health club, shops, laundry service, business services. AE, DC, MC, V. BP. Metro: Picoas.*

$$ 🏨 **Eduardo VII.** Beyond the anonymous, 1930s exterior of this hotel, which is near the park of the same name, you'll find 10 floors of ship-shape rooms that are short on space, but smart and comfortable. The hotel's singular attraction is the view of the Lisbon skyline from the top-floor restaurant and bar. ⊠ *Av. Fontes Pereira de Melo 5, Saldanha, 1060-114,* ☎ *21/356–8800,* FAX *21/356–8833,* WEB *www.eduardovii.pt. 136 rooms, 4 suites. Restaurant, bar, some in-room data ports, in-room safes, cable TV, minibars, billiards, Internet, business center, meeting rooms. AE, DC, MC, V. BP, MAP. Metro: Marquês de Pombal.*

NIGHTLIFE AND THE ARTS

Lisbon has a thriving arts-and-nightlife scene, and there are listings of concerts, plays, and films in the monthly *Agenda Cultural* and the quarterly *Unforgettable Lisboa* booklets, both available from the tourist office. Also, the Friday editions of both the *Diário de Notícias* and *O Independente* newspapers have separate magazines with entertainment listings. Although written in Portuguese, listings are fairly easy to decipher.

It's best to buy tickets to musical and theatrical performances at the box offices, but you can also get them at several agencies including the FNAC at the Colombo mall, the Valentim Carvalho music store in the Grandes Armazéns do Chiado shopping complex on Rua do Carmo, and the Virgin Megastore on Praça dos Restauradores. A special ticket office—called ABEP—on Praça dos Restauradores, near the main post office, also sells tickets to sporting events.

Nightlife

Lisbon bars and discos open late (10 PM). On weekends the mobs are shoulder to shoulder in the street, as each passing hour heralds a move to the next trendy spot. Many places are dark and silent on Sunday; Monday, Tuesday, and (sometimes) Wednesday are also popular nights to close. For a less boisterous evening out, visit a café-bar or an *adega típica* (traditional wine cellar) that has fado shows. Still other venues host a variety of live events, from rock and roll to African music.

Bars

The Bairro Alto, long the center of Lisbon's nightlife, is the best place for barhopping. Most bars here are fairly small and idiosyncratic, and stay open until 3 AM or so. Larger, designer bars started opening a few years ago along and around Avenida 24 de Julho, where—because this isn't a residential area as the Bairro Alto is—bars can stay open until 5 or 6 AM. The latest hot neighborhood is farther along the riverbank, next to the bridge in Alcântara, where the Doca do Santo Amaro and the Doca de Alcântara have fashionable terrace-bars and restaurants, some converted from old warehouses.

Whichever district you choose, note that not all bars have signs outside; to find the latest places you may have to follow the crowds or try a half-open door. Don't expect to have a quiet drink: the company is generally young and excitable.

Apollo XIII (⊠ Travessa da Cara 8, Bairro Alto, ☎ 21/342–4952) draws students into its tiny drinking den. **Bartis** (⊠ Rua Diário de Notícias 95, Bairro Alto, ☎ 21/342–4795) is a laid-back meeting place for jazz and movie buffs. If you prefer a quiet drink in an older part of town, seek out **Cerca Moura** (⊠ Largo das Portas do Sol 4, Alfama, ☎ 21/887–4859), which has outdoor seating and river views. **Doca de Santo** (⊠ Doca do Santo Amaro, Alcântara, ☎ 21/396–3522) has a great palm-lined esplanade.

Heading down toward Avenida 24 de Julho, the late-night crew stops off at **O'Gillin's** (⊠ Rua das Remolares 8–10, Cais do Sodré, ☎ 21/342–1899), an Irish bar across the road from the train station. It regularly hosts bands at night; Sunday afternoon sees a jazz group. **Pavilhão Chinês** (⊠ Rua Dom Pedro V 89, Bairro Alto, ☎ 21/342–4729) is a comfortable 1900s-style bar with bric-a-brac—statues, tankards, ceramics, baubles, toys—from around the world. At **Portas Largas** (⊠ Rua da Atalaia 105, Bairro Alto, ☎ 21/846–1379), a tiled tavern with barn doors, a mostly (but not exclusively) gay crowd spills out into the street; sangria is the house drink.

Rock City (⊠ Rua Cintura do Porto de Lisboa, Armazém 255, Santos, ☎ 21/342–8640), a riverside bar-restaurant, is terrific in summer with a tropical garden and bands. The most refined place to start off your evening is the relaxed **Solar do Vinho do Porto** (⊠ Rua de São Pedro de Alcântara 45, Bairro Alto, ☎ 21/347–5707), a formidable old building where you can sink into an armchair and sample port. **A Tasca** (⊠ Travessa de Queimada 13–15, Bairro Alto, ☎ 21/342–4910) is a bright bar with tequila as its specialty drink. At **Trifásica** (⊠ Av. 24 de Julho 66, Cais do Sodré, ☎ 21/395–7576) the music—loud though it is—takes second place to the snooker tables.

Café-Bars and Pastelarias

Many of Lisbon's cafés are glorious: the old-timers often have rich interiors of burnished and carved wood, mirrors, and tiles. Many also have outdoor seating, so you can order a coffee, beer, or snack and watch the city pass by. Those that specialize in pastries and cakes are known as *pastelarias* (pastry shops), and their offerings are among the city's greatest contributions to the gastronomic arts: be sure to sample some. Most cafés remain open for at least the early part of the evenings on weekdays; a few have become late-night drinking haunts. Some cafés close early on Saturday and altogether on Sunday, however.

In the heart of the shopping district, **Café A Brasileira** (⊠ Rua Garrett 120, Chiado) is the most famous of Lisbon's old haunts. A bronze statue of Portugal's poet-writer Fernando Pessoa sits just outside. For a feel of bygone days and enjoyment of the literary and art memorabilia on the walls, come before dark: at night every table is taken over by beer-drinking young people. **Café Martinho da Arcada** (⊠ Praça do Comércio 3, Baixa) is a welcome stop for a *pastéis de nata* (cream cake) before catching your tram to Belém. Tradition oozes from the tiled walls, and the waiters rush to and fro while bakers prepare scrumptious pastries. Note that it's closed on Sunday.

With its grand interior and suitably aloof waiters, the traditional **Café Nicola** (⊠ Praça Dom Pedro IV 24, west side of Rossío, Baixa) is one of the pricier spots for sitting down and taking in downtown. All who wander into the small **Confeiteria Cister** (⊠ Rua da Escola Politécnica 107, Rato) feel they have discovered it. Choose an enticing cake or sandwich, then find a spot at one of the polished wood tables, where patrons, young and old, linger with a friend, a newspaper, or just a large cup of coffee. There's not much that **Galeto** (⊠ Av. da República 14, Saldanha) doesn't serve, from cakes and sandwiches to full meals, from early to late every day. Pull up a stool at one of the long wooden counters.

As its name suggests, **Leiteria A Camponeza** (⊠ Rua dos Sapateiros 155–157, Baixa) is an old-fashioned *leiteria* (specializing in milk products and pastries) with blue-tiled walls that display bucolic scenes. You can enjoy its coffee, cakes, and sandwiches any day but Sunday, when the café is closed. The **Pastelaria Suíça** (⊠ Rossío 96, east side, Baixa) stretches all the way back to the adjacent Praça da Figueira. Outdoor tables are at a premium, but the relaxed ambience (even a single beer or coffee can hold your table for an hour) makes them worth the wait and slightly higher prices. Founded in 1929, the **Versailles** (⊠ Av. de República 15, Saldanha) has retained its grand furnishings. Massive mahogany display cases groan with chocolates, port wines, and liqueurs. Homemade cakes and hot chocolate are specialties.

Dance Clubs

Most clubs are in the Bairro Alto and along the Avenida 24 de Julho, though more and more cool, upscale places are opening in the Santos and Alcântara districts. Most places charge a cover of about €10–€15 (perhaps more on weekends), which usually includes one drink. Some clubs have strict door policies; bouncers may scrutinize you and your clothes. Clubs are open from about 10 or 11 PM until 4 or 5 AM; few get going until after midnight.

The ritzy **Alcântara Mar** (⊠ Rua da Cozinha Econômica 11, Alcântara, ☎ 21/363–6432) has over-the-top decor and a well-heeled clientele. **Fragil** (⊠ Rua da Atalaia 126, Bairro Alto, ☎ 21/346–9578) is a long-standing favorite that attracts a partly gay crowd. **Kapital** (⊠ Av. 24 de Julho 68, Santos, ☎ 21/395–5963) is typical of the high-fashion, high-price venues down on the avenida; its terrace is its nicest feature. **Keops** (⊠ Rua da Rosa 157–159, Bairro Alto, ☎ 21/342–8773) raises eyebrows with its funky Egyptian theme.

Kremlin (⊠ Escadinhas da Praia 5, Santos, ☎ 21/360–8768) attracts the trendiest Lisboetas, although no one turns up much before 2 AM (it stays open until 7 AM). It's rumored that John Malkovich is one of the owners of the hot club **Lux** (⊠ Av. Infante D. Henrique, near Sta. Apolónia, Alfama, ☎ 21/882–0890), which is in a remodeled riverside warehouse. For a mixture of funk, pop, and soul, **Três Pastorinhos** (⊠ Rua da Barroca 111–113, Bairro Alto, ☎ 21/346–4301) is still a groovy joint after two decades.

Fado Clubs

Fado is a haunting music rooted in African slave songs. During colonial times it was exported to Portugal; later, Lisbon's Alfama was recognized as the birthplace of the style, and today most performances occur in the Bairro Alto. In the adegas típicas food and wine are served, and fado plays late into the night: the singing starts at 10 or 11, and the adegas often stay open until 3 AM. It's becoming increasingly difficult to find an authentic adega; ask around for a recommendation. Note that some establishments charge (according to the night and who is playing) a minimum food and drink consumption charge, usually around €10–€15.

One of the oldest fado clubs, **Adega do Machado** (⊠ Rua do Norte 91, Bairro Alto, ☎ 21/322–4640), is busy every night but Monday, when it's closed. For fado at budget prices, consider a meal in the **Adega do Ribatejo** (⊠ Rua Diário de Notícias 23, Bairro Alto, ☎ 21/346–8343), a popular local haunt, where there's live entertainment nightly. **Clube de Fado** (⊠ Rua S. João de Praça 92–94, Alfama, ☎ 21/885–2704) is popular with locals who come to hear the guitar playing of both established performers and rising stars.

Parreirinha d'Alfama (⊠ Beco do Espírito Santo 1, Alfama, ☎ 21/886–8209) is a little club owned by Fado legend Argentina Santos. She doesn't sing very often herself these days but the club hires many other highly rated singers. **Senhor Vinho** (⊠ Rua do Meio à Lapa 18, Lapa, ☎ 21/397–2681) is an institution and attracts some of Portugal's most accomplished fado singers. It's closed on Sunday. **Timpanas** (⊠ Rua Gilberto Rola 24, Alcântara, ☎ 21/390–6655), which is closed on Wednesday, is one of the city's best fado clubs. This explains why it's popular with tour groups even though it's so far from the center of town.

Gay and Lesbian Clubs

Lisbon has a well-established gay and lesbian scene, concentrated primarily in and around the Bairro Alto. **Finalmente** (⊠ Rua da Palmeira 38, Bairro Alto, ☎ 21/372–6522) has one of the best sound systems in town and attracts a high-camp crowd. **Fragil** (⊠ Rua da Atalaia 126, Bairro Alto, ☎ 21/346–9578), although not exclusively gay, does attract a good, mixed crowd. **Memorial** (⊠ Rua Gustavo de Matos Sequeira 42, Rato, ☎ 21/396–8891) is popular with both gay and lesbian visitors and can get packed on the weekends. **Trumps** (⊠ Rua Imprensa Nacional 104b, Rato, ☎ 21/397–1059) is the city's biggest gay disco.

Music Clubs

Plenty of places have live rock, pop, and jazz performances. Big-name American and British bands, as well as the superstar Brazilian singers so beloved in Portugal, often play in Lisbon's large concert halls and stadiums. African music is also immensely popular here, with touring groups from Cabo Verde and Angola playing regularly alongside homegrown talent.

The city's best jazz joint is the **Hot Clube de Portugal** (✉ Praça da Alegria 39, Rato, ☎ 21/346–7369), which puts on a wide variety of gigs every night but Sunday and Monday, starting at about 11. **Pê Sujo** (✉ Largo de São Martinho 6, Alfama, ☎ 21/886–5929) specializes in live Brazilian music, which goes down smoothly with its potent caipirinhas. The **Ritz** (✉ Rua da Glória 55, Bairro Alto, ☎ 21/342–5140) is Lisbon's biggest African club. It's on the edge of the Bairro Alto, in a rather seedy area, but is renowned as a friendly place where you can dance to live music.

The Arts

Classical music concerts are staged from about October through June by the Fundação Calouste Gulbenkian. Of particular interest is the Early Music and Baroque Festival, held in churches and museums around Lisbon every spring. You may also be in town during a performance of the Nova Filarmonica, a national orchestra that gives concerts around the country throughout the year. The Orquestra Metropolitana de Lisboa performs a regular program at various city venues.

Concert Halls and Theaters

The **Centro Cultural de Belém** (✉ Praça do Império, Belém, ☎ 21/361–2400, WEB www.ccb.pt) puts on a full range of reasonably priced concerts and exhibitions, featuring national and international artists and musicians. There's a major concert and exhibition program mounted at **Culturgest** (✉ Caixa Geral de Depósitos, Rua Arco do Cego 1, Campo Pequeno, ☎ 21/790–5454), an auditorium and exhibition center sponsored by a Portuguese bank.

The main venue for rock concerts is the **Estádio de Alvalade** (✉ Rua Francisco Stromp, Alvalade, ☎ 21/751–4000), a large and uninteresting stadium. The prime mover behind Lisbon's artistic and cultural scenes is the **Fundação Calouste Gulbenkian** (✉ Av. de Berna 45, São Sebastião, ☎ 21/793–5131, WEB www.gulbenkian.pt), which not only presents exhibitions and concerts in its buildings but also sponsors events throughout the city.

The **Pavilhão Atlântico** (✉ Parque das Nações, ☎ 21/891–9333), the country's biggest indoor arena, hosts large-scale classical concerts, pop and rock bands, dance performances, and sporting events. Plays are performed in Portuguese at the **Teatro Nacional de Dona Maria II** (✉ Praça Dom Pedro IV, Baixa, ☎ 21/347–2246), Lisbon's principal theater. Performances are given August–June, and there's the occasional foreign-language production, too. The **Teatro Nacional de São Carlos** (✉ Rua Serpa Pinto 9, Baixa, ☎ 21/346–8408) hosts an opera season September–June.

Film

All films shown in Lisbon appear in their original language accompanied by Portuguese subtitles, and you can usually find the latest Hollywood releases playing around town. Ticket prices are around €3.50–€5 and even cheaper on Monday; it's best to get to the movie theater early on any day to be assured a seat. There are dozens of movie houses throughout the city, including a couple on Avenida da Liberdade. Some theaters are in preserved art deco buildings and are attractions in their own right.

A modern cinema complex in the **Amoreiras** (✉ Av. Eng. Duarte Pacheco, Amoreiras, ☎ 21/383–1275) shopping complex has 10 screens. There's a multiscreen cinema at the **Colombo** (✉ Av. Col. Militar, Benfica, ☎ 21/711–3200) mall. Portugal's national film theater, the **Instituto da Cinemateca Portuguesa** (✉ Rua Barata Salgueiro 39,

Marquês de Pombal, ☎ 21/354–6279), has screenings Monday through Saturday at 6:30 and 9:30. This is the place to catch contemporary Portuguese films and art-house reruns.

Galleries

The Centro Cultural de Belém has an ever-changing program of art exhibitions, and Lisbon's major art museums and commercial buildings often put on temporary exhibitions alongside their permanent collections. In addition, the city's gallery count has passed 100 and is growing. If you're staying at the Meridien Park Atlantic, Altis, or Hotel Dom Pedro Lisboa, you needn't even step outside to peruse their galleries. Most galleries are closed Sunday and daily 1–3, and will insure and ship whatever you buy.

The **Galeria de Arte Cervejaria Trindade** (⊠ Rua Nova da Trindade 20, Bairro Alto, ☎ 21/342–3506), at the back of the famous beer-hall restaurant is only open for exhibitions, though the splendid tiled walls of the cervejaria are a show in their own right. At the Centro Cultural de Belém, **Galeria Arte Periférica** (⊠ Praça do Império, Belém, ☎ 21/362–5072) is a good source of contemporary art, particularly by younger artists. **Galeria Barata** (⊠ Av. de Roma 11A, Campo Grande, ☎ 21/842–8350) is a modern art gallery that doubles as a bookshop—or vice versa.

If you're looking for contemporary Portuguese art that has yet to catch the eye of critics or collectors, try **Galeria Novo Século** (⊠ Rua do Século 23A, Bairro Alto, ☎ 21/342–7712). You might spot works of London-based Paula Rego at **Galeria 111** (⊠ Campo Grande 113-A, Alvalade, ☎ 21/797–7418), arguably Portugal's best known gallery. In Lisbon's historic cathedral area, **Loja da Calçada** (⊠ Calçada de S. Vicente 96, Alfama, ☎ 21/886–2780) is a small shop that concentrates on individual discoveries.

Movimento Arte Contemporânea (⊠ Rua do Sol ao Rato 9, Rato, ☎ 21/385–0789; ⊠ Av. Álvares Cabral 58, Rato, ☎ 21/386–7215) is a collective venture of three artists—from Portugal, the former Yugoslavia, and Spain—who produce paintings, sculptures, and jewelry. The homegrown talent of the trio, António de Carmo, paints beautiful dreamy, intensely colored fantasy forms and figures; his work has appeared on Lisbon tourist board literature.

OUTDOOR ACTIVITIES AND SPORTS

Participant Sports

Boating
Clube Naval (⊠ Cais do Gás, Letra H, Cais do Sodré, ☎ 21/346–9354), where you can arrange to sail and canoe, is directly on the river. The office is open weekdays 10–1 and 3–7.

Bowling
Bowling Internacional de Lisboa (⊠ Alameda dos Oceanos, near Oriente Station, Parque das Nações, ☎ 21/892–2521) is worth the ride north. It's large, noisy, and popular, with 30 lanes in high demand on weekends.

Golf
There are at least nine top-quality golf courses in Lisbon's environs, most of which are concentrated along the Estoril Coast. Indeed, if you're planning to play golf and plan no city-style dining, fado, or nightlife, consider staying at one of the hotels outside Lisbon with golf packages.

The 18-hole, par 69 golf course at **Lisboa Sport Clube** (✉ Casal da Carregueira, Belas, ☎ 21/431–0077) is about 20 minutes by car from the city at Queluz. Greens fees are €45 weekdays and €52 weekends.

Swimming

The **Altis** (✉ Rua Barata Salgueiro 52, Rato, ☎ 21/355–4110 or 21/314–2496) hotel opens its its indoor lap pool to nonguests for about €15 an hour. The **Lisboa Sport Clube** (✉ Casal da Carregueira, Belas, ☎ 21/431–0077) in Queluz has a swimming pool as well as a golf course. The central **Piscina do Ateneu** (✉ Rua Portas de Santo Antão 102, Baixa, ☎ 21/342–2365) is open to the public at certain hours; call in advance.

Tennis

The two public tennis courts making up **Campos de Tennis do Campo Grande** (✉ Jardim do Campo Grande, Campo Grande) are amid gardens. The **Centro de Tennis de Monsanto** (✉ Parque Florestal de Monsanto, Estrada do Alvita, Monsanto, ☎ 21/363–8073) is in Lisbon's large, lovely public park. The **Lisbon Racquet Center** (✉ Rua Alferes Malheiro, Alvalade) has nine courts.

Spectator Sports

Bullfighting

Bullfights are held on Thursday (and some Sundays) between Easter and September in the ornate Praça de Touros (bullring) at **Campo Pequeno.** Some people defend the Portuguese bullfight as entertainment because the bull isn't killed in the ring but rather is wrestled to the ground by a group of *forçados* (a team of eight men who fight the bull) dressed in traditional red-and-green costumes. Nonetheless, any bull injured during the contest is later killed. The first-class riding skills displayed by the *cavaleiro* (horseback fighter) during the event are undeniable. After the cavaleiro performs, the forçados goad the bull into charging them, and one man throws himself across the horns (which have been padded) while the other men pull the bull down by grabbing hold of whatever they can, including the beast's tail. Performances start at 10 PM and seats cost €15–€45. ✉ *Praça de Touros do Campo Pequeno, Av. da República, Campo Pequeno,* ☎ *21/793–2093. Metro: Campo Pequeno.*

Soccer

Soccer is by far Portugal's most popular sport, and Lisbon has three teams, which play at least weekly during the September–May season. Although you can buy tickets on the day of a game at the stadiums, it's best to get them in advance from the booth in the Praça dos Restauradores. Plan to arrive early, because there's usually a full program of entertainment first, including children's soccer, marching bands, and fireworks. (Note: always be wary of pickpockets in the crowd.)

The most famous of Lisbon's soccer teams is Benfica, which plays in the northwest part of the city at the **Estádio da Luz** (✉ Av. Gen. Norton Matos, Benfica, ☎ 21/726–0321), one of Europe's biggest stadiums. A great rival of the famous Benfica soccer team, the Sporting Clube de Portugal plays at the **Estádio José Alvalade** (✉ Rua Francisco Stromp, Alvalade, ☎ 21/758–9021), near Campo Grande in the north of the city.

SHOPPING

Small, independently owned stores are still quite common in Lisbon, and salespeople are courteous almost everywhere. Handmade goods, such as leather handbags, shoes, gloves, embroidery, ceramics, and basketwork, are sold throughout the city. Apart from top designer fashions and high-end antiques, prices are moderate. Most shops are open weekdays 9–1 and 3–7 and Saturday 9–1; malls and supermarkets often remain open until at least 10. Some are also open on Sunday. Credit cards—Visa in particular—are widely accepted.

Although fire destroyed much of Chiado in 1988, Lisbon's smartest shopping district, a good portion of the area has been restored. The neighborhood has a large new shopping complex as well as many small stores with considerable cachet, particularly on and around Rua Garrett. The Baixa's grid of streets from the Rossío to the Rio Tejo have many small shops selling jewelry, shoes, clothing, and foodstuffs. The Bairro Alto is full of little crafts shops with stylish, contemporary ceramics, wooden sculpture, linen, and clothing. Excellent stores continue to open in the residential districts north of the city, at Praça de Londres and Avenida de Roma.

Malls

Amoreiras (⊠ Av. Eng. Duarte Pacheco, Amoreiras), west of Praça Marquês de Pombal, contains a multitude of shops that sell clothes, shoes, food, crystal, ceramics, and jewelry. It also has a hairdresser, restaurants, and 10 movie screens; it's open daily 9 AM–11 PM.

Colombo (⊠ Av. Col. Militar, Benfica), one of the largest malls on the Iberian peninsula, has 19 department stores, more than 400 stores and restaurants, and a multiscreen cinema. The Col. Militar–Luz metro station has an exit right inside the complex, which is open daily 9 AM–11 PM.

As it rose from ashes of a fire that destroyed much of the Chiado district, the **Grandes Armazéns do Chiado** (⊠ main entrance on Rua do Carmo, Chiado) has been compared to a phoenix. Behind the restored facade of what was the city's main department store is a stylish complex of shops—designed by acclaimed Portuguese architect Álvaro Siza Vieira—just steps from the Avenida da Liberdade.

Portuguese suburbanites shop or catch a movie at the **Vasco da Gama** (⊠ Av. D. João II, Parque das Nações) complex, which is open 10 AM to 11 PM Sunday through Friday and 10 to midnight on Saturday. A shopping excursion here (take the metro to the Oriente stop) teams well with a visit to the Oceanário de Lisboa or a few strings in the bowling center.

Markets

The best-known flea market is the **Feira da Ladra** (⊠ Campo de Santa Clara, Graça), held on Tuesday morning (8 AM–1 PM) and all day Saturday. For food, kitchenware, and household items head to the covered **Mercado do Arroios** (⊠ Praça do Chile, Alto da Pina) at the Arroios metro station. It's open Monday–Saturday 7–2. Alfama locals shop at the **Mercado do Chão do Loureiro** (⊠ Calçada do Marq. do Tancos, off Costa do Castelo, Alfama), open Monday–Saturday 8–2.

At the **Mercado da Ribeira** (⊠ Av. 24 de Julho, Cais do Sodré), opposite the Cais do Sodré station, the vendors are entertainment in themselves. The market is open Monday–Saturday 6–2. The **Mercado 31 de Janeiro** (⊠ Rua E. V. da Silva, Saldanha) sells a little of everything, including produce, Monday–Saturday 8–2. It's near the Picoas metro stop and the Sheraton hotel. The **Praça de Espanha** (⊠ São Sebastião) market, near the metro stop of the same name, sells mostly clothes; it's open Monday–Saturday 9–5.

Specialty Stores

Antiques

Most of Lisbon's antiques shops are in the Rato and Bairro Alto districts along one long street, which changes its name four times as it runs southward from Largo do Rato: Rua Escola Politécnica, Rua Dom Pedro V, Rua da Misericórdia, and Rua do Alecrim. Look on the nearby Rua de São Bento for more stores. There's also a cluster of antiques shops on Rua Augusto Rosa, between the Baixa and Alfama districts.

Cunha Rosa E. Fernandes (⊠ Rua Augusta 18, Baixa, ☎ 21/886–7474) is packed with furniture, ceramics, and art. The bilingual owners of **Ferroelo Antiquidades** (⊠ Rua Nova de S. Mamede 6, Rato, ☎ 21/396–3122) will guide you through their collection, which includes some silver items and fine furnishings. **Françoise Baudry** (⊠ Rua Augusto Rosa 4, Baixa, ☎ 21/886–9691) has framed landscapes and other paintings in its collection.

Ricardo Hogan (⊠ Rua Augusto Rosa 11, Baixa, ☎ 21/395–4102) has an eclectic collection of carvings, pictures of saints, and pieces in marble that lends itself to serendipitous discovery. One of the best-known antiques shops is **Solar** (⊠ Rua Dom Pedro V 68–70, Bairro Alto, ☎ 21/346–552).

Ceramics

The **Fábrica Sant'Ana** (⊠ Rua do Alecrim 95, Chiado, ☎ 21/342–2537), founded in the 1700s, sells wonderful hand-painted ceramics and tiles based on antique patterns; the pieces sold here may be the finest in the city.

Portugal's most famous porcelain producer, **Vista Alegre** (⊠ Largo do Chiado 18, Chiado, ☎ 21/346–1401), established its factory in 1824. A visit to the flagship store is a must even though you can buy perfect reproductions of their original table services and ornaments at dozens of shops. There are also eight other Vista Alegre–owned stores in the city, including at the Parque das Nações, the Colombo mall, and the airport. **Viuva Lamego** (⊠ Largo do Intendente 25, Graça, ☎ 21/885–2408; ⊠ Calçada do Sacramento 29, Chiado, ☎ 21/346–9692) sells the largest selection of tiles and pottery in Lisbon—and at competitive prices.

Clothing

Although Lisbon isn't on the cutting edge of clothing design, the city is becoming increasingly fashion-aware and according celebrity status to a rising tide of designers. ModaLisboa is an annual fashion event that promotes the creations of such Portuguese designers as Ana Salazar, Maria Gambina, and Miguel Viera. Their creations are sold alongside the more established labels in a variety of stores. Praça de Londres and Avenida de Roma—both in the modern city—form one long run of haute-couture stores and fashion outlets. Designer-clothes stores are also starting to creep into the Bairro Alto.

For women's designer clothes (at designer prices!) visit **Ana Salazar** (⊠ Rua do Carmo 87, Chiado, ☎ 21/347–2289). **Augustus** (⊠ Centro Comercial Roma, Loja 36, Av. de Roma, Alvalade, ☎ 21/795–5224) is one of the city's most famous names in women's fashions. **David and Monteiro** (⊠ Av. de Roma 9A, Alvalade, ☎ 21/840–4296) has top-quality, mid-range Portuguese and international fashions, such as Tommy Hilfiger and Lacoste. **Eldorado** (⊠ Rua do Norte 23–25, Bairro Alto, ☎ 21/342–3935) sells a mix of new and secondhand clothing.

José António Tenente (⊠ Travessa do Carmo 8, Chiado, ☎ 21/342–2560) has some great collections of women's clothing. If there isn't a little girl in your life, the dresses in saucy prints at **Maison Louvre** (⊠ Rossío 106, Baixa, ☎ 21/342–8619) will make you want to adopt one. **Outra Face da Lua** (⊠ Rua do Norte 86, Bairro Alto, ☎ 21/347–1570) is about as unconventional as Lisbon shopping gets. Is it named "Other Side of the Moon" because it doesn't open until late in the evening or because of its eclectic mix of retro clothes, music, gadgets, tea, and tattoos?

Food and Wine

Several excellent delicatessens in the Baixa sell fine foods, including regional cheeses and wines, especially varieties of port—one of Portugal's major exports. Supermarkets also sell local wines, and so do—oddly enough—shops that purvey dried cod, which you'll see stacked outside on the sidewalk or hanging in the window. Rua do Arsenal has several such stores. Other popular gourmet items are the fresh chocolates, marzipan, dried and crystallized fruits, and pastries that are on sale in pastelarias.

The **Instituto do Vinho do Porto** (⊠ Rua de São Pedro de Alcântara 45, Bairro Alto, ☎ 21/347–5707) has more than 100 varieties to sample and bottles to buy. It also has a well-stocked duty-free store at the airport. **Manuel Tavares** (⊠ Rua da Betesga 1a, Baixa, ☎ 21/342–4209), just off the Rossío, has cheese, chocolate, vintage ports, and wine.

At **Napoleão** (⊠ Rua dos Fanqueiros 70, Baixa, ☎ 21/887–2042) the helpful staff speaks English and can recommend vintages. For sweets, try the **Pastelaria Suiça** (⊠ Rossío 96, Baixa, ☎ 21/321–4090), which has a particularly large selection.

Handicrafts

A showroom for traditional carpets is **Almoravida** (⊠ Rua da Senhora da Glória 130, Graça, ☎ 21/346–8967). **Arameiro** (⊠ Praça dos Restauradores 62, Baixa, ☎ 21/347–7875) is a place for lace, especially the spidery *rendas de bilros* variety made in Portugal's north. Near the Castelo de São Jorge, you'll find **A Bilha** (⊠ Rua do Milagre de Santo António 10, Alfama, ☎ 21/888–2261), which sells embroidery, lace, copper, gold, and silver. For embroidered goods and baskets from the Azores, stop by **Casa Regional da Ilha Verde** (⊠ Rua Paiva de Andrade 4, Baixa, ☎ 21/342–5974). At **Francesinha** (⊠ Rua da Barroca 96–98, Bairro Alto, ☎ 21/347–4687), hand-painted ceramics sit alongside fabrics, wrought ironwork, and simple jewelry.

Pais Em Lisboa (⊠ Rua do Teixeira 25, Bairro Alto, ☎ 21/342–0911) has wares from all over Portugal. **Pessoa de Carvalho** (⊠ Costa do Castelo 4, Alfama, ☎ 21/886–2413) is an old Alfama house and sells candles, glassware, jewelry, and handicrafts. **Au Petit Peintre** (⊠ Rua de S. Nicolau 104, Baixa, ☎ 21/342–3767), which has been around since 1909, has paper, art supplies, and small engravings and watercolors. **Tricana** (⊠ Av. Casal Ribeiro 15, Estefânia, ☎ 21/315–5002) specializes in Oriental and French carpets and tapestries, including 19th-century Aubussons.

Jewelry

The Baixa is a good place to look for jewelry. What is now called Rua Aurea was once Rua do Ouro (Gold Street), named for the goldsmiths' shops installed on it under Pombal's 18th-century city plan. The trade has flourished here ever since.

For antique silver and jewelry visit **António da Silva** (⊠ Praça Luís de Camões 40, Chiado, ☎ 21/342–2728). **Sarmento** (⊠ Rua Aurea 251, Baixa, ☎ 21/342–6774), one of the city's oldest goldsmiths, produces characteristic Portuguese gold- and silver-filigree work.

Leather Goods

Although there are shoe shops all over the city, they may have limited selections of large sizes because the Portuguese tend to have small feet. The better shops, however, can make shoes to order. Gloves are sold or custom-made in specialty shops on Rua do Carmo and Rua Aurea.

You'll find fine leather handbags and luggage at **Casa da Sibéria** (⌧ Rua Augusta 254, Baixa, ☎ 21/342–5679). **Coelho** (⌧ Rua da Conceição 85, Baixa, ☎ 21/342–5567) is excellent for leather belts and can also make leather-back fabric belts from your own material.

A reliable shoe store, with a good range of sizes and brands, is **Sapateria Bandarra** (⌧ Rua de Santa Justa 78, Baixa, ☎ 21/342–1178). Visit **Ulisses** (⌧ Rua do Carmo 87, Chiado, ☎ 21/342–0295) for leather gloves.

Music

If you want to take home some soulful fado music, check out the CDs at **Valentim de Carvalho** (⌧ Rossío 59, Baixa, ☎ 21/324–1570). For chart hits and music from just about everywhere in the world, head to the **Virgin Megastore** (⌧ Praça dos Restauradores, Baixa, ☎ 21/346–2148) inside the art deco Eden building.

LISBON A TO Z

To research prices, get advice from other travelers, and book travel arrangements, visit www.fodors.com.

AIR TRAVEL

CARRIERS

TAP, the Portuguese national airline, flies to Lisbon from New York (Newark Liberty International Airport); it also links Lisbon with other European capitals. Continental has a daily service between Newark and Lisbon. Air France, British Airways, and Alitalia also fly to Lisbon.

➤ AIRLINES AND CONTACTS: **Air France** (☎ 21/356–2171). **Alitalia** (☎ 21/353–6141). **British Airways** (☎ 21/346–0931). **Continental** (☎ 21/383–4000). **TAP** (☎ 21/841–5000).

AIRPORTS AND TRANSFERS

International and domestic flights land at Lisbon's small, modern Aeroporto de Lisboa, also known as Aeroporto de Portela, 7 km (5 mi) north of the city. There's a tourist office here as well as a currency exchange bureau.

➤ AIRPORT INFORMATION: **Aeroporto de Portela** (☎ 21/841–3500 or 21/841–3700).

AIRPORT TRANSFER

Car-rental firms and the tourist-information office at the airport provide free maps of Lisbon and its environs. The trip to the city center takes 20–30 minutes, depending on traffic. There are no trains or subways between the airport and the city, but getting downtown by bus or taxi is simple and inexpensive.

A special bus, Aerobus 91, runs every 20 minutes, 7 AM–9 PM, from outside the airport into the city center. Tickets, which you buy from the driver, cost €2.29 or €5.49 and allow one or three days of travel, respectively, on all Lisbon's buses and trams; TAP passengers can claim a free ride by showing their boarding pass. The bus stops close to all the major hotels at several useful points, including Praça Marquês de Pombal, Avenida da Liberdade, the Rossío, Praça do Comércio, and the Cais do Sodré train station. As you board the bus the driver will ask your hotel, note it on a sheet of paper, and call you when it's your stop.

City Buses 44 and 45 cost only €0.90 one-way and depart every 15–30 minutes 5 AM–1:40 AM from the main road in front of the terminal building. They pass through Praça dos Restauradores en route to the Cais do Sodré train station (from here you can continue by rail to Estoril and Cascais).

Taxis in Lisbon are relatively cheap, and the airport is so close to the city center, that many visitors make a beeline straight for a cab (lines form at the terminal). To avoid any hassle over fares you can buy a prepaid voucher (which includes gratuity and luggage charges) from the tourist office booth in the arrivals hall. Expect to pay €11–€14 to most destinations in the city center and around €33 if you're headed for Estoril or Sintra.

BUS TRAVEL

Lisbon's main bus terminal is the Gare do Oriente, adjacent to Parque das Nações, which also includes a railway and metro station. Most travel agents can sell you a bus ticket in advance; if you buy from the company ticket office at the main terminal, give yourself plenty of time to purchase before you depart. In summer it's wise to reserve a ticket at least a day in advance for destinations in the Algarve. There are four daily departures from Lisbon for the Algarve and Oporto; towns closer to the capital have more frequent service. Most international buses and domestic express buses, including those to and from the Algarve, operate from within the Arco do Cego bus terminal, very near Praça Duque de Saldanha. The Saldanha and Picoas metro stations are just a few minutes' walk away.

Terminals at Praça de Espanha and Campo Pequeno—both of which have metro stops with the same name—serve Setúbal-Sesimbra and Portugal's northwest coast, respectively; the terminal at Campo das Cebolas, at the end of Rua dos Bacalhoeiros and east of Praça do Comércio, is for destinations in the Minho and the Algarve; buses to and from Mafra operate from Largo Martim Moniz, northeast of Praça da Figueira.

City buses are operated by the public transportation company Carris and run 6:30 AM to midnight. Each stop is posted with full details of routes. For a spectacular journey across the Ponte 25 de Abril over the Rio Tejo take a bus from Praça de Espanha to Costa da Caparica or Setúbal. You can buy tickets for buses, elevadors, and funiculars at Carris kiosks in the Praça de Figueira, at the foot of the Elevador de Santa Justa, in the Santa Apolónia and Cais do Sodré railway stations, and elsewhere around town. If you pay with cash (have small change on hand if possible) it's twice the price. Either pay when boarding or simply insert your ticket in the ticket-punch machine behind the driver and wait for the pinging noise.

➤ CONTACTS: **Arco do Cego bus terminal** (☎ 21/354–5439). **Carris** (☎ 21/361–3054, WEB www.carris.pt).

CAR RENTAL

It's often much cheaper to arrange car rental in conjunction with your airline ticket or by contacting a car company directly before you arrive. But if you've left it until get to Portugal, all the major car-rental companies have offices at the airport and at Santa Apolónia station. In central Lisbon you'll find Avis, Budget, Europcar, and Hertz. Smaller local car-rental companies are also represented in Lisbon; the tourist office has full details.

➤ Major Agencies: **Avis** (✉ Av. Praia da Vitória 12c, Saldanha, ☎ 21/351–4560; 21/843–5550 airport branch; or 0800/201002). **Budget** (✉ Av. Visconde Valmor 36B, Saldanha, ☎ 21/797–1377 or 21/847–8803 airport branch). **Europcar** (✉ Av. António Agusto de Aguiar 24, Saldanha, ☎ 21/353–5115; 21/847–3181 airport; 21/886–1573 Santa Apolónia station). **Hertz** (✉ Rua do Castilho 72 Rato, ☎ 21/381–2430; 21/849–2722 airport branch; or 0800/221231).

CAR TRAVEL

Lisbon sees some of the most reckless driving in all of Portugal. Add to this the notoriously difficult parking situation in the city center and the cramped older quarters, and there's much to be said for not using a car in the capital. Nevertheless, most of the country's highways originate in Lisbon, including the fast roads west to Estoril (A5/IC15), south to Setúbal (A2/IP1, via the Ponte 25 de Abril), and north to Oporto (A1/IP1). Crossing via the spectacular Ponte Vasco da Gama, north of the city center, is an alternative route to Setúbal and provides easier access for the main highways east to Spain.

EMBASSIES

➤ Contacts: **Canada** (✉ Av. da Liberdade 196, Baixa, ☎ 21/347–4892). **United Kingdom** (✉ Rua São Bernardo 33, Rato, ☎ 21/392–4000). **United States** (✉ Av. das Forças Armadas, Alvalade, ☎ 21/727–3300).

EMERGENCIES

DOCTORS AND DENTISTS

If you need medical attention, many doctors speak English. Ask the staff at your hotel or at the embassy to recommend a reliable one.

EMERGENCY SERVICES

For general problems or in case of theft, the tourism police have an office open 24 hours. If you need to make a claim against your travel insurance, you must file a report there.
➤ Contacts: **Ambulance** (☎ 21/321–7777). **Fire** (☎ 21/342–2222). **General emergencies** (☎ 112). **Police** (☎ 21/346–6141). **Tourism Police** (✉ Rua Capelo 13, near Teatro de São Carlos, Chiado, ☎ 21/346–6141).

HOSPITALS

One clinic with English-speaking staff is Clínica Médica Internationale de Lisboa. Also, you can contact the British Hospital. Other hospitals include Hospital São José, Hospital de São Francisco Xavier, and Hospital Santa Maria.
➤ Contacts: **British Hospital** (✉ Rua Saraiva de Carvalho 49, Campo de Ourique, ☎ 21/395–5067 or 21/397–6329). **Clínica Médica Internationale de Lisboa** (✉ Rua António Augusto de Aguiar 40, São Sebastião, ☎ 21/351–3310). **Hospital Santa Maria** (✉ Av. Prof. Egas Moniz, Alto do Pina, ☎ 21/797–5171 or 21/793–2762). **Hospital de São Francisco Xavier** (✉ Est. Forte A. Duque, Belém, ☎ 21/797–5171). **Hospital São José** (✉ Rua José A. Serrano, Saldanha, ☎ 21/886–2131).

PHARMACIES

Hours of operation and listings of druggists that stay open late are posted on most pharmacy doors. Local newspapers also carry a current list of pharmacies that have extended hours. In town, useful pharmacy addresses include those of Farmácia Azevedo Filhos, Farmácia Barral, and Farmácia Durão.
➤ Contacts: **Farmácia Azevedo Filhos** (✉ Rossío 31, Baixa, ☎ 21/342–7428). **Farmácia Barral** (✉ Rua Augusta 225, Baixa, ☎ 21/342–5372). **Farmácia Durão** (✉ Rua Garrett 92, Chiado, ☎ 21/347–6185).

ENGLISH-LANGUAGE BOOKSTORES

Many bookstores downtown carry at least a few English-language novels and guidebooks. Livraria Bertrand has a broader selection than most. The English-language selection at Livraria Buchholz far exceeds most vacation needs. CDs are downstairs, books up, and classical music plays throughout. Livraria Britânica, across from the British consulate, specializes in English-language books. For American and European newspapers, go to one of the several small newsstands at the bottom of Praça dos Restauradores or on the Rossío. Livraria Barata is another good bet.

➤ BOOKSTORES: **Livraria Barata** (⊠ Rua da Roma 11A, Campo Pequeno ☎ 21/842–8350). **Livraria Bertrand** (⊠ Rua Garrett 73, Chiado, ☎ 21/346–8646). **Livraria Britânica** (⊠ Rua Luis Fernandes 14, Bairro Alto, ☎ 21/342–8472). **Livraria Buchholz** (⊠ Rua Duque de Palmela 4, Amoreiras, ☎ 21/315–7358).

FERRY TRAVEL

Ferries still cross the Rio Tejo, although there are fewer now that Lisbon has two great bridges rather than one. For details of Lisbon-area destinations accessible by ferry, *see* Lisbon's Environs A to Z *in* Chapter 3.

FUNICULAR AND ELEVADOR TRAVEL

Small funicular-railway systems and an ingenious vertical elevator (both are called "elevador") link some of the high and low parts of Lisbon. All are operated by Carris, the public transportation company, whose kiosks sell tickets (the fare is double the price if you pay in cash instead of with a ticket). Of the funicular railways, the most useful are the Elevador da Glória, which runs from Calçada da Glória, just behind Praça dos Restauradores, to Rua de São Pedro de Alcântara in the Bairro Alto, and the Elevador da Bica, which runs from Rua do Loreto down to Rua Boavista, northwest of Cais do Sodré. At this writing, the Elevador de Santa Justa functioned only as a tourist attraction—the walkway at the top leading to the Largo do Carmo in the Bairro Alto was closed for renovations. Departures on all three services are every few minutes from 7 AM to 11 PM.

➤ INFORMATION: **Carris** (☎ 21/361–3054, WEB www.carris.pt).

MAIL

The *correio central* (main post office) on Praça do Comércio receives *poste restante* (general delivery) mail and is open Monday–Saturday 8:30–6. You'll need your passport to collect your mail. The post office on the eastern side of Praça dos Restauradores, at Number 58, is open Monday–Saturday 8 AM–10 PM and Sunday 9–6.

METRO TRAVEL

The metro is modern and efficient. At the northeasterly tip of the service, Gare do Oriente connects the hugely popular Parque das Nações to the rest of the city, and you'll also find the metro useful for transport to and from the Fundação Calouste Gulbenkian and to Praça de Espanha for the bus across the Ponte 25 de Abril to Setúbal; there are stops en route along Avenida da Liberdade and at the Parque Eduardo VII. The metro operates 6:30 AM to 1 AM. Individual tickets cost €0.55; a 10-ticket strip, a *caderneta*, costs €4.50. There's also a one-day (€1.40) or seven-day (€4.80) Pase Metropolitano (Metro Pass) for use just on the metro system. Insert your ticket in the ticket-punch machine at the barrier.

➤ CONTACT: **Metro information** (☎ 21/355–8457, WEB www.metrolisboa.pt).

MONEY MATTERS

Most major banks have offices in the Baixa, and there are currency-exchange facilities at the airport (open 24 hours) and at Santa Apolónia train station (open daily 8:30–8:30). Large hotels and some travel agencies also offer exchange facilities, but the rates are usually poor. Few savvy travelers use them anyway; ATMs are ubiquitous and have better rates.

SIGHTSEEING TOURS

Beware of unauthorized guides who approach you outside popular monuments and attractions: they're usually more concerned with "guiding" you to a particular shop or restaurant. This is not to suggest that persons offering you a tour of the interior of a church or museum should be ignored—knowledgeable people associated with the particular institution often volunteer their services for a tip of €2–€3 or so.

BUS TOURS

Many companies organize half-day tours of Lisbon and its environs and full-day trips to more distant places of interest. Reservations can be made through any travel agency or hotel; some tours will pick you up at your door. A half-day tour of Lisbon will cost about €27. A full-day trip north to Obidos, Nazaré, and Fátima will run about €75 (including lunch), as will a full day east on the "Roman Route" to Évora and Monsaraz.

➤ OPERATORS: **Citirama** (✉ Av. Praia da Vitória 12-B, Saldanha, ☎ 21/355–8564). **Gray Line Tours** (✉ Av. Praia da Vitória 12-B, Saldanha, ☎ 21/352–2594). **Top Tours** (✉ Av. Duque de Loulé 108, Estefânia, ☎ 21/352–1217).

PRIVATE GUIDES

For names of personal guides, contact Lisbon's main tourist office or the Syndicate of Guide Interpreters. It can provide an English-speaking guide for half-day (around €55) or full-day (around €95) tours; the price remains the same for up to 20 people. Office hours are weekdays 9–1 and 2–5:30.

➤ CONTACT: **Syndicate of Guide Interpreters** (✉ Rua do Telhal 4, Campo de Santana, ☎ 21/346–7170).

TAXIS

Taxis are plentiful and relatively cheap. Drivers use meters but can take out-of-towners for a ride, literally, by not taking the most direct route. If you book a cab from a hotel or restaurant, have someone speak to the driver so there are no "misunderstandings" about your destination. The meter starts at €1.75 during the day and €2.09 at night. The price per kilometer during the day on weekdays is €0.32; it rises to €0.37 evenings and weekends. Supplementary charges are added for luggage and if you phone for a cab (€0.75). The meter generally isn't used for journeys outside Lisbon, so you'll have to agree on a fare.

You may hail cruising vehicles, but it's sometimes difficult to get drivers' attention; there are taxi stands at most main squares. Remember that when the green light is on, it means the cab is already occupied. Tips—10% or so—for reliable drivers are appreciated.

➤ TAXI COMPANIES: **Autocoope** (☎ 21/793–2756). **Rádio Táxis** (☎ 21/811–9300). **Télétaxi** (☎ 21/811–1100).

TELEPHONES

COUNTRY AND AREA CODES

The area code for Lisbon and its surrounding area (including Cascais, Estoril, and Sintra) is 21. To access Lisbon from abroad, dial

351 (Portugal's country code), then 21 plus the number. From within Portugal, you need just 21 plus the number.

For information, dial 118; operators often speak English or will find a colleague who does.

If you have an AT&T, MCI, or Sprint calling card, you can enter the appropriate access number from your hotel phone (and some public phones) to be connected with an English-speaking operator to make an international call. Be aware that you cannot get this service from all phones in the city. The phone office at the post office in Praça dos Restauradores is the best place to make long-distance calls, but expect to take a numbered ticket and wait your turn in line. There's another office on the northwestern corner of the Rossío, at Number 65, that's open daily 8 AM–10 PM. At both locations you can use your Visa card. You can also make direct-dial long-distance calls from most phone booths on the street, although it's easiest if you use a phone card.

Pay phones are abundant and either take coins only or coins and phone cards. Cards are available at post offices (€6–€9) as well as some news vendors and other shops.

TRAIN TRAVEL

International trains from France and Spain and long-distance domestic trains from Oporto and the north arrive at and depart from the Santa Apolónia station, on the riverfront to the east of Lisbon's center. One daily train runs to and from Paris; two daily trains to and from Madrid; and frequent daily trains to and from Oporto from 7 AM to midnight. Santa Apolónia station is also connected to the metro network and links directly to Avenida da Liberdade. To reach the Rossío, change at Baixa-Chiado. Buses 9, 12, and 46 also run from outside Santa Apolónia to the center of town. Some long-distance and suburban trains stop at the Oriente station at the Parque das Nações, which is also connected to the metro system.

Local trains to Sintra and all destinations in Estremadura use the central Rossío station, an unmistakably neo-Manueline building that stands between Praça dos Restauradores and the Rossío itself. Trains to Sintra run daily every 15 minutes from 6 AM to 2:40 AM; three trains daily run to towns in Estremadura. For information, tickets, and platforms take the escalators through the station building to the top floor.

Trains along the coast to Estoril and Cascais arrive at and depart from the waterfront Cais do Sodré station, a 10-minute walk west of the Praça do Comércio. Departures both ways are regular—every 15–30 minutes, 5:30 AM–2:30 AM. Buses 45 and 58 run between Cais do Sodré and the central Lisbon squares; Cais do Sodré metro station provides easy access, or, if you prefer, there's a taxi stand outside the station.

Traveling by train to the Algarve and the south of the country is somewhat more complicated than train travel to other destinations. The Barreiro station is on the opposite side of the Rio Tejo but is linked to Lisbon by a ferry that docks at the Terminal Fluvial (also known as Sul e Sueste), adjacent to Praça do Comércio. The fare is included in the train-ticket price. There are seven daily trains to the Algarve, the first of which leaves at 6:40 AM and the last one—an overnight service—at about midnight.

The Caminhos de Ferro Portugueses (CP) has general information lines that are really only helpful if you speak Portuguese. Your best bet is to check out the Web site.

➤ FARES AND RESERVATIONS: **CP** (☎ 21/888–4025, 800/200904, or 808/ 208208, WEB www.cp.pt). **Rail Europe** (☎ 800/942–4866 or 800/274– 8724; 0870/584–8848 U.K. credit-card bookings; WEB www.raileurope. com).

➤ STATIONS: **Estação Barreiro** (☎ 21/207–3028). **Estação Rossío** (☎ 21/346–5022). **Estação Santa Apolónia** (☎ 21/888–4142).

TRAM TRAVEL

Lisbon's elétrico system, operated by the public transportation company Carris, is one of the most amusing and enjoyable ways to get around, especially if you can board one of the clunky old wooden ones (and remember to secure your bag and wallet against pickpockets) rather than the sleek new supertrams, emblazoned with ads. For a taste of the old days, catch Tram 28 for an inexpensive tour of the city from the Alfama; Tram 15 will take you to Belém, passing by or near many of that district's sights; Tram 18 runs right to the Palácio de Ajuda, also in Belém. Stops are indicated by PARAGEM (stop) signs on the sidewalks, and every stop has a route indicator for each tram that passes that way. Buying tickets in advance at Carris kiosks will cost you half as much as paying the fare in cash when you board. The system operates 6:30 AM to midnight; insert your ticket in the ticket-punch machine by the driver.

➤ INFORMATION: **Carris** (☎ 21/361–3054, WEB www.carris.pt).

TRANSPORTATION AROUND LISBON

The best way to see central Lisbon is on foot. It's a small city by any standard, and most of the points of interest are within the well-defined older quarters. Just remember that the city is hilly and has cobblestone sidewalks that can make walking tiring (especially in the hot summer), even when you wear comfortable shoes. At some point you'll probably want to use the public-transportation system, if only to experience the old trams and funicular railways and elevators.

If you're staying in Lisbon for more than a few days, buy one of the various transport passes. A pass for unlimited rides on a tram, bus, funicular, or elevator costs €2.55 for one day's travel; four-day passes are €9.25; seven-day passes cost €13.10.

All buses, trams, and elevators are operated by Carris, the city's public transportation company; the metro has a different ticketing system. You can buy passes or tickets at the Cais do Sodré station, Restauradores metro station, and Carris kiosks throughout the city. If you decide not to use a pass, opt for advance tickets at €0.45 a ride; if you pay cash, the fare is €0.90 a ride.

Another option is the Lisboa Card, a special pass that allows free travel on all public transportation and free entry into 27 museums, monuments, and galleries—including all the major city attractions. You can buy cards that are valid for 24 hours (€10.97), 48 hours (€17.97), or 72 hours (€22.94). They're sold at the airport (in well-signed kiosks), at the Mosteiro de Jerónimos, in the Lisboa Welcome Centre, at the tourist office in the Palácio Foz, and other places around the city.

A note of warning: avoid using public transportation, especially on the metro, during rush hours. Pickpockets ply their trade on crowded trains, buses, and trams. Keep an eye on your possessions, and carry wallets in inside pockets and bags and backpacks with the fastening facing your body. If your hotel lacks a convenient safe, consider stashing some documents and cash in a fashion-defying money belt.

➤ FARES AND PASSES: **Carris information line** (☏ 21/361–3054, WEB www. carris.pt).

TRAVEL AGENCIES

You can save yourself a lot of time by buying train or bus tickets from travel agencies, which often employ English-speaking staffers. Major agencies include Abreu, American Express/Top Tours, and Marcus & Harting.

➤ LOCAL AGENCIES: **Abreu** (✉ Av. da Liberdade 158–160, Baixa, ☏ 21/323–0200). **American Express/Top Tours** (✉ c/o Top Tours, Av. Duque de Ávila 185, Saldanha, ☏ 21/352–1217). **Marcus & Harting** (✉ Rossío 45–50, Baixa, ☏ 21/346–9271).

VISITOR INFORMATION

The Lisbon branch of Portugal's tourist office—Investimentos, Comércio e Turismo de Portugal (ICEP)—is open daily 9–8. It's in the Palácio Foz, at the Baixa end of Avenida da Liberdade. There's also a branch at the airport that's open daily 6 AM to midnight. A much more rewarding place to get information is the Lisboa Welcome Centre, though you may have to wait patiently in a long line. The good news is that the information desk, which is open daily 9–8, is in a small complex with a café, a restaurant, a gallery, and a few shops. For general inquiries, you can try the Linha Verde Turista toll-free number.

For information on all the facilities and events at the Parque das Nações, stop at the information desk on Alameda dos Oceanos, in front of the Vasco da Gama center. The desk is open daily 9:30 to 8.

➤ TOURIST INFORMATION: **ICEP** (✉ Palácio Foz, Praça dos Restauradores, Baixa, ☏ 21/346–3314 or 21/845–0660 to airport branch). **Lisboa Welcome Centre** (✉ Praça do Comércio, Baixa, ☏ 21/031–2810). **Linha Verde Turista** (☏ 0800/296296). **Parque das Nações Information** (☏ 21/891–9333, WEB www.parquedasnacoes.pt).

3 LISBON'S ENVIRONS

Lisbon's backyard is rich in possibilities: drive coastal roads that thread their way along breathtaking seaside cliffs, or laze about on a sandy beach or leafy mountainside, sipping a glass of the delicious local wine. Enjoy the active nightlife of the region's resort towns or retire to a room in a converted palace, castle, or country mansion.

Updated by
Paul Murphy

S UCH FAMOUS DESTINATIONS AS the Estoril Coast, Sintra, the palace at Queluz, even the city of Setúbal and its Manueline church, are all within an hour of Lisbon. You can see the greater part of Lisbon's environs by using the capital as a base. Within a 50-km (31-mi) stretch north and south of the Rio Tejo (Tagus River) you'll find a succession of attractive coastal resorts and important towns—each endowed with unique traditions and characteristics.

Much of the region is the most southerly part of the province of Estremadura, which reaches as far north as Alcobaça and borders on the province of Ribatejo to the east. This was the first land taken back from the Moors in the 12th century Christian Reconquest, which had originated farther north in the region of the Rio Douro: Estremadura means "farthest from the Douro River," an indication of the early extent of the Christian advance against the Moors. Although the area encompasses glistening coastline, broad river estuaries, wooded valleys, and green mountains, its proximity to Lisbon means that its beaches, restaurants, and hotels are filled with people escaping from the city, and coastal roads are often congested.

Lisbon and its environs have served each other through history. Even the country's earliest rulers appreciated the importance of one to the other. It was the Moors who first built a castle northwest of the capital at Sintra as a defense against Christian forces, which, under Dom Afonso Henriques, moved steadily southward after the victory at Ourique in 1139. The castle at Sintra fell to the Christians in 1147, a few days after they defeated the Moors in Lisbon.

Once the Christian Reconquest had been consolidated in Estremadura, there was a less pressing need for defensive measures. The early Christian kings instead adopted the lush hills and valleys of Sintra as a summer retreat and designed estates that survive today. Similarly, Lisbon's 18th- and 19th-century nobility developed small resorts along the Estoril coast; the amenities and ocean views are still greatly sought after (although the ocean itself isn't as clean as it could be). For swimming, modern Lisboetas look a little farther afield—across the Rio Tejo to the beaches and resorts of the Costa da Caparica and the southern Setúbal Peninsula. In whichever direction you travel and whatever your interests, you'll be delighted with all that Lisbon's environs have to offer.

Pleasures and Pastimes

Dining

City dwellers make a point of crossing the Rio Tejo to the suburb of Cacilhas for platefuls of *arroz de marisco* (rice with shellfish) or *linguado* (sole). One of Caparica's summer delights is the smell of grilled sardines wafting from restaurants and beachside stalls. Seafood is also the specialty along the Estoril coast—even the inland villages here and on the Setúbal Peninsula are close enough to the sea to be assured a steady supply of fish.

In Sintra *queijadas* (sweet cheese tarts) are a specialty, and in the Azeitão region of the Setúbal Peninsula, locals swear by the *queijo fresco*, a delicious white sheep's-milk cheese. Lisbon's environs also produce good wines. From Colares comes a light, smooth red, a fine accompaniment to a hearty lunch; Palmela, the demarcated wine-growing district of Setúbal, produces distinctive amber-color wines of recognized quality; and the Fonseca winery produces a splendid dessert wine called Moscatel de Setúbal.

CATEGORY	COST*
$$$$	over €21
$$$	€14–€21
$$	€7–€14
$	under €7

*per person for a main course at dinner

Golf

The superb golf courses near Lisbon attract players from far and wide. Most are the creations of renowned designers, and the climate means that you can play year-round. Many hotels offer golf privileges to guests; some places even have their own courses. Package deals abound.

Lodging

Outside Lisbon, you can stay in *pousadas,* inns that are members of the Turismo de Habitação organization. These are often in converted historic buildings, and they generally have superior facilities and restaurants. The three in this region are at Queluz, Setúbal, and Palmela. Since they typically have few rooms, availability is limited. Regardless of where you stay, in summer it's essential that you book in advance. Out of season, many places discount their prices substantially.

CATEGORY	COST*
$$$$	over €275
$$$	€175–€275
$$	€75–€175
$	under €75

*For a standard double room, including tax, in high-season (off-season rates may be lower).

Shopping

Lisbon's environs have shopping opportunities galore, from clothes sold in smart Cascais and Estoril boutiques to the ceramics and woven and leather goods at roadside stalls and at weekly village markets. Quality and prices vary greatly, so shop around before buying. Prices are fixed almost everywhere, although with a firm command of Portuguese you may be able to negotiate a small discount at markets and roadside stalls.

Exploring Lisbon's Environs

To the west of Lisbon, the Estoril coast consists of a series of small beaches and rocky coves and is at its most delightful around the towns of Estoril and Cascais. Farther north, the Atlantic makes itself felt in the windswept beaches and capes beyond Guincho. Just a few miles inland, the Sintra hills are crisscrossed by minor roads and dotted with old monastic buildings, estates, gardens, and market villages.

To the south, across the Rio Tejo, the contrast couldn't be more pronounced. The beaches of the Costa da Caparica combine to form a 20-km (12½-mi) sweep of sand, backed for the most part by the flat, wine-producing country of the Setúbal Peninsula. The landscape changes only in the south, where the peaks of the Serra da Arrábida rise above a rugged shore that shelters fishing villages and resorts. The only city of any size in the region, Setúbal, is just to the east of here, an obvious stop en route to Évora or the Algarve.

Great Itineraries

With a car you can cover the main sights north and south of the Rio Tejo in two days, although this gives you little time to linger. A week's touring wouldn't be too long to spend, particularly if you plan to soak

The Estoril Coast, Sintra, and Queluz

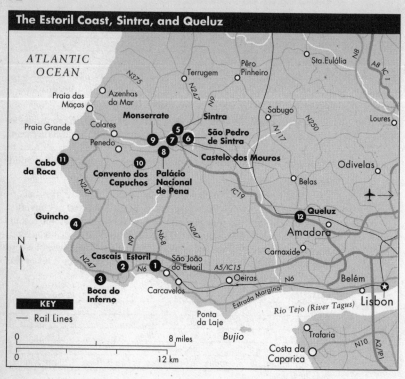

up the sun at a resort or take an in-depth look at Sintra, whose beautiful surroundings alone can fill two or three days of exploring.

All the main towns and most of the sights are accessible by train or bus from Lisbon, so you can see the entire region on day trips from the capital. This is a particularly good way to explore the resorts on the Estoril coast and the beaches of the Costa da Caparica, south across the Rio Tejo. The palace at Queluz also makes a good day trip: it's only 20 minutes northwest of Lisbon by train. Using the capital as your base, a realistic time frame for visiting the major sights is four days: one each for the Estoril coast, Queluz and Sintra, Caparica, and Setúbal.

Numbers in the text correspond to numbers in the margin and on the Estoril Coast, Sintra, and Queluz map and the Setúbal Peninsula map.

IF YOU HAVE 2 DAYS

Start in Lisbon and drive to **Estoril** ①, where you can soak up the atmosphere in the gardens and on the seafront promenade. From here, it's only a short distance to ⌘ **Cascais** ②—the perfect place for an alfresco lunch. Afterward, explore the little cove beaches, and the **Boca do Inferno** ③. The next day, it's less than an hour's ride north to **Sintra** ⑤, where before lunch you'll have time to see its palace and climb to the **Castelo dos Mouros** ⑦. After lunch, return to Lisbon, stopping in **Queluz** ⑫ to see the Palácio Nacional. For dinner, you might cross the Rio Tejo from Lisbon to **Cacilhas** ⑬ for seafood.

IF YOU HAVE 4 DAYS

From Lisbon, head for **Queluz** ⑫ and its Palácio Nacional. In the afternoon, make the short drive to ⌘ **Sintra** ⑤, where you can spend the

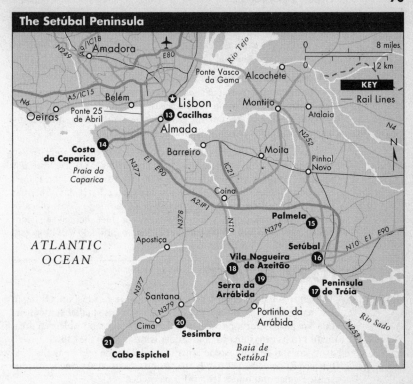

The Setúbal Peninsula

rest of the day seeing the sights in and around the town. Consider having dinner in the adjacent village of **São Pedro de Sintra** ⑥. Head out early the next day to the extraordinary **Palácio Nacional de Pena** ⑧. To contrast this haughty palace with a more humble sight, travel west to the **Convento dos Capuchos** ⑩ before continuing to the headland of **Cabo da Roca** ⑪. Wind south to the wonderful beach at **Guincho** ④ to catch the late afternoon sun and have a bite to eat. Stick to the coastal road as it heads east toward ▥ **Cascais** ②, where you can spend the night.

On the third day, drive back into Lisbon through **Estoril** ①. Cross the Rio Tejo via the mighty Ponte 25 de Abril, and detour for lunch at either **Cacilhas** ⑬ or **Costa da Caparica** ⑭. It's then only an hour's drive to the region's two attractive pousadas, one at ▥ **Palmela** ⑮, the other 10 km (6 mi) down the road in ▥ **Setúbal** ⑯. On the fourth morning drive through the **Serra da Arrábida** ⑲, stopping for lunch at an esplanade restaurant in **Sesimbra** ⑳. From here, you can return to Lisbon in around 90 minutes.

IF YOU HAVE 7 DAYS

Seven days exploring this region will allow the luxury of two nights in ▥ **Sintra** ⑤, providing time to see all the surrounding sights with ease. On the third day, drive straight to **Cabo da Roca** ⑪ and then south to **Guincho** ④, if you fancy a half day at the beach, before following the coast around to ▥ **Cascais** ②. Two nights spent here will allow you to really get to know the town and travel to and from **Estoril** ①.

From Cascais, return to Lisbon and aim for lunch at either **Cacilhas** ⑬ or **Costa da Caparica** ⑭. Spend the night at the pousada in ▥ **Palmela** ⑮ or the one in ▥ **Setúbal** ⑯. On the final day, plan to have lunch in **Vila Nogueira de Azeitão** ⑱ and continue on a drive through the **Serra da Arrábida** ⑲. If you spend the night in the attractive fishing port and resort town of ▣ **Sesimbra** ⑳, you'll have time to visit the windswept **Cabo Espichel** ㉑ before driving back to Lisbon.

When to Tour Lisbon's Environs

If you're planning to visit in summer, particularly July and August, you *must* reserve a hotel room in advance. If you can, travel to the coastal areas in spring or early fall: the crowds are much thinner, and it could be warm enough for a brisk swim in April and October.

That said, most of the region's festivals are held in the summer. In São Pedro de Sintra, the Festa de São Pedro (St. Peter's Day) celebration is on June 29; there are summer music and arts festivals in Sintra, Cascais, and Queluz; September in Palmela sees the Festa das Vindimas (Grape Harvest Festival); and the Feira de Santiago takes place in Setúbal at the end of July. Year-round markets include those in São Pedro de Sintra (second and fourth Sunday of every month) and Vila Nogueira de Azeitão (first Sunday of every month).

THE ESTORIL COAST

The Estoril coast extends for 32 km (20 mi) west of Lisbon, taking in the major towns of Estoril and Cascais as well as smaller settlements that are part suburb, part beach town. It's a favored residential area, thanks to its proximity to (and milder winters than) the capital as well as its coastal charms. Some fancifully refer to the region as the Portuguese Riviera, and certainly the casino at Estoril and the luxurious seaside villas and hotels lend the area cachet.

In summer, count on crowds. And, not only are the towns and beaches crowded, but the ocean—sparkling from a distance—suffers from a long-standing pollution problem. The quality of the water varies greatly from beach to beach, and although ongoing work is slowly rectifying the situation, avoid swimming in an area unless the water has been declared safe. Look for a blue Council of Europe flag, which signals clean water and beach; consult local tourist offices if you're unsure.

Unless you intend to tour the wider region, it's better to travel by train from Lisbon rather than driving. This section has been arranged accordingly, with coverage of Estoril first, followed by Cascais, which marks the end of the train line; from here, it's a short walk to the Boca do Inferno and a brief bus ride to the magnificent beach at Guincho. If you drive, leave Lisbon via the Estrada Marginal (follow signs for Cascais and Estoril) and take the scenic coastal route (the N6), or the faster Auto-Estrada da Oeste (A5/IC15).

Estoril

❶ *26 km (16 mi) west of Lisbon. (The train runs directly to Estoril, or get off at the previous station, São João do Estoril, and walk 2 km [1 mi] along the seafront promenade path, a fine route with excellent views.)*

In the 19th century, Estoril was preferred by the European aristocracy, who wintered here in the comfort and seclusion of mansions and gardens. Although the town has elegant hotels, restaurants, and sports facilities, reminders of its genteel history are now few. It presents its best face right in the center, where today's jet set descends on the casino, at the top of the formal gardens of the Parque do Estoril.

Across the busy main road, on the beachfront Tamariz esplanade, there are alfresco restaurants and an open-air seawater swimming pool. The best and longest local beach is at Monte Estoril, which adjoins Estoril's beach; here you'll find rest rooms and beach chairs for rent, as well as plenty of shops and snack bars.

The **Museu Exilio,** above the post office, has a collection of memorabilia relating to Portugal's mid-20th-century history. It consists mostly of black-and-white photos with captions in Portuguese, focusing on Estoril's community of aristocratic exiles who fled here from northern Europe during World War II. There's also an exhibit devoted to the Nazi persecution of the Jews. ⊠ *Av. Aida,* ☎ *21/468–4493.* ≋ *Free.* ⊙ *Weekdays 9:30–6:30, Sat. 9:30–12:30.*

In addition to gambling salons, the **Estoril Casino** has a nightclub, bars, and restaurants. Tour groups often make an evening of it here, with dinner and a floor show, but it's a pricey night out. Most visitors, however, are content to feed one of the 1,000 slot machines in the main complex and then check out the other entertainment options: art exhibits, movies, nightly cabaret performances, and concerts and ballets (in summer). To enter the gaming rooms you must pay €4 (slots are free) and show your passport to prove that you're 21. Reservations are essential for the restaurant and floor show. For €25 you can see the show and have one drink on the house; €50 buys you entrance to the show and dinner. ⊠ *Parque do Estoril,* ☎ *21/466–7700,* WEB *www. casino-estoril.pt.* ⊙ *Daily 3 PM–3 AM; floor show nightly at 11. AE, DC, MC, V.*

Dining and Lodging

$$$ ✕ **The English Bar.** Well it's not English, and it's not a bar. But get beyond the initial confusion, and you're in for a good meal. Surroundings are baronial, with plenty of burnished wood, heavy drapes, and oak beams. The menu is an international hybrid: choose from game in season, fresh fish, chicken curry, even Indonesian *saté* (skewered, charcoal-broiled meats served with a peanut sauce). ⊠ *Av. Sabóia, off Estrada Marginal,* ☎ *21/468–0413. AE, DC, MC, V. Closed Sun.*

$$–$$$$ ✕ **A Choupana.** Just east of town, this restaurant has views of Cascais Bay from its picture windows. It's a reliable establishment, where you can ask the English-speaking staff about the daily specials. Fresh seafood is the mainstay—try the *cataplana,* a tangy, typically Portuguese dish of clams and pork. Live music usually accompanies dinner, and in summer there's dancing nightly until 2. ⊠ *Estrada Marginal,* ☎ *21/468–3099. AE, DC, MC, V.*

$$–$$$ ✕ **La Villa.** Whatever you do, book a table by a window at this seaside restaurant. Although the building is a Victorian landmark, it houses an elegant modern restaurant with the area's most interesting seafood dishes. Appetizers include fresh cod with cilantro marinated in gazpacho and soft-shell crab filled with broccoli puree. For an entrée you might try monkfish braised with a pepper mustard over a baby onion and green pepper confit. Or go international with oysters, sushi, and sashimi. ⊠ *Praia do Tamariz,* ☎ *21/468–0033. AE, DC, MC, V. Closed Mon.*

$$$–$$$$ ✕▦ **Hotel Palácio.** Exiled European courts waited out World War II
★   in this luxurious 1930s hotel. Several of the well-appointed, Regency-style guest rooms have balconies, and public areas are adorned with monumental columns and chandeliers. A comfortable bar has views over the outdoor pool to the town's central park. There's no more-elegant spot in town to dine than the Four Seasons Grill ($$$; reservations and a smart outfit are essential). Golfers who stay here can tee up on the Clube de Golfe do Estoril at reduced rates. ⊠ *Rua do Parque, Parque do Estoril, 2769-504,* ☎ *21/468–0000,* FAX *21/468–4867,* WEB *www.hotel-estoril-palacio.pt. 132 rooms, 30 suites. 2 restaurants,*

3 bars, in-room data ports, in-room safes, cable TV, minibars, room service, pool, massage, sauna, golf privileges, 4 tennis courts, gym, horseback riding, squash, Internet, baby-sitting, business services, convention center, meeting rooms. AE, DC, MC, V. BP.

$$ 🏨 **Estoril Eden.** Looking for a good base with the kids? The comfortable studios and suites in this modern apartment hotel are reasonably sized and equipped with satellite TV, fold-out beds, and a basic kitchenette. Ask for one of the front rooms, which have coastal views. Children might enjoy the free summer-entertainment program and the good sports facilities; parents can keep an eye on things from the poolside café. The ocean is just a few minutes' walk away via an underpass that starts behind the Monte Estoril train station. ✉ *Av. Sabóia, 2769-502,* ☎ *21/466–7600, 800/604–4ASI, or 800/604–4274,* FAX *21/466–7601,* WEB *www.hotel-estoril-eden.pt. 162 units. Restaurant, bar, café, cable TV, kitchenettes, 2 pools (1 indoor), massage, sauna, golf privileges, health club, nightclub, baby-sitting, children's programs, convention center, meeting rooms. AE, DC, MC, V. EP.*

$$ 🏨 **Hotel Lido.** On a quiet street overlooking the green hillside above Estoril, the Lido is a modest hotel whose amenities compensate for its lack of real style. The simple rooms all look the same—strong colors, clean lines, identical furniture—but they have balconies with fine views and there's a pool, a garden, and a lounge bar. Off-season discounts are substantial. The hotel is signposted for drivers from the casino; otherwise, it's a steep 15-minute walk from the center of Estoril. ✉ *Rua do Alentejo 12, 2765-188,* ☎ *21/468–4098,* FAX *21/468–3665. 56 rooms, 6 suites. Restaurant, bar, pool, billiards, baby-sitting, meeting room. AE, DC, MC, V. BP.*

Nightlife

At night, the casino is a big draw, though there are several well-known bars and clubs. Most of places are open 10 PM–3 AM. In summer, try the **Absurdo Bar** (✉ Praia do Tamariz, ☎ 21/467–5498), where you can dance to Brazilian music. **Bauhaus** (✉ Estrada Marginal, ☎ 21/468–0965), next to the Estoril Eden hotel, attracts a lively clientele. The young and the restless head to **Forte Velho** (✉ Estrada Marginal, ☎ 21/468–1337), a medieval fort on the edge of town that has been converted into a dance club.

Outdoor Activities and Sports

GOLF

Clube de Golfe do Estoril (✉ Av. da República, ☎ 21/468–0176) has an immaculate 18-hole championship course as well as a 9-hole course. The standard greens fee for 18 holes is €48.6, but guests of the Hotel Palácio receive special rates and privileges. Note that on weekends only members can play here. On the Estoril–Sintra road, 7 km (4 mi) north of Estoril at Linhó, the **Estoril Sol** (☎ 21/923–2461) has a scenic 9-hole course on the fringes of the Serra de Sintra. The greens fee is €21. **Penha Longa** (✉ Estrada da Lagoa Azul, Linhó, ☎ 21/924–9011), 9 km (5 mi) north of Estoril, has superb views, an 18-hole course, a 9-hole course, putting greens, and golf clinics. The greens fee for 18 holes is €75.8.

TENNIS

Many of the larger hotels in Estoril have tennis courts, or contact the **Clube de Tenis do Estoril** (✉ Av. Amaral, ☎ 21/468–1675 or 21/466–2770), which has 18 courts and hosts international championships.

Shopping

Each July and August sees the **Feira do Artesanato,** an open-air crafts fair near the casino. Every evening from 5 until midnight stalls sell local arts, crafts, and food. The town of **Carcavelos,** 7 km (4 mi) southeast of Estoril, has a busy Thursday market that sells food, clothes, and crafts; you can reach it by local train.

Cascais

★ ❷ *3 km (2 mi) west of Estoril; the train runs directly here, or you can walk along the seafront promenade.*

Once a mere fishing village, the town of Cascais—with three small, sandy bays—is now a heavily developed resort packed with shops, restaurants, and hotels. Despite the masses of people, though, Cascais has retained some of its small-town character. This is most visible around the harbor, with its fishing boats and yachts, and in the old streets and squares off Largo 5 de Outubro, where you'll find lace shops, cafés, and restaurants. The beaches are very attractive, too, although bear in mind the pollution problems here: unless signs indicate otherwise, stay out of the sea.

The **Igreja de Nossa Senhora da Assunção** (Church of Our Lady of the Assumption), with its plain white facade, is the most graceful church in Cascais. Inside is an elegant golden altar and fine paintings by 17th-century Portuguese artist Josefa de Óbidos—a rare instance of a female artist of that day gaining an international reputation. ⊠ *Largo da Assunção,* ☎ *no phone.* ☜ *Free.* ☉ *Daily 9–1 and 5–8.*

One of Cascais's 19th-century town houses serves as the **Museu dos Condes Castro Guimarães,** with displays of 18th- and 19th-century paintings, ceramics, and furniture as well as artifacts from nearby archaeological excavations. ⊠ *Av. Rei Humberto II de Itália,* ☎ *21/482–5407.* ☜ *€1.30, free Sun.* ☉ *Tues.–Sun. 10–5.*

For an understanding of development in Cascais, visit the modern, single-story **Museu do Mar** (Museum of the Sea). Here, the town's former role as a fishing village is traced through model boats and fishing gear, period clothing, analysis of local fish, paintings, and old photographs. ⊠ *Av. da República,* ☎ *21/486–1377.* ☜ *€1.30, free Sun.* ☉ *Tues.–Sun. 10–5.*

☼ The most relaxing spot in Cascais, apart from the beach, is the municipal **Parque do Marechal Carmona,** open daily 9–6, where there are a shallow lake, a café, a small zoo, and tables and chairs under the trees for picnickers.

Dining and Lodging

$$–$$$ ✕ **Beira Mar.** One of several well-established and unpretentious restaurants behind the fish market, the Beira Mar has a comfortable, tiled interior. An impressive display of the day's catch shows you the best of the seafood, although as ever, you can end up paying top-dollar for dinner if you're not careful since it's all sold by weight. Make sure you know the price first, or stick to the dishes with fixed prices—rice with clams or steaks cut from swordfish or tuna are always worth trying. ⊠ *Rua das Flores 6,* ☎ *21/483–0152. AE, DC, MC, V. Closed Tues.*

$$–$$$ ✕ **O Pescador.** Fresh seafood fills the menu at this folksy restaurant, where a cluttered ceiling and maritime-related artifacts distract the eye. Sole is a specialty, and this is also a good place to try *bacalhau* (dried salt cod); it's often baked here, either with cream or with port wine and onions. ⊠ *Rua das Flores 10,* ☎ *21/483–2054. AE, DC, MC.*

$–$$ ✕ **Dom Manolo.** The surroundings aren't sophisticated in this Spanish-owned grill-restaurant, but for down-to-earth fare it's a good choice. The waiters charge back and forth delivering excellent spit-roasted chicken to a largely local clientele. Whatever your main dish, order potatoes or fries on the side; avoid the poor, overpriced salads and factory-made desserts. ✉ *Estrada Marginal 13,* ☎ *21/483–1126. No credit cards.*

$ ✕ **Pizza Itália.** There are plenty of other pizza joints in Cascais, but Pizza Itália is probably the best of the bunch. In its indoor dining rooms or on its sunny terrace you can choose from a range of authentic pies and pastas. ✉ *Rua do Poço Novo 1,* ☎ *21/483–0151. MC, V. Closed Wed. No lunch.*

$$$ ✕🏠 **Hotel Albatroz.** On a rocky outcrop above the crashing waves, ★ this gorgeous hotel was once the summer residence of the dukes of Loulé. Although expanded and modernized, its character has been retained, particularly in the fabric-lined corridors and the cozy terrace bar. The guest rooms combine elegance (old prints and floral drapes) with comfort (good beds and spacious bathrooms); it's worth paying extra for a sea view. The small pool and the terrace overlook the ocean. A fine buffet breakfast is served in the Albatroz restaurant ($$–$$$$; reservations and dressy-casual attire are essential), where fish dishes are the specialty. ✉ *Rua Frederico Arouca 100, 2750–353,* ☎ *21/484–7380,* ⨳ *21/484–4827,* 🌐 *www.albatrozhotels. com. 37 rooms, 3 suites. Restaurant, bar, cable TV, minibars, room service, saltwater pool, golf privileges, shops, Internet, baby-sitting, meeting rooms. AE, DC, MC, V. EP.*

$$$ 🏠 **Estalagem Villa Cascais.** If Portugal's 18th-century writer Maria Amália de Carvalho could return today to her house on the harbor at Cascais Bay, she would surely check in and open up her laptop. Each light-filled room is individually furnished; some have balconies or fireplaces, and all have sea views. In the bathroom, the hair dryer, the phone, and the view of the greatly changed marina might surprise Dona Maria, but the huge tubs wouldn't. ✉ *Rua Fernandes Tomas 1, 2750-342,* ☎ *21/486–3410,* ⨳ *21/484–4680,* 🌐 *www.albatrozhotels.com. 10 rooms. Restaurant, bar, cable TV, minibars, meeting room. AE, DC, MC, V. EP.*

$$ 🏠 **Hotel Baia.** This modern stone hotel fronted with white balconies overlooks fishing boats on the quayside and Cascais Bay. Your choice of rooms is straightforward: the 66 front rooms have balconies and sea views but are plain in the extreme; the rest face the town at the back but have been decorated with a bit more imagination. There's a private esplanade along the ground floor, with a lounge, restaurant, grill, café, and bar. ✉ *Estrada Marginal, 2754-509,* ☎ *21/483–1033,* ⨳ *21/483–1095,* 🌐 *www.portugalvirtual.pt/hotelbaia. 114 rooms. Restaurant, bar, café, grill, cable TV, pool, golf privileges, convention center. AE, DC, MC, V. BP, MAP, FAP.*

$ 🏠 **Casa da Pérgola.** Set back from the road amid gardens, this intimate town house has been in the hands of the same family for more than 100 years. The painted-and-tiled facade sets a refined, solidly 19th-century tone that's continued inside by the heavy drapes, impressive stairway, period furniture, and art. In cooler weather you eat breakfast in the dining room surrounded by cabinets of old porcelain; on warmer days you can enjoy the day's first meal in the garden. Book well in advance to secure a room here. ✉ *Av. de Valbom 13, 2750-508,* ☎ *21/484–0040,* ⨳ *21/483–4791,* 🌐 *www.ciberguia.pt/casa-da-pergola. 6 rooms. Dining room, some air-conditioning; no room TVs. No credit cards. BP. Closed Nov.–Feb.*

Nightlife and the Arts

Cascais has plenty of bars on and around the central pedestrian street, Rua Frederico Arouca, and in Largo Luís de Camões. The marina is also a lively place to barhop with a wide choice of places that stay open until around 2 AM.

Chequers (✉ Largo Luís de Camões 7, ☎ 21/483–0926) blasts rock music into the square nightly in summer. **Coconuts** (✉ Av. Rei Humberto II de Itália, ☎ 21/484–4109), a popular disco close to the marina, has seven bars, two dance floors, and nice sea views from a terrace. Nothing much happens before midnight, but the action doesn't finish until 4 AM.

You can hear fado, the mournful Portuguese folk music, at **Forte D. Rodrigo** (✉ Rua de Birre 961, ☎ 21/487–1373). On hot summer nights, customers of the English-style pub, **John Bull** (✉ Largo Luís de Camões 8, ☎ 21/483–3319), spill out into the square.

Outdoor Activities and Sports

FISHING

The **Clube Naval de Cascais** (✉ Esplanada Príncipe Luís Filipe, in front of Hotel Baia, ☎ 21/483–0125) organizes deep-sea fishing outings.

GOLF (AND MORE)

Belas Clube de Campo (✉ Alameda do Aqueducto, Belas Clube de Campo, ☎ 21/962–6640, WEB www.belas-clube-de-campo.pt) is a prestigious 18-hole course designed by Rocky Roquemor. It makes good use of lakes and water courses, and it has a nice clubhouse. Greens fees are €72–€83. **Quinta da Marinha** (✉ 4 km [2½ mi] west of Cascais, ☎ 21/468–0100 for golf; 21/468–0180 for tennis; 21/486–9433 for horseback riding; WEB www.marinhagolf.com) has an 18-hole course designed by Robert Trent Jones, Jr. Green fees are €61–€76. There are also tennis courts, a pool, and an exceptional equestrian center where you can arrange horseback rides year-round.

SURFING

You can rent surfing equipment from **Equinócio** (✉ Varandas de Cascais 3, ☎ 21/483–5354).

Shopping

Cascais is the best shopping area on the Estoril coast, with pedestrian streets lined with stores and small market stalls. For smart fashions, gifts, and handmade jewelry, browse around Rua Frederico Arouca. Markets are held north of town at Rua Mercado (off Avenida 25 de Abril) on Wednesday and Saturday; you'll find fruit, vegetables, cheese, bread, and flowers. On the first and third Sunday of each month, a large market is held at the Praça de Touros (Bull Ring) on Avenida Pedro Álvares, west of the center.

Near the church, in **Ceramicarte** (✉ Largo da Assunção 3–4, ☎ 21/484–0170), Fátima and Luís Soares present their carefully executed, modern ceramic designs alongside more traditional jugs and plates. There's also a small selection of tapestries and artworks.

Boca do Inferno

❸ *2 km (1 mi) west of Cascais.*

The most visited attraction in the area around Cascais is the forbiddingly named Mouth of Hell, one of several natural grottoes in the rugged coastline. It's best to visit at high tide or in stormy weather, when the waves are thrust high onto the surrounding cliffs. You can walk along the fenced paths to the viewing platforms above the grotto and peer down into the abyss. A path leads down to secluded spots on the rocks below, where fishermen cast their lines. Afterward, shop for lace, leather items, and other handicrafts at roadside stalls, and stop in one of the nearby cafés.

NEED A
BREAK?

On the coastal road west of Cascais, the café-terrace **Esplanada Santa Marta** (✉ Estrada da Boca do Inferno, ☎ 21/483–7779) overlooks the tiny Santa Marta Beach and a lighthouse. This is a perfect spot for a cool drink on the way to or from the Boca do Inferno, a 20-minute walk beyond.

Guincho

❹ *9 km (5½ mi) north of Boca do Inferno.*

There's a wide beach at Guincho, where Atlantic waves pound onto the sand even on the calmest of days, providing perfect conditions for windsurfing (the annual world championships are often held here during the summer). The undertow here is notorious; even the best swimmers should take heed. Whether you surf or not, savor some fresh fish served at one of the restaurant terraces overlooking the beach. And if you don't want to drive—perhaps you would rather wash the meal down with wine and a glass of port?—it's a simple matter to come by bus, which leaves from outside Cascais's train station every two hours (7:45 AM–5:45 PM, journey time 25 minutes).

Dining and Lodging

$–$$ ✗▥ **Estalagem do Forte Muchaxo.** This inn is nestled in the rocks over Guincho beach. Although most of the rooms have ocean views, those at the back overlook the nearby hills; the beach itself is just steps away. Much of the building is rustic, with stone floors, wood paneling, and maritime bric-a-brac. In the well-known restaurant ($$–$$$), fish specialties such as *caldeirada* (fish stew) are the order of the day. Meals are a little overpriced, and service isn't always top-notch, but what you're ultimately paying for is the unrivaled view through picture windows. ✉ *Praia do Guincho, 2750-642,* ☎ *21/487–0221,* ℻ *21/487–0444. 60 rooms. Restaurant, bar, some air-conditioning, cable TV, minibars, saltwater pool, Internet, meeting rooms. AE, DC, MC, V. BP, MAP, FAP.*

SINTRA, SINTRA ENVIRONS, AND QUELUZ

The lush woods and valleys on the northern slopes of the Serra de Sintra (Sintra Mountains) have been inhabited since prehistoric times, although the Moors were the first to build a castle on the peaks. Later Sintra became the summer residence of Portuguese kings and aristocrats, and its late medieval palace is the greatest expression of royal wealth and power of the time. In the 18th and 19th centuries English travelers, poets, and writers—including an enthusiastic Lord Byron—were drawn by the region's beauty. The poet Robert Southey described Sintra as "the most blessed spot on the whole inhabitable globe." Its historic importance has been recognized by UNESCO, which designated it as a World Heritage Site in 1995.

Sintra is a good base for visiting the surrounding countryside. Driving is the easiest way to explore the area, but you could also take a guided tour (arranged through the tourist office) or see the sights by taxi. The nearest attractions are within walking distance or are accessible by bus or horse-drawn carriages.

Sintra

★ **⑤** *30 km (18 mi) northwest of Lisbon, 13 km (8 mi) north of Estoril.*

The palaces, gardens, wooded paths, and viewpoints of Sintra are as enchanting as its horse-drawn carriages and old hotels. Even at the height of summer the region exudes its famous charm: tour buses are largely banned from the main square, and with a little effort you can escape any crowds by taking one of several walks in the countryside. To explore Sintra, you might start at the tourist office and—armed with local walking information—begin your discoveries.

★ The conical twin chimneys of the **Palácio Nacional de Sintra** (Sintra Palace), also called the Paço Real, are the town's most recognizable landmarks. There has probably been a palace here since Moorish times, although the current structure dates from the 14th century. The property was the summer residence of the House of Avis, Portugal's royal line, and it displays a fetching combination of Moorish, Gothic, and Manueline architectural styles. Some of its rooms are exceptional, and bilingual descriptions in each of them let you enjoy the palace at your own pace. The kitchen, with its famous chimneys, is an intriguing stop, not least because of its sheer size (imagine the life of a scullery maid here). It's still used today when official banquets are held at the palace. The chapel has Mozarabic (Moorish-influenced) *azulejos* (tiles) from the 15th and 16th centuries. The ceiling of the Sala das Armas is painted with the coats of arms of 72 noble families, and the grand Sala dos Cisnes has a remarkable ceiling of painted swans. One of the oldest rooms, the Sala das Pegas, figures in a well-known tale about Dom João I (1385–1433) and his dalliance with a lady-in-waiting. The king had the room painted with as many magpies as there were chattering court ladies, thus satirizing the gossips as loose-tongued birds. ✉ *Largo Rainha D. Amélia*, ☎ *21/910–6840.* ⊡ *€3, free Sun. 10–2.* ⊙ *Thurs.–Tues. 10–5:30 (last admission at 5).*

NEED A BREAK?

Well placed in Sintra's central square—with fine views of the palace—**Café Paris** (✉ Largo Rainha D. Amélia, ☎ 21/923–2375) makes a pleasant, if pricey, stop for a drink or even a meal. Outside seating can be difficult to score; the lucky ones can soak up the bustling street scenes.

The tourist office's building also contains an art gallery, the **Galeria do Museu Municipal,** specializing in works associated with Sintra. ✉ *Praça da República 23,* ☎ *21/924–4772.* ⊡ *Free.* ⊙ *Tues.–Fri. 9–noon and 2–6, weekends 2:30–7.*

The former fire station headquarters has been transformed into the **Museu do Brinquedo** (Toy Museum). Based on the collection of João Arbués Moreira, who began hoarding his toys when he was 14, the museum occupies more than four floors. Pick out your favorites from the thousands of toy planes, trains, and automobiles; dolls' furniture; rare lead soldiers; puppets; and a zillion-and-one other Christmas gifts and birthday presents—including some given to royal children. There's a café here, too. ✉ *Rua Visconde de Monserrate,* ☎ *21/924–2171,* WEB *www.museo-do-brinquedo.pt.* ⊡ *€3.* ⊙ *Tues.–Sun. 10–6.*

The steep, wooded slopes that rise from Sintra are home to many grand houses, including the intriguing **Quinta da Regaleira,** a five-minute walk along the main road past the tourist office. You have to call ahead to book a tour, and the entrance fee is high, but it's worth it. The estate was built in the early 20th century for a Brazilian mining magnate with a vivid imagination and a keen interest in freemasonry and the

Knights Templars (who made their 11th-century headquarters on this very site). The main part of the tour takes in the gardens, where almost everything—statues, water features, grottoes, lookout towers—is linked to freemasonry or the Knights Templars. By the time you reach the spooky, 100-ft-deep Poço do Iniciáto (Initiation Well)—an inverted underground "tower"—you may be wondering what strange events might have gone on here (none did). From the well, you pass through inky tunnels, cross a small lake via stepping stones and emerge, gratefully, back into the light. Though the house—with its fantastic mix of styles, among them Gothic and Manueline—is flamboyant, it's something of an anticlimax after the garden tour. There's an uninspired exhibit on freemasonry, a café, and a restaurant. ⊠ *Rua Consigliéri Pedroso,* ☎ *21/910–6650,* WEB *www.regaleira.pt.* ☎ *€9.98.* ☉ *June–Sept. tours daily 10–5, every 30 mins; tours less frequent Oct.–May.*

If your stay is longer than a day or so, the **Museu Arqueológico de São Miguel di Odrinhas** is worth a visit. Its displays include locally found ancient and medieval objects. ⊠ *Av. Professor Dr. D. Fernando da Almeida,* ☎ *21/961–3574.* ☎ *€2.50.* ☉ *Wed.–Sun. 10–1 and 2–6.*

Dining and Lodging

$$–$$$$ ✕ **Tacho Real.** Sintra locals come to this restaurant, at the top of a steep flight of steps, for a celebratory night out. They can count on confident, traditional dishes cooked with panache. Lamb, *leitão* (suckling pig), steaks, and game in season are all on the menu. ⊠ *Rua do Ferraria 4,* ☎ *21/923–5277. AE, MC, V. Closed Wed.*

$–$$ ✕ **Alcobaça.** The friendly owner bustles around to make sure guests are well served in this simple restaurant on a town-center side street. Try the excellent grilled chicken, arroz de marisco, or tasty fresh clams *bulhão pato* (in garlic sauce). ⊠ *Rua das Padarias 7–11,* ☎ *21/923–1651. MC, V.*

$$$$ ✕ฌ **Hotel Palácio de Seteais.** Built in the 18th-century as a home for
★ the Dutch consul to Portugal, this hotel is surrounded by pristine grounds 1 km (½ mi) or so from the center of Sintra. You enter under an arch that joins the building's two wings. In them, public rooms have period furnishings, delicate frescoes, and Arraiolos carpets, and guest rooms are individually styled, some with hand-painted wallpapers. The restaurant ($$–$$$; reservations essential; dressy attire requested) serves set, four-course, Continental meals. In summer, having coffee or tea on the terrace is a delight. ⊠ *Rua Barbosa do Bocage 8, 2710–517,* ☎ *21/923–3200,* FAX *21/923–4277,* WEB *www.tivolihotels.com. 30 rooms, 1 suite. Restaurant, bar, cable TV, pool, tennis court, horseback riding, Internet, meeting rooms. AE, DC, MC, V. BP*

$$$ ✕ฌ **Lawrence's Hotel.** When this 18th-century inn reopened as a luxury hotel late in the 20th century, the U.S. secretary of state and the Netherlands' Queen Beatrix were among the first guests. The intimate rooms are bathed in light from French windows, and deluxe touches such as heated towel racks and crested linens abound. The staff can arrange anything from jeep tours to baby-sitting. At Lawrence's Restaurant ($$$–$$$$; reservations recommended) specialties—served on Portugal's Vista Alegre porcelain—might include fish soup *en croûte* (served in hollowed-out bread) with coriander, roast duck, and a dessert flambéed at your table. ⊠ *Rua Consigliéri Pedroso 38–40, 2710-550,* ☎ *21/910–5500,* FAX *21/910–5505,* WEB *portugalvirtual.pt/lawrences. 11 rooms, 5 suites. Restaurant, bar, in-room safes, cable TV, library, Internet, meeting rooms. AE, DC, MC, V. BP.*

$$ ฌ **Casa Miradouro.** Count yourself lucky if you've managed to book
★ a room at this candy-striped 1890s house at the edge of Sintra. Its Swiss owner, the charming Mr. Kneubühl, has a keen eye for style and com-

fort. Rooms have grand views, wrought-iron bedsteads, and polished tile floors. Breakfast is served in the downstairs dining room, which opens onto a terrace; although no other meals are served, you're only a (steep) five-minute walk from Sintra's restaurants. ⊠ *Rua Sotto Mayor 55, 2710,* ☎ *21/923–5900,* FAX *21/924–1836,* WEB *www.casa-miradouro.com. 6 rooms. Breakfast room. AE, DC, MC, V. BP. Closed mid-Jan.–Feb.*

$$ ⊡ **Quinta da Capela.** Built by the dukes of Cadaval, this long, low, 16th-century manor house has spacious rooms filled with period furniture. The grounds also contain a garden, a chapel, and a tree-shaded pool. The views stretch over to the Pena Palace. As the manor house is 3 km (2 mi) west of Sintra, off the road to Colares, a car is essential. ⊠ *Estrada de Monserrate, 2710,* ☎ *21/929–0170,* FAX *21/929–3425. 8 rooms, 2 suites. Dining room, pool, sauna, gym; no room TVs, no air-conditioning. MC. BP. Closed Nov.–Feb.*

$$ ⊡ **Quinta das Sequóias.** This 19th-century manor house on 40 wooded
★ acres underwent inspired renovations to transform it into a hotel. One of the bathrooms was cleverly built around monolithic boulders, and a tower was chosen as a place for a guest room as well as a flower-filled, ground-floor sitting area. Antique touches proliferate: here an old parasol, there a period jewelry box. Buffet breakfasts (and light dinners on request) are served in a large, galleried dining room. The gardens include a pool, a Jacuzzi, and a terrace. (Note there's a two-night minimum stay in peak season.) ⊠ *2 km (1 mi) from Sintra, past the Palácio de Seteais (Box 4), 2710-801,* ☎ *21/924–3821 or 21/923–0342,* FAX *21/910–6065,* WEB *www.quintadassequoias.com. 6 rooms. Bar, dining room, pool, hot tub, billiards; no room TVs, no smoking. AE, DC, MC, V. BP.*

$$ ⊡ **Tivoli Sintra.** The Tivoli makes the most of its location: in each room, balconies afford valley and ocean views. Do whatever it takes to score one of the superior rooms, where enormous balconies provide even more tremendous vistas. Rooms are dark and have reproduction country-style antiques and tiled baths. ⊠ *Praça da República, 2710–616,* ☎ *21/923–7200,* FAX *21/923–7245,* WEB *www.tivolihotels.com. 77 rooms. Restaurant, bar, in-room data ports, in-room safes, cable TV, minibars, Internet center, convention center, meeting rooms. AE, DC, MC, V. BP.*

Outdoor Activities and Sports

Sintra's pretty surroundings positively beg to be seen at a leisurely pace on horseback. The **Centro Hípico da Costa do Estoril** (⊠ Estrada da Charneca 186, Cascais, ☎ 21/487–2064) offer rides in the Sintra hills and elsewhere. The equestrian center at the **Penha Longa Country Club** (⊠ Estrada da Lagoa Azul, Linhó, ☎ 21/924–9033) can arrange a variety of rides in the area.

Shopping

Sintra is a noted center for antiques, curios, and ceramics, although you'll need to choose carefully: prices are on the high side, and there's a fair amount of poor-quality goods. Keep an eye out for special in-store displays of hand-painted ceramics, many of them reproductions of 15th- to 18th-century designs, signed by the artists.

Vintage port wines are on sale in **Camélia** (⊠ Praça da República 2, ☎ 21/923–1704), whose owners can recommend vintages; you can buy local cheese here, too. For hand-embroidered linen tablecloths, bedspreads, towels, and sheets, visit **Violeta** (⊠ Rua das Padarias 19, ☎ 21/923–4095).

The small town of **Pêro Pinheiro** is known for its marble, and several shops here sell stacks of cachepots, plaques, and other garden objects. The town is on route N9, 9 km (5½ mi) northeast of Sintra.

São Pedro de Sintra

6 *2 km (1 mi) southeast of Sintra.*

This little hillside village is most famous for its fair, the Feira de São Pedro, held every second and fourth Sunday of the month in the vast Praça Dom Fernando II (also called the Largo da Feira), where stalls are set up under the plane trees. Dating from the time of the Christian Reconquest, the fair is one of Portugal's best, with livestock and agricultural displays as well as local crafts, antiques, and food for sale. Even on nonfair days, it's worth coming to São Pedro to see the village church in its own enclosed little square. There are also several good restaurants in São Pedro, which makes it an attractive lunch stop.

The steep walk to São Pedro de Sintra along the main road from Sintra isn't much fun, although you can cut out much of the distance by climbing up through the gardens of the **Parque Liberdade** (☉ June–Sept., daily 9–8; Oct.–May, daily 9–6), which starts just east of Sintra. Otherwise, local buses leave from outside the Sintra train station (weekdays every 30–40 minutes, reduced service on weekends), and you can catch one as it passes the tourist office; or take a taxi.

Dining

$$-$$$ ✕ **Cantinho de São Pedro.** Imaginative Portuguese cuisine with a French twist is served at this busy, rustic restaurant in a small courtyard of artisans' workshops, just off the main square. Locals consider the food well worth the wait for a table. Try the trout with almonds and cream or look for the fresh shellfish on the list of *pratos do dia* (dishes of the day). ⊠ *Praça Dom Fernando II 18,* ☎ *21/923–0267. AE, DC, MC, V. Closed Mon.*

Shopping

The **Lojas do Picadeiro** (⊠ Praça Dom Fernando II) is a row of artisans' workshops that sell everything from wooden toys to rustic furniture and local art; a couple of taverns help restore flagging spirits.

Castelo dos Mouros

★ **7** *3 km (2 mi) southwest of Sintra.*

Only the battlemented ruins of the 9th-century Moorish Castle still stand today, but the extent of these gives a fine impression of the solid fortress that finally fell from Moorish hands when it was conquered by Dom Afonso Henriques in 1147. It's visible from various points in Sintra itself—the steps of Sintra Palace is a favored vantage point—but for a closer look follow the steps that lead up to the ruins from the back of the town center, a walk that will take around 40 minutes going up and 25 minutes coming down. Buses run this way, too, or rent one of the horse-drawn carriages outside Sintra Palace for a more romantic trip. Panoramic views from the castle's serrated walls help explain why Moorish architects chose the site, and eagle-eyed visitors can also trace the remains of a mosque within the walls. ⊠ *Estrada da Pena,* ☎ *21/923–7300,* 🌐 *www.parquedesintra.pt.* 🎫 *€3, guided tours €3.* ☉ *June–Sept., daily 9–8; Oct.–May, 9–7. Last admission 1 hr before closing.*

Palácio Nacional de Pena

★ **8** *4 km (2½ mi) south of Sintra.*

The Disney-like, drawbridged Pena Palace is a glorious conglomeration of turrets and domes awash in pastels. There are various ways to get here: you can take a local bus or a horse-drawn carriage, sign up for a tour, or make the long but very pleasant walk up from the center of Sintra (about 1½ hours). However you choose to arrive, note that the walk back down to Sintra is delightful: you travel through shaded woods and can rest at viewpoints under the cork trees.

Commissioned by Maria II's consort, Ferdinand of Saxe-Coburg, in 1840 and finished in 1885 when he was Fernando II, Pena Palace is a collection of styles that range from Arabian to Victorian. The surrounding park is filled with trees and flowers from every corner of the Portuguese empire. A tram takes you from the park gate up to the palace. Note an enormous statue on a nearby crag; it's thought to be Baron Eschwege (the building's German architect) cast as a medieval knight. A path beyond the Baron Eschwege statue leads to the **Cruz Alta,** a 16th-century stone cross that's 1,782 ft above sea level. It's an arduous climb, especially in the summer sun, but the views from this altitude are stupendous.

The final kings of Portugal lived in the Pena Palace, the last of whom— Dom Manuel II—went into exile in England in 1910 after a republican revolt. The pseudo-medieval structure, with its ramparts, towers, and great halls, has a rich, sometimes vulgar, and often bizarre collection of Victorian and Edwardian furniture, ornaments, and paintings. Although there are placards explaining each room, it's not a bad idea to take a guided tour (9:30, 11:30, 2, 4:30). ⊠ *Estrada da Pena,* ☎ *21/ 910–5340.* 🖃 *Palace: €5, free Sun. 10–2. Tram: €1.50.* ☼ *Mid-Sept.– mid-June, Tues.–Sun. 10–5, last admission 4:30; mid-June–mid-Sept., Tues.–Sun. 10–7, last admission 6:15.*

Monserrate

❾ *4 km (2½ mi) west of Sintra.*

The **gardens** here were laid out by Scottish gardeners in the mid-19th century at the behest of a wealthy Englishman, Sir Francis Cook. The grounds' centerpiece—the Moorish-style, domed pavilion—is closed to visitors, but the gardens, with their streams, waterfalls, and Etruscan tombs, are worth a stop for their array of tree and plant species, though labels are few and far between. This is a popular picnic spot; it's easy to find your own glade somewhere along the winding paths. ⊠ *Estrada da Monserrate,* ☎ *21/923–7300,* 🖳 *www.parquedesintra.pt.* 🖃 *€3, guided tours €3.* ☼ *June–Sept., daily 9–8; Oct.–May, daily 9–7. Last admission 1 hr before closing.*

En Route   Past Monserrate the road leads west for 3 km (2 mi) to the small village of **Colares,** associated with the locally produced red wine. The town, its winding streets alive with colorful flowers and trees, is also known for its parish church, which is adorned with ceramic tiles, and its main square, bordered by 18th-century houses. For terrific views of the sea and surrounding mountains, take the winding road that climbs up to the village of **Penedo,** less than 2 km (1 mi) away from Colares.

Convento dos Capuchos

★ **❿** *13 km (8 mi) southwest of Sintra.*

The main entrance to this extraordinarily austere convent, with its simple tiled roof and wooden beams lined with cork (to keep in what little warmth there might be), sets the tone for the severity of the ascetic living conditions. From 1560 until 1834, when it was abandoned, seven monks—never any more, never any less—inhabited the bare cells; prayed in the tiny chapel hewn out of the rock; and perhaps found some comfort in the washroom, kitchen, and refectory. Impure thoughts meant a spell in the Penitents' Cell, an excruciatingly small space. The 45-minute tour is obligatory, but, to their credit, the guides bring the history of the place to life with zest and humor. No vehicles are allowed close to the convent, so the peace is disturbed only by birdsong. ⊠ *Convento dos Capuchos,* ☎ *21/923–7300,* WEB *www.parquedesintra.pt.* ⊠ *€3.* ⊙ *June–Sept., daily 9–8 (last admission 7); Oct.–May, daily 9–6 (last admission 5).*

Cabo da Roca

★ ⓫ *15 km (9 mi) west of Sintra, 20 km (12½ mi) northwest of Cascais.*

Between enchanting, culturally rich Sintra and the beach resort of Cascais you'll discover a totally different face of Lisbon's environs in this protected natural park. The windswept Cabo da Roca and its lighthouse mark continental Europe's westernmost point and are the main reason that most people make the journey. As with many such places, stalls purvey shell souvenirs and other gimmicks; an information desk and gift shop sells a certificate that verifies your visit. Even without the certificate, though, the memory of this desolate granite cape will linger. The cliffs tumble to a frothing sea below, and on the cape a simple cross bears an inscription by Portuguese national poet Luís de Camões. You can reach the cape from Cascais (30 minutes) or Sintra (40 minutes) by local bus, with regular departures from outside either town's train station.

OFF THE BEATEN PATH

THE ATLANTIC COAST – North of Cabo da Roca, the protected national parkland extends through the successive Atlantic-facing resort villages of Praia Grande, Praia das Maças, and Azenhas do Mar. The first two have good beaches, and all have public swimming pools and small restaurants. A fun way to reach Praia das Maças is on the 19th-century Elétrico de Sintra, a tram that departs hourly from Ribeira de Sintra, 4 km (2½ mi) north of town, every day but Monday (the fare is €2.50). It passes through Banzão and offers engaging views as it approaches the beach. The park's many contrasts are readily apparent as you ride or drive through the microclimate of Serra de Sintra. ☎ *21/867–7681 for Elétrico de Sintra information.*

Queluz

⓬ *15 km (9 mi) east of Sintra, 15 km (9 mi) northwest of Lisbon.*

Halfway between Lisbon and Sintra (just off route N249/IC19) is the town of Queluz, dominated entirely by its magnificent palace. The drive from Lisbon takes about 20 minutes, making this a good half-day option or a fine stop on the way to or from Sintra. It's also easy to take the train: get off at the Queluz-Belas stop, turn left outside the station, and follow the signs for the 1-km (½-mi) walk to the palace.

★ The **Palácio Nacional de Queluz** (Queluz National Palace) was inspired, in part, by the palace at Versailles. Intended as a royal summer residence, the salmon-pink rococo edifice was ordered by Dom Pedro III in 1747, and work began under the supervision of architect Mateus Vicente de Oliveira. Within five years it was fit to receive its first royal inhabitants, but it took another 40 years and the artistic endeavors of Frenchman Jean-Baptiste Robillon for Queluz to acquire its famous romantic appearance. The building is fronted by a huge cobbled square and surrounded by Robillon's formal landscaping and waterways. The trees (brought from Amsterdam), statues (imported from London), ponds, canal, fountains, hedges—and the palace—all fit a carefully executed baroque plan that implies harmony and wholeness. After a

1934 fire, the palace was restored. It's used today for banquets, music festivals, official meetings attended by world leaders, and as accommodations for visiting heads of state.

You can tour the apartments and elegant state rooms, including the frescoed Music Salon, the Hall of Ambassadors, and the mirrored Throne Room with its crystal chandeliers and gilt trim. Room furnishings and details—often of fine woods and precious metals from around the globe—are truly fit for a king. Walks in the formal gardens take you through orange groves and down avenues of oaks to azulejo-lined fountains and canals. ⊠ *Rte. IC19,* ☎ *21/435–0039.* ⌖ *€3, free Sun. 10–2.* ⊙ *Wed.–Mon. 10–5, last admission 4:30.*

Dining and Lodging

$$ ✕⌂ **Pousada de Dona Maria I.** The Royal Guard quarters beneath the
★ clock tower opposite the palace have undergone a stunning transformation: marble hallways lined with prints of old Portugal give way to crisp, high-ceilinged rooms furnished with exacting 18th-century reproductions. Only breakfast is served in the pousada itself, but the cooking hits the mark across the road in the old palace kitchens, now the Restaurante de Cozinha Velha ($$$–$$$$; reservations essential), with its imposing open fireplace and a vast oak table. The Portuguese specialties on the ever-changing menu are occasionally tempered by a French touch. ⊠ *Rte. IC19, 2745-191,* ☎ *21/435–6158,* ℻ *21/435– 6189,* ⅦⅢ *www.pousadas.pt. 24 rooms, 2 suites. Restaurant, bar, cable TV, meeting rooms. AE, DC, MC, V. BP.*

THE SETÚBAL PENINSULA

The Setúbal Peninsula, south of the Rio Tejo, is popular for its Costa da Caparica beaches, which provide the cleanest ocean swimming closest to Lisbon. Other attractions include the major port of Setúbal, some Roman ruins, and the scenic mountain range—the Serra da Arrábida—that separates the port from the peninsula's southernmost beaches and fishing villages.

If you're intent on eating seafood at Cacilhas, spending the day at a beach, or simply touring the town of Setúbal, traveling by public transportation from Lisbon is easiest. If you want to see most of the sights covered in this section, however—and particularly if you want to tour the southern coastal and mountainous region—you should rent a car. Apart from the ferry ride to Cacilhas, connections between the Setúbal Peninsula and Lisbon are via the capital's two bridges. Returning on the impressive suspension bridge, the Ponte 25 de Abril, you're guaranteed terrific views of Lisbon. Avoid crossing during rush hour and on Friday and Sunday evenings, when the traffic can be horrendous. If you're heading directly for Setúbal, take the northern route across the Rio Tejo via the Ponte Vasco da Gama, from which the fast A12 highway cuts south and avoids the bottleneck over the Ponte 25 de Abril.

Cacilhas

⑬ *6 km (4 mi) south of Lisbon.*

Although a town in its own right, Cacilhas appears little more than a suburb of Lisbon, albeit one with the bonus of several reliable seafood restaurants along its main street, Rua do Ginjal. The town is immediately across the Rio Tejo from the capital; at night, and especially on weekends, it's a popular destination. Waiters armed with menus linger outside their doors, ready to pounce on passersby who can't decide where to eat; once inside, you're tempted with the best of the day's catch. The ferries run frequently from Terminal Fluvial, adjacent to Praça do Comércio, and from Cais do Sodré. One-way tickets cost €0.75, and the journey takes about 15 minutes.

The **Cristo Rei**—a huge, white statue of Christ, built in 1959—was modeled on the famous statue of Christ the Redeemer in Rio de Janeiro. The figure stands proudly above Cacilhas, its outstretched arms seemingly embracing the city of Lisbon across the water. Take the elevator to the platform beneath the statue's feet for panoramic city views. If your schedule is tight, though, opt for the vista from Lisbon's Torre Vasco da Gama. Buses from Cacilhas dockside can take you directly to the Cristo Rei statue every 20–30 minutes, daily 8 AM–9 PM. If you're driving, cross the Ponte 25 de Abril and follow the signs. ☎ 21/275–1000. ☒ €1.50. ☉ Daily 9–6.

Costa da Caparica

★ ⑭ *14 km (8½ mi) southwest of Lisbon; 8 km (5 mi) west of Cacilhas; take the minor N377, a slower, more scenic route than the main IC20 route (off the A2/IP1).*

When Lisbon's inhabitants want to go to the beach, their preferred spot is the Costa da Caparica, a 20-km (12-mi) stretch of sand on the northwestern coast of the Setúbal Peninsula. The coastal strip centers on the lively resort of Caparica itself, at the northern end of the beach, less than an hour from the capital. Formerly a fishing village, it's now packed in summer with Portuguese tourists who come to enjoy the relatively unpolluted waters, eat grilled sardines, and stroll the seafront promenade. You may be able to avoid the crowds by heading south toward the less accessible dunes and coves at the end of the peninsula. From June through September, a small narrow-gauge train departs from Caparica and travels along an 8-km (5-mi) coastal route, making stops along the way; a one-way ticket to the end of the line costs €2.50. Each beach is different: the areas nearest Caparica are family oriented, whereas the more southerly resorts tend to attract a younger crowd (there are some nudist beaches as well).

Palmela

⑮ *38 km (24 mi) southeast of Lisbon.*

The small town of Palmela lies in the center of a prosperous wine-growing area, and every September, the community holds a good-natured Festa das Vindimas (Grape Harvest Festival) that draws inhabitants from their whitewashed houses and into the cobbled streets. The village is dominated by the remains of a 12th-century castle that was captured from the Moors and enlarged by successive kings. In the 15th century the monastery and church of Sant'Iago were built within the castle walls. The structures were damaged in the 1755 earthquake and lay abandoned for many years. After extensive restoration, a pousada was opened in the monastic buildings. From this height, on a clear day, you can see Lisbon.

Dining and Lodging

$$–$$$ ✕🏨 **Pousada de Palmela.** On a hill at the eastern end of the Arrábida range, this building was originally a medieval fortress and later a monastery. In 1979 it was converted into a luxury pousada, and the designers made inspired use of the flagstone corridors and old cloister (now a lounge). Most rooms have views of the valley and the sea; bathrooms are well equipped, and beds are comfortable. There's little trace of monastic asceticism in the monks' former refectory, now a dependable restaurant ($$$–$$$$) that serves traditional Portuguese

food and a good range of wines. ⊠ *Castelo de Palmela, 2950-997,* ☎ *21/235–1226,* FAX *21/233–0440,* WEB *www.pousadas.pt. 28 rooms. Restaurant, bar, cable TV, meeting rooms. AE, DC, MC, V. BP*

Setúbal

⑯   *10 km (6 mi) south of Palmela, 50 km (31 mi) southeast of Lisbon.*

At the mouth of the Rio Sado, Setúbal is the country's third-largest port and one of its oldest cities. A significant industrial town in Roman times, it became one again during Portugal's Age of Discovery and took off during the 19th century. Its center remains an attractive blend of medieval and modern, and the handsome Igreja de Jesus in itself makes the city worth a stop. Many travelers also use Setúbal as a spot to spend the night before driving on to the Algarve, since the Castelo de São Filipe has been converted into an exceptional pousada. Even if you decide to go on, you may want to dine here, or just pause to take in the views from the lofty castle.

Better still, spend half a day in the city, strolling cobbled pedestrian streets that open into pretty squares with cafés. The tourist office is built atop Roman ruins discovered during (and saved from) a construction project. Inside, you'll be standing above and peering down through the glass floor into a 5th-century fish-processing room. Near the port, an agreeable clutter of boats and warehouses is fronted by gardens, where you can stock up for a picnic at a huge, indoor fish-and-produce market (open Tuesday–Sunday 7–2).

★   The 15th-century **Igreja de Jesus** (Church of Jesus), perhaps Portugal's earliest example of Manueline architecture, was built with local marble and later tiled with simple but affecting 17th-century azulejos. The architect was Diogo de Boitaca, whose work here predates his contribution to Lisbon's Mosteiro dos Jerónimos (Jerónimos Monastery). Six extraordinary twisted pillars support the vault; climb the narrow stairs to the balcony for a closer look. These details would soon become the very hallmark of Manueline style. Outside, you can still admire the original, although badly worn, main doorway and deplore the addition of a concrete expanse that makes the church square look like a roller-skating rink.

The church's original monastic buildings and Gothic cloister—on Rua Balneário Paula Borba—house the **Museu de Setúbal**, a museum with a fascinating collection of 15th- and 16th-century Portuguese paintings, several by the so-called Master of Setúbal. Other attractions include azulejos, local archaeological finds, and a coin collection. ⊠ *Praça Miguel Bombarda,* ☎ *265/524772.* ✆ *Free, but €1 suggested donation to church.* ☉ *Tues.–Sun. 9–noon and 2–5.*

Dining and Lodging

$$–$$$ ✕ **Rio Azul.** This *marisqueira* (seafood restaurant) is hidden on a side street off Rua Luisa Todi, on the way to the castle and west of the harbor. Although it's signposted from the main road, it's a little tricky to find. As you'd expect, the dishes to go for are the fresh fish grilled to perfection and the arroz de marisco. ⊠ *Rua Placido Stichini 1,* ☎ *265/522828. AE, DC, MC, V. Closed Wed.*

$–$$ ✕ **Alforge.** Rough slabs of marble hang on the wall like old masters at this funky little bar-diner near the market (parallel to the main avenue). At lunchtime, office workers hunker down to an excellent selection of daily grills—steaks to squid—accompanied by ceramic jugs of *vinho verde* (green wine). At night it's open until 2 AM for full meals or just drinks and sandwiches at the bar. ⊠ *Rua Regimento Infantaria 14,* ☎ *265/37675. No credit cards. Closed Sun.*

$$–$$$ ✕⊞ **Pousada de São Filipe.** From the ramparts of this 16th-century
★ castle-cum-pousada, the views of the town and the Rio Sado are fantastic. The approach to the main entrance takes you up a tunneled flight
of stairs and past an 18th-century chapel decorated with azulejos depicting the life of São Filipe. The traditional guest rooms have carved
headboards, tile floors, rugs, and white walls. The interior is also
awash with azulejo tiling, especially in the bar. The restaurant ($$$–
$$$$) is strong on Portuguese cuisine, with such dishes as fish broth,
stewed broad beans with cuttlefish, roast veal with Muscatel wine, and
orange tart. ⊠ *Castelo de São Filipe, Estrada de São Filipe, 2900-300,*
☎ *265/523844,* ℻ *265/532538,* WEB *www.pousadas.pt. 16 rooms.
Restaurant, bar, cable TV, meeting rooms. AE, DC, MC, V. BP.*

$$ ⊞ **Quinta do Patricio.** Open fireplaces and brightly colored rugs and
paintings fill this homey manor house. From the large garden you'll
get some nice views of the town. There are also two separate apartments for rent on the grounds, one with a kitchen, the other romanti-
cally converted from a former windmill. Breakfast is served, other
meals are available on request, and reservations made well in advance
are essential. Note that the wedding parties staged here most weekends can make things noisy. ⊠ *Estrada de São Filipe, 2900,* ☎ ℻ *265/
233817,* WEB *www.hafesta.com. 3 rooms, 2 with bath; 2 apartments.
Bar, pool. No credit cards. BP.*

Peninsula de Tróia

⑰ *20 mins from Setúbal by boat.*

Across the estuary from Setúbal is the Peninsula de Tróia, a long spit
of land blessed with fine beaches and clean water. The peninsula has
been much developed, and the large Tróia Tourist Complex here includes the famous Tróia Golf Course. The area has managed to retain a little of its history, though: the peninsula is the site of the
Roman town of Cetobriga, destroyed by a tidal wave in the 5th century. You can visit its scant ruins, opposite the marina. Car and passenger ferries to the peninsula run every 30–60 minutes (24 hours a
day), from Setúbal's port.

Outdoor Activities and Sports

The Tróia Golf Course, an 18-hole championship course designed by
Robert Trent Jones Sr., is considered by many to be Portugal's most
difficult. It's on the coast, with small, narrow, well-protected greens
and wide fairways. The main challenge is reaching the green. The
course is part of the **Complexo Turístico de Tróia** (⊠ Carvalhal, Grândola, ☎ 265/494112), which has a driving range, putting greens,
bunker and chipping areas, tennis courts, a restaurant, and a bar.
Green fees are €60 weekends and €50 weekdays.

Vila Nogueira de Azeitão

⑱ *14 km (8½ mi) west of Setúbal.*

The region around the small town of Vila Nogueira de Azeitão, on the
western side of the Serra da Arrábida, retains a disproportionately large
number of fine manor houses and palaces. In earlier times, many of
the country's noblemen maintained country estates here, deep in the
heart of a wealthy wine-making region. Wines made here by the José
Maria da Fonseca Company are some of the most popular in the country (and one of Portugal's major exports); the best known is the dessert
wine called Moscatel de Setúbal.

For a close look at the wine business, seek out the headquarters of the
José Maria da Fonseca Company, which stands on the main road

through town. The intriguing tours (which must be booked in advanced) allow you to see all stages of production, and take around 20–40 minutes depending on the size of the group. ⊠ *Rua José Augusto Coelho 11,* ☏ *21/219–8940,* WEB *www.jmf.pt.* ☑ *Free.* ☉ *Daily tours throughout the year; call for times.*

Vila Nogueira de Azeitão's agricultural traditions are trumpeted on the first Sunday of every month, when a **country market** is held in the center of town. Apart from the locally produced wine, you can buy the goats' milk *queijo fresco*—a good choice for a picnic lunch—as well as excellent fresh bread from one of the market's bakery stalls.

Although it's not open to the public, the 16th-century Palácio de Tavora (Tavora Palace), on the central **Praça da República,** has an interesting history. In the 18th century, the Marquês de Pombal accused the Duke of Aveiro, who owned the palace, of collaborating in the assassination plot against the king, Dom José. Subsequently the duke was executed by the marquês, and the Tavora coat of arms was erased from the Sala das Armas in Sintra's National Palace.

NEED A BREAK?	The 16th-century **Quinta das Torres** (☏ 21/208–0001), at Vila Fresca de Azeitão, 2 km (1 mi) east of Vila Nogueira de Azeitão, is now an inn with a restaurant. Set in beautiful gardens, the fine old building has antique furniture and tapestries at every turn. The food served here is well prepared and moderately priced.

The pride and joy of the **Quinta da Bacalhoa,** a late-16th-century L-shape mansion, is its box-hedged garden and striking azulejo-lined paths. You can't tour the villa, which is a private house, but the garden is open to the public and contains a pavilion with three pyramidal towers—the so-called Casa do Fresco, which houses the country's oldest azulejo panel. Dating from 1565, it depicts the story of Susannah and the Elders. Scattered elsewhere are Moorish-influenced panels, fragrant groves of fruit trees, and enough restful spots to while away an afternoon. ⊠ *4 km (2½ mi) east of Vila Nogueira de Azeitão on N1,* ☏ *21/218–0011.* ☑ *€1.* ☉ *Mon.–Sat. 1–5.*

Serra da Arrábida

⑲ *West of Setúbal, with access along the main N10 or minor N379; Portinho da Arrábida is 14 km (8½ mi) southwest of Setúbal.*

Occupying the entire southern coast of the Setúbal Peninsula is the Parque Natural da Arrábida, dominated by the Serra da Arrábida, a 5,000-ft-high mountain range whose wild crags fall steeply to the sea. There's profuse plant life at these heights, particularly in the spring, when the rocks are carpeted with wildflowers. The park is distinguished by a rich geological heritage and numerous species of mammals, birds, butterflies, and other insects.

The main road through the park is the N10, which you can leave at Vila Nogueira de Azeitão to travel south toward the small fishing village of **Portinho da Arrábida,** at the foot of the mountain range. The village is a popular destination for Lisboetas, who appreciate the good local beaches. In summer, when the number of visitors makes parking nearly impossible, leave your car above the village and make the steep walk down to the water, where you'll find several modest seafood restaurants that overlook the port.

From Portinho da Arrábida, the lower, coastal road hugs the shore nearly all the way to Setúbal; the upper road leads to the ramshackle, white-walled **Convento de Arrábida,** an atmospheric 16th-century monastery built into the hills of the Serra da Arrábida. The views from here are glorious, but you'll have to contact the tourist office in Setúbal in advance to arrange a visit to the monastery.

Sesimbra

20 *40 km (25 mi) south of Lisbon, 30 km (19 mi) southwest of Setúbal.*

Sesimbra, a lively fishing village surrounded by mountains and isolated bays and coves, owes its popularity to its proximity to the capital. And, despite high-rise apartments that now mar the approaches to the town, its few surviving narrow, central streets reflect a traditional past. Moreover, the long beach is lovely, if a little crowded in summer, and perfectly fine for swimming. The waterfront is guarded by a 17th-century fortress and overlooked by outdoor restaurants serving fresh-fish meals. A short walk along the coast to the west takes you to the main port, littered with nets, anchors, and coils of rope and packed with fishing boats—which unload their catches at entertaining auctions. You can also take a 40-minute walk to the hilltop remains of a Moorish castle northwest of town.

Dining

$$–$$$ ✕ **Café Filipe.** Set in a line of sidewalk restaurants overlooking the waterfront, the Filipe is always busy with diners digging into the terrific grilled fish—cooked outside on a charcoal grill—or arroz de marisco. There's no nicer spot for lunch, but you may have to wait in line for a table. It's worth it. ✉ *Av. 25 de Abril,* ☎ *no phone. MC, V.*

Outdoor Activities and Sports

Sesimbra, a deep-sea fishing center, is renowned for the huge swordfish that are landed in the area. The **Clube Naval de Sesimbra** (✉ Porto de Abrigo, ☎ 21/223–3451, offers coastal fishing trips most Saturdays.

Cabo Espichel

21 *12 km (7 mi) west of Sesimbra.*

Espichel Cape, a salt-encrusted headland with a number of 18th-century pilgrim rest houses and a forsaken church, is the southwestern point of the Setúbal Peninsula. It's a rugged and lonely place, where the cliffs rise hundreds of feet out of the stormy Atlantic. To the north, unsullied beaches extend as far as Caparica, with only local roads and footpaths connecting them. There are six buses a day here from Sesimbra.

LISBON'S ENVIRONS A TO Z

To research prices, get advice from other travelers, and book travel arrangements, visit www.fodors.com.

BOAT AND FERRY TRAVEL

LisboFerries cross the river to Cacilhas (7 AM–9 PM) from Fluvial terminal, adjacent to Praça do Comércio. One-way tickets cost €0.50, and the journey takes about 15 minutes. For information on car ferries from Cais do Sodré, check with the Lisbon tourist office. From Setúbal there's 24-hour ferry service for cars (€4.25) and foot passengers (€1) across to the Tróia Peninsula; the journey takes about 20 minutes. Departures are every 30–60 minutes.

➤ CONTACT: **LisboFerries** (☎ 21/322–4000, WEB www.transtejo.pt).

BUS TRAVEL

Although the best way to reach Sintra and most of the towns on the Estoril Coast is by train from Lisbon, there are some useful bus connections between towns. Tickets are cheap (less than €3.50 for most journeys), and departures are generally every hour (less frequent on weekends); local tourist offices have timetables.

At Cascais, the bus terminal outside the train station has regular summer service to Guincho (15 minutes) and Sintra (one hour). From the terminal outside the Sintra train station, there are half-hourly departures in summer to the resorts of Praia das Maças and Azenhas do Mar (30 minutes) in the west, and north to Mafra in Estremadura (one hour). There's also regular year-round service from Sintra to Cascais and Estoril (one hour). The most useful Sintra service, however, is the circular Stagecoach/Scotturb Bus 434 (daily, every 20–30 minutes, 10:20–5:45; €3.20 ticket valid all day), which connects Sintra station, the town center (the stop is outside the tourist office), Castelo dos Mouros, and the Pena Palace.

Buses to Caparica (45 minutes) depart from Praça de Espanha (Metrô: Palhavã) in Lisbon, traveling over the Ponte 25 de Abril. Regular buses to Caparica also leave from the quayside bus terminal at Cacilhas, the suburb immediately across the Rio Tejo from Lisbon, which you can reach by ferry from the Fluvial terminal, adjacent to Praça do Comércio. Bus departures on both routes are as frequent as every 15 minutes in the summer, and services run from 7 AM until well after midnight, but can be very crowded. There's also a special beach bus (No. 75) that runs to Caparica every 15–30 minutes from the beginning of June to the beginning of September; pick it up in Lisbon at Campo Grande, Saldanha, or Marquês de Pombal metrô stations, or outside the Amoreiras shopping center.

Express buses to Setúbal (45 minutes) leave every hour from Lisbon's Praça de Espanha (Metrô: Palhavã); a local service also calls at Vila Nogueira de Azeitão (45 minutes) before traveling on to Setúbal (one hour). At Setúbal bus station you can connect with local services north to Palmela (20 minutes) and southwest to Sesimbra (30 minutes). Six buses daily run a 30-minute trip from Sesimbra bus station to the southwestern Cabo Espichel.

➤ CONTACTS: **Cacilhas bus terminal** (✉ Largo Alfredo Diniz, ☎ no phone). **Cascais bus terminal,** ☎ 21/483–6357). **Palmela bus station** (✉ Largo do Chafariz D. Maria I, ☎ 21/235–0078). **Sesimbra bus station** (✉ Av. da Liberdade, ☎ 21/223–3071). **Setúbal bus station** (✉ Av. 5 de Outubro 44, ☎ 265/525051).

CAR RENTAL
There are better choices for car rentals in Lisbon, although the tourist offices in Cascais, Estoril, Sintra, and Setúbal can advise you of the local possibilities.
➤ MAJOR AGENCIES: **Avis** (✉ Tamariz Esplanade, Estoril, ☎ 21/468–5728; ✉ Av. Luisa Todi 96, Setúbal, ☎ 265/538710). **Europcar** (✉ Estrada Marginal, Centro Comércial Cisne, Bloco B, Lojas 4 and 5, Cascais, ☎ 21/486–4438). **Hertz** (✉ Av. Luisa Todi 277, Setúbal, ☎ 265/527653).

CAR TRAVEL
Fast highways connect Lisbon with Estoril (A5/IC15) and Setúbal (A2/IP1), and the quality of other roads in the region is generally good. Take care on hilly and coastal roads, though, and if possible, avoid driving out of Lisbon at the start of a weekend or public holiday or back in at the end. Both Rio Tejo bridges—especially the Ponte 25 de Abril but also the dramatic Ponte Vasco da Gama—can be very slow. Parking can be problematic, too, especially in the summer along the Estoril Coast.

When you do park, *never* leave anything visible in the car, and it's wise to clear out the trunk as well.

Lisbon is the initial point of arrival for almost all the destinations covered here; from the city, it's easy to take public transportation or drive to all the surrounding towns. Driving south from Peniche-Óbidos, you can take the N8/IC1, rather than the main highway, if you prefer to see Sintra before Lisbon. If you're traveling north from the Algarve, then you reach the city of Setúbal and its peninsula before arriving in Lisbon.

EMERGENCIES
In all the towns, a notice on the door of every *farmácia* (drugstore) indicates the name and address of the nearest all-night pharmacy.
➤ EMERGENCY SERVICES: **General emergencies** (☎ 112). **Police** (☎ 21/483–1127 in Cascais; 21/468–1396 in Estoril; 265/522022 in Setúbal; 21/923–0761 in Sintra).
➤ HOSPITALS: **Cascais hospital** (✉ Av. Ultramar and Rua Padre J. M. Loureiro, ☎ 21/484–4071). **Setúbal hospital** (✉ Rua Camilo Castelo Branco, ☎ 265/522133). **Sintra Health Center** (✉ Rua Visconde de Monserrate 2, ☎ 21/923–3400).

MAIL
➤ POST OFFICES: **Cascais** (✉ Rua Manuel J. Avelar, ☎ 21/483–3175). **Setúbal** (✉ Av. 22 de Dezembro, ☎ 265/522778). **Sintra** (✉ Praça da República 26, ☎ 21/924–9825).

TAXIS
If you don't have your own car, it may pay—at least in time and convenience—to take a taxi to the towns around Lisbon. Cabs are relatively inexpensive, and you can usually agree on a fixed price that will include the round-trip to an attraction (the driver will wait for you to complete your tour). Tourist offices can give you an idea of what fares are reasonable for local trips.
➤ CONTACT: **Central taxi lines** (☎ 21/466–0101, 21/468–7096, or 21/465–9500).

TELEPHONES
The area code for Setúbal is 265; for all other places it's 21, the same as for Lisbon. You'll find public phones in city centers and in most resort areas. They're generally reliable, and accept phone cards that are sold by news vendors and in other shops.

DIRECTORY AND OPERATOR ASSISTANCE
For information, dial 118; operators speak English or will transfer you to one who does.

TOURS AND PACKAGES
ORIENTATION TOURS
Most travel agents and large hotels in Lisbon or its environs can reserve you a place on a guided tour. Cityrama has half-day trips to Queluz, Sintra, and Estoril and a tour of the area's royal palaces (each €44.39); nine-hour tours of Mafra, Sintra, and Cascais (€69.83 including lunch); and even an evening visit to Estoril's famous casino (€82.3 including dinner). Gray Line Tours has half-day trips into the Arrábida Mountain range and to local craft centers for around €50.

For guided tours of the Sintra area, ask at the tourist information center, which has current schedules and can sell tickets. Half-day tours typically encompass visits to all the principal sights and a wine tasting in Colares.

➤ CONTACTS: **Citirama** (✉ Av. Praia da Vitória 12-B, Saldanha, Lisbon, ☎ 21/355–8564). **Gray Line Tours** (✉ Av. Praia da Vitória 12-B, Saldanha, Lisbon, ☎ 21/352–2594).

HORSE AND CARRIAGE TOURS

Sintratur offers old-fashioned horse-and-carriage rides in the Sintra area. A short tour of Sintra costs €30; longer trips run between €60 and €100 and go as far afield as Pena Palace and Monserrate.
➤ CONTACT: **Sintratur** (✉ Rua João de Deus 82, Sintra, ☎ 21/924–1238).

TRAIN TRAVEL

Electric commuter trains travel the entire Estoril Coast, with departures every 15–30 minutes from the waterfront Cais do Sodré station in Lisbon, west of the Praça do Comércio. The scenic trip to Estoril takes about 30 minutes, and four more stops along the seashore bring you to Cascais, at the end of the line. A one-way ticket to either costs €1.10; service operates daily 5:30 AM–2:30 AM. Trains from Lisbon's Rossío station, between Praça dos Restauradores and the Rossío, run every 15 minutes to Queluz (a 20-minute trip) and on to Sintra (40 minutes total). The service operates 6 AM–2:40 AM, and one-way tickets cost €0.90 to Queluz, €1.10 to Sintra.

Fertagus trains from Lisbon's Sete Rios and Entre Campos stations cross the Rio Tejo via the Ponte 25 de Abril. Passengers on the double-decker railcars benefit from fine views, air-conditioning, and background music during the seven-minute crossing. Taxis at stations across the river can take you on to Cacilhas, Setúbal, and other towns on the Setúbal Peninsula. Trains run between 5:30 AM and 2 AM. From June through September a narrow-gauge railway runs for 8 km (5 mi) along the Costa da Caparica from the town of Caparica, on the Setúbal Peninsula. It makes 20 stops at beaches along the way, and a one-way ticket to the end of the line costs €2.50.
➤ CONTACTS: **Fertagus** (☎ 21/294–9700). **Rail information line** (☎ 21/888–4025, WEB www.cp.pt).

VISITOR INFORMATION

ICEP, the Portuguese national tourist office with its main Lisbon office in the Palácio Foz, has information on the city's environs. Local tourist offices are usually open June–September, daily 9–1 and 2–6, sometimes later in the tourist-resort areas. Hours are greatly reduced after peak season, and most offices are closed Sunday.
➤ NATIONAL TOURIST INFORMATION: **ICEP (Portugal national tourist office)** (✉ Palácio Foz, Praça dos Restauradores, Baixa, Lisbon, ☎ 21/346–3314, WEB www.portugalinsite.pt).
➤ REGIONAL TOURIST INFORMATION: **Cabo da Roca** (✉ Azóia, ☎ 21/928–0892). **Caparica** (✉ Ave. da República 18, ☎ 21/290–0071). **Cascais** (✉ Rua Visconde da Luz 14, ☎ 21/486–8204). **Estoril** (✉ Arcadas do Parque, ☎ 21/466–3813). **Palmela** (✉ Castelo de Palmela, ☎ 21/233–2122). **Queluz** (✉ Palácio Nacional de Queluz, ☎ 21/436–3415). **Sesimbra** (✉ Largo da Marinha 26, off Av. dos Naufragios, ☎ 21/223–5743). **Setúbal** (✉ Travessa Frei Gaspar 10, ☎ 265/553–9120). **Sintra** (✉ Praça da República 23, ☎ 21/923–1157 or 21/924–1700; ✉ Sintra train station, ☎ 21/924–1623).

4 ESTREMADURA AND THE RIBATEJO

Estremadura's rolling hills and glorious coastline contain some of the country's most famous towns and monuments. Bordering Estremadura on either side of the Rio Tejo is the Ribatejo—a famous bullfighting area and home to the shrine at Fátima—whose mainly flat lands fade into the vast plains of the southern Alentejo region.

Updated by
Emmy de la
Cal, Justine de
la Cal, Martha
de la Cal, and
Peter Collis

WATER SHAPES THE CHARACTER OF THESE PROVINCES. Estremadura occupies a narrow stretch of land along the coast, extending north from Lisbon to include the onetime royal residence of Leiria, 119 km (74 mi) from the capital. Closely tied to the sea, the province is known for its fine beaches, coastal pine forests, and picturesque fishing villages. Some of these have evolved, for better or worse, into popular resorts. Fruits and vegetables grow in fertile coastal valleys, and livestock contentedly graze in rich pastures, but Estremadura hasn't always been so peaceful. During the Wars of Reconquest, which raged from the 8th through the 13th centuries, it was the scene of a series of bloody encounters between Christians and Moors. In the aftermath of the wars, Portuguese sovereignty was secured with the defeat of the Spanish at Aljubarrota in 1385 and the turning back of Napoléon's forces in 1810 at Torres Vedras. The bloodshed left behind masterpieces of religious architecture—such as those at Alcobaça and Batalha—which commemorate Portuguese triumphs.

The Ribatejo developed along both sides of the Rio Tejo (Tagus River), and it is this waterway, born in the mountains of Spain, that has shaped and sustained the province. In the north, inhabitants tend groves of olive and fig trees, and the peaceful landscape has changed little since the Romans settled.

Over the centuries Romans, Visigoths, Moors, and Christians built and rebuilt various castles and fortifications to protect the strategic Tejo. You'll see fine examples along the river at Belver, Abrantes, and Almourol. Tomar, spanning the banks of the Rio Nabão (a tributary of the Tejo), is dominated by the hilltop Convento de Cristo (Convent of Christ), built in the 12th century by the Knights Templar. In the brush-covered hills at the province's western edge lies Fátima, one of Christendom's most important pilgrimage sites. As it flows south approaching Lisbon, the Tejo expands, often overflowing its banks during the winter rains, and the landscape changes to one of rich meadows and pastures and broad, alluvial plains, where grains grow in abundance.

The Ribatejans are said to be more reserved than their fellow Portuguese—that is, until they step into the arena to test their mettle against a ton or so of charging bull. This is bullfighting country, the heartland of one of Portugal's richest and most colorful traditions. On the vast plains along the east bank of the Tejo, you'll encounter men on horseback carrying long wooden prods and often wearing the traditional waistcoats and stocking caps of their trade. These are *campinos,* the Portuguese "cowboys," who tend the herds of bulls and horses bred and trained for arenas throughout the country.

Pleasures and Pastimes

Beaches

Starting with Ericeira and extending north to São Pedro de Moel by Marinha Grande, there are a number of pleasant sandy beaches at convenient intervals along the coast. Some of the more popular stretches—with the customary range of facilities, hotels, and restaurants—are in Nazaré, Peniche, and Foz do Arelho.

Dining

In Estremadura restaurants, the emphasis is on fish, including the ubiquitous *bacalhau* (dried salt cod) and *caldeirada* (a hearty fish stew). The seaside resorts of Ericeira, Nazaré, and Peniche are famous for lobster. In Santarém and other spots along the Rio Tejo, an *açorda* (thick bread porridge) made with *savel,* a shadlike river fish, is popular, as are *en-*

guias (eels) prepared in a variety of ways. Pork is a key component in Ribatejo dishes, and roast lamb and kid are widely enjoyed. Perhaps the result of a sweet-making tradition developed by nuns in the region's once-numerous convents, dessert menus abound with colorful-sounding—although often cloyingly sweet and eggy—dishes such as *queijinhos do céu* (little cheeses from heaven). The straw-color white wines from the Ribatejo district of Bucelas are among the country's finest.

Between mid-June and mid-September reservations are advised at upscale restaurants. Most moderate or inexpensive establishments, however, don't accept reservations. They also have informal dining rooms, where sharing a table with other diners is common. Dress is casual at all but the most luxurious places.

CATEGORY	COST*
$$$$	over €21
$$$	€14–€21
$$	€7–€14
$	under €7

*per person for a main course at dinner

Lodging

Estremadura has plenty of good-quality lodgings, especially along the coast. In summer, you'll need reservations. Most establishments offer substantial off-season discounts. The best accommodations in the Ribatejo are the government-run inns called *pousadas*. The pousadas are small, some with as few as six rooms, so reserving well in advance is essential. There's also a number of high-quality, government-approved private guest houses. Look for signs reading TURISMO RURAL or TURISMO DE HABITAÇÃO.

CATEGORY	COST*
$$$$	over €275
$$$	€175–€275
$$	€75–€175
$	under €75

*For a standard double room, including tax, in high season (off-season rates may be lower).

Shopping

The regions around Alcobaça and Leiria are well known for their high-quality crystal and handblown glass. Traditional hand-painted ceramics are sold at shops and roadside stands throughout Estremadura. Caldas da Rainha, a large ceramics-manufacturing center, produces characteristic cabbage-leaf and vegetable-shape pieces. Traditional cable-stitch Portuguese fishermen's sweaters are for sale in towns all along the coast.

Water Sports

The clear waters and bizarre rock formations along Estremadura's coast make it a favorite with anglers, snorkelers, and scuba divers. A wet suit is recommended for diving and snorkeling, as the chilly waters don't invite you to linger long, even in summer. The area's most commonly caught fish are sea bass, bream, and red mullet.

Exploring Estremadura and the Ribatejo

The sea is never far from sight in coast-hugging Estremadura, though seafaring days are but a memory in such places as Óbidos, where the harbor that once lapped against the village walls has long since silted up. Nazaré, however, still makes its living from the ocean—from fishing as well as from sunseekers. The same is true of the old town of Ericeira, where sunbathers and surfers alike can indulge in their favorite pastimes. Coastal valleys once witnessed many a bloody fight between rival groups, including the Moors. These battles nonetheless left at least one positive legacy—extraordinary monasteries, such as the one at Batalha, built to celebrate Portuguese victories.

The Rio Tejo flows through the Ribatejo, where vast plains spread out from the riverbanks. Although fortifications line the river, the most famous monument is Fátima, where the Virgin Mary allegedly appeared to three young shepherds; millions of pilgrims still flock here every year to pay homage. In Tomar, the impressive Convento do Cristo, an amalgam of 12th- to 16th-century styles that was once the headquarters of the Knights Templars, is a reminder of the religious struggles that have defined the region.

Great Itineraries

Three days will give you a sense of the region, five days will allow you to include a visit to the shrine at Fátima and the Convento de Cristo, and a full week will give you enough time to cover the major attractions as well as explore the countryside. With additional days you can easily extend your itinerary to include Évora and the Alentejo or head north to Coimbra and the Beiras. It's best to explore these regions by car, unless you have a great deal of time and patience: trains don't serve many of the most interesting towns, and bus travel is slow.

Numbers in the text correspond to numbers in the margin and on the Estremadura and the Ribatejo map.

IF YOU HAVE 3 DAYS

Start with a visit to the imposing monastery and palace at **Mafra** ①, then head for the coast, with a stop at the resort and fishing village of **Ericeira** ②. Continue north along the shore to **Peniche** ④, with its imposing fortress. Head inland to spend the night in the enchanting walled city of ⊞ **Óbidos** ⑥. The next morning continue north, stopping at ceramics shops in **Caldas da Rainha** ⑦. En route to ⊞ **Nazaré** ⑧, tour the church and cloister at **Alcobaça** ⑨. On your third day head inland to the soaring, multispired monastery church in **Batalha** ⑩. Return to Lisbon along N1/IC2 with a stop in **Vila Franca de Xira** ⑫ (after joining the A1 toll road at Aveiras da Cima) to visit the bullfighting museum. Alternatively, you could take N356 east from Batalha and then A1 down to Vila Franca from the Fátima junction.

IF YOU HAVE 5 DAYS

Follow the three-day itinerary to **Batalha** ⑩, and then continue north to **Leiria** ⑪ and its hilltop castle. Take N113 east to the A1 and drive down to ⊞ **Fátima** ⑰, one of Christendom's most renowned destinations. The next morning, continue east on N113 to **Tomar** ⑱, an attractive town dominated by its hilltop convent. Later in the day, follow N110 south and then take N358-2, a scenic road that follows the Rio Zêzere (Zêzere River), to its union with the Rio Tejo. Just west of their confluence, on an island in the Tejo, is the **Castelo de Almourol** ⑲, one of Portugal's finest. From here, follow N118 southwest along the Tejo, stopping in **Alpiarça** ⑮ to visit the Casa dos Patudos, a large country house containing the art collection of its former owner, and in **Almeirim** ⑬ to see the winery at the Quinta da Alorna. Spend the night in ⊞ **Santarém** ⑭, an important farming and livestock center with many fine sights. The next day return to Lisbon with a drive along the Tejo on N118 through the region of marshy plains known as the Lezíria.

IF YOU HAVE 7 DAYS

Leave Lisbon and head north to **Mafra** ①, then visit **Ericeira** ②. From here continue north along the coast, turning inland to **Torres Vedras** ③

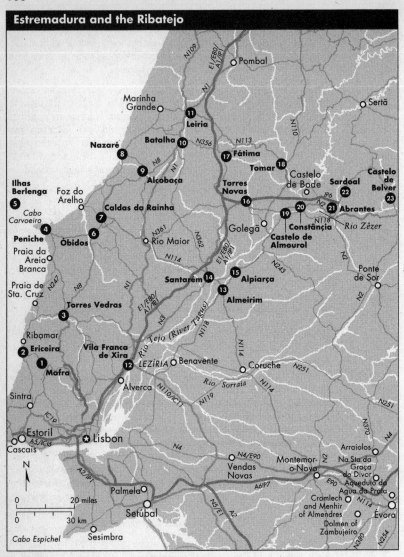

to have a look at the castle and the fortifications erected during the Peninsular War. Continue on to **Peniche** ④. If the weather is good, take the boat ride out to the **Ilhas Berlenga** ⑤. From Peniche drive inland a few miles to 🏛 **Óbidos** ⑥ before heading north through **Caldas da Rainha** ⑦ and **Alcobaça** ⑨ to 🏛 **Nazaré** ⑧. The next morning visit 🏛 **Leiria** ⑪ and the glassworks at Marinha Grande. Stay in Leiria for two nights and use the town as a base to visit **Fátima** ⑰ and explore the Parque Natural das Serras de Aire e Candeeiros, where there are marvelous limestone grottoes at Mira de Aire, Alvados, and Santo António as well as hundreds of fossilized dinosaur footprints at Bairro.

Leaving Leiria continue to **Tomar** ⑱. If you have time, stop in Ourem to visit its medieval castles before continuing to the lake at Castelo de Bode. To fully experience the countryside and visit a charming, out-of-the-way village, take N244-3 from 🏛 **Abrantes** ㉑ to **Sardoal** ㉒, an attractive backcountry hamlet. From Sardoal, N244-3 traces a broad loop through a heavily forested region before returning to the Tejo and joining the main highway N118 at the hilltop **Castelo de Belver** ㉓. Return on N118 to spend the night in Abrantes. In the morning visit the **Castelo de Almourol** ⑲ and continue to ⛫ **Santarém** ⑭ by way of **Alpiarça** ⑮ and **Almeirim** ⑬. The next morning return to Lisbon with a stop in **Vila Franca de Xira** ⑫.

When to Tour Estremadura and the Ribatejo

To avoid the busloads of visitors who inundate these places during July and August, visit the major monuments and attractions such as Óbidos and Mafra in the early morning. This also helps to beat the oppressive summer heat, particularly inland. The best time of year for touring is in early spring and from mid-September until late October. The climate during this period is pleasant, and attractions and restaurants aren't crowded. If throngs of people don't bother you, time your visit to Fátima to coincide with May 13, when between 500,000 and 1 million pilgrims overwhelm this otherwise sleepy country town. Less spectacular pilgrimages take place year-round.

ESTREMADURA

The narrow province surrounding Lisbon and extending north along the coast for approximately 160 km (100 mi) is known as Estremadura, referring to the extreme southern border of the land the Portuguese reconquered from the Moors. This is primarily a rural region characterized by coastal fishing villages and small farming communities that mostly produce fruit and olives. A tour through region includes visits to towns with some of Portugal's most outstanding architectural treasures, including Mafra, Alcobaça, Óbidos, Tomar, and Batalha.

Mafra

❶ *28 km (17 mi) northwest of Lisbon.*

In 1711, after nearly three years of a childless union with his Hapsburg queen, Mariana, a despairing King João V vowed that should the queen bear him an heir, he would build a monastery dedicated to St. Anthony. In December of that same year, a girl—later to become queen of Spain—was born; João's eventual heir, José I, was born three years later.

★ True to his word, King João V built the enormous **Mosteiro Palácio Nacional de Mafra** (Monastery and Royal Palace), which looms above the small farming community of Mafra. The original project—entrusted to the Italian-trained German architect Friedrich Ludwig—was to be a modest facility that could house 13 friars. What emerged after 18 years of construction was a rectangular complex containing a monastery large enough for hundreds of monks as well as an imposing basilica and a grandiose palace that has been compared to El Escorial outside Madrid, Spain. The numbers involved in the construction are mind-boggling: at times 50,000 workers toiled. There are 4,500 doors and windows, 300 cells, 880 halls and rooms, and 154 stairways. Perimeter walls that total some 19 km (12 mi) surround the park.

The one-hour guided tours are enlightening; those conducted by English-speaking docents take place at 11 AM and 2:30 PM. The highlight is the magnificent baroque library: the barrel-vaulted, two-tiered hall holds some 40,000 volumes of mostly 16th-, 17th-, and 18th-century works and a number of ancient maps. The basilica contains 11 chapels and was patterned after St. Peter's in the Vatican. The balcony of the connecting corridor overlooks the high altar and was a favorite meeting place for Dom João and Mariana. This midway point between the "his" and "hers" royal bedrooms was considered neutral territory.

When you're in the gilded throne room, notice the life-size renditions of the seven virtues, as well as the impressive figure of Hercules, by Domingos Sequeira. On display in the games room is an early version of a pinball machine. Note the hard-planked beds in the monastery infirmary; the monks used no mattresses. You'll be fortunate if you arrive on a Sunday afternoon between 4 and 5, when the sonorous tones of the 92-bell carillon ring out. ✉ *Largo Cândido dos Reis,* ☎ *261/817550.* ✉ *€3, including tour.* ☉ *Mon. and Wed.–Sun. 10–1 and 2–5.*

NEED A
BREAK?
The **Pastelaria Fradinho** (☎ 261/815738), just across from the monastery, is a welcome respite from the rigors of sightseeing. Light, cheerful, and adorned with tiles, it specializes in little, homemade, friar-shape, egg-and-almond pastries called, predictably, *fradinhos* (little friars).

☮ The royal game reserve, the **Tapada Nacional de Mafra,** is in a forest behind and about 2 km (1 mi) from the Mosteiro Palácio Nacional de Mafra. The huge, wall-enclosed area was once the private hunting ground of João V and is stocked with deer and other local fauna. You can wander about on your own or take part in general walking tours or those geared toward photography or bird-watching. If your feet are tired, opt for a guided tour by minitrain, in a horse-drawn carriage, or on horseback. (Note that on weekdays minitrains leave only when they have 20 passengers; horseback tours must always be booked a day in advance.) You can also practice your archery skills—with a bow and arrows or with a crossbow—at the shooting range. ☎ *261/814240,* WEB *www.tapadademafra.pt.* ✉ *Grounds: €4 on foot, €5 on a walking tour, €8.50 by minitrain, €30 by carriage, €20–€30 on horseback. To shooting range: €15 plus €50 deposit for equipment.* ☉ *Grounds: daily 10–4. Minitrain and horseback tours: weekdays 10 AM and 2 PM; weekends 10 AM, 3 PM, and 4 PM. Shooting-range sessions: 9:30 AM and 4 PM.*

Lodging

$ 🏨 **Hotel Castelão.** A convenient location in the center of Mafra and budgets rates are the draws. The large, modern hotel also has a traditional wine cellar and a restaurant that serves regional fare. ✉ *Av. 25 de Abril, 2640-456,* ☎ *261/816050,* FAX *261/816059. 19 rooms. Restaurant, minibars, cable TV, bar, recreation room. AE, DC, V. BP.*

Ericeira

❷ *11 km (7 mi) northwest of Mafra.*

Ericeira, an old fishing town tucked into the rocky coast, is a popular seaside resort. Its core fans out from the sheer cliff, beneath which boats are hauled up onto a small, sheltered beach. The growth of summer tourism has caused a proliferation of bars, pubs, discos, pizzerias, and the like in the increasingly gentrified but still attractive town center. But along the waterfront there are a number of traditional seafood restaurants that are popular with both locals and visitors. Either end of the town has good sand for sunbathing, but the south end is preferred by surfers.

Lodging

$ 🏨 **Hotel Pedro O Pescador.** If you prefer your hotels on the small side, then you'll like this intimate, pastel blue, family-run place near the beach. Cheerful rooms have plank floors, floral print fabrics, and Alentejo furniture. The small, modern restaurant is frequented mostly by hotel guests but has a reputation for simple but excellent cooking. ✉ *Rua Dr. Eduardo Burnay 22, 2655-33,* ☎ *261/869121,* FAX *261/862321. 25 rooms. Restaurant, bar. AE, DC, MC, V. CP.*

Torres Vedras

❸ *20 km (12 mi) northeast of Ericeira.*

A bustling commercial center crowned with the ruins of a medieval castle, Torres Vedras is best known for its extensive fortifications—a system of trenches and fortresses erected by the Duke of Wellington in 1810 as part of a secret plan for the defense of Lisbon. It was here, at the Lines of Torres Vedras, that the surprised French army under Napoléon's Marshal Masséna was routed. You can see reconstructed remnants of the fortifications on a hill above town and throughout the area.

Lodging

$$ 🏨 **Hotel Golf Mar.** The idyllic location—on a rise overlooking a broad, sandy beach—and the golf course are the main reasons to stay here: the huge, concrete-block facade is hardly alluring, and the interior lacks imagination. The hotel is near the town of Lourinhã, 16 km (10 mi) northwest of Torres Vedras. ✉ *Praia do Porto Novo, 2560-100,* ☎ *261/984157,* 𝔽𝔸𝕏 *261/984621,* 𝕎𝔼𝔹 *www.eav.pt. 220 rooms, 7 suites. Restaurant, 9-hole golf course, 2 tennis courts, 3 pools (1 indoor), hair salon, massage, sauna, billiards, horseback riding, 2 bars, dance club, video game room, meeting rooms. AE, DC, MC, V. BP.*

$ 🏨 **Hotel Império Jardim.** This bright, cheerfully appointed hotel is a good deal. It has several on-site eateries and shops, and it's right in the center of town as well. ✉ *Praça 25 de Abril 17, 2560-285,* ☎ *261/ 314232,* 𝔽𝔸𝕏 *261/321901,* 𝕎𝔼𝔹 *www.imperio-online.com/hotel. 47 rooms. Restaurant, café, patisserie, room service, minibars, cable TV, bar, shops, laundry service, meeting rooms, free parking. AE, MC, V. BP.*

Outdoor Activities and Sports

The nine-hole **Clube do Golfe do Vimeiro** (✉ Praia do Porto Novo, ☎ 261/314232), designed by Frank Pennink, is on the beach and is part of the Hotel Golf Mar. Guests of the hotel golf for free; both guests and nonguests must reserve greens in advance. Fees range from €20 to €25.

En Route For the most scenic drive to Peniche, return to the coast and follow N247 north for 43 km (27 mi) to Cabo Carvoeiro. About 3 km (2 mi) north of Torres Vedras is the archaeological site Castro do Zambujal, the remains of an Iron Age settlement of people who worked the copper mines that once existed here. Farther on, the jagged coast is interrupted by fine beaches at Ribamar, Santa Cruz, and Areia Branca.

Peniche

❹ *32 km (20 mi) northwest of Torres Vedras.*

In the lee of a rocky peninsula, Peniche is a major fishing-and-canning port that's also a popular summer resort known for its fine lace. The busy harbor is watched over by a sprawling 16th-century **Fortaleza Museu** (Fort Museum). At one time the fort's dungeons were full of French troops captured by the Duke of Wellington's forces. During Portugal's dictatorship, which ended in 1974, it was a prison for opponents of the regime. With the restoration of democracy, it became a museum. You can tour the former cells and take in a small archaeological exhibit. For a good view of the fortress and the harbor, drive out to Cabo Carvoeiro; the narrow road winds around the peninsula, along the rugged shore, and past the lighthouse and bizarre rock formations. 🎟 €1. ☉ *Tues.–Sun. 10:30–12:30 and 2–6.*

The most interesting of the area's several churches is the 13th-century **Igreja de São Leonardo** (Church of St. Leonard) in the village of Atouguia da Baleia. ☎ *262/759142 to town council office.* ☉ *Apr.–Oct., daily 9–noon and 2–5:30.*

Dining and Lodging

$$–$$$$ ✕ **Nau dos Corvos.** On the Cabo Carvoeiro cliffs with a dramatic view of the sea and the lighthouse, this restaurant specializes in traditionally prepared seafood dishes. Be sure to try the *tamboril na canoa com gambas* (monkfish with tomato and shrimp served in an earthenware pot). ⊠ *Cabo Carvoeiro,* ☎ 262/789004. *AE. Closed Thurs. No lunch Wed.*

$$$ 🏨 **Hotel Atlântico Golfe.** Even if you're not a golfer, the views from your balcony (all rooms have them) over the links and the long, beach will appeal. The hotel is on a sandy stretch famed for the health-giving properties of its waters, which are attributed to the local rock. The rooms are spacious and well equipped. ⊠ *Praia da Consolacão, 2525-150,* ☎ *262/757700,* 𝖥𝖠𝖷 *262/750717,* 𝖶𝖤𝖡 *www.atlanticogolfehotel.com. 90 rooms. Restaurant, in-room safes, minibars, cable TV, 9-hole golf course, tennis court, indoor-outdoor pool, health club, hot tub, sauna, bar, meeting rooms. AE, DC, MC, V. BP.*

$ 🏨 **Hotel Praia Norte.** This well-equipped, modern hotel is on a green lawn near the sea at the outskirts of Peniche. Guest rooms aren't very large, but they're light, pleasantly furnished, and well appointed. ⊠ *Av. Monsenhor Manuel Bastos, 2520-206,* ☎ *262/780500,* 𝖥𝖠𝖷 *262/780509,* 𝖶𝖤𝖡 *www.hotelpraianorte.com. 89 rooms. Restaurant, golf privileges, tennis court, 2 pools (1 indoor), hot tub, sauna, Turkish bath, volleyball, bar, dance club, playground, meeting rooms. AE, DC, MC, V. BP.*

Outdoor Activities and Sports

Peniche Sportagua is a large water-park complex with slides and separate adults' and children's swimming pools. The park also has a restaurant, snack bar, and live music shows. ⊠ *Av. Monsenhor M. Basto,* ☎ *262/789125.* 🎫 *€9.* ☉ *Mid-July–mid-Sept., daily 9–7.*

Ilhas Berlenga

❺ *10 km (6 mi) northeast of Cabo Carvoeiro.*

The harbor at Peniche is the jumping-off point for excursions to the Berlenga Islands. These six islets are part of a nature reserve and a favorite place for fishermen and divers. Berlenga, the largest of the group, is the site of the Forte de São João Baptista, a 17th-century fortress built to defend the area from pirates. There's a campground on the island, and a limited number of rooms are available. For information about accommodations, contact the Peniche tourist office.

The company Viamar operates regular summer boat services from Peniche to Berlenga. From May 15 to June 30 and again September 1 to September 15 there is one round-trip daily leaving at 10 AM and returning at 4:30 PM. In July and August there are two round-trips daily at 9:30 AM and 11:30 AM, plus an evening boat that leaves at 5:30 PM and returns the following morning.

Outdoor Activities and Sports

FISHING

The most commonly caught fish are sea bass, bream, and red mullet. A fishing license isn't required. The charter-boat company **Nautipesca** (⊠ Largo Ribeira Velha, Peniche, ☎ 936/222658 or 917/588358) offers deep-sea fishing excursions. Boats leave when conditions permit and when there's a minimum of 10 people interested in heading out. Per-person rates are €28 on weekdays, €35 on weekends.

SCUBA DIVING

The clear (and somewhat chilly) waters and bizarre rock formations off the Ilhas Berlenga are popular with scuba divers and snorkelers. The **Mergulhão** (⊠ Porto de Pesca de Peniche, Armazen 4, ☎ 966/008487, 𝖶𝖤𝖡 www.scubaportugal.com/mergulhao/diveshop) dive center has two boats that its staff uses to take groups of six people out to explore underwater shipwrecks and caverns. One-tank trips cost €45–€55, depending on the destination. Be sure to book in advance.

Óbidos

★ **6** *20 km (12 mi) east of Peniche.*

Once a strategic seaport, Óbidos is now high and dry—and 10 km (6 mi) inland—owing to the silting of its harbor. On the approach to town, you can see bastions and crenellated walls standing like sentinels over the now-peaceful valley of the Ria Arnoia. It's hard to imagine fishing boats and trading vessels docking in places that are today filled by cottages and cultivated fields.

As you enter town through the massive, arched gates, it seems as if you've been transported into medieval Portugal. The narrow Rua Direita, lined with boutiques and white, flower-bedecked houses, runs from the gates to the foot of the castle: you may want to shop for ceramics and clothing on this street. The rest of the town is crisscrossed by a labyrinth of stone footpaths, tiny squares, and decaying stairways. Each nook and cranny offers its own reward. Cars aren't permitted inside the walls except to unload luggage at hotels. Parking is provided outside town.

Óbidos has a long association with prominent Portuguese women. So enchanted was the young Queen Isabel with Óbidos—which she visited with her husband, Dom Dinis, shortly after their marriage in 1282—that the king gave it to her as a gift, along with Abrantes and Porto de Mós; the town remained the property of the queens of Portugal until 1834. In the 14th century Inês de Castro sought refuge in the castle here, and Queen Leonor (the wife of João II) came here in the 15th century to recuperate after the death of her young son; the town pillory bears her coat of arms.

The walls of the fine, medieval **castelo** (castle) enclose the entire town, and it's great fun to climb them and appreciate the view of the countryside. Extensively restored after suffering severe damage in the 1755 earthquake, the multitower complex has both Arabic and Manueline elements. Since 1952 parts of the castle have been a pousada.

The 17th-century artist Josefa de Óbidos came as a small child and lived here until her death in 1684. You can see some of her work in the *azulejo*-lined (tile-lined) **Igreja de Santa Maria** (St. Mary's Church), which was a Visigoth temple in the 8th century. The church is in a square off Rua Direita. ☎ *No phone.* ☉ *Daily 9:30–12:30 and 2:30–7.*

Dining and Lodging

$$–$$$ ✕ **Alcaide.** From the upstairs dining room and terrace of this rustic tavern you can enjoy a lovely view of town. The Alcaide is often jammed with hungry sightseers, especially from May through October; this isn't a quiet hideaway. The food, however, is always carefully prepared, and the service is attentive. Try the bacalhau *á casa* (with chestnuts and roasted apples). ✉ *Rua Direita,* ☎ *262/959220. AE, DC, MC, V. Closed Wed. Nov.–June.*

$$–$$$ ✕ **A Ilustre Casa de Ramiro.** The motifs at this restaurant in an old building outside the castle walls are Moorish, but the food is authentically regional. You could do worse than try the *pato de arroz* (rice with duck). ✉ *Rua Porta do Vale,* ☎ *262/959194. AE, MC, V. Closed Thurs.*

$$–$$$ ✕▥ **Pousada do Castelo.** Except for the electric lights and the relatively modern plumbing, the style of the Middle Ages prevails in this pousada, which occupies parts of the castle that Dom Dinis gave to his young bride, Isabel, in 1282. Room 2, in one of the massive stone

towers, is especially evocative of ancient times; other rooms are individually furnished with 16th- and 17th-century reproductions. The restaurant's ($$–$$$$) food and service are worthy of royalty; there's a curtained alcove where you can dine in privacy and still enjoy a view of the castle walls and valley below. Try the *cabrito assado* (roast kid). ⊠ *Paço Real, 2510-999,* ☎ *262/959105,* ℻ *262/959148,* 🕸 *www.pousadas.pt. 6 rooms, 3 suites. Restaurant, bar. AE, DC, MC, V. BP.*

$–$$ ✕🏨 **Albergaria Josefa d'Óbidos.** This flower-bedecked inn is built into the hillside at the main gate. Rooms have comfortable 18th-century reproductions, including massive wooden pieces that greatly mask the fact that the place was built in 1983. Several reproductions of Josefa d'Óbidos's works hang in the bar. The large, rustic restaurant ($$) has an open, brick grill and serves regional specialties: try the *arroz de tamboril* (casserole with monkfish and rice) or one of the bacalhau dishes. The peace in the dining room is sometimes disturbed by large tour groups. ⊠ *Rua D. João de Ornelas, 2510-074,* ☎ *262/959228,* ℻ *262/959533. 34 rooms, 2 suites. Restaurant, bar. AE, DC, MC, V. EP.*

Caldas da Rainha

❼   *5 km (3 mi) north of Óbidos.*

Caldas da Rainha (Queen's Baths), the hub of a large farming area, is best known for its sulfur baths. In 1484 Queen Leonor, en route to Batalha, noticed people bathing in a malodorous pool. Having heard of the healing properties of the sulfurous water, the queen interrupted her journey for a soak and became convinced of the water's beneficial effects. She had a hospital built on the site and was reputedly so enthusiastic that she sold her jewels to help finance the project. There's a bronze statue of Leonor in front of the hospital.

The expansive wooded park surrounding the spa contains the **Museu Malhoa,** a museum with works mostly by the local 19th- and 20th-century painter José Malhoa. ⊠ *Parque D. Carlos I,* ☎ *262/831984.* 🎟 *€2.* ⊙ *Tues.–Sun. 10–12:30 and 2–5.*

The **Museu de Cerâmica** (Ceramics Museum) in the house of the noted 19th-century artisan, Rafael Bordalo Pinheiro. The collection contains ceramic works from all over the region, as well as works by Bordalo Pinheiro himself. ⊠ *Rua Dr. Ilídio Amado,* ☎ *262/840280.* 🎟 *€2.* ⊙ *Tues.–Sun. 10–12:30 and 2–5.*

Dining and Lodging

$$ ✕ **Adega Típica do Coto.** This popular local restaurant on the main street in Coto, 2 km (1 mi) north of Caldas, has a mainly Portuguese menu. If it's in season, try the *javali* (wild boar). The bread is baked fresh each day in a brick oven. ⊠ *Rua Principal 14, Coto,* ☎ *262/844898. No credit cards.*

$$ 🏨 **Quinta da Foz.** This large manor house dates from the 16th cen-
★   tury and is surrounded by lawns at the edge of the Óbidos Lagoon, some 15 minutes' walk from the beach. It's a quiet base from which to explore Caldas da Rainha, only 9 km (5½ mi) away, and other towns. The bedrooms are large and comfortably furnished, with lots of flowers about. ⊠ *Largo do Areial, Foz do Arelho 2500-457,* ☎ *262/979369,* ℻ *262/979369. 5 rooms, 2 apartments. Horseback riding. No credit cards. EP.*

$ 🏨 **Hotel Cristal.** Business travelers choose this modern eight-story hotel because it's near the town center. In public areas, marble floors and wooden details are polished to perfection. Rooms are comfortable, though there aren't many details to indicate you're in Portugal. ⊠ *Rua António Sergio 31, 2500-130,* ☎ *262/840260,* ℻ *262/842621,* 🕸 *www.*

hoteiscristal.pt. 111 rooms, 2 suites. Restaurant, in-room safes, mini-bars, cable TV, pool, sauna, bar, free parking. AE, DC, MC, V. EP.

Outdoor Activities and Sports

The **Laguna de Óbidos** at Foz do Arelho is a lagoon that's popular with windsurfers. You can rent equipment at the beach: the cost for just the rig is about €10 per hour; rental and lessons cost about €20 per hour.

Shopping

Caldas da Rainha is famous for its cabbage-leaf and vegetable-shape ceramic pieces produced in several of the town's factories and work-shops, which you can visit if you reserve ahead of time. **Fábrica Rafael Bordalo Pinheiro** (⊠ Rua Rafael Bordalo Pinheiro, ☎ 262/842353), a factory named after the artist who made the Caldas da Rainha–style ceramics famous, is worth touring. **SECLA** (⊠ Rua São João de Deus, ☎ 262/824151) is one of the area's leading ceramics workshops.

Nazaré

8 *24 km (15 mi) northwest of Caldas da Rainha. For the most interest-ing route, head west from Caldas along the lagoon to the beach town of Foz do Arelho, then take the coast road 26 km (16 mi) north.*

Not so long ago you could mingle on the beach with black-stocking-capped fishermen and even help as the oxen hauled boats in from the crashing surf. But Nazaré is no longer a village and has long ceased to be quaint. The boats now motor comfortably into a safe, modern harbor, and the oxen have been put to pasture. The beachfront boulevard is lined with restaurants, bars, and souvenir shops, and in summer the broad, sandy beach is covered with a multicolor quilt of tents and awnings.

To find what's left of the Nazaré once hailed by many as "the most picturesque fishing village in Portugal," come in the winter, and either climb the precipitous trail or take the funicular to the top of the 361-ft cliff called **Sitio.** Clustered at the cliff's edge overlooking the beach is a small community of fishermen who live in tiny cottages and seem unaffected by all that's happening below.

Dining and Lodging

$–$$ ✕🍽 **Adega Oceano.** Balconies overlook the beach at this white, pleas-antly appointed hotel. The restaurant ($–$$$$), which has an outdoor seating area, serves typical Portuguese cuisine, including noteworthy caldeiradas. ⊠ *Av. da República 51, 2450-101,* ☎ *262/561161,* 𝔽𝔸𝕏 *262/561790. 30 rooms. Restaurant, beach, bar. AE, DC, MC, V. EP.*

$–$$ ✕🍽 **Albergaria Mar Bravo.** This modern guest house is right on the beach, just steps from both the sea and the center of town. The classy restaurant ($$–$$$$) serves regional and international dishes; the seafood is always very fresh. ⊠ *Praça Sousa Oliveira 7, 2450-159,* ☎ *262/569160,* 𝔽𝔸𝕏 *262/569169. 16 rooms. Restaurant, snack bar, cable TV, beach, bar, meeting rooms, free parking, no-smoking rooms. AE, DC, MC, V. CP.*

$$ 🍽 **Hotel Maré.** The Maré is right in the town center and just a few strides from the beach. If you can't get a room with a view, head for the fifth-floor terrace to take in the panoramic vistas. ⊠ *Rua Mouzinho de Al-buquerque 8, 2450-254,* ☎ *262/561226,* 𝔽𝔸𝕏 *262/561750,* 𝕎𝔼𝔹 *www. hotel-mare.com. 36 rooms. Restaurant, snack bar, minibars, billiards, bar, shops, baby-sitting, meeting rooms. AE, DC, MC, V. CP.*

$–$$ 🍽 **Albergaria Miramar.** The sea and town views from this inn are fan-tastic: it's about 1 km (½ mi) *above* Nazaré, in the village of Pederneira. The inn's smooth white facade is contrasted by its terra-cotta-tile roof, turquoise-blue swimming pool, and emerald-green lawns. ⊠ *Rua Abel da Silva, Pederneira 2450-060,* ☎ *262/550000,* 𝔽𝔸𝕏 *262/550001,* 𝕎𝔼𝔹 *www.h-miramar.com. 41 rooms. Restaurant, cable TV, pool, bar, free parking. AE, DC, MC, V. CP.*

Shopping

The many shops and stands along the beachfront promenade have a good selection of traditional fishermen's sweaters as well as a wide array of caps and plaid shirts (the best are made of wool rather than acrylic blends). It pays to shop around: prices vary widely, and bargaining is the order of the day.

Alcobaça

⑨ *10 km (6 mi) southeast of Nazaré, 20 km (12 mi) northeast of Caldas da Rainha.*

★ Alcobaça is known for its crystal and is the site of a museum devoted to wine making. But the town is known best for its impressive church and monastery. Like the monastery at Mafra, the **Mosteiro de Alcobaça** was built as the result of a kingly vow, this time in gratitude for a battle won. In 1147, faced with stiff Muslim resistance during the battle for Santarém, Portugal's first king, Afonso Henriques, promised to build a monastery dedicated to St. Bernard and the Cistercian Order. The Portuguese were victorious, Santarém was captured from the Moors, and shortly thereafter a site was selected. Construction began in 1153 and was concluded in 1178. The church, the largest in Portugal, is awe inspiring. The unadorned, 350-ft-long structure of massive granite blocks and cross-ribbed vaulting is a masterpiece of understatement: there's good use of clean, flowing lines, with none of the clutter of the later rococo and Manueline architecture. At opposite ends of the transept, placed foot-to-foot some 30 paces apart, are the delicately carved tombs of King Pedro I and Inês de Castro. The story of Pedro and Inês, one of the most bizarre love stories in Portuguese history, was immortalized by Luís de Camões in the epic poem *Os Lusiads*.

Pedro, son of King Afonso IV and heir to the throne, fell in love with the beautiful young Galician Inês de Castro, a lady-in-waiting to Pedro's Castilian wife, Constança. Fearful of the influence of Inês's family on his heir, the king banished her from the court. Upon the death of Constança, Pedro and Inês secretly married, and she lived in Coimbra, in a house later known as the Quinta das Lagrimas (the House of Tears); two sons were born of this union. King Afonso, ever wary of foreign influence on Pedro, had Inês murdered. Subsequently, Pedro took the throne and had Inês's murderers pursued: two of the three were captured and executed, their hearts wrenched from their bodies. Pedro publicly proclaimed that he had been married to Inês and arranged an elaborate and macabre funeral for his wife. Before the procession, Inês's body, in royal garb, was enthroned beside him, and the courtiers were forced to kiss her lifeless hand. She was then placed in the tomb in Alcobaça that Pedro had designed, which lay, according to his wishes, opposite his own—so that on Judgment Day the lovers would ascend to heaven facing each other.

The graceful twin-tiered cloister at Alcobaça was added in the 14th and 16th centuries. The Kings Hall, just to the left of the main entrance, is lined with a series of 18th-century azulejos illustrating the construction of the monastery. ⊠ *Praça 25 de Abril,* ☎ *no phone.* 🎫 *€6.* ☉ *Daily 10–7.*

While in Alcobaça, you may want to visit the interesting **Museu Nacional do Vinho** (National Wine Museum) to see wine-making implements and presses. The museum is in an old winery, on N8 heading north and just from the edge of town. ⊠ *Rua de Leiria,* ☎ *262/*

582222. ⊡ *€1.50.* ⊙ *Tues.–Fri. 9–12:30 and 2–5:30, weekends 10–12:30 and 2–6.*

Dining and Lodging

$ ✕ **Trindade.** The intimate dining room of this unpretentious restaurant is lined with old photos of local scenes that reveal some of Alcobaça's history. Try the specialty, *açorda de marisco* (with shellfish), and for dessert, the homemade pastry. ⊠ *Praça D. Afonso Henriques 22,* ☎ *262/582397. AE, DC, MC, V. Closed Thurs. Oct.–May.*

$–$$ ⌂ **Casa da Padeira.** This family-run guest house 5 km (3 mi) outside of Alcobaça is named after a baker who fought the Spaniards with a wooden shovel—and pushed them into her oven—during the Battle of Aljubarrota. You're free to wander the well-tended gardens and mingle with the family. The large guest rooms are furnished with period reproductions. Homemade bread, fresh from the oven, is the highlight of breakfast; dinner is available on request. ⊠ *Hwy. N8, 19, Aljubarrota 2460-711,* ☎ *262/505240,* ꜰᴀˣ *262/505241. 8 rooms, 2 suites. Breakfast room, miniature golf, pool, gym, billiards, bar. AE, DC, MC, V. EP.*

$–$$ ⌂ **Hotel Santa Maria.** Gardens surround this hotel, and the monastery faces it. Some rooms have balconies; all rooms are simply furnished, comfortable, and, according to the manager, "good for the soul." There's no restaurant, but the wood-paneled bar is agreeable. ⊠ *Rua Dr. Francisco Zagalo 20-22, 2460-041,* ☎ *262/590160,* ꜰᴀˣ *262/590161. 75 rooms. Minibars, cable TV, bar, free parking. AE, DC, MC, V. EP.*

Shopping

Casa Lisboa (⊠ Praça 25 de Abril, ☎ no phone), across from the monastery, has a good selection of fine lead crystal.

Batalha

★ ❿ *18 km (11 mi) northeast of Alcobaça.*

Batalha, which means "battle" in Portuguese, is the site of another of the country's religious structures—this one classified as a UNESCO World Heritage Site—that memorialize victory in battle.

The church monastery **Santa Maria da Vitória** (St. Mary of Victory) was built to commemorate a decisive Portuguese victory over the Spanish on August 14, 1385, in the battle of Aljubarrota. In this engagement the Portuguese king, João de Avis, who had been crowned only seven days earlier, took on and routed a superior Spanish force. In so doing he maintained independence for Portugal, which was to last until 1580, when the crown finally passed into Spanish hands. The heroic statue of the mounted figure in the forecourt is that of Nuno Álvares Pereira, who, along with João de Avis, led the Portuguese army at Aljubarrota.

The monastery, a masterly combination of Gothic and Manueline styles, was built between 1388 and 1533. Some 15 architects were involved in the project, but the principal architect was Afonso Domingues, whose portrait, carved in stone, graces the wall in the chapter house. In the great hall lie the remains of two unknown Portuguese soldiers who died in World War I: one in France, the other in Africa. Entombed in the center of the Founder's Chapel, beneath the star-shape, vaulted ceiling, is João de Avis, lying hand-in-hand with his English queen, Philippa of Lancaster. The tombs along the south and west walls are those of the couple's children, including Henry the Navigator. Perhaps the finest parts of the entire project are the Unfinished Chapels, seven chapels radiating off an octagonal rotunda, started by Dom Duarte in 1435 and left roofless owing to lack of funds. Note the intricately filigreed detail of the main doorway. ⊡ *€3.* ⊙ *Daily 9–6.*

On N8, 5 km (3 mi) south of Batalha's monastery, a small **Museu Militar** documents conflicts with Spain from the early Middle Ages through the early 15th century. ⊠ *Campo Militar de São Jorge,* ☎ 244/482087. ☎ €2. ⊘ *Tues.–Sun. 10–noon and 2–5.*

Dining and Lodging

$$ ✕⊞ **Pousada do Mestre Afonso Domingues.** Named for the architect
★ who designed the famous Batalha monastery, this pousada is full of modern comforts in a two-story, white-stucco building. The good-size guest rooms have patterned wallpaper and are furnished in 17th- and 18th-century style; several look out on the monastery, as does the first-floor restaurant ($$–$$$$), with its polished *calçada* (pavement with small black stones on a white background) and wooden ceiling. The menu includes several types of bacalhau, and there's an extensive wine list. ⊠ *Largo Mestre Afonso Domingues 6, 2440-102,* ☎ 244/765260, ☒ 244/765240, 🌐 *www.pousadas.pt. 19 rooms, 2 suites. Restaurant, bar. AE, DC, MC, V. BP.*

OFF THE   **PARQUE NATURAL DAS SERRAS DE AIRE E CANDEEIROS –** This sparsely pop-
BEATEN PATH ulated region straddles the border between Estremadura and the Ribatejo and is roughly midway between Lisbon and Coimbra. Within its 75,000 acres of scrublands and moors are small settlements, little changed in hundreds of years, where farmers barely eke out a living. In this rocky landscape, stones are the main building material for houses, windmills, and the miles of walls used to mark boundary lines. In the village of Minde, you can see women weaving the rough patchwork rugs for which this region is known. The park is well suited for leisurely hiking or cycling. If you're driving, the N362, which runs for approximately 45 km (28 mi) from Batalha in the north to Santarém in the south, is a good route.

Leiria

⑪ *11 km (7 mi) north of Batalha.*

Leiria is a pleasant, modern, industrial town at the confluence of the Rios Liz and Lena, overlooked by a wonderfully elegant medieval castle. The region is known for its handicrafts, particularly the fine hand-blown glassware from nearby Marinha Grande. Leiria's **castelo,** built in 1135 by Prince Afonso Henriques (later Portugal's first king), was an important link in the chain of defenses along the southern border of what was at the time the Kingdom of Portugal. When the Moors were driven from the region, the castle lost its significance and lay dormant until the early 14th century, when it was restored and modified and became the favorite residence of Dom Dinis and his queen, Isabel of Aragon. With these modifications the castle became more of a palace than a fortress and remains one of the loveliest structures of its kind in Portugal. Within the perimeter walls you'll encounter the ruins of a Gothic church, the castle keep, and—built into the section of the fortifications overlooking the town—the royal palace. There's also a museum. Lined by eight arches, the balcony of the palace affords lovely views. ☎ 244/813982. ☎ *Castle: €1. Castle and museum: €2.* ⊘ *Apr.–Sept., Tues.–Fri. 9–6:30, weekends 10–5:30; Oct.–Mar., Tues.–Fri. 9–5:30, weekends 10–5:30.*

Marinha Grande, just west of Leiria, is known for its fine-quality lead crystal, which has been produced in the region since the 17th century. The former Royal Glass Factory, founded in the 18th century, is now the site of a **Museu do Vidro,** with a collection of glass and crystal from several periods and factories. ⊠ *Praça Gulhereme Stevens, Marinha*

Grande, ☎ *244/56307.* 🎫 *€1.* ⊙ *June–Sept., Tues.–Sun. 10–7; Oct.–May, Tues.–Fri. 10–6.*

Dining and Lodging

$$ ✕ **O Casarão.** Five kilometers (3 miles) south of Leiria, in Azoia at the
★ Nazaré turnoff, O Casarão occupies a large country house surrounded by gardens. The service and presentation are flawless without being pretentious, and the extensive menu includes several ancient recipes from nearby monasteries. One of the best dishes is bacalhau *tibarna* (with olive oil, corn bread, and potatoes). Be sure to leave room for the *bolo pinão* (pine-nut cake). The comprehensive wine list displays the labels of 120 varieties. ✉ *Cruzamento de Azoia,* ☎ *244/871080. AE, DC, MC, V. Closed Mon.*

$$ ✕ **Casinha Velha.** An old house—just 1 km (½ mi) from downtown—with rustic Portuguese furniture is the site of this restaurant. The menu includes a noteworthy bacalhau as well as cabrito assado. ✉ *Rua Professores Portelas 23,* ☎ *244/855355. AE, DC, MC, V. Closed Tues.*

$ ✕▥ **Best Western Hotel Dom José III.** Although this deluxe hotel is near the center of town, the area surrounding it is quiet. The panoramic restaurant ($$–$$$$) serves excellent Portuguese and international fair with a splendid view of the castle. ✉ *Av. Dom José III, 2400-164,* ☎ *244/817888,* 𝔽𝔸𝕏 *244/811780,* 𝚆𝙴𝙱 *www.bestwestern.com. 54 rooms, 10 suites. Restaurant, minibars, cable TV, laundry service, free parking. AE, DC, MC, V. BP.*

$ ▥ **Eurosol.** A pair of modern, mid-rise hotels, the Eurosol and Eurosol Jardim, occupy a hilltop that's about a 15-minute walk from the town center. The lobbies and bedrooms are spacious and smart, with contemporary lines and furnishings. The eighth-floor restaurant is ringed with picture windows that give bird's-eye views of town. ✉ *Rua Dom José Alves Correia da Silva, 2400-010,* ☎ *244/812201,* 𝔽𝔸𝕏 *244/811205,* 𝚆𝙴𝙱 *www.eurosol.pt. 128 rooms, 7 suites. Restaurant, minibars, cable TV, pool, health club, massage, sauna, bar, shops, meeting rooms, free parking. AE, DC, MC, V. EP.*

Shopping

The **Santos Barrosa Vidros** (✉ Zona da Estão–Cumeira, ☎ 244/570100), a factory museum, displays all types of glass products. Call ahead of time to arrange for a tour as hours are erratic. Admission is free.

THE RIBATEJO

To the east of Estremadura, straddling both banks of the Rio Tejo, the Ribatejo is a placid, flat, fertile region known for its vegetables and vineyards. It's also famous for its horses and bulls; you may well see campinos in red waistcoats and green stocking caps moving bulls along with long wooden poles. As a consequence of its strategic location, the Ribatejo is home to a number of imposing castles as well as such diverse sights as the bullfighting centers of Vila Franca de Xira and Santarém and the shrine at Fátima.

Vila Franca de Xira

⑫ *30 km (18 mi) north of Lisbon via the A1.*

Vila Franca de Xira is an excellent place to see Portuguese bullfights, which are held from Easter through October. For more information call the tourist office. The bullring here, one of Portugal's finest, also contains a small museum with a collection of bullfighting memorabilia; it's open Tuesday–Sunday 10–12:30 and 2–6, and admission is free.

The Portuguese bullfight—known as the *tourada*—is different from any version of this ancient spectacle in Mexico or Spain. Here the bull's principal opponent isn't a sword-carrying matador but a *cavaleiro*—a horseman elegantly attired as an 18th-century nobleman, with plumed hat and embroidered coat. Using exceptional equestrian skills, he provokes the bull and, just inches away from the animal's padded horns, deftly places a colorfully festooned *bandarilha* (dart) in a designated part of the bull's back. With each pass of an ever shorter bandarilha, the danger to horse and rider increases—in spite of the bull's blunted horns. At the proper moment, when the bull is sufficiently fatigued, the final dart is placed, and with a flourish the cavaleiro exits the arena. (Following a decree by the Marquês de Pombal in the 18th century, bulls aren't killed in Portuguese rings.)

The stage is now set for the *pega,* an audacious display of bravery with burlesque overtones. A group of eight men—called the *forcados*—dressed in bright-crimson vests and green stocking caps parades into the arena, and the leader, hands on hips, confronts the tired but still-enraged bull. When the bull charges, the leader meets him head on with a backwards leap and literally seizes the bull by the horns. While he tries to hang on to the furious bull's head, suspended between its horns, the other men rush in and, with one of them hanging on to its tail, try to force the animal to a standstill. At times this can be an amusing sight, but there's an ever-present element of danger (forcados have been killed during the pega). At the end of the spectacle, a few cows are led in to lure the bull from the ring. If he has shown exceptional bravery, the bull will be spared for stud purposes; otherwise, he will be slaughtered for the meat.

Had Hemingway and his buddies taken a wrong train and wound up in Vila Franca de Xira some 60 years ago, perhaps Pamplona would have remained an unsung, grimy industrial town, and the world would have flocked instead to the Ribatejo each year for one of Portugal's greatest parties. The first week of July sees the **Festa do Colete Encarnado** (Festival of the Red Waistcoat), during which the downtown streets are cordoned off, and the bulls are let loose as folks try their luck at dodging the charging beasts. At night the streets are alive with fado music and flamenco dancing. The running of the bulls also takes place during an autumn fair that's held in early October.

Not all the area sights are related to bullfighting. The **Museu do Ar** (Air Museum), in nearby Alverca, has a captivating collection of old airplanes. ⊠ *At airport, 8 km (5 mi) south of Vila Franca de Xira,* ☏ *219/581294.* 🎫 *€1.50.* ☉ *Oct.–June, Tues.–Sun. 10–5; July–Sept., Tues.–Sun. 10–6.*

Dining and Lodging

$$–$$$$ ✕ **Redondel.** This restaurant inside the walls of the famous bullring
★   sees a lot of action. It's considered Vila Franca's top eatery, with a menu full of regional dishes. There are high-vaulted brick ceilings, and in keeping with the theme, the dining room is adorned with bullfight posters and memorabilia. ⊠ *Arcadas da Praça de Touros,* ☏ *263/272973. Reservations essential. AE, DC, MC, V. Closed Mon.*

$$–$$$ ✕ **O Sultão.** Named for a famous white horse, this establishment in the Lezíria Grande Equestrian Center serves very good Portuguese food, especially the cabrito assado. The dining room also affords an excellent view of the riding ring. ⊠ *Centro Equestro, off EN1, Lezíria Grande,* ☏ *263/273961. AE, DC, MC, V. Closed Sun.*

$ ✕🏨 **Residencial Flora.** For simple but well-maintained budget accommodations, try this contemporary hotel in the center of town. Its small, homey restaurant ($$–$$$$) and wine cellar make a stay here

BULLFIGHTING

Although the two spectacles differ widely now, Portuguese and Spanish bullfights have a common origin. Both forms were born in the Middle Ages in the struggle between Moors and Christians for the Iberian Peninsula; both were essentially arts of the nobility; and both were practiced by horsemen.

The horse was an important instrument of war in the Christian Reconquest, and the rider and his mount were both highly trained in the martial arts. As part of their training, Portuguese and Spanish knights honed their equestrian skills and developed the dexterity of their horses in combat with the notoriously belligerent and agile Iberian fighting bulls. Long after these dangerous exercises lost their military utility, the noblemen continued to practice them for their own amusement. These displays of skill and courage, staged in castle courtyards and town squares, gradually evolved into today's spectacles.

During a bullfight the horse must make precisely timed movements to avoid being gored and to best position its rider for placing the darts. This equestrian science developed out of fighting maneuvers, but over the years has been refined, most notably by the 18th-century Portuguese nobleman, Dom Pedro Alcántara e Meneses, fourth marquis of Marialva. The marquis, who held the rank of Master of the Horse to the Portuguese Court, established the rules that still govern the art of Portuguese equestrian bullfighting.

Bullfighting remained essentially the same in Portugal and Spain until the middle of the 18th century. Its subsequent development into two separate styles, the matador on foot becoming protagonist in Spain and the horseman continuing to play the leading role in Portugal, was due to the disapproval of Bourbon monarch Felipe V, who ascended to the Spanish throne in 1700. The king's French sensibilities were offended by the gore and violence of bullfighting and he soon prohibited the practice. Spain's noblemen were forced to comply. Bullfighting, however, had become too popular to disappear. The horsemen had always been assisted by a retinue of grooms and other helpers, and these lowly workers now took the art over for themselves.

In Spain, the evolution of bullfighting has produced the dramatic figure of the *matador,* a solitary figure who fights a deadly duel with his opponent from a proletarian position, on the ground. In Portugal, however, the aristocratic tradition of the horseman bullfighter has remained intact. The star of the show is the elegantly costumed *cavaleiro,* and the aim of the fight is not to kill the bull but to show off the courtly skills of the horse and its rider. Even today, horseback bullfighters tend to come from the wealthy and aristocratic segments of society, whereas the greatest matadors have typically come from more humble origins.

all the more worthwhile: the food is excellent food. If you're not a guest of the hotel, it's best to make reservations. (Note that the restaurant is closed on Sunday and from mid-August to mid-September.) ✉ *Rua Noel Perdigão 12, 2600,* ☏ *263/271272,* ℻ *263/276538. 19 rooms. Restaurant, bar. MC, V. EP.*

$$ 🏨 **Lezíria Parque Hotel.** This modern, four-story, hotel-and-apartment
★ complex off the main Lisbon–Oporto road is a comfortable base from which to explore the bull- and horse-breeding region across the Rio Tejo. Rooms are small and plainly furnished, but the ground-floor coffee shop is quite pleasant. ✉ *Hwy. N1, Povos 2600,* ☏ *263/276670,* ℻ *263/276990. 71 rooms. Restaurant, coffee shop, bar. AE, DC, MC, V. EP.*

$$ 🏨 **Quinta do Alto.** Once you drive through the massive iron gates of this hotel, you may have a hard time leaving. On 50 choice acres of orchards, gardens, and vineyards in the hills high above the Tejo, just 30 minutes from the Lisbon airport, the Quinta do Alto was once the summer residence of a prominent Portuguese family. Red brick adorns the vaulted ceilings, and the tile floors are enhanced with Arraiolos carpets. ✉ *Estrada de Monte Gordo, 2600-065,* ☏ *263/276850,* ℻ *263/ 276027. 10 rooms, 1 apartment. Tennis court, pool, gym, sauna, squash. AE, DC, MC, V. EP.*

En Route   On the Rio Tejo's east bank, between Vila Franca de Xira and Santarém, is a region of marshy plains and rich pasturelands known as the Lezíria. The area contains many stud farms, where Portugal's best bulls and horses are bred. As you drive through the town of Benavente and the surrounding countryside, look for campinos in the fields working the bulls and horses.

Almeirim

⑬   *40 km (25 mi) northeast of Vila Franca de Xira, 4 km (2½ mi) east of Santarém.*

Almeirim is visited mostly because it has a number of restaurants that serve a local delicacy called *sopa da pedra* (stone soup). It also has a working stud farm and a winery that can be visited.

The **Quinta da Alorna** is a 500-acre farm and winery that was established in 1723 by the Marquês de Alorna, a viceroy of India. You can stop in for tastings (it has marvelous chardonnay) on Friday or Sunday, when the winery is open most of the day. For visits on other days, you must make an appointment. ✉ *EN 118 at Km 73,* ☏ *243/570700.* 🎟 *Tastings: €5. Tours: free.* ☉ *Fri. 9–noon and 2–6, Sun. 9:30–6.*

Santarém

⑭   *7 km (4 mi) northwest of Almeirim.*

Present-day Santarém, high above the Tejo, is an important farming and livestock center. Some historians believe that its beginnings date from as early as 1200 BC and the age of Ulysses. Its strategic location led several kings to choose it as their residence, and the Cortes (parliament) frequently met here. Thanks to its royal connections, Santarém is more richly endowed with monuments than other towns of its size. The Portuguese refer to it as their "Gothic capital."

Walk up to the **Portas do Sol,** a lovely park within the ancient walls. From this vantage point you can look down on a sweeping bend in the river and beyond to the farmlands that stretch into the neighboring Alentejo.

The **Museu de Arte e Arqueologia Medievais–Museu Municipal** (Museum of Medieval Art and Archaeology–Municipal Museum), in the

Romanesque church of São João de Alporão, has interesting relics, including the finely sculpted tomb of Duarte de Meneses, which according to legend contains a single tooth, all that remained of the nobleman after his brutal murder by the Moors in Africa. The museum is directly across from the bell tower known as the Torre das Cabaças. ⊠ *Rua Figueiredo Leal,* ☎ *243/304462.* ⌨ *€2.* ⊙ *Tues.–Wed. and weekends 9:30–12:30 and 2–5:30, Thurs.–Fri. 10–12:30 and 2–5:30.*

The 14th-century, Gothic **Igreja da Graça** (Graça Church) contains the gravestone of Pedro Álvares Cabral, the discoverer of Brazil. There's also a tomb of the explorer in Belmonte, the town of his birth, but no one is really sure just what (or who) is in which tomb. Note the delicate rose window whose setting was carved from a single slab of stone. ⊠ *Largo Pedro Álvares Cabral,* ☎ *no phone.* ⊙ *Tues.–Wed. and weekends 9:30–12:30 and 2–5:30; Thurs.–Fri. 10–12:30 and 2–5:30.*

Dining and Lodging

$$ ✗ **Adiafa.** Excellent grilled meats and good service are the norm at this large typically Ribatejo restaurant by the bullring. In winter, a fire in the fireplace may well welcome you. ⊠ *Campo da Feira,* ☎ *243/ 324086. No credit cards. Closed Tues.*

$$ ✗ **Taberna da Quinzena.** Photos of patrons vie for your attention with bullfighting posters at this restaurant in a former house. It's run by the great-grandson of the original owner. Specialties include spareribs and açorda *com bacalhau assado* (with roast codfish). ⊠ *Rua Pedro de Santarém 93,* ☎ *243/322804. No credit cards.*

$$ ⌂ **Quinta de Vale de Lobos.** Trees, gardens, and ponds surround this two-story, 19th-century farmhouse 6 km (4 mi) from Santarém. You can lounge in the large, comfortable living rooms and stroll in the adjacent woods; you also have access to a 600-acre hunting estate. The generously sized bedrooms and apartments are comfortably furnished. ⊠ *Hwy. N3, Azoia de Baixo 2000,* ☎ *243/429264,* ⠛ *243/429313. 4 rooms, 2 apartments. Pool. No credit cards. EP.*

$–$$ ⌂ **Corinthia Santarém Hotel.** Rooms at this contemporary hotel overlook the plains or the town. Some rooms have balconies, complimentary morning newspapers, and bathrobes; all are equipped with such gadgets as hair dryers, alarm clocks, and trousers presses. ⊠ *Av. Madre Andaluz, 2000-210,* ☎ *243/309500,* ⠛ *243/309509,* ⬚ *www. corinthiahotels.com. 105 rooms, 5 suites. Restaurant, coffee shop, snack bar, room service, in-room safes, minibars, cable TV with movies, 3 pools (1 indoor), health club, sauna, bar, lounge, laundry service, meeting rooms, airport shuttle, free parking. AE, DC, MC, V. EP.*

$ ⌂ **Beirante.** The Beirante is near Santarém's historic center, with easy access to the toll road. Accommodations here are plain but comfortable; room rates are truly budget. ⊠ *Rua Alexandre Herculano 5, 2000-149,* ☎ *243/322547,* ⠛ *243/333845. 32 rooms. No credit cards. EP.*

Alpiarça

⑮ *10 km (6 mi) northeast of Santarém.*

Alpiarça is a pleasant little town where you'll have the chance to see how a wealthy country gentleman lived at the beginning of this century. The **Casa dos Patudos,** now a museum, was the estate of José Relvas, a diplomat and gentleman farmer. This unusual three-story manor house with its zebra-striped spire is surrounded by gardens and vineyards and filled with an impressive assemblage of ceramics, paintings, and furnishings—including Portugal's foremost collection of Arraiolos carpets. ⊠ *On N118,* ☎ *243/558321.* ⌨ *€2.50.* ⊙ *Tues.–Sun. 10– noon and 2–5.*

En Route   About 20 km (12 mi) northeast of Alpiarça, on the way to Torres Novas, is the town of Golegã, one of Portugal's most notable horse-breeding centers. During the first two weeks of November, this is the site of the colorful Feira Nacional do Cavalo (National Horse Fair), the most important event of its kind in the country. It has riding displays, horse competitions, and stalls that sell handicrafts.

Torres Novas

⑯ *39 km (24 mi) northwest of Alpiarça.*

Torres Novas is best known for its crenellated, 14th-century hilltop **castelo,** which encloses a delightful garden. At the foot of the structure stands a caricature statue of Dom Sancho I—son and royal successor of Afonso Henriques—created by João Cutiliero, a prominent contemporary sculptor.

Dining and Lodging

$ ✕🏨 **Hotel dos Cavaleiros.** Facing the main square, this modern three-story hotel blends in well with the surrounding 18th-century buildings. Rooms are of a decent size and have plain, light-wood furnishings; ask for one on the third floor with a terrace. In spite of its sterile, coffee-shop appearance, the restaurant ($) serves generous portions of well-prepared traditional dishes. Try the *espetada mista* (grilled pork, squid, and shrimp on a spit). ✉ *Praça 5 de Outubro, 2350-418,* ☎ *249/819370,* 📠 *249/819379. 57 rooms, 3 suites. Restaurant, bar, free parking. AE, DC, MC, V. EP.*

Fátima

⑰ *20 km (12 mi) northwest of Torres Vedras, 16 km (10 mi) southeast of Batalha, 20 km (12 mi) southeast of Leiria.*

On the western flanks of the Serra de Aire lies Fátima, an important Roman Catholic pilgrimage site that is, ironically, named after the daughter of Mohammed, the prophet of Islam. If you visit this sleepy little Portuguese town in between pilgrimages, it will be difficult to imagine the thousands of faithful who come from all corners of the world to make this religious affirmation, cramming the roads, squares, parks, and virtually every square foot of space. Many of the pilgrims go the last miles on their knees.

When Pope John Paul II visited in 1991, it was estimated that more than 1 million people flocked to Fátima. Where there are so many people, there are bound to be opportunists, and Fátima is no exception—as shown by places like the "Virgin Mary Souvenir Shop" and the "Pope John Paul II Snack Bar."

It all began on May 13, 1917, when three young shepherds—Lucia dos Santos and her cousins Francisco and Jacinta—reported seeing the Virgin Mary in a field at Cova de Iria, near the village. The Virgin promised to return on the 13th of each month for the next five months, and amid much controversy and skepticism, each time accompanied by increasingly larger crowds, the three children reported successive apparitions. This was during a period of anticlerical sentiment in Portugal, and after the sixth reputed apparition, in October, the children were arrested and interrogated. But they insisted the Virgin had spoken to them, revealing three secrets. Two of these, revealed by Lucia in 1941, were interpreted to foretell the coming of World War II and the spread of communism and atheism. In a 1930 Pastoral Letter, the Bishop of Leiria declared the apparitions worthy of belief, thus approving the "Cult of Fátima."

In May 2000, Francisco and Jacinta were beatified in a ceremony held at Fátima by Pope John Paul II. Lucia is still alive and is a Carmelite nun. The third secret, which was revealed after the beatification, foretold an attempt on the life of the Pope. On the 13th of each month, and especially in May and October, the faithful flock here to witness the passing of the statue of the Virgin through the throngs, to participate in candlelight processions, and to take part in solemn masses.

At the head of the huge esplanade is the large, neoclassical **basílica** (built in the late 1920s), flanked on either side by a semicircular peristyle. ✉ *Albergaria Nossa Senhora das Dores,* ☎ *249/539600,* WEB *www.santuario-fatima.pt.* 🖷 *Free.* ◷ *Easter–Oct., 7:30 AM–9 PM; Nov.–Easter 7:30 AM–8 PM.*

The **Capela das Aparições** (Chapel of Apparitions) is built where the appearances of the Virgin Mary are said to have taken place. A marble pillar and statue of the Virgin mark the exact spot. ✉ *Albergaria Nossa Senhora das Dores,* ☎ *249/539600,* WEB *www.santuario-fatima. pt.* 🖷 *Free.* ◷ *Easter–Oct. 7:30 AM–9 PM; Nov.–Easter 7:30 AM–8 PM.*

☉ The **Museu de Cera** (Wax Museum), in the center of town, has 30 tableaux depicting the events that took place in Fátima when the little shepherds first saw the apparitions. ✉ *Rua Jacinto Marto,* ☎ *249/ 539300,* WEB *www.mucefa.pt.* 🖷 *€4.* ◷ *Apr.–Oct., daily 9:30–6:30; Nov.–Mar., daily 10–5.*

The **Casa dos Pastorinhos** is a cottage in the nearby hamlet of Aljustrel, where the three shepherd children who saw the Virgin Mary were born. To reach it, turn off Avenida Papa João XXIII and take the N356 to Aljustrel. The cottage is looked after by a local family and has no set opening hours. To be safe, visit before lunch or early in the afternoon.

☉ The hills to the south and west of Fátima are honeycombed with limestone **caves.** Within about a 25-km (15-mi) radius of town are four major caverns—São Mamede, Mira de Aire, Alvados, and Santo António—equipped with lights and elevators. Here you can see the subterranean world of limestone formations, underground rivers and lakes, and multicolor stalagmites and stalactites. The Fátima tourist office can assist you with further details, including open hours, which vary by season. ☎ *244/704302 to São Mamede; 244/440322 to Mira de Aire; 244/440787 to Alvados; 249/841876 to Santo António.* 🖷 *€4 to each cavern.*

Dining and Lodging

$$–$$$ ✕ **Retiro dos Caçadores.** A big brick fireplace, wood paneling, and stone walls set the mood in this cozy hunter's lodge, where the food is simple, but portions are hearty and the quality good. This is the best place in town for fresh game, especially coelho *com arroz* (with rice) and *perdiz* (partridge). ✉ *Lombo Egua,* ☎ *249/531323. MC, V. Closed Wed.*

$$–$$$ ✕ **Tia Alice.** Considered the area's best restaurant, Tia (Aunt) Alice is
★ concealed in an inconspicuous old house with French windows, across from the parish church near the sanctuary at Cova de Iria. A flight of wooden stairs inside leads to an intimate dining area with a wood-beam ceiling and stone walls. The cabrito assado is worth trying as is the *Tia Alice especial* (codfish with béchamel sauce and shrimp), which serves two. ✉ *Rua do Adro,* ☎ *249/531737. AE, DC, MC, V. Closed Mon. and July. No dinner Sun.*

$$ 🏨 **Hotel de Fátima.** The closest hotel to the sanctuary is a modern four-story structure, generally considered Fátima's top lodging establishment. Light-wood furniture complements royal blue fabrics in the guest rooms, which have many amenities. ✉ *Rua João Paulo II (Apartado 11, 2496-908),* ☎ *249/533351,* FAX *249/532691,* WEB *www.hotelfatima.*

com. 126 rooms, 7 suites. Restaurant, cable TV, minibars, bar, shops, meeting rooms, free parking. AE, DC, MC, V. EP.

$ 🖬 **Casa Beato Nuno.** This large pink-stucco inn just a few minutes' walk from the sanctuary, is run by the Carmelites but is open to visitors of all faiths. The austere rooms are clean and comfortable. ⊠ *Av. Beato Nuno 51, 2496,* ☎ ℻ *249/530230. 136 rooms. Restaurant. MC, V. EP.*

Tomar

⓲ *24 km (15 mi) east of Fátima, 20 km (12 mi) northeast of Torres Novas.*

Tomar is an attractive town laid out on both sides of the Rio Nabão, with the new and old parts linked by a graceful, arched stone bridge. The river flows through a lovely park with weeping willows and an old wooden waterwheel.

In the Old Town, walk along the narrow, flower-lined streets, particularly Rua Dr. Joaquim Jacinto, which takes you to the heart of the Jewish Quarter and the modest **Museu–Sinagoga Luso-Hebraico Abraham Zacuto Sinagoga de Tomar.** Built in the mid-15th century, this is Portugal's oldest synagogue, though it's no longer used as such. Inside is a small museum with exhibits chronicling the Jewish presence in the country. The once-sizable community was considerably reduced in 1496 when Dom Manuel issued an edict ordering the Jews either to leave the country or convert to Christianity. Many, who became known as *marranos,* converted but secretly practiced their original religion. ⊠ *Rua Dr. Joaquim Jacinto,* ☎ *249/322427.* 🖃 *Donations accepted.* ☉ *Daily 10–1 and 2–6.*

★ Atop a hill rising from the Old Town is the remarkable **Convento de Cristo** (Convent of Christ). You can drive to the top of the hill or hike for about 20 minutes along a path through the trees before reaching a formal garden lined with azulejo-covered benches. This was the Portuguese headquarters of the Knights Templar, from 1160 until the order was forced to disband in 1314. Identified by their white tunics emblazoned with a crimson cross, the Templars were at the forefront of the Christian armies in the Crusades and during the struggles against the Moors. King Dinis in 1334 resurrected the order in Portugal under the banner of the Knights of Christ and reestablished Tomar as its headquarters. In the early 15th century, under Prince Henry the Navigator (who for a time resided in the castle), the order flourished. The caravels of the era of discovery even sailed under the order's crimson cross.

The oldest parts of the complex date from the 12th century, including the towering castle keep and the fortresslike, 16-sided Charola, which, like many Templar churches, is patterned after the Church of the Holy Sepulchre in Jerusalem and has an octagonal oratory at its core. The paintings and wooden statues in its interior, however, were added in the 16th century. The complex's medieval nucleus acquired its Manueline church and cluster of magnificent cloisters during the next 500 years. To see what the Manueline style is all about, stroll through the church's nave with its many examples of the twisted ropes, seaweed, and nautical themes that typify the style, and be sure to look at the chapter house window, probably the most photographed one in Europe. Its lichen-encrusted sculpture evokes the spirit of the great Age of Discovery. ☎ *249/313481.* 🖃 *€3.* ☉ *May–Sept., daily 9–6; Oct.–Apr., daily 9–5:30.*

In the gardens by the Rio Nabão there's an enormous working **waterwheel.** It's typical of those once used in the region for irrigation and thought to be of either Arabic or Roman origin. ⊠ *Av. Marquês Tomar.*

Across the Rio Nabão is the 13th-century **Igreja de Santa Maria do Olival,** where the bones of several Templar knights are interred, including those of Gualdim Pais, founder of the order in Portugal. Popular belief—supported by some archaeological evidence—has it that the church was once connected with the Convent of Christ by a tunnel. ⊠ *Rua Prof. Andrade,* ☎ *no phone.* 🎫 *Free.* ⊘ *Weekdays 10–5, weekends 11–5.*

In Pegões, some 5 km (3 mi) northwest of Tomar, is a 5-km-long (3-mi-long) **aqueduct,** built in the 16th century to bring water to Tomar. It joins the walls of the Convento de Cristo.

Dining and Lodging

$–$$ ✕ **A Bela Vista.** The date on the calçada reads "1922," which was when
★ the Sousa family opened this attractive little restaurant next to the old arched bridge. For summer dining there's a small, rustic terrace with views of the river and the Convento de Cristo. Carrying on the family tradition, Eugenio Sousa presides over the kitchen, which turns out great quantities of hearty regional fare. Try the cabrito assado or the *dobrada com feijão* (tripe with beans), and wash it down with a robust local red wine. ⊠ *Rua Marquês de Pombal 68,* ☎ *249/312870. No credit cards. Closed Tues. No dinner Mon.*

$$ ✕🏨 **Hotel dos Templários.** A large, modern hotel in a tranquil park along
★ the Rio Nabão, the Templários has many units with views of the Convento de Cristo. The big, airy dining room ($$) has picture windows facing the park and serves interesting regional dishes. With its spacious grounds, reasonable rates, and many amenities, the hotel makes a good base for exploring the whole area. ⊠ *Largo Candido dos Reis 1, 2304-909,* ☎ *249/310100,* ᖴᴬˣ *249/322191,* ᴡᴱᴮ *www.hoteldostemplarios.pt. 171 rooms, 5 suites. Restaurant, in-room safes, minibars, cable TV, tennis court, 3 pools (1 indoor), hair salon, health club, hot tub, sauna, billiards, bar, video game room, baby-sitting, playground, meeting rooms, free parking, no-smoking rooms. AE, DC, MC, V. EP.*

$$ ✕🏨 **Pousada de São Pedro.** Built in 1946 to house engineers building
★ the dam on the Rio Zêzere, this pousada overlooks a man-made lake that fans out northward near the town of Castelo de Bode. It's on a wooded hill 13 km (8 mi) from Tomar on the N358 and in one of Portugal's most popular water-sports areas. The restaurant ($$–$$$) serves high-quality regional fare. ⊠ *Castelo de Bode 2300,* ☎ *249/ 381159,* ᖴᴬˣ *249/381176,* ᴡᴱᴮ *www.pousadas.pt. 25 rooms. Restaurant, minibars, bar. AE, DC, MC, V. BP.*

Castelo de Almourol

★ ⑲ *16 km (10 mi) south of Tomar, 16 km (10 mi) east of Torres Novas.*

For a close look at the **Castelo de Almourol,** a storybook edifice on a craggy island in the Rio Tejo, take the 1½-km-long (1-mi-long) dirt road leading down to the water. The riverbank in this area is practically deserted, making it a wonderful picnic spot. (In summer you can take a boat to the island.) It could hardly be more romantic: an ancient castle with crenellated walls and a lofty tower sits on a greenery-covered rock in the middle of a gently flowing river. The stuff of poetry and legends, Almourol was the setting for Francisco de Morais's epic *Palmeirim da Inglaterra* (*Palmeirim of England*).

Dining

$–$$ ✕ **Restaurante Almourol.** A good lunch stop on the N3, this restaurant is in a lovely old house with gardens, orange trees, and a terrace overlooking the castle. It specializes in river fish dishes, especially savel (shad) and enguias. ⊠ *Av. Cais de Tancos, Vila Nova da Barquinha,* ☎ *249/720100. AE, DC, MC, V.*

Constância

⑳ *4 km (2½ mi) east of Castelo de Almourol.*

Peaceful little Constância is at the confluence of the Zêzere and the Tejo. It's best known as the town where Luís de Camões was exiled in 1548, the unfortunate result of his romantic involvement with Catarina de Ataide, the "Natercia" of his poems and a lady-in-waiting to Queen Catarina. There's a bronze statue of the bard in a reflective pose at the riverbank.

Dining and Lodging

$ ★ ✕🏨 **Quinta de Santa Barbara.** If you're looking for a place to immerse yourself in the Portuguese countryside, look no farther. The Quinta, a short drive from town, has several sprawling buildings—a few of which date from the 16th century—on some 45 acres of farmland and pine forests overlooking the Tejo. Each of the six spacious rooms in the main house is individually decorated with 18th-century Portuguese reproductions and has a modern tiled bathroom. The small restaurant ($$), with a barrel-vault ceiling and stone walls, specializes in local dishes. ✉ *2 km (1 mi) east of Constância on IP6; follow directions on sign at traffic circle, 2250,* ☎ *249/739214,* FAX *249/739373. 6 rooms. Restaurant, tennis court, pool, horseback riding, bar. MC, V. EP.*

Abrantes

㉑ *16 km (10 mi) east of Constância.*

Abrantes became one of the country's most populous and prosperous towns during the 16th century, when the Rio Tejo was navigable all the way to the sea. With the coming of the railroad and the development of better roads, the town's commercial importance waned. Walk up through the maze of narrow, flower-lined streets to the 16th-century **castelo.** Much of it is in disrepair, but with a bit of imagination you can conjure visions of what an impressive structure this must have been. The attractive garden that has been planted between the twin fortifications is a wonderful place to watch the sun set: the play of light on the river and the lengthening shadows along the olive groves provide an stirring setting for an evening picnic.

Dining and Lodging

$–$$ ✕🏨 **Hotel de Turismo.** The hotel's hilltop location is so spectacular that it's a shame the architect couldn't have come up with something more innovative than an exterior of pink stucco. Inside is a different story: there's an inviting, clubby lounge with a fireplace and comfy leather chairs. Guest rooms are small but comfortable; some have terraces with wonderful vistas. The dining room ($–$$$) also has intoxicating views and is an excellent place to sample *palha de Abrantes* (straw of Abrantes), a dessert consisting of a thick egg and almond paste topped with yellow threadlike wisps made of eggs and sugar. ✉ *Largo de Santo António, 2200-349,* ☎ *241/361271,* FAX *241/325218,* WEB *www. hotelabrantes.pt. 41 rooms. Restaurant, room service, minibars, cable TV, 2 tennis courts, pool, bar, laundry service, meeting rooms, free parking, no-smoking rooms. AE, DC, MC, V. BP.*

Sardoal

㉒ *12 km (7 mi) north of Abrantes on N244-3, 20 km (12 mi) northeast of Constância on N358-2.*

Sardoal, an island of white houses with yellow trim and red-tile roofs in a sea of wooded hills, is an enchanting place of narrow streets paved with pebbles from nearby streams. There seems to be flowers everywhere—hanging from windows and balconies and lining the winding lanes and alleys. In such a spot you might expect art to flourish, and the 17th-century parish church *does* contain a collection of fine 16th-century paintings by the "Master of Sardoal," an unknown painter whose works have been found in other parts of the country and whose influence on other artists has been noted.

Castelo de Belver

㉓   *30 km (19 mi) southeast of Sardoal. Follow N244-3 through the pine-covered hills to Chão de Codes; take N244 south toward Gavião.*

A fairy-tale castle planted on top of a cone-shape hill, the fortress of Belver was built in the last years of the 12th century by the Knights Hospitallers under the command of King Sancho I. The castle commands a superb view of the Tejo. In 1194 this region was threatened by the Moorish forces who controlled the lands south of the river, except for Évora. The expected attack never took place, and the present structure is little changed from its original design. The walls of the keep, which stands in the center of the courtyard, are some 12 ft thick, and on the ground floor is a great cistern of unknown depth. According to local lore, an orange dropped into the well will later appear bobbing down the river.

ESTREMADURA AND THE RIBATEJO A TO Z

To research prices, get advice from other travelers, and book travel arrangements, visit www.fodors.com.

AIR TRAVEL

Estremadura and the Ribatejo are served by Lisbon's Aeroporto de Portela, 7 km (5 mi) north of the city.
➤ AIRPORT INFORMATION: **Aeroporto de Portela** (☎ 21/841–3500 or 21/841–3700).

BUS TRAVEL

There are few, if any, places in this region that aren't served by at least one bus daily. Express coaches run by several regional lines travel regularly between Lisbon and the larger towns such as Santarém, Leiria, and Abrantes. If you have the time and patience, bus travel is an inexpensive way to get around. It's best to do your booking through a travel agent.
➤ BUS COMPANY: **Rede Nacional de Expressos** (☎ 707/223344).
➤ BUS STATIONS: **Fátima** (✉ Av. D. José Alves Correia Silva, ☎ 249/531611). **Leiria** (✉ Av. Herois de Angola, ☎ 244/811507). **Santarém** (✉ Av. Brasil 41, ☎ 243/333200). **Tomar** (✉ Varzea Grande, ☎ 249/9312738).

CAR RENTAL

There are major car-rental agencies in Leiria and Nazaré, as well as in Lisbon.
➤ MAJOR AGENCIES: **Avis** (☎ 262/561928 in Nazaré). **Hertz** (☎ 244/826781 in Leiria).

CAR TRAVEL

It's easy to reach Estremadura and the Ribatejo from Lisbon, since both provinces begin as extensions of the city's northern suburbs. There are two principal access roads from the capital: the A1 (also called E80 and IP1), which is the Lisbon–Oporto toll road, provides the best inland access; the A8 (also called IC1) is the fastest route to the coast. From Oporto there's easy access via the A1 tollway.

The roads are generally good, and traffic is light, except for weekend congestion along the coast. There are no confusing big cities in which to get lost, although parking can be a problem in some of the towns. However, drive with extreme caution. Affable as they are on foot, the Portuguese are among Europe's most aggressive drivers.

EMERGENCIES

All sizable towns have at least one pharmacy open weekends, holidays, and after normal store hours. Local newspapers usually keep a schedule, and notices are posted on the door of every pharmacy.

➤ EMERGENCY SERVICES: **General emergencies** (☎ 112).

➤ HOSPITALS: **Caldas da Rainha Hospital Distrital** (✉ Rua Diário de Notícias, ☎ 262/830300). **Leiria Hospital Distrital** (✉ Largo D. Mel. Aguiar, ☎ 244/817000). **Tomar Hospital Distrital** (✉ Av. Dr. Candido Madureira, ☎ 249/321100).

MAIL

➤ POST OFFICES: **Fátima** (✉ Rua Conago Dr. M. Formigão, ☎ 249/539080). **Leiria** (✉ Rua Sá de Miranda, Lote 1, ☎ 244/830980). **Tomar** (✉ Av. Marquês de Tomar, ☎ 249/323094).

TELEPHONES

Area codes in the region include 262 for Caldas da Rainha, 249 for Fátima, 244 for Leiria, 243 for Santarém, and 249 for Tomar.

DIRECTORY AND OPERATOR ASSISTANCE

For information, dial 118; operators often speak English.

TOURS AND PACKAGES

ORIENTATION TOURS

Few regularly scheduled sightseeing tours originate within the region, but many of the major attractions are covered by a wide selection of one-day tours from Lisbon. For information contact Gray Line Tours or Citirama.

➤ CONTACTS: **Citirama** (✉ Av. Praia da Vitória 12-B, Saldanha, Lisbon, ☎ 21/355–8564). **Gray Line Tours** (✉ Av. Praia da Vitória 12-B, Saldanha, Lisbon, ☎ 21/352–2594).

BOAT TOURS

Boat trips along the Rio Zêzere, depart at noon in summer from a dock at the Estalagem Lago Azul, upstream from the Castelo de Bode dam. The four-hour cruises cost €37 including a buffet lunch with wine, but they take place only when there are enough passengers; this is most likely to happen on weekends and national holidays. For reservations and information, contact Hotel dos Templários in Tomar.

➤ CONTACTS: **Estalagem Lago Azul** (✉ Hwy. N378, Ferreira do Zêzere, Castanheira, ☎ 249/361445). **Hotel dos Templários** (✉ Largo Candido dos Reis 1, Tomar, ☎ 249/310100).

TRAIN TRAVEL

Travel by train within central Portugal isn't for people in a hurry. Service to many of the more remote destinations is infrequent—and in some cases nonexistent. Even major attractions such as Nazaré and Mafra have no direct rail links. Nevertheless, trains will take you to most of the strategic bases for touring the towns in this chapter.

The Lisbon–Oporto line (Santa Apolónia station) provides reasonably frequent service to Vila Franca de Xira, Santarém, Torres Novas, Tomar, and Fátima. Towns in the western part of the region, such as

Torres Vedras, Caldas da Rainha, Óbidos, and Leiria, are served on another line from Lisbon's Rossío station.

If your Portuguese is good you can try calling one of the general information lines of the Caminhos de Ferro Portugueses (CP) for schedule and other information. Otherwise, you're better off checking out the CP Web site.

➤ TRAIN INFORMATION: **CP** (☎ 21/888–4025, 800/200904, or 808/208208, WEB www.cp.pt).

TRAVEL AGENCIES

Many travel agencies in the region are small, with limited services and no one who speaks English. However, Meliá Europa, in Leiria, has English-speaking personnel and a full range of services.

➤ CONTACT: **Meliá Europa** (✉ Av. Cidade Maringá 25, Leiria, ☎ 244/833850).

VISITOR INFORMATION

ESTREMADURA

➤ TOURIST OFFICES: **Alcobaça** (✉ Praça 25 de Abril, ☎ 262/582377). **Batalha** (✉ Praça Mouzinho de Albuquerque, ☎ 244/765180). **Caldas da Rainha** (✉ Rua Eng. Duarte Pacheco, ☎ 262/831003). **Ericeira** (✉ Rua Eduardo Burnay 46, ☎ 261/863668). **Leiria** (✉ Jardim Luís de Camões, ☎ 244/823773). **Mafra** (✉ Av. 25 de Abril, ☎ 261/812023). **Nazaré** (✉ Av. República 17, ☎ 262/561194). **Óbidos** (✉ outside town walls, at entrance to parking lot, ☎ 262/959231). **Peniche** (✉ Rua Alex. Herculano, ☎ 262/789571). **Torres Vedras** (✉ Rua 9 de Abril, ☎ 261/314094).

THE RIBATEJO

➤ TOURIST OFFICES: **Abrantes** (✉ Largo 1 de Maio, ☎ 241/362555). **Constância** (✉ Câmara Municipal, ☎ 249/730050). **Fátima** (✉ Av. José A. Correia da Silva, ☎ 249/531139). **Santarém** (✉ Rua Capelo e Ivens 63, ☎ 243/391512). **Tomar** (✉ Rua Serpa Pinto 1, ☎ 249/329000). **Torres Novas** (✉ Largo dos Combatentes da Segunda Guerra Mundial, ☎ 249/813019). **Vila Franca de Xira** (✉ Rua Almirante Cándido dos Reis 147, ☎ 263/276053).

5 ÉVORA AND THE ALENTEJO

Known as the granary of Portugal, the
Alentejo is a thinly populated, largely
agricultural region of grainfields and cork
and olive trees. The landscape ranges from
the breezy Atlantic beaches of the littoral to
the fortress-crowned hills and rolling plains
of the dry, inland areas. Ancient Évora, at
the center of the region, is rich in history and
architectural treasures.

THE ALENTEJO, WHICH MEANS "THE LAND BEYOND THE RIO TEJO (Tagus River)" in Portuguese, is a vast, sparsely populated area of heath and rolling hills punctuated with stands of cork and olive trees. It's the country's largest region, stretching from the rugged west-coast beaches all the way east to Spain and from the Tejo in the north to the low mountains on the border of the Algarve, Portugal's southernmost region. Its central hub, Évora, is rich with traditional Portuguese architecture. Over the centuries the pastoral countryside has been the scene of innumerable battles: between Romans and Visigoths, Moors and Christians, Portuguese and Spaniards, Portuguese and French, and finally (in the 1830s) between rival Portuguese factions in a civil war. Few hilltops in the region are without at least a trace of a castle or fortress.

Updated by Emmy de la Cal, Justine de la Cal, Martha de la Cal, and Peter Collis

One of the Alentejo's major industries is cork, of which Portugal is the world's largest producer. This is not, however, an industry for people in a hurry. It takes two decades before the trees can be harvested, and they can be carefully stripped only once every nine years. The numbers painted on the trees indicate the year of the last harvest. Exhibits at several regional museums chronicle this delicate process and display associated tools and handicrafts.

The undulating fields of wheat and barley surrounding Beja and Évora, the rice paddies of Alcácer do Sal, and the vineyards of Borba and Reguengos de Monsaraz are representative of this region, Portugal's breadbasket. Traditions here are strong. Herdsmen tending sheep and goats wear the *pelico* (traditional sheepskin vest), and women in the fields wear broad-brim hats over kerchiefs and colorful, patterned dresses over trousers. Dwellings are dazzling white; more elegant houses have wrought-iron balconies and grillwork. The windows and doors of modest cottages and hilltop country *montes* (farmhouses) are trimmed with blue or yellow, and colorful flowers abound. The best time to visit the Alentejo is spring, when temperatures are pleasant and the fields are carpeted with wildflowers. Summer can be brutal, with the mercury frequently topping 37°C (100°F). As the Portuguese say, "In the Alentejo there is no shade but what comes from the sky."

Pleasures and Pastimes

Beaches

Some of Europe's finest and least crowded beaches are on the rugged stretch of Portugal's west coast that extends from the southern extreme of the Alentejo at Odeceixe north to the tip of the Tróia Peninsula. Some beaches—such as Praia do Carvalhal and Praia Grande at Almograve—don't have any facilities and are uncrowded even in July and August, when most of Europe's shores are packed elbow to elbow. You can also find solitude by heading west on unmarked tracks along the coast. The beaches at Vila Nova de Milfontes and at Porto Covo have restaurants and the usual beach facilities. Exercise great care when swimming on the west coast: the surf is often high, and strong undertows and riptides are common.

Castles

In much of the Alentejo, you can't drive far without seeing a castle or a fortress crowning one of the hills. Some, such as the castles at Estremoz and Alvito, have been restored and converted into luxurious *pousadas* (government-run inns). Others, including those at Castelo de Vide and Viana do Alentejo, are open for you to clamber about their battlements.

Dining

In the Alentejo, the country's granary, bread is a major part of most meals. It's the basis of a popular dish known as *açorda,* a thick, stick-to-the-ribs porridge to which various ingredients such as fish, meat, and eggs are added. Açorda *de marisco*—bread with eggs, seasonings, and assorted shellfish—is one of the more popular varieties. Another version, açorda *alentejana,* consists of a clear broth, olive oil, garlic, slices of bread, and poached eggs.

Pork from the Alentejo is the best in the country and often is combined with clams, onions, and tomatoes in the classic dish *carne de porco à alentejana.* One of Portugal's most renowned sheep's milk cheeses—tangy, but mellow when properly ripened—is made in the Serpa region. Elvas, near the Spanish border, is known for its tasty sugar plums. Alentejo wines—especially those from around Borba and Reguengos de Monsaraz—are regular prizewinners at national tasting contests.

Between mid-June and mid-September reservations are advised at upscale restaurants. Many moderate or inexpensive establishments, however, don't accept reservations and have informal dining rooms where you share a table with other diners. Dress at all but the most luxurious restaurants is casual; any exceptions to the dress code or reservation policy are noted in the reviews.

CATEGORY	COST*
$$$$	over €21
$$$	€14–€21
$$	€7–€14
$	under €7

*per person for a main course at dinner

Horseback Riding

The sparse population and minimal automobile traffic make this region a delight for equestrian outings. Whether for a few hours or a few days, you'll get an authentic perspective of the Alentejo on horseback. Overnight tours are organized, with lodging at bed-and-breakfasts and meals both on the trail and at local restaurants. Trails provide a variety of backdrops—including castles, villages, and prehistoric sites.

Lodging

The best accommodations in this region are the pousadas. Indeed, some of the finest in the country are in the Alentejo, including one in the old Lóios convent in Évora and another in the castle at Estremoz. Many of the pousadas are small, some with as few as six rooms, so reserving well in advance is essential. There are also a number of high-quality, government-approved private guest houses in the region. Look for signs that say TURISMO RURAL or TURISMO DE HABITAÇÃO.

CATEGORY	COST*
$$$$	over €275
$$$	€175–€275
$$	€75–€175
$	under €75

*For a standard double room, including tax, in high season (off-season rates may be lower).

Shopping

The brightly colored hand-painted plates, bowls, and figurines from the upper Alentejo are popular throughout Portugal. The best selection of this distinctive type of folk art is in and around Estremoz, where the terra-cotta jugs and bowls are adorned with chips of marble from local quarries. Saturday morning the *rossio* (town square) is chock-full of vendors displaying their wares. Redondo and the village of São Pedro do Corval, near Reguengos de Monsaraz, are also good sources of this type of pottery, as is Évora. The village of Arraiolos, near Évora, is famous for its hand-embroidered wool rugs.

Swimming

In addition to swimming in the ocean at the many beaches along the west coast, many towns have modern municipal swimming pools—so even in the middle of the dry Alentejo, you'll never be very far from a refreshing dip. Water sports are also available, unlikely as it may seem, on some of the region's artificial reservoirs.

Exploring Évora and the Alentejo

The Alentejo, Portugal's largest region, contains a wide variety of attractions—from the rugged west-coast beaches to the architectural treasures of Évora. The area is divided roughly into two parts: the more mountainous region north of Évora, and the flatter Lower Alentejo, in the southern part of the region.

Great Itineraries

You can make convenient loops starting and finishing in Lisbon, or you can extend your travels by continuing south to the Algarve from Beja or Santiago do Cacém. You should allow 10 days to get a feel for the region, exploring Évora and visiting some outlying attractions such as Monsaraz, Castelo de Vide, and Mértola. This will also allow time for a day or two of sunbathing on a west-coast beach. If you skip the beach, you can cover the most interesting attractions at a comfortable pace in seven days. Three days will give you time to explore Évora and its surroundings along with one or two additional highlights.

Numbers in the text correspond to numbers in the margin and on the Évora, the Upper Alentejo, and the Lower Alentejo maps.

IF YOU HAVE 3 DAYS

Be sure to include ⊞ **Évora** ①–⑱, one of Portugal's most beautiful cities, in your first day of exploring. The following morning visit the rug-producing town of **Arraiolos** ㉒ and then continue on to **Estremoz** ㉖ and its imposing fortress, which doubles as a pousada. Head east past Borba and its marble quarries to **Vila Viçosa** ㉕, site of the Paço Ducal. Then continue south to the whitewashed village of ⊞ **Terena** ㉔. In the morning visit the fortified hilltop town of **Monsaraz** ㉓ before returning to Lisbon.

IF YOU HAVE 7 DAYS

From Lisbon head for ⊞ **Évora** ①–⑱. The next day explore the **Aqueduto da Agua da Prata** ⑲ and the prehistoric sites just outside town, which include the **Cromlech and the Menhir of Almendres** ⑳ and the **Dolmen of Zambujeiro** ㉑. On the way to ⊞ **Estremoz** ㉖, stop at **Arraiolos** ㉒. From Estremoz head east to the fortified town of ⊞ **Elvas** ㉘, stopping en route at the Paço Ducal in **Vila Viçosa** ㉕. The following day continue to **Monsaraz** ㉓, with a stop along the way at **Terena** ㉔. From Monsaraz head south to ⊞ **Beja** ㊲, inspecting the Roman ruins at **São Cucufate** ㉟ en route. The next day head west to ⊞ **Santiago do Cacém** ㊶ for more Roman ruins and a few hours at the beach. On your seventh day return to Lisbon, stopping along the way to see the castle at **Alcácer do Sal** ㊷.

IF YOU HAVE 10 DAYS

Spend two nights in ⊞ **Évora** ①–⑱ to visit the town and its **Aqueduto da Agua da Prata** ⑲, the nearby prehistoric sites of **Cromlech and the Menhir of Almendres** ⑳ and the **Dolmen of Zambujeiro** ㉑, and neigh-

The Upper Alentejo

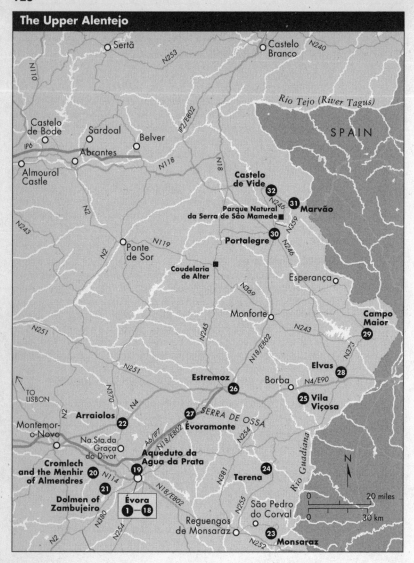

boring **Arraiolos** ㉒. Then head for ⊞ **Estremoz** ㉖, with a stop along the way to visit the castle and enjoy the view at **Évoramonte** ㉗. The next morning head north to the Coudelaria de Alter outside Alter do Chão. Continue north and then west to ⊞ **Castelo de Vide** ㉜, a friendly, whitewashed town known for its spa and healing waters. From here you can visit ⊞ **Marvão** ㉛, a fortified cliff-top town, and the Parque Natural da Serra de São Mamede.

From Marvão drive south through the low mountains of the Serra de São Mamede to **Portalegre** ㉚. Spend a few hours here and continue to ⊞ **Elvas** ㉘, with its extensive fortifications and Manueline cathedral. Stop en route at **Campo Maior** ㉙, a town distinguished by its hilltop castle and tiny whitewashed houses with wrought-iron grillwork. The next morning, drive south through the wine-growing and marble-quarry region to **Vila Viçosa** ㉕ and its Paço Ducal. Continue south by

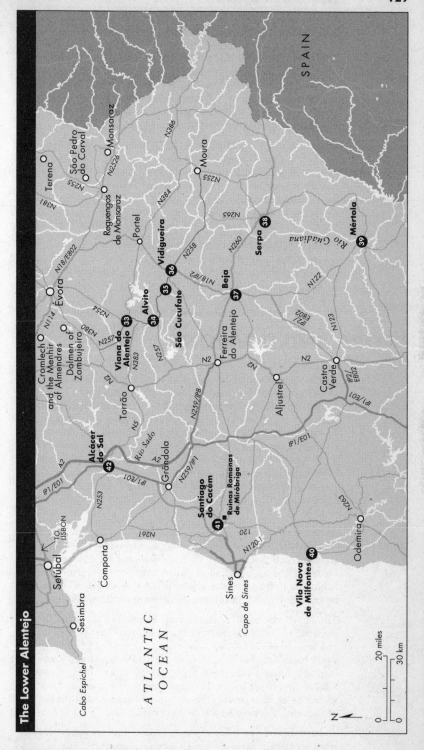

The Lower Alentejo

way of **Terena** ㉔ to spend the night in **Monsaraz** ㉓. The next day visit **Beja** ㊲, a fortified town whose center still retains a Moorish character, stopping to see the Roman ruins at **São Cucufate** ㉟ en route. From Beja, head southeast to **Serpa** ㊳. Spend a couple hours walking around the town, perhaps visiting one of the famed cheese makers, before driving south to **Mértola** ㊴ on the Rio Guadiana. Spend two days exploring the museums and other sights in this former Roman river port before driving west to **Santiago do Cacém** ㊶. Two days here will give you the chance relax on a beach and tour some Roman ruins.

From Santiago do Cacém you can either head south to the Algarve or return to Lisbon. The most scenic route to Lisbon is the N261, which runs along the coast to the tip of the Tróia Peninsula; from there you can take the ferry across the Rio Sado estuary. You can also drive through the Reserva Natural do Sado by turning off at Comporta and following N253 to **Alcácer do Sal** ㊷. Visit the hilltop castle here and continue on to Lisbon via the A2 toll highway.

When to Tour Évora and the Alentejo

Spring comes early to this part of Portugal. Early April to mid-June is a wonderful time to tour, when the fields are full of colorful wildflowers. July and August are brutally hot, with temperatures in places such as Beja often reaching 37°C (100°F) or more. By mid-September things cool off sufficiently to make touring this region a delight.

ÉVORA AND ENVIRONS

Dressed in traditional garb, shepherds and farmers with faces wizened by a lifetime in the baking sun stand about Praça do Giraldo; a group of college girls dressed in jeans and T-shirts chat animatedly at a sidewalk café; a local businessman in coat and tie purposefully hurries by; and clusters of tourists, cameras in hand, capture the historic monuments on film—all this is part of a typical summer's day in Évora. The flourishing capital of the central Alentejo and is also a university town with an astonishing variety of inspiring architecture. Atop a small hill in the heart of a vast cork-, olive-, and grain-producing region, Évora stands out from provincial farm towns the world over: the entire inner city is a monument and was declared a UNESCO World Heritage site in 1986.

Although the region was inhabited some 4,000 years ago—as attested to by the dolmens and menhirs in the countryside—it was during the Roman epoch that the town called Liberalitas Julia in the province of Lusitania first achieved importance. A large part of present-day Évora is built on Roman foundations, of which the Temple of Diana, with its graceful Corinthian columns, is the most conspicuous reminder.

The Moors also made a great historical impact on the area. They arrived in 715 and remained more than 450 years. They were driven out in 1166, thanks in part to a clever ruse perpetrated by Geraldo Sem Pavor (Gerald the Fearless). Geraldo tricked Évora's Moorish ruler into leaving a strategic watchtower unguarded. With a small force, Geraldo took control of the tower. To regain control of it, most of the Moorish troops left their posts at the city's main entrance, allowing the bulk of Geraldo's forces to march in unopposed.

Toward the end of the 12th century Évora's fortunes increased as the town became the favored location for the courts of the Burgundy and Avis dynasties; less than 164 km (102 mi) from Lisbon. It attracted many of the great minds and creative talents of Renaissance Portugal. Some of the more prominent residents at this time were Gil Vicente, the founder of Portuguese theater; the sculptor Nicolas Chanterene; and Gregorio Lopes, the painter known for his renderings of court life. Such a concentration of royal wealth and creativity superimposed upon the existing Moorish town was instrumental in the development of the delicate Manueline-Mudéjar (elaborate, Moslem-influenced) architectural style. You can see fine examples of this in the graceful lines of the Palácio de Dom Manuel and the turreted Ermida de São Bras.

Évora is, above all, a town for walking. Wherever you glance as you stroll the maze of narrow streets and alleys of the Cidade Velha (Old Town), amid arches and whitewashed houses, you'll come face to face with reminders of the town's rich architectural and cultural heritage. The area surrounding Évora is a rich agricultural region with scattered small villages and some of Portugal's earliest inhabited sites.

Note that, of the churches mentioned below, only the Sé and the Igreja de São Francisco have regular visiting hours. To view the interiors of the others you may have to sit in on a mass (times for services are usually posted on church doors) and look around afterward.

Évora

★ **①**–**⑱** *164 km (102 mi) southeast of Lisbon.*

★ **①** **Praça do Giraldo,** the arcade-lined square in the center of the old walled city, is named after Évora's liberator, Gerald the Fearless. During Caesar's time the square, marked by a large arch, was the Roman forum. In 1571 the arch was destroyed to make room for the fountain, a graceful, flattened sphere made of white Estremoz marble and designed by the Renaissance architect Afonso Álvares.

② Note the striking white Renaissance facade of the **Igreja de Santo Antão,** which stands near the fountain at the north end of Praça do Giraldo. A medieval hermitage of the Knights Templar was razed in 1553 to make way for this church, which has massive round pillars and soaring vaulted ceilings. The marble altar in bas-relief is a holdover from the primitive hermitage.

NEED A BREAK? The **Café Arcada,** opposite the fountain on Praça do Giraldo, is an Évora institution. The large hall, divided into snack bar and restaurant sections, is decorated with photos of the big bands that played here in the 1940s. Tables on the square are just the place from which to watch the city on parade.

The narrow, cobblestone **Rua 5 de Outubro,** a pedestrian thoroughfare lined with shops and whitewashed houses with wrought-iron balconies, is one of the town's most attractive streets and connects the Praça do Giraldo and the cathedral.

★ **③** Two, massive, asymmetrical towers and battlement-ringed walls give the **Sé** a fortresslike appearance. The transitional Gothic-style cathedral was constructed in 1186 from huge granite blocks. It has been enhanced over the centuries with an octagonal, turreted dome above the transept; a blue-tile spire atop the north tower; a number of fine Manueline windows; and several Gothic rose windows. At the entrance, Gothic arches are supported by marble columns bearing delicately sculpted statues of the apostles. With the exception of a fine baroque chapel, the granite interior is somber. The cloister, a 14th-century Gothic addition with Mudéjar vestiges, is one of the finest of its type in the country. Statues of the evangelists decorate the corners. Housed in the Sé's towers and chapter room is the **Museu de Arte Sacra da Sé** (Sacred Art Museum). Of particular interest is a 13th-century ivory *Vir-*

132

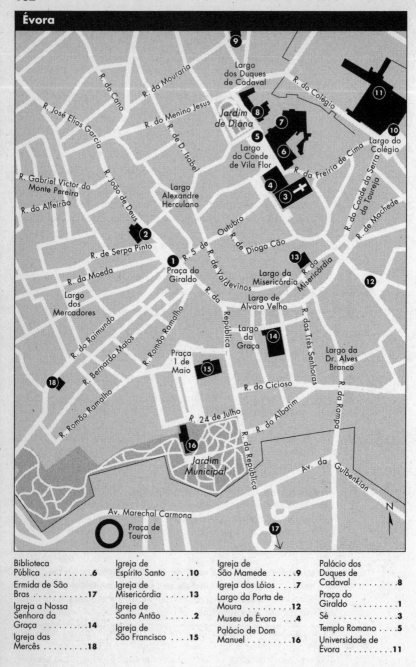

Évora

gin of Paradise, whose body opens up to show exquisitely carved scenes of her life. Her head is a 16th-century wooden replacement, strangely out of proportion with her figure. ⊠ *Largo Marquês de Marialva,* ☎ 266/759330. ▣ *Museum and cloisters: €3.* ☉ *Daily 9–noon and 2–5.*

❹ The **Museu de Évora** (Évora Museum) is in a stately, late-17th-century baroque building between the Sé and the Largo do Conde de Vila Flor, a plaza that's the site of several important structures. The museum, once a palace that accommodated bishops, contains a rich collection of sculpture and paintings as well as interesting archaeological and architectural artifacts. The first-floor galleries, arranged around a pleasant garden, include several excellent carved pillars and a fine Manueline doorway. Among the early Portuguese paintings on display in the upstairs gallery are works attributed to the 16th-century Master of Sardoal. ⊠ *Largo do Conde de Vila Flor,* ☎ 266/702604. ☉ *Tues. 2–5:30, Wed.–Sun. 9:30–12:30 and 2–5.*

★ ❺ The well-preserved ruins of the **Templo Romano,** or Roman Temple, dominate Largo do Conde de Vila Flor. The edifice, considered one of the finest of its kind on the Iberian Peninsula, was probably built in the 1st to 2nd centuries AD. Although it has long been referred to as the Temple of Diana, historians believe that the use of the Corinthian order of architecture in its columns and entablature indicates that it was dedicated to an emperor. The temple, largely destroyed during the invasions of the barbarian tribes in the early 5th century, was later used for various purposes, including that of municipal slaughterhouse in the 14th century. It was restored to its present state in 1871.

❻ The **Biblioteca Pública** (Public Library) occupies the former town hall and contains an outstanding collection of rare books and manuscripts. These aren't routinely on display, however. Bibliophiles need to obtain a reader's card to enter, a process that takes at least a day. ⊠ *Largo do Conde de Vila Flor.* ☉ *Weekdays 9–12:30 and 2–5.*

❼ The **Igreja dos Lóios** is adjacent to the former Convento dos Lóios, which is now the Pousada dos Lóios. To enter the church go down several steps and through a portal framed by a series of fan-shape arches in the flamboyant Gothic style. The sanctuary, dedicated to St. John the Evangelist, was founded in the 15th century by the Venetian-based Lóios Order. Its interior walls are covered with 18th-century *azulejo* (tile) panels created by Oliveira Bernardes, the foremost master of this unique Portuguese art form. The blue-and-white tiles depict scenes from the life of the church's founder, Rodrigo de Melo, who, along with members of his family, is buried here. The bas-relief marble tombstones at the foot of the high altar are the only ones of their kind in Portugal. Note the two metal hatches on either side of the main aisle: one covers an ancient cistern, which belonged to the Moorish castle that predated the church (an underground spring still supplies the cistern with potable water); and beneath the other hatch lie the neatly stacked bones of hundreds of monks. This bizarre ossuary was uncovered in 1958 during restoration work. Enhanced by the 16th-century Renaissance gallery, the cloister is now an integral part of the Pousada dos Lóios. ⊠ *Largo Conde de Vila Flor,* ☎ 266/744307. ▣ *€2.25.* ☉ *Tues.–Sun. 10–12:30 and 2–5.*

❽ The **Palácio dos Duques de Cadaval** is readily identified by two massive stone towers that have pointed battlements. These towers, once part of a medieval castle that protected the town, were later incorporated into the Palace of the Dukes of Cadaval, a former residence of kings João I and João IV. A small gallery contains historic documents, paintings, and the unusual Flemish-style bronze tomb of Rui de Sousa, a signatory of the Treaty of Tordesillas. In 1494 the treaty divided the world into two spheres of influence: Spanish and Portuguese. Today, much of the palace is used by the city, but the ground-floor gallery is open to the public. ⊠ *Largo Conde de Vila Flor,* ☎ *266/704714.* 🖾 *€2.25.* 🕓 *Daily 10–12:30 and 2–5.*

NEED A BREAK? Opposite the Templo Romano, the restful, tree-lined **Jardim de Diana** (Diana Garden) looks out over the aqueduct and the plains from the modest heights of what is sometimes grandiosely referred to as "Évora's Acropolis." From this park—in one sweeping glance that encompasses the temple, the spires of the Gothic Sé, the Igreja dos Lóios, and the 20th-century pousada housed in the convent—you can take in nearly 2,000 years of Portuguese history. A snack bar at the corner of the park is a great spot to reflect on the architectural marvels before you. ⊠ *Largo do Conde de Vila Flor.*

---

9 The small **Igreja de São Mamede** (St. Mamede's Church) contains a vaulted ceiling decorated with baroque frescoes. Note the fine azulejos that cover the nave's wall. The marble bust of Renaissance humanist Andre de Resende on the east wall was created by João Cutileiro, a well-known contemporary Portuguese sculptor. ⊠ *Rua da Mouraria,* ☎ *no phone.*

10 The 16th-century **Igreja de Espírito Santo** is a squat structure with five arches in front. The church was originally a part of the ancient Évora University. The interior contains some fine azulejos and paintings, including artist Gregorio Lopes's painting of the *Last Supper.* As you explore the surrounding streets, you'll have a good view of the ancient town walls; in some places, vestiges of the Roman foundations are visible. ⊠ *Largo do Colégio,* ☎ *no phone.*

From 1555 until its closure by the Marquis de Pombal in 1759, the **Universidade de Évora** was a Jesuit college; in 1979, after a lapse of more than 200 years, Évora University resumed classes. Although the enrollment is small, the college's presence enlivens this ancient city. The large courtyard is flanked on all sides by graceful buildings with double-tier, white-limestone, arched galleries in Italian Renaissance style. From the main entrance you'll see the imposing baroque facade of the gallery, known as the Sala dos Actos (Hall of Acts), which is crowned with allegorical figures and coats of arms carved in white marble quarried in the region. Lining the gallery's interior are azulejo works depicting historical, mythological, and biblical themes. ⊠ *Rua do Colégio.*

12 The **Largo da Porta de Moura**—perhaps Évora's most beautiful square—is characterized by paired stone towers that guard one of the principal entrances to the walled old city. The spires of the Sé rise above the towers, and in the center of the square is an unusual Renaissance fountain. The large white-marble sphere, supported by a single column, bears a commemorative inscription in Latin dated 1556. Overlooking the fountain is the Cordovil Mansion (closed to the public), on whose terrace are several particularly attractive arches decorated in the Manueline-Mudéjar style. ⊠ *Bounded by Ruas D. Augusto Eduardo Nunes, Enrique da Fonseca, Mendes Esteves, de Machede, and Miguel Bombarda, a 5-min walk southeast of the Sé.*

13 The interior of the 16th-century **Igreja de Misericórdia** (Mercy Church) is lined with large azulejo panels depicting scenes from the life of Christ; the unsigned 18th-century tiles are thought to be the work of António de Oliveira de Bernardes. ⊠ *Rua da Misericórdia,* ☎ *no phone.*

⑭ The **Igreja a Nossa Senhora da Graça** (Our Lady of Grace Church) is a splendid piece of classic Italian-style architecture, the first breath of the Renaissance in provincial Portuguese architecture. Note the massive figures on columns at either side of the portal. According to local legend, these four figures represent the first victims put to death in the Inquisition in Évora in 1543. Note that the church is closed for interior restoration works. The adjacent Largo de Alvaro Velho is an inviting square lined with metalsmith shops. ⊠ *Largo da Graça,* ☎ *no phone.*

⑮ After the Sé, the **Igreja de São Francisco** is the grandest of Évora's churches. Its construction in the early 16th century, on the site of a former Gothic chapel, involved the greatest talents of the day, including Nicolas Chanterene, Oliver of Ghent, and the Arruda brothers, Francisco and Diogo. The magnificent architecture notwithstanding, the bizarre Capela dos Ossos (Chapel of the Bones) is the main attraction. The translation of the chilling inscription over the entrance reads: WE BONES WHO ARE HERE ARE WAITING FOR YOURS. The bones of some 5,000 skeletons dug up from cemeteries in the area line the ceilings and supporting columns. With a flair worthy of Charles Addams, a 16th-century Franciscan monk placed skulls jaw-to-cranium so they form arches across the ceiling; arm and leg bones are neatly stacked to shape the supporting columns. ⊠ *Praça 1 de Maio,* ☎ *266/704521.* ⊠ €1. ☉ *Sun.–Fri. 9–1 and 2:30–5:30.*

NEED A BREAK? Off Rua 24 de Julho, a few steps from the Igreja de São Francisco, the **Jardim Municipal** (Municipal Gardens) is a pleasant place to rest after the rigors of sightseeing. The extensive and verdant gardens are landscaped with plants and trees from all over the world.

---

⑯ At the entrance to the Jardim Municipal is the **Palácio de Dom Manuel.** Only a part of the former royal palace remains—restored after a fire in 1916. The existing wing displays a row of paired, gracefully curved Manueline windows, and on the building's south side there's a notable arcade of redbrick sawtooth arches. Currently used as an art gallery, the palace has witnessed a number of historic events since its construction in the late 15th century. It was here, for instance, in 1497, that Vasco da Gama received his commission to command the fleet that would discover the sea route to India.

⑰ The **Ermida de São Bras** (St. Blaise Chapel), a curious structure built in the late 15th century, was the first important building in the Alentejo to join Gothic and Moorish elements and form the Gothic-Mudéjar style. The fortified church, a few hundred feet south of the city walls, is characterized by massive battlement-topped walls and a series of round towers crowned with steep spires. ⊠ *Rua da República,* ☎ *no phone.*

⑱ The **Igreja das Mercês** is a late-17th-century building with good examples of azulejos depicting scenes from the life of St. Augustine, the patron saint of the founding order of this church. There are also two unusual confessionals concealed behind tile panels. ⊠ *Rua do Raimundo,* ☎ *266/702604.* ⊠ *Free.* ☉ *Tues.–Sun. 10–12:30 and 2–5.*

Dining and Lodging

$$–$$$ ✕ **Fialho.** Amor and Gabriel Fialho are the third generation of Fialhos to operate this popular, traditional restaurant. It may be rustic—with a beamed ceiling and painted plates hung on its walls—but the food is quite sophisticated. Start with the excellent *salada de polvo* (marinated octopus salad) and, as a main course, try the *coelho de convento a cartuxa* (roast rabbit with potatoes and carrots), which is made according to a recipe from a nearby monastery. There's a wide selection of Alentejo wines. ⊠ *Travessa das Mascarenhas 16,* ☎ *266/703079. AE, MC, V. Closed Mon.*

$$ ✕ **Cozinha de Santo Humberto.** One of Évora's oldest restaurants was
★ once a wine cellar. Try the *sopa de peixe alentejana* (a mixed fish soup) or the *carne de porco com ameijoas* (small pieces of pork sautéed with clams). Game dishes such as grouse and partridge are particularly good in season (Santo Humberto, is, after all, the patron saint of hunters). The list of Alentejo wines is excellent. ⊠ *Rua da Moeda 39,* ☎ *266/704251. AE, MC, V.*

$$ ✕ **Tasquinha do Oliveira.** Nobody has gone to any pains decorating this tiny restaurant, but the food is something else. Such game dishes as *arroz de lebre* (hare cooked with rice) and Alentejan classics like *pézinhos de coentrada* (pigs' trotters with coriander) are superbly prepared. ⊠ *Rua Cándido dos Reis 45-A,* ☎ *266/744841. AE, MC, V. Closed Sun. and 15 days in Aug.*

$–$$ ✕ **Adega do Alentejano.** The food is hearty and simple in this pleasantly rustic Alentejo wine cellar. Stick to the very reasonable local wine from the barrel, and you'll be agreeably surprised by the bill. ⊠ *Rua Gabriel Vito do Monte Pereira 21-A,* ☎ *266/744447. No credit cards.*

$$$ ✕⌂ **Pousada dos Lóios.** This luxurious pousada is in the 15th-century
★ monastery opposite the Templo Romano. Except for the small size of the rooms, which were formerly the monks' cells, and the need for anyone over 5 ft 2 inches to duck when entering, there's no trace of monastic austerity here. Opulent period furnishings compensate for the cramped quarters, and elegant public rooms deserve a visit even if you don't plan to spend the night. Superbly prepared Alentejo specialties are served in the restaurant ($$–$$$), a marvel of Manueline details. ⊠ *Largo Conde de Vila Flor, 7000-804,* ☎ *266/704051,* ℻ *266/707248,* 🌐 *www.pousadas.pt. 31 rooms, 1 suite. Restaurant, bar, pool. AE, DC, MC, V. BP.*

$$ ✕⌂ **Évora Hotel.** On the route to Montemor-o-Novo, just outside town, you'll find this pleasant, modern establishment. Guest rooms are generous in size and have small balconies. Public areas are light and spacious, as is the dining room ($$), which presents a delicious buffet of regional specialties. ⊠ *Quinta do Cruzeiro (N114), 7000-171,* ☎ *266/748800,* ℻ *266/748806. 166 rooms, 4 suites. Restaurant, bar, pool, tennis court. AE, DC, MC, V. MAP, FAP.*

$$ ⌂ **Hotel da Cartuxa.** Building a two-story hotel—one that's simultaneously rustic *and* modern—inside a 14th-century walled city is no small feat. This establishment, just steps from Praça do Giraldo in the old part of town, proves that it can be done successfully, though. The comfortable public areas are furnished with antiques, and the large guest rooms and have tile baths. Ask for a room at the back for a view of the garden, pool, and Roman walls. ⊠ *Travessa da Palmeira 4/6, 7000-546,* ☎ *266/739300,* ℻ *266/739305,* 🌐 *www.hoteldacartuxa. com. 91 rooms. Restaurant, bar, pool, parking (fee). AE, DC, MC, V. MAP, FAP.*

$$ ⌂ **Hotel D. Fernando.** Most of the airy, well-equipped rooms in this modern hotel have balconies overlooking the lawn-surrounded swimming pool, which is very inviting after a day of summer sightseeing. Public areas are pleasant and spacious. The hotel is just outside Évora's old walls, a short stroll from the historic center. ⊠ *Av. Dr. Barahona 2, 7000-756,* ☎ *266/741717,* ℻ *266/741716. 101 rooms, 2 suites. Restaurant, bar, pool. AE, DC, MC, V. EP.*

$$ ⌂ **Solar de Monfalim.** In a historic building with a delightful arched gallery overlooking the street, this comfortable, family-run guest house provides quiet, old-fashioned hospitality in the heart of the old city.

The rooms, although small, are comfortably furnished, as is the TV lounge. ⊠ *Largo da Misericórdia 1, 7000-646,* ☎ *266/750000,* FAX *266/742367,* WEB *www.monfalimtur.pt. 26 rooms. Bar. AE, MC, V. EP.*

$ ⬚ **Santa Clara.** What this unpretentious hotel lacks in facilities it makes up for in location—it's close to Praça do Giraldo and the center of Évora. Rooms are on the small side but are attractively furnished and adequately equipped. ⊠ *Travessa da Milheira 19, 700-545,* ☎ *266/704141,* FAX *266/706544. 43 rooms. Bar. AE, DC, MC, V. EP.*

Outdoor Activities and Sports

BALLOONING AND FOUR-WHEEL DRIVING

Turibalão Lda. (⊠ Largo Luis de Camões 14, ☎ FAX 266/706323) conducts hot-air balloon flights and four-wheel-drive excursions through the Alentejo.

GO-CARTS

Lucena Karting (⊠ Quinta Lucena, ☎ 266/896680), a go-cart track on the outskirts of Évora (take N114 toward Montemor-o-Novo), provides an outlet for pent-up youthful energy. It costs €5 to take a five-minute spin; for €37 you can ride around for an hour. The track is open Tuesday through Sunday from 10 to 7.

HORSEBACK RIDING

The **Equeturi** (⊠ Quinta do Bacêlo, ☎ 266/742884, WEB www.equeturi. com) horseback-riding center is about 2 km (1 mi) from Évora on the road to Montemor-o-Novo. It gives lessons and conducts escorted rides in the countryside. Reservations are advised.

Aqueduto da Agua da Prata

⑲ *Extends 18 km (11 mi) north of Évora.*

The graceful arched Silver Water Aqueduct, which once carried water to Évora from the springs at Graça do Divor, is best seen along the road to Arraiolos. You can also see a section of it within Évora, along the Rua do Cano in the city's northwest corner. Constructed in 1532 under the patronage of Dom João III, the aqueduct was designed by the famous architect Francisco de Arruda. Extensive parts of the system remain intact and can be seen from the road.

Cromlech and the Menhir of Almendres

⑳ *15 km (9 mi) west of Évora.*

A trip through the countryside surrounding Évora will take you to some of the earliest inhabited sites in Portugal. In Guadalupe, the site of a 17th-century chapel, near the grain-storage bins of the agricultural cooperative, is the Menhir of Almendres, an 8-ft-tall, Neolithic, stone obelisk. Several hundred yards away is the cromlech, 95 granite monoliths arranged in an oval in the middle of a large field.

Dolmen of Zambujeiro

㉑ *12 km (7 mi) southwest of Évora. From N380 (the Évora–Alcaçovas road) take the turnoff to Valverde.*

The 20-ft-high Dolmen of Zambujeiro is the largest of its kind on the Iberian Peninsula. This prehistoric monument is typical of those found throughout Neolithic Europe: several great stone slabs stand upright, supporting a flat stone that serves as a roof. These structures were designed as burial chambers.

Arraiolos

㉒ *22 km (14 mi) northwest of Évora.*

Arraiolos, dominated by the ruins of a once-mighty fortress, is a typical hilltop Alentejo village of whitewashed houses and narrow streets. What distinguishes it is its worldwide reputation as a carpet-producing center. In the 16th century, as Portuguese trade with the East grew, an interest developed in the intricate designs of the carpets from India and Persia, and these patterns served as models for the earliest hand-embroidered Arraiolos carpets. The colorful rugs aren't mass-produced in factories but are handmade by locals in their homes and cottages. An authentic Arraiolos rug, made of locally produced wool, has some 44,000 ties per square meter. To discourage imitations, in 1992 the town council designed a blue seal of authenticity to be affixed to each carpet. There's a permanent exhibition of Arraiolos carpets in the **Câmara Municipal** (Town Hall). Contact the tourist office, which is in the Town Hall, for more information. ⊠ *Praça Lima e Brito 27,* ☎ *266/490240 for tourist office.* ⊡ *Free.* ☉ *Weekdays 9–12:30 and 2–5:30, weekend hrs vary.*

Dining and Lodging

$$–$$$ ✕▥ **Pousada da Nossa Senhora da Assunção.** If you need to sleep on your decision about which carpet to buy, consider an overnight stay in this picturesque pousada. It's a little more than a kilometer outside of town in the Convento dos Lóios, an old convent that has been restored and tastefully padded with modern comforts. The restaurant ($$) decor is contemporary, but the menu favors traditional regional dishes. ⊠ *Val das Flores (take E-370 to Pavia), 7044-176,* ☎ *266/419340,* FAX *266/419280,* WEB *www.pousadas.pt. 30 rooms. Restaurant, bar, pool, tennis court. AE, DC, MC, V. BP.*

Shopping

The main street of Arraiolos is lined with showrooms and workshops featuring the town's famous hand-embroidered wool rugs. One of the town's best rug selections can be found at **Calántica** (⊠ Rua Alexandre Herculano 20, ☎ 266/499356). **Condestavel** (⊠ Rua Bombeiros Voluntários 7, ☎ 266/499587) is a large rug shop with branches in Évora and Lisbon.

THE UPPER ALENTEJO

The Upper Alentejo is the hillier, rockier half of the great Alentejo plain and has the region's highest mountain ranges—the Serra de São Mamede and the Serra de Ossa. Neither is very lofty though, and the undulating fields, heaths, and cork plantations that make up most of the landscape leave you in no doubt about where you are. Quarries scar the landscape around Borba, Estremoz, and Vila Viçosa, but they produce Portugal's finest marble. Modern wine-making techniques have revolutionized production in the Upper Alentejo's vineyards, and some of Europe's finest wines are now produced in areas like Borba, Reguengos de Monsaraz, and Portalegre.

Monsaraz

★ **㉓** *50 km (31 mi) southeast of Évora.*

The entire fortified hilltop town of Monsaraz is a living museum of narrow, stone-surfaced streets lined with ancient white houses. The town's 150 or so permanent residents (mostly older people) live mainly from tourism, and because they do so graciously and unobtrusively, Monsaraz has managed to retain its essential character.

Old women clad in black still sit in the doorways of their cottages and chat with neighbors, their ever-present knitting in hand. At the southern end of the walls stand the well-preserved towers of a formidable castle. The view from atop the pentagonal tower sweeps across the plain to the west and to the east over the Rio Guadiana (Guadiana River) to Spain. Within the castle perimeter is an unusual arena with makeshift slate benches at either end of an oval field. Bullfights are held here several times a year and always in the second week of September (during the festival of Senhora Jesus dos Passos, the village's patron saint).

The small **Monsaraz Museum,** next to the parish church, displays religious artifacts and the original town charter, signed by Dom Manuel in 1512. The former tribunal contains an interesting 15th-century fresco that depicts Christ presiding over figures of Truth and Deception. ⊠ *Praça Nuno Álvares Pereira,* ☎ *no phone.* ☒ €1. ☉ *Daily 9–6.*

The area around Monsaraz is dotted with megalithic monuments. The **Menhir of Outeiro,** 3 km (2 mi) north of town, is one of the tallest ever discovered.

Dining and Lodging

$–$$ ✕ **Casa do Forno.** The labor of love of two ambitious women (Gloria
★ and Mariana), Casa do Forno is an upscale restaurant. At the entrance is a huge, rounded oven with an iron door, hence the name (*forno* is Portuguese for "oven"). Picture windows line the dining room and afford a spectacular view over the rolling plains. The Alentejan menu appropriately features roasts; one special dish worth trying is the *borrego Convento Orado* (roast lamb prepared according to an ancient recipe obtained at the nearby monastery). ⊠ *Travessa da Sanabrosa,* ☎ *266/557190. AE, MC, V. Closed Tues.*

$–$$ ✕ **Lumumba.** This little restaurant in one of the old village houses has a devoted clientele that hails from both sides of the Portuguese–Spanish border. The dining room is small, but there is an attractive terrace for outside dining with views over the valley to distant mountains. The menu is classic Alentejo, with good lamb and kid roasts and casseroles. The grilled fish dishes are also excellent; try the *chocos grelhados* (grilled squid) or the *peixe espada grelhada* (charcoal-grilled blade fish). ⊠ *Rua Direita,* ☎ *266/557121. No credit cards. Closed Mon.*

$$ ▥ **Horta da Moura.** A working farm is the site of this hotel. The main house, whose white-stucco facade has blue trim and an arched portico, is typical of Alentejo-style architecture. The cozy interior has vaulted brick ceilings with wooden beams and traditional furnishings. The outlying buildings include stables, a riding school, a crafts room, a winery, and a recreation center with a large fireplace. The helpful staff eagerly arranges walking, horseback riding, and cycling trips along the river, as well as four-wheel-drive and canoe excursions and fishing trips. ⊠ *Reguengos de Monsaraz 7200,* ☎ *266/550100,* FAX *266/ 550108,* WEB *www.hortadamoura.pt. 6 rooms, 7 suites, 1 apartment. Pool, 2 tennis courts, horseback riding, fishing, bicycles, recreation room. AE, DC, MC, V. EP.*

$ ▥ **Estalagem Dom Nuno.** This small, rustic guest house—a true romantic hideaway—occupies an old, restored, white home on the main street of the walled town. The clean guest quarters have modern furnishings and fantastic valley views—the sunsets alone are worth the price of a room. ⊠ *Rua do Castelo 6, 7200,* ☎ *266/557146,* FAX *266/557400. 8 rooms. AE, DC, MC, V. EP.*

Shopping

Reguengos de Monsaraz, 16 km (10 mi) west of Monsaraz, is a sleepy little Alentejo town often simply called Reguengos. It's center of a large wine-producing region and is also known for its handwoven rugs. The tiny hamlet of **São Pedro do Corval,** 5 km (3 mi) northeast of Reguengos, is one of Portugal's major centers for inexpensive hand-painted pottery.

Terena

㉔ *28 km (17 mi) north of Reguengos.*

Terena has a charter dating from 1262 and a castle on a hill and is a place where tourists are still a curiosity. Drive—or better yet, stroll—along the narrow Rua Direita past the white houses, some with Gothic doorways, others with baroque or Renaissance ones. The small, well-preserved castle was one of several built in this area to defend the border with Spain, which lies across the Rio Guadiana, 11 km (7 mi) east.

Lodging

$ ☒ **Casa de Terena.** A restored 18th-century house in out-of-the-way
★ Terena has been turned into a charming inn. It has six comfortably furnished guest quarters, all with period reproductions. ☒ *Rua Direita 45, 7250-065,* ☎ *268/459132,* ℻ *268/459155. 5 rooms, 1 suite. Bar. MC, V. EP.*

Vila Viçosa

㉕ *18 km (11 mi) northeast of Terena.*

A quiet town with a moated castle, Vila Viçosa is in the heart of the fertile Borba plain. It has been closely linked with Portuguese royalty since the 15th century, but this association hasn't always been a happy one: in 1483 King João II, seeking to strengthen his grip on the throne, moved to eliminate the second Duke of Bragança, his brother-in-law and most formidable rival, who from Vila Viçosa controlled more than 50 cities, castles, and towns. After much intrigue and counterintrigue, the unfortunate Duke was beheaded in Évora's main square.

Court life in Vila Viçosa flourished in the late 16th and early 17th centuries, when the huge palace constructed by the fourth Duke of Bragança (Jaime) was the scene of great royal feasts, theater performances, and bullfights. This all came to an abrupt end in 1640, when King João IV, the eighth Duke of Bragança and the first Portuguese to occupy the throne after 60 years of Spanish domination, elected to move his court to Lisbon. Thereafter, Vila Viçosa slipped into relative oblivion. In more recent times Portugal's second-to-last king, Carlos I, and the young Prince Luís Filipe spent their last night in the palace. The following day, February 1, 1908, in response to a royal decree that mandated exile for "political" crimes, they were assassinated by members of a secret political society while they were in an open carriage.

The **Paço Ducal** (Ducal Palace) and the nearby *castelo* (castle) draw a great many visitors. Built of locally quarried marble, the palace's main wing extends for some 360 ft and overlooks the expansive Palace Square and the bronze equestrian statue of Dom João IV. At the north end of the square note the Porta do Nó (Knot Gate) with its massive stone ropes—an intriguing example of the Manueline style.

The palace's interior was extensively restored in the 1950s and contains all you'd expect to find: azulejos, Arraiolos rugs, frescoed ceilings, priceless collections of silver and gold objects, Chinese vases, Gobelin tapestries, and a long dining hall adorned with antlers and other hunting trophies. The enormous kitchen's spits are large enough to accommodate several oxen, and there's enough gleaming copper to keep a small army of servants busy polishing. Dom Carlos, the nation's penultimate king, spent his last night here before being assassinated in 1908;

AZULEJOS

It's difficult to find an old building of any note in Portugal that isn't adorned somewhere or other with the predominantly blue-toned ceramic tiles called *azulejos*. The centuries-old marriage of glazed ornamental tiles to Portuguese architecture is one of those matches that seem to have been made in heaven.

After the Gothic period, large buildings made entirely of undressed brick or stone became a rarity in Portuguese architecture. Most structures had extensive areas of flat plaster on their facades and interior walls that cried out for some form of decoration. The compulsion to fill these empty architectural spaces produced the art of the fresco in Italy; in Portugal, it produced the art of the azulejo.

The medium is very well suited to the deeply rooted Portuguese taste for intricate, ornate decoration. And, aesthetics aside, glazed tiling is ideally suited to the country's more practical needs. Durable, waterproof, and easily cleaned, the tile provides cool interiors during Portugal's hot summers and exterior protection from the damp onslaughts of Atlantic winters.

The term azulejo comes not from the word *azul* (blue in Portuguese), but from the Arabic word for tiles, *az-zulayj*. But despite the long presence of the Moors in Portugal, the Moorish influence on early Portuguese azulejos was actually introduced from Spain in the 15th century, well after the Christian reconquest. No examples of tile work from the time of the Moorish occupation have survived in Portugal.

The very earliest tiles on Portuguese buildings were imported from Andalusia. They're usually geometric in design and were most frequently used to form panels of repeated patterns. As Portugal's prosperity increased in the 16th century, the growing number of palaces, churches, and sumptuous town and country mansions created a demand for more tile ornamentation. Local production was small at first, and Holland and Italy were the main suppliers. The superb Dutch-made azulejos in the Paço Ducal in Vila Viçosa are famous examples from this period. The first Portuguese-made tiles had begun to appear in the last quarter of the 15th century, when a number of small factories were established, but three centuries were to pass before Portuguese tile making reached its peak.

The great figure in 18th-century Portuguese tile making is António de Oliveira Bernardes, who died in 1732. The school established by the master tile maker spawned the series of monumental panels depicting hunting scenes, landscapes, battles, and other historical motifs that grace many of the stately Portuguese homes and churches of the period. Some of the finest examples can be seen in the Alentejo—in buildings such as the old university in Évora and the parish church in Alcácer do Sal—as well as at the Castelo de São Felipe in Setúbal. In Lisbon's Museu do Azulejo you can trace the development of tiles in Portugal from their beginnings to the present.

Portuguese tile making declined in quality in the 19th century, but a revival occurred in the 20th century, spearheaded by leading artists such as Almada Negreiros and Maria Keil. Today, some notable examples of the use of tile by contemporary artists can be seen in many of the capital's metrô stations.

his rooms have been maintained as they were. Carlos was quite an accomplished painter—some say a better painter than he was a monarch—and many of his works (along with private photos of Portugal's last royal family) line the walls of the apartments. The palace itself as well as its armory, its treasury, and the castle and hunting museum can each be visited in separate guided tours. ⊠ *Terreiro do Paço,* ☎ 268/ 980659. ⌨ *Palace: €5. Armory, treasury, castle, porcelain collection: €2.50 each.* ◷ *Apr.–Sept., Tues.– Fri. 9:30–1 and 2:30–5:30, weekends 9:30–1 and 2:30–6; Oct.–Mar., Tues.–Sun. 9:30–1 and 2–5.*

Following the tour of the Paço Ducal you can visit the nearby **Museu dos Coches** (Coach Museum), its collection of horse-drawn conveyances and antique automobiles. Note that if you've seen or plan to see Lisbon's coach museum, you can skip this one; it's interesting but isn't in the same league as the one in the capital. ⊠ *Terreiro do Paço,* ☎ 268/ 980659. ⌨ *€1.50.* ◷ *Apr.–Sept., Tues.– Fri. 9:30–1 and 2:30–5:30, weekends 9:30–1 and 2:30–6; Oct.–Mar., Tues.–Sun. 9:30–1 and 2–5.*

Dining and Lodging

$$$ ✕⌨ **Pousada de D. João IV.** If you're hooked on Vila Viçosa's history, this state inn next door to the palace has all the atmosphere you'll need. It's in a restored 16th-century convent that's furnished with period reproductions. Its restaurant ($$–$$$$) even serves you dishes based on old convent recipes. ⊠ *Terreiro do Paço, 7160,* ☎ *268/980742,* ℻ *268/980747,* ⛚ *www.pousadas.pt. 33 rooms, 3 suites. Restaurant, bar, pool. AE, DC, MC, V. BP.*

En Route On the main road between Vila Viçosa and Estremoz, you'll see dirt-and-rock piles strewn about the countryside. These tailings are the residue of centuries of extracting high-quality marble from the region's many quarries. The town of Borba, about 4 km (2½ mi) northwest of Vila Viçosa, has a pleasant conglomeration of modest whitewashed houses, noble mansions, and small churches—all beautifully decorated with marble. Borba is one of the Alentejo's major wine producers, and the town's vintners have won many national prizes.

Estremoz

㉖ *31 km (19 mi) northwest of Vila Viçosa.*

Estremoz, which lies on the ancient road that connected Lisbon with Mérida, Spain, has been a site of strategic importance since Roman times, and the castle, which overlooks the town, was a crucial one of the Alentejo's many fortresses. Estremoz is most closely associated with Isabel of Aragon, although she spent only a short time here. Married to Dom Dinis—a Portuguese king—in 1282, she arrived in 1336 and after a brief stay became ill and died. The luxurious Pousada da Rainha Santa Isabel, which occupies the castle, was named for her. It was also in Estremoz in 1367 that the queen's grandson Pedro, the lover and secret husband of Inês de Castro, died. The Portuguese people loved Queen Isabel and over the ages have handed down many tales and legends of her humility and charity. She was beatified in the 16th century, then canonized in 1625 by Pope Urban VIII. A statue in the castle square commemorates her. From atop the castle tower you'll have a magnificent view over the Alentejo plains.

The **Museu Municipal** (Municipal Museum) is in a 16th-century almshouse across from the castle. Its displays chronicle the development of the region and range from Roman artifacts to contemporary pottery, including a collection of the brightly colored figurines for which Estremoz is famous. ⊠ *Largo D. Dinis,* ☎ *268/339200.* ⌨ *€1.*

⊙ *Apr.–Sept., Tues.–Sun. 9–12:30 and 3–7; Oct.–Mar., Tues.–Sun. 10–12:30 and 3–5.*

The lower town, a maze of narrow streets and white houses, radiates from the **Rossio,** a huge, unpaved square. Stands lining it sell the town's famous colorful pottery. In addition to the multicolored, hand-painted plates, pitchers, and dolls, note the earthenware jugs decorated with bits of local white marble.

NEED A BREAK?	There are several refreshment stands and snack bars along the Rossio, but for more substantial fare try the **Café Alentejano.** From this popular 60-year-old café and its first-floor restaurant, you can watch the goings-on in the square.

Dining and Lodging

$–$$ ✕ **Adega do Isaias.** Hidden away on a narrow side street a few min-
★   utes' walk from the square, this is the best place in town for hearty, no-nonsense roasts and grilled meats. The front part of the former wine cellar is a rough-looking bar; walk through to the dining area—a sloping, cement-floor cave that's lined with huge terra-cotta wine jugs. During your meal you sit on benches at planked tables; expect the service to be casual, at best. But the food will be great, and the place will probably be packed. ⊠ *Rua do Almeida 21,* ☎ *268/322318. No credit cards. Closed Sun.*

$$$ ✕▥ **Pousada da Rainha Santa Isabel.** One of Portugal's most luxuri-
★   ous pousadas is in Estremoz's hilltop castle. The sumptuous lobby and other public rooms display literally tons of gleaming Estremoz marble as well as 15th-century tapestries, Arraiolos rugs, and original paintings. The generous-size bedrooms are furnished with 17th- and 18th-century reproductions; some rooms have elaborate four-poster beds. Just to sit in the baronial dining hall ($$–$$$$) is a treat, and the food and service are fit for a queen. The accent is on traditional Alentejo dishes and old-fashioned recipes. The *perdiz caçador* (partridge in red wine) is very good in the autumn. ⊠ *Largo D. Dinis 1, 7100,* ☎ *268/ 332075,* FAX *268/332079,* WEB *www.pousadas.pt. 30 rooms, 3 suites. Restaurant, bar, pool. AE, DC, MC, V. BP.*

$$–$$$ ▥ **Estalagem Páteo dos Solares.** This modern hotel occupies a large old house that has been restored using traditional materials and lots of marble. It's near the old walls in the center of town. ⊠ *Rua Brito Capelo, 7100-562,* ☎ *268/338400,* FAX *268/338419,* WEB *www. maisturismo.pt/psolares. 42 rooms, 1 suite. Restaurant, bar, pool. AE, DC, MC, V. BP.*

Évoramonte

❷ *17 km (10 mi) southwest of Estremoz, 42 km (26 mi) northeast of Évora.*

Évoramonte is a medieval town that sits along the western flank of the Serra de Ossa at an altitude of 1,550 ft. Drive up to the castle for a view that extends as far as the Serra da Estrela. The castle here, built in Italian Renaissance style, is distinguished by a massive round tower at each of its four corners. Also note the heavy Manueline ropes that run, like ribbons on a Christmas package, around the exterior; they're joined at the entrance with two tidy cement knots.

The famous sopa alentejana is said to have originated in Évoramonte. The convention held here in 1834 to end the civil war between the Liberals and the Miguelists took so long that by the end only stale bread was left to eat—and thus was born the popular Alentejo soup, made with stale bread, garlic, olive oil, coriander, and water.

Elvas

28 *40 km (25 mi) east of Estremoz, 15 km (9 mi) west of Spain.*

Another of the fortified Alentejo towns, Elvas—because of its proximity to the Spanish town of Badajoz—was from its founding an important bastion in warding off attacks from the east. The extensive fortifications, 17th-century Portugal's most formidable, are characterized by a series of walls, moats, and reinforced towers. The size of the complex can be best appreciated by driving around the periphery of the town.

The distinguished, 8-km (5-mi) **Aqueduto Amoreira** (Amoreira Aqueduct), which took more than a century to build, is still in use today. It was started in 1498 under the direction of one of the era's great architects, Francisco de Arruda—who also designed the Aqueduto da Agua da Prata north of Évora—but not until 1622 did the first drops of water flow into the town fountain.

The 16th-century **Igreja da Nossa Senhora da Assunção** (Church of Our Lady of the Assumption) at the head of the town square, the Praça da República, has an impressive triple-nave interior lined with 17th-century blue-and-yellow azulejos. The church was designed by Francisco de Arruda, architect of the Elvas aqueduct, but underwent subsequent modifications. It was a cathedral until the diocese was moved to Évora in the 18th century. ☒ *Praça da República,* ☏ *no phone.*

From the Igreja da Nossa Senhora da Assunção, walk up the hill past a pillory and two stone towers (spanned by a graceful Moorish loggia) to the **castelo.** At the battlements you'll have a sweeping view of the town and its fortifications. ☒ *Praça da República,* ☏ *no phone.* ☎ *Free.* ☉ *Daily 9–12:30 and 2–5:30.*

Dining and Lodging

$$ ✕▥ **Pousada de Santa Luzia.** Portugal's first pousada is in a two-story,
★   Moorish-style building 12 km (7 mi) from one of the major border crossings between Spain and Portugal. The cheerful, decent-size guest rooms have bright floral fabrics, hand-painted Alentejo furniture, and modern tiled bathrooms that are small but adequate. The large restaurant ($$–$$$$) has arched windows overlooking a garden and is a favorite with Elvas residents. One of the most popular dishes is *bacalhau dourado* (cod sautéed with eggs, potatoes, and onions). ☒ *Av. de Badajoz, 7350-097,* ☏ *268/637470,* ⬛ *268/622127,* 🆆🅴🅱 *www.pousadas.pt. 25 rooms. Restaurant, bar, pool, 2 tennis courts. AE, DC, MC, V. BP.*

Campo Maior

29 *19 km (12 mi) northeast of Elvas.*

Surrounded by rows of gentle hills covered with the Alentejo's ubiquitous cork and olive trees, Campo Maior is a quiet, sparsely populated corner of the country where little has changed over the years. You may notice the smell of roasting coffee lingering in the air: it isn't coming from a nearby café but from the several coffee-roasting plants in the area.

Try to make it to this town during the first week of September, when nearly 100 streets and squares are covered with a rainbow-color mantle of paper flowers and decorations. The decorations for each neighborhood are a closely held secret for months, as the women nimbly assemble the paper flowers and the men construct the wooden framing. When the festival opens, all is revealed in a blaze of color. Check with the local or regional tourist office for exact dates.

At the top of the hill is a castle that was reconstructed after a disastrous explosion in 1732. As you walk around the fortifications, you'll notice some tiny whitewashed dwellings with laundry fluttering about like flags in the breeze. The little buildings are the old army barracks, the only part of the military complex still occupied. Before leaving Campo Maior, stroll through the lower part of town, where the narrow streets are lined with many fine examples of wrought-iron grillwork and balconies, giving the town a Spanish appearance.

Portalegre

 47 km (29 mi) northwest of Campo Maior.

Portalegre is the gateway to the Alentejo's most mountainous region as well as to the Parque Natural da Serra de São Mamede. The town is at the foot of the Serra de São Mamede, where the parched plains of the south give way to a greener, more inviting landscape. Although Portalegre lacks the charm of the whitewashed hamlets in the south of the province, it has long been noted worldwide for the quality of its handmade tapestries, which currently fetch prices of around €5,000 per square meter.

From the park in the center of the lower town and walk uphill past a maze of shops and old houses to the twin-towered **Sé** (Cathedral). The 18th-century facade of this, the town's most prominent landmark, is highlighted with marble columns and wrought-iron balconies. ⊠ *Praça do Município,* ☎ *245/21082.* ☉ *Mon.–Sat. 8:30–noon and 3–6, Sun. 9–noon.*

The **Museu Municipal,** in a former seminary next to the cathedral, contains a wealth of religious art, including a gilded, 16th-century Spanish pietà. ⊠ *Rua José Maria da Rosa,* ☎ *245/300120.* ▨ *€1.80.* ☉ *Wed.–Mon. 9:30–12:30 and 2–6.*

From the cathedral square, head east about 400 yards to the ruins of a once-formidable **castelo,** whose tower walls afford a splendid view of the cathedral and its surroundings.

The **Casa-Museu José Regio** (José Regio House and Museum), just off Avenida Poeta José Regio, roughly midway between the cathedral and the castle, was named for a local poet who died in 1969. He bequeathed his varied collection of religious and folk art to the museum, which is in his former home. ⊠ *Largo de Boa Vista,* ☎ *245/203625.* ▨ *€1.20.* ☉ *Tues.–Sun. 9:30–12:30 and 2–6.*

The **Museu de Tapeçaria Guy Fino** (Guy Fino Tapestry Museum) displays 46 tapestries designed by Portugal's most famous artists of the last half century. ⊠ *Rua do Figueiro,* ☎ *245/307980.* ▨ *€1.80.* ☉ *Mon.–Tues. and Thurs.–Sun. 9:30–1 and 2:30–6.*

You can enter the **Parque Natural da Serra de São Mamede** roughly 5 km (3 mi) northeast of Portalegre. The nature park extends north to the fortified town of Marvão and the spa town of Castelo de Vide, and south to the little hamlet of Esperança on the Spanish border. The sparsely inhabited 80,000-acre park region is made up of small family plots, and sheepherding is the major occupation. The area is rich in wildlife, including many rare species of birds, as well as wild boars, deer, and wildcats. This isn't a spectacularly scenic park but rather a quiet place for hiking, riding, or simply communing with nature. For information about activities, contact the park office. ⊠ *Praceta Herois da India 8,* ☎ *245/203631.*

OFF THE
BEATEN PATH

COUDELARIA DE ALTER – If you're interested in horses, you must visit the Coudelaria de Alter (Alter Stud Farm), 22 km (14 mi) southwest of Portalegre. It was founded by Dom João V in 1748 to furnish royalty with high-quality mounts. Dedicated to preserving and developing the extraordinarily beautiful Alter Real (Royal Alter) strain of the Lusitania breed, the farm has had a long, turbulent history. After years of foreign invasion and pillage, little remains of its original structures. Fortunately, the equine bloodline, one of Europe's noblest, has been preserved, and you can watch these superb horses being trained and exercised on the farm (phone ahead to make sure a visit is practical on the day you want to go). There are also three small but interesting museums here: one documents the history of the farm, one has a collection of horse-drawn carriages, and one has displays on the art of falconry. You can also watch falcons going through their daily training sessions. The town of Alter do Chão itself, with the battlements of a 14th-century castle overlooking a square, is also worth a stroll. ⊠ *The farm is on a dusty track 3 km (2 mi) northwest of Alter do Chão,* ☎ *245/610080.* ⊠ *Free.* ☉ *Farm daily 9:30–noon and 2–4:30.*

Dining and Lodging

$ ✕ **O Abrigo.** On a quiet street around the corner from the cathedral you'll find this small, husband-and-wife–run restaurant. You enter the cork-lined dining area through a snack bar. One of the best dishes on the menu is the *migas alentejanas* (a tasty fried-pork-and-bread-crumbs concoction), served on a terra-cotta platter. ⊠ *Rua de Elvas 74,* ☎ *245/ 331658. MC, V. Closed Tues.*

$–$$ ✕▥ **Dom João III.** This modern multistory hotel is across from the city park. Although the lobby and hallways are somewhat institutional, the rooms are pleasant; many have balconies overlooking the park. The large top-floor restaurant, a favorite with local businessmen, is ringed with picture windows overlooking the town. The menu has international dishes as well as regional specialties. ⊠ *Av. da Liberdade, 7300-065,* ☎ *245/330192,* ℻ *245/330444. 58 rooms, 2 suites. Restaurant, bar, pool. AE, DC, MC, V. EP.*

En Route For the most scenic approach to Marvão and the Serra de São Mamede from Portalegre, take N359 18 km (11 mi) to Marvão. The narrow but well-surfaced serpentine N359 rises to an elevation of 2,800 ft, past stands of birch and chestnut trees and small vegetable gardens bordered by ancient stone walls. At Portagem take note of the well-preserved Roman bridge.

Marvão

★ ㉛ *25 km (16 mi) northeast of Portalegre.*

The views of the mountains as you approach the medieval fortress town of Marvão are spectacular, and the town's castle, atop a sheer rock cliff, commands a 360-degree panorama. The village, with some 300 mostly older inhabitants, is laid out in several long rows of tidy, white-stone dwellings terraced into the hill. Although you can drive through the constricted streets, Marvão is best appreciated on foot.

You can climb the tower of the **castelo** and trace the course of the massive Vauban-style stone walls (characterized by concentric lines of trenches and walls, a hallmark of the 17th-century French military engineer Vauban), adorned at intervals with bartizans, to enjoy breathtaking vistas from different angles. Given its strategic position, it's no surprise that Marvão has been a fortified settlement since Roman times or earlier. The present castle was built under Dom Dinis in the late 13th century and modified some four centuries later, during the reign of Dom João IV.

At the foot of the path leading to the castle is the **Museu Municipal,** in the 13th-century Church of Saint Mary. The small gallery contains a diverse collection of religious artifacts, azulejos, costumes, ancient maps, and weapons. ✉ *Largo de Santa Maria,* ☎ *245/909132,* WEB *www. estgp.pt/museu.* 🎫 *€1.* ☉ *Daily 9–12:30 and 2–5:30.*

Scattered among the chestnut groves at **Santo António das Areias,** 5 km (3 mi) northeast of Marvão, are some two dozen prehistoric dolmens.

Dining and Lodging

$$ ✕🏨 **Pousada de Santa Maria.** In 1976 several old houses within the
★ city walls were joined to create the Pousada de Santa Maria. The rooms are decorated with traditional Alentejo furnishings, and the restaurant ($$) serves some of the best regional dishes in the village. ✉ *Rua 24 de Janeiro 7, 7330,* ☎ *245/993201,* FAX *245/993440,* WEB *www. pousadas.pt. 29 rooms. Restaurant, bar. AE, DC, MC, V. BP.*

$ ✕🏨 **Albergaria El Rei Dom Manuel.** A house inside the castle walls was completely renovated to create this inn. Five of its rooms have fantastic cliff-side views. The restaurant ($$) serves regional fare. ✉ *Largo da Olivença, 7330,* ☎ *245/909150,* FAX *245/909159,* WEB *www. tourismarvao.pt. 15 rooms. Restaurant, bar, cable TV. AE, DC, MC, V. BP.*

Outdoor Activities and Sports

Five kilometers (3 miles) northwest of Marvão on N246-1 is the **Ammaia Clube de Golfe de Marvão** (✉ Quinta do Prado, Marvão, ☎ 245/ 993755), an 18-hole golf course with stunning views of the São Mamede mountain range. Greens fees range from €25 a day on weekdays to €30 a day on weekends.

En Route An intriguing backcountry lane connects Marvão with Castelo de Vide. About halfway down the hill from Marvão, turn to the right toward Escusa (watch for the sign) and continue through the chestnut- and acacia-covered hills to Castelo de Vide.

Castelo de Vide

32 *8 km (5 mi) west of Marvão.*

A quiet, hilltop spa town, Castelo de Vide is graced with flowers that sprout from nearly every nook and cranny. The town's beauty has evidently reached the hearts of its residents, who have kind and gentle natures. As you walk along, notice the many houses with Gothic doorways and their various designs. (The tourist brochures proclaim that Castelo de Vide has the largest number of Gothic doorways of any town in Portugal.)

The large, baroque Praça Dom Pedro V is bordered by the Igreja de Santa Maria (St. Mary's Church) and the town hall. An alleyway to the right of the church leads to the village fountain, which taps one of the many springs in the area. (The waters are alleged to cure a wide variety of disorders ranging from diabetes to dermatitis.) The canopied, 16th-century marble fountain is the town symbol. A cobblestone alley leads from the fountain up to a Juderia (Jewish Quarter).

A bare little room in a modest one-story cottage is all that remains of a medieval **sinagoga** (synagogue) that was once the center of a thriving Jewish community. In the Middle Ages, as the town prospered, many Jews and Marranos (Jews forced to convert to Christianity) settled here.

✉ *Rua da Juderia,* ☎ *no phone.* 🎫 *Free.* ☉ *June–Sept., daily 10–8; Oct.–May, daily 10–5:30.*

From the Juderia it's a short climb to the ruins of the **castelo.** Go up into the tower and inside the well-preserved keep to the large Gothic hall, which has a picture window looking down on the town square and the church. 🎫 *Free.* ☉ *June–Sept., daily 10–8; Oct.–May, daily 10–5:30.*

Dining and Lodging

$$–$$$ ✗ **Sr. Marinos.** This comfortable, wood-paneled restaurant in the center of town has an unusually eclectic menu for this part of the country. It includes a number of French and Italian plates alongside some outstanding regional fare. The multilingual host will help out with translations. The wine list is as long as your arm. ✉ *Praça Dom Pedro 6,* ☎ *245/901408. AE, MC, V. Closed Sun. No lunch Mon.*

$$ ✗🖭 **Sol e Serra.** The large rooms in this three-story Mediterranean-style hotel—just a 10-minute walk from the castle—have balconies looking over the park. The spacious bar, which overlooks the pool, is one of the town's most popular gathering places, and the restaurant ($$–$$$$), with its wooden beams, is one of the few places in Portugal that has a kosher menu. It also has live music and folk-dancing performances every Friday June–September. ✉ *Estrada de São Vincente, 7320,* ☎ *245/900000,* 𝖥𝖠𝖷 *245/900001,* 🖳𝖤𝖡 *www.portugal/info.net/soleserra. 51 rooms. Restaurant, bar, pool. AE, DC, MC, V. EP, MAP, FAP.*

$–$$ ✗🖭 **Hotel Garcia d'Horta.** Named after a notable 16th-century Jewish doctor and naturalist who lived in Castelo de Vide (his bust by modern sculptor João Cutileiro is in the garden), this tastefully appointed hotel is one of the area's best values. Its restaurant, A Castanha ($$), is renowned for great Alentejan cooking and polished service. A stay here gets you a discount at the 18-hole Ammaia Golf Course, just a few miles away. ✉ *Estrada de São Vincente, 7320,* ☎ *245/901100,* 𝖥𝖠𝖷 *245/901200,* 🖳𝖤𝖡 *www.hgo.8m.pt. 52 rooms, 1 suite. Restaurant, bar, pool, golf privileges. AE, MC, V. EP, MAP, FAP.*

THE LOWER ALENTEJO

Extending south of Évora and from the rugged west-coast beaches east to the border with Spain, the Lower Alentejo is a vast, mostly flat region of wheat fields, cork oaks, and olive trees. It rains very little here, and the summer months are particularly hot. Shepherds wearing broad-brimmed hats and sheepskin vests still tend their sheep in the fields. Gypsies still set up camp, with makeshift tents, horse carts, and open fires. These scenes from a rapidly disappearing way of life contrast sharply with the modernization taking place in the region.

Viana do Alentejo

③③   *37 km (23 mi) southeast of Évora.*

The attractive castle at Viana do Alentejo—with its rough stone walls, brick battlements, and round turrets—was constructed in 1313 to the very specific orders of Dom Dinis. He decreed that the pentagonal walls should be tall enough that a horseman with a lance measuring 9 *côvados* (an ancient unit of measure equal to 66 centimeters [26 inches]) couldn't injure anyone on the battlements. The fortified parish church within the walls of the castle—designed by the famous Diogo de Arruda—has a pleasing combination of battlements, spires, and ornate Manueline elements. Below the castle a delightful Renaissance fountain enhances the town square. Viana do Alentejo is also noted for a primitive-style pottery, sold in several small shops in town.

Dining

$–$$ ✕ **S. Luis.** In the vaulted rooms of what was a medieval hospital adjoining the castle, this little family-run restaurant serves some of area's best food. It's packed on weekends (and the staff gets somewhat overstretched). The menu is short, simple, and composed entirely of local dishes. Try the *carne de porco assado com puré de patatas* (roast pork with mashed potatoes). ⊠ *Rua António Isidoro de Sousa 36,* ☎ *266/953116. No credit cards.*

Alvito

❸❹ *12 km (7 mi) south of Viana do Alentejo.*

Alvito is a typical, sleepy Alentejo town on a low hill above the Rio Odivelas. Noted for its fortresslike 13th-century parish church, the town also has a 16th-century castle converted into a pousada and a number of modest houses with graceful Manueline doorways and windows.

Dining and Lodging

$$–$$$ ✕🏨 **Pousada do Castelo de Alvito.** This pousada is within the walls of the fortress at the edge of the village. The essential architectural elements of a castle, including crenellated battlements and massive round towers, have been retained, and there's a large garden and courtyard. The cozy restaurant ($–$$$) serves a variety of Alentejo specialties, including an excellent bacalhau *caldeirada* (stew). ⊠ *Largo do Castelo, 7920,* ☎ *284/485343,* 𝖥𝖠𝖷 *284/485383,* 𝖶𝖤𝖡 *www.pousadas.pt. 20 rooms. Restaurant, bar, pool. AE, DC, MC, V. BP.*

São Cucufate

❸❺ *11 km (7 mi) southwest of Alvito.*

It's believed that these 2,000-year-old ruins of a two-story Roman villa were part of an extensive Roman settlement. Coins and other artifacts that have turned up indicate a 1st-century Roman presence here. The villa's ground floor was probably used as a barn, with the living quarters above it. Remnants of the original heating and drainage systems are visible. The building was later adapted and used in the 13th-century as a monastery. The frescoes in the little chapel that still stands on the site were painted in the late 15th and early 16th centuries. There's an information center and a café. ⊠ *Free (donations accepted).* ☉ *Chapel: Tues.–Sun. 9–12:30 and 2–5:30; other parts of site are always open.*

Vidigueira

❸❻ *5 km (3 mi) southeast of São Cucufate.*

Vidigueira, a quiet farm town in the middle of the Alentejo plain, is best known as the onetime home of Vasco da Gama, the Portuguese explorer whose voyage in 1497 opened the sea route to India. A statue of him stands in the main square. At the edge of town, in a setting of gardens and ponds, is a Carmelite chapel where the explorer's body lay from the time it was returned from India in 1539 until it was moved in 1898 to Lisbon's Mosteiro de Jerónimos (Jerónimos Monastery).

Beja

❸❼ *23 km (14 mi) southeast of Vidigueira.*

Spread across a small knoll midway between Spain and the sea is Beja, the Lower Alentejo's principal agricultural center. Much of the oldest part of town retains a significantly Arabic flavor—students of Portuguese even claim that the local dialect has Arabic characteristics—the legacy of more than 400 years of Moorish occupation.

Beja, founded by Julius Caesar and known as Pax Julia, was an important town in the Roman province of Lusitania during the first century. The name Pax Julia was chosen because it was here, after a long struggle, that peace was finally established between the Lusitanian chiefs and Julius Caesar. You can see Roman artifacts and other tokens of Beja's long history at the regional museum in the Convento da Conceição and at the excavations in nearby Pizões.

Many of the town's most interesting monuments were destroyed in the 19th century during the population's fury against the church's domination. In spite of that, Beja has an important valuable heritage that should be explored on foot.

Facing a broad plaza in the center of the oldest part of town, the **Convento da Conceição** was founded in 1459 by the parents of King Manuel I. Favored by the royal family, this Franciscan convent became one of the richest of the period. It now houses the Museu Regional Rainha Dona Leonor (Queen Leonor Regional Museum), whose exhibits are of more interest to scholars of local history than to casual visitors. The church and cloisters display some fine azulejos from the 16th and 17th centuries, including panels depicting scenes from the life of St. John the Baptist, and a section of multicolored Moorish tiles. At the far end of the second-floor gallery is the famous Mariana Window, named after a young Beja nun, Mariana Alcoforado. As the story goes, Mariana fell in love with a French count named Chamilly, who was in the Alentejo fighting the Spaniards. When he went back to France, the nun waited longingly and in vain at the window for him to return. The 1669 publication in France of five passionate love letters, known as the *Portuguese Letters,* written by Mariana to the count, documented the scandalous affair and brought a measure of lasting international literary fame to this provincial Alentejo town. ⊠ *Largo da Conceição,* ☎ *no phone.* ▦ *€0.50 (includes admission to Museu Visigótico).* ◷ *Tues.– Sun. 9:30–12:30 and 2–5:15.*

The **Igreja de Santa Maria** (St. Mary's Church), across the square from the Convento da Conceição, was once a mosque, and can be easily recognized by its massive round pillars, Mudéjar arches, and its bell tower similar in design to that of the famed Giralda Tower in Seville. ⊠ *Largo da Conceição,* ☎ *284/328438.*

NEED A
BREAK?   **Café Pastelaria Santa Maria** (⊠ Rua dos Açoutados), opposite the Igreja de Santa Maria, has outside tables looking out on the convent square and is a pleasant spot for cake and coffee or a light lunch.

Castelo de Beja (Beja Castle) is an extensive system of fortifications, whose crenellated walls and towers chronicle the history of the town from its Roman occupation through its 19th-century battles with the French. ⊠ *Largo de Santo Amaro.* ▦ *€1.* ◷ *June–Sept., Tues.–Sun. 10–1 and 2–6; Oct.–May, Tues.–Sun. 9–noon and 1–4.*

The **Museu Visigótico** (Visigoth Museum), next to the Castelo de Beja in a 6th-century church, houses an impressive collection of tombstones, weapons, and pottery that documents the Visigoth presence in the region. ⊠ *Largo de Santo Amaro,* ☎ *284/321465.* ▦ *€0.50 (includes admission to Convento da Conceição).* ◷ *Tues.–Sun. 10–12:30 and 2–5:30.*

Dining and Lodging

$$–$$$$ ✕ **Os Infantes.** You sit under vaulted ceilings while dining on traditional Alentejan fare in this agreeable restaurant. The food is basic, but skillfully prepared. The *ensopado de borrego* (lamb stew) and the migas alentejanas are recommended. ⊠ *Rua dos Infantes 14,* ☎ *284/322789. AE, MC, V. Closed Wed.*

$–$$ ✕ **A Esquina.** Good, plain local cooking—served with care in pleasant surroundings—is the attraction here. There are few better places to try *lebre com feijão* (hare with beans) in season. The wine list is short, but there's usually a good selection of Serpa cheeses. ⊠ *Rua Infante D. Henrique 26,* ☎ *284/389238. AE, V. Closed Sun.*

$$ ✕🏨 **Pousada do Convento de São Francisco.** Surrounded by spacious gardens is an old convent that has been tastefully converted into this comfortable pousada. The former chapel has been preserved and incorporated into the complex. In the restaurant ($$–$$$$) Alentejo dishes fill the menu, but the *bacalhau com natas* (salt cod cooked with a cream sauce) is delicious. ⊠ *Largo Dom Nuno Álvares Pereira, 7801-901,* ☎ *284/328441,* 𝔽𝔸𝕏 *284/329143,* 𝕎𝔼𝔹 *www.pousadas.pt. 34 rooms, 1 suite. Restaurant, bar, pool, 2 tennis courts. AE, DC, MC, V. BP, MAP.*

$ 🏨 **Cristina.** This comfortable *pensão* (pension) occupies a modern five-story building on one of the main shopping streets. Guest rooms are light and airy, albeit a bit sterile. ⊠ *Rua de Mértola 71, 7800,* ☎ *284/323035,* 𝔽𝔸𝕏 *284/329874. 28 rooms, 3 suites. Bar. AE, DC, MC, V. EP.*

$ 🏨 **Monte Horta do Cano.** A kilometer and a half (1 mi) from Beja on the road to Ferreira do Alentejo, this rustic inn—once a farming estate—has six handsome rooms. On tap for the energetic are tennis, swimming, and clay-pigeon shooting. For those otherwise inclined there's an old wine cellar converted into a bar where you can linger over fine Alentejo wines and snacks of regional bread, cheeses, and cured sausage. ⊠ *Santiago Maior (Apartado 1018, 7800-249),* ☎ 𝔽𝔸𝕏 *284/326156. 6 rooms. Bar, pool, tennis court, mountain bikes. No credit cards. EP.*

Serpa

③⑧ *27 km (17 mi) southeast of Beja.*

In this sleepy agricultural town, men pass the time by gathering together in the compact Praça da República under the shadow of an ancient stone clock tower. Unemployment is high, and there's little else for many to do. In cubbyholes along narrow, cobbled streets, carpenters, shoemakers, basket weavers, and other craftsmen work in much the same manner as their forefathers. One of Portugal's most renowned sheep's milk cheeses is still made in small factories around the town.

An aqueduct forms an integral part of the walls of the 13th-century **castelo,** from which there's a stunning view of town. The huge ruined sections of wall tottering precariously above the entrance are the result of explosions ordered by the Duke of Ossuna during the 18th-century War of the Spanish Succession.

Within the castle walls there's a small **Museu Etnográfico** (Ethnographic Museum) with archaeological and ethnographic exhibits. ☎ *284/540100.* ☒ *Free.* ⊙ *Tues.–Sun. 9–12:30 and 2–5:30.*

The **Museu do Relógio** displays a collection of 1,100 clocks in the domed rooms of the former Convento do Mosteirinho (Mosteirinho Convent). ⊠ *Praça da República,* ☎ *284/543194,* 𝕎𝔼𝔹 *www.museudorelogio. pa-net.pt.* ☒ €2. ⊙ *Tues.–Fri. 2–6, weekends 10–6.*

Dining and Lodging

$$–$$$ ✕ **Molha o Bico.** Huge wine barrels sit at the entrance to this restaurant in a restored wine cellar near Praça da República. In winter, the

specialty is grilled pork; in summer try the gazpacho to start, followed by the fried fish. The Serpa cheese and the Alentejo wines are good at any time of year. ⊠ *Rua Quente 1,* ☎ *284/549264. AE, DC, MC, V. Closed Wed.*

$$ ⓣ **Pousada de São Gens.** On a hill above Serpa's fortifications, this
★   modern, white-domed, Moorish-style pousada is relaxed and informal. The Arabic influence continues as you walk through the green-tile entrance to the lobby, with its many arches and vaulted ceilings. Each of the rooms has a small terrace; bright, cheery fabrics nicely offset the white walls and ceilings. ⊠ *2 km (1 mi) south of Serpa (off N260 to Spain), 7830,* ☎ *284/544724,* ℻ *284/544337,* ⓌⒺⒷ *www.pousadas.pt. 16 rooms, 2 suites. Restaurant, bar, pool. AE, DC, MC, V. BP.*

Mértola

㊴ *81 km (50 mi) south of Serpa.*

The ancient walled-in town of Mértola is on a hill overlooking the Rio Guadiana and its Roman quay. Its occupiers have included the Phoenicians, Carthaginians, the Romans, and the Arabs. Under the Romans, it was an important copper-mining center, and it was the capital of the Moorish kingdom in Portugal until 1238, when the Christians—under Santiago "Mata Mouros" (Moor Killer)—seized it.

Mértola has seen several archaeological excavations in recent years. The artifacts from these digs are all part of the Museu Arqueológico (Archaeology Museum), which has branches—each with displays from different periods—in several locations around town. At any one of them you can buy a special ticket that gives you access to the others as well as to the castelo and the Igreja Matrix.

Built in 1292, the **Castelo de Mértola** contains carved stone from the Roman, Moorish, and Christian periods. Note the very deep cistern in the center of the courtyard. ☎ *no phone.* ⊡ *€3 (ticket gains entrance to castle, several museums, and the Igreja Matrix).* ☉ *Oct.– June, Tues.–Sun. 10–12:30 and 2–5:30; July–Sept., Tues.–Sun. 10–1 and 3–7.*

The 12th-century **Igreja Matrix** (Parish Church), with its 12 white towers, rises from the slopes above the river. It was once a mosque and retains many of its original Islamic features, including a mihrab (prayer niche that indicates the direction of Mecca). ⊠ *Rua da Igreja,* ☎ *286/ 611101.* ⊡ *€3 (ticket gains entrance to church, castle, and several museums).* ☉ *Wed.–Sun. 10–12:30 and 2–5:30.*

Amid displays of jewels and metal items, the **Núcleo Islâmico** (Islamic Branch of the Museu Arqueológico) has an important collection of ceramics that date from the 9th to the 13th centuries. ⊠ *Rua da Igreja,* ☎ *no phone.* ⊡ *€3 (ticket gains entrance to this museum and several others as well as church and castle).* ☉ *Oct.–June, Tues.–Sun. 10–12:30 and 2–5:30; July–Sept., Tues.–Sun. 10–1 and 3–7.*

You'll find statues, vases, and other Roman-period artifacts in the **Núcleo Romano,** the Roman Branch of the Museu Arqueológico. It's in the basement of the Câmara Municipal (City Hall). ⊠ *Praça Luís Vaz de Camões,* ☎ *no phone.* ⊡ *€3 (ticket gains entrance to this museum and several others as well as the church and the castle).* ☉ *Weekdays 9–12:30 and 2–5:30.*

At the **Núcleo Visigótico–Basílica Paleocristã** (Visigoth Branch–Paleo-Christian Basilica) division of the Museu Arqueológico you can see Paleo-Christian writings on tombstones. ⊠ *Praça Rossio do Carmo,* ☎ *no phone.* ⊡ *€3 (ticket gains entrance to this museum and several others*

When you pack your MCI Calling Card, it's like packing your loved ones along too.

Your MCI Calling Card is the easy way to stay in touch when you travel. Use it to call to and from over 125 countries. Plus, every time you call, you can earn frequent flier miles. So wherever your travels take you, call home with your MCI Calling Card. It's even easy to get one. Just visit **www.mci.com/worldphone** or **www.mci.com/partners**.

EASY TO CALL WORLDWIDE

1. Just enter the WorldPhone® access number of the country you're calling from.

2. Enter or give the operator your MCI Calling Card number.

3. Enter or give the number you're calling.

Austria ◆	0800-200-235
Belgium ◆	0800-10012
Czech Republic ◆	00-42-000112
Denmark ◆	8001-0022
Estonia ★	0800-1122
Finland ◆	08001-102-80
France ◆	0-800-99-0019
Germany	0800-888-8000
Greece ◆	00-800-1211

Hungary ◆	06▼800-01411
Ireland	1-800-55-1001
Italy ◆	800-17-2401
Luxembourg	8002-0112
Netherlands ◆	0800-022-91-22
Norway ◆	800-19912
Poland ✢	00-800-111-21-22
Portugal ✢	800-800-123
Romania ✢	01-800-1800
Russia ◆ ✢	747-3322
Spain	900-99-0014
Sweden ◆	020-795-922
Switzerland ◆	0800-89-0222
Ukraine ✢	8▼10-013
United Kingdom	0800-89-0222
Vatican City	172-1022

◆ Public phones may require deposit of coin or phone card for dial tone.   ★ Not available from public pay phones.
▼ Wait for second dial tone.   ✢ Limited availability.

EARN FREQUENT FLIER MILES

Find America *with a Compass*

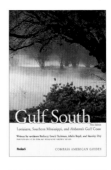

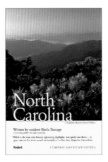

Written by local authors and illustrated throughout
with spectacular color images, Compass American
Guides reveal the character and culture of more than
40 of America's most fascinating destinations. Perfect
for residents who want to explore their own backyards
and for visitors who want an insider's perspective
on the history, heritage, and all there is to see and do.

Fodor's COMPASS AMERICAN GUIDES

At bookstores everywhere.

as well as church and castle). ⊙ *Oct.–June, Tues.–Sun. 10–12:30 and 2–5:30; July–Sept., Tues.–Sun. 10–1 and 3–7.*

Lodging

$ 🏠 **Residencial Beira Rio.** What was once a mill is now a small guest house. Some guest rooms have balconies overlooking the Rio Guadiana; others face town. There are also two sitting rooms and a dining room. A buffet-style breakfast is served on the terrace. ⊠ *Rua Dr. Afonso Costa 108, 7750-352,* ☎ *286/611190,* ℻ *286/611192,* 🌐 *www. beirario.co.pt. 13 rooms. Dining room, cable TV, free parking. AE, DC, MC, V. EP.*

Vila Nova de Milfontes

⓴ *162 km (101 mi) northwest of Mértola.*

This small resort town is at the broad mouth of the Rio Mira, which is lined on both sides by soft, sandy beaches. Overlooking the sea is an ivy-covered fortress built on Moorish foundations in the late 16th century to protect Milfontes from the Algerian pirates who regularly terrorized the Portuguese coast. It was built on ancient foundations, for it was believed that the spirits there would ward off the pirates. It has been restored and converted into a small guest house.

Dining and Lodging

$$–$$$$ ✗ **Restaurante O Pescador.** Locals fondly refer to this bustling, air-conditioned *marisqueira* (seafood restaurant) as *"o Moura"* (Moura's place, a reference to the owner's name). Mouro and his wife started off as fish sellers in the nearby market, so you know the seafood dishes will be good. ⊠ *Largo da Praça 18,* ☎ *283/996338. No credit cards. Closed Thurs. Oct.–Apr.*

$$ 🏠 **Castelo de Milfontes.** In the town's restored castle, this inn is run along the lines of an old-fashioned guest house: the door closes at midnight, and dinner (included in the room rate) is served at a set time with the guests seated around a common table. Guest rooms are comfortable; ask for one with a sea view. ⊠ *Vila Nova de Milfontes 7645,* ☎ *283/998231,* ℻ *283/997122. 7 rooms. Bar, dining room. No credit cards.*

$$ 🏠 **Duna Parque.** This two-story apartment-hotel complex is a 10-minute walk from town and a 5-minute walk from the beach. Guest quarters are in apartments and semidetached villas, all of which have living-room areas, kitchens, and open fireplaces. Some have balconies or roof terraces. The bar-restaurant, with its rustic beams and stonework, serves regional cooking. Note that there's a three-night minimum stay in July and August. ⊠ *Eira da Pedra, 7645-291,* ☎ *283/996451,* ℻ *283/996459,* 🌐 *www.dunaparque.com. 45 units. Restaurant, bar, cable TV, kitchens, indoor-outdoor pool, sauna, hot tub, 2 tennis courts, miniature golf, exercise equipment. AE, MC, V. MAP, FAP.*

Santiago do Cacém

㊶ *40 km (25 mi) northeast of Vila Nova de Milfontes.*

Santiago do Cacém, about 16 km (10 mi) inland at the junction of N120 and N261, is a quiet regional market town. The castle, built by the Knights of the Order of Santiago (St. James) on the site of Moorish ruins, dominates the community and affords sweeping views to the sea, marred only by the oil refineries at Sines. Inside the parish church, you can see a sculpture of St. James battling the Moors. The oldest part of town, just below the castle, is a maze of narrow streets with several well-preserved 17th- and 18th-century manor houses.

The **Museu Municipal** (Municipal Museum), in a former prison at the center of town, has several exhibits on Alentejo life, including one that shows the stages of and implements used in cork production. ⊠ *Praça do Município*, ☎ *269/827375.* ⊠ *Free.* ☉ *Tues.–Fri. 10–noon and 2–5, weekends 2–4.*

Just outside of town, off N121 to Ferreira do Alentejo, you can explore the excavations of the city of **Miróbriga.** Originally this site was settled by the Celts in the 4th century BC; in the 1st century AD, it became a Roman town. The ruins, although not nearly as extensive or well preserved as those at Conímbriga near Coimbra, contain the interesting sanctuaries of Venus and Esculapius (god of medicine). ⊠ *Cumeadas.* ⊠ *€1.50.* ☉ *Tues.–Sat. 9–12:30 and 2–5:30, Sun. 9–noon and 2–5:30.*

Dining and Lodging

$$ ✕ **Cerro da Inês.** The regional food is excellent, and so are the vistas.
★ The restaurant atop a water tower with views of the historic town and the countryside. ⊠ *Rua Machado dos Santos 8,* ☎ *269/823883. AE, MC, V. Closed Mon.*

$$ ✕🏠 **Quinta da Ortiga.** This lovely old estate, just 5 km (3 mi) from
★ Santiago do Cacém, is amid 10 acres of trees and farmland. With wood-panel ceilings and Arraiolos carpets, it evokes life in a rural villa—rustic but with touches of luxury. The intimate restaurant ($$), which serves cuisine of the region, is more like a family dining room than a commercial establishment. ⊠ *Off IP8 to Sines (Apartado 67, 7540),* ☎ *269/822074,* FAX *269/822073. 14 rooms. Restaurant, bar, pool. AE, DC, MC, V. CP.*

Outdoor Activities and Sports

For instruction and for riding on the beach at Sines, contact **Centro Equestre de Santo André** (⊠ Monte V. Cima, Santo André, ☎ 269/761235).

Alcácer do Sal

42 *52 km (32 mi) northeast of Santiago do Cacém.*

Because of its favored location and its salt, Alcácer do Sal was one of Portugal's first inhabited sites; parts of the castle foundations are around 5,000 years old. The Greeks were here, and, later, the Romans, who established the town of Salatia Urbs Imperatoria—a key intersection in their system of Lusitanian roads. During the Moorish occupation, under the name of Alcácer de Salatia, this became one of the most important Muslim strongholds in all of Iberia. In the 16th century Alcácer prospered as a major producer of salt, and a brisk trade was conducted with the northern European countries, which used it to preserve herring. The hilltop castle is the town's most prominent attraction. Red-tile-roof buildings descend from the castle to the riverbank in long, horizontal rows.

The marshlands and the estuary of the Rio Sado that extend to the west of Alcácer form the **Reserva Natural do Sado.** The riverbanks are lined with salt pans and rice paddies, and the nature reserve gives shelter to wildlife such as dolphins, otters, white storks, and egrets. From the beach town of Comporta, Route N261 runs south along the coast through a mostly deserted stretch of dunes and pine trees with some undeveloped sandy beaches.

Dining and Lodging

$$ ✕ **Porto Santana.** You can take your lunch outside with a view of the Rio Sado. Dinner is served indoors as at night the outdoor area be-

comes a bar. The specialty here is *sopa de cação* (baby shark soup). ✉ *Rua Senhora Santana,* ☎ *265/622344. AE, DC, MC, V. Closed Tues.*

$$ 🏠 **Pousada de Dom Afonso II.** In the ancient castle that overlooks the Rio Sado, this very attractive member of pousada looks out over the rooftops of the town and the green plain across the river. Guest rooms are comfortable and tastefully appointed. ✉ *Castelo de Alcácer, Alcácer do Sal 7580,* ☎ *265/613070,* FAX *265/613074,* WEB *www.pousadas.pt. 33 rooms, 2 suites. Restaurant, bar, pool. AE, DC, MC, V. BP, MAP, FAP.*

ÉVORA AND THE ALENTEJO A TO Z

To research prices, get advice from other travelers, and book travel arrangements, visit www.fodors.com.

AIR TRAVEL

You can fly into Lisbon's Portela Airport or the airport in Faro and then take ground transportation into the region. Évora is roughly 160 km (99 mi) from Lisbon and about 245 km (152 mi) from Faro.
➤ AIRPORTS: **Faro Airport** (☎ 289/800617 or 289/800801). **Portela Airport** (☎ 21/841–3500 or 21/841–3700).

BUS TRAVEL

There are few places in this region that aren't served by at least one bus daily. Express coaches run by several regional lines travel regularly between Lisbon and the larger towns such as Évora, Beja, and Estremoz. Since several companies leave for the Alentejo from different terminals in Lisbon, it's best to have a travel agent do your booking.
➤ CONTACTS: **Belos Transportes S.A.** (✉ Terminal Rodoviário, Évora, ☎ 266/769410; ✉ Rossio do Marquês de Pombal 88, Estremoz, ☎ 268/322282). **Eva Transportes** (✉ Rua Tavares 2, Beja, ☎ 284/313620). **Rede Nacional de Expressos** (✉ Av. Duque D'Avila, Arco do Cego, Lisbon, ☎ 21/354–5439).

CAR RENTAL

➤ MAJOR AGENCIES: **Europcar** (✉ Rua Angola 3–5, Beja, ☎ 284/328128). **Hertz** (✉ Dona Isabel 7/13, Évora, ☎ 266/701767).

CAR TRAVEL

Driving will give you access to many out-of-the-way beaches and villages. Although you'll encounter construction on many of the region's main routes, the roads are generally good, and traffic is light. There are no confusing big cities in which to get lost, although parking can be a problem in some of the towns such as Évora

The toll highway A6, which branches off A2 running south from Lisbon, takes you as far as the Spanish border at Caia, where it links up with the highway from Madrid. This road provides easy access to Évora and the Upper Alentejo. The A2 runs south to the Algarve as does the nontoll IP1/E01. Farther inland and south of Évora, the IP2/E802 is the best access for Beja and the southeastern Alentejo. The N521 runs 105 km (65 mi) from Caceres, Spain, to the Portuguese border near Portalegre. To the south, the N433 runs from Seville, Spain, to Beja, 225 km (140 mi) away.

EMERGENCIES

Beja and Évora have hospitals with emergency rooms, and their approaches are marked HOSPITAL; the emergency room is marked URGÊNCIAS. All sizable towns have at least one drugstore that's open weekends, holidays, and after normal store hours. Local newspapers usually keep a schedule, and notices are posted on all pharmacy doors.

➤ EMERGENCY SERVICES: **Évora Police** (☎ 266/702022). **General emergencies** (☎ 112).
➤ HOSPITALS: **Hospital Distrital** (✉ Rua Dr. António F. C. Lima, Beja, ☎ 284/310200). **Hospital Distrital Espirito Santo** (✉ Largo Sr. da Pobreza, Évora, ☎ 266/740100).

MAIL

➤ POST OFFICES: **Beja** (✉ Largo dos Correios, ☎ 284/326135). **Évora** (✉ Rua de Olivença, ☎ 266/745480).

TAXIS

Cabs within Évora's city limits for a fixed price (€2.60). Outside the city limits, the charge is €0.33 per kilometer. Note that if you travel to another town, such as Beja, you'll have to pay for the taxi's return trip to Évora. To get a cab, head for one of the many taxi stands around town, such as the one in Praça do Giraldo (you can't hail them on the street) or call Radio Taxis Évora.
➤ TAXI COMPANY: **Radio Taxis Évora** (☎ 266/734734).

TELEPHONES

Area codes in the region include 266 for Évora, 284 for Beja, 265 for Alcácer do Sal, and 288 for Estremoz.

DIRECTORY AND OPERATOR ASSISTANCE

For information, dial 118; operators often speak English.

TOURS AND PACKAGES

ORIENTATION TOURS

Few regularly scheduled sightseeing tours originate within the region, but many of the major attractions are covered by a wide selection of one-day tours from Lisbon. For information in Lisbon, contact Gray Line Tours or Citirama.
➤ CONTACTS: **Cityrama** (✉ Av. Praia da Vitória 12-B, Saldanha, Lisbon, ☎ 21/355–8564). **Gray Line Tours** (✉ Av. Praia da Vitória 12-B, Saldanha, Lisbon, ☎ 21/352–2594).

WALKING TOURS

Walking tours of Évora are available through Mendes and Murteira, and the company can also organize bus tours of the district's archaeological sites.
➤ CONTACT: **Mendes and Murteira** (✉ Rua 31 de Janeiro 15-A, Évora, ☎ 266/703616).

TRAIN TRAVEL

Travel by train in the vast Alentejo is not for people in a great hurry. Service to the more remote destinations is infrequent—and in some cases nonexistent. A couple towns, including Évora and Beja, are connected with Lisbon by several trains daily. The trains leave from Barreiro station across the river, reached by a ferryboat connection from the river station in Praça do Comércio.
➤ CONTACTS: **Beja CP Train Station** (✉ Largo da Estação ☎ 284/326135). **Évora CP Train Station** (✉ Largo da Estação, ☎ 266/742336).

TRAVEL AGENCIES

Many travel agencies in the region are small, with limited services and no English-speaking personnel. In Évora, Touralentejo has a full range of services and staff members who speak English.
➤ CONTACT: **Touralentejo** (✉ Rua Miguel Bombarda 78, Évora, ☎ 266/702717).

VISITOR INFORMATION

➤ TOURIST OFFICES: **Arraiolos** (⊠ Câmara Municipal, ☎ 266/490240). Évora (⊠ Praça do Giraldo, ☎ 266/702671). **Região de Turismo de Évora** (⊠ Rua de Aviz 90, Évora, ☎ 266/742534).

➤ TOURIST OFFICES: **Campo Maior** (⊠ Rua Major Talaja, ☎ 268/688936). **Castelo de Vide** (⊠ Rua Bartolomeu Álvares da Santa 81, ☎ 245/901361). **Estremoz** (⊠ Rossio do Marquês de Pombal, ☎ 268/333541). **Marvão** (⊠ Rua Dr. António Matos Magalhães, ☎ 245/933886). **Portalegre** (⊠ Palácio Póvoas-Rossio, ☎ 245/331359). **Região de Turismo de São Mamede** (⊠ Estrada de Santana 25, Portalegre, ☎ 245/300770). **Vila Viçosa** (⊠ Câmara Municipal, ☎ 268/881101).

➤ TOURIST OFFICES: **Alcácer do Sal** (⊠ Rua da República 66, ☎ 265/622565). **Beja** (⊠ Rua Capitão João Francisco de Sousa, ☎ 284/311913). **Mértola** (⊠ Rua Alonso Gômes, ☎ 286/612573). **Região de Turismo da Planície Dourada** (⊠ Praça da República 12, Beja, ☎ 284/310150). **Santiago do Cacém** (⊠ Praça do Mercado Municipal, ☎ 269/826696). **Serpa** (⊠ Largo D. Jorge, ☎ 284/544727).

6 THE ALGARVE

The southern coast is broken by extraordinary rock formations in some places and by sprawling resorts in others. Just as enticing as the sand and surf, though, are the less-trammeled reaches: ancient ruins that evince the Romans, inland hill towns that recall the Moors, coastal villages that evoke great mariners. Along the way are simple pleasures—perhaps a plate of grilled sardines or a sunset viewed from old battlements.

By Jules Brown

Updated by
Paul Murphy

PPEALING, YES—PERHAPS TOO APPEALING for its own good. The Algarve is deservedly popular with millions of annual vacationers who throng here for sun, sandy beaches, superb golf, and all the other trappings of the seaside resorts. Along with the region's popularity has come progress, and during the past two decades, the Algarve has been heavily developed, with parts of the once pristine, 240-km (149-mi) coastline now overbuilt. In some areas the shore is almost wall-to-wall with villa complexes, hotels, discos, and bars.

Until the construction of the airport at Faro in the '60s, the Algarve was rarely visited by tourists, and for centuries before that it remained isolated from the rest of Europe. Phoenicians, Romans, and Visigoths established fishing and trading communities here, but it wasn't until the arrival of the Moors in the 8th century that the region became an important strategic settlement. It was the Moors who gave the province its name—El Gharb (the Land to the West)—and who established their capital at the inland town of Silves (then called Chelb). In those days it had direct access to the sea and at its peak was a grand city with a population of more than 30,000.

Silves fell to the Christians in 1189, but the Moors weren't completely out of the region until the middle of the 13th century, leaving many tangible reminders of their 500-year rule: Arabic place-names; the white, cubelike houses in the coastal fishing villages; the popular fruits and sweets of the region; and the physical features of many of the people. In the 15th century Prince Henry the Navigator established a town and a pioneering navigation school near Sagres, where principles were developed that would enable 16th-century Portuguese mariners to explore much of the world. After this flurry of activity, though, the Algarve once again settled into obscurity.

The Algarve measures a mere 40 km (25 mi) north to south, bordered on the north by the Serra de Monchique (Monchique Mountains) and the Serra de Caldeirão (Caldeirão Mountains) and on the east by the Rio Guadiana (Guadiana River). Its location in the south, protected by hills, makes the Algarve much warmer than any other place in the country. The vegetation is far more luxuriant; the land, originally irrigated by the Moors, supports a profusion of fruits, nuts, and vegetables; and the fishing industry has always flourished.

Even where development is at its heaviest, construction takes the form of landscaped villas and apartment complexes, which are generally made of local materials and which blend well with the scenery. And there are still small, undeveloped fishing villages and secluded beaches, particularly in the west. The west is also home to extraordinary rock formations and idyllic grottoes. In the east a series of isolated sandbar islands and sweeping beaches balance the crowded excesses of the middle. To see the Algarve at its best, though, you may have to abandon the shore for a drive inland. Here, rural Portugal still survives in hill villages, market towns, and agricultural landscapes, which, although only a few miles from the coast, seem a world away in attitude.

Pleasures and Pastimes

Beaches

The Algarve's beaches are generally clean and impressive—some of the finest in Europe. There are hundreds from which to choose on the long stretch of coast. Most (especially those in the main resorts) have snack bars and showers, and many have water-sports equipment for rent. Although you can wade out for a swim from most shores, heed local warnings about currents and steeply sloping seabeds.

The best cove beaches are at Lagos. Interesting stretches with enormous rock formations include those at Albufeira and Praia da Rocha. If you require more breathing space, particularly if you're traveling with young children, try the strands near Olhão and Tavira; these and the beaches near Sagres are less populated than those at major resorts.

Bullfights

Unlike the Spanish, the Portuguese don't kill their bulls at the end of the fight, although the severely injured ones are slaughtered immediately afterwards, out of sight of the public. You can attend fights in the towns of Albufeira and Lagos; aficionados of the sport recommend attending the events held in August, which are fought by the country's top matadors (at other times, smaller bulls are used). Bullfights are held every Saturday at 5:30 PM April–June and September–October; in July and August they're held at 10 PM, when the day's heat has dissipated.

Dining

Algarvian cooking makes good use of local seafood. The most unusual of regional appetizers, *espadarte fumada* (smoked swordfish), is sliced thin, served with a salad, and best when accompanied by a dry white wine. Restaurants generally serve their own version of *sopa de peixe* (fish soup) as well as a variety of succulent shellfish: *perceves* (barnacles), *santola* (crab), and *gambas* (shrimp). Main courses often depend on what has been landed that day, but there's generally a choice of *robalo* (sea bass), *pargo* (bream), *atum* (tuna), and espadarte.

At simple beach cafés and harbor stalls the unmistakable smell of *sardinhas assadas* (charcoal-grilled sardines) permeates the air—they make a tempting lunch served with fresh bread and smooth red wine. Perhaps the most famous Algarvian dish is *cataplana*—a stew of clams, pork, onions, tomatoes, and wine, which takes its name from the lidded utensil used to steam the dish. You have to wait for cataplana to be specially prepared, but once you've tasted it, you won't mind waiting again and again.

In inland rural areas, game highlights most menus, with many meat dishes served *o forno* (oven roasted). Specialties include *cabrito* (kid), *leitão* (suckling pig), and *codorniz* (quail), as well as *ensopado de borrego* (lamb stew).

The Algarve is known for its almonds, oranges, and figs, but these rarely appear in restaurants, where the choice of dessert is often limited to flan, ice cream, and perhaps a fresh fruit salad. Typical Algarvian sweets include rich egg, sugar, and almond custards that reflect the Moorish influence, including *doces de amendoa* (marzipan cakes in the shapes of animals and flowers), *bolos de Dom Rodrigo* (almond sweets with egg-and-sugar filling), *bolo Algarvio* (cake made of sugar, almonds, eggs, and cinnamon), and *morgado de figos do Algarve* (fig-and-almond paste). You will find these on sale in *pastelarias* (cake shops) and in some cafés.

Unless otherwise noted, casual dress is acceptable throughout the Algarve. Reservations are not needed off-season, but in summer, you'll need them at most of the better restaurants.

CATEGORY	COST*
$$$$	over €21
$$$	€14–€21
$$	€7–€14
$	under €7

per person for a main course at dinner

Fishing

The best fishing waters are those off the western shores, particularly around Sagres, and local fishermen recommend October through January as the most fruitful—or, rather, *fishful*—months. You're likely to catch gray mullet, sea bass, moray eels, scabbard fish, and bluefish. Individuals and charter companies have organized trips from various ports. Check the boards on quaysides for prices and departure times or consult local tourist offices.

Golf

Golf is a year-round game here, and you'll find some of Europe's best courses, designed by the likes of Henry and William Cotton and Frank Pennink. All courses have a clubhouse with a bar and restaurant, practice grounds, and equipment rentals. Many Algarve hotels promote the area's golf facilities, and although greens fees are never included in room rates, they're often discounted, and guests at certain hotels are given preference when it comes to booking tee times.

Lodging

There are busy beachside hotels and secluded retreats in luxuriant country estates. Apartment and villa complexes with luxurious amenities are also options. Some properties—built on the most beautiful parts of the coast—are truly fancy. They may be a good distance from major towns, but most have bars, restaurants, shops, and other facilities. Budget lodgings are also available.

In most towns and resorts, you'll be approached by people offering very reasonably priced *quartos* (rooms) in private houses, which are almost always clean and cheerful, if small and with shared bathrooms. Don't expect to pay less than around €25 for a reasonable double room per night. Also don't agree to take a room without seeing it first; it may be farther from the town center than you were led to believe.

In summer, reservations at most places are essential, and rates often rise by as much as 50% above off-peak prices. Since the weather from September through May is still good, you might want to consider an off-peak trip to take advantage of the lower prices.

CATEGORY	COST*
$$$$	over €275
$$$	€175–€275
$$	€75–€175
$	under €75

For a standard double room, including tax, in high season (off-season rates may be lower).

Nightlife

In the major resorts you'll find plenty of bars, discos, and clubs. If you prefer a quieter evening, the Algarve's open-air cafés are perfect for a drink and people-watching, and sometimes a musician will stroll by. Many hotels also put on performances of fado and other traditional music. To gamble, head for one of the Algarve's three casinos—at Praia de Rocha, Vilamoura, and Monte Gordo—and remember to bring your passport as well as your wallet.

Shopping

All the main towns and villages have regular food markets, usually open daily from 8 until around 2. Among the best are those in Olhão, Tavira, Lagos, and Silves. Larger weekly and monthly markets, where a wider variety of produce and goods is sold, are held in Albufeira, on the first and third Tuesday of the month; in Loulé, every Saturday; in Lagos, on the first Saturday of the month; in Portimão, on the first Monday; in Sagres, on the first Friday; and in Silves, on the third Monday. Most major towns hold annual country fairs, where alongside the market stalls you'll find crafts and entertainment. Dates vary from year to year; check with tourist offices for details.

Probably the best town in which to shop is Portimão, where you can spend at least a half day browsing. In summer, the main resorts have a lot of roadside stalls (a good area is outside the lighthouse at Cabo São Vicente), at which you can buy jewelry, handicrafts, art, and clothes. Look for reasonably priced hand-knit sweaters in stores throughout the Algarve. The best places to look for handmade copper items and other metal crafts are Portimão, Lagos, and Loulé. Small woven sisal baskets make good souvenirs and are available nearly everywhere.

Water Sports

There are anchorage and harbor facilities at Faro, Lagos, Olhão, Portimão, Praia da Rocha, Sagres, and Vila Real. Snorkeling and scuba diving are especially good in the western Algarve, where certified, experienced divers can explore caves and rock formations. Wind- and board surfing are popular at a number of spots as well. In fact, several of the more remote west-coast beaches attract surfers from all parts of Europe.

Exploring the Algarve

The Algarve's main roads—the N125 and the IP1/E1—and its train line connect towns and villages along the entire coast, though rail travelers should beware that the train service is very slow and stations are often some way from the center of the town, resort, or village they purport to serve. If you rent a car, you can see all of the region in a week, albeit at a fairly brisk pace. Even if you plan to stay at one resort for several days, make an effort to see both the eastern and western ends of the province and an inland town or two; each has a very distinct character.

For touring purposes, the province can conveniently be divided into four sections, starting with Faro—the Algarve's capital—and the nearby beaches and inland towns. The second section encompasses the region east to the border town of Vila Real de Santo António, from which you can cross into Spain. The most built-up part of the coast, and the section with the most to offer vacationers, runs from Faro west to Portimão. The fourth section covers Lagos, the principal town of the western Algarve, and extends to Sagres and Cabo São Vicente.

Great Itineraries

Give yourself at least three days to take in the more important sights. In five days you can see the sights, have a little time at the beach, linger over a delicious seafood lunch (or two) at a beachfront restaurant, and still have time to get away from the built-up coastal strip to some of the more remote inland villages. A seven-day stay will allow you to, perhaps, get in a game of golf or spend a few days simply relaxing on some of the many excellent beaches. After all, it was the discovery of these sandy stretches by sun-starved northern Europeans that transformed this sleepy province into one of the continent's most popular vacation spots.

Numbers in the text correspond to numbers in the margin and on the Algarve, Faro, and Lagos maps.

IF YOU HAVE 3 DAYS
Begin with a day exploring the provincial capital, ⊞ **Faro** ①–⑧, and its surroundings. The following morning, head west to the lighthouse at **Cabo São Vicente** ㉜ and the fortress and exhibition center at

Sagres ㉛, where you can have lunch overlooking the cliffs. In the afternoon, return to Faro, stopping along the way in **Lagos** ㉕–㉙ or **Portimão** ㉑. On day three, drive east to **Vila Real de Santo António** ⑭, at the border with Spain. En route you can explore **Olhão** ⑨, with its Moorish-style architecture, and **Tavira** ⑫, one of the Algarve's most attractive towns.

IF YOU HAVE 5 DAYS

After a day in and around ⊞ **Faro** ①–⑧, drive west to visit **Portimão** ㉑ and the nearby beach resort of **Praia da Rocha** ㉒. Continue west to overnight in ⊞ **Lagos** ㉕–㉙, an attractive city whose origins go back to Carthaginian times. After seeing the sights in Lagos, head to **Cabo São Vicente** ㉜ for views from the lighthouse and then to ⊞ **Sagres** ㉛. The next morning, follow N268 along the west coast to Aljezur, where you take N267 through a remote part of the Algarve to the hill town of **Monchique** ㉔. Enjoy lunch at one of the terrace restaurants that afford views across the countryside to the sea. After lunch, head down the mountain on N266 to the coastal road N125 and swing east to **Olhão** ⑨ and ⊞ **Tavira** ⑫. On your last day, visit the border town of **Vila Real de Santo António** ⑭.

IF YOU HAVE 7 DAYS

With a week, you can see the main attractions at a leisurely pace and still have a few days left to bask on the fine beaches. Simply pick a spot and spend an extra night nearby. In keeping with the five-day itinerary, you could simply stay a day or two longer near ⊞ **Praia da Rocha** ㉒ or ⊞ **Praia da Luz** ㉚. If you like your beaches long and flat, you could head to the sands of the Sotavento—the region extending east from Faro—instead. The strands off ⊞ **Tavira** ⑫ and **Olhão** ⑨ are the best. The beaches of the Barlavento, west of Faro, often have dramatic cliffs and bizarre rock formations as a backdrop.

When to Tour the Algarve

Winter is mild: if you seek solitude and don't mind limiting your swimming to heated hotel pools, it's the perfect time to visit. There are plenty of bargains to be had as well. Algarvian springs, with their rolling carpets of wildflowers, are delightful. Late in the season, you can just about take a dip in the ocean, and there's plenty of space to lay out your beach blanket. Summer (July–August) is high season, when lodging is at a premium, prices are at their highest, and crowds are at their thickest. But summer also brings warmer seas, piercing blue skies, and golden sands at the foot of glowing ocher-red cliffs.

FARO AND ENVIRONS

Many people fly in to Faro and pass straight through on their way to beaches east and west, which is unfortunate. The city's harbor and Cidade Velha (Old Town) are both worthy of a night's stay or more, and its many facilities make it a fine base for touring the region. The towns that ring Faro contain their own sights worth seeing, from beaches and markets to churches and ruins.

Faro

❶–❽ *300 km (186 mi) southeast of Lisbon.*

The Algarve's prosperous provincial capital has around 100,000 residents. Founded by the Moors, the city was taken by Afonso III in 1249, at the end of the Arab domination. Much of its early architecture was lost in the late 16th century, when it was sacked by the English under the earl of Essex. It was further damaged by two 18th-century earthquakes, the latter of which, in 1755, also destroyed Lisbon. Remnants

The Algarve

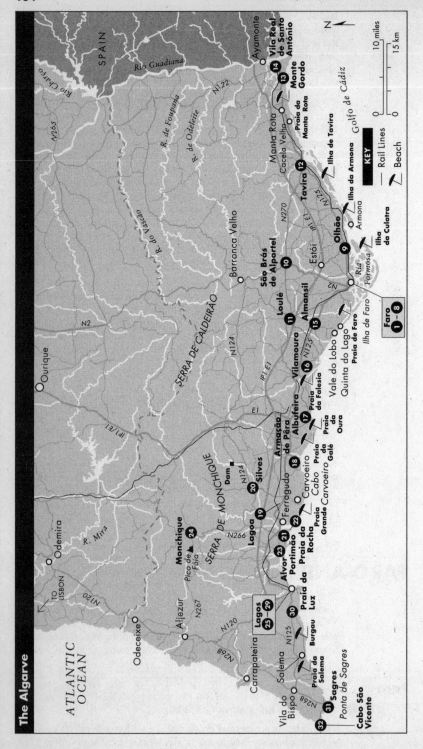

SPAIN

Rio Guadiana

ATLANTIC
OCEAN

SERRA DE CALDEIRÃO

SERRA DE MONCHIQUE

Golfo de Cádiz

KEY
— Rail Lines
⌐ Beach

N ↖

10 miles
15 km

Ayamonte
Vila Real de Santo António **14**
Monte Gordo **13**
Praia da Manta Rota
Cacela Velho
Manta Rota
Tavira **12**
Ilha de Tavira
Ilha da Armona
Olhão **9**
Armona
Ilha da Culatra
Estói
São Brás de Alportel **10**
Loulé
Almansil
Vilamoura **11**
15
Vale do Lobo **16**
Quinta do Lago
Praia de Faro
Ilha de Faro
Ria Formosa
Faro 1 – 8
Praia da Falesia
Albufeira **17**
Praia da Oura
Armação de Pêra
Carvoeiro **18**
Praia Cabo Carvoeiro
Praia Grande Carvoeiro Galé
Silves **20**
Ferragudo **22**
Lagoa **19**
Dam
Monchique **24**
Pico de Fóia
Alvor **23**
Portimão **21**
Praia da Rocha
Praia da Luz
Lagos 25 – 29
Burgau **30**
Salema
Praia da Salema
Sagres **31**
Vila do Bispo
Cabo São Vicente
Ponta de Sagres
32
Carrapateira
Odeceixe
Aljezur
Odemira
Ourique
Barranco Velho
R. Mira
R. de Foupana
R. de Odeleite
R. do Vascão
TO LISBON

N125
N264
N268
N267
N266
N124
N2
N270
N2
N122
N265
IP1/E1
E1

of the medieval walls and some historic buildings, however, can still be seen in the delightful Cidade Velha (Old Town). Here, quiet streets and squares, where balconies and tile work adorn even the most unappealing facade, are perfect for a stroll.

① You enter the Cidade Velha through an 18th-century gate, the **Arco da Vila,** which stands in front of the central Jardim Manuel Bivar (Manuel Bivar Garden). Note the white-marble statue of St. Thomas Aquinas in a niche at the top and the storks that nest here permanently.

② The squat, mostly Renaissance-style **Sé** (Cathedral) faces the Largo da Sé, a grand square bordered by orange trees and whitewashed palace buildings. The cathedral retains a Gothic tower but is mostly of interest for its interior full of 17th- and 18th-century *azulejos* (tiles). On one side of the nave is a red chinoiserie organ, dating from 1751. Best of all, however, is the view from the top of the church tower, looking out over Cidade Velha rooftops and across the lagoon. ⌂ *Largo da Sé,* ☎ *no phone.* ◷ *Mon.–Sat. 10–5 or 6, Sun. 8–1 for services.*

③ The 16th-century Convento de Nossa Senhora da Assunção (Convent of Our Lady of the Assumption) houses the **Museu Arqueológico** (Archaeological Museum). The conversion makes fine use of the convent's two-story cloister. The best displays are the Roman artifacts from local settlements predating Moorish Faro as well as Roman statues from the excavations at Milreu. ⌂ *Praça Afonso III 14,* ☎ *289/897400.* ▧ *€2.* ◷ *Mon.–Sat. 10–6:30.*

④ The plain facade of the **Igreja de São Francisco** (Church of St. Francis) gives no hint of the richness of its baroque interior. Inside are glorious 18th-century blue-and-white azulejos and a chapel adorned with gilt work. There aren't any set visiting hours. Ask at the tourist office or push the bell by the church's door; late afternoon is usually the best time to try. ⌂ *Largo de São Francisco,* ☎ *no phone.*

⑤ The small *doca* (dock)—flanked by Faro's main square, the Praça Dom Francisco Gomes, and the Jardim Manuel Bivar—is filled with small pleasure craft rather than working fishing boats. A good time to come here is at dusk when the sun sets dramatically over the lagoon.

NEED A
BREAK?
The **Café Aliança** (⌂ Rua Francisco Gomes 7–11, ☎ 289/801621) is a time-worn coffeehouse, between Rua Francisco Gomes and Rua Marinha. Service is somewhere between slow and dead slow (wave vigorously to catch a waiter's attention), but it's worth it to see a glimpse of the Faro of an earlier time.

⑥ At the dockside **Museu Marítimo** (Maritime Museum), models of local fishing craft are displayed alongside full-size boats of war and exploration. ⌂ *Capitania do Porto de Faro,* ☎ *289/803601.* ▧ *€1.* ◷ *Weekdays 9:30–noon and 2:30–5.*

East of the harbor, in the pedestrian shopping streets around **Rua de Santo António,** you'll find much of what makes Faro tick as a tourist town: bars, restaurants, shops, and sidewalk hawkers touting souvenirs and snacks.

⑦ Providing a bit of culture in an area otherwise dominated by stores and eateries, the **Museu Etnográfico Regional** (Regional Ethnographical Museum) sheds light on local agricultural and fishing practices through models and diagrams. Crafts and reconstructions of typical house interiors are displayed, too. ⌂ *Praça da Liberdade 2,* ☎ *289/827610.* ▧ *€1.50.* ◷ *Weekdays 9–12 and 2–5.*

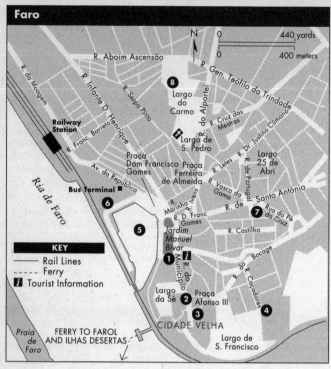

8 Just northwest of the city center, the baroque **Igreja do Carmo** (Carmo Church), looking very out of place amid the modern buildings surrounding it, is flanked by twin bell towers. Inside, a door to the right of the altar leads to the Capela dos Ossos (Chapel of the Bones), whose walls are covered in more than 1,000 skulls and bones of parishioners and monks—an eerie sight, to say the least. ⊠ *Largo do Carmo,* ☎ *no phone.* ☞ *€0.60.* ☉ *Weekdays 10–1 and 3–5, Sat. 10–1.*

Beach

Although thick with crowds in peak season and on weekends, the long, sandy **Praia de Faro,** on the Ilha de Faro (Faro Island), a sandbar 5 km (3 mi) southwest of Faro, is the stretch closest to town. It's near the airport and is a 25-minute ride from town on Bus 16, which runs every hour 8 AM–10 PM. You can catch it at the harbor or opposite the bus terminal.

Dining and Lodging

$–$$ ✗ **Adega Nova.** Expertly prepared Portuguese dishes are served at long wooden tables lined by benches, a seating arrangement that keeps things lively at this down-to-earth *adega* (wine cellar). You'll find more good cheer, as well as drinks, in the tile-covered bar. It's a good thing, too, as this place is close to the train station in an otherwise dreary area. ⊠ *Rua Francisco Barreto 24,* ☎ *289/813433. No credit cards.*

$–$$ ✗ **Dois Irmãos.** In business since 1925, this large, central restaurant (one of several good places on this street) specializes in cataplana, as evidenced by the utensils that hang from its wood-beam ceiling. Almost any of the other seafood dishes are worth trying, too. Just save room for the flan. Choose your wine from one of the hundreds of bottles that line the upper walls. ⊠ *Largo do Terreiro do Bispo 14–15,* ☎ *289/823337. AE, DC, MC, V.*

$–$$ ✗ **Mesa dos Mouros.** The Moors' Table occupies an ancient stone house right by the Sé. You can either eat indoors or dine alfresco on a raised wooden terrace looking across the cobbled square, which is fringed with orange trees. Despite the antiquity of its surroundings, this is a very stylish restaurant that serves good fish dishes and also Spanish tapas. ✉ *Largo da Sé,* ☎ *289/878873. MC, V.*

$$ ★ 🏨 **Hotel Eva.** From this well-appointed hotel on the main square, you have views of the yacht-filled harbor and the Cidade Velha. There's a bar with occasional evening entertainment, as well as a rooftop pool and top-floor restaurant. Rooms are modern and comfortably furnished; ask for one overlooking the front. There's also a courtesy bus to the town beach on nearby Ilha de Faro. ✉ *Av. da República 1, 8000–0078,* ☎ *289/803354,* 𝔽𝔸𝕏 *289/802304. 150 rooms. Restaurant, bar, coffee shop, snack bar, in-room safes, cable TV, minibars, pool, hair salon, laundry service, convention center. AE, DC, MC, V. BP, MAP, FAP.*

$ ★ 🏨 **Residencial Algarve.** The original building was constructed in the 1880s for a wealthy maritime family. It was renovated to mirror the original style and is now one of Faro's nicest budget hotels. Even the bathrooms recall those in much more upscale establishments. The hotel is just a few steps from the center of town. ✉ *Rua Infante Dom Henrique 52, 8000–0078,* ☎ *289/895700,* 𝔽𝔸𝕏 *289/895703,* 𝕎𝔼𝔹 *www.residencialalgarve.com. 14 rooms. Breakfast room, cable TV. MC, V. BP.*

Nightlife

Faro's central pedestrian streets are filled at night with throngs of café goers. Rua do Prior, in particular, is known for its wide selection of late-closing bars. Friday night is the best time for barhopping. **Gothic Bar** (✉ Rua da Madalena 38, off Rua do Prior, ☎ 289/807887) is a reliable stalwart. Don't be put off by the silly name: **Kingburger** (✉ Rua do Prior 40, ☎ 289/828085) rocks until well into the morning. If you're after a full-fledged disco, visit trendy **24 Julho** (✉ Rua do Prior 38, ☎ 289/282468), which is patronized almost exclusively by the locals on weekends when it stays open until 7 AM.

Olhão

❾ *8 km (5 mi) east of Faro.*

During the Napoleonic Wars, the inhabitants of this 18th-century port town on the Ria Formosa (a *ria* is a briny river) defied the French blockade on trade with Britain and profited from smuggling. With the proceeds, they built North African–style, cube-shape whitewashed houses. In 1808, local fishermen reputedly sailed to Brazil to inform the exiled Dom João VI that the French had departed from Portugal. Because of their loyalty and courage (they sailed without navigational aids), the fishermen's home town was granted a town charter. Although modern construction has destroyed much of its charm, Olhão's port is still colorful, and its intricate Cidade Velha is appealing. To get a bird's-eye view climb the parish church's bell tower.

The **Roman ruins** at Milreu, about 10 km (6 mi) northwest of Olhão, were first excavated in 1876. The settlement was once known as Roman Ossonoba, and the remains—including a temple (later converted into a Christian basilica) and mosaic fragments adorning some of the 3rd-century baths—date from the 2nd through the 6th centuries. A few of the more portable pieces are on display in Faro's Municipal Museum. 🎫 €1.25. ☾ *May–Sept., Tues.–Sun. 9:30–12:30 and 2–6; Oct.–Apr., Tues.–Sun. 9:30–12:30 and 2–5.*

Beaches

Adding to the allure of this area's beaches is the designation of this entire section of coastline, including islands and river inlets, as a nature reserve, thanks to the great number of migratory birds that flock to the area on their way south for the winter. To reach beaches on the nearby islands, take a ferry from the jetty east of town. From June to September, ferries run hourly each day; from October through May there are three or four trips daily. Schedules are available at the tourist office. The fare is about €1. If the kiosk at the jetty is closed, you can buy tickets on board.

The island of **Armona,** about 15 minutes east of Olhão, has some fine, isolated stretches of sand as well as vacation villas and café-bars. The sandy island of **Culatra,** 40 minutes east of Olhão, has several ramshackle fishing communities; at the southern village of Farol, you'll find agreeable beaches.

Shopping
One of the Algarve's best food markets, the **Mercado dos Pescadores** (☉ Mon.–Sat. 7–2) is held in the riverfront buildings in the town gardens. Feast your eyes on the shellfish for which Olhão is renowned; mussels, in particular, are a local specialty.

São Brás de Alportel

🔟 *18 km (11 mi) northwest of Olhão.*

São Brás is a regional center for the processing of cork from the surrounding countryside. It's an unremarkable place, but there are two reasons why it makes a refreshing break from the developed coastline: its museum of traditional dress and its pousada.

Just a short walk from the center of town is the **Museu Etnográfico do Traje Algarvio** (Ethnographic Museum of Algarvian Costume), a charmingly old-fashioned collection of local costumes and various other regional rural bygones. ⊠ *Rua Dr. José Dias Sancho 61,* ☏ *289/840100.* 🎫 *€1.* ☉ *Weekdays 10–1 and 2–5, weekends 2–5.*

Dining and Lodging

$$ ✕🏨 **Pousada de São Brás.** The Algarve's only inland pousada is atop a hill where the air is pure, and the views are splendid. It was built in the 1940s and though it has been lavishly refurbished for the 21st century, most of the original look has been kept intact. In public areas bright yellow rattan furniture has splashy green upholstery, and lattice-work dividers provide a sense of privacy. Guest rooms and their tile baths are well appointed. In the restaurant ($$–$$$$) look for such Portuguese fare as clams with coriander or roast kid with rosemary; the quality of the food is variable. ⊠ *Estrada de Lisboa, 8150,* ☏ *289/842305,* FAX *289/841726,* WEB *www.pousadas.pt. 31 rooms, 2 suites. Restaurant, bar, cable TV, pool, tennis court. AE, DC, MC, V. BP, MAP.*

Loulé

⓫ *13 km (8 mi) west of São Brás de Alportel.*

This little town is known for its crafts and its vibrant Saturday-morning fair, held in and around the landmark, onion-dome, central market. The tiny, cobbled streets—particularly Rua da Barbacã—around the castle and the church are lined with whitewashed houses and workshops (closed Saturday afternoons and Sunday) where a few artisans still make lace, leather, and copper items. Note the many houses with very finely sculpted (or filigreed) plasterwork on their white chimneys—a typical old Algarve sight. The rest of Loulé is overwhelmed by the main boulevard and modern buildings, but there's a pleasant municipal park at the top of town.

Once a Moorish stronghold, Loulé has preserved the ruins of the medieval **Castelo de Loulé** (Loulé Castle), which houses the historical museum and archives as well as the tourist office. ⊠ *Largo Dom Pedro I,* ☎ *289/400642.* 🎟 *Free.* ☉ *Weekdays 9–5:30, Sat. 10–5:30.*

The restored 13th-century **Igreja Matriz** (Parish Church) has handsome tiles, wood carvings, and an unusual wrought-iron pulpit. ⊠ *Largo Pr. C. da Silva,* ☎ *no phone.* ☉ *Mon.–Sat. 9–noon and 2–5:30.*

Lodging

$ 🏨 **Loulé Jardim Hotel.** Portuguese business types are drawn to this hotel, which is well off the main road on a small square in the old part of town, yet only a short drive (8 km [5 mi]) from the coast. Rooms are modest and clean; prices leave you with extra money to buy some of those items crafted in town. ⊠ *Praça Manuel D'Arriaga, 8100-665,* ☎ *289/413094,* 𝔽𝔸𝕏 *289/463177,* 𝕎𝔼𝔹 *www.loulejardimhotel.com. 52 rooms. 2 bars, lounge, in-room safes, cable TV, pool, laundry service, meeting room; no air-conditioning. AE, MC, V. BP*

THE EASTERN ALGARVE

The eastern portion of the province, known as the Sotavento, is a region of flat, sandy beaches. Although there has been some development along the coast, this is primarily a quiet, low-key area, though its principal town, Tavira, is an important fishing port.

Tavira

★ ⑫ *30 km (19 mi) east of Loulé, 28 km (17 mi) east of Faro.*

At the mouth of the quiet Rio Gilão (Gilão River), Tavira is immediately endearing with its castle ruins, riverfront gardens, and old streets. Many of the town's white, 18th-century houses retain their original doorways and coats-of-arms; others have peculiar four-sided roofs; and still others are completely covered in tiles. The town also has more than 30 churches, most dating from the 17th and 18th centuries. One of two river crossings—the low bridge adjacent to the arcaded Praça da República—is of Roman origin, although it was rebuilt in the 17th century and again a few years ago after sustaining damage from floodwaters

Since Tavira is a tuna-fishing port, you'll find plenty of local color and fresh fish; tuna steaks, often grilled and served with onions, are on restaurant menus all over town at remarkably low prices. In the harbor area, you can sample no-frills dining at its best, alongside the fishermen, at any of the café-restaurants across from the picturesque tangle of boats and nets.

From the battlemented walls of the ruined central **castelo** you can look down over Tavira's many church spires and across the river delta to the sea. ⊠ *Stepped street off Rua da Liberdade.* 🎟 *Free.* ☉ *Weekdays 8–4:30, weekends 10–5:30.*

One of the town's two major churches, **Santa Maria do Castelo** (St. Mary of the Castle) was built on the site of a Moorish mosque in the 13th century. Although it was almost entirely destroyed by the 1755 earthquake, the church retains its original Gothic doorway. ⊠ *Alto de Santa Maria (next to castelo),* ☎ *no phone.* ☉ *Daily 10–5.*

The **Igreja da Misericórdia** (Misericórdia Church) is a Renaissance structure with a portal that dates from 1541. On Good Friday, a 10 PM candlelight procession begins here. From May through July, the church occasionally hosts musical performances during the Algarve International Classical Music Festival. ⊠ *West of Praça da República,* ☎ *no phone.* ⊙ *Daily 9:30–1 and 2–5:30.*

Beaches

Directly offshore and extending west for some 10 km (6 mi) is the **Ilha de Tavira,** a long sandbar with several good beaches. Ferries run to the island every half hour in July and August and every hour May through June and September through mid-October. The fare is about €1 round-trip. In summer a bus (marked QUATRO ÁGUAS) runs between the center of town and the jetty 2 km (1 mi) east.

About 12 km (7½ mi) east of Tavira is Manta Rota, a small community with a few bars, restaurants, hotels, and the **Praia de Manta Rota.** At this exceptional beach, sandbars merge with the shore. A particularly nice strand is the offshore sandbar at the village of Cacela Velha. Note that, from Manta Rota to Faro, the underwater drop-offs are often steep and you can quickly find yourself in deep water.

Dining and Lodging

$$–$$$ ✕ **Restaurante Imperial.** This restaurant behind the riverside gardens is well known for its fish: clams, tuna, a tasty mixed fried-fish plate—you name it. In summer, there's seating on the sidewalk. Waiters are good at their job but a little aloof: after 40 years of service, the Imperial doesn't have to try hard to attract customers. Desserts are a tad disappointing. ⊠ *Rua José Pires Padinha 22–24,* ☎ *281/322306. MC, V. Closed Wed. Oct.–May.*

$–$$ ✕ **Beira Rio.** Named for it's riverbank location, the Beira Rio offers the best water views in town. Locals tend to eat in the azulejo-lined dining room; visitors are often drawn to the peaceful terrace, where watching the moon rise over the Roman bridge is alone worth the price of dinner. Well-prepared Portuguese specialties such as pork with port-wine sauce share the menu with steaks, pizzas, and pasta. ⊠ *Rua Borda de Agua de Assêca 46–48,* ☎ *281/323165. AE, DC, MC, V. No lunch.*

$–$$ ✕ **Ponto de Encontro.** Cross the Roman bridge to this typical Portuguese restaurant beside a small square abloom with flowers and closed to traffic in summer. Dine inside amid tile walls and tables immaculately draped with linens. Or relax at outside tables to a view of the passing scene. Algarve-style swordfish grilled with garlic, tuna fried with onion, and other fresh fish dishes are specialties. ⊠ *Praça Dr. António Padinha 39,* ☎ *281/323730. AE, DC, MC, V.*

$$ ✕🏠 **Marés Residencial e Restaurante.** Only a stone's throw from the waterfront (and the summer ferry to the Ilha de Tavira), this tiny hotel is above an excellent Portuguese restaurant ($$–$$$$). Some of the rooms have balconies that offer river or town views; all provide basic comforts and have bathrooms decorated with rustic tilework. A rooftop terrace looks out over Tavira's distinctive pyramid-shape roofs. ⊠ *Rua José Pires Padinha 1134/140, 8800,* ☎ *281/325815,* FAX *281/ 325819. 15 rooms. Restaurant. AE, DC, MC, V. BP.*

$ 🏠 **Residencial Princesa do Gilão.** Across the river from the main square, this small, gleaming white hotel stands on the quayside, with fine views of both the river and the castle walls. All the rooms are modern and compact; request one that faces the front and has a balcony. ⊠ *Rua Borda de Água de Aguiar 10–12, 8800,* ☎ FAX *281/325171. 22 rooms. No air-conditioning. No credit cards. BP.*

Monte Gordo

🔞 *22 km (14 mi) east of Tavira.*

Pine woods and orchards break up the flat landscape around this large resort area, just 4 km (2½ mi) from the Spanish border. Relentlessly modern, Monte Gordo has plenty of hotels, restaurants, and nightspots but falls well short on charm and character.

Beach

The flat, 12-km-long (7-mi-long) **Praia de Monte Gordo** is a very popular beach. The seawater here has the highest average temperature in the country.

Dining and Lodging

$–$$ ✕ **Mota.** Large, lively, and unpretentious, this well-established restaurant is on the sands of the Praia de Monte Gordo. Seating is on a large covered terrace facing the ocean. During the day you can drop in for a snack or salad if you don't want a full meal; in the evening you're served regional dishes while live music plays in the background. ⊠ *Praia de Monte Gordo,* ☎ *281/512340. No credit cards.*

$$ ▥ **Alcázar.** Outside, white balconies contrast with a redbrick facade; inside, sinuous arches and low, molded ceilings recall a cave's interior—or that of an Arab tent. Rooms have their own terraces and window boxes. The staff is accommodating, and the location—two blocks from the beach—is convenient. ⊠ *Rua de Ceuta 9, 8900–435,* ☎ *281/510140,* ℻ *281/510149. 119 rooms. Restaurant, bar, coffee shop, piano bar, some in-room data ports, in-room safes, some in-room hot tubs, cable TV, some minibars, 2 pools, tennis court, shops, dance club, recreation room, playground, laundry service. AE, DC, MC, V. BP, MAP.*

$$ ▥ **Casablanca Hotel.** Not being on the main drag is a major advantage at this cozy hotel with a strong Moorish feel. The solarium and the heated indoor pool help ward off any out-of-season chill. ⊠ *Rua Sete, 8900,* ☎ *281/511444,* ℻ *281/511999. 42 rooms. 2 pools (1 indoor). AE, DC, MC, V. BP, MAP.*

Nightlife

In addition to a wealth of nightclubs and discos, Monte Gordo has a **casino** (⊠ Av. Infante, ☎ 281/530800) with blackjack and roulette, among other games, as well as a slot-machine room. From July through September, you can have dinner and see a cabaret show for €75; from October through June the cost is €50. You must be 18 or older to enter (bring your passport), and dressy-casual attire is best.

Vila Real de Santo António

⑭ *4 km (2½ mi) east of Monte Gordo, 47 km (29 mi) east of Faro.*

This community on the Rio Guadiana is the last stop before Spain. The original town was destroyed by a tidal wave in the 17th century and wasn't rebuilt until the late 18th century, when the Marquês de Pombal constructed a new, gridded town. Consequently, Vila Real, which took only five months to complete, is a showpiece of 18th-century planning. Like most border towns, it's a lively place, with plenty of bars and restaurants and some traffic-free central streets that encourage evening strolls.

The company Riosul Viagens e Turismo arranges day-long river cruises that include lunch, a stop for a swim, and a final stop in the timeless village of Foz de Odeleite before returning by boat to Vila Real. The company has shuttle service from all eastern and central Algarve hotels to the Vila Real de Santo António dock. The cost is €35 to €42.50, depending on pickup location.

THE CENTRAL ALGARVE

The central Algarve, between Faro and Portimão, has the heaviest concentration of resorts. Nevertheless, in between built-up areas you can still discover quiet bays and amazing rock formations as well as exclusive, secluded hotels and villas. With a car it's easy to travel the few miles inland that make all the difference: minor roads lead into the hills and to towns that have resisted the changes wrought upon the coast.

Almansil

⑮ *10 km (6 mi) northwest of Faro.*

Almansil, which straggles along the N125, is near two of the region's biggest draws: the seaside resort areas of Quinta do Lago, roughly 5 km (3 mi) to the south, and Vale do Lobo, about 5 km (3 mi) to the southwest. Wealthy Europeans love these complexes for their superb hotels and sports facilities. Golf is the thing here, but tennis and horseback riding are also popular. Almansil's biggest draw is the **Igreja de São Lourenço** (Church of St. Lawrence), built in 1730. Notable are the church's blue-and-white, floor-to-ceiling azulejo panels and its intricate gilt work. ⊠ *São Lourenço,* ☎ *no phone.* ☑ *€3.* ☉ *Mon. 2:30–6, Tues.–Sat 10–1 and 2:30–5.*

A pair of 200-year-old cottages downhill from the Igreja de São Lourenço have been transformed into the **Centro Cultural de São Lourenço.** The center has exhibits of contemporary Portuguese works, and it holds occasional classical music concerts. Don't miss the delightful sculpture garden to the rear. ⊠ *São Lourenço.* ☎ *289/395475.* ☑ *Free.* ☉ *Mon. 2:30–6, Tues.–Sat. 10–1 and 2:30–5.*

Atlantic Park is the smallest of the region's water parks but is still full of fun chutes and flumes. ⊠ *N125, Quatro Estradas, Celões,* ☎ *289/397282.* ☑ *€11 full day; €9 after 2 PM.* ☉ *Daily mid-Apr.–mid-Oct. 10–6.*

Dining and Lodging

$–$$$ ✕ **Sr. Franco.** The finger-lickin' chicken that's grilled over charcoal pits in this large, spotless restaurant has won awards for owner Joaquim Guerréiro (he concocts a special seasoning of local herbs). For an even better dining experience order a side salad (with tomatoes, onions, and ample fresh oregano) and top everything off with a bottle of Portuguese *vinho verde,* a fruity, faintly sparkling wine. The food is well worth the 5-km (3-mi) trip southwest from Almansil. ⊠ *Estrada de Quarteira, Escanxinas,* ☎ *289/393756. AE, DC, MC, V.*

$$$$ ✕🏨 **Hotel Quinta do Lago.** With 1,680 acres of hilly pine woods—surrounded by opulent private villas and sparkling, blue waters—this Almansil resort is secluded. Golf is the main focus; a stay here gets you substantial discounts at area courses. Numerous other sporting activities, from horseback riding to clay-pigeon shooting, can be arranged. The beach and sandbar are accessed via a wooden bridge. Superb Venetian dishes are served in the elegant Ca d' Oro restaurant ($$$–$$$$); the equally classy Brisa do Mar ($$$–$$$$) focuses on more local culinary matters. ⊠ *Quinta do Lago, 8135–024,* ☎ *289/350350,* ℻ *289/396393,* 🌐 *www.quintadolagohotel.com. 132 rooms, 9 suites. 2 restaurants, 3 bars, in-room data ports, in-room safes, cable TV, in-room VCRs, minibars, no-smoking floor, room service, 2 pools (1 indoor), massage, sauna, golf privileges, 2 tennis courts, gym, health club, Ping-Pong, beach, bicycles, billiards, Internet, shops, laundry service, business services, convention center, meeting rooms. AE, DC, MC, V. BP, MAP.*

$$$$ ✕🏨 **Le Meridien Dona Filipa & San Lorenzo Golf Course.** Rooms at this
★ striking hotel are pleasant and have balconies, most of which overlook the sea. The service is superb, and the landscaped grounds are extensive. Although the hotel has its own tennis courts, it's also very close to the locally renowned Vale do Lobo Tennis Center. A stay here gets you reduced greens fees and preferential tee times at the prestigious San

Lorenzo Golf Club, which is owned by the hotel. Dining choices ($$$–$$$$) include the Dom Duarte restaurant, which has a Portuguese menu; the Primavera, which serves Italian cuisine; and the Grill, which offers local and international fare. ✉ *Vale do Lobo (Almansil 8135–901),* ☎ *289/357200,* ℻ *289/357201,* 🌐 *www.lemeridien-donafilipa. com. 147 rooms. 2 restaurants, 2 bars, grill, in-room safes, cable TV, minibars, no-smoking floors, room service, pool, 18-hole golf course, miniature golf, 3 tennis courts, shops, Internet, children's programs, playground, laundry service, business services, meeting rooms. AE, DC, MC, V. BP.*

Nightlife and the Arts

In the center of the Quinta do Lago resort area, you'll find **Allegro and Pátio Disco Bar** (✉ Rotunda 6a, ☎ 289/394627 or 289/396751). Allegro is a lounge where good taste blends with the sounds of a piano. The Pátio Disco Bar has several rooms for dancing or just chilling out. **T Clube and Trigonometria Music Café** (✉ Buganvilia Plaza, ☎ 289/396751), in the Quinta do Lago resort, have something for everyone. T Clube is a year-round disco, with a restaurant and gardens, for thirtysomethings. The state-of-the-art Trigonometria Music Café attracts younger ravers with three indoor and three outdoor bars as well as a snooker table. It's only open from mid-April to August, though the doors also swing wide on New Year's Eve and during Carnival and Easter holidays.

Outdoor Activities and Sports

GOLF

The Portuguese Open Championship has been held seven times at the **Campo de Golfe da Quinta do Lago** (☎ 289/390700), which has two 18-hole courses on the superb Quinta do Lago estate. Greens fees cost up to €124. The Hotel Le Meridien Dona Filipa's **Campo de Golfe San Lorenzo** (✉ Vale do Lobo, ☎ 289/396522) has 18 of Europe's finest holes. If you're not a guest of the hotel, the greens fee is €140; hotel guests pay €60. The **Vale do Lobo Golf Club** (✉ take N396 off N125 to Quarteira; continue to Vale do Lobo and follow signs, ☎ 289/393939) has two 18-hole courses: the Royal (greens fees €115–€135) and the Ocean (greens fees €98–€115).

HORSEBACK RIDING

At **Horses Paradise** (✉ Rua Cistoval Tires Norte, ☎ 289/394189) riding rates range from €19 to €40. There are fully equipped riding centers at **Quinta dos Amigos** (✉ Escanxinas, ☎ 289/395269), where many locals keep their horses. Rates start at €19.

TENNIS

The **Vale do Lobo Tennis Center** (✉ Vale do Lobo, ☎ 289/396991) has 14 all-weather courts, a bar, a pro shop, a pool, gym, steam room, and a restaurant. Court fees start at €7.

Vilamoura

16 *10 km (6 mi) west of Almansil.*

What was once a prosperous Roman settlement is today a prosperous resort community with the Algarve's biggest marina—an enormous, self-contained, 1,000-berth complex with apartments, hotels, bars, cafés, restaurants, shops, and sports facilities. The town of Vilamoura and the area surrounding it also have several luxury hotels and golf courses as well as a major tennis center a casino.

Just off a corner of the marina, the excavations of Roman ruins at the site known as Cêrro da Vila, where Vilamoura was first established, have revealed an elaborate plumbing system as well as several mosaics.

The small, well-laid-out **Museu de Cêrro da Vila** gives access to the site and exhibits pieces found here. ⊠ *Av. Cerro do Vila.* ☎ *289/312153.* ≅ *€2.* ☉ *Nov.–mid-Apr., daily 9:30–12:30 and 2–6; mid-Apr.–Oct., daily 10–1 and 3–7.*

Dining and Lodging

$$$$ ✕▥ **Tivoli Marinotel.** The luxurious Marinotel overlooks Vilamoura's marina. It's rooms are well equipped and its facilities are wide ranging, and activities available at the marina include sailboat and motorboat excursions, deep-sea fishing trips, and scuba diving. Many people think this hotel has the best places to eat ($$$–$$$$) in town: the Grill Sirius, overlooking the boats, specializes in fish and has live music; the Aries restaurant faces the hotel gardens and serves top-quality international dishes. ⊠ *Vilamoura Marina, 8126–901,* ☎ *289/303303,* ℻ *289/303345,* ⠧⠑⠃ *www.tivolihotels.com. 393 rooms. 2 restaurants, 2 bars, grill, in-room safes, cable TV, in-room VCRs, minibars, room service, 2 pools (1 indoor), golf privileges, 2 tennis courts, health club, marina, boating, shops, dance club, recreation room, Internet, laundry service, business services, convention center, meeting rooms. AE, DC, MC, V. BP, MAP, FAP.*

$$$ ▥ **Hotel Dom Pedro Golf.** Part of a highly successful vacation complex, the Dom Pedro is close to the casino, not far from a splendid beach, and five minutes from the marina. Rooms are attractively furnished, and there's a garden in which to relax. The hotel also has a comprehensive range of facilities. ⊠ *Rua Atlântico, 8125–478,* ☎ *289/300700,* ℻ *289/300701,* ⠧⠑⠃ *www.dompedro.com. 261 rooms. Restaurant, bar, in-room safes, cable TV, minibars, room service, 2 pools, hot tub, golf privileges, 3 tennis courts, shops, baby-sitting, Internet, convention center, meeting rooms. AE, DC, MC, V. BP, MAP, FAP.*

Nightlife

A big part of Vilamoura's nightlife scene is its **Casino Vilamoura** (⊠ set back from marina, behind Marinotel hotel, ☎ 289/302999), open nightly 4 PM–3 AM. You'll find two restaurants, a disco, and the usual selection of games, including slot machines. For €12.50 you can see the nightly show and have a free drink. Dress is smart-casual, and you must be 18 to enter.

Outdoor Activities and Sports

GOLF

Vilamoura Golf Club has four superb 18-hole championship courses: the **Old Course** (☎ 289/310341), **Laguna** (☎ 289/310180), **Pinhal** (☎ 289/310390), and the **Millennium course** (☎ 289/310333). Greens fees range from €60 to €110, depending on the course and the season.

HORSEBACK RIDING

Horses are available for lessons and for trail rides at the **Centro Hípico da Estalagem de Cegonha** (⊠ Estalagem de Cegonha, ☎ 289/302577). Rates start at €18.

SAILING

To rent a sailboat, just walk around Vilamoura Marina and enquire at any of the various kiosks that deal with water sports. If you'd like to relax and let someone else do the work, book a cruise on the **Condor de Vilamoura** (⊠ Vilamoura Marina, ☎ 289/314070), which sails toward Albufeira. The cost is €18 for three hours or €35 for seven hours, including lunch.

TENNIS

The **Vilamoura Ténis Center** (⊠ off Av. Eng. João Meireles, ☎ 289/302369) has 12 courts and a pro shop, restaurant, and bar. Court fees start at €6.

Albufeira

★ ⑰ *12 km (7½ mi) west of Vilamoura.*

Brash Albufeira has mushroomed from a fishing village into the Algarve's largest and busiest resort. The town beach attracts thousands of visitors daily, and the noisy center is full of cafés, bars, restaurants, discos, and souvenir shops. Albufeira ages a bit during the shoulder seasons when it draws older (often retired) visitors, mainly from northern Europe.

One of the last Algarve towns to hold out against the Christian army in the 13th century, Albufeira still has a distinctly Moorish flavor, most apparent in the steep, narrow streets and whitewashed houses snuggled on the hill that marks the center of the Cidade Velha. (A few words of caution: streets leading into the older parts of town may be difficult for some visitors to climb.)

♻ **Zoo Marine,** 6 km (4 mi) northwest of Albufeira, is a popular marine park with low-key rides, swimming pools, performing parrots, and dolphin and sea lion shows. Hotel pickups are available. ⊠ *N125, Km 65, Guia,* ☎ *289/560300,* Ⓦ*ᴇʙ* *www.zoomarine.com.* ⊠ *€16.19.* ☯ *Nov.–Mar., daily 10–5; Apr.–June and mid-Sept.–Oct., daily 10–6; July–mid-Sept., daily 10–7:30.*

Beaches

On most summer days, the **town beach,** which is reached by tunnel from Rua 5 de Outubro, is so crowded that it may be hard to enjoy its interesting rock formations, caves, and grottoes, not to mention sand and sea. If you want more space, you'll have to move farther afield. **Praia da Oura,** just 2 km (1 mi) east of Albufeira, is pretty but extremely crowded throughout most of the year. The beautiful **Praia da Galé,** 4 km (2½ mi) west of Albufeira, has the classic Algarve rock formations; just don't expect it to be deserted.

Dining and Lodging

$$–$$$ ✕ **La Cigale.** This beachfront restaurant, 9 km (5 mi) east of Albufeira, is renowned among locals for its excellent French and Portuguese cooking. The terrace is the most sought-after place to dine; reserve a table on it well in advance. ⊠ *Praia de Olhas d'Agua,* ☎ *289/501637. DC, MC, V. Closed Dec.–Feb.*

$$–$$$ ✕ **A Ruina.** For charcoal-grilled seafood, especially sardines or tuna
★ steaks, this big, rustic restaurant is the place to go. Start with a shellfish salad and choose your main course from the display. You can sit on the beach or in one of two simple but attractively furnished dining rooms. There's a roof terrace and a top-floor bar, too. ⊠ *Cais Herculano, Praia dos Pescadores,* ☎ *289/512094. MC, V.*

$$ ✕ **Cabaz da Praia.** You'll have views of the beach from the cliff-side
★ terrace of this long-established restaurant. Its name means "beach basket," and it has been converted from an old fisherman's cottage. There's fine French-Portuguese cooking here—fish soup, grilled fish served imaginatively, and chicken with seafood. Try the soufflé, perhaps the restaurant's most popular dish. ⊠ *Praça Miguel Bombarda 7,* ☎ *289/512137. AE, MC, V. Closed Thurs. No lunch Sat.*

$$ ✕🛏 **Hotel Montechoro.** In the resort area of Montechoro, 4 km (2½ mi) north of Albufeira, this modern development is ideal for those who like to have lots of facilities and to be where all the action is. Guest rooms are rather outdated, but most enjoy fine views out over the countryside or onto "the strip," a long street leads straight to Praia d'Oura and is lined with boisterous bars and tacky shops. The hotel's dining

choices ($$$–$$$$) include the Montechoro Restaurant, and the rooftop Amendoeiras Grill, from which the views are stupendous. ⊠ *Av. Dr. Francisco Sá Carneiro, Montechoro 8200–912,* ☎ *289/589423,* FAX *289/589947,* WEB *www.maisturismo.pt/hmontech.html. 362 rooms. Restaurant, 3 bars, piano bar, grill, snack bar, in-room safes, cable TV with movies, minibars, room service, 2 pools, hair salon, Turkish bath, golf privileges, 8 tennis courts, gym, health club, squash, shops, billiards, baby-sitting, playground, Internet, laundry service, convention center, meeting rooms. AE, DC, MC, V. BP, MAP, FAP.*

$$$$ ⊞ **Sheraton Algarve Hotel.** An exterior elevator takes you down to the
★ beach from this cliff-top hotel 8 km (5 mi) east of Albufeira. Traditional Moorish-style courtyards, fountains, and terraces mix well with fine Portuguese tiles and furnishings. Facilities are comprehensive, up-to-the-minute, and particularly good for sports lovers. Service is superb. ⊠ *Praia da Falésia, 8200–909,* ☎ *289/500100,* FAX *289/501950,* WEB *www.luxurycollection.com. 215 rooms. 2 restaurants, 3 bars, snack bar, in-room safes, cable TV, minibars, 3 pools (1 indoor), hot tub, sauna, golf privileges, 3 tennis courts, exercise equipment, gym, children's programs, Internet, laundry service, convention center, meeting rooms. AE, DC, MC, V. BP, MAP, FAP.*

$$ ⊞ **Hotel Vila Galé Cerro Alagoa.** One of Albufeira's most comfortable lodgings is just a 10-minute walk from the main square. Smart, well-equipped rooms have private balconies; be sure to ask for one with a sea view, or you may end up facing the busy main road. A courtesy bus runs you to nearby beaches. Book well in advance for summer stays here as package-tour operators tend to book whole blocks of rooms. ⊠ *Via Rápida, 8200–916,* ☎ *289/583100,* FAX *289/583199,* WEB *www. vilagale.pt. 310 rooms. Restaurant, pub, in-room safes, cable TV, minibars, 2 pools (1 indoor), hot tub, golf privileges, gym, health club, recreation room, shop, meeting rooms. AE, DC, MC, V. BP, MAP.*

Nightlife

The owner, the music, and the clientele are all mellow at the cliff-side **Bizarro's** (⊠ Rua Latino Coelho, ☎ 289/512824). It's the perfect bar from which to watch the sun go down. Though its dress code is on the strict side, **Club 7½** (⊠ Rua São Gonçalo de Lagos 5, ☎ no phone) stays open for drinking and dancing until dawn. The long-established club **Kiss** (⊠ Off Av. Dr. Francisco Sá Carneiro, Montechoro, ☎ 289/ 515639) is crowded and glitzy and often has DJs. It's not for the fainthearted or the prudish, though.

Shopping

Every night in the height of summer, stalls with fairy lights wind their way through the center, selling handicrafts and tourist trinkets. It's fun to browse and you may pick up the occasional interesting piece. For high-quality Portuguese ceramics, crystal and porcelain go to **La Lojas** (⊠ Rua Candido dos Reis 20, ☎ 289/513168).

Armação de Pêra

⑱ *14 km (9 mi) west of Albufeira.*

At this bustling resort, it's best to reserve your room near the sea, rather than behind the main road where apartment-hotels are crammed together. Year-round, local boats can take you on two-hour cruises to caves and grottoes west along the shore, past the Praia Nossa Senhora da Rocha (Beach of Our Lady of the Rocks)—a beach named after the Romanesque chapel above it. To arrange tours, head to Praia Armação de Pêra—a wide sandy beach with a promenade—or Praia Nossa Senhora da Rocha and speak with the fishermen directly.

Aside from ferrying vacationers to and from adjacent cove beaches, the fishermen no longer work from the shores of **Carvoeiro**, 6 km (4 mi) west of Armação de Pêra. Still, it has just about maintained the character of a fisherman's settlement. The town has a picturesque harbor with shell-shape beaches, and a short walk or boat journey away—at Algar Seco—are interesting rock formations.

Lodging

$$$$ 🏨 **Vila Vita Parc.** The pampering begins as soon as the wrought-iron gates open to welcome you. Gentle colors, dark-wood details, fireplaces, and Mediterranean-Moorish touches make this resort an exclusive oasis. From its cliff-top setting, landscaped gardens wind down to two sequestered beaches. All rooms have either a sea or garden view or both. ✉ *Armação de Pêra 8365-911,* ☎ *282/310100,* FAX *282/320333,* WEB *www.vilavitaparc.com. 91 rooms, 74 suites. 6 restaurants, 8 bars, in-room safes, cable TV, minibars, room service, 3 pools (1 indoor), hot tub, Japanese baths, massage, sauna, spa, steam room, Turkish bath, driving range, 9-hole golf course, golf privileges, miniature golf, putting green, 5 tennis courts, boccie, health club, squash, volleyball, beach, windsurfing, boating, waterskiing, fishing, dance club, shops, Internet, baby-sitting, children's programs, playground, laundry service, concierge, business services, convention center, meeting rooms, travel services, car rental, helipad. AE, DC, MC, V. BP, MAP, FAP.*

$$–$$$ 🏨 **Hotel Garbe.** The bar, lounge, and restaurant—all with terraces that provide unhindered sea views—maximize the superb location of this squat, white complex. It's atop a low cliff at the western end of the beach and is built on several levels, with steps to the sands below. Public rooms are bright and appealing; guest rooms have modern furnishings. ✉ *Av. Marginal, 8365-909,* ☎ *282/315187,* FAX *282/315087,* WEB *www.nexus-pt.com/hotelgarbe. 152 rooms. 2 restaurants, 2 bars, cable TV, room service, hair salon, pool, recreation room, shop. AE, MC, V. BP, MAP, FAP.*

$$–$$$ 🏨 **Hotel Viking.** About 1 km (½ mi) west of town, the Viking stands directly above the beach. Its manicured grounds include swimming pools (one for children) and bars that are between the main building and the cliff top. ✉ *Praia Nossa Senhora da Rocha, 8400-450,* ☎ *282/314876,* FAX *282/314852,* WEB *www.hotel-viking.com. 184 rooms. 3 restaurants, 4 bars, in-room safes, cable TV, minibars, room service, 2 pools, hair salon, hot tub, massage, sauna, tennis court, health club, squash, beach, boating, shops, dance club, recreation room, children's programs, playground, laundry service, convention center, meeting rooms, car rental. AE, DC, MC, V. BP, MAP.*

Outdoor Activities and Sports

The **Carvoeiro Clube de Ténis Club** (✉ Vale Currais, ☎ 282/356904) has 12 courts as well as a fitness center, a swimming pool, and a restaurant.

Lagoa

⑲ *10 km (6 mi) northwest of Armação de Pêra.*

This market town is primarily known for its wine, *vinho Lagoa*; the red is particularly good. The principal winery, **Cooperativa de Lagoa** (☎ 282/342181), is on the main road just after the Carvoeiro junction, on the left. Call if you're interested in joining a prearranged group tour. At any time during normal working hours you can pop in to the office (at the side of the building) to sample the wine and buy a bottle or two.

🄲 The biggest of the Algarve's several water parks is **Slide & Splash,** east of Lagoa. The rides are also the most exciting of their kind in the region. The park is open daily at 10 AM from Easter through October; closing times vary greatly, so call ahead to confirm. ⊠ *Vale de Deus, just off the N125 (signposted), Estombar,* ☎ *282/341685.* 🄳 *€12.50.*

Shopping

Along N125 in nearby Porches, you can stop at roadside shops that sell both mass-produced and handmade pottery. **Olaria Pequena** (⊠ N125, between Porches and Alcantarilha, ☎ 282/381213), which means "the small pottery," is owned and run by a friendly young Scot, Ian Fitzpatrick, who has worked in the Algarve for years. He sells his handmade pieces at very reasonable prices. The shop is open Monday through Saturday from 10 to 1 and 3 to 6.

Silves

★ ⑳ *7 km (4 mi) northeast of Lagoa.*

Once the Moorish capital of the Algarve, today Silves is one of the region's most intriguing inland towns. Rich and prosperous in medieval times, it remained in Arab hands until 1249, although not without attempts by Christian forces to take it. In 1189, following a siege led by Sancho I, the city was sacked by Crusaders, who subsequently put thousands of Moors to the sword. Silves finally lost its importance after its almost complete destruction by the 1755 earthquake. Today it's an enjoyable excursion from the coast; trains, buses, and a river service using traditional Portuguese gondola-like boats make the 20-km (12-mi) trip north from Portimão.

In the 12th century the Moors built a sandstone **fortaleza** (fortress) that survived untouched until the Christian sieges. Its impressive parapets were restored in 1835 and still dominate the upper part of town. You can walk around the fort's remaining walls or clamber about its crenellated battlements, taking in the views of Silves and the hills. (Keep an eye open: some places have no guardrails.) Its gardens are watched over by a statue of King Dom Sancho I, and its capacious water cistern is now a gallery space devoted to temporary exhibitions, some of which have nothing to do with the fort. ☎ *282/445624.* 🄳 *€1.25.* 🕑 *June–Sept., daily 9–8 (last admission 7:30); Oct.–May, daily 9–6 (last admission 5:30).*

The 12th- to 13th-century **Santa Maria da Sé** (Cathedral of St. Mary), built on the site of a Moorish mosque, saw service as the principle cathedral of the Algarve until the 16th century. The 1755 earthquake and indifferent restoration have left it rather plain inside, but its tower—complete with gargoyles—is still a fine sight. ⊠ *Rua da Sé,* ☎ *no phone.* 🄳 *Free; donations accepted.* 🕑 *Mon.–Sat. 9–6:30, Sun. 8:30–1.*

Although the labels are in Portuguese, the items on display at Silves's **Museu Arqueologia** (Archaeology Museum) still give interesting insights into the area's history. A primary attraction is an Arab water cistern, preserved in situ, with a 30-ft-deep well. The museum is a few minutes' walk below the cathedral, off Rua da Sé. ⊠ *Rua das Portas de Loulé,* ☎ *282/444832.* 🄳 *€1.50.* 🕑 *Daily 9–6.*

Silves's **mercado** (produce market), liveliest in the morning, is at the foot of town, close to the medieval bridge. If you arrive at lunchtime, you can have a delicious meal of spicy grilled chicken or fish from the outdoor barbecue at one of the simple restaurants facing the river that runs through town. The market is closed Sunday.

Dining

$–$$$ ✕ **Rui Marisqueira.** The fish and shellfish are remarkably good value, which is the main reason why the crowds from the coast come up into the hills to dine here. Grilled sea bream and bass are usually available, and there's locally caught game—wild boar, rabbit, and partridge—in season. ✉ *Rua Comendador Vilarinho 27,* ☎ *282/442682. AE, MC, V. Closed Tues.*

$–$$ ✕ **Churrasqueira Valdemar.** At this grill room on the riverfront behind the market, whole chickens are barbecued outside over charcoal. Eat under the stone arches and enjoy your *piri-piri* (spicy) chicken with salad, fries, and local wine. ✉ *Facing the river, behind the market,* ☎ *no phone. No credit cards.*

Portimão

㉑ *15 km (9 mi) southwest of Silves.*

Portimão is the Algarve's most important fishing port. Even before the Romans arrived, there was a settlement here, at the mouth of the Rio Arade (Arade River). Devastated in the 1755 earthquake, the town was revived by the fish-canning industry in the 19th century. Although colorful boats now unload their catch at a modern terminal across the river, contemporary Portimão, sprawling with concrete high-rise buildings, remains a cheerful, busy place.

Rather than staying in Portimão, most visitors choose one of the excellent local beach resorts and visit Portimão as a day trip, especially to shop. If you prefer to stay in town, the local tourist office can help you find accommodations at one of the hotels or *pensões* (pensions), which are of reasonable quality.

Beach

Across the bridge from and 5 km (3 mi) east of Portimão is the former fishing hamlet of Ferragudo. Despite its fine beach, **Praia Grande,** Ferragudo shows no sign of going down the mass-market tourist route. Right on the beach is the restored 16th-century Castelo de São João (St. John's Castle), built to defend Portimão and now privately owned. There are plenty of restaurants and bars near the beach as well as places to rent sailboards.

Dining

Lunch outdoors at Portimão's "sardine dock" is a must. You sit at one of many inexpensive establishments, eating the excellent charcoal-grilled sardines (a local specialty), chewy fresh bread, and simple salads and drinking local wine while around you the air is thick with barbecue smoke and the tang of the sea.

$$ ✕ **A Lanterna.** On the main road just over the bridge from Portimão, this well-run restaurant serves exceptional fish soup and smoked swordfish, both genuine Algarvian treats. Other seafood specialties are worthy, too. ✉ *Parchal,* ☎ *282/414429. MC, V. Closed Sun.*

$–$$ ✕ **Flor da Sardinha.** This is one of several open-air eateries next to the bridge, by the fishing harbor, whose staff grills fresh sardines on quayside stoves and serves them to crowds seated at plastic tables. A plateful of these delicious fish, with boiled potatoes (never fries!) and a bottle of the local wine, is one of Portugal's best treats. ✉ *Cais da Lota,* ☎ *282/424862. No credit cards.*

$–$$ ✕ **Kibom.** On a narrow pedestrian street in a typical Algarvian house, Kibom has represented the town in gourmet food competitions. The traditional Portuguese food here is highly recommended. Dishes include *arroz de marisco* (shellfish with rice), *feijoada de choco* (octopus with beans), and cataplana de *lagosta* (a spiny lobster). ✉ *Rua Damião L.*

Faria e Castro, off Rua Judice Biker, ☎ *282/414623. AE, DC, MC, V. Closed Sun.*

Shopping

Portimão's main shopping street is Rua do Comércio. Shops on Rua de Santa Isabel specialize in crafts, leather goods, ceramics, crystal, and fashions. The enormous **Modelo Shopping Center** (⊠ N124 at Av. Miguel Bombarda, toward Praia da Rocha), open daily 10–10, has a plethora of shops and restaurants under one roof.

For ceramics, porcelain, crystal, and handmade copper items, visit **O Aquario** (⊠ Rua Vasco da Gama 42, ☎ 282/426673; ⊠ Rua Vasco da Gama 41, ☎ no phone). **Gabys** (⊠ Rua Direita 5, ☎ 282/411988) sells good-quality leather items. There are high-class shoes and leather goods at **St. James** (⊠ Rua de Santa Isabel 26, ☎ 282/424620).

Praia da Rocha

22 *3 km (2 mi) southeast of Portimão.*

Praia da Rocha was one of the first resorts in the Algarve to undergo a transformation for the mass market, and it's now dominated by high-rise apartments and hotels. Its excellent beach is made all the more interesting by a series of huge colored rocks worn into strange shapes by the wind and sea. Buses run throughout the day between the town and Portimão.

The 16th-century **Fortaleza de Santa Catarina** (Fortress of St. Catharine; ⊠ Av. Tomás Cabreira, ☎ no phone) was a defensive castle and provides wonderful views out to sea and across the Rio Arade to Ferragudo. Directly below the fortress, on the river side, is one of the Algarve's growing number of marinas. On the other side a long cement jetty extends into the Atlantic.

Dining and Lodging

$$ ✕ **Cabassa.** On a grassy terrace close to the Fortaleza de Santa Catarina, this restaurant is far removed from the resort's frenetic activity. It's known for its innovative Italian cooking, great-value Portuguese barbecue nights, and friendly young staff. ⊠ *Av. Tomás Cabreira,* ☎ *282/424307. MC, V. No lunch.*

$–$$ ✕ **Safari.** This lively cliff-top restaurant has a distinctly African flavor. Seafood and Angolan dishes are the best choices: try the chicken curry or one of the charcoal grills. Enjoy your meal on the terrace. ⊠ *Rua António Feu,* ☎ *282/423540. AE, DC, MC, V.*

$$$ 🏨 **Hotel Algarve-Casino.** The sea vistas from this classy hotel are spectacular, so be sure to book a room with a view. The Moorish-style public rooms are bright, the spacious guest rooms have tile floors and balconies, and the casino has a restaurant as well as shows. ⊠ *Av. Tomás Cabreira, 8500–802,* ☎ *282/415001,* ℻ *282/415999,* 🌐 *www.solverde. pt. 209 rooms. 3 restaurants, cable TV, minibars, room service, 2 pools, hair salon, 2 tennis courts, shops, casino, convention center, meeting rooms, car rental. AE, DC, MC, V. BP, MAP.*

$$ 🏨 **Bela Vista.** Once a private house, this small beachfront hotel has azulejos, leaded stained-glass panels, a wonderful staircase, and a large fireplace. These and many other remarkable features make it popular. Early reservations are essential for high-season stays. ⊠ *Av. Tomás Cabreira, 8500–802,* ☎ *282/450480,* ℻ *282/415369,* 🌐 *www.hotelbelavista. net. 14 rooms, 2 suites. Bar, minibars; no air-conditioning. AE, DC, MC, V. BP.*

Alvor

㉓ *5 km (3 mi) west of Praia da Rocha.*

Characterized by a maze of streets, lanes, and alleys that intersect one another, the handsome old port of Alvor is one of the Algarve's best examples of an Arab village. In summer, many vacationers are attracted to Alvor's excellent beaches.

Beach

If the small, covelike **Praia dos Três Irmãos** is too crowded, there's always space to spare on one of the beaches to either side.

Dining and Lodging

$$$ ✕🏨 **Carlton Alvor Hotel.** Rooms at this split-level hotel have views of
★ the sea or the Serra de Monchique. The dining room has picture windows overlooking the coast, and there's a deck with a snack bar. Although it's an easy walk to the pleasant sands below, there's an elevator that can take you down. All of the restaurants ($$$) are first class: O Almofariz serves Algarvian specialties, Sale e Pepe offers Tuscan cuisine, and Harira has Moroccan fare. ⊠ *Praia dos Três Irmãos, 8500–904,* ☎ *282/400900,* 𝖥𝖠𝖷 *282/400999,* 𝖶𝖤𝖡 *www.pestana.com. 180 rooms, 18 suites. 4 restaurants, 3 bars, snack bar, in-room safes, cable TV, minibars, room service, saltwater pool, hair salon, massage, sauna, driving range, golf privileges, miniature golf, 7 tennis courts, beach, shops, children's programs, playground, Internet, laundry service, convention center, meeting rooms. AE, DC, MC, V. BP, MAP.*

$$$ ✕🏨 **Le Meridien Penina.** The Meridien has attentive service, elegant
★ public spaces, and tastefully furnished rooms—many with balconies and some with views of the Serra de Monchique. A stay here gives you access to (and reduced greens fees at) the superlative Henry Cotton–designed golf course. A bus shuttles you to and from the hotel beach, which has a restaurant (reservations essential) and water-sports facilities. A supervised children's village has its own pool and restaurant. There's a choice of five restaurants ($$$–$$$$), including the Grill Room, which serves excellent Portuguese dishes, and the Sagres Restaurant, with its lively theme evenings. ⊠ *Montes de Alvor, Penina 8501–952,* ☎ *282/420200,* 𝖥𝖠𝖷 *282/420300,* 𝖶𝖤𝖡 *www.lemeridien-penina.com. 196 rooms. 5 restaurants, 2 bars, grill, in-room safes, cable TV, minibars, no-smoking rooms, room service, pool, sauna, driving range, one 18-hole and two 9-hole golf courses, 6 tennis courts, gym, horseback riding, beach, windsurfing, boating, shops, Internet, children's programs, playground, laundry service, concierge, business services, convention center, meeting rooms, travel services, car rental, helipad. AE, DC, MC, V. BP, MAP, FAP.*

Monchique

㉔ *25 km (15½ mi) northeast of Alvor, 20 km (12½ mi) north of Portimão.*

This tiny market town is known for the lovely ride up to reach it. Although handicrafts, particularly carving and woodworking, are available, the quality isn't top-notch. A short drive west on N266–3 brings you to the highest point in the Serra de Monchique. At 2,959 ft, the Pico de Fóia affords panoramic views—weather permitting—over the western Algarve. There's also a café here.

Dining and Lodging

$–$$ ✕ **Teresinha.** Just west of Monchique, modest Teresinha has good
★ country cooking, a simple interior, and an outdoor terrace that overlooks a valley as well as the coast. The ham and the grilled chicken are particularly tasty. ⊠ *Estrada da Fóia,* ☎ *282/912392. MC, V.*

$ ✕🅜 **Estalagem Abrigo da Montanha.** This pleasant, rustic inn—in the heart of the Serra de Monchique—has magnolia trees, a camellia-filled garden, and panoramic views. A leisurely lunch in the restaurant ($$–$$$$), where dependable regional dishes are prepared, makes for an enjoyable afternoon. If you want to stay longer to take in the scenery, be sure to reserve in advance for one of the welcoming rooms (all with views). ✉ *Corto Pereiro, Estrada da Fóia, 8550,* ☎ *282/912131,* 🄵🄰🄭 *282/913660,* 🆆🅴🅱 *www.abrigodamontanha.com. 15 rooms. Restaurant, bar, pool. AE, DC, MC, V. BP.*

LAGOS AND THE WESTERN ALGARVE

From the bustling town of Lagos, the rest of the western Algarve is easily accessible. This is the most unspoiled part of the region, with some genuinely isolated beaches and bays along an often wind-buffeted route that reaches to the southwest and the magnificent Cabo São Vicente.

Lagos

★ ㉕–㉙ *13 km (8 mi) west of Portimão, 70 km (43 mi) northwest of Faro.*

An attractive, busy fishing port with some cove beaches nearby, Lagos draws an international crowd. And yet, the inhabitants seem to follow a way of life that goes beyond catering to visitors.

The town has a venerable history. Its deep-water harbor and wide bay have made it a natural choice for various groups of settlers, starting with the Carthaginians, who founded the town around 400 BC. Under the Moors, Lagos was a center for trade between Portugal and Africa. Even after the town fell to the Christians in 1241, trade continued and was greatly expanded under Prince Henry the Navigator, who used Lagos as his base. It later became capital of the Algarve, a role it lost in 1756, after the great earthquake reduced much of it to rubble. Nonetheless, some interesting buildings remain, as does the circuit of defensive walls, built between the 14th and 16th centuries over older, Moorish bastions. Some of the best-preserved sections can be seen from near the expansive Praça da República, at the southwest end of Avenida dos Descobrimentos. The main pedestrian streets leading off the central Praça Gil Eanes are lined with stores (including several good antiques shops), restaurants, cafés, and bars—all of which do a roaring business in summer.

㉕ In the 15th century, the first African slave market in Europe was held under the arches of the old **Casa da Alfandega.** The building now contains an art gallery with changing exhibits and is sometimes used for concerts and theater productions. It's only open during exhibitions and shows; ask at the tourist office for details. ✉ *Praça da República,* ☎ *no phone.* 🎫 *Free.*

㉖ It was from the Manueline window of the old **Castelo dos Governadores** (Governor's Palace) that the young king, Dom Sebastião, is said to have addressed his troops before setting off on his crusade of 1578. The palace is long gone, though the section of wall with the famous window remains and can be seen in the northwest corner of the Praça da República. The crusade was one of Portugal's greatest ever disasters, with the king and some 8,000 men killed in Morocco at Alcácer-Quibir. (Dom Sebastião is further remembered by a much maligned, modernistic statue that stands in Praça Gil Eanes.)

㉗ The **Museu Regional** (Regional Museum) houses an amusing jumble of exhibits, including mosaics, archaeological and ethnological items, and a town charter from 1504—all arranged haphazardly. ✉ *Rua Gen-*

eral Alberto Silveira, ☎ *282/762301.* 🎫 *€1.95; includes entry to Igreja de Santo António.* ☉ *Tues.–Sun. 9:30–12:30 and 2–5.*

Lagos's most extraordinary building is the early 18th-century baroque
★ ㉘ **Igreja de Santo António** (Church of St. Anthony). Its interior is a riot of gilt extravagance made possible by the import of gold from Brazil. Dozens of cherubs and angels clamber over the walls, among fancifully carved woodwork and azulejos. ⊠ *Entrance via Museu Regional on Rua General Alberto Silveira,* ☎ *282/762301.* 🎫 *€1.95; includes entry to Museu Regional.* ☉ *Tues.–Sun. 9:30–12:30 and 2–5.*

㉙ The 17th-century fort, **Forte Ponta da Bandeira,** defended the entrance to the harbor in bygone days. From inside the fort you can look out at sweeping ocean views. For an interesting perspective on the rock formations and grottoes of the area's shoreline, take one of the short boat trips offered by the fishermen near the Ponta da Bandeira. Check for departure times on the quayside boards. ⊠ *Av. dos Descobrimentos,* ☎ *282/761410.* 🎫 *€1.85.* ☉ *Tues.–Sun. 9:30–12:30 and 2–5.*

Beaches

The largest beach near town and one of the best centers for water sports is the 4-km (2½-mi) stretch of **Meia Praia,** to the northeast. You can walk to it in less than five minutes simply by crossing the footbridge. If you want to go farther along, however, you can take a bus from the riverfront Avenida dos Descobrimentos, and in summer there's a ferry service a few hundred yards from Forte Ponta da Bandeira.

You can reach the prettiest beach south of town—**Praia de Dona Ana**—by car (follow the signs for the Hotel Golfinho) or on an enjoyable, 30-minute walk along a cliff top. If you hoof it, pass the fort, turn left at the fire station, and follow the footpaths, which go to the most southerly point, A short way beyond Praia de Dona Ana, is the attractive **Praia do Camilo.** Just beyond this beach is the Ponta da Piedade, a much-photographed group of rock arches and grottoes.

Dining and Lodging

$$–$$$ ✕ **No Patio.** This cheerful restaurant with an attractive inner patio is run by a Danish couple, Bjarne and Gitte. The outstanding fare is best described as international with a Scandinavian accent. Specialties include herring, duck-liver mousse, and tenderloin of pork with a Madeira and mushroom sauce. ⊠ *Rua Lançarote de Freitas 46,* ☎ *282/763777. AE, MC, V. Closed Sun.–Mon.*

$–$$ ✕ **Dom Sebastião.** Portuguese cooking, especially charcoal-grilled fish
★ specials, and unobtrusive service are the draws here. You can dine inside at elegant candlelit tables on a cobblestone floor or outside on a sidewalk terrace. You may wish to start your meal with smoked swordfish, followed by grilled tuna or the cataplana—all extremely good. ⊠ *Rua 25 de Abril 20,* ☎ *282/762795. AE, DC, MC, V. Closed Sun. Oct.– May.*

$–$$ ✕ **Mirante.** Just south of the town center and above the Praia de Dona Ana, Mirante shouts its fishermen's credentials loudly: a cork ceiling, ropes, and nets decorate the narrow interior. It makes an excellent lunch stop or a place for an early dinner, particularly in summer. Try the tuna steak stewed with onions and, for dessert, the homemade cream tart. The staff is friendly and efficient. ⊠ *Praia de Dona Ana,* ☎ *282/762713. MC, V.*

$–$$ ✕ **O Galeão.** Tucked away on a backstreet is this bustling, informal, local restaurant—it's so popular that you'll wait in line unless you've made a reservation. The food is first-rate, particularly the steaks—for once, fish, although well cooked, isn't the main event. A reasonably priced wine list encourages you to sample regional choices. ⊠ *Rua da Laranjeira 1,* ☎ *282/763909. AE, DC, MC, V.*

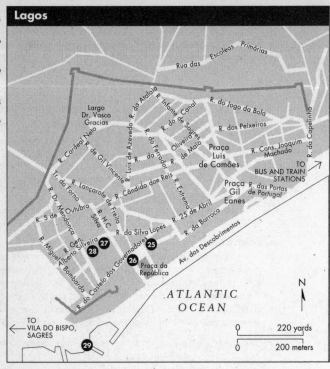

Lagos

Rua das Escoleas Primárias

R. do Jogo da Bola

Largo
Dr. Vasco
Gracias

R. Cardeal Neto

R. de Gil Vincente

R. da Atalaia

R. Infante de Canal

R. do de Sogres

R. do Ferrador

Oliveira

R. Luis de Azevedo

Praça
Luis
de Camões

R. dos Peixeiros

R. Cons. Joaquim
Machado

R. da Capelinha

Tr. do Forno

R. Lançarote de Freita

R. Cándido doe Reis

R. R. de Maio

Praça
Gil
Eanes

R. das Portas
de Portugal

TO
BUS AND TRAIN
STATIONS

R. Dr. Mendonça

R. 5 de Outubro

R. H. C.

Silva

R. Extrema

R. 25 de Abril

R. da Barroca

R. da Silva Lopes

R. Gen.
Alberto Silveira

Av.s Descobrimentos

R. Miguel
Bombarda

R. do Castelo dos Governadores

Praça da
República

28 **27** **25**

26

ATLANTIC
OCEAN

N

TO
VILA DO BISPO,
SAGRES

29

0 ——— 220 yards

0 ——— 200 meters

$–$$ ✕ **Piri-Piri.** On one of the main streets this small, low-key restaurant—
done in understated pastels—has an inexpensive but extensive menu.
The long list of Portuguese dishes includes a variety of market-fresh
fish, but the specialty is the zesty piri-piri chicken that gives the restaurant its name. ⊠ *Rua Afonso d'Almeida 10,* ☏ *282/763803. MC, V.*

$$ ⌂ **Hotel Golfinho.** The Golfinho is large and modern, but its rooms
are done in traditional Portuguese style, with attractive wood and
leather furniture. Balconies afford views of the sea and inland reaches.
A bus shuttles guests—often part of tour groups—to and from town,
and cliff-top paths lead to nearby coves. ⊠ *Praia de Dona Ana, 8600–
500,* ☏ *282/769900,* 𝐅𝐀𝐗 *282/769999,* 𝐖𝐄𝐁 *www.hotelgolfinho.com. 262
rooms. 2 restaurants, bar, coffee shop, in-room safes, cable TV, room
service, pool, golf privileges, shops, Internet, meeting rooms. AE, DC,
MC, V. BP, MAP, FAP.*

$$ ⌂ **Tivoli Lagos.** At the eastern edge of the Cidade Velha and an easy
★ walk from the town center, this state-of-the-art hotel has an attractive
and unusual design: it's strung across several levels in between gardens,
lounges, and patios. Guest rooms are large and elegantly appointed,
with attractive tiling everywhere, even on lamps and tabletops. A bus
shuttles you to Meia Praia, where the hotel has very good beach and
water-sports facilities. ⊠ *Rua António Crisógno dos Santos, 8600–678,*
☏ *282/790079,* 𝐅𝐀𝐗 *282/790345,* 𝐖𝐄𝐁 *www.tivolihotels.com. 324 rooms.
3 restaurants, 2 bars, piano bar, in-room safes, cable TV, some minibars, room service, 2 pools (1 indoor), golf privileges, 3 tennis courts,
gym, health club, recreation room, shops, meeting rooms. AE, DC, MC,
V. BP, MAP.*

$ ⌂ **Pensão Mar Azul.** It's not hard to befriend fellow travelers in the
comfortable community lounge of this simple, central pension. Rooms—
some with a terrace—are clean and cheerful, though not all have full
private baths (some just have a shower with shared toilet outside the

room). Avoid guest quarters that face the pedestrian thoroughfare, which can be noisy in high season. ⊠ *Rua 25 de Abril 13–1, 8600,* ☎ *282/ 769749,* FAX *282/769960. 18 rooms, some share bath. Lounge, cable TV; no air-conditioning. No credit cards. EP.*

Nightlife

There are a number of bars at the end of Rua 25 de Abril, most playing music that's brutally loud. Perhaps the most refined of these is **Bon Vivant** (⊠ Rua 25 de Abril, ☎ 282/768329), with a roof-top terrace way above the din. An excellent bar is **Mullens** (⊠ Rua Cândido dos Reis 86, ☎ 282/761281), whose enthusiastic staff helps to keep things swinging until 2 AM; full meals are served, too. For dancing or cuddling on couches by a fireplace, try **Phoenix** (⊠ Rua 5 de Outubro 11, ☎ 282/760503), which plays disco and pop until 5 AM. The classy **Stevie Ray's Blues Jazz Bar** (⊠ Rua Senhora da Graça, ☎ 282/760683) serves imported beers and French champagne.

Outdoor Activities and Sports

The 18 holes of the **Campo de Golfe de Palmares** (⊠ Monte Palmares, Meia Praia, ☎ 282/762953) overlook Lagos Bay. Green fees range from €45 to €70.

Praia da Luz

㉚ *6 km (4 mi) west of Lagos.*

There was once an active fishing fleet here, and a favorite pastime was to watch the boats being hauled onto the broad sandy beach that lends the community its name. The boats are gone, but this is still an agreeable destination—despite the development that has hit it. At the western edge of town a little church faces an 18th-century fortress that once guarded against pirates and is now a restaurant. Many of the accommodations available in Luz are in private villas and apartments; the tourist office in Lagos may be able to advise about them.

For a break from the coast and its buzz, you can head inland to the small, quiet town of **Vila do Bispo** at the western terminus of the N125 highway. The interior of its parish church, in the Praça do Igreja at the center of town, is covered with 18th-century azulejos. To see it, come on a Sunday morning; the church is only open for services at 11:30.

Beaches

Four kilometers (2 miles) west of Praia da Luz is **Burgau,** a fishing village with narrow, steep streets leading to it. Although the town has partly succumbed to the wave of tourism that has swept over the Algarve, its fine beach remains unchanged. The relaxed, low-key village of **Salema,** 5 km (3 mi) west of Burgau, is blessed with a 1,970-ft-long beach at the foot of green hills.

Dining and Lodging

$$–$$$ ✕ **Fortaleza.** This restaurant does an admirable job of preparing in-
★ ternational and local specialties. It's in a fortress whose foundations date from Moorish times. A classical guitarist often plays on Tuesday evenings; on summer Sundays there's a jazz barbecue during which you can enjoy the grounds, the terrace, and the sea views. ⊠ *Rua da Igreja 3,* ☎ *282/789926. MC, V.*

$–$$ ✕ **Café Correia.** Favorites at this rustic family-run restaurant in the inland town of Vila do Bispo are the stuffed squid and the rabbit cooked with beer and an onion sauce. The wine list, presented in a well-worn ledger, contains 180 varieties. ⊠ *Rua José Cardoso 34, Vila do Bispo,* ☎ *282/442455. No credit cards. Closed Sat.*

$$ ⊞ **Bela Vista.** This family-owned hilltop hotel's horseshoe configura-
★   tion gives all the spacious guest quarters a great sea view. Rooms and
suites have terraces as well as many modern conveniences. The restau-
rant is excellent, and the nearby beach is fine. ⊠ *Praia da Luz, 8600,*
☎ *282/788655,* FAX *282/788656,* WEB *www.belavistadaluz.com. 39*
rooms, 6 suites. Restaurant, bar, in-room safe, cable TV, 2 pools, ten-
nis court, aerobics, gym, health club, playground. AE, DC, MC, V. BP.

$$ ⊞ **Ocean Club.** You can rent these well-appointed one-, two-, or three-
bedroom apartments (with daily maid service) for short or long stays,
but you must reserve well in advance. The Ocean Club blends well with
the old village surroundings, yet still provides a high level of comfort
in its carefully decorated units. They're all near the beach, where the
water-sports facilities are excellent. ⊠ *Rua Direita 20, 8600–160,* ☎
282/788764, FAX *282/789763,* WEB *www.algarve-holiday.co.uk. 210*
apartments. 2 restaurants, kitchens, cable TV, 3 pools, 5 tennis courts,
playground. V. BP.

Outdoor Activities and Sports

GOLF

Ten kilometers (6 miles) west of Praia da Luz you'll find the 18-hole
course at **Campo de Golfe Parque da Floresta** (⊠ Budens, ☎ 282/
690000). Greens fees are €60–€70.

SCUBA DIVING

Lessons by certified instructors, wreck dives, and night dives are available at **Blue Ocean Divers** (⊠ Center Motel Ancora, Estrada de Porto
de Mós, ☎ FAX 282/782718).

WINDSURFING

Praia da Luz's broad bay provides an excellent venue for this exciting
sport. Instruction and equipment rental are available directly on the
beach.

Sagres

③ *30 km (19 mi) southwest of Praia da Luz, 3 km (2 mi) southeast of*
Cabo São Vicente.

In the 19th century, this village, amid harsh, barren moorland, was rebuilt over earthquake ruins. Today there's little of note apart from a
fort and a series of fine, sweeping beaches.

★ ☾ Views from the **Fortaleza de Sagres** (Sagres Fortress), an enormous run
of defensive walls high above the crashing waves, are spectacular. Its
massive walls and battlements make it popular with young visitors. (It's
about a 15-minute walk from the village to the tunnel-like entrance;
three buses a day also run this way on weekdays.) The fortress was rebuilt in the 17th century, and although some historians have claimed
that it was the site for Prince Henry's house and famous navigation
school, it's more likely that Henry built his school at Cabo São Vicente.
But this doesn't detract from the powerful atmosphere. Certainly the
Venta da Rosa (Wind Compass, or compass rose) dates from Prince
Henry's period. Only uncovered this century, this large circular construction made of stone and packed earth is in the courtyard just inside the fortress. Of the same age is the restored simple Graça Chapel.

A stark, modern building within the fort houses an **exhibition center**
with revolving exhibits documenting the region's history, flora, fauna,
and nautical themes. ☎ *282/620140.* ⌑ *€3.* ☉ *May–Sept., daily 10–*
8:30; Oct.–Apr., daily 10–6:30.

Dining and Lodging

$$ ✕🏨 **Fortaleza do Beliche.** In a lonely setting between Sagres and Cabo
★ São Vicente the remnants of an isolated cliff-top fortress have been converted into the Fortaleza do Beliche, a restaurant and very small hotel that are an annex of the Pousada do Infante. The furnishings are smart, and the rooms are comfortable. This is also an excellent spot for high-quality regional cooking ($$–$$$)—perhaps amid the flicker of fire in the fireplace and the sparkle of the old chandeliers. ⌧ *2 km (1 mi) past Sagres on coastal road to Cabo São Vicente, Sagres 8650– 385,* ☎ *282/624124,* 𝖥𝖠𝖷 *282/624225,* 𝖶𝖤𝖡 *www.pousadas.pt. 4 rooms. Restaurant, bar. MC, V. BP. Closed Nov.–Mar.*

$$ ✕🏨 **Pousada do Infante.** In a two-story country house across the bay
★ from the Fortaleza de Sagres, this pousada has a glorious view of the sea and the craggy cliffs. Guest rooms are homey, and public areas are comfortable—particularly the terrace bar, which is a perfect place to watch sunsets. Throughout the pousada are Moorish embellishments such as minarets and arches alongside the pool. The service and the Portuguese food in the well-respected restaurant ($$–$$$$) are accomplished; expect seafood specials such as fried squid or clams with pork, and, for dessert, perhaps almond cake. ⌧ *On headland between fishing harbor and Praia da Mareta, Sagres 8650–385,* ☎ *282/624222,* 𝖥𝖠𝖷 *282/624225,* 𝖶𝖤𝖡 *www.pousadas.pt. 39 rooms. Restaurant, bar, cable TV, pool, tennis court, meeting rooms. AE, DC, MC, V. BP.*

Nightlife

Sagres is a well-known haunt of young travelers, and there are several music bars near the village square. The loud, lively **Last Chance Saloon** (⌧ road to Praia da Mareta, ☎ no phone) is on the pub-crawl route for most young merrymakers passing through Sagres. **A Rosa dos Ventos** (⌧ Praça da República, ☎ 282/624480) is the town's most popular bar, attracting a motley crowd of European travelers. It also serves local snacks, burgers, and salads.

Cabo São Vicente

★ ❸❷ *6 km (4 mi) northwest of Sagres, 95 km (59 mi) west of Faro, 30 km (19 mi) southwest of Lagos.*

At the southwest tip of Europe, where the land juts starkly into the rough Atlantic waters, is Cabo São Vicente, called *O Fim do Mundo* (The End of the World) by early Portuguese mariners. Legends attach themselves easily to this desolate place, which the Romans once considered sacred (they believed it was where the spirits of the light lived because with sunset the light disappeared). It takes its modern name from the martyr St. Vincent, whose relics were brought here in the 8th century; it's said that they were transported to Lisbon 400 years later in a boat piloted by ravens.

Most historians agree that it was here in the 15th century that Prince Henry built his house and the school of navigation where he trained his captains—including Vasco da Gama and Ferdinand Magellan—before they set out on their voyages of discovery. The ancient buildings were long ago destroyed by pirates and earthquakes.

The keeper of the isolated **Faro de São Vicente** (St. Vincent Lighthouse) opens it to visitors at his discretion. The beacon is said to have the strongest reflectors in Europe—they cast a beam 96 km (60 mi) out to sea. The views from the lighthouse are remarkable. Turquoise water whips across the base of the rust-color cliffs below, the fortress at Sagres is visible to the east, and in the distance lies the immense Atlantic.

THE ALGARVE A TO Z

To research prices, get advice from other travelers, and book travel arrangements, visit www.fodors.com.

AIR TRAVEL

TAP Air Portugal has regular daily service from Lisbon and Oporto. Flying time from Lisbon to Faro is 45 minutes; from Oporto, 90 minutes.
➤ AIRLINE: **TAP Air Portugal** (☎ 289/818538).

AIRPORTS AND TRANSFERS

International and domestic airlines use Faro Airport, which is 6 km (4 mi) west of town. It's easy to find your way into Faro: after around 4 km (2½ mi) signs along the road from the airport direct you right into town.
➤ AIRPORT INFORMATION: **Faro Airport** (☎ 289/800617 or 289/800801 for flight information).

AIRPORT TRANSFER
From mid-May to the end of October there's free Aerobus service from Faro Airport to the town center. It runs every 45 minutes from 8 to 8 every day but Tuesday; just show your airplane ticket when boarding. A taxi from the terminal building to the center of Faro costs around €8 (there's a small extra charge for baggage). Ask the staff at the airport tourist office for a list of prices for rides to other destinations in the region. Always make sure that you agree on a price with the taxi driver before setting off. Buses 14 and 16 shuttle between Faro town and the airport hourly, 8 AM–9 PM (until 11 PM July–mid-September); buy tickets on board (€1).

BUS TRAVEL

Various companies run daily express buses between Lisbon and Lagos, Portimão, Faro, Tavira, and Vila Real de Santo António. Allow for 3½–4½ hours' travel time for all these destinations. Generally this is more comfortable than traveling by train, and some of the luxury coaches have a toilet, TV, and food service. Any travel agency in Lisbon can reserve a seat for you; in summer, book at least 24 hours in advance.

The main form of public transportation in the Algarve is the bus, and every town and village has its own terminal. You may have to walk from the main road to the more isolated beach areas, however. Tickets are relatively inexpensive, although a bus ride always costs more than the comparable train journey. Most ticket offices have someone who speaks at least a little English. The booklet *Guia Horário*, which costs €3 and is available at main terminals, lists every bus service, with timetables and information in English. Some local services are infrequent or don't run on Sunday.
➤ MAIN BUS TERMINALS: **Albufeira** (✉ Parque Ribeira, ☎ 289/589755). **Faro** (✉ Av. da República, ☎ 289/899760). **Lagos** (✉ Rossío de São João, ☎ 282/762944). **Portimão** (✉ Av. Guanaré, ☎ 282/418120). **Vila Real de Santo António** (✉ Av. da República, ☎ 281/511807).

CAR RENTAL

Most of the major international firms have offices at Faro Airport, and many have branches elsewhere in the Algarve, too.
➤ MAJOR AGENCIES: **Auto Jardim** (✉ Av. da Liberdade, Albufeira, ☎ 289/589688; ✉ Faro Airport, ☎ 289/800881). **Avis** (✉ Rua da Igreja Nova 13, Albufeira, ☎ 289/512678; ✉ Faro Airport, ☎ 289/810120; ✉ Largo das Portas de Portugal 11, Lagos, ☎ 282/763691; ✉ Alto do Quintão, Praia da Rocha, ☎ 282/490250). **Budget** (✉ Faro Airport, ☎ 289/818888). **Hertz** (✉ Faro Airport, ☎ 289/818248).

CAR TRAVEL

To reach the Algarve from Lisbon—an easy 300-km (186-mi) drive south—cross the Ponte 25 de Abril and take the toll road to Setúbal. Beyond here, the main IP1 highway runs via Alcácer do Sal, Grândola, and Ourique, eventually joining N125, the main east–west thoroughfare near Guia, north of Albufeira. To reach Portimão, Lagos, and the western Algarve, turn right; go straight to reach Albufeira; and turn left for Faro and the eastern Algarve. The drive from Lisbon to Faro, Lagos, or Albufeira takes about three hours, longer in the summer, on weekends, and on holidays.

In the east, a suspension bridge crosses the Rio Guadiana between Ayamonte in Spain and Vila Real de Santo António in Portugal. The east–west N125 extends 165 km (102 mi) from the Spanish border all the way west to Sagres. It runs parallel to the coast but slightly inland, with clearly marked turnoffs to the beach towns. Be very careful on this route as it's one of Europe's most dangerous. In summer expect traffic jams in several places along it. In addition, portions of highway are under construction everywhere, and roadwork and diversions add to the traffic near the busy resorts. The high-speed IP1 extends from the Spanish border to Alcantarilha, just west of Albufeira; eventually it will run to Sagres.

Beware that Portugal has some of the worst accident statistics in Europe. Always drive defensively. In inland areas, minor country roads aren't always well maintained; when driving at night in rural areas, look out for mopeds without lights. Signage throughout the region can be very confusing, but don't despair. Local officials have started replacing older tangles of signs with streamlined versions.

EMERGENCIES

Each region has a health center for primary medical (outpatient) treatment; local tourist offices can supply addresses and phone numbers. There are hospitals in Faro, Lagos, and Portimão. Each town has at least one pharmacy that stays open all night; consult the notice posted on every pharmacy's door for current schedules.

EMERGENCY SERVICES

➤ CONTACTS: **General Emergencies** (☎ 112). **Police** (✉ Rua Serpa Pinto, Faro, ☎ 289/804924; ✉ Rua General Alberto Silveira, Lagos, ☎ 282/762930).

HOSPITALS

➤ CONTACTS: **Faro** (✉ Rua Leão Penedo, ☎ 289/803411). **Lagos** (✉ Rua do Castelo dos Governadores, ☎ 282/763034). **Portimão** (✉ Av. São João de Dios, ☎ 282/415115).

MAIL

In Faro, there's a post office in Largo do Carmo. In Lagos, there's a branch in Praça Gil Eanes. Both are open Monday through Saturday from 8:30 to 6:30.

SAFETY

LOCAL SCAMS

The Algarve is one of Europe's most popular sites for vacation and retirement homes. In towns such as Albufeira and Praia da Rocha an entire industry exists to persuade visitors to tour apartment developments and proposed sites in the hopes that they'll sign on the dotted line. You may be approached by agents offering all sorts of inducements (such as free gifts, meals, and drinks) to encourage you to visit time-share properties and villa complexes. Even if you do agree to go on a tour, *never* sign anything, regardless of the promises made.

TAXIS

If you intend to take a cab from Faro Airport, look for the board in the arrivals hall with information on all the regulated areas to major tourist destinations. You can call for taxis or hail them on the street, and around €4–€5 will get you across town (traffic permitting). Beware however a significant number of drivers will have meters that are mysteriously "not working"; always agree on a fare before you set off.

TELEPHONES

Officially there are no area codes in the Algarve: in practice 281 is the prefix for numbers east of Faro, 289 for numbers from Faro as far west as Albufeira, and 282 for numbers from (approximately) Armação de Pêra westwards. Public phones are readily available in tourist areas; they're simple and cheap to operate using prepaid cards.

DIRECTORY AND OPERATOR ASSISTANCE

For information, dial 118; operators often speak English.

TOURS AND PACKAGES

Many companies and individual fishermen along the coast hire out boats for excursions. These range from one-hour tours of local grottoes and rock formations to full-day trips that often involve a stop at a beach for a barbecue lunch. Main centers for coastal excursions are Albufeira, Vilamoura, Portimão, Tavira, Lagos, Sagres, Vila Real, and Armação de Pêra. Consult the tourist offices in these towns for details or simply wander down to the local harbor, where the prices and times of the next cruise will be posted.

Jeep "safaris" are a unique way to see fascinating inland villages. Lunch is usually included in the price. Algarve operators include Megatur and Zebra Safari. Riosul Viagens arranges cruises up the Rio Guadiana, which runs between Portugal and Spain. It also has half-day overland tours by jeep and full-day cruise-jeep tours that take you off the beaten path up to the village Foz de Odeleite. Turinfo can organize boat trips, jeep tours, and other activities around the Sagres Peninsula.

► CONTACTS: **Megatur** (⊠ Rua Conselheiro Bivar 80, Faro, ☎ 289/807485). **Riosul Viagens e Turismo Lda.** (⊠ Rua Tristão Vaz Teixeira 15 C, Monte Gordo, ☎ 281/510201). **Turinfo** (⊠ Praça da República, Sagres, ☎ 282/620003). **Zebra Safari** (⊠ Arcadas de S. João, Albufeira, ☎ 289/583300).

TRAIN TRAVEL

There are regular daily departures to the Algarve from Lisbon's Barreiro station on the south banks of the Tagus. Purchase your ticket for a boat ride at Terminal Fluvial in front of the Praça do Comércio, which takes you across the river to the train station for all trains traveling in a southerly direction. The route runs through Setúbal to the rail junction of Tunes (3 hours from Barreiro) and continues on to Albufeira (another 10 minutes), Faro (another 40 minutes), and all stations east to Vila Real de Santo António (another 2 hours). For the western route to Silves (another 20 minutes) and Lagos (another hour), you must change trains at Tunes.

The railroad connects Lagos in the west with Vila Real de Santo António in the east—running close to N125. Several trains a day run the entire often-scenic route, which takes three to four hours; tickets are very reasonably priced, and the trip is pleasant. Some of the faster trains don't stop at every station, and some of the stations are several miles from the towns they serve, although there's usually a connecting bus. The main train stations generally have someone who speaks some En-

glish, but it's easier to get information at tourist offices. At the Faro
and Lagos offices, timetables are posted.

➤ TRAIN STATIONS: **Faro** (⊠ Largo da Estação, ☎ 808/208208). **Lagos**
(⊠ Largo da Estação, ☎ 282/762987).

TRAVEL AGENCIES

There are travel agencies on practically every corner in every town in
the Algarve. Most of these can book guided sightseeing tours. Abreu
is one of the largest and oldest in the country.

➤ LOCAL AGENCIES: **Abreu** (⊠ Av. da República 124, Faro, ☎ 289/
870900; ⊠ Rua Infante Dom Henrique 83, Portimão, ☎ 282/460560).
Space (⊠ Rua Conselheiro Bivar 36, Faro, ☎ 289/805525; ⊠ Rua Judice Biker 26A, Portimão, ☎ 282/416063).

VISITOR INFORMATION

FARO AND ENVIRONS

➤ TOURIST OFFICES: **Faro** (⊠ Airport, ☎ 289/818582; ⊠ Rua da Misericórdia 8–12, ☎ 289/803604). **Loulé** (⊠ Edifício do Castelo, ☎ 289/
463900). **Olhão** (⊠ Largo Sebastião Martins Mestre 6A, ☎ 289/
713936).

EASTERN AND CENTRAL ALGARVE

➤ TOURIST OFFICES: **Albufeira** (⊠ Rua 5 de Outubro, ☎ 289/585279).
Armação de Pêra (☎ 282/312145). **Monchique** (⊠ Largo dos Choroes,
☎ 282/911189). **Monte Gordo** (⊠ Av. Marginal, ☎ 281/544495). **Portimão** (⊠ Av. Zeca Afonso, ☎ 282/531800). **Praia da Rocha** (⊠ Av.
Tomás Cabreira, ☎ 282/419132). **Silves** (⊠ Rua 25 de Abril, ☎ 282/
442255). **Tavira** (⊠ Rua da Galeria 9, ☎ 281/322511).

LAGOS AND THE WESTERN ALGARVE

➤ TOURIST OFFICES: **Lagos** (⊠ Sitio de São João, ☎ 282/763031). **Sagres**
(⊠ Rua Comandante Matoso, ☎ 282/624873).

7 COIMBRA AND THE BEIRAS

From the dune-lined beaches and wide, shallow lagoon of the Atlantic coast to the mountains and fortified towns near the Spanish frontier, the face of the Beiras is constantly changing. Lacing everything together is the Rio Mondego, the region's lifeblood and the most Portuguese of all rivers.

Updated by
Emmy de la
Cal, Justine de
la Cal, Martha
de la Cal, and
Peter Collis

T'S NOT FAR FROM ONE POINT IN THE BEIRAS TO ANY OTHER. In fact, you can drive from the Atlantic shore to the lonely fortified towns along the Spanish border—only 160 km (100 mi)—in the time it takes many residents of Los Angeles or London to commute to work. But within this small area there's tremendous diversity.

To the east Portugal's highest mountains, the Serra da Estrela, rise to nearly 6,600 ft and provide a playground of alpine meadows, wooded hills, and clear streams. High in this range's granite reaches, a tiny trickle of an icy stream begins a tortuous journey to the sea. This is the Rio Mondego, praised in song and poetry as the most Portuguese of all rivers. The longest river entirely within the country and the lifeblood of the Beiras, it provides vital irrigation to fruit orchards and farms as it flows through the region's heart. Coimbra, the country's first capital and home to one of Europe's earliest universities, rises above its banks. Closer to the sea, under the imposing walls of Montemor Castle, the river widens to nurture rice fields before merging with the Atlantic at the popular beach resort of Figueira da Foz.

This region has played an important role in Portugal's development. The Romans built roads, established settlements, and in 27 BC incorporated into their vast empire the remote province known as Lusitania, which encompassed most of what is now central Portugal, including the Beiras. They left many traces of their presence, including the well-known and well-preserved ruins at Conímbriga, near Coimbra. The Moors swept through the territory in the early 8th century and played a leading role for several hundred years. Many of the region's elaborate castles and extensive fortifications show a strong Moorish influence. The towns along the Spanish frontier have been the scene of many fierce battles—from those during the Wars of Christian Reconquest to those during the fledgling Portuguese nation's struggle against invaders from neighboring Castile.

The Beiras also played a part in Portugal's golden Age of Discovery. In 1500 Pedro Álvares Cabral, a nobleman from the town of Belmonte on the eastern flank of the Serra da Estrela, led the first expedition to what is now Brazil. Much of the wealth garnered during this period, when tiny Portugal controlled so much of the world's trade, financed the great architectural and artistic achievements of the Portuguese Renaissance. Throughout the region there are fine examples of the Manueline style, the uniquely Portuguese art form that reflects the nation's nautical heritage. The cathedrals at Guarda and Viseu, the Igreja e Mosteiro de Santa Cruz (Church and Monastery of Santa Cruz) in Coimbra, and the Convento de Jesus (Convent of Jesus) in Aveiro are especially noteworthy.

During the 19th-century Peninsular War, between Napoléon's armies and Wellington's British and Portuguese forces, a decisive battle was fought in the tranquil forest of Buçaco. Later in the same century, this area witnessed a much more peaceful invasion, as people from all corners of Europe came to take the waters at such well-known spas as Luso, Curia, and Caramulo. Around the turn of the 20th century, when the now tourist-packed Algarve was merely a remote backwater, Figueira da Foz was coming into its own as an international beach resort.

Pleasures and Pastimes

Beaches

There's a virtually continuous stretch of good sandy beach along the entire coastal strip known as the Beira Litoral—from Praia de Leirosa in the south to Praia de Espinho in the north. One word of caution: if your only exposure to Portuguese beaches has been the Algarve's southern coast, be careful here. West-coast beaches tend to have heavy surf and strong undertows and riptides. If you see a red or yellow flag, do *not* go swimming. The water temperature on the west coast is usually a few degrees cooler than it is on the south coast.

You have your choice of beaches. There are fully equipped resorts, such as Figueira da Foz and Buarcos, or if you prefer sand dunes and solitude, you can lay your mat down at any one of the beaches farther north. Just point your car down one of the unmarked roads between Praia de Mira and Costa Nova and head west. The beaches at Figueira da Foz, Tocha, Mira, and Furadouro (Ovar) are well suited to children; they all have lifeguards and have met the European Union standards for safety and hygiene.

Dining

At almost any of the ubiquitous beach bar–restaurants, you can't go wrong by ordering the *peixe do dia* (fish of the day). In most cases it will have been caught only hours before and will be prepared outside on a charcoal grill. You'll usually be served the whole fish along with boiled potatoes and a simple salad. Wash it down with a chilled white Dão wine, and you have a tasty, healthy, relatively inexpensive meal. In Figueira da Foz and in the Aveiro region, *enguias* (eels), *lampreia* (lamprey), and *caldeirada* (a fish stew that's a distant cousin of the French bouillabaisse) are popular.

The inland Bairrada region, between Coimbra and Aveiro, and in particular the town of Mealhada are well known for *leitão assado* (roast suckling pig). In Coimbra the dish to try is *chanfana*; this is traditionally made with tender young kid braised in red wine and roasted in an earthenware casserole. In the mountains, fresh *truta* (trout) panfried with bacon and onions is often served, as is *javali* (wild boar). *Bacalhau* (salt cod) in one form or another appears on just about every menu in the region. Bacalhau *à brás* (fried in olive oil with eggs, onions, and potatoes) is one of many popular versions of this ubiquitous dish.

The Beiras contain two of Portugal's most notable wine districts: Bairrada and Dão. The reds from these districts generally benefit from a fairly long stay in the bottle; 1983 and 1985 are particularly good years, and if you see a 1983 Porta dos Cavaleiros Reserva *tinto* (red) on a wine list, grab it. The full-bodied Dão goes wonderfully with chanfana or leitão assado. The flowery whites from around here should be drunk much younger.

This region is also justly famous for its contribution to the country's dessert menus, although many of these pastry delights, such as Coimbra's *arrufada* (a small cinnamon-flavor pastry), are rarely found far from home. The tangy sheep's cheese of the Serra da Estrela is popular throughout the country.

With the exception of some luxury hotel dining rooms, restaurants are casual in dress and atmosphere, although a bit less casual than in the southern parts of the country. The emphasis is generally more on the food than on the trappings. Except for pizza, foreign food is virtually nonexistent.

CATEGORY	COST*
$$$$	over €21
$$$	€14–€21
$$	€7–€14
$	under €7

per person for a main course at dinner

Fishing

There's excellent trout fishing in the Rio Vouga (Vouga River) and in the rivers and lakes of the Serra da Estrela—particularly in the Rio Zêzere, which cuts through one of Europe's deepest glacial valleys—and in the Comprida and Loriga lakes. The Beira Litoral is full of beaches and rocky outcroppings where you can try your luck with a variety of fish, including bass, bream, and sole. Check with the local tourist offices for information about obtaining permits. No permit is required for ocean fishing.

Lodging

There are plenty of high-quality accommodations in the western reaches of the Beiras, but the options thin the farther inland you move; make reservations in advance if you plan to travel during the busy summer months. That said, the Beiras has a great variety of lodging choices, ranging from venerable old luxury hotels to gleaming, modern hostelries. Though small, the region's seven *pousadas* (inns that are members of the Turismo de Habitição organization) make the perfect bases for exploring the entire region. In addition, there are several government-approved private manor houses that take guests. Most establishments offer substantial off-season discounts. (High season varies by hotel but generally runs July 1–September 15.)

CATEGORY	COST*
$$$$	over €275
$$$	€175–€275
$$	€75–€175
$	under €75

For a standard double room, including tax, in high season (off-season rates may be lower).

National Parks

The rugged Parque Natural da Serra da Estrela is Portugal's largest national park, encompassing its highest mountains. It's frequented by hikers, anglers, and those who just like to drink up its craggy alpine scenery. The smaller and less crowded Parque Natural da Serra da Malcata was created to protect the endangered Iberian lynx.

Shopping

The Beiras are rich in artisans' traditions, but much of what is made is only available within a limited geographic area. The region around Aveiro produces Portugal's finest china, including the well-known Vista Alegre brand. In the Serra da Estrela, the famous Serra cheese and *presunto* (cured ham) are available in most towns, along with hand-carved wooden kitchen implements and wicker baskets.

Exploring Coimbra and the Beiras

The Beiras region encompasses the provinces of the Beira Litoral (Coastal Beira), the Beira Baixa (Lower Beira), and the Beira Alta (Upper Beira), which together make up roughly one-quarter of continental Portugal's landmass. On the verge of being discovered, the Beiras contain some of the last remaining areas in Europe unscathed by mass tourism.

Portugal's first capital, the ancient university town of Coimbra, provides a good introduction to this part of the country. The region's western portion contains the seaside resort of Figueira da Foz and the canals and lagoons in and around Aveiro. Farther inland it includes Viseu, with its wonderful parks and historic old quarter. The mountain resort of Caramulo and the belle epoque towns of Luso and Curia are some of the country's most popular spas. The region's eastern area includes Portugal's highest mountains—the Serra da Estrela—and a chain of ancient fortified towns along the Spanish border.

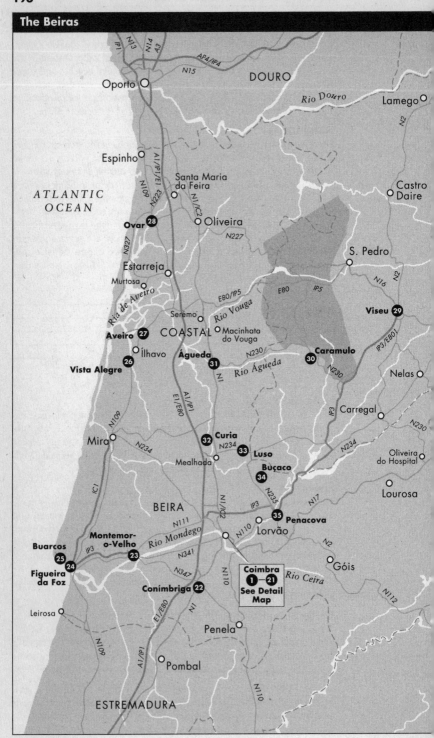

ATLANTIC
OCEAN

DOURO

Oporto

Lamego

Espinho

Santa Maria
da Feira

Castro
Daire

Ovar 28

Oliveira

S. Pedro

Estarreja

Murtosa

Serémo

Rio Vouga

Viseu 29

Aveiro 27

COASTAL

Macinhata
do Vouga

Caramulo

Vista Alegre 26

Ílhavo

Águeda 31

Rio Águeda

30

Nelas

Mira

Carregal

Curia 32

Luso 33

Oliveira
do Hospital

Mealhada

Buçaco 34

Lourosa

BEIRA

Penacova 35

Buarcos

Montemor-
o-Velho 23

Rio Mondego

Lorvão

Góis

Figueira
da Foz 24 25

Coimbra
1 — 21
See Detail
Map

Rio Ceira

Conímbriga 22

Leirosa

Penela

ESTREMADURA

Pombal

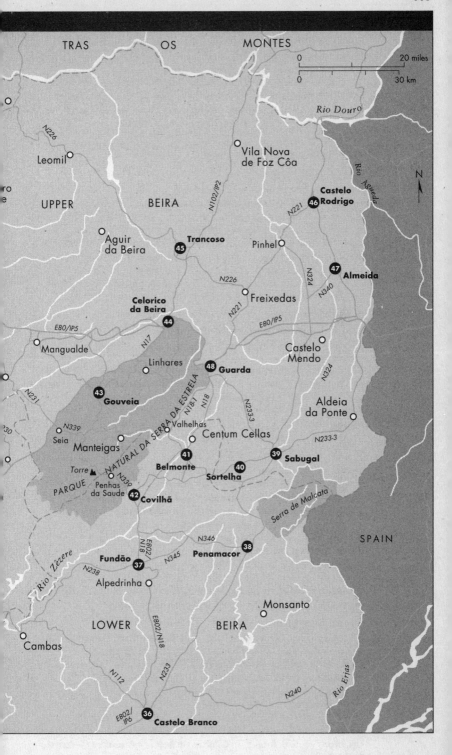

Great Itineraries

If you have just three days, you can visit Coimbra and the main towns and, if you keep moving, include a stretch of the coast and the mountains. A week is enough time to get the feel of Coimbra, visit a spa and the coast, and explore the Serra da Estrela. If you have 10 days, you can explore the region's winding back roads and remote mountain hamlets at a comfortable pace and still have time to take in Coimbra and the beach resorts. In any case, traveling by car is the best way to explore this part of Portugal and to capture its essence.

Numbers in the text correspond to numbers in the margin and on the Beiras map and the Coimbra map.

IF YOU HAVE 3 DAYS

Spend your first morning in ⌖ **Coimbra** ①–㉑, with a stroll through the Cidade Velha (Old Town) and the university. In the afternoon visit the Roman ruins at **Conímbriga** ㉒. The next day, follow the Rio Mondego to the beach resort of **Figueira da Foz** ㉔, head up the coast, and move inland to visit the china factory in **Vista Alegre** ㉖ and the nearby Museu do Mar. Explore **Aveiro** ㉗ and the famous Ria de Aveiro, and end the day by taking IP5 east to ⌖ **Viseu** ㉙. On your third morning, visit Viseu's cathedral, and then continue east on IP5 to **Guarda** ㊽, before returning to Coimbra through the Parque Natural da Serra da Estrela.

IF YOU HAVE 7 DAYS

Start in ⌖ **Coimbra** ①–㉑ and **Conímbriga** ㉒, as above. The next day, explore the coast with visits to the beach resorts of ⌖ **Figueira da Foz** ㉔ and **Buarcos** ㉕, stopping on the way to visit the castle at **Montemor-o-Velho** ㉓. In the evening drive out to Cape Mondego to enjoy the view and the sunset. Continue along the dune-lined coast on the third day, and after a stop in **Vista Alegre** ㉖ and a visit to the nearby Museu do Mar, explore ⌖ **Aveiro** ㉗. The following morning, take a boat trip through the narrow waterways and marshlands that make up the Ria de Aveiro and after lunch continue on to ⌖ **Viseu** ㉙ by way of **Ovar** ㉘ and the castle at Santa Maria da Feira.

On your fifth day, continue east from Viseu and make a loop that includes visits to the fortified towns of **Celorico da Beira** ㊹, **Trancoso** ㊺, **Castelo Rodrigo** ㊻, and **Almeida** ㊼—a pleasant drive through the sparsely settled countryside over little-traveled roads. Spend the night in the mountain bastion of ⌖ **Guarda** ㊽. The next morning, after visiting the cathedral and museum, drive through the mountainous Parque Natural da Serra da Estrela, exiting at Seia. Continue by way of **Penacova** ㉟ to the forest of ⌖ **Buçaco** ㉞, just north of Coimbra. Be sure to visit the opulent Palace Hotel and, if it's within your budget, spend the night; there are more modest accommodations in the nearby spa town of ⌖ **Luso** ㉝. On your last day, return to Coimbra.

IF YOU HAVE 10 DAYS

After exploring ⌖ **Coimbra** ①–㉑ and **Conímbriga** ㉒, head for the coast, with a stop at **Montemor-o-Velho** ㉓. Spend two nights at ⌖ **Figueira da Foz** ㉔ so you can enjoy a day relaxing on the beach here or at **Buarcos** ㉕. In the evening take in the casino's show and the next morning follow the coast north to ⌖ **Aveiro** ㉗, detouring inland to pause at **Vista Alegre** ㉖ and the nearby Museu do Mar. On the fifth day, after touring the Ria de Aveiro and stopping in **Ovar** ㉘ and Santa Maria da Feira, take the scenic route (N227) to ⌖ **Viseu** ㉙. From here, drive a circuitous route that takes in **Celorico da Beira** ㊹, **Trancoso** ㊺, **Castelo Rodrigo** ㊻, and **Almeida** ㊼ and ends at ⌖ **Guarda** ㊽ for the night.

Continue south from Guarda to **Belmonte** ㊶ and trace an arc that includes the fortified mountain towns of **Sortelha** ㊵, **Sabugal** ㊴, and **Pe-**

namacor ㊳. Overnight in the quiet provincial capital of ⌑ **Castelo Branco** ㊱. In the morning, after seeing the gardens and exploring the town, head north through **Fundão** ㊲ to **Covilhã** ㊷, and spend a few hours exploring the Parque Natural da Serra da Estrela. Overnight at the pousada outside the town of Manteigas or continue on for the 26 km (16 mi) to ⌑ **Gouveia** ㊸. Leave the park via N17 southwest to **Penacova** ㉟, and drive to the forest of ⌑ **Buçaco** ㉞. You can spend the night here (at the Palace Hotel) or in nearby ⌑ **Luso** ㉝ before returning to Coimbra.

When to Tour Coimbra and the Beiras

Although the Beiras' coastal beaches are popular in summer, the crowds are nothing like those in the Algarve. The water along this shore isn't as warm as it is farther south, and as a consequence the season is considerably shorter. Plan your beach time here between early June and mid-September.

With the exception of the eastern regions, the interior isn't subject to the blazing heat of the Alentejo or the Algarve's interior and so is well suited for summertime touring. Aside from occasional showers, the weather is comfortable between early April and mid-November. Winters, especially in the eastern mountain towns, are harsh.

COIMBRA AND ENVIRONS

Since its emergence as the Roman settlement of Aeminium, this city on the banks of the Rio Mondego has played an influential and often crucial role in the country's development. In Roman times, it was an important way station, the midway point on the road connecting Lisbon with Braga to the north, and a rival of the city of Conímbriga, across the river to the south. But by the beginning of the 5th century the Roman administration was falling apart, and Aeminium fell under the dominance of Alans, Swabians, and Visigoths in turn. Beset by constant tribal warfare, the riverside settlement had little chance to develop. But by the middle of the 7th century, under Visigoth rule, its importance was such that it had become the regional capital and center of the bishopric of Conímbriga. Upstart Aeminium had finally gained ascendancy over its rival Conímbriga.

The Moorish occupation of Coimbra is believed to have occurred around the year AD 714, and it heralded an era of economic development: for the next 300 years or so, Coimbra was a frontier post of Muslim culture. North of the city there are no traces of Moorish architecture, but Coimbra has retained tangible fragments of its Muslim past—remains of old walls as well as a small gate, the Arco de Almedina, once an entrance to a medina—and the surrounding country is full of place-names that betray a Moorish origin.

After a number of bloody attempts, the reconquest of Coimbra by Christian forces was finally achieved in 1064 by Ferdinand, King of León, and Coimbra went on to become the capital of a vast territory extending north to the Rio Douro and encompassing much of what are now the Beiras. The city was the birthplace and burial place of Portugal's first king, Dom Afonso Henriques, and was the capital from which he launched the attacks against the Moors that were to end in the conquest of Lisbon and the birth of a nation. Coimbra was also the capital of Portugal until the late 13th century, when the court was transferred to Lisbon.

The figure who has remained closest to the heart of the city was the Spanish-born wife of King Dinis, Isabel of Aragon. During her life, while her husband and son were away fighting wars, sometimes against each other, Isabel occupied herself with social works, battling prostitution and fostering education and welfare schemes for Coimbra's young women. She helped found a convent, and had her own tomb placed in it. She bequeathed her jewels to the poor girls of Coimbra to provide them with wedding dowries. She died on a peacemaking mission to Estremoz in 1336. Her body was brought back to Coimbra, and almost immediately the late queen became the object of a local cult. Isabel was beatified in the 16th century, then canonized in 1625 by Pope Urban VIII after it was determined that her body had remained undecayed in its tomb.

Nowadays, Coimbra is best known for its university. Although it was first established in Lisbon by King Dinis I in 1290 and subsequently transferred back and forth between Coimbra and Lisbon, it was finally installed on its present site in 1537. Since then the university has played an important role in the life of both the city and the nation. During the 1960s, it was a center of the unrest preceding the 1974 revolution. Many current political leaders were educated here, and Dr. António Salazar, the country's dictator from 1932 until 1968, once taught economics in its lecture halls. Today, the students add much life to the city. They proudly wear the traditional black capes and adorn their briefcases with colored ribbons denoting which faculty they attend (red for law and yellow for medicine, for example). After final exams in May, they burn their ribbons with great exuberance in a ceremony called Queima das Fitas (Burning of the Ribbons).

To devotees of fado, that uniquely Portuguese music, Coimbra has a special significance. The second great style of fado was born here, and performances are more about personal expression than entertainment. In contrast to the brasher Lisbon version, the Coimbra fado, performed only by men, is softer and gentler. During the student demonstrations of the 1960s, this music was used as a form of protest in much the same manner as the folk song was in the United States. Wandering the narrow, steep passageways of the old university quarter, you may well hear plaintive sounds drifting through the night air. Musical accompaniment is played on a heart-shape, 12-string guitar, and tradition dictates that you don't applaud.

In a bucolic setting southwest of Coimbra, you'll find Conímbriga, one of the Iberian Peninsula's most important archaeological sites. It began as a small settlement in Celtic or possibly pre-Celtic times. In 27 BC, during his second Iberian visit, the emperor Augustus established a Roman province that came to be called Lusitania. It was in this period that, as the Portuguese historian Jorge Alarcão wrote, "Conímbriga was transformed by the Romans from a village where people just existed into a city worth visiting." It still is.

Coimbra

★ ❶–㉑ *165 km (102 mi) northeast of Lisbon.*

❶ The triangular plaza at the foot of the Ponte Santa Clara, on the riverfront perimeter of Coimbra's Baixa (Lower Town) district is the **Largo da Portagem.** The statue of Joaquim António de Aguiar, with pen in hand, represents the signing in 1833 of a decree banning religious orders throughout Portugal (the result of an anticlerical liberalism that had infused political thought throughout Europe at this time).

NEED A
BREAK?   Why not succumb to the temptation of the pastry-filled windows of the cafés along the Rua Ferreira Borges? The **Café Nicola** (✉ Rua Ferreira Borges 35, Baixa) is a good choice for sampling arrufada, Coimbra's

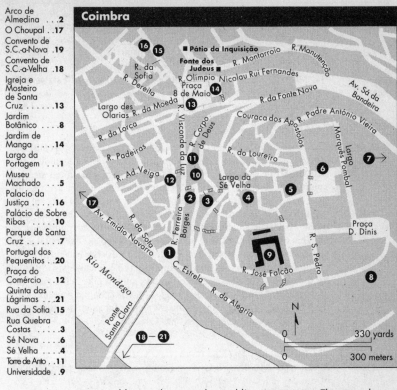

Coimbra

most notable contribution to the world's great pastries. This curved confection is said to represent the Rio Mondego's tortuous course.

2 On the Baixa district's Rua Ferreira Borges, one of the city's principal shopping streets, the **Arco de Almedina** is a tall, graceful opening in a massive stone wall. The 12th-century arch is one of the last vestiges of the medieval city walls, and above it are a Renaissance carving of the Virgin and Child and an early Portuguese coat of arms. The adjacent tower houses the city's historical archives and the *sino de correr* (warning bell), used from the Middle Ages until 1870 to signal the populace to return to the safety of the city walls. The tower is also used as an art gallery.

3 **Rua Quebra Costas** is the main pedestrian link between the Baixa district and the Sé Velha. The street name translates to "back-breaker"; try carrying a heavy load of groceries up this steep incline, and you'll understand why it's an apt name.

★ **4** The **Sé Velha** (Old Cathedral) was constructed in the 12th century. Made of massive granite blocks and crowned by a ring of battlements, it looks more like a fortress than a house of worship. (Engaged in an ongoing struggle with the Moors, the Portuguese, who were building and reconstructing castles for defense purposes throughout the country, often incorporated fortifications in their churches.) The harsh exterior is softened somewhat by graceful 16th-century Renaissance doorways. The somber interior has a gilded wooden altarpiece, a late-15th-century example of the Flamboyant Gothic style, created by the Flemish masters Olivier of Ghent and Jean d'Ypres. The walls of the Chapel of the Holy Sacrament are lined with the touching, lifelike sculptures of Jean de Rouen, whose life-size Christ figure is flanked by finely detailed representations of the apostles and evangelists. The cloisters (closed 1 PM–

2 PM), built in the 13th century, are distinguished by a well-executed series of transitional Gothic arches. ✉ *Largo da Sé Velha,* ☎ *239/ 825273.* 🎫 *Cathedral free, cloisters €0.75.* ⊙ *Mon.–Thurs. 10–6, Fri. 10–2, Sat. 10–5.*

NEED A
BREAK?

The cathedral square is ringed with cafés and restaurants. **Café Sé Velha** (✉ Rua da Joaquim António Aguiar 136), decorated with *azulejos* (painted and glazed ceramic tiles) depicting local scenes, is one of the most inviting.

★ ❺ The **Museu Machado de Castro** (Machado de Castro Museum) contains a fine collection of sculpture, including works by Jean de Rouen and Master Pero, and an intriguing little statue of a mounted medieval knight. The Bishop's Chapel, adorned with 18th-century azulejos and silks, is a highlight of the upstairs galleries, which also contain a diverse selection of Portuguese paintings and furniture. The building, itself a work of art, was constructed in the 12th century to house the prelates of Coimbra; it was extensively modified 400 years later and was converted to a museum in 1912. Don't miss the basement's well-preserved vaulted passageways—built by the Romans as storerooms for the forum that was once here—and be sure to take in the view from the terrace of the Renaissance loggia. As you exit the museum, note the large 18th-century azulejo panel depicting Jerónimo translating the Bible. ✉ *Largo Dr. José Rodrigues,* ☎ *239/823727.* 🎫 *€3, free Sun. morning.* ⊙ *Tues.–Sun. 9:30–12:30 and 2–5:30.*

❻ The 17th-century Jesuit **Sé Nova** (New Cathedral) was patterned after the baroque church of Il Gesù in Rome, as were many such churches of the day. ✉ *Largo da Sé Nova.* 🎫 *Free.* ⊙ *Tues.–Sat. 9:30–12:30 and 2–6:30.*

❼ **Parque de Santa Cruz** (Santa Cruz Park), east of the old city on Praça da República, is a pleasant mixture of luxuriant vegetation, ornate fountains, and meandering walking paths.

❽ You'll find relief from Coimbra's oppressive summer heat in the shade and greenery of the **Jardim Botânico** (Botanical Garden), not far from the university on Alameda Dr. Júlio Henriques.

★ ❾ The **Universidade Velha** (Old University) is steeped in tradition. Although there are modern dormitories and apartments, many of the 20,000 students, some because of tradition and some for economic reasons, prefer the old *repúblicas* (student cooperatives) scattered around the university quarter. Those who live in these ramshackle houses—with the bare minimum of creature comforts—share costs and chores, allowing themselves the one indulgence of a cook. The dwellings were hotbeds of anti-Salazar activity during the years of the dictatorship, and they historically attract people who lean to the left of the political spectrum. The repúblicas aren't open to the public, but if you can get an invitation to step inside one, don't pass up the opportunity for a glimpse of student life. The **República Bota-Abaixo** (✉ Rua São Salvador 6), near the Museu Machado de Castro, is a typical example of this Portuguese-style cooperative.

Built in 1634 as a triumphal arch, the **Porta Férrea** (✉ Praça Porta Férrea) is adorned with the figures of the kings Dinis and João III. It marks the entrance to the principal university courtyard, with its statue of Dom João III; it was during his reign that the university moved permanently to Coimbra. Walk to the far end of the courtyard for a view of the Mondego and across it to the Convento de Santa Clara-a-Nova. The double stairway rising from the courtyard leads to the graceful colonnade framing the Via Latina (Latin Way), the scene of colorful student processions at graduation time. Amid much pomp and ceremony, doctoral degrees are presented in the Ceremonial Hall's **Sala dos Capelos,** which is capped with a fine paneled ceiling and lined with a series of portraits of the kings of Portugal. Admission to it is €3.

The 18th-century **clock-and-bell tower,** rising above the courtyard, is one of Coimbra's most famous landmarks. The bell, which summons students to class and in centuries past signaled a dusk-to-dawn curfew, is derisively called the *cabra* (she-goat; an insulting term common in other parts of Europe, particularly the Mediterranean, and used here to express the students' dismay at being confined to quarters). In the courtyard's southwestern corner is a building with four huge columns framing massive wooden doors: behind them is one of the world's most beautiful libraries, the baroque **Biblioteca Joanina.** Constructed in the early 18th century, it has three dazzling book-lined halls and a large painting of the monarch responsible for its construction—Dom João V. The library is open Monday through Saturday from 10 to noon and from 2 to 5; admission is €3. Next to the Biblioteca Joanina is the **Capela de São Miguel,** with a fine 16th-century Manueline portal opening onto the courtyard. Begun in 1517, the chapel's glories are nevertheless from the 18th century. Its baroque organ, mannerist main altar, and rococo side altars are stunning.

🔟 The **Palácio de Sobre Ribas** (Palace above the Riverbanks) occupies a tower in the ancient walls on Rua Sobre Ribas, in the lower part of the Cidade Velha. The building's exterior is graced by several Manueline doorways and windows.

⑪ Now containing a regional handicrafts center, the **Torre de Anto** (Tower of Anto) was named in honor of Portuguese poet António Nobre, who lived in it during the 19th century. ⊠ *Rua Sobre Ribas.* ☼ *Crafts center: weekdays 9–12:30 and 2–5:30.*

⑫ One of the Baixa district's busiest and most attractive plazas, the **Praça do Comércio,** was the site of the circus in Roman times. Today it's ringed with fashionable shops in 17th- and 18th-century town houses, and street vendors sell everything from combs to carpets on its corners. The Rua Eduardo Coelho, which fans out from the square, is lined with shoe stores and was once known as the Street of the Shoemakers. Closed to the public, the Igreja de Sant'Iago, on the square's northeast corner, is a small, late-13th-century stone structure with finely carved Romanesque columns. On the opposite corner, the Igreja de São Bartolomeu dates from 957. Destroyed several times, it was rebuilt in its present form in 1756.

⑬ The stark, 12th-century stone facade of the **Igreja e Mosteiro de Santa Cruz** (Church and Monastery of Santa Cruz) is enhanced by a Renaissance entrance, added as part of renovations in 1507. Inside, the high altar—whose delicate carvings were done by Nicolas Chanterene in 1521—is flanked by the intricately detailed tombs of Portugal's first two kings, Dom Afonso Henriques and his son, Dom Sancho I. In the sacristy are several notable examples of 16th-century Portuguese painting. The lower portions of the interior walls are lined with azulejos depicting various religious motifs. From the sacristy, a door opens to the Casa do Capitulo (Silent Cloister); this double-tier Manueline cloister contains scenes from the Passion of Christ, attributed to Chanterene. ⊠ *Praça 8 de Maio,* ☎ *239/822941.* ⊠ *Church: free. Sacristy, chapter room, and cloister: €1.* ☼ *Daily 9–noon and 2–5.*

NEED A
BREAK?

The **Café Santa Cruz** (✉ Praça 8 de Maio, ☎ 239/833617) is one of the most unusual watering holes north of Lisbon. Until its conversion to more pedestrian uses in 1927, this was an auxiliary chapel for the monastery. Now its high-vaulted Manueline ceiling, stained-glass windows, and wood paneling make it a great place in which to indulge a favorite Portuguese pastime: sitting in a café with a strong, murky *bica* (Portugal's answer to espresso) and a brandy, reading the day's newspaper. It's closed Sunday.

⑭ A small park with an odd assortment of domed, rose-color turrets grouped around a fountain, the **Jardim de Manga** (Manga Garden) on Rua Olímpio Fernandes was designed by Jean de Rouen in the 16th century and once belonged to the cloisters of the Mosteiro de Santa Cruz. The fountain symbolizes the fountain of life, and the eight pools radiating from it represent the rivers of paradise. Across from the Jardim de Manga on Rua Olímpio Fernandes is the impressive **Fonte dos Judeus** (Jewish Fountain). It dates from 1725 and marks one of the boundaries of the old Jewish quarter. A small alley leads from the Fonte dos Judeus into the notorious **Pátio da Inquisição** (Courtyard of the Inquisition) on Rua Pedro da Rocha. This once-feared site is now home to the local Red Cross.

⑮ The broad, busy **Rua da Sofia** is one of the city's main thoroughfares. Developed in the 16th century, the road is famous for its many fine religious monuments, including the Carmo, Graça, São Pedro, and Santa Justa churches. The entire street has been classified as a national monument.

⑯ The **Palácio da Justiça** (Hall of Justice) occupies a stately 16th-century building that was once the College of St. Thomas. To the left of the main entrance is a large azulejo panel depicting the goddess of justice watched over by a Knight Templar. The three panels in front read WORK, JUSTICE, and ORDER. Gracing the interior is a two-tier cloister, decorated with azulejo panels depicting historical themes associated with Coimbra. ✉ *Rua da Sofia.* 🎫 *Free.* ⊘ *Weekdays 9–12:30 and 2–5:30.*

⑰ **O Choupal** is a pleasant wooded area along the river at the city's west end. Originally a poplar grove planted as a buffer against floods, the park has a place in Coimbra's history as a setting for student serenades and poetic meditation. It's now used more by joggers than romantics.

⑱ On Rua de Baixo, across the river from the Largo da Portagem, is the **Convento de Santa Clara-a-Velha** (Old Santa Clara Convent), a ruined Gothic church, presently being excavated from centuries-old flood deposits by restorers. Founded as a Poor Clairs convent in the early 14th century by Queen Isabel, widow of King Dinis and patron saint of Coimbra, the building was beset by periodic flooding and was finally abandoned in 1677. Both Queen Isabel and the tragic Inês de Castro were originally interred here.

⑲ On the hill overlooking the Old Santa Clara Convent is the **Convento de Santa Clara-a-Nova** (New Santa Clara Convent), built in the 17th century to house the Poor Clair nuns who were forced from their old convent by floods. The remains of Queen Isabel were also moved here. Don't be put off by the barrackslike exterior. The sumptuous baroque church and noble cloisters—the only parts of the convent open to visitors—shouldn't be missed. Queen Isabel's silver shrine is behind the main altar in the church, installed there by Coimbra townspeople in 1696. The queen's original tomb—she ordered it for herself in 1330—stands in the lower choir at the other end of the church. Carved out of a single block of stone, the splendid Gothic sarcophagus is deco-

FADO

The dramatic image of a black-shawled fado singer, head thrown back, eyes closed with emotion, has become an emblem of Portugal; the swelling, soulful song with the plaintive guitar accompaniment seems to embody Portugal's romantic essence. Fado's importance is such that when the great *fadista* Ámalia Rodrigues died in 1999, the government declared three days of national mourning and awarded her a state funeral. When the singing begins in a fado house, all talking ceases and a reverent silence descends on the tables.

But for all that, fado isn't an extremely old tradition. The genre, probably an outgrowth of a popular sentimental ballad form called the *modinha,* seems to have emerged some time in the first half of the 19th century in the poor quarters of Lisbon. At first, fado was essentially a music of the streets, a bohemian art form born and practiced in the alleys and taverns of Lisbon's Mouraria and Alfama quarters. By the end of the century, though, fado had made its way into the drawing rooms of the upper classes. Portugal's last king, Dom Carlos I, was a fan of the form, and a skilled guitar player to boot.

Strictly an amateur activity in its early years, fado began to turn professional in the 1930s with the advent of radio, recording, and the cinema. The political censorship exercised at the time by Portugal's long-lasting Salazar dictatorship also contributed to the development of fado. Wary of the social comments *fadistas* might be tempted to make in their lyrics, the authorities leaned on them heavily. Fado became increasingly confined to fado houses, where the singers needed professional licenses and had their repertoires checked by the official censor.

Nowadays, although the tradition of fado sung in taverns and bars by amateurs (called *fado vadio* in Portuguese) is still strong, the place to hear fado—the Lisbon form of it, at least—is in a professional fado house. Called *casas de fado,* the houses are usually restaurants, too, and some of them mix the pure fado with folk dancing shows. The word "fado" means "fate" in Portuguese, and like the blues, fado songs are full of the fatalism of the poor and the deprived; laments of abandoned or rejected lovers; and tales of people oppressed by circumstances they cannot change.

There are two basic styles of fado: Coimbra and Lisbon. In both forms the singer is typically accompanied by three, or sometimes more, guitarists, at least one of whom plays the Portuguese guitar, a pear-shape 12-string descendant of the English guitar introduced into Portugal by the British port wine community in Oporto in the 19th century. It is the Portuguese guitar that gives the musical accompaniment of fado its characteristically plaintive tone, as the musician plays variations on the melody. The other instruments are usually classical Spanish guitars, which the Portuguese call *violas.*

Although the greatest names of Lisbon fado have been women, and the lyrics often deal with racy, down-to-earth themes, Coimbra fado is always sung by men, and the style is more lyrical than that of the capital. The themes tend to be more erudite, too—usually serenades to lovers or plaints about the trials of love. Coimbra fado is also a largely amateur expression, typically sung by university students.

rated with sculpted polychrome figures of Franciscan friars and nuns. An effigy of the queen herself dressed in her Poor Clair habit lies on top. During the Peninsular War, the French general Massena used the convent as a hospital for 300 troops wounded during the battle of Buçaco. The carefully hidden convent treasures escaped the desecration inflicted on so many Portuguese monuments during this period. ⊠ *Rua Santa Isabel,* ☎ *no phone.* ▨ *Church: free. Cloisters: €0.75.* ⊙ *Daily 9–12:30 and 2:30–5:30.*

☾ ⑳ At Coimbra's small, open-air theme park, **Portugal dos Pequenitos** (Portugal of the Little Ones), children will have great fun poking around the models of Portugal's most important buildings, built to the scale of a five-year-old child. Then they can compare them with what they've seen firsthand. ⊠ *Rossío de Santa Clara,* ☎ *239/441225.* ▨ *€4.* ⊙ *Sept.–Apr., daily 9–5:30; May–Oct., daily 9–7.*

㉑ Popular history has it that Dom Pedro and Inês de Castro lived with their children on this estate, which came to be known as **Quinta das Lágrimas** (House of Tears). It was here on a black January night in 1355 that Inês was killed by agents of Dom Pedro's father, Afonso IV. The 18th-century manor house on the grounds—which has nothing to do with the Inês tragedy—has been turned into a hotel. You can visit the gardens and the celebrated Fonte dos Amores (Fountain of Love), whose waters are said to be Dona Inês's tears. ⊠ *Estrada das Lages,* ☎ *239/802380.* ▨ *€0.75.* ⊙ *Daily 9–5.*

Dining and Lodging

$$ ✕ **Dom Pedro.** The entrance to this restaurant—just a few steps along
★ the riverfront from the tourist office and next to a car dealer—is hardly impressive, but inside it's a different story. A tasteful blend of arches, tile, and wood makes this just the right place in which to enjoy the excellent chanfana and *açorda de mariscos* (a sort of bread porridge mixed with eggs and mounds of fresh shellfish). There's an extensive list of Portuguese wines, and the service is efficient without being stuffy. ⊠ *Av. Emídio Navarro 58,* ☎ *239/829108. AE, MC, V.*

$$ ✕ **Trovador.** Seasoned travelers know well that the rule of thumb is to stay away from restaurants near major sights. But Trovador—just a step away from the old cathedral—has good service and regional food as well as a manor house decor. On Friday and Saturday you can listen to fado at dinner. ⊠ *Largo da Sé Velha 15–17,* ☎ *239/825475. MC, V.*

$ ✕ **Democrática.** Wine barrels add a touch of rustic Portugal to the otherwise functional interior of this popular old establishment. The students and locals who frequent it come for the food and the conviviality, however. The fare is simple and inexpensive. A tasty *caldo verde* (potato soup with shredded cabbage and sausage) and fresh grilled fish make a typical meal. ⊠ *Travessa da Rua Nova 7,* ☎ *239/823784. MC, V. Closed Sun.*

$ ✕ **Zé Manel.** It's just a back-alley hole-in-the-wall with simple wooden tables and chairs, an open kitchen with a jumble of pots and pans, and walls plastered with an odd assortment of yellowing paper announcements. But the food is great and cheap, so don't pass up of the chance for a meal here—if you can get in (it's a favorite with students). For such a small place, it has an amazing choice of dishes, including a wonderful *sopa da pedra* (a rich vegetable soup served with hot stones in the pot to keep it warm). ⊠ *Beco do Forno 10/2,* ☎ *239/823790. Reservations not accepted. No credit cards. Closed 1st 2 wks in Aug.*

$$ ✕▨ **Astoria.** The domed, triangular Astoria faces the Rio Mondego and has been a Coimbra landmark since its construction in 1927. If you like your hotels with old-world charm and almost-state-of-the-art comforts, then you'll like this veteran. Ask for a room facing the river.

The wood-paneled L'Amphitryon Restaurant ($$–$$$) is one of the city's finest for Portuguese fare and Buçaco wines. ✉ *Av. Emídio Navarro 21, 3000-150,* ☎ *239/853020,* ⅀ *239/822057,* Ⓦ *www. almeidahotels.com. 75 rooms. Restaurant, bar, room service, concierge, meeting rooms. AE, DC, MC, V. BP, CP, MAP, FAP.*

$$ ✕⊡ **Quinta das Lágrimas.** This small hotel is on the grounds of the
★ estate where Inês de Castro was supposedly killed at the order of her husband's father. Guest rooms are furnished simply but adequately. At the Arcadas da Capela restaurant ($$$–$$$$), German-born chef Joachim Koerper sometimes uses recipes dating from the 18th century and often uses homegrown herbs, fruits, and vegetables. ✉ *Rua António Augusto Gonçalves, 3040-901,* ☎ *239/802380,* ⅀ *239/441695,* Ⓦ *www.supernet.pt/hotelagrimas. 35 rooms, 4 suites. Restaurant, bar, pool, golf course, tennis court. AE, DC, MC, V. BP, CP, MAP, FAP.*

$$ ✕⊡ **Tivoli.** Favored by businesspeople, the Tivoli is sleek, outfitted with all the latest gadgets, and near the main railway station in Coimbra's modern business district. The only thing lacking is a sense of place: once in your comfortable room, you could be anywhere. The Porta Férrea restaurant ($$$–$$$$) has excellent international and regional dishes and subdued surroundings. ✉ *Rua João Machado 4–5, 3000-226,* ☎ *239/826934,* ⅀ *239/826827,* Ⓦ *www.tivoli.pt. 90 rooms, 10 suites. Restaurant, bar, in-room safes, cable TV, minibars, room service, pool, health club, laundry service, business services, meeting rooms, car rental. AE, DC, MC, V. BP, CP, MAP, FAP.*

$$ ⊡ **Dona Inês.** This modern glass-and-marble hotel is on the banks of the Mondego, just a few minutes' walk from the business district. Although simply furnished, the rooms are light and airy. ✉ *Rua Abel Dias Urbano 12, 3000-001,* ☎ *239/855800,* ⅀ *239/855805,* Ⓦ *www. hotel-dona-ines.pt. 72 rooms, 12 suites. Restaurant, bar, cable TV, tennis court, meeting rooms. AE, DC, MC, V. BP, MAP, FAP.*

$$ ⊡ **Meliá Confort.** As its modern glass facade suggests, this hotel is contemporary, uncluttered, and equipped to meet all your needs. Rooms are done in beiges, browns, and oranges and have lightwood furniture. The hotel is in a quiet residential zone, a 20-minute walk from the city center. You can also hop on the bus that stops outside the hotel's door every half hour or so. ✉ *Av. Armando Gonçalves 20, 3000-059,* ☎ *239/480800,* ⅀ *239/484300,* Ⓦ *www.solmelia.com. 126 rooms, 14 suites. Restaurant, bar, cable TV, minibars, room service, sauna, shops, meeting room. AE, DC, MC, V. BP.*

$ ⊡ **Ibis.** If you've been in one of this chain's properties, you've been in them all; but for the money, the service is hard to beat. This pleasant, comfortable hotel also has a prime riverfront location in the center of Coimbra and not too far from its more distinguished rivals. ✉ *Av. Emídio Navarro 70, 3000-150,* ☎ *239/852130,* ⅀ *239/852140,* Ⓦ *www. ibishotel.com. 110 rooms. Restaurant, bar. AE, DC, MC, V. EP.*

Outdoor Activities and Sports

BOATING

O da Barca (☎ 239/491900) offers leisurely hour-long boat trips on the river approximately every two hours, starting at 10 AM, daily from mid-June through September. Boats department from the pier in Parque Dr. Manuel Braga, just upriver from the Santa Clara Bridge. The cost is €8.

April through mid-October 15, the student-run **O Pioneiro do Mondego** (☎ 239/478385) conducts kayak trips on the Rio Mondego. You're picked up at 10 AM in Coimbra and taken by minibus to Penacova, a peaceful little river town 25 km (16 mi) to the north. The descent takes about three hours, but plan on a day for the whole outing. Call the English-speaking staff for information and reservations. Trips cost €14.96 per person, including kayak rental.

EcoAction (☎ 239/781727) will provide English-speaking guides for nature hikes and cultural rambles in the surrounding countryside.

HORSEBACK RIDING

You can arrange to horseback ride for an hour or two or take longer equestrian excursions at the **Centro Hípico de Coimbra** (✉ Mata do Choupal, ☎ 239/837695). It's on the right bank of the Rio Mondego, 2 km (1 mi) or so downstream from the Santa Clara Bridge.

TENNIS

At the **Clube Tenis de Coimbra** (✉ Av. Urbano Duarte, Quinta da Estrela, ☎ 239/403469), nonmembers pay a €6-per-hour court fee that covers two to four players. Rackets are available for free, but you'll have to bring your own balls or buy them from the club.

Shopping

Numerous stores sell the ceramics produced in and around Coimbra, mostly blue-and-white reproductions of delicate 17th- and 18th-century patterns. The Baixa district by the river is crowded with shops; major shopping streets include Rua Ferreira Borges, Praça do Comércio, Rua Eduardo Coelho, Rua Fernão de Magalhães, and Rua Visconde da Luz.

Conímbriga

★ ㉒ *16 km (10 mi) southwest of Coimbra.*

You enter Conímbriga, an important archaeological site, via a brick reception pavilion with pools and gardens surrounding a museum. Exhibits chronicle the development of the site from its Iron Age origins, through its heyday as a prosperous Roman town, to its decline following the 5th-century barbarian conquests. The museum also contains artifacts unearthed at the site; it's best to tour it after seeing the excavations.

At the site's entrance is a portion of the original Roman road that connected Olissipo (as Lisbon was then known) and the northern town of Braga. If you look closely, you can make out ridges worn into the stone by cart wheels. The uncovered area represents just a small portion of the Roman city, but within it are some wonderful mosaic floors. The 3rd-century House of the Fountains has a large, macabre mosaic depicting Perseus offering the head of Medusa to a monster from the deep, an example of the amazing Roman craftsmanship of the period.

Across the way is the Casa do Cantaber (House of Cantaber), named for a nobleman whose family was captured by invading barbarians in 465. A tour of the house reveals the comfortable lifestyle of Roman nobility at the time. Private baths included a *tepidarium* (hot pool) and *frigidarium* (cold pool). Remnants of the central heating system that was beneath the floor are also visible. Fresh water was carried 3 km (2 mi) by aqueduct from Alcabideque; parts of the original aqueduct can still be seen. A bus that leaves from Rua João de Ruão 18—in the center of Coimbra and close to the river—drops you off right by the entrance to the ruins. The one-way fare is €1.50. ✉ *Condeixa-a-Velha,* ☎ *239/941177.* ▣ *Ruins and museum €3.* ☺ *Ruins: daily sunrise–sunset. Museum: Mid-Mar.–mid-Sept. Tues.–Sun. 10–8; mid-Sept.–mid-Mar. Tues.–Sun. 10–6.*

Dining and Lodging

$$ ✕▥ **Pousada de Santa Cristina.** This pousada in the delightful town of
★ Condeixa-a-Nova makes an ideal base for visiting the Roman ruins at Conímbriga, 1 km (½ mi) to the south, and Coimbra, 15 km (9 mi) to the northeast. The pousada occupies a converted palace and contains

spacious, comfortably furnished bedrooms and one of the area's best traditional restaurants ($$–$$$). ✉ *Rua Francisco Lemos, Condeixa-a-Velha 3150-142,* ☎ *239/944025,* 🖷 *239/943097,* 🌐 *www.pousadas. pt. 45 rooms. Restaurant, bar, pool, tennis court. AE, DC, MC, V. BP.*

THE WESTERN BEIRAS

The western Beiras encompass shore and mountain, fishing villages and country towns, wine country and serene forest. Sights to see range from castles to cathedrals, monasteries to museums. You can also just lie in the sun by the Atlantic or sample the restorative powers of the air and water in any of a cluster of inland towns.

On the gentle-faced coast, long, sandy beaches and sunbaked dunes stretch from Figueira da Foz north toward the great lagoon at Aveiro, with its colorful kelp boats. A bit farther inland are the vineyards of the Dão region, the Serra do Caramulo range, the lush forests of Buçaco, and the sedate spa resorts of Curia and Luso.

Montemor-o-Velho

㉓ *20 km (12 mi) west of Coimbra, 16 km (10 mi) northwest of Conímbriga; the most scenic route, N341, runs from Coimbra along the Rio Mondego's south bank.*

On a hill overlooking the fertile Mondego basin between Coimbra and Figueira da Foz, Montemor-o-Velho figures prominently in the region's history and legends. One popular story tells how the castle's besieged defenders cut the throats of their own families to spare them a cruel death at the hands of the Moorish invaders; many died before the attackers were repulsed. The following day the escaping Moors were pursued and thoroughly defeated. Legend has it that all those slaughtered at Montemor were resurrected but forever carried a red mark on their necks as a reminder of the battle.

The castle walls and tower are largely intact, although little remains inside the impressive ramparts to suggest this was a noble family's home that once garrisoned 5,000 troops. Archaeological evidence indicates the hill has been fortified for more than 2,000 years. Although the castle played an important role in the long-standing conflict between the Christians and Moors, changing hands many times, the structure seen today is primarily of 14th-century origin. The two churches on the hill are also part of the castle complex; the Igreja de Santa Maria de Alcaçova dates from the 11th century and contains some well-preserved Manueline additions.

Here again are threads of the story of Inês de Castro, for in January 1355 Dom Afonso IV, meeting in the castle with his advisers, made the decision to murder her. In 1811 during the Napoleonic invasions, the castle was badly damaged. 🎫 *Free.* ☉ *Tues.–Sun. 10–12:30 and 2–5.*

Figueira da Foz

㉔ *14 km (9 mi) west of Montemor-o-Velho.*

There are various theories as to the origin of the name Figueira da Foz. The consensus around the busy fishing harbor at this seaside resort favors the literal translation: "the fig tree at the mouth of the river." The belief is that when this was just a small settlement, oceangoing fishermen and traders from up the river would arrange to meet at the big fig tree to conduct their business. Although today there are no fig trees to be seen, the name has stuck.

Shortly before the turn of the last century, with the improvement of road and rail access, Figueira, with its long, sandy beach and mild climate, developed into a popular resort. Today, although the beach is little changed, a broad four-lane divided boulevard runs along its length. The town side is lined with the usual mélange of apartments, hotels, and restaurants, but the beachfront has been spared from development.

One of Figueira da Foz's more curious sights is the 18th-century **Casa do Paço** (Palace House), the interior of which is decorated with about 7,000 Delft tiles. These Dutch tiles were salvaged from a shipwreck at the mouth of the harbor. ⊠ *Largo Prof. Vitor Guerra 4, around corner from main post office,* ☎ *233/401320.* ▨ *Free.* ☉ *Weekdays 9:30–12:30 and 2–5.*

The triangular 17th-century **Fortaleza da Santa Catarina** (Santa Catarina Fortress), adjacent to the beachfront tennis courts, was occupied by the French during the early days of the Peninsular War.

NEED A BREAK?
There are a number of brightly painted wooden-shack restaurants on the beach. These are wonderful places for fresh grilled fish or just a cold drink. **A Plataforma** is one of the best.

Palácio Sotto Mayor, an elegantly furnished, French-style manor house, was constructed as part of the wave of development in the late 19th and early 20th centuries that made Figueira da Foz a world-class resort. Long in the hands of one of Portugal's leading families, the building now belongs to the owners of the casino, and local gossip has it that it was "donated" as payment for gambling debts. Its collection includes paintings and fine furnishings. ⊠ *Rua Joaquim Sotto Mayor,* ☎ *233/422121.* ▨ *€1.* ☉ *Sept.–June, weekends 2–6; July–Aug., daily 2–6.*

Dining and Lodging

$–$$$ ✕ **Quinta de Santa Catarina.** The fish dishes at this popular restaurant—in a garden on the outskirts of the town—are outstanding. The menu varies depending on the catch of the day, but ask if one of the *tambril* (monkfish) dishes is available. The house also does a really good *rojões á minhota* (Minho-style sautéed pork). ⊠ *Rua Joaquim Sotto Mayor 92,* ☎ *233/423468. AE, MC, V. Closed Mon.*

$$ ✕ **O Peleiro.** In the quiet village of Paião, 10 km (6 mi) from Figueira, ★ this restaurant—all wood and tiles—was once a tannery, and that's what the name means. Heavy on regional specialties, the menu includes sopa da pedra—a must. Grilled pork or veal on a spit are also excellent, and there's a good wine selection. ⊠ *Largo Alvideiro 3, Paião,* ☎ *233/940159. AE, MC, V. Closed Sun. and 1st 2 wks of May and Sept.*

$$ ✕🏨 **Mercure.** Tour groups favor this five-story, 1950s-vintage hotel, perhaps because it overlooks a broad, sandy beach. Public and guest rooms are spacious and airy. Seafront rooms have small balconies, and the large pool has a view of the beach. The restaurant ($$–$$$) serves international dishes as well as regional specialties. ⊠ *Av. 25 de Abril 22, 3080-086,* ☎ *233/403900,* ℻ *233/403901,* 🕸 *www.accorhotel. com. 102 rooms. Restaurant, piano bar, minibars, pool, baby-sitting, meeting room. AE, DC, MC, V. EP.*

$$ 🏨 **Aparthotel Atlântico.** In this high-rise tower at the beach, the accommodations—apartments with kitchenettes—are small but adequate, with plain, functional furnishings. Some apartments have wonderful sea views. ⊠ *Av. 25 de Abril 20, 3080-086,* ☎ *233/403910,* ℻ *233/ 403901. 70 apartments. Bar, kitchenettes, pool. AE, DC, MC, V. EP.*

$
★ 🖫 **Ibis.** On a quiet street just a five-minute walk from the beach, this small hotel has all the reasonably priced modern appointments Ibis fans expect, but unusually for the chain (which likes to construct new hotels), it's in a remodeled stone building built in 1914. ⊠ *Rua da Liberdade 20, 3080-168,* ☎ *233/422051,* FAX *233/420756,* WEB *www.ibishotel. com. 50 rooms. Bar, breakfast room. AE, DC, MC, V. EP.*

$ 🖫 **Pensão Esplanada.** This turn-of-the-last-century corner house is across from the beach. The floors creak, and the rooms have seen better days, but things are clean and the price is right. Ask for a room with a sea view. ⊠ *Rua Engenheiro Silva 86, 3080-150,* ☎ *233/422115,* FAX *233/429871. 19 rooms. No credit cards. EP.*

Nightlife

The 1886 gaming room of the **Casino da Figueira** has frescoed ceilings, chandeliers, and a variety of table games, including blackjack and American and Continental roulette. Banks of slot machines lie in wait in a separate room. Within the same building there's also a belle epoque show room—site of a nightly revue at 11—as well as two cinemas and a piano bar. Although dress is casual, jeans and T-shirts aren't permitted. The minimum age to enter is 18; bring your passport. ⊠ *Av. Bernado Lopes,* ☎ *233/408400.* 🖭 *Gaming room: free. Show: €5.50.* ☉ *Table games: daily 5 PM–3 AM. Slot machines: daily 3 PM–3 AM.*

Outdoor Activities and Sports

Activity centers on the water here. The fishing for sea bream, bass, and mullet is good at Costa de Lavos and Gala beaches, just south of town, and you can rent windsurfers and other water-sports gear from most resorts on the shore.

BIKING

In summer, you can rent bikes and mopeds by the day and week at the **AFGA Travel Agency** (⊠ Rua Miguel Bombarda 79, ☎ 233/402222).

TENNIS

There are good hard courts at the **Figueira da Foz Tennis Club** (⊠ Av. 25 de Abril 1, ☎ 233/422287). Fees—per hour, per court—are €6 from 9 AM to 11 AM, €4 from 2 PM to 5 PM, and €9 from 11 AM to 2 PM and from 5 PM to 9 PM. Lessons with a pro are available, and you can rent rackets.

Buarcos

㉕ *2 km (1 mi) north of Figueira da Foz.*

This town, with its fine sandy beach, has retained some of the character of a Portuguese fishing village in spite of a heavy influx of tourists. Here colorfully painted boats are still pulled up onto the beach, and fishermen sit around mending nets.

OFF THE **FAROL DE CABO MONDEGO –** Drive out to the cape where the Cape
BEATEN PATH Mondego Lighthouse stands for a wonderfully uncluttered view of the coastline. The road traces a loop and returns to Buarcos.

Dining

$$–$$$ ✕ **Teimoso.** Although the menu choices are varied, seafood—sold by weight—is what put this seaside restaurant on the map. Locals and visitors alike gather in the dining room, which has large picture windows, to order the shellfish that comes fresh from huge saltwater tanks. ⊠ *Estrada do Cabo Mondego,* ☎ *233/402720. MC, V. Closed Wed.*

Outdoor Activities and Sports

Cape Mondego has good fishing for sea bream, bass, and mullet. Carp and barbel are caught in the Quiaios Lakes, northeast of town. The bay here is a popular windsurfing location, as are the Quiaios Lakes. Board surfers often find 10- to 12-ft waves at Quiaios Beach (just north of Cape Mondego).

En Route　The most scenic route north from Buarcos is a winding road that climbs through a wooded area to the little village of Boa Viagem (Good Journey). From here you can trace the course of the Rio Mondego as it flows into the sea and then head north, following a narrow road that runs along the sand dunes to Aveiro, or turn inland to Vagos and pick up N109 to Vista Alegre.

Vista Alegre

㉖　*50 km (31 mi) northeast of Buarcos.*

Portugal's finest china is produced here by a business that was started in 1824 as a sort of commune. Housing was furnished for workers from all parts of the country, training was provided by French master craftsmen, and the clay came from the nearby town of Ovar. Today the settlement's large, tree-filled square is bordered by the factory, a china museum and gift shop, and a small 17th-century chapel with the delicately carved tomb of the chapel's founder.

Through its collection of hundreds of magnificent pieces, the **Museu Histórico da Vista Alegre** (Vista Alegre Historical Museum) traces the development of fine porcelain at the factory from the 1850s to the present day. ✉ *Off N109,* ☎ *234/320755.* ⌑ *Free.* ☉ *Tues.–Fri. 9–12:30 and 2–5:30, weekends 2–5.*

Two kilometers (1 mile) northeast of Vista Alegre is the small town of Ílhavo, with its brightly tiled art nouveau houses and its **Museu do Mar** (Museum of the Sea). Housed in a drab concrete building next to a fish-processing plant, the museum has an interesting collection documenting the region's close relationship with the sea. It also has some good early pieces of Vista Alegre china. ✉ *Rua Vasco da Gama, Ílhavo,* ☎ *234/321797.* ⌑ €2. ☉ *Wed.–Sat. 9–12:30 and 2–5:30, Sun. and Tues. 2–5:30.*

Aveiro

㉗　*5 km (3 mi) northeast of Vista Alegre.*

Aveiro's traditions are closely tied to the sea and to the Ria de Aveiro, the vast, shallow lagoon that fans out to the north and west of town. Salt is extracted from the sea here, and kelp is harvested for use as fertilizer. Swan-necked *moliceiros* (kelp boats) still glide along canals that run through Aveiro's center. In much of the older part of town, sidewalks and squares are paved with *calçada* (traditional Portuguese hand-laid pavement) in intricate nautical patterns. The town's most attractive buildings date from the latter half of the 15th century.

The **Ria de Aveiro,** a 45-km (28-mi) hydralike delta of the Rio Vouga, was formed in 1575, when a violent storm caused shifting sand to block the river's flow into the ocean. The unique combination of fresh and salt water, narrow waterways, and tiny islands is bordered by salt marshes and pine forests, and the ocean side is lined with sandy beaches. This is the tranquil realm of colorful moliceiros that glide gracefully along, their owners harvesting seaweed.

Although you can drive through the Ria on back roads, the best way to see the area is by boat. From mid-June to mid-September, large excursion vessels depart daily from the main canal just in front of the tourist office at 11 AM; they return at 5 PM. A stop is made along the way for lunch, which is included in the €17.50 ticket. The boats can carry up to 80 passengers, but will leave with a minimum of 30. You can also take one- or two-hour trips on moliceiro boats (six passengers maximum) that leave four times a day from the same spot. The fare is €7.

In 1472 Princess Joana, daughter of King Afonso V, retired against her father's wishes to the **Convento de Jesus** (Convent of Jesus)—established by papal bull in 1461—where she spent the last 18 years of her life. This royal presence gave impetus to the Aveiro's economic and cultural development. After nearly four centuries of religious life, the Convento de Jesus was closed in 1874 upon the death of its last nun. It now contains the **Museu de Aveiro,** which encompasses an 18th-century church whose interior is a masterpiece of baroque art. The elaborately gilded wood carvings and ornate ceiling by António Gomes and José Correia from Oporto are among Portugal's finest. Blue-and-white azulejo panels have scenes depicting the life of Princess Joana, who was beatified in 1693 and whose tomb is in the lower choir. Her multicolor inlaid-marble sarcophagus is supported at each corner by delicately carved angels. Note also the 16th-century Renaissance cloisters, the splendid refectory lined with camellia-motif tiles, and the chapel of São João Evangelista (St. John the Evangelist). Items on display, many brought from other convents, include sculpture, coaches and carriages, artifacts, and paintings—including a particularly fine 15th-century portrait of Joana by Nuno Gonçalves. ⊠ *Rua Santa Joana Princesa,* ☎ *234/423297.* ▨ *€1.50.* ⊙ *Tues.–Sun. 10–5:30.*

NEED A BREAK?	Looking onto the canal, just down the road from the tourism office, are several little **coffee houses** that specialize in regional *doces* (sweets) such as *ovos moles* (egg-yolk sweets) and biscuits and wafers of various sorts.

On the **Praça da República,** look for the graceful, three-story Câmara Municipal (Town Hall), which has a pointed bell tower. The plaza's 18th-century **Igreja da Misericórdia** (Mercy Church; ☎ 234/426732) has an imposing baroque portal; the walls of the otherwise sober interior are resplendent with blue-and-white azulejos. There's a small museum here with vestments and other religious articles. It's only open in July and August, Monday through Saturday 9–12:30 and 2–5.

The best place for viewing Aveiro's brightly decorated boats is along the **Canal de São Roque.** To the west of the canal are huge, glistening mounds of white salt, recovered by evaporation from the lagoon. At Aveiro's northeast edge, on Rua João de Moura, the **Estação de Caminhos de Ferro** (Railway Station) displays some lovely azulejo panels depicting regional traditions and customs. For restless youngsters, the large **Parque Municipal** (City Park), south of Aveiro's center on Avenida Artur Ravara, has a well-equipped playground.

Dining and Lodging

$$ ✕ **A Barca.** Devoted diners pack this small, family-run restaurant to
★ feast on its fish dishes. Although the style is homey, the cooking has won national gastronomical prizes. Try the *fritada de peixe* (fish fry) and the *amêijoas á bulhão pato* (clams in a garlic and coriander sauce). ⊠ *Rua José Rabumba 5,* ☎ *234/426024. MC, V. Closed Sun.*

$–$$ ✕ **O Mercantel.** This restaurant is the brainchild of Senhor Costa (a.k.a. Costa da Lota), who spent 13 years working at the nearby *lota* (fish market). His skill with fish is locally renowned, and people have applauded his change of career. Specialties include fresh fish, fish stew, and *arroz de marisco* (shellfish with rice). ⊠ *Rua António dos Santos Le 16*, ☎ *234/428057. AE, DC, MC, V. Closed Mon.*

$–$$ ✕ **Porterhouse.** Although the kitchen is good with fish and shellfish, its top dishes are *bife porterhouse* (a juicy, grilled, porterhouse steak) and *espeitada de carne* (skewered meat grill). A fireplace lends warmth and cheer when Atlantic mists are blowing in. ⊠ *Rua João Afonso 13/15*, ☎ *234/428156. V.*

$$ ✕🗔 **Pousada da Ria.** Midway down the narrow, pine-covered penin-
★ sula that separates the Ria da Aveiro from the sea, this two-story inn is about a 30-minute drive southwest of Aveiro. It's filled with and surrounded by plants and flowers, and the wood-and-tile entry has a loft sitting area. Through picture windows in 10 of the cheerfully furnished rooms you can watch the colorfully painted moliceiros glide along the water. The spacious restaurant ($$) has equally lovely views, a summer terrace, and a highly recommended *ensopada de cabrito* (kid stew). ⊠ *Murtosa 3870-301*, ☎ *234/860180*, ⅎ*A*Ⅹ *234/838333*, 🕸 *www.pousadas.pt. 18 rooms, 1 suite. Restaurant, bar, pool, tennis court. AE, DC, MC, V. BP.*

$–$$ ✕🗔 **Hotel Imperial.** The efficient, modern Imperial is in the heart Aveiro. Its rooms lack charm but are comfortable; some on the upper floors have small balconies and nice views. The restaurant ($$–$$$$) is luxurious without being ostentatious and is popular with the business community. Specialties include *enguias fritas* (fried eels) and *bacalhau com natas* (dried salt cod with cream). The breakfast buffet is the best in town. ⊠ *Rua Dr. Nascimento Leitão, 3810-108*, ☎ *234/380150*, ⅎ*A*Ⅹ *234/380151*, 🕸 *www.bestwestern.pt. 100 rooms, 8 suites. Restaurant, 2 bars, cable TV, minibars, laundry service, meeting rooms. AE, DC, MC. BP.*

$$ 🗔 **Hotel As Américas.** This hotel blends modern comforts with art nouveau style. A building from the 1920s has been converted into a bar, breakfast room, and games room. An attached modern building houses the well-equipped guest rooms. ⊠ *Rua Engenheiro Von Hafe 20–22, 3800-176*, ☎ *234/384640*, ⅎ*A*Ⅹ *234/384258. 70 rooms, 2 suites. Bar, breakfast room, in-room data ports, in-room safes, cable TV, minibars. AE, MC, V. BP.*

$ 🗔 **Arcada.** At the foot of the bridge over the central canal, the loca-
★ tion of this arched, four-story building couldn't be more convenient. It's a comfortable, family-owned classic with old-fashioned, no-frills comfort. Furnishings in the well-kept rooms vary from traditional Portuguese to blond-wood 1950s pieces. The lounge and bar recall a gentleman's club, albeit one that's slightly past its prime. ⊠ *Rua Viana do Castelo 4, 3800-275*, ☎ *234/421885*, ⅎ*A*Ⅹ *234/421886. 43 rooms, 6 suites. Bar, breakfast room. AE, DC, MC, V. EP.*

$ 🗔 **Residencial do Alboi.** This small, modern hotel is on a quiet back-street a few blocks from the main canal. Rooms are comfortable, the bar is attractive, and the breakfasts are excellent. ⊠ *Rua da Arrochela 6, 3810-052*, ☎ *234/380390*, ⅎ*A*Ⅹ *234/380391. 22 rooms. Bar, break-fast room. AE, MC, V. EP.*

Outdoor Activities and Sports

BIKING

Near the tourist office on Rua João Mendonça and at other spots around town you'll find racks with bikes that you can use to tour Aveiro and its surroundings. To free a bike, insert a €1 coin; when you return the bike, you get your money back.

HORSEBACK RIDING

Escola Equestre de Aveiro (⊠ Quinta do Chão d'Agra, Vilarinho, ☎ 234/912108), about 6 km (4 mi) north of Aveiro on N109, gives classes for all levels and offers rides (reservations are necessary) into the wetlands around Aveiro. Prices range from €10 an hour for a group trek to €20 an hour for a single rider.

Shopping

The **Armazéms de Aveiro** (✉ Rua Conselheiro Luís de Magalhães 1, ☎ 234/422107) sells leading Portuguese brands of high-quality ceramics and china, including Vista Alegre, Quinta Nova, and Artebus. The staff will ship purchases as well. The mall **Forum Aveiro** (✉ Rua Batalhão Caçadores 10, ☎ no phone), beside the main canal in the center of town, has dozens of little shops and restaurants.

Ovar

28 *24 km (15 mi) north of Aveiro; head north on N109 from Aveiro to Estarreja, then turn west and follow N109-5 through quiet farmlands, and after crossing the bridge over the Ria, continue north on N327 to Ovar.*

At Ria de Aveiro's northern end, Ovar is a good jumping-off point for the string of beaches and sand dunes to the north. This small town, with its many tiled houses, is a veritable showcase of azulejos. The **Câmara Municipal** (Town Hall), built in the 1960s, is adorned with some unusually beautiful multicolor tile panels. The exterior of the late-17th-century **Igreja Matriz** (Parish Church) is completely covered with blue-and-white azulejos. ✉ *Av. do Bom Reitor and Rua Gomes Freire,* ☎ *no phone.* ☉ *Mon.–Sat. 9–12:30 and 2:30–5:30.*

The small **Museu de Ovar,** in an old house in the town center, has displays of traditional tiles, regional handicrafts, and costumes and tableaux recreating scenes from provincial life in the past. There's also a small collection of mementos of popular 19th-century novelist Júlio Dinis, a native of Ovar and its most famous son. ✉ *Rua Heliodoro Salgado 11,* ☎ *256/572822.* ▣ *€1.50.* ☉ *Mon.–Sat. 9:30–12:30 and 2:30–5:30.*

The fairy-tale-like **Castelo de Santa Maria da Feira** (Castle of Santa Maria da Feira) is 8 km (5 mi) northeast of Ovar. Its four, square towers are crowned with a series of conical turrets in a display of Gothic architecture more common in Germany or Austria than in Portugal. Although the original walls date from the 11th century, the present structure is the result of modifications made 400 years later. From atop the tower you can make out the sprawling outlines of the Ria de Aveiro. ✉ *Largo do Castelo,* ☎ *no phone.* ▣ *€1.50.* ☉ *Tues.–Sun. 9–12:30 and 2–6.*

Viseu

29 *82 km (51 mi) southeast of Ovar, 71 km (44 mi) southeast of Aveiro; you can take the scenic but twisting and bone-jarring N227 across the Serra da Gralheira or the smoother, faster, but much less interesting IP1 and IP5.*

A thriving provincial capital in one of Portugal's prime wine-growing districts, the Dão region, Viseu has remained a country town in spite of its obvious prosperity. Its newer part is comfortably laid out, with parks and wide boulevards that radiate from a central traffic circle.

The tree-lined **Praça da República,** also known as the Rossío, is framed at one end by a massive azulejo mural depicting scenes of country life. The heroic figure in bronze, standing sword in hand, is Prince Henry the Navigator, the first duke of Viseu. The stately building across from the tile mural is the Câmara Municipal. Walk inside to admire the colorful Aveiro tiles and fine woodwork, and be sure to see the courtyard. Just to the south of the square, a graceful stairway leads to the 18th-century, baroque Igreja dos Terceiros de São Francisco (Church of the Brotherhood of St. Francis), behind which is a large, wooded park with paths and ponds.

Almeida Moreira, the first director of the Museu de Grão Vasco, bequeathed his Moorish-style mansion and his diverse collection of paintings, furniture, and ceramics to the city. Today it's the **A Casa-Museu de Almeida Moreira** (Almeida Moreira House and Museum). The hilltop house alone is worth the admission price. ⊠ *Rua Soar Cima,* ☎ *232/423769.* ◪ *€1.50.* ☉ *Tues.–Sun. 9:30–12:30 and 2–5:30.*

★   One of Portugal's most impressive squares, the **Largo da Sé,** is bounded by three imposing edifices—the cathedral, the palace housing the Museu de Grão Vasco, and the Igreja da Misericórdia.

The **Sé,** a massive stone structure with twin bell towers, lends the plaza a solemn air. Construction on this cathedral was started in the 13th century and continued off and on until the 18th century. Inside massive Gothic pillars support a network of twisted, knotted forms that reach across the high, vaulted roof; a dazzling, gilded, baroque high altar contrasts with the otherwise somber stone. The lines of the 18th-century upper level are harsh when compared with the graceful Italianate arches of the 16th-century lower level. The walls here are adorned with a series of excellent azulejo panels that depict various religious motifs. To the right of the mannerist main portal is a double-tier cloister, which is connected to the cathedral by a well-preserved Gothic-style doorway. Admission to the cathedral, which is open daily 9:30–12:30 and 2–5:30, is free.

The white, rococo **Igreja da Misericórdia** (Church of Mercy) has soft lines that contrast sharply with the severe, gray lines of the Sé, which stands directly opposite. At this writing the Museu de Grão Vasco was closed for refurbishments that were slated to last until 2004. The church was temporarily displaying the museum's star pieces: Flemish-influenced works—appreciated for their naturalistic style and use of landscape—by 16th-century painter Vasco Fernandes (Grão Vasco). The church is open Tuesday 2 to 6 and Wednesday through Sunday 10 to 6; admission is €1.50.

★   The **Praça de Dom Duarte** is one of those rare places where just the right combination of rough stone pavement, splendid old houses, wrought-iron balconies, and views of an ancient cathedral (it's just below the Largo da Sé) come together to produce a magical effect. Try to be here at night, when the romance is further enhanced by the soft glow of the streetlights.

A statue of a warrior stands on a rock at the edge of town, on the road to Aveiro. It's a **monument to Viriáto,** the leader of the Lusitanian resistance to the Roman invasion in the 2nd century BC. Some historians believe this was the site of his encampment.

Dining and Lodging

$–$$ ✕ **O Cortiço.** Viseu's most celebrated restaurant is known for the some-
★   times comical names of its dishes as well as for its intelligent use of old local recipes. Try the *coelho bêbedo* (drunk rabbit), which is rabbit stewed in red wine, or the bacalhau *podre* (rotten), which is actually a savory dish of salt cod braised in a tomato and wine sauce. ⊠ *Rua Augusto Hilario 47,* ☎ *232/423853. AE, DC, MC, V.*

$$ ⊞ **Meliá Confort Grão Vasco.** For many years the Grão Vasco has
★   been Viseu's leading hotel. Its location in a wooded park just steps from the main square gives you the convenience of the city and the quiet of the countryside. Many of the rooms have balconies that look out on

an oval pool. The restaurant serves a wide variety of principally Portuguese dishes; if it's in season, try the wild boar. ✉ *Rua Gaspar Barreiros, 3510-032,* ☎ *232/423511,* FAX *232/426444,* WEB *www.solmelia.com. 111 rooms. Restaurant, bar, in-room safes, cable TV, minibars, pool, baby-sitting, meeting rooms. AE, DC, MC, V, EP.*

$$ 🏨 **Montebelo.** Several elongated, glass cylinders with bone-white exoskeletons curve around the circular, solarium-like entrance of this enormous hotel. The effect is both curvaceous and linear—not to mention breathtaking. The modern architecture belies the formal gardens as well as the interior's classic touches. Public areas and guest rooms have brass details, rich wood furniture, and luxurious fabrics and carpets in deep reds, golds, and greens. ✉ *Urbanização Quinta do Bosque, 3510-020,* ☎ *232/420000,* FAX *232/415400,* WEB *www.grupovisabeira.pt. 100 rooms, 16 suites. Restaurant, bar, pool, tennis court, health club, golf privileges. AE, DC, MC, V. BP.*

$ 🏨 **Bela Vista.** This comfortable *residencial* (accommodation in what was once a private home) on a quiet street about 1½ km (1 mi) from the center of town has rooms that are small but comfortable. ✉ *Rua Alexandre Herculano 510, 3510-035,* ☎ *232/422026,* FAX *232/428472. 44 rooms. No credit cards. EP.*

Shopping

A walk along the Rua Direita, in the old part of town, can be rewarding. The narrow street is lined with shops displaying locally made wood carvings, pottery, and wrought iron.

En Route Driving to Caramulo from Viseu takes you through the heart of the Dão region. Here you'll see many vineyards, some carefully terraced. The wines pressed from these grapes are some of Portugal's finest.

Caramulo

③⓪ *24 km (15 mi) southwest of Viseu.*

In the early part of the last century, when tuberculosis was rife, people came here for the beneficial effects of the fresh mountain air. Although tuberculosis is no longer the problem it once was, Caramulo hasn't lost its appeal. People still come to enjoy the heather-clad wooded slopes and to walk through the parks and gardens. Mineral water bottled at the nearby spring is popular throughout the country.

The unusual museum in the **Museu do Caramulo–Fundação Abel de Lacerda** (Caramelo Museum–Abel de Lacerda Foundation) was established and supported by a local doctor. Its varied collections, all from donations, include jewels, ceramics, and a fine assortment of paintings that represent such diverse artists as Salvador Dali, Pablo Picasso, and Grão Vasco. Next door to the Fundação Abel de Lacerda is the **Museu do Automóvel**, whose collection of perfectly restored antique cars includes such rare items as a 1902 Darracq. Also on exhibit are vintage bicycles and motorcycles. ✉ *Av. Abel de Lacerda,* ☎ *232/861270 (both museums),* WEB *www.museu-caramulo.net.* 🎫 *€5 (valid for both museums).* ☉ *June–Sept., daily 10–1 and 2–6; Oct.–May, daily 10–1 and 2–5.*

OFF THE **CARAMULINHO** – From the trailhead on N230-3, it's about a 30-minute BEATEN PATH climb to Caramulinho, at an elevation of 3,500 ft. Here at the tip of the Serra do Caramulo, you can look out across a vast panorama taking in the coastal plain to the west and the Serra da Estrela to the southeast.

Dining and Lodging

$$ ✕🏨 **Pousada de São Jerónimo.** The exterior is reminiscent of an alpine ★ chalet, which seems appropriate given this small pousada's location in

the Serra do Caramulo. In the reception area, Arraiolos carpets hang on knotty-pine walls. The lounge, restaurant, and bar are divided by a see-through partition, and there's an inviting open fireplace. Rooms are small but adequate, and each has a marble bathroom and a small balcony. Views throughout the property are exceptional. The restaurant's ($$) fare is country style, with chanfana *de borrego* (roast lamb, instead of the more usual kid, with red wine) one of the favorites. ⊠ *1 km (½ mi) from Caramulo on N230 (Oliveira do Hospital 3400),* ☎ *232/861291,* FAX *232/861640,* WEB *www.pousadas.pt. 12 rooms. Restaurant, bar, pool, badminton. AE, DC, MC, V. BP.*

Águeda

① *25 km (15½ mi) west of Caramulo, 18 km (11 mi) southeast of Aveiro.*

This center for the production of paper products has an attractive parish church and several well-preserved manor houses. Although Águeda itself isn't particularly appealing, the peaceful greenery of the surrounding countryside makes a visit to this area worthwhile.

☾ The **Museu Ferroviário** (Railway Museum) is 10-km (6-mi) north of Águeda on IC2 in the village of Macinhata do Vouga. Part of the village railway station, the museum contains exhibits that include four steam locomotives dating from 1886. ⊠ *Estação de Caminhos de Ferro,* ☎ *234/521123.* ☜ *€1.50.* ☾ *Weekdays 9–1 and 2–5.*

Dining and Lodging

$$ ✕▣ **Estalagem da Pateira.** The name *pateira* comes from *pato,* the Por-
★ tuguese word for duck, and this modern inn is on Portugal's largest lake, which was the private duck reserve of King Manuel I in the 16th century. If you fancy the idea of being serenaded to sleep by croaking frogs after watching a spectacular lake sunset, this place—7 km (4 mi) west of Águeda off Route 333—is for you. The restaurant ($–$$) serves some excellent fare including a very good bacalhau. ⊠ *Rua da Pateira 84, Fermentelos 3750-439,* ☎ *234/721219,* FAX *234/722181. 56 rooms, 1 suite. Restaurant, bar, café, pool, gym, boating. AE, DC, MC, V. MAP, FAP.*

Curia

② *16 km (10 mi) south of Águeda, 20 km (12 mi) north of Coimbra.*

This small but popular spa is in the heart of the Bairrada region, an area noted for its fine wines and its roast suckling pig. The waters, with their high calcium and magnesium-sulfate content, are said to help in the treatment of kidney disorders. Curia is a quiet retreat of shaded parks—with a small lake and grand belle epoque hotels—just a half hour's drive from the clamor of the summer beach scene. Coimbra, Aveiro, Figueira da Foz, the Serra do Caramulo, and Viseu are all within an hour's drive.

Dining and Lodging

$$ ✕ **Pedro dos Leitões.** Of the several restaurants specializing in suck-
★ ling pig, on the N1 from Coimbra to Oporto, "Suckling Pig Pete" is the most popular. Having a meal here is just one of those things everyone does on a trip to Portugal. The size of the parking lot is a dead giveaway that this is no intimate bistro, and Pedro's spitted pigs pop out of the huge ovens at an amazing rate, especially in summer. In spite of the volume, quality is maintained. ⊠ *N1, Mealhada,* ☎ *231/202062. MC, V. Closed Mon.*

$$ ✕▣ **Grande Hotel de Curia.** One of fanciest hotels in the vicinity of
★ Curia's thermal springs was built in the 1890s. Everything seems pol-

ished to perfection, from the marble floors to the mahogany furniture and paneling; fine carpets and fabrics abound. The restaurant ($$–$$$), with its wood-plank floors and soft draperies, typifies the subdued elegance throughout. The menu is primarily international, with a few regional specialties. Medical staff in the state-of-the-art health center can help you with diet and exercise programs. ✉ *Curia (Tamengos 3780-541),* ☎ *231/515720,* ℻ *231/515317. 84 rooms, 6 suites. Restaurant, bar, in-room safes, cable TV, 2 pools (1 indoor), hot tub, massage, sauna, Turkish bath, health club, library, meeting rooms. AE, DC, MC, V. BP.*

$$ ✕⛺ **Hotel Palace de Curia.** The approach down a tree-lined drive is
★ like the beginning of an old movie. In fact, parts of the *Buster Keaton Story* were filmed at this four-story hotel. Its centerpiece of 15 acres of gardens, vineyards, and orchards—all of which supply things to the kitchen. The marble-floored reception area transports you to the 1920s; corridors with names like Avenue of the Roses lead to large guest rooms. Touring a small collection of antique cars, wandering in the aviary or the deer park, and dining on outstanding Portuguese fare in the enormous restaurant ($$–$$$$) are just some of the activities here. ✉ *Curia (Tamengos 3780-541),* ☎ *231/510300,* ℻ *231/515531. 114 rooms. Restaurant, bar, in-room safes, pool, 9-hole golf course, tennis court, billiards, playground, meeting rooms. AE, DC, MC, V. BP. Closed Nov.–Mar.*

$$ ⛺ **Quinta de São Lourenço.** This delightful 18th-century manor—surrounded by vineyards and pine groves—is in the tiny village of São Lourenço do Bairro. The house has six comfortable-size bedrooms with wooden floors, period furniture, and modern bathrooms. There's also a small apartment. Meals can be arranged upon request. ✉ *3 km (2 mi) from Curia on N1 to Mugofores, São Lourenço do Bairro 3780-179,* ☎ *231/528168,* ℻ *231/528594. 6 rooms, 1 apartment. Bar, billiards, recreation room, library. No credit cards. CP.*

Luso

㉝ *8 km (5 mi) southeast of Curia, 18 km (11 mi) northeast of Coimbra.*

This charming town, built around the European custom of "taking the waters," is on the main Lisbon–Paris train line, in a little valley at the foot of the Buçaco Forest. Like Curia, it has an attractive park with a lake, elegant hotels, and medicinal waters. Slightly radioactive and with a low-sodium and high-silica content, the water—which emerges from the Fonte de São João, a fountain in the center of town—is said to be effective in the treatment of kidney and rheumatic disorders.

Dining and Lodging

$–$$ ✕ **O Cesteiro.** At the western edge of town just past the Luso bottling plant, this popular local restaurant serves simple fare that includes several types of salt cod, roast kid, and fresh fish. ✉ *Rua Dr. Lúcio Abranches,* ☎ *231/939360. MC, V.*

$$ ✕⛺ **Grande Hotel de Luso.** This hotel is a large, yellow-stucco complex in a park at the center of town. The buildings, constructed in 1945, are an architectural zero, but the interior is attractive. Rooms are large and airy, with modern, tiled bathrooms; some bedrooms have terraces that overlook the Olympic-size pool. The hotel is adjacent to the renowned Luso Spa, with its many therapeutic programs. The restaurant ($–$$) serves a good selection of international and regional foods in a pleasant environment with a view of the pool. ✉ *Rua Dr. Cid de Oliveira, 3050-230,* ☎ *231/937937,* ℻ *231/937930,* ⟨WEB⟩ *www.hoteluso. com. 143 rooms. Restaurant, bar, 2 pools (1 indoor), sauna, miniature golf, dance club. AE, DC, MC, V. MAP, FAP.*

$ ⊡ **Pensão Alegre.** On a hill overlooking the park, this 19th-century
★ manor house has been receiving guests since 1931. Filled with colorful tiles and rich wood, it exudes old-world hospitality. Rooms have
high ceilings and plank floors; ask for Number 103, which has a large
terrace. Home-cooked meals are available on request. ⊠ *Rua Emídio
Navarro 2, 3050,* ☎ *231/930256,* ℻ *231/930556. 20 rooms. Dining
room, pool. No credit cards. EP.*

Buçaco

③④ *3 km (2 mi) southeast of Luso, 16 km (10 mi) northeast of Coimbra.*

In the early 17th century, the head of the Order of Barefoot Carmelites,
searching for a suitable location for a monastery, came upon an area
of dense virgin forest. Having rejected an offer to settle in Sintra because there were too many distractions, he chose instead the tranquil
forest of Buçaco. A site was selected halfway up the slope of the green-
est hill, and by 1630 the simple stone structure was occupied. To preserve their world of isolation and silence, the monks built a wall
enclosing the forest. Their only link with the outside world was through
one door facing toward Coimbra, which one of them watched over.
The Coimbra Gate, still in use today, is the most decorative of the eight
gates constructed since that time.

So concerned were the Carmelites for the well-being of their forest that
they obtained a papal bull in 1643 calling for the excommunication
of anyone caught cutting down even a single tree. They planted a
number of exotic varieties, and the forest flourished. Attracted by the
calm and tranquility of the forest, individual monks left the monastery
to be alone with God and nature. They built simple hermitages, where
they would stay, without human companionship, for several months
at a time. You can still see vestiges of these hermitages as you walk
through the forest.

In 1810 this serenity was shattered by a fierce battle in which the
Napoleonic armies under Massena were repulsed by Wellington's
British and Portuguese troops. An obelisk marks the site of the Battle
of Buçaco, a turning point in the French invasion of the Iberian Peninsula. In 1834, owing to the rise in anticlerical sentiment and the country's need for money to rebuild the economy after the war of succession
between the two sons of King John VI, the government issued a decree ordering the confiscation of all monasteries and convents. The
monastery was virtually abandoned.

In the early years of the last century, much of the original structure was
torn down to construct—under the supervision of Italian architect
Luigi Manini—an opulent, multiturreted, pseudo-Manueline extrav-
aganza that was to be a royal hunting lodge. With the exception of
one brief vacation and a dubious romantic fling, this "simple hunting
lodge" was never used by the royal family. It became a prosperous hotel—
now the Palace Hotel do Buçaco—and in the years between the two
world wars it was one of Europe's most fashionable vacation addresses. Tales told in local villages have it that during World War II,
when neutral Portugal was a hotbed of espionage, Nazi agents ensconced
in the tower rooms beamed radio signals to submarines off the coast.
Today many come to Buçaco just to view this unusual structure, to stroll
the shaded paths that wind through the forest, and to climb the hill
past the Stations of the Cross to the Alta Cruz (High Cross), their efforts rewarded by a view that extends all the way to the sea.

The small **Museu Militar de Buçaco** (Buçaco Military Museum) houses
uniforms, weapons, and various memorabilia from the Battle of Buçaco.

⊠ *On the left of N234, just outside forest grounds,* ☎ *231/93931.* ▣ *€1.* ☉ *Tues.–Sun. 10–noon and 2–5.*

Dining and Lodging

$$–$$$ ╳▥ **Palace Hotel Buçaco.** A former royal hunting lodge in a 250-acre
★ forest, the Palace is an architectural hodgepodge that includes everything from Gothic to neo-Manueline to early Walt Disney. There's an
elevator, but who can resist walking up the grand, red-carpeted stairway, its walls lined with azulejo panels, and past the suit of armor?
It's worth the steep price for the restaurant's prix-fixe meals ($$$$)
just to sit at a finely laid table and take in the carved-wood ceiling, inlaid hardwood floors, and Manueline windows. The fine Buçaco wines
laid down in the cellars, which contain some 200,000 bottles, are only
available here. *Buçaco (Luso 3050-261),* ☎ *231/937970,* 🅵🅰🆇 *231/
930509,* 🆆🅴🅱 *www.almeidahotels.com. 53 rooms, 6 suites. Restaurant,
bar. AE, DC, MC, V. MAP, FAP.*

Penacova

❸❺ *12 km (7½ mi) southeast of Buçaco, 12 km (7½ mi) northeast of Coimbra; from Buçaco, the most scenic route is N235, through wooded countryside along the foot of the Serra do Buçaco; from Coimbra, take N110
along the Rio Mondego.*

A little town on a hill at the junction of three low mountain ranges,
Penacova affords panoramic views wherever you look and wonderful
hikes. The attractive parish church in the town square was built in 1620.

Just outside Penacova, in a small wooded valley, is the village of Lorvão
and the **Mosteiro de Lorvão.** This monastery is worth visiting not just
to see what's still standing, but also to feel the vibes of a departed epoch.
Its origins are obscure, but there's archaeological evidence of monastic life here dating as far back as the 6th century. In the 13th century
Lorvão became a convent for Cistercian nuns and was the custodian
of a famed library of 12th-century illuminated manuscripts. The convent was closed down by government order in the 19th century. By that
time, the impoverished nuns were partly supporting themselves by
making the forerunners of the exquisitely carved willow toothpicks that
you can buy in Penacova and in handicraft shops around the country.
(The nuns originally used them to decorate the little cakes they made
for sale.) Still standing is a baroque church that dates primarily from
the 18th century and has beautifully carved choir stalls and an ornate
wrought-iron choir grille. The adjacent museum contains archaeological pieces recovered from the site as well as several illuminated
manuscripts. ⊠ *Lorvão, turnoff on N110, 2 km (1 mi) south of Penacova,* ☎ *no phone.* ▣ *Free.* ☉ *Wed.–Sun. 9:30–12:30 and 2–6.*

Dining and Lodging

$$–$$$ ╳ **O Panorâmico.** It's easy to see how this small, family-run restau-
rant got its name: there's a wonderful panoramic view of the Rio
Mondego as it snakes its way along to Coimbra. Be sure to try the house
specialty, *lampreia à mode de Penacova* (lamprey cooked with rice).
⊠ *Largo Alberto Leitão,* ☎ *239/477333. MC, V.*

$$ ▥ **Palacete do Mondego.** The pink-and-yellow paint job and art nou-
veau–style architecture may seem out of place given the bucolic, hill-
top setting. But this hotel has a lot going for it and makes a good base
for exploring the countryside. It's on a site where a castle is believed
to have stood when the Moors and the Christians were facing off in
these territories during the 11th and 12th centuries. The all-round views
command both the Mondego and Alva rivers, giving some credence
to the castle theory. Guest rooms are well equipped, attractively fur-

nished, and comfortable. ⊠ *Av. Dr. Vissaya de Barreto 3, 3000-360,* ☎ *239/470700,* ℻ *239/470701. 38 rooms. Restaurant, bar, pool. AE, DC, MC, V. BP.*

Outdoor Activities and Sports

HIKING

Several paths lead over the hills to the monastery in Lorvão or through the vineyards and fields down to the Rio Mondego.

KAYAKING

Between April 1 and October 15, there are kayak trips down the Rio Mondego from Penacova to Coimbra. For more information contact the student-run **O Pioneiro do Mondego** (☎ 239/478385) or the local tourist office.

THE EASTERN BEIRAS

Life is difficult in the mountains and along the frontier with Spain. Winters are cold and harsh, and summers are broiling hot. The rugged mountains of the Serra da Estrela and the sparse vegetation of the stone-strewn high plateau present a sharp contrast to the sandy beaches, lush valleys, and densely forested peaks along the coast. As you drive east, the red-tile roofs and brightly trimmed white-stucco houses are replaced by stone-and-slate structures, reflecting the more somber environment.

As crops don't flourish here, many inhabitants have supplemented their meager farming incomes by smuggling contraband across the Spanish border. Between 1950 and 1970, many of the villages lost their ablest workers to the factories of northern Europe; a half million Portuguese went to France alone. As a consequence, many towns are populated primarily by senior citizens.

Still, it's worth visiting this region to stand atop a centuries-old castle wall and look out on the landscape's rugged beauty. And in this part of the country, where visitors are still something of a curiosity, you'll find perhaps the warmest welcome.

Castelo Branco

③⑥ *150 km (93 mi) southeast of Coimbra.*

The provincial capital of Beira Baixa is a modern town of wide boulevards, parks, and gardens. Lying just off the main north–south IP2 highway, it's easily accessible from all parts of the country.

Of course there's an older section of town, where you'll find the **Praça Luís de Camões,** the town's best-preserved medieval square. The building with the arched stone stairway is the 16th-century **Câmara Municipal** (Town Hall). At the top of the town's hill are the ruins of the 12th-century **Castelo Templario** (Templar's Castle). Not much remains of the series of walls and towers that once surrounded the entire community. Adjoining the Castelo Templario is the flower-covered **Miradouro de São Gens** (St. Gens Terrace), which provides a fine view of the town and surrounding countryside.

A small regional museum, the **Museu Francisco Tavares Proença Junior** is housed in the old Paço Episcopal (Episcopal Palace). In addition to the usual Roman artifacts and odd pieces of furniture, the collection contains some fine examples of the traditional *bordado* (embroidery) for which Castelo Branco is well known. Adjacent to the museum is a workshop where embroidered bedspreads in traditional patterns are made and sold. ⊠ *Rua Bartolomeu da Costa,* ☎ *272/ 344277.* ▨ *€1.50, free Sun.* ⊘ *Daily 10–12:30 and 2–5:30.*

★ Take a stroll through the **Jardim do Antigo Paço Episcopal** (Garden of the Old Episcopal Palace). These 18th-century gardens are planted with rows of hedges cut in all sorts of bizarre shapes and contain an unusual assemblage of sculpture. Bordering one of the park's five small lakes are a path and stairway lined on both sides with granite statues of the apostles, the evangelists, and the kings of Portugal. The long-standing Portuguese disdain for the Spanish is graphically demonstrated here; the kings who ruled when Portugal was under Spanish domination are carved at a noticeably smaller scale than the "true" Portuguese rulers. Unfortunately, many statues were damaged by Napoléon's troops when the city was ransacked in 1807. ⊠ *Rua Bartolomeu da Costa,* ☎ *no phone.* 🎫 *€0.50.* ☉ *May–Sept., daily 9–8; Oct.–Apr., daily 9–5.*

Dining and Lodging

$$ ✕ **Praça Velha.** In a stone building on a lovely square (the plaque out-
★ side reads 1685), this is by far the best restaurant in town. Of the two dining rooms, the older section with the beamed ceiling and stone floors is best. One intriguing specialty is *bife na pedra* (steak served still cooking on a hot stone slab). ⊠ *Largo Luís de Camões 17,* ☎ *272/328640. AE, DC, MC, V.*

$$ 🏨 **Meliá Confort Colina do Castelo.** This modern hotel atop a hill over-looking the town has all the conveniences you could wish for in addition to exceptionally good views. ⊠ *Rua da Piscina, 6000-453,* ☎ *272/349280,* FAX *272/329759,* WEB *www.solmelia.com. 97 rooms, 6 suites. Restaurant, bar, snack bar, in-room safes, cable TV, minibars, room service, hot tub, massage, sauna, Turkish bath, indoor pool, 3 tennis courts, gym, health club, squash, meeting rooms. AE, DC, MC, V. BP.*

$ 🏨 **Rainha Dona Amelia.** The Dona Amelia is a graceful, modern, five-story hotel in the center of the town. The no-frills rooms are pleasant, functional, and airy. Because of its proximity to the Serra da Estrela, this hotel is busiest between November and May. ⊠ *Rua de Santiago 15, 6000-179,* ☎ *272/326315,* FAX *272/326390. 64 rooms. Restaurant, bar. AE, MC, V. MAP, FAP.*

Shopping

Tradition in Castelo Branco dictates that a new bride make an embroidered bedspread for her wedding night. This custom is still followed, and these delicately patterned, hand-embroidered linen-and-silk spreads are among the finest examples of Portuguese craftsmanship. There's a display-and-sales room next to the Museu Francisco Tavares Proença Junior.

En Route As you travel north on IP2, you cross a landscape of broad plains dotted with olive trees and with the peaks of the Serra da Estrela as a distant backdrop. Thirty kilometers (19 miles) north of Castelo Branco you'll come to the village of Alpedrinha, known for its fine fountains and well-preserved remnants of the Roman road that connected this fertile agricultural region with the Spanish town of Mérida.

Fundão

③⑦ *36 km (22 mi) north of Castelo Branco, 16 km (10 mi) south of Covilhã.*

The pears and cherries grown in this region are the best in Portugal, and Fundão is the principal market town for the area's many orchards. It's also a convenient gateway to the fortified towns along the Spanish border. The 18th-century **Igreja Matriz** (Parish Church) is noted for its azulejos and decorative ceiling. ⊠ *Largo da Igreja,* ☎ *no phone.* ☉ *Daily 9 –7.*

Dining and Lodging

$–$$ ✕ **O Casarão.** This quiet neighborhood restaurant's three small dining areas have beamed ceilings and are divided by brick pillars. Owner José Pereira proudly proclaims that he serves the best food in Fundão, and in this restaurant-poor town he's probably right. Try the Oporto-style tripe. ⊠ *Rua José Germano da Cunha 2/4*, ☎ *275/752844. No credit cards. Closed Sat.*

$ ✕🖼 **Estalagem da Neve.** Rooms in this tiny Victorian-style inn are small but comfortably furnished. The restaurant ($–$$), with its beamed ceiling and tiled walls, is an inviting place in which to enjoy a fine Portuguese meal. Try the trout or roast kid. ⊠ *Calçada de São Sebastião, 6230-347*, ☎ *275/751299*, 🖷 *275/752215. 5 rooms. Restaurant, bar, pool. AE, DC, MC, V. EP.*

Penamacor

㊳ *28 km (17 mi) east of Fundão, 28 km (17 mi) southeast of Covilhã.*

Like many of the towns in this region, Penamacor is a mix of old and new. Dominated by the ruins of an ancient castle, it was a key link in the chain of strategically placed fortified communities. On its outskirts are newer stucco houses, many built by Portuguese emigrants with money earned working in France and Germany.

The **Castelo de Penamacor** (Penamacor Castle) once guarded the northern approaches to the Rio Tejo. In the wake of the 11th- and 12th-century campaigns to reconquer this region from the Moors, Penamacor lay in ruins. In 1180 Dom Sancho I ordered the reconstruction of the fortifications. Although you can still find traces from that period, much of what you now see, including the solitary watchtower, dates from the early 16th century. If the castle is closed, ask for the key at the tourist office.

The 16th-century **Igreja da Misericórdia** (Church of Mercy) is distinguished by a fine Manueline entrance. A rare octagonal **pillory** in front of the old town hall is worth a look.

The small but interesting **Museu Municipal** (Town Museum) is in a building that was a political prison until the 1974 revolution. One of the original cells has been kept intact, and among the other exhibits is the only complete Roman crematorium on the Iberian Peninsula. ⊠ *Largo ex Quartel*, ☎ *no phone.* 🎫 *Free.* ☉ *Daily 9–12:30 and 2– 5:30.*

Lodging

$$ 🖼 **Estalagem Vila Rica.** This 19th-century converted farmhouse is sur-
★   rounded by trees and gardens and is adjacent to a popular hunting area. The large guest rooms are simple but comfortable. ⊠ *N233, 6090-535*, ☎ *277/394311*, 🖷 *277/394321. 11 rooms. Bar. No credit cards. EP.*

Sabugal

㊴ *20 km (12 mi) northeast of Penamacor, 36 km (22 mi) northeast of Covilhã; from Penamacor, follow N233 north across the high plateau.*

The main attraction here is the 13th-century **Castelo de Sabugal** (Sabugal Castle), which sits majestically atop a grassy knoll and is noted for its unusual pentagonal tower. Some historians maintain that the five sides represent the five shields of the Portuguese national coat of arms. Climb the stone stairs in the courtyard and walk around the battlements. The castle overlooks the Rio Côa, an important tributary of the Douro. Admission is free, and the hours are Monday through Saturday from 10 to 5. Still, the castle might be closed at these times; if so, ask for the key at the tourist office.

OFF THE BEATEN PATH

PARQUE NATURAL DA SERRA DA MALCATA – The 50,000-acre park along the Spanish border between Penamacor and Sabugal was created to protect the natural habitat of the Iberian lynx, which was threatened with extinction. Although this isn't a place of rugged beauty and spectacular vistas, it's nevertheless an attractive, quiet region of heavily wooded, low mountains with few traces of human habitation. In addition to the lynxes, the park shelters wildcats, wild boars, wolves, and foxes.

Sortelha

★ ④ *10 km (6 mi) southwest of Sabugal, 26 km (16 mi) east of Covilhã.*

If you only have time to visit one fortified town, then this should be it. From the moment you walk through its massive ancient stone walls, you feel as if you're experiencing a time warp. Except for a few TV antennas, there's little to evoke the 21st century. The streets aren't littered with souvenir stands, nor is there a fast-food outlet in sight. Stone houses are built into the rocky terrain and arranged within the walls roughly in the shape of an amphitheater.

☾ Above the village are the ruins of a small but imposing **castelo** (castle). The present configuration dates back mainly to a late-12th-century reconstruction, done on Moorish foundations; further alterations were made in the 16th century. Note the Manueline coat of arms at the entrance. Wear sturdy shoes so that you can walk along the walls (you can circle the entire village this way). Children of all ages can let their fantasies run wild while taking in views of Spain to the east and the Serra da Estrela to the west. The three holes in the balcony projecting over the main entrance were used to pour boiling oil on intruders. Just to the right of the north gate are two linear indentations in the stone wall. One is exactly a meter (roughly a yard) long, and the shorter of the two is a *côvado* (66 centimeters [26 inches]). In the Middle Ages, traveling cloth merchants used these markings to ensure an honest measure.

Dining and Lodging

$$–$$$ ✕ **Restaurante Dom Sancho.** This pleasant little restaurant in a restored
★ stone house in the main square began life as a bar that was the pet project of a local engineer. Since then it has become one of the area's more presentable restaurants. It specializes in game dishes like roast wild boar and venison. ⊠ *Largo do Corro,* ☎ *271/388267. No credit cards. Closed Tues.*

There aren't any hotels or pousadas in this medieval town, but several ancient stone houses offer comfortable, although not luxurious, accommodations at very low rates. They don't accept credit cards.

Casas do Campanário (⊠ Rua da Mesquita, 6320-536, ☎ 271/388198), next to the church, just inside the village walls, consists of two apartments; one can accommodate two people, the other eight people. **Casa da Vila** (⊠ Rua Direita, 6320-536, ☎ 271/388113) has two double rooms.

Belmonte

④ *14 km (9 mi) northwest of Sortelha, 20 km (12 mi) southwest of Guarda.*

Three things catch your eye on the approach to Belmonte. The first two, the ancient castle and the church, represent the historic past; the third structure, an ugly water tower, symbolizes the new industry of the town, now a major clothing-manufacturing center. Belmonte's importance can be traced back to Roman times, when it was a key outpost on the road between Mérida, the Lusitanian capital, and Guarda. You can still see elements of this road.

Ask a Portuguese, or better yet a Brazilian, what Belmonte is best known for, and the answer will undoubtedly be Pedro Álvares Cabral. In 1500 this native son "discovered" Brazil and in doing so helped to make Portugal one of the richest and most powerful nations of that era. The **monument to Cabral,** in the town center, is an important stop for Brazilians visiting Portugal.

Of the mighty complex of fortifications and dwellings that once made up the **Castelo de Belmonte** (Belmonte Castle) only the tower and battlements remain. As you enter, note the scale-model replica of the caravel that carried Cabral to Brazil. On one of the side walls is a coat of arms with two goats, the emblem of the Cabral family (in Portuguese, *cabra* means "goat"). Don't miss the graceful but oddly incongruous Manueline window incorporated into the heavy fortifications. ⊠ *On a rocky hill overlooking town from the north.* 🎫 *Free.* ⊙ *Mon.–Sat. 10–12:30 and 2–5:30.*

Adjacent to the Castelo de Belmonte, a cluster of old houses makes up the **Judería** (Jewish Quarter). Belmonte had (and, in fact, still has) one of Portugal's largest Jewish communities. Many present-day residents are descendants of the Morranos, the Jews who were forced to convert to Christianity during the Inquisition. For centuries, many kept their faith in secret, pretending to be Christians while practicing their true religion behind closed doors. Such was their fear of repression, that Belmonte's secret Jews didn't emerge fully into the open until the end of the 1970s. The community remained without a synagogue until 1995.

The 12th-century stone **Igreja de São Tiago** (Church of St. James) contains fragments of original frescoes and a fine pietà carved from a single block of granite. The tomb of Pedro Cabral is also in this church. Actually there are two Pedro Cabral tombs in Portugal, the result of a bizarre dispute with Santarém, where Cabral died. Both towns claim ownership of the explorer's mortal remains, and no one seems to know just who or what is in either tomb. If the church is closed, see if someone at the tourist office can help you gain entrance. ⊠ *Adjacent to Castelo de Belmonte,* ☎ *no phone.* 🎫 *Free.* ⊙ *Daily 10–6.*

OFF THE BEATEN PATH   **CENTUM CELLAS –** A short way outside Belmonte, on a dirt track leading off N18, is a strange archaeological sight that has kept people guessing for years: a massive, solitary, three-story framework of granite blocks. The building is thought to be of Roman origin, but experts are unable to explain its original function convincingly or provide many clues about its original appearance. Some archaeologists believe it was part of a much larger complex. Excavations of the surrounding area are planned.

Dining and Lodging

$ ✕🏠 **Belsol.** Owner João Pinheiro is an enterprising hotelier who has opted for quality and good service over ostentation. In the guest rooms, rosy wood furniture and floors make a nice counterpoint to the white walls and striped, contemporary fabrics and area rugs in white, taupe, and lavender; several rooms have balconies with views of the Rio Zêzere. Stone terraces lead to swimming pools and landscaped areas. Local businesspeople favor the restaurant ($–$$) for its excellent Portuguese food. Try the trout fresh from local waters. ⊠ *Quinta do Rio, off IP2/N18 (Belmonte 6250),* ☎ *275/912206,* ℻ *275/912315,* 🖳

www.hotelbelsol.com. 55 rooms. Restaurant, bar, cable TV, 3 pools, playground. AE, DC, MC, V. BP.

$$–$$$ ⌂ **Convento de Belmonte.** Just over a kilometer (½ mi) from Belmonte on the slopes of the Serra da Esperança, this attractive pousada is in a restored Franciscan monastery founded in 1563 by a descendant of Pedro Álvares Cabral, the first European to reach Brazil. The blend of ancient and modern has been accomplished with finesse. Rooms are well equipped, handsome, and have balconies with views of the surrounding hills. ✉ *Serra da Esperança (Apartado 35, Belmonte 6250),* ☎ *275/910300,* FAX *275/910310,* WEB *www.pousadas.pt. 23 rooms, 1 suite. Restaurant, bar, pool, fishing. AE, DC, MC, V. BP.*

Covilhã

42 *16 km (10 mi) southwest of Belmonte, 48 km (30 mi) north of Castelo Branco.*

Although its origins go back to Roman times, there's little in present-day Covilhã of historic significance. The town is closely linked to sheep raising—it's Portugal's most important wool-producing center—and is a convenient gateway to the Serra da Estrela.

Dining and Lodging

$$ ✕⌂ **Hotel Turismo.** This hotel may be simple, modern, and functional but it's far from spartan, with exercise facilities and a dance club. Guest rooms are pleasant and well equipped. Among the local specialties served in the panoramic rooftop restaurant ($–$$) is fresh trout from nearby mountain streams. ✉ *Acesso a Variante, Quinta da Olivosa (Covilhã 6200-909),* ☎ *275/330400,* FAX *275/330440,* WEB *www.imb-hotels. com. 60 rooms. Restaurant, bar, sauna, massage, health club, squash, dance club, meeting rooms. AE, DC, MC, V. BP.*

$ ⌂ **Covilhã Parque Hotel.** On a tree-lined street near the center of town, this large, modern hotel has the same owners—and style—as the Hotel Turismo. Its comforts are basic, and its amenities are few, but its hard to find lower room rates. ✉ *Av. Frei Heitor Pinto, Bloco A, 6200-909,* ☎ *275/327518,* FAX *275/327519,* WEB *www.imb-hotels.com. 134 rooms. Bar, laundry service. AE, DC, MC, V. CP.*

Parque Natural da Serra da Estrela

Until the end of the 19th century, this mountainous region was little known except by shepherds and hunters. The first scientific expedition to the Serra da Estrela was in 1881, and since then it has become one of the country's most popular recreation areas. In summer the high, craggy peaks, alpine meadows, and rushing streams become the domain of hikers, climbers, and trout fishermen. The lower and middle elevations are heavily wooded with deciduous oak, sweet chestnut, and pine. Above the tree line, at about 4,900 ft, is a rocky, subalpine world of scrub vegetation, lakes, and boggy meadows that, in late spring, are transformed into a vivid, multicolored carpet of wildflowers. The Serra da Estrela Natural Park is home to many species of animals, the largest of which include wild boar, badger, and, in the more remote areas, the occasional wolf.

If you prefer to take in the scenery by car, the roads through the Serra da Estrela, although hair-raising at times, are well maintained. The drive between Covilhã and Seia on N339, the country's highest road, affords a breathtaking view of the Zêzere Valley. Along the way you'll pass a small fountain marking the source of the Rio Mondego. It's in this region that Portugal's noblest cheese, the tangy *queijo da Serra,* is made from the milk of ewes pastured on the rugged mountain slopes.

Dining and Lodging

$–$$ ✕ **Cabana do Pastor.** A cozy mountain restaurant with a fireplace and
★   panoramas, this is a good place to try some Serra cheese. If you're lucky,
the restaurant may have some at its optimum stage of maturity. The
fine, locally cured presunto is also good here, and the place is famed
for its *cabrito no forno,* a succulent dish of roast kid. The restaurant
is 12 km (7½ mi) southwest of Gouveia. ✉ *Behind souvenir shop on
N339, Seia,* ☎ *238/311316. V.*

$$ ✕⊞ **Pousada de Santa Barbara.** In the pines high on the Serra da Es-
★   trela's western flank, 20 km (12 mi) southwest of Gouveia, this moun-
tainside pousada is a restful and cool respite from the summer heat.
Many of the rooms have balconies supported by massive stone columns.
The restaurant ($$) serves a variety of tasty local dishes. ✉ *N17,
Povoa das Quartas (Oliveira do Hospital 3404-909),* ☎ *238/609551,*
FAX *238/609645,* WEB *www.pousadas.pt. 16 rooms. Restaurant, bar,
pool, tennis court. AE, DC, MC, V. BP.*

$$ ✕⊞ **Pousada de São Lourenço.** At an elevation of 4,231 ft, this gran-
★   ite mountain lodge is in the heart of the Serra da Estrela, 13 km (8 mi)
from the spa town of Manteigas. The cozy lounge has plush seating
by a fireplace, and rooms are both elegant and rustic with dark wood
furniture and fabrics in deep colors. Ask for Room 207; it has a loft
for sleeping and one of the best views. If you're just driving through,
stop for lunch at the restaurant ($$) and try the unusual but delicious
bacalhau *á lagareiro* (with corn bread, olive oil, and potatoes). ✉ *On
E232 to Gouveia (Manteigas 6260-200),* ☎ *275/982450,* FAX *275/
982453,* WEB *www.pousadas.pt. 21 rooms, 1 suite. Restaurant, bar. AE,
DC, MC, V. BP.*

$$ ⊞ **Albergaria Senhora do Espinheiro.** Next to the Cabana do Pastor
★   restaurant, 12 km (7½ mi) from Gouveia, this inn is owned and run
by António Mora, a big, gentle bear of a man who will enhance your
stay with his knowledge of the region. The use of wood and tile
throughout gives the inn a warm feeling. Rooms are small and fur-
nished in pine; ask for one at the back, where the views are best. ✉
N339, Seia 6270, ☎ FAX *238/312073. 23 rooms. Bar. AE, DC, MC,
V. EP.*

$$ ⊞ **Hotel Serra da Estrela.** Built in the early part of the last century as
a tuberculosis sanitorium, this hotel 12 km (7½ mi) from Covilhã has
been completely renovated. Rooms are large, and those in the front
have good valley views. At an elevation of 3,936 ft, the hotel provides
an excellent base for a few days in the mountains. ✉ *Penhas da Saude
(on road to Torre) (Covilhã 6203-073),* ☎ *275/310300,* FAX *275/
310309. 38 rooms. Restaurant, bar, snack bar, 2 tennis courts. AE, DC,
MC, V. MAP, FAP.*

Outdoor Activities and Sports

CAMPING

There are several official campsites within the park, but you must bring
your own camping gear.

HIKING

This is a hiker's paradise, and there are plenty of well-marked trails.
A comprehensive trail guide is available at tourist offices in the region,
and, although it's in Portuguese, the maps, elevation charts, and pictures are useful.

SKIING

With the coming of winter and the first snows, the area becomes a winter playground, offering many Portuguese their only exposure to winter sports. In Manteigas you can ski and snowboard year round thanks
to the synthetic run at the **Ski Parque** (☎ 275/982870) complex. The

weekday rates (which include lift tickets and equipment) run from €10 for two hours to €20 for seven hours; rates are slightly higher on weekends and at night. Although there are five ski lifts at **Torre** (☎ 275/334933)—the highest point in continental Portugal, with an elevation of 6,539 ft—the conditions and facilities aren't on a par with ski resorts in the rest of Europe. Still you'll find a restaurant and sports-equipment shops, and you can rent gear. Lift tickets cost €12.50 a day during the week, and €15 a day on weekends.

Gouveia

43 *28 km (17 mi) northwest of Covilhã.*

Nestled into the western side of the Mondego Valley, this quiet town of parks and gardens is a popular base from which to explore the Serra da Estrela. The exterior of the baroque **Igreja Matriz** (Parish Church) is covered with blue-and-white tiles, and well-executed azulejos depicting the Stations of the Cross line the inside walls of the small, dimly lighted chapel across the street. ⊠ *Praça de São Pedro,* ☎ *no phone.* ☉ *Daily 9–6.*

The **Museu Abel Manta,** in an 18th-century manor house, displays a good collection of the paintings by this artist, one of the country's most distinguished. He was born in Gouveia in 1888 and died in Lisbon in 1982. ⊠ *Rua Direita,* ☎ *238/490219.* ☒ *Free.* ☉ *Tues.–Sun. 9:30–12:30 and 2:30–6.*

OFF THE BEATEN PATH

CANIL MONTES HERMÍNIOS – Gouveia is the principal center for the Serra da Estrela sheepdogs, which are famous for their loyalty and courage. In earlier days, when marauding wolf packs were an ever-present menace, the dogs wore metal collars with long spikes to protect their throats. To learn more about the dogs, you can visit the Montes Hermínios Kennels, one of the major breeding kennels in the Vale do Rossim. ⊠ *N232 between Gouveia and Manteigas, Solar do Cão da Serra, Estrada da Serra,* ☎ *238/492426.* ☉ *Visits by appointment.*

Dining and Lodging

$–$$ ✕ **O Júlio.** Thanks to the talents of its chef, owner, and namesake, Júlio, ★ those who love good food travel to this unassuming restaurant from miles around. Try the *truta frita do Mondego* (fried trout from the Rio Mondego) or the *javali no forno* (roast wild boar). ⊠ *Travessa do Loureiro 1,* ☎ *238/498016. MC, V. Closed Tues.*

$ ⊞ **Hotel Gouveia.** This small, modern hotel on one of the main approaches to the Serra da Estrela has comfortable rooms furnished in traditional style. Several have small balconies. The ground-floor O Foural restaurant is popular with local businesspeople; service is attentive, and although the menu (and the prices) changes daily, a good bet is the roast kid. If you like tennis, there are two courts you can use for free in the nearby city park. ⊠ *Av. 1 de Maio, 6290,* ☎ *238/491010,* 𝔽𝔸𝕏 *238/494370. 45 rooms, 3 suites. Restaurant, bar. AE, DC, MC, V. EP.*

En Route The fortified hamlet of Linhares—atop a rocky outcrop at an elevation of 2,625 ft and 16 km (10 mi) northeast of Gouveia—is a good place to take in Serra da Estrela views. The village's stone houses, church, and shops are encircled by walls, much of which remain intact, as do two square, crenellated towers from the time of King Dinis. There's a 16th-century pillory in front of the church.

Celorico da Beira

44 *23 km (14 mi) northeast of Gouveia, 16 km (10 mi) northwest of Guarda.*

Celorico da Beira is a major producer of Serra cheese and the site of one of Europe's largest cheese markets, held every other Friday. The cheese is made from the best quality ewe's milk, using traditional methods. Production takes place between December and March.

Celorico has the requisite **castelo** (castle) watching over it from a hilltop. A large portion of the walls and an impressive tower are intact. Before visiting the castle, be sure to stop by the town hall for the key. ✉ *Follow Rua Fernão Pacheco from main road up through remnants of the old town.* 🎫 *Free.* ⊙ *Mon.–Sat. 10–12:30 and 2–5*

Trancoso

45 *18 km (11 mi) northeast of Celorico da Beira, 26 km (16 mi) northwest of Guarda.*

This town reached its pinnacle in 1282, when King Dinis chose it as the site for his marriage to Isabel of Aragon. Portions of its well-preserved castle walls and towers date from the 9th century. Above one of the gates, the **Porta do Carvalho,** you can make out the figure of a knight. This was a local lad who, during one of the many battles with the Spanish, left the safety of the castle walls to capture the Spanish flag. He was caught, but before being spirited away, he defiantly hurled the flag over the wall.

En Route The most scenic route from Trancoso is the tortuous N226 to Friexedas and the N221 to Pinhel, 38 km (24 mi) to the east. Atop a hill in the Marofa range, Pinhel was a key bastion during the wars of restoration. Its most striking 17th-century remnants are two solitary towers. On one of them, below the balcony facing the town, you can make out the graceful form of a Manueline window. Taking N221 north, you'll cross the Serra da Marofa and a desolate, rocky moonscape. Now much improved, this stretch was once known as the Accursed Road, because of its many bends.

Castelo Rodrigo

46 *60 km (37 mi) northeast of Trancoso.*

This old fortified town is now mostly deserted, many of its former residents having emigrated to France and Germany. The ruins of the **fortaleza** (fortress) afford a panoramic view of the surrounding countryside. In neighboring Figueira de Castelo Rodrigo, the 18th-century **Igreja Matriz** (Parish Church) contains several attractive gilded wooden altars. It's open daily 9–6.

Almeida

47 *18 km (11 mi) southeast of Castelo Rodrigo.*

Enclosed within a star-shape perimeter of massive stone walls, moats, and earthen bulwarks lies the quiet little town of Almeida. Less than 10 km (6 mi) from the Spanish border, it has been the scene of much fighting over the centuries. This is a place for walking, clambering along the walls and bulwarks, and giving your imagination free rein—perhaps to conjure up ghosts of battles past.

Dining and Lodging

$$ ✕▥ **Pousada Senhora das Neves.** Portuguese architect Cristiano Mor-
★ eira eloquently integrated a modern hotel into historic fortress walls.
Public areas and guest rooms are spacious and light, and large terraces
look out across the high tablelands into Spain. You can sip your af-
ternoon glass of chilled white port and imagine Wellington's troops
facing Napoléon's armies on this very spot. The restaurant ($$), divided into two plank-floor dining rooms, serves regional dishes, including
sopa de peixe do Rio Côa (a rich tomato-based soup made with fish
from the nearby Côa River). The wine list has more than 60 selections.
✉ *Rua das Muralhas, 6350,* ☎ *271/574283,* ℻ *271/574320,* ⅦⒺⒷ
*www.pousadas.pt. 20 rooms, 1 suite. Restaurant, bar, fishing. AE, DC,
MC, V. BP.*

$ ✕▥ **A Muralha.** This modern residencial, just outside the fortifications,
is the creation of former English teacher Manuel Dias, who manages
the hotel, and his wife, Eliza, who runs the restaurant ($–$$). Cork-
paneled hallways lead to homey, simply furnished rooms with cork floors.
The restaurant's specialties include cabrito no forno and an excellent
bacalhau. ✉ *Bairro de São Pedro, 6350-211,* ☎ *271/574357,* ℻ *271/
574760. 24 rooms. Restaurant, bar. AE, MC, V. EP.*

Guarda

㊽ *38 km (24 mi) southwest of Almeida, 36 km (22 mi) northeast of Covilhã, 60 km (37 mi) east of Viseu.*

At an elevation of about 3,300 ft, Guarda is Portugal's highest city and
is aptly referred to by the four Fs: *forte, feia, fria, e farta* (strong, ugly,
cold, and wealthy). A somber conglomeration of austere granite buildings in a harsh, uncompromising environment, Guarda is no charming mountain hamlet. The winters are cold and gloomy, often cutting
into the short springtime.

From pre-Roman times, Guarda has been a strategic bastion on the
northeastern flank of the Serra da Estrela, protecting the approaches
from Castile. The town is thought to have been a military base for Julius
Caesar. Following the fall of the Roman Empire, the Visigoths and later
the Moors gained control. Guarda was liberated in the late 12th century by Christian forces and, along with a number of towns in the region, enlarged and fortified by Dom Sancho I.

The **Torre de Menagem** (Castle Keep), on a small knoll above the
cathedral, and a few segments of wall are all that remain of Guarda's
once extensive fortifications. From atop the ruins is an impressive
view across the rock-strewn countryside toward the Castilian plains.

Construction on the fortresslike **Sé** (Cathedral) started in 1390 but
wasn't completed until 1540. As a consequence, the imposing Gothic
building also shows Renaissance and Manueline influences. Although
built on a smaller and less majestic scale, the cathedral shows similarities to the great monastery at Batalha. Inside, a magnificent four-
tier relief contains more than 100 carved figures. The work is attributed
to the 16th-century sculptor Jean de Rouen. ✉ *Praça Luís de Camões,*
☎ *no phone.* ☉ *Tues.–Sun. 9–12:30 and 2–5:30.*

The Sé occupies the north side of the **Praça Luís de Camões,** which is
also the site of some fine 16th- and 18th-century houses and arcades.
The statue standing in the center of the square is of Dom Sancho I.

The **Museu da Guarda** (Guarda Museum), in a stately early 17th-cen-
tury palace adjacent to the 18th-century Igreja da Misericórdia (Church
of Mercy), is worth a visit. It documents the region's history with a

collection of prehistoric and Roman objects, old paintings, documents, arms, and ecclesiastical art. ⊠ *Rua Frei Pedro Roçadas 30,* ☎ *271/ 213460.* 🎟 *€1.50.* 🕐 *Tues.–Sun. 10–12:30 and 2–5:30.*

Dining and Lodging

$–$$ ✕ **Belo Horizonte.** Guarda isn't noted for its good restaurants, but this modest establishment in the old quarter is one of the few exceptions. It serves hearty regional fare and a different type of bacalhau daily. ⊠ *Largo de São Vicente 2,* ☎ *271/211454. AE, MC, V. Closed Sat.*

$ ✕🏨 **Hotel Turismo.** Since it opened in 1940 in a stately, country-style
★ manor house, the Turismo has been Guarda's leading hotel. The extensive use of wood and leather in the bar and lounges makes it comfortable and clubby. Bedrooms are adequate in size and furnished in traditional style. The quiet, refined, Portuguese restaurant ($–$$) serves the best food in town. ⊠ *Praça do Município, 6300-736,* ☎ *271/223366,* FAX *271/223399,* WEB *www.bestwestern.com/hotelturismodaguarda. 100 rooms, 2 suites. Restaurant, bar, pool. AE, DC, MC, V. EP.*

$ 🏨 **Filipe.** This residencial has plain but comfortable rooms and little else. In an under-equipped town like Guarda it's a good choice if you don't plan to stay long and are looking for something inexpensive. ⊠ *Rua Vasco da Gama 9, 6300-772,* ☎ *271/223658,* FAX *271/221402. 40 rooms. AE, DC, MC, V. EP.*

$ 🏨 **Solar de Alarcão.** To absorb Guarda's history, book a room in this 17th-century granite house just around the corner from the Sé. Accommodations are comfortable and furnished with antiques; the only concessions to modernity are TVs and well-fitted bathrooms. There's also a small family chapel. ⊠ *Rua Dom Miguel de Alarcão 25, 6300-684,* ☎ FAX *271/214392. 3 rooms. No credit cards. EP.*

COIMBRA AND THE BEIRAS A TO Z

To research prices, get advice from other travelers, and book travel arrangements, visit www.fodors.com.

AIR TRAVEL

Lisbon is the preferred gateway to the region for most international travelers. Coimbra is 160 km (99 mi) northeast of Lisbon's airport via the A1 highway.

BUS TRAVEL

Buses of various vintages can take you to almost any destination within the region, and unlike train stations, which are often some distance from the town center, bus depots are central. Although this is a great way to travel and get close to the local people, it requires a great deal of time and patience.

Regional and local bus schedules are posted at terminals, and you can also get information at local tourist offices. Rede Nacional de Expressos provides comfortable bus service between Lisbon, Oporto, and Coimbra, and to other parts of the Beiras. International as well as regional services are available at the Rodoviário da Beira Litoral bus station in Coimbra and at the Rodoviário da Beira Interior stations in Castelo Branco and Covilhã.

Coimbra's yellow municipal buses make regular stops around the city from 6 AM to midnight. The tourist office in Praça da Portagem has maps of the bus routes.

➤ CONTACTS: **Rede Nacional de Expressos** (☎ 21/354–5775 in Lisbon). **Rodoviário da Beira Interior** (⊠ Rodrigo Rebelo 3, Castelo Branco, ☎ 272/340120; ⊠ Central de Camionagem, Covilhã, ☎ 275/334914).

Rodoviário da Beira Litoral (⊠ Av. Fernão de Magalhães, Coimbra, ☎ 239/855270). Serviços Municipais de Transportes de Coimbra (SMTUC; ☎ 239/941441).

CAR RENTAL

If you don't get a car from one of the numerous agencies in Lisbon, try Hertz, which has offices in Coimbra and Viseu. Avis also has offices in Coimbra and Viseu as well as Aveiro.

➤ MAJOR AGENCIES: **Avis** (⊠ Av. Dr. Lourenço Peixinho 181–B, Aveiro, ☎ 234/371041; ⊠ Av. Emídio Navarro, Coimbra, ☎ 239/834786; ⊠ Hotel Grão Vasco, Rua Gaspar Barreiros, Viseu, ☎ 232/435750). **Hertz** (⊠ Rua Padre Estevão Cabral, Loja 6, Coimbra, ☎ 239/834750; ⊠ Rua da Paz 21, Viseu, ☎ 232/421846).

CAR TRAVEL

The Beiras, with their many remote villages, are suited to exploration by car. Distances between major points are short; there are no intimidating cities to negotiate; and except for the coastal strip in July and August, traffic is light. Roads in general are good and destinations well marked; however, parking is a problem in the larger towns.

Although you can zip from Lisbon to Coimbra on the A1 toll highway in less than two hours or drive from Oporto to Coimbra in under an hour, resist the temptation. The heart and soul of the Beiras are along the many miles of more minor roads—those squiggly little lines lacing Portugal's map.

EMERGENCIES

In all sizable towns, pharmacies operate on a rotating system for staying open after normal closing hours, including weekends and holidays. Consult a local newspaper or the notice posted on the door of every pharmacy. If you require medical assistance, hospitals in Castel Branco, Coimbra, Figueira da Foz, and Guarda have *urgências* (emergency rooms).

➤ EMERGENCY SERVICES: **General** (☎ 112).
➤ HOSPITALS: **Hospital Amato Lusitano** (⊠ Av. Pedro A. Cabral, Castelo Branco, ☎ 272/322133). **Hospital Distrital da Figueira da Foz** (⊠ Gala, Figueira da Foz, ☎ 233/402000). **Hospital Sousa Martins** (⊠ Av. Reinha Dona Amalia, Guarda, ☎ 271/222133). **Hospital da Universidade de Coimbra** (⊠ Praça Prof. Mota Pinto, Celas, Coimbra, ☎ 239/400400).

MAIL

Coimbra's central post office, the CTT Estação Central, is adjacent to the train station and is the center for *poste restante* (general delivery). Most other towns have just one central post office, where poste restante is received.

➤ POST OFFICES: **CTT Estação Central** (⊠ Av. Fernão de Magalhães 223, Coimbra).

TELEPHONES

The area code for Coimbra is 239. Area codes for western Beiras communities covered in this chapter range from 231 to 234 (though Ovar's code is 256); in the eastern Beiras, the codes include 271, 272, 275, and 277.

DIRECTORY AND OPERATOR ASSISTANCE

For telephone directory assistance, dial 118; operators often speak English.

TOURS AND PACKAGES

There are very few regularly scheduled guided tours originating in the Beiras. The Departamento Cultural (Cultural Department) in Coimbra's town hall organizes excellent one-day bus excursions to areas around Coimbra, but they take place once a month only. If you can catch one of these, the experience is worthwhile as the tours usually include a rewarding introduction to regional home cooking. The Coimbra town hall tourist offices can supply details. Other than that, the only regular tours of the Beiras originate either in Lisbon or in Oporto. For further information contact a travel agency.

➤ CONTACT: **Coimbra tourist office** (☎ 239/832591 or 239/833202).

TRAIN TRAVEL

Although the major destinations in the Beiras are linked by rail, service to most towns, with the exception of Coimbra, is infrequent. Using Coimbra as a hub, there are three main rail lines in the region. Line 110, the Beira Alta line, goes northeast to Luso, Viseu, Celorico da Beira, and Guarda. Line 100 extends south through the Ribatejo to intersect with Line 130, the Beira Baixa line, which runs from Lisbon northeast through Castelo Branco and Fundão to Covilhã, the gateway to the Serra da Estrela. Going north from Coimbra, Line 100 serves Curia, Aveiro, and Ovar and continues north to Oporto and Braga.

Coimbra, Luso, Guarda, Ovar, and Aveiro are on the main Lisbon–Oporto and Lisbon–Paris lines. Two trains arrive from and depart for Paris daily, and in summer a daily car-train operates between Paris and Lisbon. There are also regular trains linking the principal cities in the Beiras with Madrid, Lisbon, and Oporto. There are three stations in Coimbra: Coimbra A (Estação Nova), along the Mondego River, a five-minute walk from the center of town (for domestic routes), Coimbra Parque (also for domestic routes), and Coimbra B (Estação Velha), 5 km (3 mi) west. International trains and trains from Lisbon and Oporto arrive at Coimbra B, where there's a free shuttle to Coimbra A. There are also bus links between stations. Schedules for all trains are posted at all three stations.

➤ CONTACT: **Train information** (☎ 808/208208).

TRAVEL AGENCY

➤ LOCAL AGENCY: **Abreu** (✉ Rua da Sota 2, Coimbra, ☎ 239/855520).

VISITOR INFORMATION

COIMBRA AND THE WESTERN BEIRAS

➤ TOURIST OFFICES: **Águeda** (✉ Largo Dr. João Elísio Sucena, ☎ 234/601412). **Buarcos** (✉ Largo Tomas de Aquino, ☎ 233/433019). **Caramulo** (✉ Av. Dr. Jerónimo de Lacerda, ☎ 232/861437). **Ovar** (✉ Edifício da Câmara Municipal, Rua Elias Garcia, ☎ 256/572215). **Penacova** (✉ Câmara Municipal, Largo Alberto Leitão 5, ☎ 239/470300). **Região de Turismo do Centro** (✉ Largo da Portagem, Coimbra; ☎ 239/833019). **Região de Turismo do Centro** (✉ Praceta Dr. Marcos Viana, Av. 25 de Abril, Figueira da Foz, ☎ 233/402820). **Região de Turismo de Dão-Lafões** (✉ Av. Gulbenkian, Viseu, ☎ 232/420950). **Região de Turismo da Rota da Luz** (✉ Rua João Mendonça 8, Aveiro, ☎ 234/423680).

THE EASTERN BEIRAS

➤ TOURIST OFFICES: **Belmonte** (✉ Praça da Republica, ☎ 275/911488). **Castelo Branco** (✉ Câmara Municipal, Alameda da Liberdade, ☎ 272/330339). **Fundão** (✉ Av. da Liberdade, ☎ 275/752770). **Gouveia** (✉ Av. dos Bombeiros Voluntários, ☎ 238/492185). **Guarda** (✉ Câmara Municipal, Largo do Município, ☎ 271/221817). **Penamacor** (✉ Av. 25 de Abril, ☎ 277/394316). **Região de Turismo da Serra da Estrela** (✉ Av. Frei Heitor Pinto, Covilhã, ☎ 275/319569).

8 OPORTO AND THE NORTH

The vibrant city of Oporto is famous for the wine that bears its name, but the rest of the north is undiscovered country for most visitors. The Minho region has beaches along its Atlantic coast and a lush inland dotted with ancient towns. New roads have penetrated the northeastern Trás-os-Montes region, whose dramatic landscape is rich in wildlife and populated by castles, fortresses, and medieval villages.

T HE REMOTE CORNERS OF NORTHERN PORTUGAL seem far away in Oporto, a trading center since pre-Roman times and still a vibrant, cosmopolitan city. The Moors never had the same strong foothold here that they did farther south, and the city remained largely unaffected by the great earthquake of 1755; as a result, Oporto shows off a baroque finery lacking in Lisbon. Its grandiose granite buildings were financed by the trade that made the city wealthy: wine from the upper valley of the Rio Douro (Douro River, or River of Gold) was transported to Oporto, from where it was then exported. You can follow that trail today by boat or on the beautiful Douro rail line.

By Jules Brown

Updated by Emmy de la Cal, Justine de la Cal, Martha de la Cal, and Peter Collis

The north can be beautiful, as it is in the valley of the Rio Douro and the deep, rural heartland of the Minho, the coastal province north of Oporto; it can also be rugged, as in the Terra Fria (Cold Land), the remote uplands of the northern Trás-os-Montes (Beyond the Mountains). From here come the mysterious, prehistoric *porcas* (stone pigs), reminders of early tribes who scratched a living from the cold earth. Some towns, such as Chaves (Keys), bear curious names and complicated histories. Festivals such as the Holy Week parade at Braga (complete with a torchlight procession through dark, old streets) evoke an earlier time.

The Minho, which takes its name from the river forming Portugal's northern border with Spain, is bounded by the Atlantic in the west and cut by the long, peaceful Rios Lima and Cávado. The Minho coast is advertised as the Costa Verde (Green Coast), a sweeping stretch of beaches and fishing villages named for its lush, green landscape. Some locations have been appropriated as resorts by the Portuguese, but there are still plenty of places where you can find solitary dunes or splash in the brisk Atlantic away from crowds. Inland you can lose yourself in villages with country markets and fairs that have hardly changed for hundreds of years. You'll also see that little of the green countryside is wasted. Vines are trained on poles and in trees high above cultivated fields, forming a natural canopy, for this is *vinho verde* country. This refreshing "green wine"—so called because it's drunk young—is a true taste of the north, one to which you'll quickly become accustomed as you sit, glass in hand, by a river or the coast and reflect upon the day's events.

To the northeast there's adventure at hand, in the winding mountain roads and remote towns and villages of the Trás-os-Montes region. After centuries of isolation, the area is being accessed by ever more and ever better roads, but there's still great excitement in getting off the beaten track and taking rattling bus rides into the far northeastern corners. The imposing castle towers and fortress walls of this frontier region are a great attraction, but—unusual in such a small country—it's often the journey itself that's the greatest prize: traveling past voluminous man-made lakes, through forested valleys rich in wildlife, across bare crags and moorlands, and finally down to coarse, stone villages where TV aerials sit oddly in almost medieval surroundings.

Pleasures and Pastimes

Beaches

The Atlantic is very cold, even at the height of summer, and beaches along the Costa Verde are notoriously windswept. More pleasant is a dip in the Rio Lima or Rio Minho, although you should heed local advice about currents and pollution before plunging in. Ponte de Lima has a particularly nice wide, sandy beach. Espinho, south of Oporto, and the main resorts to the north (Póvoa de Varzim and Ofir) are the best places for water-sports enthusiasts.

Castles

There are towers, castles, and forts galore to explore in this part of the country, some of them so complete they provide a virtual medieval playground. The best include those at Guimarães, Monção, Bragança, and Chaves. Don't miss the region's two vast ornamental staircases at the pilgrimage sights of Lamego and Bom Jesus do Monte.

Dining

The cooking in Oporto is rich and heavy. It's typified by the city's favorite dish, *tripas á moda do Porto* (Oporto tripe), a concoction of beans, chicken, sausage, vegetables, and spices. Elsewhere in Portugal residents of Oporto are known as *tripeiros* (tripe eaters)—a nickname earned when the city was under siege during the Napoleonic Wars, and tripe was the only meat available. However, tripe doesn't dominate the menu in Oporto, and dishes tend to resemble those served in the Minho region. *Caldo verde* (literally "green soup") is ubiquitous; it's made of potato and shredded kale (cabbage) in a broth and is usually served with a slice or two of *chouriço* sausage. Fresh fish is found all the way up the coast, and every town has a local recipe for *bacalhau* (dried cod); in the Minho it's often cooked with potatoes, onions, and eggs. *Lampreias* (lampreys)—eel-like fish—are found in Minho rivers from February through April and are a specialty of Viana do Castelo and Monção. Pork is the meat most often seen on menus, appearing in inventive stews and sausages. For adventurous palates a typically *Minhoto* dish is *papas de sarrabulho*, a hearty stew of shredded pork in a flour-thickened, cumin-scented, pig's-blood soup. Roast *cabrito* (kid) is very popular, too.

In the mountains wonderful *truta* (trout) is available at any town or village close to a river. Trás-os-Montes menus are enlivened by hearty meat stews, which usually include parts of the pig you may wish had been left out (an ear or a trotter, for example). Sausages are a better bet, particularly *alheira* (a legacy of the Sephardic Jews, who devised this mock sausage of chicken and spices to fool religious authorities) or chouriço, the spicy, smoked variety. The other smoked specialty of the region is *presunto de Chaves,* a delicious smoked ham from the town of Chaves. Most dishes will be served with *batatas* (potatoes) or *arroz* (rice), both fine examples of staples being raised to an art form. Spuds here, whether roasted, boiled, or fried, have an irresistibly nutty and sweet flavor. Rice is lightly sautéed with chopped garlic in olive oil before adding water, resulting in a side dish that could easily be devoured as a main course.

The wine available throughout the north is of very high quality. The Minho region's vinho verde is a light, young, slightly sparkling red or white wine. The taste is refreshing, both fruity and acid. Both reds and whites are served chilled (most people prefer the white), and vinho verde goes exceptionally well with fish and shellfish. Vinho verde made from the *Alvarinho* grape in the region of Monção is prized throughout the country. Port enjoys the most renown of the local wines (ask for *vinho do Porto*), but the Douro region, where port comes from, also produces some of Portugal's finest table wines. Other good regions for wine include the area around Chaves, particularly at Valpaços, which produces some excellent, full-bodied, and almost creamy reds.

On the whole, restaurants in Oporto and the north offer extremely good value, although the smaller ones often don't accept credit cards. Dress throughout the region is informal, and reservations are usually unnecessary.

CATEGORY	COST*
$$$$	over €21
$$$	€14–€21
$$	€7–€14
$	under €7

*per person for a main course at dinner

Fishing

Inland, especially in the northeast, fishing is a traditional leisure activity. The best freshwater fishing is in the Lima and Minho rivers, where trout can be caught. Local tourist offices can assist with fishing licenses.

Lodging

In Oporto hotel rates rival those in Lisbon, and you should reserve rooms well in advance to avoid disappointment. Lodgings in the Minho and Trás-os-Montes regions are very reasonably priced compared to their counterparts elsewhere in the country. The Turismo no Espaço Rural (Manor House Tourism) network allows you to spend time at a variety of historic manor houses, country farms, and little village cottages scattered throughout the Minho. Many of these converted 17th- and 18th-century buildings are found in the lovely rural areas around Ponte de Lima. The government-run group of *pousadas* (inns) offers a variety of settings in the north, from a 12th-century monastery in Guimarães to more rustic, hunting-lodge digs high on a hill in Bragança.

CATEGORY	COST*
$$$$	over €275
$$$	€175–€275
$$	€75–€175
$	under €75

*For a standard double room, including tax, in high season (off-season rates may be lower).

Shopping

The north is an excellent region in which to shop for folk art and crafts. Oporto, of course, has the best selection of shops, but don't miss the smaller towns of the Minho, which often specialize in particular handicrafts; Vila do Conde, for example, is known for its lace. The region's weekly and monthly markets are also famous throughout Portugal for having the best local crafts at very reasonable prices.

Exploring Oporto and the North

The north of Portugal can be divided into three basic regions—Oporto and its immediate environs (the nearby coastal resorts and the Douro Valley), the evergreen Minho and Costa Verde to the north, and the somewhat remote and untamed Trás-os-Montes area to the east, a region still slightly short on amenities yet long on spectacular scenery and superb country cooking.

Great Itineraries

Oporto is just 3½ hours north of Lisbon by highway or express train, so even a short trip to Portugal can include a night or two here. From Oporto, it's only another two hours through the Minho and along the Costa Verde coastline up to the Spanish border, or another three–four hours east to the less visited Trás-os-Montes and the eastern border with Spain.

It takes only a day or two to experience the more urban pleasures of Oporto and its wine lodges and the nearby coastal resorts. Several more days would permit a visit to the history-rich towns of Braga or Guimarães or a trip through the lovely Douro Valley. A full week

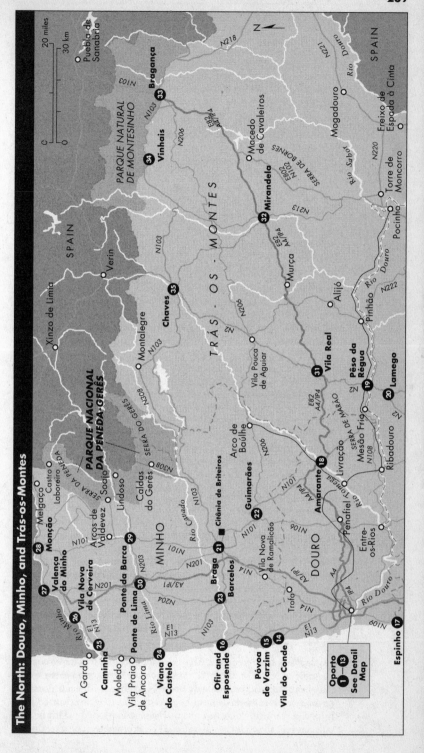

239

The North: Douro, Minho, and Trás-os-Montes

would allow you to cover all of this and the peaceful inland towns and villages along the rivers Lima and Minho, or you could set off for the remote northeastern Trás-os-Montes and its fascinating towns of Bragança and Chaves. Two weeks would give you the opportunity to do the complete circuit and return sated on the riches of the north.

Numbers in the text correspond to numbers in the margin and on the North: Douro, Minho, and Trás-os-Montes map and the Oporto map.

IF YOU HAVE 3 DAYS

Devote the first morning to ⊞ **Oporto** ①–⑬, followed by an afternoon tour of the port-wine lodges in Vila Nova de Gaia, across the Rio Douro. Before turning in, spend time enjoying the riverside cafés and restaurants. In the morning, drive north through the sandy coastal towns of **Vila do Conde** ⑭, **Póvoa de Varzim** ⑮, and **Ofir and Esposende** ⑯. After the bracing air, shopping to the sound of the waves, and a seafood lunch, head inland to the ancient city of ⊞ **Braga** ㉑, with its profusion of churches. Overnight here or in the delightfully medieval ⊞ **Guimarães** ㉒, which you should explore on day three. Worth a side trip from either town is the fascinating Citânia de Briteiros, the hilltop site of an ancient Iron Age settlement.

Alternatively, you could spend your second two days savoring the pastoral Douro Valley. Follow the winding N108 east from Oporto along the river's north bank. Don't miss the view at Entre-os-Rios, where the Douro and Tâmega rivers converge. Head back up toward ⊞ **Amarante** ⑱, one of the north's most picturesque towns, its halves joined by a narrow 18th-century bridge. It's worth overnighting here. On day three, wind your way southeast along the N101, passing through Mesão Frio, to the Douro, where you can follow the river east to **Pêso da Régua** ⑲, heart of the port-wine country, and tour a wine cellar or two. Across the river and a bit farther south is **Lamego** ⑳, with its impressive 18th-century pilgrimage shrine of Nossa Senhora dos Remédios. From either of these towns, it's not far to **Vila Real** ㉛, gateway to the remote and beautiful region of Trás-os-Montes. You could spend the night here and head east the next day, or return to Oporto.

IF YOU HAVE 5 DAYS

Spend a day and night in ⊞ **Oporto** ①–⑬, then head inland and north. Take two days to explore ⊞ **Braga** ㉑, including the Citânia de Briteiros, and ⊞ **Guimarães** ㉒. On day four go west to **Barcelos** ㉓, folk-art center of the country; try to arrive on a Thursday, when the large weekly market is filled with purveyors of everything from live pigs to hand-painted pottery. Continue north to graceful ⊞ **Viana do Castelo** ㉔, along the Rio Lima. Wander its narrow stone streets and stay the night in the art deco pousada on a hill overlooking town or drive up along the Costa Verde to **Caminha** ㉕ or one of the other partially walled castle towns along the Spanish border: ⊞ **Vila Nova de Cerveira** ㉖, **Valença do Minho** ㉗, and **Monção** ㉘.

On day five, head to quaint Arcos de Valdevez and rent a rowboat for a couple of hours on the river, then continue on to two nearby towns with beautiful bridges, **Ponte da Barca** ㉙, with its 15th-century arched passageway, and **Ponte de Lima** ㉚, graced with a long, low Roman footbridge. If you're in Ponte de Lima on the second Monday of the month, you can visit the country's oldest market. From here, return to Oporto or Lisbon.

IF YOU HAVE 7 DAYS

Oporto ①–⑬ is the ideal first day and night for your explorations. On day two, head inland for ⊞ **Amarante** ⑱, where you can have dinner in the romantic old part of town and spend the night. The next day, continue to ▦ **Vila Real** ㉛, the capital and first sizable town in the Trás-os-Montes region. On day four, head northeast—passing through Murça, with its giant, granite porca (Iron Age fertility symbol)—to the attractive town of **Mirandela** ㉜. Visit the 17th-century Palácio dos Tavoras and then continue on the IP4 into the Serra de Nogueira toward the country's northeastern corner. Eventually you'll see the great castle at ▦ **Bragança** ㉝ rising in the distance; plan on spending two nights here. On day five, visit the sights of the city, which dates from about 600 BC. The next day, head west along the N103, one of the country's most spectacular drives. You'll pass through **Vinhais** ㉞ on the way to **Chaves** ㉟, originally a Roman military base and popular today for its thermal springs. From Chaves, you could head back toward Vila Real and on to a final night in Oporto.

Another alternative would be to stay on the N103 and continue west until you reach the lake and hydroelectric dam system along the Rio Cávado. The winding road allows for marvelous views and has several access points into the **Parque Nacional da Peneda-Gerês** where you could quite understandably choose to stay overnight (the São Bento Pousada overlooks the Caniçada dam) for a bit of hiking in the woods, or you could continue down the road to ▦ **Braga** ㉑, spend the night, and then return to Oporto.

When to Tour Oporto and the North

It's best to visit the north in summer, when Oporto and the Costa Verde have a generally warm climate, but be prepared for drizzling rain at any time. Coastal temperatures are a few degrees cooler than in the south. Inland, and especially in the northeastern mountains, it can be very hot in summer and cold, hard going in winter.

OPORTO

Industrious Oporto—Portugal's second city, with a population of a half million and a location 321 km (199 mi) north of Lisbon—considers itself the north's capital and, more contentiously, the country's economic center. Locals support this claim by quoting a typically down-to-earth maxim: "Coimbra sings, Braga prays, Lisbon shows off, and Oporto works." Certainly wherever you look, there's evidence of a robust city. Massive developments on the outskirts give way to a fashionable commercial area in the heart of town; shops and restaurants bustle with big-spending locals; and the city's buildings, churches, and monuments—both old and new—impress with their solid construction. There's poverty here, of course, primarily down by the river in the ragged older areas, parts of which are positively medieval. But in the shopping centers, the stately stock exchange building, and the affluent port-wine industry, Oporto oozes confidence.

This emphasis on worth rather than beauty has created a solid city rather than a graceful one. The public buildings tend to be sober. Gray and ocher tones often dominate facades. But the city abounds in fine structures and interesting perspectives. It's quite impressive at first sight if you approach from the south, and its glorious location on a steep hillside above the Rio Douro affords exhilarating views.

The river has influenced the city's development since pre-Roman times, when the town of Cale on the left bank prospered sufficiently to support a trading port, called Portus, on the site of today's city. Under the Romans this twin town of Portus-Cale became a thriving commercial center, and it continued to be successful despite the later ravages of Moorish occupation and Christian reconquest. Given the outward-looking nature of its inhabitants, it's fitting that Henry the Navigator—the great explorer king—was born here at the end of the 14th century.

The importance of the river trade to the city is reflected in its current name, whose use began in early medieval times. Porto, as the city is called in Portuguese, means simply "port," and over the centuries the city has traded widely in fish, salt, and wine. As the result of an agreement with England in 1703, the region's most notable product—wine, made from the grapes of the Douro's vineyards—found a new market and was shipped out of the city in ever-increasing quantities. The port-wine trade is still big business, based just over the river in the suburb of Vila Nova de Gaia (site of the Roman town of Cale).

Exploring Oporto

You can walk around most of central Oporto, taking buses or taxis to the few outlying attractions. Be prepared for the hills, which can prove tiring in the summer heat. The city is very congested, so leave your car at your hotel. Central parking is difficult to find, and much of the downtown area (in particular, the riverside and the winding streets of the Old Town below the cathedral) isn't accessible to cars.

★ ☞ ❶ The **Torre dos Clérigos,** the tower of the Igreja dos Clérigos, is a distinct feature on the Oporto skyline and a good place to get your bearings before a walking tour of the city. Designed by Italian architect Nicolau Nasoni and begun in 1754, it reaches an impressive height of 249 ft. There are 225 steep stone steps to the belfry, and the considerable effort required to climb them is rewarded by stunning views of the Old Town, the river, and beyond to the mouth of the Douro. The church itself, also built by Nasoni, predates the tower and is an elaborate example of Italianate baroque architecture. ⊠ *Rua dos Clérigos,* ☎ *22/ 200–1729.* ☎ *Tower: €1. Church: free.* ☉ *Tower: Sept.–May, daily 10– noon and 2–5; June–July, daily 10–7; Aug., daily 10–10. Church: Mon.– Thurs. and Sat. 10–noon and 2–5, Sun. 10–1 and 8–10:30.*

❷ Just east of the Torre dos Clérigos, Rua dos Clérigos runs into the city's commercial heart: the **Avenida dos Aliados,** an imposing boulevard lined with bright flower beds and grand buildings. At one end of it is the broad Câmara Municipal (Town Hall). A tall bell tower sprouts from the roof of this palacelike, early 20th-century building, inside of which an impressive Portuguese wall tapestry is displayed. Praça da Liberdade—the hub from which Oporto radiates—is at the other end of the avenue. Two statues adorn the square: a cast of Dom Pedro IV sitting on a horse and a modern statue of the great 19th-century Portuguese poet and novelist Almeida Garrett.

NEED A
BREAK?

Many of Oporto's old-style coffeehouses—which once rivaled Lisbon's in opulence and literary legend—have disappeared. Two notable ones have survived and are perfect places to sit and imbibe both a *cimbalino* (espresso) and the city. The ornate **Majestic Café** (⊠ Rua de Santa Catarina 112, ☎ 22/208–7673) has piano music and temporary art exhibitions. It's on a busy pedestrian shopping street, a short walk from Avenida dos Aliados. Just around the corner from the Majestic Café is the attractively restored **Confeitaria do Bolhão** (⊠ Rua Formosa 339, ☎ 22/339–5220).

❸ Use the pedestrian underpass from the Praça da Liberdade to cross to the **Estação de São Bento,** Oporto's central railroad station. The main hall is decorated with enormous *azulejos* (tiles) depicting the history of Portuguese transportation. From the steps of the train station, you can look across to the city's cathedral.

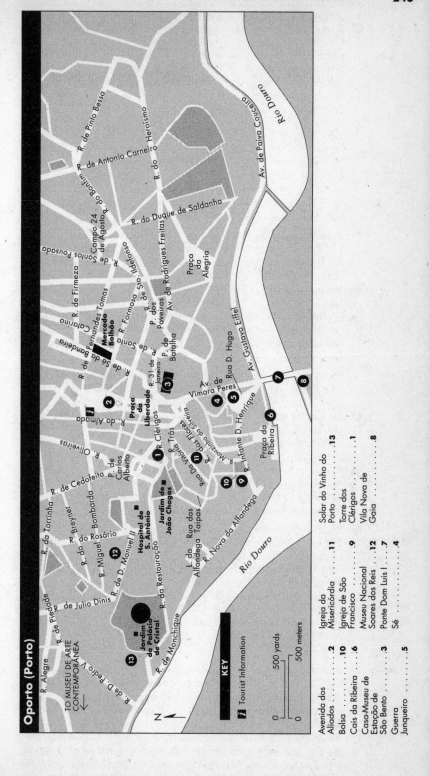

243

Oporto (Porto)

TO MUSEU DE ARTE
CONTEMPORÂNEA

KEY

ℹ️ Tourist Information

0 — 500 yards
0 — 500 meters

Avenida dos
Aliados **2**
Bolsa **10**
Cais da Ribeira . . . **6**
Casa-Museu de
Estação de
São Bento **3**
Guerra
Junqueiro **5**

Igreja da
Misericórdia . . . **11**
Igreja de São
Francisco **9**
Museu Nacional
Soares dos Reis . . **12**
Ponte Dom Luís I . . **7**
Sé **4**

Solar do Vinho do
Porto **13**
Torre dos
Clérigos **1**
Vila Nova de
Gaia **8**

❹ Originally constructed in the 12th century by the parents of Afonso Henriques (Portugal's first king), Oporto's granite **Sé** (Cathedral) has been rebuilt twice: first in the late 13th century and again in the 18th century, when the architect of the Torre dos Clérigos, Nicolau Nasoni, was among those commissioned to work on its expansion. Despite the renovations, it remains a fortresslike structure—an uncompromising testament to medieval wealth and power. Size is the only exceptional thing about the interior; when you enter the two-story, 14th-century cloisters, however, the building comes to life. Decorated with gleaming azulejos, a staircase added by Nasoni leads to the second level and into a richly furnished chapter house, from which there are fine views through narrow windows. Nasoni also designed the Paço dos Arcebispos (Archbishops' Palace), behind the cathedral. It has been converted to offices so you can only admire its 197-ft-long facade. ⊠ *Terreiro da Sé,* ☎ 22/205–9028. 🎫 *Cathedral: Free. Cloisters: €1.25.* ☉ *Mon.–Sat. 9–12:30 and 2:30–6, Sun. 2:30–6.*

❺ **Casa-Museu de Guerra Junqueiro** (Guerra Junqueiro House and Museum), another of the city's 18th-century buildings attributed to architect Nicolau Nasoni, is on a narrow street that curves around the cathedral's eastern side. This white mansion was home to the poet Guerra Junqueiro (1850–1923). Although furnishings, sculptures, and paintings are labeled in Portuguese, English, and French (and there are brochures in English), the short tour of the elegant interior is less than enlightening if you don't speak Portuguese. ⊠ *Rua de Dom Hugo 32,* ☎ 22/200–3689. 🎫 *Tues.–Fri. €0.75; free weekends.* ☉ *Tues.–Sat. 10–12:30 and 2–5, Sun. 2–5.*

If you follow Rua de Dom Hugo, its steep steps will take you to surviving sections of the medieval city's walls. Tangled alleys in this area eventually emerge at the riverfront quayside of the Ribeira District. Along **❻** the **Cais da Ribeira** (Ribeira Pier) a string of fish restaurants and *tascas* (taverns) are built into the street-level arcade of timeworn buildings. In the Praça da Ribeira, people sit and chat around an odd, modern, cubelike sculpture; farther on, steps lead to a walkway that's backed by tall houses and runs above the river. The pier also provides the easiest access to the lower level of the middle bridge across the Douro. Boats docked at Cais da Ribeira offer various cruises around the bridges and up the river to Régua and Pinhão.

❼ The two-tier **Ponte Dom Luís I** (Dom Luís I Bridge) was built in 1886 and leads directly to the suburb of Vila Nova de Gaia. Its real glory, however, is not its practical calling but the nearly magical vistas it affords of downtown Oporto. A jumble of red-tile roofs on pastel-color buildings mixes with gray-and-white Gothic and baroque church towers, and all is reflected in the majestic Douro; if the sun is shining just right, everything appears to be washed in gold. You can take in the views while heading to Vila Nova de Gaia along the narrow walkway on the bridge's upper level; if you don't like heights, stay on the lower level.

★ ☙ **❽** **Vila Nova de Gaia,** a suburb across the Rio Douro from central Oporto, has been the headquarters of the port-wine trade since the late 17th century, when import bans on French wine led British merchants to look for alternative sources. By the 18th century, the British had established companies and a regulatory association in Oporto. The wine was transported from vineyards on the upper Douro to port-wine *adegas* ("lodges" or warehouses) at Vila Nova de Gaia, where it was allowed to mature before being exported. Very little has changed in the relationship between Oporto and the Douro since those days, as wine is still transported to the city, matured in the warehouses, and bottled.

Instead of traveling down the river on *barcos rabelos* (flat-bottom boats), however, the wine is now carried by truck. A couple of the traditional boats are moored at the quayside on the Vila Nova de Gaia side.

Of the more than 13 companies with adegas in Vila Nova de Gaia, many are still foreign-owned. They include such well-known names as Sandeman, Croft, and Cockburn and such lesser-known Portuguese firms as Ferreira, Calem, and Borges. All are signposted and within a few minutes' walk of each other; their names are also displayed in huge white letters across their roofs. Each company offers free guided tours of its facility, which always end with a tasting of one or two wines and an opportunity to buy bottles from the company store. Children are usually welcome and are often fascinated by the huge warehouses and all sorts of interesting machinery. The major lodges are open weekdays 9–12:30 and 2–7, Saturday 9–12:30, from June though September; the rest of the year, tours end at 5 and are conducted only on weekdays. Tours begin regularly, usually when enough visitors are assembled. The tourist office at Vila Nova de Gaia offers a small map of the main lodges and can advise you on hours of the smaller operations.

Vila Nova de Gaia isn't solely devoted to the port-wine trade. Combine a tour of the wine lodges with a visit to the **Casa-Museu de Teixeira Lopes**, the home of the sculptor António Teixeira Lopes (1866–1942), who was born here. It contains some excellent sculpture as well as a varied collection of paintings by Teixeira Lopes's contemporaries. The collection of books, coins, and ceramics is also interesting. ⊠ *Rua Teixeira Lopes 32, Vila Nova de Gaia,* ☎ *22/370–2095.* 🎫 *Free.* 🕑 *Tues.–Sat. 9–12:30 and 2–5:30.*

From Vila Nova de Gaia you can cross back to the city, using the narrow footway on the upper level of the Dom Luís I Bridge, which puts you on Avenida de Vimara Peres, close to the cathedral. But at 200 ft above the river and with traffic thundering past, this is not a crossing for the faint of heart or for those who have tasted of the port "not wisely but too well." If you fall in one of these categories, take the lower level.

Away from the water, Rua do Infante Dom Henrique, once known as Rua dos Ingleses (English Street), contains shipping offices and warehouses. Where it meets Rua de São João stands the granite Feitoria Inglêsa (Factory House of the British Association), built at the end of the 18th century as the headquarters of the Port Wine Shippers' Association. (It's not open to the public.) A statue of Prince Henry stands in the nearby Praça do Infante Dom Henrique, which is also home to the ⑨ late-14th-century **Igreja de São Francisco** (Church of St. Francis). It may be an undistinguished Gothic building on the outside, but it has an astounding interior: gilded carving—added in the mid-18th century—runs up the pillars, over the altar, and across the ceiling. An adjacent museum houses furnishings from the Franciscan monastery that once stood here. ⊠ *Rua do Infante Dom Henrique,* ☎ *22/206–2100.* 🎫 *€3.* 🕑 *Daily 9–6.*

⑩ The **Bolsa**, Oporto's 19th-century, neoclassical stock exchange, is behind the Igreja de São Francisco and takes up much of the site of the old Franciscan monastery. Guided tours (the only way to see the interior) stroll around the huge, showy edifice, much of it in questionable taste. The Arab-style ballroom, in particular, has critics as numerous as the glowing adjectives with which the guides describe it. ⊠ *Rua Ferreira Borges,* ☎ *22/339–9000.* 🎫 *Tours €5.* 🕑 *Apr.–Oct., daily 9–7; Nov.–Mar., daily 9–12:30 and 2–5:30.*

North of the Bolsa, at Largo de São Domingos, is Rua das Flores—a street known for its silversmiths and striking wrought-iron balconies.
⓫ It leads to the **Igreja da Misericórdia** (Mercy Church) as well as the Estação de São Bento. Although the church dates from the 16th century, it was largely remodeled two centuries later by Nicolau Nasoni. Call at the adjacent offices, and you'll be shown the *Fons Vitae* (Fountain of Life), a vibrant, anonymous, Renaissance painting, depicting the founder of the church, Dom Manuel I, his queen, and their eight children kneeling before a crucified Christ. ⊠ *Rua das Flores*, ☎ *22/207–4710.* ⊡ *Church: free. Fons Vitae painting: €1.50.* ☉ *Weekdays 9–12:30 and 2–5:30.*

A former royal palace northwest of the Igreja da Misericórdia is now
⓬ the **Museu Nacional Soares dos Reis,** a museum named for the 19th-century Portuguese sculptor whose works are contained within. The large art collection includes several Portuguese primitive works of the 16th century as well as superb collections of silver, ceramics, glassware, and costumes. Bus 78 runs here from Praça da Liberdade. ⊠ *Rua de Dom Manuel II,* ☎ *22/339–3770.* ⊡ *Tues.–Sat. €3; free Sun.* ☉ *Tues. 2–6, Wed.–Sun. 10–12:30 and 2–6.*

Rua de Dom Manuel II leads to the Jardim do Palácio de Cristal (Crystal Palace Gardens), named for a 19th-century palace that once stood here—it was replaced in the 1950s by an enormous domed pavilion used for sports and exhibitions. On the far side of the gardens is the a 19th-century country house called the Quinta da Macierinha, whose ground
★ ⓭ floor is home to the **Solar do Vinho do Porto** (Port Wine Institute). It offers relaxed tastings of Oporto's famous wine in much the same fashion as its counterpart in Lisbon, but it has a much friendlier reputation—and the wine has only had to travel across the river before being served. Tasting prices start at €0.50 per glass. The Quinta da Macierinha is home to the **Museu Romântico** (Romantic Museum), with displays of period furniture ⊠ *Rua de Entre Quintas 220,* ☎ *22/609–4749 Port Wine Institute; 22/605–7033 museum; 22/606–6207 for guided tours.* ⊡ *Port Wine Institute: free; tasting prices vary. Museum: Tues.–Fri. €0.75; free weekends.* ☉ *Port Wine Institute: Mon.–Sat. 2–midnight. Museum: Tues.–Sat. 10–12:30 and 2–5:30, Sun. 2–6.*

OFF THE   **MUSEU DE ARTE CONTEMPORÂNEA –** In western Oporto, the Museum of
BEATEN PATH   Contemporary Art is housed in the Serralves Mansion, which is surrounded by gardens. It displays the work of contemporary Portuguese painters, sculptors, and designers. Exhibitions change regularly, and the museum sometimes closes for two weeks at a time for rehanging. Check with the tourist office for the latest information. You can take either a taxi or Bus 3, 19, 21, 35, or 78. The journey takes about 30 minutes from the center of town. ⊠ *Rua de Serralves 977,* ☎ *22/615–6500,* WEB *www.serralves.pt.* ⊡ *€4.* ☉ *Tues.–Wed. and Fri.–Sun. 10–7, Thurs. 10–10.*

Dining

$$$–$$$$ ✕ **Bull and Bear.** Chef-owner Miguel Castro Silva gives his northern Portugal dishes touches of French, Italian, and even Japanese flavors at his comfortable, modern restaurant in the Oporto stock exchange building. The result is such unusual and successful combinations as *ameijoas com feijão manteiga* (clams with butter beans) and *linguado com molho de amêndoa* (sole with almond sauce). ⊠ *Av. da Boavista 3431,* ☎ *22/610–7669. AE, DC, MC, V. Closed Sun. No lunch Sat.*

$$$–$$$$ ✕ **Portucale.** Atop a modern building, the Portucale is known equally
★ for the excellence of its food and the citywide views from its windows.
The tripe and game dishes are rich and imaginative; if it's available,
the roast cabrito is a good bet. After dinner, sip some port from the
impressive selection. ⊠ *Rua da Alegria 598*, ☎ *22/537–0717. Reservations essential. AE, DC, MC, V.*

$$–$$$$ ✕ **Dom Tonho.** Seafood is the specialty of this restaurant, which is on
the riverfront in a house that's weathered two centuries. Try one of
the codfish dishes, the *robalo* (rock bass), or the *cherne ao sal* (turbot
baked in salt). Each dish is named after a historical Portuguese person. ⊠ *Cais da Ribeira 13*, ☎ *22/200–4307. AE, DC, MC, V.*

$$$ ✕ **O Escondidinho.** A tiled entrance announces a country-house decor
in this restaurant on a central shopping street. The menu has French-
influenced dishes as well as high-quality Douro dishes. Steak is prepared no less than six ways (try the woodsy-smoky version with
truffles), and the sole is always deliciously fresh. The *pudim flan* (egg
custard) is outstanding. ⊠ *Rua dos Passos Manuel 144*, ☎ *22/200–1079. Reservations essential. DC, MC, V. Closed Sun.*

$$$ ✕ **O Tripeiro.** This spacious restaurant is just the place to try Oporto-
style tripe, which is nearly always on the menu in one form or another.
In case you don't appreciate the city's favorite food, the menu has several meat and bacalhau specialties, too. Along with the typically Portuguese food comes typically Portuguese details: wooden ceiling beams,
whitewashed walls, and potted plants throughout. ⊠ *Rua de Passos
Manuel 195*, ☎ *22/200–5886. AE, DC, MC, V. Closed Sun.*

$$–$$$ ✕ **Casa Nanda.** This restaurant is the epitome of a Portuguese tasca:
★ a small, cozy, tavern that offers home cooking. The cook and co-
owner, Fernanda Maria, learned her skills from a legendary figure in
the history of Oporto restaurants, a tasca keeper of great fame. The
experience shows. This is a great place to try *cozido à Portuguesa* (a
monumental dish of boiled meats and vegetables), but phone first to
see if it's available that day. ⊠ *Rua da Alegria 394*, ☎ *22/537–0575.
No credit cards. Closed Sun. and 2 wks in July.*

$$–$$$ ✕ **O Macedo.** A 10-minute drive from the center of town, this agree-
able little restaurant is in a restored old building overlooking the
Douro estuary. The wine list is exceptionally good, and the menu has
a tempting selection of meat and fish dishes. Try the *goraz assado no
forno* (oven-baked sea bream) or the *bife de fillet mignon com natas
à Macedo* (house-style filet mignon with cream sauce). ⊠ *Rua do Passeio Alegre 552*, ☎ *22/617–0166. AE, MC, V. Closed Sun. and 2 wks
in Aug.*

$$–$$$ ✕ **Majestic Café.** One of Oporto's grand old coffeehouses doubles as
★ a reasonably priced grill-restaurant. Sit amid the sculpted wood, carved
nymphs, and mirrors and choose from a fair list of omelets, sandwiches,
salads, burgers, and steaks. Or just have coffee and a pastry. The enclosed patio is the perfect place to dine on a summer's eve; if you come
on Friday or Saturday night, your meal will be accompanied by piano
music. There's also an art gallery downstairs. ⊠ *Rua de Santa Catarina 112*, ☎ *22/208–7673. AE, DC, MC, V. Closed Sun.*

$–$$$ ✕ **Casa Filha da Mãe Preta.** The pleasant first-floor dining room of
this well-known Cais da Ribeira restaurant is decorated with azulejos
and has arched windows that look across the river to the port-wine
lodges of Vila Nova de Gaia. Stick with such simple fish specialties as
lulas grelhadas (grilled squid) or *pez espada* (grilled blade fish). Most
of the grilled dishes come with an ample serving of rice; unless you're
sharing with someone else, ask for a *meio dose* (half serving). Reser-
vations are a good idea in summer. ⊠ *Cais da Ribeira 39–40*, ☎ *22/
208–6066. AE, DC, MC, V. Closed Sun.*

$$ ✕ **Bule.** In addition to some of the best cooking in town, Bule has a pretty little terrace with tables shaded by umbrellas, a spacious and comfortable interior dining room, and impeccable service throughout. The *pato assado* (roast duck) is a succulent specialty, as is the bacalhau *à lagareiro* (baked with onions and garlic in olive oil). ⊠ *Rua de Timor 128,* ☎ *22/618–8777. AE, DC, MC, V. Closed 1st 2 wks Aug.*

$$ ✕ **Chez Lapin.** At this Cais da Ribeira restaurant overlooking the river, the service may be slow and the folksy decor may be overdone, but the food is excellent, and the outdoor terrace is attractive. The menu has such traditional but sometimes uncommon Oporto dishes as bacalhau *e polvo assado no forno* (baked and with octopus) and *caldeirada de peixe* (fish stew), all served in generous portions. The restaurant also offers trips aboard its five traditional rabelo boats docked at the quay out front. ⊠ *Rua Canastreiros 48,* ☎ *22/200–6418. Reservations essential. AE, DC, MC, V.*

$–$$ ✕ **Pedro dos Frangos.** It's hard to bypass this popular restaurant, where chicken is grilled temptingly in the window. If you're in a hurry, sit at the bar, although it's more comfortable upstairs in the plain dining room. Order a *meia frango* (half chicken and fries) with a side of the delicious *esparregado* (greens, usually spinach or turnip tops, sautéed with olive oil and garlic, then pureed), and you'll have plenty of energy to go out and see the rest of the city. ⊠ *Rua do Bonjardim 219–223,* ☎ *22/200–8522. No credit cards. Closed Tues.*

$–$$ ✕ **Traçadinho.** A long bar invites you to take an aperitif before descending to the vaulted dining room of this popular traditional restaurant, where many dishes are cooked over an open wood fire. The bacalhau *à Traçadinho* (baked with onions and tomatoes) is legendary, as is the cozido à Portuguesa. ⊠ *Rua da Madeira 186,* ☎ *22/200–5624. No credit cards. Closed Sun.*

Lodging

$$$ 🏨 **Hotel Infante de Sagres.** Visiting royalty have been happy to stay at
★ Oporto's first luxury hotel, which was built after World War II. It does, indeed, provide service fit for a king; it also has a great location close to Avenida dos Aliados. Intricately carved wood details, rare area rugs and tapestries, stained-glass windows, and 18th- and 19th-century antiques fill the public areas. In guest rooms, shades of beige, cream, and white complement dark-wood furnishings and lend a contemporary character; bathrooms are marble from floor to ceiling and have sophisticated lighting. ⊠ *Praça D. Filipa de Lencastre 62, 4050-259,* ☎ *22/ 339–8500,* FAX *22/339–8599,* WEB *www.hotelinfantesagres.pt. 83 rooms. Restaurant, bar, cable TV, minibars, room service. AE, DC, MC, V. EP.*

$$$ 🏨 **Tivoli Porto Atlântico.** This small hotel is west of the city center, off Avenida da Boavista, in a residential area near the Museum of Contemporary Art. The comfortable interior is unobtrusively modern. Rooms share a terrace and have every little amenity you could possibly want—right down to a shoe-shine kit. Bathrooms are marble-clad and luxurious. ⊠ *Rua Afonso Lopes Vieira 66, 4100-020,* ☎ *22/607– 7900,* FAX *22/607–7045,* WEB *www.tivolihotels.com. 58 rooms. Restaurant, bar, in-room safes, cable TV, minibars, room service, pool, laundry service, business services, meeting rooms, car rental, free parking. AE, DC, MC, V. EP.*

$$ 🏨 **Grande Hotel do Porto.** The staff is efficient, and the rates are rea-
★ sonable at the stately Grande, which is on the city's best shopping street. The hotel has just the right mix of old and new. Public areas are full of turn-of-the-last-century details; streamlined guest rooms are loaded with modern amenities. ⊠ *Rua de Santa Catarina 197, 4000-450,* ☎ *22/207–6690,* FAX *22/207–6699,* WEB *www.grandhotelporto.com. 100 rooms. Restaurant, bar, in-room safes, cable TV, minibars, no-smok-*

ing rooms, room service, baby-sitting, laundry service, meeting rooms, free parking. AE, DC, MC, V. EP.

$$ 🏨 **Hotel Boa-Vista.** Overlooking the Douro estuary and the sea, this hotel is a 10- to 15-minute taxi ride or 20-minute bus ride west of town. The handsome mid-19th-century building has small guest rooms that are attractively appointed and well equipped. Ask for one with a sea view. ⊠ *Esplanada do Castelo 58, 4150-196,* ☎ *22/532–0020,* 𝖥𝖠𝖷 *22/617–3818. 71 rooms. Restaurant, bar, snack bar, in-room safes, cable TV, minibars, 2 pools (1 indoor), meeting rooms, free parking. AE, MC, V. EP.*

$$ 🏨 **Hotel Dom Henrique.** The Dom Henrique attracts business travelers who want a central base and an attentive staff. The ground-floor restaurant of this octagonal downtown tower has modern lines and furnishings; the 17th-floor bar has classic birds'-eye views. The floors in between are full of spacious, well-appointed guest quarters. ⊠ *Rua Guedes de Azevedo 179, 4049-009,* ☎ *22/340–1616,* 𝖥𝖠𝖷 *22/340–1600,* 𝖶𝖤𝖡 *www.hotel-dom-henrique.pt. 112 rooms. Restaurant, bar, cable TV, minibars, no-smoking rooms, baby-sitting, meeting rooms. AE, DC, MC, V. EP.*

$$ 🏨 **Ipanema Park Hotel.** This elegant tower of a hotel may be a 15-minute taxi ride from the center of town, but it has loads of on-site facilities. Rooms are equipped with every modern convenience, and although the decor doesn't tell you you're in Portugal, the views—of the Douro estuary and the Atlantic—do. ⊠ *Rua de Serralves 124, 4150-702,* ☎ *22/532–2100,* 𝖥𝖠𝖷 *22/610–2809,* 𝖶𝖤𝖡 *www.ipanemaparkhotel.pt. 281 rooms. Restaurant, bar, in-room data ports, in-room safes, cable TV, minibars, no-smoking rooms, 2 pools (1 indoor), barbershop, hair salon, massage, sauna, Turkish bath, health club, squash, shops, baby-sitting, business services, meeting rooms, free parking. AE, DC, MC, V. EP.*

$$ 🏨 **Mercure Batalha.** This attractive, modern hotel is a block or two from Avenida dos Aliados. Rooms are elegantly appointed and have the customary comforts. You can get sweeping views over the city from a wide terrace at the top of the building. ⊠ *Praça da Batalha 116, 4050-453,* ☎ *22/204–3300,* 𝖥𝖠𝖷 *22/204–3499,* 𝖶𝖤𝖡 *www.mercure.com. 141 rooms, 8 suites. Restaurant, bar, minibars, baby-sitting, concierge, meeting rooms, airport shuttle. AE, DC, MC, V. EP.*

$$ 🏨 **Pestana Porto Carlton Hotel.** Right in Oporto's historic heart, the Pestana is in a restored old building that's abutted by a medieval wall and surrounded by other old structures, some of which date from as far back as the 16th century. Rooms have city or sea views; all are contemporary, cozy, and almost cluttered with vibrant fabrics, plush carpets, throw pillows, and upholstered chairs. Bathrooms are sleek spaces, where the marble is polished to a high gloss. ⊠ *Praça da Ribeira 1, 4050-453,* ☎ *22/340–2300,* 𝖥𝖠𝖷 *22/340–2400,* 𝖶𝖤𝖡 *www.pestana.com. 48 rooms, 3 suites. Restaurant, bar, in-room safes, cable TV, minibars, no-smoking rooms, room service, laundry service, meeting rooms. AE, DC, MC, V. EP.*

$–$$ 🏨 **Pensão dos Aliados.** The well-equipped, comfortable rooms in this excellent *pensão* (pension) are usually in great demand, partly because the location is bang in the center of town. The delightfully ornate turn-of-the-last-century building that houses the place is a listed city landmark. ⊠ *Rua Elisio de Melo 27, 4000-186,* ☎ *22/200–4853,* 𝖥𝖠𝖷 *22/200–2710. 45 rooms. Restaurant, bar. AE, MC, V. EP.*

$–$$ 🏨 **Pensão Pão de Açúcar.** Just off the Avenida dos Aliados, this art nouveau pensão offers a lot for its relatively modest rates. You can choose from among simple rooms, suites, or a top-floor room opening onto a terrace with tables and chairs. ⊠ *Rua do Almada 262, 4050-032,* ☎ *22/200–2425,* 𝖥𝖠𝖷 *22/205–0239. 44 rooms, 6 suites. Bar, minibars. AE, MC, V. EP.*

$ ⊞ **Hotel Nave.** This moderately priced modern hotel is functional rather than charming. It is, however, a mere 10-minute walk from the center, and its rooms are comfortable and well equipped. ⊠ *Av. Fernão de Magalhães 247, 4300-190,* ☎ *22/589–9030,* FAX *22/589–9039,* WEB *www.maisturismo.pt/hnave. 81 rooms. Restaurant, bar, cable TV, free parking. AE, DC, MC, V. EP.*

$ ⊞ **Pensão Estoril.** The Estoril offers functional but comfortable rooms at very reasonable rates. It's in a quiet location near the city center and has a terrace, a bar, and metered parking in a nearby square. Ask for a room with a balcony overlooking the back garden area. ⊠ *Rua de Cedofeita 193, 4050-179,* ☎ *22/200–2751,* FAX *22/208–2468. 18 rooms. Bar, cable TV. MC, V. EP.*

Nightlife and the Arts

Noted as a center for modern art, Oporto enjoys regular exhibitions at the Museu de Arte Contemporânea, as well as at a variety of galleries, many of which are on Rua Miguel Bombarda. Check local newspapers or with the tourist board for listings of current exhibitions as well as concerts.

Bars

Anikibóbó (⊠ Rua da Fonte Taurina 36, ☎ 22/332–4619), down on the Ribeira waterfront, is where Oporto's intellectual and artistic crowd hang out until the early hours (it's open from 10 PM to about 4 AM daily). The odd name was the title of a film made by Portugal's famed director, Manuel de Oliveira. The decor is old stone, set off by modern paintings; the little garden out back is great on warm nights. The nicest places for an evening drink are the old-style cafés; try the **Majestic Café** (⊠ Rua de Santa Catarina 112, ☎ 22/208–7673), open Monday to Saturday until around 10 PM. For a glass of port, the best place is the **Solar do Vinho do Porto** (⊠ Rua de Entre Quintas 220, ☎ 22/609–4749), which is open until midnight every day but Sunday.

Dance and Music Clubs

Oporto has a number of fashionable discos west of the city center in the commercial developments along the Douro estuary; these clubs usually open around 11 PM and close at 4 AM. A very funky, very hip crowd shows up late at **Indústria** (⊠ Av. do Brasil 843, ☎ 22/617–6806), in the Centro Comercial da Foz. The **Mal Cozinhado** (⊠ Rua do Outeirinho 13, ☎ 22/208–1319) is a lively restaurant with traditional folk music and dancing, including the plaintive sounds of fado, Monday–Saturday. Music from the 1960s and '70s is the draw at **Twins** (⊠ Rua do Passeio Alegre 994, ☎ 22/618–5740).

Spectator Sport

Soccer

The main sporting obsession in Oporto is *futebol* (soccer), and the city has one of the country's best teams, FC Porto, which rivals Lisbon's Benfica for domestic fame and fortune. Futebol matches are played September through May at the **Antas Stadium** (⊠ Av. de Fernão de Magalhães 4350, ☎ 22/557–0400) in the east of the city; Buses 6, 78, and 88 run past it. Other good regional teams are Guimarães and Boavista.

Shopping

The best shopping streets are those off the Praça da Liberdade, particularly Rua 31 de Janeiro, Rua dos Clérigos, Rua de Santa Catarina, Rua Sá da Bandeira, Rua Cedofeita, and Rua das Flores. Traditionally, Rua das Flores has been the street for silversmiths. Gold-plated filigree is also a regional specialty, and examples are numerous along the same street and along Rua de Santa Catarina. Rua 31 de Janeiro and nearby streets are the center of the shoe trade, and many shops create made-to-measure shoes upon request.

You'll see port on sale throughout the city. But first taste the wine at either the Solar do Vinho do Porto or the lodges at Vila Nova de Gaia. You may want to buy a bottle of the more unusual white port, drunk as an aperitif, as it's not commonly sold in North America or Britain. Try a Portonic, half tonic water and half white port served in a special glass sold in most shops.

Crafts

The **Artesanato Centro Regional de Artes Tradicionais** (Center for Traditional Arts; ✉ Rua da Reboleira 37, ☎ 22/332–0201) has an excellent selection of regional arts and crafts. For a general handicrafts emporium, try **Artesanato dos Clérigos** (✉ Rua da Assunção 33, next to Torre dos Clérigos, ☎ 22/200–0257). **Pedro A. Baptista** (✉ Rua das Flores 237, ☎ 22/200–2880) deals in antique and modern silver.

Market and Malls

For a good general market, visit the **Mercado Bolhão,** held Monday through Saturday at Rua Formosa and Rua Sá da Bandeira. Afterward stop at the Confeitaria do Bolhão, a delicious-smelling pastry shop.

One of the best shopping centers is **Via Catarina Shopping** (✉ Rua Santa Catarina). Unlike most, this mall is centrally located in an old restored building. The top floor is occupied by little restaurants. The **Centro Comercial de Brasília** (✉ Av. da Boavista), in the city's northwest, is a popular mall. **Shopping Center Cidade do Porto** (✉ Rua do Bom Sucesso) is like many of Oporto's contemporary malls.

OPORTO'S ENVIRONS: THE COAST AND THE DOURO

There are relaxing resorts both north and south of Oporto. Espinho, south of Oporto, and the main resorts to the north—Vila do Conde, Póvoa de Varzim, Ofir, and Esposende—are the best places for watersports enthusiasts, with equipment rental establishments often right on the beaches. Inland, the beautiful Douro Valley awaits, with its carefully terraced vineyards dotted with farmhouses stepping down to the river's edge. Drives along the river lead to romantic ancient towns. This is also the heart of prizewinning wine country, and every town has charming bars where you can pull up a chair, order a bottle and a plate of *petiscos* (mixed appetizers), and watch small-town life go by.

Vila do Conde

★ ⑭ *27 km (17 mi) north of Oporto.*

Vila do Conde has a long sweep of fine sand, a fishing port, a lace-making school, and a struggling shipbuilding industry that has been making wooden boats since the 15th century. The yards are probably Europe's oldest, and the traditional boat-making skills used in them have changed surprisingly little over the centuries. It was here that the replica of Bartolomeu Dias's caravel was made in 1987 to commemorate his historic voyage around the Cape of Good Hope 500 years earlier. Urban and industrial sprawl mars the outer parts of town, but the center has winding streets and centuries-old buildings.

Vila do Conde has been known for its lace since the 17th century, and it remains the center of a flourishing lace industry. The tourist office can give you information about the Escola de Rendas (Lace-Making School), where you can see how the famed *rendas de bilros* (bone lace) is made. Local artisans also produce excellent sweaters.

The **Convento de Santa Clara** (Convent of St. Claire), now a center for children with disabilities, overwhelms the north bank of the Rio Ave (Ave River), on which the Vila do Conde is situated. Dom Afonso Sanches and his wife, Dona Teresa Martins, established the convent in the 14th century, and it retains its original cloister and the beautiful tombs of its founders. The 16th-century **Igreja Paroquial** (Parish Church), in the center of town near the market, has a superb Gothic-style portal. ✉ *Av. Doutor Artur Cunha Araújo 46,* ☎ *252/638730.*

Póvoa de Varzim

⑮ *4 km (2 mi) north of Vila do Conde, 31 km (20 mi) north of Oporto.*

Póvoa de Varzim has a long beach, but the town has little of Vila do Conde's charm—except, perhaps, for the many shops and roadside stalls that sell similarly beautiful and reasonably priced hand-knit sweaters. It is, instead, a major resort, with high-rise hotels used mostly by vacationing Portuguese. The waterfront casino, which is open daily 3 PM–3 AM, attracts much attention. It has an outstanding restaurant, a disco, and nightly floor shows; you must be 18 to enter (take along your passport), and smart-casual dress is your best bet.

Ofir and Esposende

⑯ *17 km (11 mi) north of Póvoa de Varzim, 46 km (29 mi) north of Oporto.*

Ofir, on the south bank of the Rio Cávado, has a lovely beach with sweeping white sands, dunes, pinewoods, and water sports—a combination that has made it a popular resort. On the opposite bank of the river, Esposende, which also has a beach, retains elements of the small fishing village it once was. You'll have to drive here to appreciate these twin towns: the train line runs inland at this point, passing through Barcelos.

Espinho

⑰ *18 km (11 mi) south of Oporto.*

Frequent trains and the N109 run past a string of quiet family beaches to Espinho, which has become an increasingly fashionable resort over the years. It has plenty of leisure facilities and a good selection of shops. Its casino, open daily throughout the year 3 PM–3 AM, has dining, dancing, and cabaret in addition to gaming tables; foreign visitors must present their passports (18 is the minimum age), and although there's no formal dress code, smart and casual is most appropriate. The long, sandy beach is very popular in summer, but you can find some space by walking through the pinewoods to less developed areas to the south.

Outdoor Activities and Sports

The **Clube de Golfe de Miramar** (✉ Praia de Miramar, ☎ 22/762–2067) has nine holes and is 5 km (3 mi) north of Espinho. If you're an accredited golfer in your own country, you can play here weekdays for €25 (nine holes) or €50 (18 holes). On weekends, it's open only to club members. The 18-hole **Oporto Golf Club** (✉ Espinho-Paramos, ☎ 22/734–2008), founded in 1890 by members of the Port Wine Shippers' Association, is just 2 km (1 mi) south of Espinho. Greens fees are €40 on weekdays and €50 weekends, when nonmembers can play only until 10 AM.

OFF THE
BEATEN PATH

THE DOURO TRAIN LINE – Even if you're driving, it's worth considering at least a day trip on the Douro train. The main route runs 40 km (25 mi) inland from Oporto and then swings south to the Rio Douro, following the river's north bank to Pêso da Régua, a 2½-hour journey. From here it continues east to the end of the line at Pocinho, providing a glorious 70-km (43-mi) ride that hugs the river all the way. At Livração, the Tâmega line branches off the main line and runs northeast up the Rio Tâmega tributary to Amarante. This 25-minute ride is well worth taking. The little single-carriage diesel train ambles along the meandering Tâmega Valley high above the river, and the views at every twist and turn are enchanting. You can make trip arrangements through the Oporto-based tour operator, Douro Azul.

Amarante

★ ⑱ *78 km (48 mi) northeast of Espinho, 60 km (37 mi) northeast of Oporto.*

Small, agreeable Amarante is the one place in Oporto's environs that really demands an overnight stop. Straddling the Rio Tâmega, its halves are joined by a narrow 18th-century bridge that stretches above tree-shaded banks. Although the river is polluted (which precludes swimming), it's beautiful to look at. Rowboats and pedal boats are for hire at several points along the riverside paths. The riverbank is also the site of the local market, held every Wednesday and Saturday morning; at these times, the usually peaceful town is disturbed by manic traffic racing along the main street and over the bridge.

★ The imposing, 16th-century **Igreja de São Gonçalo** (St. Gonçalo Church) is on the Rio Tâmega's north side. The effigy of the saint, in a room to the left of the altar, is reputed to guarantee marriage to anyone who touches it. His features have almost been worn away over the years, as desperate suitors try and, perhaps, try again. ⊠ *Praça da República,* ☎ *255/437425.* ⚏ *Free.* ⊗ *Daily 8–6.*

NEED A
BREAK?

Along Rua 31 de Janeiro, the narrow main road leading to the bridge, several small cafés and restaurants have terraces that overlook the river. Enjoy a drink, a snack, or a meal as you soak up the views. On the other side of the river, the big, modern **São Gonçalo Café** in the square beside the Igreja de São Gonçalo has outside tables in summer, ideal for a restful break. It also has lunch and dinner service.

The cloisters and associated buildings of a convent now house the tourist office and the **Museu Municipal Amadeo de Souza-Cardoso.** The museum has an excellent collection of modern Portuguese art, including important works by Cubist painter Souza-Cardoso, who was born in the area, moved to Paris—where he shared an apartment with Amadeo Modigliani—in 1906, returned to Portugal in 1914, and died four years later at the age of 31. The museum also hosts temporary exhibitions and has some interesting archaeological pieces. The star attractions are the *diabos* (devils), a pair of 19th-century carved wooden figures connected with ancient fertility rites. They were venerated on St. Bartholomew's Day (August 24), when the devil was thought to run loose. The originals were destroyed by the French in the Peninsular War. In 1870, the Archbishop of Braga ordered the present two burned because of their pagan function. The São Gonçalo friars didn't feel free to go that far, but they did emasculate the male diabo. ✉ *Alameda Teixeira de Pascoães,* ☎ *255/420236.* ☒ *€1.* ☉ *Tues.–Sun. 10–noon and 2–5.*

Dining and Lodging

$$–$$$$ ✕ **Restaurante Amaranto.** This spacious, well-appointed restaurant is atop the Amaranto Hotel on the river and near the center of town. The views are spectacular, and the menu has excellent regional fare with French touches. Try the *febras de porco à transmontana* (pork filled with smoked ham). ✉ *Edifício Amaranto, Rua Acácio Lino,* ☎ *255/422006. AE, DC, MC, V.*

$$ ✕ **A Quelha.** The restaurants along or near Rua 31 de Janeiro may have
★ river views, but they don't necessarily serve the best food. This friendly, ham-and-garlic-bedecked place—behind a service station off a square at the end of the main street—has no views, but the regional fare served on its wooden tables is fantastic. The menu changes daily. Come early, because it gets packed. ✉ *Rua da Olivença,* ☎ *255/425786. No credit cards. No dinner Mon.*

$$ ✕▥ **Casa da Calçada.** Next to the old bridge and overlooking the Rio Tâmega are the carefully restored buildings of this hotel, which was once a nobleman's manor. Its ground-floor lounges are comfortable, and its guest rooms are elegant and individually furnished. The restaurant ($$–$$$) serves regional, international, and vegetarian dishes. The gardens contain a swimming pool, a tennis court, and vineyards, and a stay here gets you a 25% discount at the Golfe de Amarante course, a 10-minute drive away. ✉ *Largo do Paço 6, 4600-017,* ☎ *255/410830,* 🖷 *255/426670,* 🕸 *www.manorhouses.com/hotels/calcada. html. 30 rooms, 4 suites. Restaurant, bar, cable TV, minibars, pool, wading pool, golf privileges, tennis court, free parking. AE, DC, MC, V. EP.*

$$ ✕▥ **Pousada de São Gonçalo.** The modern São Gonçalo pousada— 20 km (12 mi) east of Amarante—is in the Serra do Marão at an altitude of nearly 3,000 ft. The rugged terrain and stone exterior are matched by a rustic interior, with lovely wood furniture, a large fireplace, and tile floors. The restaurant ($$–$$$) serves such satisfying regional fare as *cabrito da montanha* (mountain goat stew). A bottle of red wine from the carefully chosen list and a serving of the creamy, cinnamon-scented *arroz doce* (rice pudding) and you'll feel that all's right with the north of Portugal. ✉ *Curva do Lancete, Serra do Marão, 4604-909,* ☎ *255/460030,* 🖷 *255/461353,* 🕸 *www.pousadas.pt. 15 rooms. Restaurant, bar, minibars. AE, DC, MC, V. BP.*

$ ▥ **Albergaria Dona Margarita.** Rooms here are simple but comfortable; some have French windows that open onto a long balcony with splendid views of the river and adjacent gardens. There's also a pretty terrace, where breakfast is served in summer. ✉ *Rua Cândido dos Reis 53, 4600,* ☎ *255/432110,* 🖷 *255/437977. 22 rooms. Breakfast room. No credit cards. EP.*

Outdoor Activities and Sports

Golfe de Amarante (☎ 255/446060), at Quinta da Devesa, 5 km (3 mi) southwest of Amarante, is an 18-hole golf course with superb mountain views. The facilities include a bar, a restaurant, a golf shop, and a driving range. Greens fees are €30 on weekdays and €42.50 on weekends. A handicap certificate is required.

Pêso da Régua

⑲ *35 km (22 mi) southeast of Amarante, 108 km (67 mi) east of Oporto.*

This small river port is in the heart of port-wine country, and through it passes all the wine from the vineyards of the Upper Douro Valley on its way to Oporto. Local wine lodges offer tours of their cellars, which make a nice contrast to the large-scale operations in Vila Nova de Gaia. To arrange a tasting with lunch or dinner (€50) and/or stays (€65–€176) at an inn, contact the **Gabinete da Rota do Vinho do Porto** (✉ Rua dos Camilos 90, ☎ 254/320145 or 254/320146).

Lamego

⑳ *13 km (8 mi) south of Pêso da Régua, 121 km (75 mi) southeast of Oporto.*

A prosperous wine-producing town, Lamego is rich in baroque churches and mansions. The town's most famous monument is the 18th-century **Santuário de Nossa Senhora dos Remédios** (Our Lady of Cures Church and Shrine), which is on a hill west of the center of town and in a park of the same name. To reach it, you climb a marvelous granite staircase whose 686 steps are decorated with azulejos. Landings along the way have statues and chapels. At the top, rest under the chestnut trees and enjoy the views. During the Festas de Nossa Senhora dos Remédios, the annual pilgrimage to the shrine, many penitents climb the steps on their knees, just as they do at the shrine of Bom Jesus, near Braga. The main procession is September 8, but the festivities start at the end of August and include concerts, dancing, parades, a fair, and torchlight processions. ✉ *Monte de Santo Estevão,* ☎ *254/614392.* ✇ *Free.* ☉ *Nov.–May, daily 7:30–6; June–Oct., daily 7:30–8.*

THE MINHO AND THE COSTA VERDE

The coastline of Minho Province, north of Oporto, is known as the Costa Verde, a largely unspoiled stretch of small towns and sandy beaches that runs all the way to the border with Spain. The weather in this region is more inclement than elsewhere, a fact hinted at in its name: the Costa Verde is green because it sees a disproportionate amount of rain. It's a land of emerald valleys, endless pine-scented forests, and secluded beaches that are beautiful but not for fainthearted swimmers. Summers can be cool, and swimming in the Atlantic is bracing at best. "These are real beaches for real people," is the reply when visitors complain about the water temperature.

You break up your time on the coast with trips inland to medieval towns along the Rio Lima or through the border settlements along the Rio Minho. The remains of ancient civilizations are everywhere; you'll encounter dolmens, Iron Age dwellings, and Celtic and Roman towns. Old traditions are carefully incorporated into modern-day hustle and bustle. Up here, you'll see more than the occasional oxcart loaded with some sort of crop, being led by a long-skirted, wooden-shoed woman on both highway and country lane.

Braga

㉑ *53 km (33 mi) northeast of Oporto.*

Braga is one of northern Portugal's outstanding surprises. It first prospered in the 6th century—under the Visigoths—when it became an important bishopric. Braga's later archbishops often wielded greater power than the Portuguese kings themselves. In the 16th century, the city was beautified with churches, palaces, and fountains, many of which were altered in the 18th century.

Today Braga feels like the religious capital it is. Shops that sell religious items line the pedestrian streets around the cathedral. The Semana Santa (Holy Week) festivities here, including eerie torchlight processions of hooded participants, are impressive. There are also several interesting historical sights—most of them religious in nature—a short distance from the city. You can visit all of them by bus from the center of town; inquire at the tourist office for timetables.

The huge **Sé** (Cathedral) was originally Romanesque but is now an impressive blend of styles. The delicate Renaissance stone tracery on the roof is particularly eye-catching. Enter from Rua do Souto through the 18th-century cloister; the cathedral interior is on your left, and there are various interesting chapels. Steps by the entrance to the cathedral lead to the Museu de Arte Sacra (Museum of Religious Art), which has a fascinating collection of religious art and artifacts, including a 14th-century crystal cross set in bronze. From the magnificent *coro alto* (upper choir), which you cross as part of the tour, there are views of the great baroque double organ. Across the cloister, you'll see the Capela dos Reis (Kings' Chapel), a 14th-century chapel containing the tombs of Afonso Henriques's parents, Henry of Burgundy and his wife, Teresa. ⊠ *Rua do Souto,* ☎ *253/263317.* ☜ *Cathedral: free. Museum: €2 (includes tour).* ☉ *Nov.–May, daily 8:30–5:30; June–Oct., daily 8:30–6:30.*

Across narrow Rua do Souto from the Sé is Largo do Paço, a park flanked by the well-proportioned **Paço dos Arcebispos** (Archbishops' Palace), which overlooks an attractive, castellated fountain. Parts of the building date from the 14th century. Today it's occupied by faculties from the city's university and functions as the public library, one of the country's most impressive, with more than 300,000 volumes.

The pedestrian Rua Diogo de Sousa leads down from the cathedral and Paço dos Arcebispos to one of the city's former gateways, the 18th-century Arco do Porta Nova. Beyond it and to the right is the **Palácio dos Biscainhos** (Biscainhos Palace), a baroque mansion typical of many in the city. The elegant rooms are furnished in 18th-century style and display silver and porcelain collections. The ground floor of the palace is flagstone, which allowed carriages to run through the interior to the stables beyond. At the back of the palace is a formal garden with decorative tiles. ⊠ *Rua dos Biscainhos,* ☎ *253/204650.* ☜ *€2.* ☉ *Tues.–Sun. 10–12:15 and 2–5:30.*

Past the garden gateway of the Palácio dos Biscainhos, you'll find the **Zona Arqueológica** (Archaeological Zone), which contains the excavations of an old Roman city known as Bracara Augusta. (The site isn't usually open to the public.) To the east, the Roman city stretched as far as the large Largo de São Tiago.

The city center is found at the **Praça da República,** the square at the head of Braga's elongated central gardens. The west side of the square is arcaded, and behind it stands the dominating 14th-century tower, the Torre de Menagem.

NEED A BREAK?	There are two inexpensive cafés in the arcade at the Praça da República. The **Café Astoria** (☎ no phone) has mahogany-paneled walls, mirrors, marble tables, and a molded ceiling. **Café Viana** (☎ 253/262336) has been in business since 1871 and serves a wide variety of snacks. It's also a good place for breakfast and offers views of the fountain and gardens.

The **Capela de São Frutuoso de Montélios,** about 4 km (2 mi) north of town on the N205-4, is one of Portugal's oldest buildings. The original chapel is believed to have been constructed in the 7th century in the form of a Greek cross. It was partially destroyed by the Moors, and rebuilt in the 11th century. Some 4 km (2 mi) northwest of Braga on the N205-4 stand the impressive and romantic ruins of the **Mosteiro de Tibães,** built as a Benedictine monastery in the 11th century and rebuilt at the end of the 19th century. You can tour four cloisters, which have some fine examples of azulejos. On a hilltop 5 km (3 mi) west of Braga on the N309 is the **Santuário Nossa Senhora do Sameiro,** after Fátima the most important Marian shrine in Portugal, visited annually by hundreds of thousands of pilgrims. The church itself is of little architectural interest.

★ Many people come to Braga specifically to see the **Bom Jesus do Monte,** a pilgrimage shrine atop a 1,312-ft-high, densely wooded hill 5 km (3 mi) east of the city. The stone staircase, a marvel of baroque art that was started in 1723, leads to an 18th-century sanctuary-church, whose terrace commands wonderful views. Many pilgrims climb up on their knees. Fountains placed at various resting places represent the five senses and the virtues, and small chapels display tableaux with life-size figures illustrating the Stations of the Cross. If you don't want to climb up the staircase (which would be a pity), you can drive up the winding road or pay €1 and take the funicular. There are restaurants, refreshment stands, and even a couple of hotels beside the sanctuary at the top. Buses run here every half hour from the center of Braga.

The **Citânia de Briteiros,** 7 km (4 mi) southeast of Braga, is the fascinating remains of a Celtic *citânia* (hill settlement). It dates from around 300 BC and was probably not abandoned until AD 300, making it one of the last Celtic strongholds against the Romans in Portugal. The walls and foundations of 150 huts and a meeting house have been excavated (two of the huts have been reconstructed to show their original size), and paths are clearly marked between them. Parts of a channeled water system also survive. The site was excavated in the late 19th century by Dr. Martins Sarmento, who gave his name to the museum in Guimarães, where most of the finds from Briteiros were transferred. If you intend to visit the site, don't miss the museum. ✉ *Free.* ☉ *Daily 9–6.*

Dining and Lodging

$$–$$$ ✕ **Restaurante Inácio.** Just outside the 18th-century town gate, this well-known restaurant serves solid regional fare. Bacalhau is a good bet, as is the roast kid. The house wine is on the raw side, but the wine list is decent so you have plenty of other options. Service in the stone-clad interior is brisk and efficient. Reservations are essential on weekends. ✉ *Campo das Hortas 4,* ☎ *253/613235. AE, DC, MC, V. Closed Tues.*

$$–$$$ ✕ **Sameiro.** A meal in this restaurant is worth a climb to the top of the hill that's home to the Santuário Nossa Senhora do Sameiro. The dining room is spacious and pleasantly furnished, and the views are superb. The menu is unadulterated northern Portuguese cuisine. Try the *arroz de vitela com pastelinhos de marisco* (a veal and rice concoction with little seafood pastries) or one of the various bacalhau dishes. ✉ *Monte Sameiro,* ☎ *253/675114. AE, DC, MC, V. Closed Mon.*

$–$$ ✕▥ **Hotel do Elevador.** Many seasoned travelers to the north have made
★ this charming hotel—in a 19th-century building on a wooded hill 3 km (2 mi) outside Braga—their top choice. It's named after the water-operated funicular that hoists the foot-weary up to the Bom Jesus do Monte sanctuary. The restaurant, Panorâmico do Elevador ($$–$$$$), scores highly for its food and for its gorgeous views. ✉ *Monte do Bom Jesus, 4710-455,* ☎ *253/603400,* FAX *253/603409,* WEB *www.hoteisbomjesus. web.pt. 23 rooms. Restaurant, bar, cable TV, minibars, meeting rooms, free parking. AE, DC, MC, V. EP.*

$ ⊡ **Albergaria Senhora-a-Branca.** This inn is in the center of town and offers very good value. Public areas are contemporary. Guest rooms are on the small side, but they're attractively furnished. ⊠ *Largo da Senhora a Branca 58, 4710,* ☎ *253/269938,* FAX *253/269937,* WEB *www.albergariasrabranca.pt. 18 rooms, 2 suites. Bar, dining room, free parking. AE, DC, MC, V. BP.*

$ ⊡ **Dona Sofia.** Close to the Sé, this pleasant, well-appointed hotel is one of Braga's best bargains. The only meal served is breakfast, but otherwise there's nothing lacking in terms of basic comforts, and the staff is friendly. ⊠ *Largo São João de Souto 131, 4700-326,* ☎ *253/ 263160,* FAX *253/611245. 34 rooms. Breakfast room. MC, V. EP.*

$ ⊡ **Hotel de Turismo.** This smart, modern hotel is on a main road just a few minutes from the center of town. Rooms are well equipped and have balconies, although the views are mostly of traffic. The restaurant is good, and there's a rooftop pool. ⊠ *Praceta João XXI, Av. da Liberdade, 4715-036,* ☎ *253/206000,* FAX *253/206010. 134 rooms. Restaurant, bar, pool. AE, DC, MC, V. EP.*

Nightlife

Braga has an active nightlife. The café-bars in the arcaded Praça da República are good places for a drink and are lively at any time of the day or night. **Populum Bar** (⊠ Campo da Vinha, ☎ 253/610966) is a dance club with two rooms: one for disco dancing and one for ballroom dancing.

Guimarães

★ ㉒ *22 km (14 mi) southeast of Braga, 51 km (32 mi) northeast of Oporto.*

Afonso Henriques was born in 1110 in Guimarães, and Portuguese schoolchildren are taught that *"aqui nasceu Portugal"* ("Portugal was born here") with him. Within 20 years he was referred to as king of *Portucale* (the united Portuguese lands between the Minho and Douro rivers) and had made Guimarães the seat of his power. From this first "Portuguese" capital, Afonso Henriques drove south, taking Lisbon back from the Moors in 1147. Today Guimarães is a town proud of its past, and this is evident in a series of delightful medieval buildings and streets. Today, the Old Town's narrow, cobbled thoroughfares pass delightful medieval buildings, small bars that open onto sidewalks, and pastel houses that overhang little squares and have flowers in their windowsills.

☾ The **castelo** (castle) was built (or at least reconstructed from earlier remains) by Henry of Burgundy; his son, Afonso Henriques, was born within its great battlements and flanking towers. Standing high on a solid rock base above the town, the castle has been superbly preserved. A path leads down from its walls to the tiny Romanesque Igreja de São Miguel de Castelo, the plain chapel where it's believed that Afonso Henriques was baptized. ⊠ *Rua D. Teresa de Noronha,* ☎ *253/ 412273.* 🎟 *Free.* ☉ *Castle: Tues.–Sun. 9:30 to 5:30. Church: irregular hrs.*

The **Paço dos Duques** (Palace of the Dukes), below the castle, is a much-maligned 15th-century palace belonging to the dukes of Bragança. Critics claim that the restoration during the Salazar regime, which turned the building into a state residence, damaged it irrevocably. Certainly the palace's brick chimneys and turrets bear little relation to the original structure, which was an atmospheric ruin for many years. You can judge for yourself on a guided tour of the interior, where you'll find much of interest—from tapestries and furniture to porcelain and paintings. You can book guided tours at the main desk. ⊠ *Rua Conde D.*

Henrique, ☎ 253/412273. 🎫 €3 *(tour included).* ⊙ *Daily 9:30–12 and 2–5.*

The **Colegiada de Nossa Senhora da Oliveira** (Church of Our Lady of the Olive Branch) is in a delightful square. The church was founded in the 10th century to commemorate one of Guimarães's most enduring legends. Wamba, elected king of the Visigoths in the 7th century, refused the honor and thrust his olive-branch stick into the earth, declaring that only if his stick were to blossom would he accept the crown—whereupon the stick promptly sprouted foliage. In the square in front of the church, an odd 14th-century Gothic canopy sheltering a cross marks the alleged spot. ✉ *Largo da Oliveira.* 🎫 *Free.* ⊙ *Daily 7:15–noon and 3:30–5:30.*

The convent buildings surrounding the Colegiada de Nossa Senhora da Oliveira house the **Museu Alberto Sampaio,** with its beautiful displays of religious art, medieval statuary, sarcophagi, and coats of arms. The highlight is a 14th-century silver triptych of the Nativity that's full of animation and power. It's said to have been captured from the King of Castile at the crucial Battle of Aljubarrota and presented to the victorious Dom João I, whose tunic, worn at the battle, is preserved in a glass case nearby. ✉ *Rua Alfredo Guimarães,* ☎ *253/423910.* 🎫 *€2; free Sun. morning.* ⊙ *Tues.–Sun. 10–12:30 and 2–5.*

Close to the Museu Alberto Sampaio, the **Museu de Arte Primitiva e Moderna** (Museum of Primitive and Modern Art) houses Portugal's most important collection of naïve art. The works are from several different countries and are attractively displayed. ✉ *Antigos Paços do Concelho, Largo da Oliveira,* ☎ *253/414186.* 🎫 *Free.* ⊙ *Weekdays 9–12:30 and 2–5:30.*

| NEED A BREAK? | You can relax over coffee and a cake every day but Sunday at **A Medieval** (☎ no phone), an inexpensive café in Largo da Oliveira. If you're really thirsty, stop in at **Secos e Molhados** (✉ Praça de Santiago 14, ☎ no phone), a classy beer house that's open from 11 AM until 2 AM. |

The Old Town's streets peter out at the southern end of Guimarães in the Almeida da Liberdade, a swath of gardens whose benches and cafés are often full. Here the **Igreja de São Francisco** (Church of St. Francis) has a chancel decorated with 18th-century azulejos depicting the life of the saint. The church also has a fine Renaissance cloister. ✉ *Largo de São Francisco,* ☎ *253/412228.* ⊙ *Daily 9–noon and 3–5.*

★ At the top of the Largo do Toural is the excellent **Museu Martins Sarmento.** Like the Museu Alberto Sampaio, it's contained within the cloister and buildings of a church, the Igreja de São Domingos. The museum has rich finds from the Celtic settlement of Citânia de Briteiros, as well as Lusitanian and Roman stone sarcophagi, a strange miniature bronze chariot, various weapons, and elaborate ornaments. Two finds stand out: the decorative, carved stone slabs known as the *pedras formosas* (beautiful stones)—one of which was found at a funerary monument at Briteiros—and the huge, prehistoric, granite *Colossus of Pedralva*, a figure of brutal power thought to have been used in ancient fertility rites. ✉ *Rua de Paio Galvão,* ☎ *253/415969.* 🎫 *€1.50.* ⊙ *Tues.–Sun. 9:30–noon and 2–5.*

Dining and Lodging

$$–$$$
★ ✕🏨 **Pousada de Santa Marinha.** This pousada is in a 12th-century monastery that was founded by the wife of Dom Afonso Henriques to honor the patron saint of pregnant women. Antiques and extraordinary azulejo wall panels fill the public rooms, and some guest rooms

used to be monks' cells. The stone dining room ($$$) serves regional and Continental dishes; the *rojões á Minhota* (pork simmered and served with pickled vegetables) is delicious; sop up the sauce with *broa* (chewy corn bread). A fitting dessert is *toucinho do céu,* which translates as "bacon from heaven" but is actually a rich egg-and-almond pudding cake. ⊠ *Largo Domingos Leite de Castro, 4810-001,* ☎ *253/514453,* FAX *253/514459,* WEB *www.pousadas.pt. 49 rooms, 2 suites. Restaurant, bar, cable TV, minibars, shops, meeting rooms, free parking. AE, DC, MC, V. BP.*

$$ ✕⌂ **Pousada da Nossa Senhora da Oliveira.** Town houses that date from the 16th and 17th centuries were remodeled and filled with antique reproductions to create this pousada. Service is courteous and efficient, and guest rooms are elegant, though not large; those facing the street can be noisy. The superb restaurant (reservations essential; $$–$$$) has a large fireplace and windows that overlook the Largo da Oliveira. The menu features Minho dishes; try the *coelho á fundador* (fricassee of rabbit with fennel and red wine). A dessert favorite is the *bolo de amêndoa* (almond cake made with flour and mashed potatoes). ⊠ *Rua de Santa Maria, 4801-910,* ☎ *253/514157,* FAX *253/514204,* WEB *www.pousadas.pt. 16 rooms. Restaurant, bar, cable TV, minibars, free parking. AE, DC, MC, V. BP.*

Shopping

Guimarães is a center for the local linen industry. The fabric is hand-spun and hand-woven, then embroidered, all to impressive effect; it is available in local shops or at the weekly Friday market. Shops owned by artisans themselves offer the best linen buys. Try **A Oficina** (⊠ Rua Paio Galvão, Loja 11, ☎ no phone).

Barcelos

㉓ *27 km (18 mi) northeast of Guimarães, 12 km (7 mi) west of Braga.*

Barcelo, which is on the banks of the Rio Cávado, is the center of a flourishing handicrafts industry, particularly ceramics and wooden toys and models. It pays to come here if you plan to carry home a host of souvenirs. The best time to visit is during the famous weekly market.

★ ☾ The **Feira de Barcelos** (Barcelos Market), held every Thursday in the central Campo da República, is one of the country's largest; with rows of covered booths, it resembles a small city. It starts very early in the morning and sells almost anything you can think of: traditional Barcelos ceramics (brown pottery with yellow-and-white decoration), workaday earthenware, baskets, rugs, glazed figurines (including the famous Barcelos cock), decorative copper lanterns, and wooden toys. There are also mounds of vegetables, fruits, cheese, fresh bread and cakes, clothes, shoes, leather, and kitchen equipment. At times—when the early mist rises off the ground, the cries of the vendors ring out, and the smell of roasting chestnuts wafts across the square—it seems almost medieval.

NEED A BREAK? There are several attractive cafés in the center of town. From the market in the Campo da República, head for the **Avenida da Liberdade** and to the front of the tourist office building on the Largo Dr. José Novais for clean, well-lighted places to sit, have a cup of coffee and a pastry, and think about heading back to the market to get an extra suitcase for all the great stuff you just bought.

From the Campo da República, Rua Dom António Barroso leads down through the Old Town toward the river. On the left, the former medieval town tower now houses the tourist office and the **Centro de Artesanato** (Artisans' Center), which has some of the best local handicrafts. Ceramic dishes and bowls, often signed by the artist, are a good buy. Figurines, too, are popular, although none approach the individuality of those made by the late Rosa Ramalho and Mistério, local potters whose work first made famous the ceramics of Barcelos. ⊠ *Torre de Menagem, Largo de Porta Nova,* ☎ *253/811882.* 🎫 *Free.* ☉ *Mon.–Sat. 9–noon and 1:30–5:30.*

The Rio Cávado, crossed by a medieval bridge, is shaded by overhanging trees and bordered by municipal gardens. High above the river stands the ruin of the medieval Paço dos Condes (Palace of the Counts), where you'll find the **Museu Arqueológico** (Archaeological Museum). Among the empty sarcophagi and stone crosses is the 14th-century crucifix known as the Cruzeiro do Senhor do Galo (Cross of the Rooster Man). According to local legend, after sentencing an innocent man to death, a judge prepared to dine on a roast fowl. When the condemned man said, "I'll be hanged if that cock doesn't crow," the rooster flew from the table and the man's life was spared. The Barcelos cock is on sale in pottery form throughout the town; indeed, it's become almost a national symbol. ⊠ *Rua Dr. Miguel Fonseca,* ☎ *253/809600.* 🎫 *Free.* ☉ *Daily 10–5:30.*

The **Museu de Olaria** (Pottery Museum), a five-minute walk from the medieval bridge, has more than 6,000 pieces. Look for selections from current and now-extinct Portuguese workshops, private donations, and excavation finds from both Portugal and all over the world. ⊠ *Rua Cónego Joaquim Gaiolas,* ☎ *253/824741.* 🎫 *€1.40.* ☉ *Tues.–Fri. 10–5:30, weekends 10–12:30 and 2–5:30.*

Dining and Lodging

$$–$$$ ✕ **Restaurante Bagoeira.** Vendors from the town's Thursday market favor this rustic restaurant, with its wooden ceiling, black-metal chandeliers, and vases of fresh flowers. *Grelhados* (grilled meats and fish) are prepared in full view of hungry customers on a huge old range that splutters and hisses. ⊠ *Av. Dr. Sidonio Pais 495,* ☎ *253/811236. AE, DC, MC, V.*

$ 🏨 **Quinta de Santa Combra.** Just 5 km (3 mi) from Barcelos on the road to Famalicão, this fine 18th-century manor house—full of wood beams and granite—offers bed and breakfast. It's a good deal for the money. ⊠ *Lugar de Crujães, 4750,* ☎ 🄵🄰🅇 *253/832101. 6 rooms. Breakfast room, pool, horseback riding. AE. BP.*

Viana do Castelo

★ ㉔ *45 km (28 mi) northwest of Barcelos, 71 km (44 mi) north of Oporto.*

At the mouth of the Rio Lima, Viana do Castelo has been a prosperous trading center since it received its town charter in 1258. Although you shouldn't miss the excellent local beach, Praia do Cabedelo (reached by ferry from the riverside at the end of the main street), it's good to stroll through town as well. Many of Viana's finest buildings date from the 16th and 17th centuries, the period of its greatest prosperity.

Viana is regarded as the region's folk capital and specializes in producing traditional embroidered costumes. Although these make colorful souvenirs, you'll also find less elaborate crafts such as ceramics, lace, and jewelry. The large Friday market is a good place to shop.

The town's best face is presented in the old streets that radiate from the **Praça da República.** The most striking building here is the Misericórdia, a 16th-century almshouse, whose two upper stories are supported, unusually, by tall caryatids (carved, draped female figures). The square's stone fountain, also Renaissance in style, harmonizes perfectly with the surrounding buildings, which include the restored town hall and its lofty arcades.

NEED A
BREAK?   **Natário** (⊠ Rua Manuel Espregueira 37, ☎ no phone), a small café right off the main drag, is a perfect place to soak up the Minho atmosphere. The proprietor makes his own pastries, cakes, and croquettes. Brazilian writer Jorge Amado was rumored to have frequented this place when he was in town.

A 10-minute walk west from the Praça da República across the town's main avenue, the Avenida dos Combatentes da Grande Guerra, takes you to the impressive mansion that houses the **Museu Municipal** (Municipal Museum). The early 18th-century interior has been carefully preserved, and the collection of 17th-century ceramics and ornate period furniture shows how wealthy many of Viana's merchants were. ⊠ *Largo de São Domingos,* ☎ *258/820678.* ☑ *€1.* ☉ *Tues.–Sun. 9:30– noon and 2–5.*

A little ways beyond the Museu Municipal are the great ramparts of the **Castelo de Santiago da Barra,** the 16th-century fortification that added the words "do castelo" to the town's name and protected Viana against attack from pirates eager to share in its wealth. Outside the walls, Viana holds a large market every Friday.

An *elevador* (funicular railway) behind the train station climbs to the modern **Basílica de Santa Luzia,** a white, domed basilica overlooking the town from wooded heights. The views from the steps are magnificent, and a staircase to the side allows access to the very top of the dome for some extraordinary coastal vistas. This steep climb, up a very narrow staircase to a little platform, is for the agile only. ⊠ *Estrada de Santa Luzia,* ☎ *no phone.* ☑ *Elevador: €0.60. Dome: €0.50.* ☉ *Elevador: every 30 mins daily 10–7. Dome: daily 10–noon and 2–6.*

Dining and Lodging

$$$ ✕ **Casa d'Armas.** This cozy, romantic restaurant is in a renovated
★   mansion near the fishing docks. Although seafood is the reason to come here, the menu also has several grilled meat dishes. ⊠ *Largo 5 de Outubro 30,* ☎ *258/827505. DC, MC, V. Closed Wed.*

$$–$$$ ✕ **Os Tres Potes.** The cellarlike dining room, converted from a 16th-century bakery, gets busy on summer weekends, when people crowd in for the folksinging and dancing sessions. Sitting at tables under stone arches or on the open-air terrace, you can choose from a fine range of regional dishes: start with the *aperitivos regionais* (a selection of cod pastries and cheeses); move on to the house bacalhau or the exceedingly tender *polvo grelhado* (grilled octopus). There's a good wine list, too. ⊠ *Beco dos Fornos 7-9, off Praça da República,* ☎ *258/829928. Reservations essential. AE, DC, MC, V.*

$$ ✕⌂ **Pousada Santa Luzia do Monte.** A 1920s mansion, on a wooded
★   outcrop behind the basilica, houses this pousada. The gardens and terrace are a delight, as are the grand public rooms—especially in winter, when the fireplaces add crackling, romantic warmth to the sometimes chilly lounges. Guest rooms are spacious and have glamorous marble baths. The restaurant ($$–$$$$) serves regional and Continental cuisine and has sweeping views of both the countryside and the Atlantic. ⊠ *Monte de Santa Luzia, 4901-909,* ☎ *258/828889 or 258/828890,* FAX *258/828892,* WEB *www.pousadas.pt. 47 rooms, 1 suite. Restaurant, bar, in-room safes, cable TV, minibars, pool, tennis court, billiards, free parking. AE, DC, MC, V. BP.*

$ ⌂ **Hotel Viana Sol.** Although the prices are low, this hotel has a few frills as well as comfortable, functional, modern rooms. It's in the center of town, not far from the river. ⊠ *Largo Vasco da Gama, 4900-322,* ☎ *258/828995,* FAX *258/823401. 65 rooms. Bar, in-room safes, cable TV, indoor pool, sauna, gym, squash, dance club. AE, DC, MC, V. EP.*

Nightlife

The motifs at the **Casting Bar** (⊠ Rua de S. Bento 120-121, ☎ 258/827209) come from the world of fashion. A young crowd flocks to **Foz Caffe** (☎ 258/332485), a Praia da Cabedelo nightspot. The popular bar **Glamour** (⊠ Rua da Bandeira 177, ☎ 258/822963) has an open-air esplanade and highly entertaining theme nights.

En Route   Leaving Viana, both the train and the N13 continue north, following the coast and passing a succession of small villages with delightful beaches. There are good stretches of sand at the resorts of Vila Praia de Âncora and Moledo, and if you keep your eyes open, you'll find some side roads that lead to fairly isolated beaches.

Caminha

㉕ *25 km (16 mi) north of Viana do Castelo, 97 km (60 mi) north of Oporto.*

At Caminha you reach the Rio Minho, which forms the border with Spain. The fortified town hall on the main square once was part of Caminha's defenses; its loggia, supported by graceful pillars, is very pleasing to the eye. There's a 16th-century clock tower in the square, too; the nearby parish church resembles a Gothic fortress and was built a century earlier, when Caminha was an important port. The rich interior of the church and the surviving mansions in the surrounding streets are reminders of the town's former wealth, but by the 17th century Caminha had lost much of its business to Viana do Castelo. Today this beautiful community is known for its nightlife.

Vila Nova de Cerveira

㉖ *12 km (7 mi) northeast of Caminha.*

Granite hills border one side of Vila Nova de Cerveira and the Rio Minho and Spain border the other. The town dates from the 13th century, when it was fortified to ward off any marauding Spaniards. Nowadays, the Spanish who come ashore on the ferry that connects Vila Nova to the Spanish town of Goian come for day trips and good shopping. Vila Nova de Cerveira is also known for its biennial art show.

Dining and Lodging

\$\$ ✕⊞ **Pousada de Dom Dinis.** Ancient, mottled buildings within the ramparts of Vila Nova de Cerveira's 14th-century castle house this pousada. Guest rooms have reproductions of traditional Minho furniture; some rooms also have private patios. The modern restaurant (\$\$–\$\$\$\$) features local Minho dishes, including *robalo grelhado com molho manteiga* (grilled bass with butter sauce). For dessert, try the pears poached in red wine. ⊠ *Praça da Liberdade, 4920,* ☎ *251/708120,* FAX *251/708129,* WEB *www.pousadas.pt. 29 rooms. Restaurant, bar. AE, DC, MC, V. BP.*

Valença do Minho

㉗ *15 km (9 mi) northeast of Caminha, 123 km (76 mi) northeast of Oporto.*

Valença do Minho is the major border crossing point in this area, with roads as well as rail service into Spain. Valença's Old Town is enclosed by perfectly preserved walls, which face the similarly defended Spanish town of Tuy. Strolling along the river and ramparts is very pleasant, especially in the evening, when the day-trippers from Spain have retreated to their own side of the river.

Monção

28　*18 km (11 mi) northeast of Valença do Minho, 144 km (89 mi) northeast of Oporto.*

The riverside town of Monção is another fortified border settlement with a long history of skirmishes with the Spanish. In town there are the remains of a 14th-century castle that withstood a desperate siege in 1368. When the Portuguese supplies ran low, a local woman baked some cakes with the last of the flour and sent them to the Spaniards with the message that there was plenty more where that came from. The bluff worked, the Spanish retreated, and the little cakes are still on sale in town. Try a glass of the local vinho verde, a noteworthy wine available in several bars.

En Route　South of Monção the N101 traverses glorious rural countryside before descending to the valley of the Rio Vez, a tributary of the Lima. **Arcos de Valdevez,** 35 km (22 mi) from Monção, makes a nice stop. It's a typically serene little river town, where you can rent rowboats. Five kilometers (3 miles) farther south you arrive at the Lima, one of the country's most beautiful rivers. It was known to the Romans as the River of Oblivion, because its blissful beauty was said to make travelers forget their home. Ask at the tourist office about walks along the ancient Roman roads.

Ponte da Barca

29　*5 km (2 mi) south of Arcos de Valdevez on N101, 39 km (24 mi) south of Monção.*

In Ponte da Barca, the *ponte* in question is a beautiful, 10-arched bridge, built in the 15th century. At the junction of four main roads, the small town has been an important commercial center for centuries, and the Tuesday market held on the riverside here is well worth catching. On other days you can spend time quite happily walking along the riverbank.

Ponte de Lima

★ **30**　*18 km (11 mi) west of Ponte da Barca on N203, 57 km (35 mi) southwest of Monção.*

Ponte de Lima's long, low, graceful bridge is of Roman origin. It's also open only to foot traffic; drivers cross a concrete bridge at the edge of town. The main square by the old bridge has a central fountain and benches and is ringed by little cafés—the perfect places to stop for a leisurely drink. The nearby square tower still stands guard over the town, while beyond, in the narrow streets, there are several fine 16th-century mansions and a busy market. Walking around town, you'll return again and again to the river, which is the real highlight of a visit. A wide beach usually displays lines of drying laundry, and a riverside avenue lined with plane trees leads down to the Renaissance Igreja de Santo António dos Capuchos. The twice-monthly Monday market, held on the riverbank, is the oldest in Portugal, dating from 1125. On market days and during the mid-September Feiras Novas (New Fairs) you'll see the town at its effervescent best.

Dining and Lodging

The Ponte de Lima region is well known for its **Turismo no Espaço Rural** (Rural Tourism; ☎ 258/742829 to Turihab) program. There are 108 manor house properties in the area, mostly along the Rio Lima's north bank, no more than several miles from town. Facilities are usually minimal; houses may have a communal lounge or bar, a pool or access to local swimming facilities, fishing, and gardens. Rates includes bed and breakfast, although some places will arrange other meals on request. Many manor houses only accept cash, but if you book through Turihab—one of the agencies that's associated with the rural tourism program—you can pay by credit card.

$$ ✕ **Restaurante Encanada.** The Encanada is adjacent to the tree-lined avenue along the riverfront. A terrace provides river views. The menu is limited, but you can count on good local cooking, with dishes that depend on what's available at the market. Try one of the Minho dishes such as rojões á Minhota accompanied by a vinho verde. ✉ *Mercado Municipal 8,* ☏ *258/941189. AE, MC, V. Closed Mon.*

Parque Nacional da Peneda-Gerês

★ *Lindoso, in the park's center section, is 30 km (19 mi) east of Ponte da Barca.*

The 172,900-acre Peneda-Gerês National Park, bordered to the north by the frontier with Spain, was created in 1970 to preserve the region's diverse flora and fauna. Even a short trip to the main towns and villages contained within the park shows you wild stretches of land framed by mountains, woods, and lakes. Access is free, and general information is available at tourist offices in Braga and Viana do Castelo. There's also an information center at Caldas do Gerês, where you can get a walking map and more specific hints.

Accommodations are mostly in the attractive spa town of Caldas do Gerês, in the southern section around the Serra do Gerês (Gerês Mountains). It's a two-hour drive from Braga; turn off the N103 just after Cerdeirinhas, along the N304; there's bus service, too, from Braga to Cerdeirinhas and Caldas do Gerês. The park's central region is accessible from Ponte da Barca, from which the N203 leads to Lindoso, or from Arcos de Valdevez, from which the minor N202 leads to the village of Soajo. Both towns offer basic accommodations and superb hiking. To see the park's northern reaches, which encompass the Serra da Peneda (Peneda Mountains), it's best to approach from Melgaço, a small town on the Rio Minho, 25 km (15½ mi) east of Monção. From Melgaço, it's 27 km (17 mi) on the N202 to the village of Castro Laboreiro, at the park's northernmost point.

TRÁS-OS-MONTES

The name means "Beyond the Mountains," and though roads built in the 1980s have made it easier to get here than in the past, exploring this beautiful region in the extreme northeast still requires a sense of adventure. Great distances separate towns, and twisting roads can test your patience. Medieval villages exist in a landscape that alternates between splendor and harshness, and the population, thinned by emigration, retains rural customs that have all but disappeared elsewhere. Many still believe in the evil eye, witches, wolf men, golden-haired spirits living down wells, and even the cult of the dead.

Having a car is the easiest way to tour the region, but making the trip by car would mean missing out on some of the finest train journeys in the country. The trip from Oporto to Mirandela provides an excellent opportunity to see the changing landscape, and you can take a bus on to Bragança. But it is slow going. Both trains and buses stop at every village, and the journey could take more than nine hours.

Vila Real

③① *116 km (72 mi) northeast of Oporto. By train from Oporto, change at Pêso da Régua to the Corgo line.*

The capital of Trás-os-Montes is superbly situated between two mountain ranges, and much of the city retains a small-town air. Although there's no great wealth of sights, it's worth stopping here to stroll down the central avenue, which ends at a rocky promontory over the gushing Rio Corgo. A path around the church at the head of the promontory provides views of stepped terraces and green slopes. At the avenue's southern end, a few narrow streets are filled with 17th- and 18th-century houses, their entrances decorated with coats of arms.

The finest baroque work in Vila Real is the **Capela dos Clérigos** (Chapel of the Clergy), also called the Capela Nova (New Chapel), a curious fan-shape building set between two heavy columns. ⊠ *Rua 31 de Janeiro and Rua Direita,* ☎ *no phone.* ⊠ *Free.* ⊙ *Daily 10–noon and 2–6.*

★ An exceptional baroque mansion believed to have been designed by Nicolau Nasoni (architect of Oporto's Clérigos Tower), the **Solar de Mateus** is 4 km (2 mi) east of Vila Real. Its U-shape facade—with high, decorated finials at each corner—is recognized worldwide as the building pictured on the Mateus Rosé wine label. Set back to one side is the chapel, with an even more extravagant facade. The elegant interior is open to the public, as are the formal gardens, which are enhanced by a "tunnel" of cypress trees that shade the path. ⊠ *N322 (road to Sabrosa), Mateus,* ☎ *259/323121.* ⊠ *House, gardens, and tour: €6. Gardens only: €3.50.* ⊙ *Dec.–Feb., daily 10–1 and 2–5; Mar.–May and Oct.–Nov., daily 9–1 and 2–6; June–Sept., daily 9–7.*

Dining and Lodging

$–$$ ✕ **O Aldeão.** The Aldeão piles its plates high with Portuguese specialties. The steak comes garnished with a bit of everything and satisfies even the largest of appetites. A regional favorite, *feijoada branca á transmontana* (a hearty white-bean-and-smoked-sausage stew), is prepared to perfection here. Service is friendly, the surroundings straightforward, and the prices unbeatable for this quality and quantity of food. ⊠ *Rua Dom Pedro de Castro 70,* ☎ *259/324794. AE, MC, V.*

$$ ✕⊞ **Pousada do Barão de Forrester.** This pousada in Alijó, some 30 km (18 mi) southeast of Vila Real, is named for Baron Forrester, a 19th-century Scotsman whose family members were successful port vintners and whose remarkable map of the Rio Douro helped open the river to navigation. Time fades away as you sit reading by the fire in the lounge, glass of port at your side. The restaurant ($$–$$$$) has two terraces for sunlit lunches and star-filled suppers. Try the river mackerel in marinade or the bacalhau *à Barão de Forrester* (fried with onion and baked potatoes). ⊠ *Rua José Rufino, Alijó 5070-031,* ☎ *259/959215,* ₣ₐ╳ *259/959215,* ᵂᴱᴮ *www.pousadas.pt. 20 rooms. Restaurant, bar, pool, tennis court, fishing. AE, MC, DC, V. BP.*

$ ⊞ **Miracorgo.** The reception area is handsome, the guest rooms are bright, and the service is good—all of which more than makes up for the unattractive, modern exterior. Request a room facing the valley, with views of the dramatic stepped terraces. ⊠ *Av. 1 de Maio 76–78, 5000-651,* ☎ *259/325001,* ₣ₐ╳ *259/325006. 166 rooms. Bar, pool, shop, dance club. AE, DC, MC, V. EP.*

En Route   The main road northeast of Vila Real (the N15) is straight for much of its length. You'll drive through exceptionally fine, high countryside; rolling, arable land continues as far as Murça, 40 km (25 mi) away. Here you'll see the most famous of the ancient zoomorphic images, and the largest of the Iron Age porcas, which are found all over the region. This particular granite boar stands on a plinth in the town's central square and is presumed to be a fertility symbol.

Mirandela

32 *72 km (45 mi) from Vila Real. Train service, via Tua from Pêso da Régua, runs through pastures and barley fields, following the course of the Rio Tua, a tributary of the Douro.*

Mirandela, an attractive town midway between Vila Real and Bragança, has a medieval castle and a Roman bridge with 20 arches of uneven sizes. The grandest monument, however, is the 17th-century Palácio dos Tavoras (Tavora Palace), right in the center of town. Its great facade has elaborate pediments and baroque ornaments. Once the residence of the prominent Tavora family, it's now used as the town hall.

Bragança

33 *60 km (37 mi) northeast of Mirandela, 255 km (158 mi) northeast of Oporto.*

This ancient town in the very northeastern corner of Portugal has been inhabited since Celtic times (from about 600 BC). The town lent its name to the noble family of Bragança (or Braganza), whose most famous member, Catherine, married Charles II of England; the New York City borough of Queens is named for her. Descendants of the family ruled Portugal until 1910; their tombs are contained within the church of São Vicente de Fora in Lisbon. Unfortunately, since improved roads have encouraged development, the approaches to Bragança have been spoiled by many ugly new buildings.

Above the modern town rises the magnificent 15th-century Castelo (Castle), found within the ring of battlemented walls that surround the Cidadela (Citadel), the country's best-preserved medieval village and one of the most thrilling sights in Trás-os-Montes. Bragança has locally made ceramics, and there's also a good crafts shop within the walls of the Citadel. Baskets, copper objects, pottery, woven fabrics, and leather goods are all well made here.

The central cathedral is small and disappointing, but the modern town center is attractive in its way, with a wide central avenue and several cafés that open onto the sidewalk in summer. You'll easily exhaust all the sights in less than day, but it's worth staying overnight for the views of the castle from the pousada on the outskirts of town.

★ ☞ Within the walls of the **Cidadela** (Citadel), you'll find the Castelo and the Domus Municipalis (City Hall), a rare Romanesque civic building dating from the 12th century. It's always open, but you may need to get a key from one of the local cottages for the Igreja de Santa Maria (Church of St. Mary), a building with Romanesque origins that has a superb 18th-century painted ceiling. A prehistoric granite boar stands below the castle keep, this one with a tall medieval stone pillory sprouting from its back. The keep, the Torre de Menagem, now contains the **Museu Militar,** which displays armament from the 12th century through to World War I. The most exciting aspect of the museum is the 108-ft-high Gothic tower, with its dungeons, drawbridge, turrets, battlements, and vertiginous outside staircase. ☎ 273/322378. 🎫 *Citadel: free. Museum: €1.50. ☼ Citadel: daily sunrise–sunset. Museum: Mon.– Wed. and Fri.–Sun. 9–noon and 2–5.*

As you leave the castle walls on your way back down to town, you'll pass the Renaissance **Igreja de São Bento,** with a fine Mudèjar (Moorish-style) vaulted ceiling and a gilded retable. The church may or may not be open.

The exhibits at the **Museu do Abade de Baçal,** housed in Bragança's former bishop's palace, were collected by a local priest with eclectic tastes. The Abade de Baçal, who died in 1947, acquired prehistoric pigs, ancient tombstones, furniture, local costumes, fine silver, coins, and paintings—anything that caught his eye. ⊠ *Rua do Consilheiro Abílio Beca 27,* ☎ *273/331595.* 🎟 *€2.* ⊙ *Tues.–Sun. 10–5.*

Dining and Lodging

$$–$$$ ✕ **La Em Casa.** This low-key but attractive restaurant is between the castle and the cathedral. It serves regional Portuguese food with a decent menu of fish and shellfish. As you might expect this far inland, however, such dishes are considerably more expensive than the meat dishes. ⊠ *Rua Marquês de Pombal 7,* ☎ *273/322111. Reservations essential. AE, DC, MC, V.*

$$ ✕🏨 **Pousada de São Bartolomeu.** On a hill just west of the town cen-
★   ter, Bragança's modern, comfortable pousada offers terrific views of the Citadel. The bar-lounge has an open fireplace and wooden furnishings, and the rustic guest rooms have balconies. It doesn't really matter that the pousada is a few miles from all the in-town restaurants: the on-site dining room ($$), serves the area's best stews and game dishes. ⊠ *Estrada do Turismo, 5300-271,* ☎ *273/331493,* 𝖥𝖠𝖷 *273/323453,* 𝖶𝖤𝖡 *www.pousadas.pt. 28 rooms. Restaurant, bar, minibars, pool, tennis court. AE, DC, MC, V. BP.*

Vinhais

③④ *31 km (19 mi) west of Bragança.*

Vinhais provides a welcome break from the beautiful although rather desolate scenery along the N103—bleak uplands with the mountains of Spain to the north and the distant mass of the Serra da Estrela (Estrela Mountains) to the south. Most probably a pre-Roman *castro* (settlement), the present town was founded in the 13th century by King Sancho II. The structure housing the former **Convento de São Francisco** (Convent of St. Francis) has a great baroque facade that incorporates two churches, one of which has a beautiful painted ceiling. ☎ *296/583532.* ⊙ *Daily 9–6.*

En Route   Shortly before reaching Chaves, you'll see the ruins of the 13th-century **Castelo do Monforte** (Monforte Castle), built upon the site of an earlier Roman fort, a remote outpost of the great empire.

Chaves

★ ③⑤ *55 km (34 mi) west of Vinhais, 96 km (60 mi) west of Bragança.*

Chaves was known to the Romans as Aquae Flaviae (Flavian's Waters), in honor of the emperor Flavian. They established a military base here and popularized the town's thermal springs. The impressive 16-arch Roman bridge across the Rio Tâmega, at the southern end of town, dates from the 1st century AD and displays two original Roman milestones. Today Chaves is characterized most by a series of fortifications built during the late Middle Ages, when the city was prone to attack from all quarters. The town lies only 12 km (7 mi) from the Spanish border. Its name means "keys"—whoever controlled Chaves held the keys to the north of the country.

The most obvious landmark is the great, blunt fortress overlooking the river, the 14th-century **Torre de Menagem** (Castle Keep). This houses a military museum, and the grounds offer grand views of the town.

The tower is surrounded by narrow, winding streets filled with elegant houses, most of which have lovely carved wood balconies on their top floors. ⊠ *Largo da Câmara Municipal de Chaves,* ☎ *276/340500.* 🖃 *Museum: €0.50 (joint admission with Museu da Região Flaviense).* ☉ *Tues.–Fri. 9:30–12:30 and 2–5, weekends 2–5:30.*

In Praça de Camões, the main square below the Torre de Menagem, the late-17th-century **Igreja da Misericórdia** (Church of Mercy) is lined with huge panels of blue-and-white azulejos that depict scenes from the New Testament. ⊠ *Praça de Camões,* ☎ *no phone.* ☉ *Daily 9–5:30.*

The **Museu da Região Flaviense** (Flaviense Regional Museum) adjacent to the Igreja da Misericórdia has a hodgepodge of local archaeological finds and relics that tell the town's history. ⊠ *Praça de Camões,* ☎ *276/340500.* 🖃 *€0.50 (joint admission with military museum in Torre de Menagem).* ☉ *Tues.–Fri. 9:30–12:30 and 2–5, weekends 2–5:30.*

Dining and Lodging

$ ✕ **O Pote.** This family-run restaurant a short ways out of town has no pretensions. It serves tasty Portuguese food to an enthusiastic local clientele. Ask about the daily specials. You can't go wrong if you choose the *entrecôte de vitela* (grilled veal). ⊠ *Estrada da Fronteira,* ☎ *276/321226. AE, DC, MC, V. Closed Mon.*

$$ ✕🏨 **Forte de São Francisco.** The ruins of a 16th-century Franciscan monastery have been transformed to create this remarkable hotel. Outside, massive walls surround extensive gardens and courtyards. The interior is a sober but attractive blend of ancient stone and modern simplicity. The Franciscan monks would no doubt have frowned on the contemporary comforts of the elegant, well-equipped guest rooms and the sumptuous food served in the restaurant ($$–$$$). They might, however, have winked at the hotel's well-stocked wine cellar installed in their old water cistern. ⊠ *Alto da Pedisqueira, 5400-435,* ☎ *276/333700,* FAX *276/333701,* WEB *www.forte-s-francisco-hoteis.pt. 58 rooms. Restaurant, bar, cafeteria, pool, tennis court. AE, DC, MC, V. EP.*

$ ✕🏨 **Hotel Trajano.** The subdued basement restaurant ($$) of the Hotel Trajano is a good place to try the presunto for which the town is famous. *Truta á transmòntana* (river trout wrapped in paper-thin slices of smoky presunto) is another good choice, served with boiled potatoes and salad. There's a reasonably priced selection of local wines to accompany your meal, which is served promptly on elegantly rustic monogrammed plates. The good service continues upstairs, where the hotel's pleasant guest rooms are cheerily decorated in Portuguese country style. ⊠ *Travessa Cândido dos Reis, 5400-164,* ☎ *276/301640,* FAX *276/327002. 39 rooms. Restaurant, bar, cable TV. AE, MC, V. EP.*

$–$$ 🏨 **Hotel Aquae Flaviae.** Although it bears the ancient Roman name for Chaves, and it's a cannon shot away from the town's fortified tower, this is a gleaming modern hotel. The facade has an art-deco touch—it looks more like an enormous movie house than a hotel—and the interior impresses with its smooth lines and polished surfaces. The rooms are as spacious as they are attractive. ⊠ *Praça do Brasil, 5400-123,* ☎ *276/309000,* FAX *276/309010. 168 rooms. Restaurant, bar, grill, in-room safes, cable TV, minibars, pool, wading pool, sauna, gym, shops, billiards, free parking, meeting rooms. AE, DC, MC, V. EP.*

En Route If you continue west along the N103 for 35 km (22 mi) you'll come to an enormous system of lakes and hydroelectric dams along the Cávado. At this point you can make a short side trip to see the ruined castle at Montalegre, which is visible from miles around. Take a right turn onto the N308 and drive for 12 km (7 mi). The views are worth the detour. Back on the N103, you'll follow along the edge of the great lake system, skirting drowned valleys in an endless series of long loops. Allow plenty of time, because you're sure to want to stop often to take in the incredible views. To the north is the Parque Nacional da Peneda-Gerês; there are occasional access points along the road. Finally, after passing the village of Cerdeirinhas, the road runs for 30 km (19 mi) through rocky heights and down tree-clad slopes to reach Braga, where you are firmly in the center of the Minho province.

OPORTO AND THE NORTH A TO Z

To research prices, get advice from other travelers, and book travel arrangements, visit www.fodors.com.

AIR TRAVEL

Oporto's Aeroporto Sá Carneiro, 13 km (8 mi) north of the city, is the gateway to all of northern Portugal. There's direct service from many European and South American cities, though not from the United States. TAP runs regular flights from Lisbon's Aeroporto Portela. Omni also has flights to regional airports in Bragança and Vila Real from Lisbon.

➤ AIRPORT INFORMATION: **Aeroporto Portela** (☎ 21/445–8600). **Aeroporto Sá Carneiro** (☎ 22/943–2400). **Bragança airport** (☎ 273/381175). **Vila Real airport** (☎ 259/336620).

➤ AIRLINES: **Omni** (☎ 218/451786). **TAP** (☎ 808/205700 or 218/415000).

AIRPORT TRANSFERS

Buses 56 and 87 run from the airport to downtown Oporto. It takes up to an hour, depending on the traffic, to reach the stop at Cordoaria, the area behind the Clérigos Tower. Taxis are available, too, outside the terminal; the fare will run €15–€18 including the €1.50 baggage charge.

BUS AND TRAM TRAVEL

Oporto has a very good public transportation system of buses and trams. The tourist office provides a city map with the routes. Main stops are at Praça da Liberdade, Praça de Dom João I, and Cordoaria, behind the Torre dos Clérigos. Bus 78 runs from Praça da Liberdade, past the Museu Nacional Soares dos Reis and the Palácio de Cristal gardens, along the main Avenida da Boavista, to the Museu de Arte Contemporânea. Trams 1 and 18 make a pleasant run along the river.

All bus rides within the inner metropolitan zone—this includes most places you'll want to see—cost €1 if you buy your ticket on the bus and €0.45 if you buy it at an STCP kiosk. The price for an outer zone ticket is €0.70 bought at the kiosk and €1 on board; €2.60 buys one day of unlimited rides, and €4.40 buys a 10-ride ticket. The tourist office issues its own Passes Turísticos, which cost €4 (one day of unlimited rides) or €5.50 (two days of unlimited rides) and includes discounts to certain museums.

Several bus companies operate in the north. Major terminals are found at Oporto, Braga, Guimarães, Vila Real, and Chaves. The best source of information about departures is the local tourist office, since bus station personnel invariably speak no English. Most bus stations do, however, have timetables that you should be able to decipher with the aid of a dictionary.

The main company operating in Trás-os-Montes is Cabanelas, whose terminal in Oporto is at Rua da Ateneu Comercial. Bus trips in this region are slow and, on some of the minor routes, uncomfortable. One useful tip is to take the bus rather than the train between the neighboring towns of Guimarães and Braga. It's only 22 km (14 mi) on the road, but the circuitous train ride involves two changes.

➤ Bus Information: **Cabanelas** (☎ 22/200–5637).

CAR RENTAL

All the major companies are represented at Oporto's Sá Carneiro Airport, and some have offices at the larger hotels throughout the region.

➤ Major Agencies: **Avis** (⊠ Rua Guedes de Azevedo 125, Oporto, ☎ 22/205–5947; ⊠ Braga train station, Largo da Estação, Braga, ☎ 253/427205). **Europcar** (⊠ Rua de Santa Catarina 1158, Oporto, ☎ 22/205–7737; ⊠ Campanhã Station, Rua da Estação, Oporto, ☎ 22/518–0723). **Hertz** (⊠ Rua de Santa Catarina 899, Oporto, ☎ 22/339–5300; ⊠ Rua Gabrial P. Castro 28, Braga, ☎ 253/616744; ⊠ Av. Conde da Carreira, Viana do Castelo, ☎ 258/822250).

CAR TRAVEL

The IP4 highway is a fast way to travel between Oporto and Bragança, and there are quick routes from Oporto to towns both north and south. The A4/E82 toll road connects Oporto to Amarante. From here the three-lane E82/IP84 passes through Vila Real, Mirandela, and Bragança en route to the Spanish border at Quintanilha. The IP3 runs from Lamego through Pêso da Régua to Vila Real. The toll road A3-IP1 runs from Oporto to Braga and on to Ponte de Lima and Valença on the Spanish boarder. The three-lane ICI/IP9 travels from Oporto to Viana de Castelo.

Given the nature of Portuguese terrain—particularly in the northeast—some journeys will never be anything but slow. Examples are the routes Bragança–Chaves–Braga (N103), Vila Real–Chaves (N2), and Bragança–Mirando do Douro (N218). It's best simply to accept the roads' limitations, slow down, and appreciate the scenery. Off the beaten track, always check with local tourist offices to make sure that the routes you wish to follow are navigable. Road work and winter landslides can cause detours and delays. In isolated regions, take special care at night, because many roads are unlighted and unpaved.

EMERGENCIES

Pharmacies take turns staying open late. Schedules and addresses are posted on the door of each establishment, and listings of late-night services are carried in the local press.

➤ Emergency Services: **General** (☎ 112).

➤ Hospitals: **Hospital Geral de Santo António** (⊠ Largo Professor Abel Salazar, Oporto, ☎ 22/207–7500). **Hospital de Santa Maria** (⊠ Rua de Camões 906, Oporto, ☎ 22/550–4844). **Hospital de São João** (⊠ Alameda Professor Hernâni Monteiro, Oporto, ☎ 22/252–7151).

MAIL

The main post office in Oporto is in Praça General Humberto Delgado. General-delivery mail (mark it POSTE RESTANTE) is received here.

➤ Post Office: **Oporto** (⊠ Praça General Humberto Delgado, ☎ 22/208–0251, ⊙ weekdays 8 AM–10 PM, Sat. 8–8).

TAXIS

In Oporto there's a taxi stand in Praça da Liberdade, or you can phone for a cab. Make sure that the driver switches on the meter. If you have phoned for the cab, the cabbie will have already done so from wherever he picked up the call. The starting charge is €1.80, and then it's €0.32 per kilometer. If you have suitcases you pay €1.50 extra, but not per bag. It's customary, but not obligatory, to tip up to 10% of the fare. Note that taxis add a surcharge for crossing the Ponte Dom Luís I to Vila Nova de Gaia, the suburb known for its port wine.

➤ CONTACT: **Radio Taxis** (☎ 22/507–3900).

TELEPHONES

At the main post office in Oporto telephones are available for local, regional, or international calls. The cashier will indicate which phone to use, and you pay afterward. Note that most of the public pay phones can be used for all types of calls. You can buy cards with 50- or 120-minute units in most tobacconists, newsstands, and phone company outlets. Area codes in the region include Braga 253, Bragança 273, Chaves 276, Guimarães 253, Oporto 22, Viana do Castelo 258, Vila Nova de Cerveira 251, and Vila Real 259.

DIRECTORY AND OPERATOR ASSISTANCE

For general information, dial 118; operators often speak English.

TOURS

ADVENTURE TOURS

In the region north along the Rio Lima from Viana do Castelo you can canoe, raft, parasail, surf, bodyboard, water-ski, hike, climb, and mountain bike. You can also take a ride in a Jeep, a hot-air balloon, or an ultralight. The Região de Turismo Alto Minho can help you make arrangements.

➤ CONTACT: **Região de Turismo Alto Minho** (✉ Castelo Santiago da Barra, Viana do Castelo, ☎ 258/820270, 258/820271, 258/820272, or 258/820273).

BOAT TOURS

Several Oporto-based companies offer cruises on the Rio Douro. These range from short trips taking in Oporto's bridges and the local fishing villages to one- and two-day cruises that include meals and accommodations. Most of the short cruises depart several times daily from the Cais da Ribeira, at the foot of Oporto's Old Town. The longer cruises, some in traditional rabelo riverboats, usually involve taking a train from the Estação de São Bento that connects with a boat farther up the Douro. These longer, upriver cruises usually leave once or twice a week from May to October.

One of the oldest companies is Endouro. Turisdouro specializes in rides on sailboats traditionally used to transport port wine downriver. Ferreira & Rayford specializes in longer cruises from the upriver town of Pêso da Régua. Gabinete da Rota do Vinho do Porto can make reservations for boat and train tours, hotels, and wine tastings.

Douro Azul organizes a variety of tours on the Douro. One of the most popular is a steam train ride up the Rio Douro to Pêso da Régua and Pinhão, with a return trip by boat on Monday, Wednesday, or Saturday; for trips on Sunday, Tuesday, and Thursday, you leave Oporto by boat and return by train. Lunch is often included in the price. Trains depart from the downtown Estação de São Bento; boats leave from the quay in Vila Nova de Gaia. Douro Azul also operates two air-conditioned hotel boats: the *Alto Douro* (37 double cabins, restaurant, and sundecks) and the *Invicta* (40 double cabins).

➤ CONTACTS: **Douro Azul** (✉ Rua de São Francisco 4, Oporto, ☎ 22/340–2500, WEB www.douroazul.com). **Endouro** (✉ Rua da Reboleira 49, Oporto, ☎ 22/332–4236). **Ferreira & Rayford** (✉ Rua de S. Francisco 4, Pêso da Régua, ☎ 22/339–3950). **Gabinete da Rota do Vinho do Porto** (✉ Rua dos Camilos 90, Pêso da Régua, ☎ 254/320145 or 254/320146). **Turisdouro** (✉ Rua Machado dos Santos 824, Oporto, ☎ 22/370–8429).

Bus tours of the city usually last a half day and take in all the principal sights, including the port-wine lodges in Vila Nova de Gaia. Contact the tourist office for more information. Citirama and SGV Viagens
e Turismo operate half- and full-day coach tours to destinations as diverse as the Douro Valley, the Costa Verde, and Parque Nacional da
Peneda-Gerês.

➤ CONTACTS: **Citirama** (☎ 21/319–1090). **SGV Viagens e Turismo** (✉
Rua Damião de Góis 425, Oporto, ☎ 22/557–4000).

If you want to get above it all Helitours offers 10-minute flights over
Oporto and 20-minute flights that take you farther upriver. The three-
hour tour includes a trip to Mesão Frio, with a stop for lunch. The he-
lioport is in Masarelos. overlooking the river and next to the Helitours
office.

➤ CONTACT: **Helitours** (✉ Alameda Basílio Teles, Oporto, ☎ 22/543–
2464, WEB www.douroazul.com).

TRAIN TRAVEL

Most trains into Oporto (including those from Lisbon) arrive at Estação de Campanhã, just east of the city center. From here, you can
take a five-minute connecting train ride to the central Estação de São
Bento; connecting trains run regularly. When leaving Oporto, be sure
to budget in plenty of time from the station to make your connection.
For the express service to and from Lisbon, reserve your seat at least
a day in advance.

Trains from Guimarães and from the coast immediately north of the
city use the Estação da Trindade. The station is a few minutes' walk
from downtown Oporto, behind the town hall at the top of Avenida
dos Aliados. From Spain, the Vigo–Porto train uses the Tuy/Valença
border crossing and runs south down the Costa Verde to Oporto via
Viana do Castelo. These trains usually stop at the Campanhã and São
Bento stations, but some only stop at Campanhã, and you'll have to
change for São Bento.

All the region's train routes originate in Oporto; from here some of
the finest lines in the country stretch out into the river valleys and mountain ranges of the northeast. Even if you've rented a car, try to take a
day trip on at least one of the beautiful lines that traverse the region.

The Douro Line runs from Estação de São Bento east to Pocinho via
Livração, Pêso da Régua, and Tua (a four-hour journey). Three narrow-
gauge lines branch off from it: the Tâmega Line, linking Livração with
beautiful Amarante (25 minutes); the Corgo Line from Pêso da Régua
to Vila Real (one hour); and the Tua Line from Tua to Mirandela (two
hours). The trains on these lines generally have just one class of car, and
the trains usually stop at every station. Journeys are slow but rewarding. Recently there have been service cuts on the minor lines, and some
route sections have been closed altogether. The lines mentioned above
should still be operational, but for reservations and current schedules
contact Estação de São Bento or the tourist office in Oporto.

Trains on the main route north along the Costa Verde depart approximately hourly from both São Bento and Campanhã stations and run
through Barcelos and Viana do Castelo, as far as Valença do Minho.
Branch lines connect with Braga and Guimarães.

➤ TRAIN STATIONS: **Estação de Campanhã** (✉ Rua da Estação, Oporto,
☎ 22/535–4141). **Estação de São Bento** (✉ Praça Almeida Garrett,
Oporto, ☎ 22/536–4141). **Estação da Trindade** (✉ Rua Alferes Malheiro, Oporto, ☎ 22/200–4833).

TRAVEL AGENCIES

In Oporto, you'll find several travel agencies around the central Avenida dos Aliados. Reliable ones include Abreu and Top Tours, agents for American Express.

➤ LOCAL AGENCIES: **Abreu** (✉ Av. dos Aliados 207, Oporto, ☏ 22/204–3500). **Top Tours** (✉ Rua Alferes Malheiro 96, Oporto, ☏ 22/207–4020).

VISITOR INFORMATION

OPORTO

➤ TOURIST OFFICES: **ICEP** (✉ Praça Dom João I 43, east of Av. dos Aliados, ☏ 22/205–7514; ✉ Rua General Torres 1141, Vila Nova de Gaia, ☏ 22/379–0994). **Posto de Turismo Municipal** (✉ Rua Clube dos Fenianos 25, at top of Av. dos Aliados, ☏ 22/339–3470; ✉ Rua Infante D. Henrique, 63, south of Praça da Liberdade, ☏ 22/200–9770; ✉ Rua Clube dos Fenianos 25, ☏ 800/200905).

OPORTO'S ENVIRONS

➤ TOURIST OFFICES: **Amarante** (✉ Rua Cândido dos Reis, ☏ 255/432980). **Espinho** (✉ Corner of Ruas 6 and 23, ☏ 227/340911). **Esposende** (✉ Rua 1 de Dezembro, ☏ 253/961354). **Lamego** (✉ Av. Visconde Guedes Teixeira, ☏ 254/612005). **Póvoa de Varzim** (✉ Praça Marquês de Pombal, ☏ 252/298120). **Vila do Conde** (✉ Rua 25 de Abril, ☏ 252/642700).

THE MINHO AND THE COSTA VERDE

➤ TOURIST OFFICES: **Arcos de Valdevez** (✉ Av. da Marginal, ☏ 258/516001). **Barcelos** (✉ Torre de Menagem, Largo da Porta Nova, ☏ 253/811882). **Braga** (✉ Av. da Liberdade 1, ☏ 253/262550). **Caminha** (✉ Rua Ricardo Joaquim Sousa, ☏ 258/921952). **Gerês** (✉ Caldas de Gerês, ☏ 253/391133). **Guimarães** (✉ Alameda S. Dâmaso 83, ☏ 253/412450). **Monção** (✉ Largo do Loreto, ☏ 251/652757). **Ponte da Barca** (✉ Largo da Misericórdia, ☏ 258/452899). **Ponte de Lima** (✉ Praça da República, ☏ 258/942335). **Valença do Minho** (✉ Av. de Espanha, ☏ 251/823374). **Viana do Castelo** (✉ Praça da Erva, ☏ 258/822620). **Vila Nova de Cerveira** (✉ Rua Dr. A. Duro, ☏ 251/795787). **Vila Praia de Âncora** (✉ Av. Dr. Ramos Pereira, ☏ 258/911384).

TRÁS-OS-MONTES

➤ TOURIST OFFICES: **Bragança** (✉ Av. Cidade de Zamora, ☏ 273/381273). **Chaves** (✉ Terreiro de Cavalaria, ☏ 276/340661). **Vila Real** (✉ Av. Carvalho Araújo 94, ☏ 259/322819).

9 MADEIRA

Floral scents and the sound of waterfalls fill Madeira's sea-washed air. Bird-of-paradise flowers grow wild; pink and purple fuchsia weave lacy patterns up pastel walls; and jacaranda trees create purple canopies over roads and avenues. The natural beauty of this island is like no other, from the cliffs that plummet seaward to mountain summits cloaked in silent fog. The magic has captivated travelers for centuries.

Updated by
Paul Murphy

W INE CONNOISSEURS THROUGH THE AGES have savored
Madeira's eponymous export, but a sip of this heady
elixir provides only a taste of the island's many delights.
Foremost among these is the balmy year-round temperature, ensured
by warm Atlantic currents. Other draws include the promise of clear
skies, the carpets of flowers, the waterfalls that cascade down green
canyons, and the great hiking paths.

Madeira is a subtropical island 900 km (558 mi) southwest of Lisbon—
at roughly the same latitude as Casablanca. In the middle of the isle is
a backbone of high, rocky peaks and the crater of a now-extinct volcano. Steep ravines fan out from the center like spokes of a wheel. Although Madeira is only 57 km (35 mi) long and 22 km (14 mi) wide,
distances seem much greater, as the roads climb and descend precipi-
tously from one ravine to the next. In the same island group are tiny
Porto Santo, about 50 km (31 mi) northeast, which has a sandy beach
popular with vacationers and its 5,000 inhabitants; the Ilhas Desertas, a chain of waterless, unpopulated islands 20 km (12 mi) southeast of Madeira; and the also-uninhabited Ilhas Selvagens, much farther
south, near Spain's Canary Islands.

Madeira was discovered and claimed for Portugal in 1419–20 by explorer João Gonçalves Zarco, whose statue stands at the main inter-
section in Funchal, the capital. Because the uninhabited island was then
covered with a nearly impenetrable forest, Zarco named it Madeira,
which means "wood" in Portuguese. In the 15th and 16th centuries
the colony grew rich from sugar plantations. Later, Madeira's wine industry sustained the island's growth, and in recent decades, tourism
has become big business.

Funchal exudes a British air, dating from the mid-16th-century marriage of the Portuguese princess, Catherine of Bragança, to England's
King Charles II, which marked the end of Spain's domination of Portugal. The marriage contract gave the English the right to live on
Madeira, plus valuable trade concessions. Charles in turn gave Madeirans
an exclusive franchise to sell wine to England and its colonies. The island's wine boom lured many British families to Funchal, and vacationers followed to enjoy the mild winters.

Today the British still flock to Madeira—many via good-value hotel
packages. It's also a popular destination for Germans and Scandina-
vians, who enjoy downtime in Funchal and hiking the island's famous
network of *levadas,* inland irrigation canals converted into superb
walking trails. A reserved crowd enjoys Madeira's magnificent blend
of sun and seascapes, good food and lodging, tranquil gardens, and
afternoon teatime. And although travelers whose priority is cosmopolitan action until dawn will be unfulfilled by Madeira, others—
of almost any age, nationality, and fitness level—are likely to be caught
in its spell.

Historically Madeira has been a winter resort, but that—like much on
the island—is changing. Christmas week, when every tree in Funchal
is decorated with lights and the main boulevard becomes an open-air
folk museum, is still the most popular time to visit, along with New
Year's Eve, when cruise ships from everywhere pull into the harbor for
an incomparable fireworks display from the hills surrounding Funchal.
But festivals—celebrating flowers in April, the island's patron saint in
August, and wine in September—are popular, too.

The island's popularity has wrought change: its airport is now international, and its numerous new roads (construction projects continue) have halved many journey times. But such developments don't seem about to overwhelm Madeira. Rather, it's the island's amazingly rugged interior that overwhelms all who experience it. Multiple microclimates, exotic topography and vegetation, and designated nature reserves create an amazing ecodestination. With this awesome heritage, Madeira has the power to keep its core a sanctuary for centuries to come.

Pleasures and Pastimes

Dining

A soft, white, deep-sea fish known as *espada* (often called "scabbard fish" because of its long, swordlike shape) is served everywhere and prepared dozens of ways—from poached à la Provençal to fried with bananas. In all the world, espada are fished commercially only in the deep, offshore waters of Madeira and Japan. The fishermen set out in the early evening in small boats, lower lines baited with specially prepared squid, and laboriously pull up the catch. Sunday is a day of rest, however, so don't look for fresh espada on Monday.

Seafood fans should also try the Portuguese version of bouillabaisse, *caldeirada de peixes variados,* a slowly simmered combination of fish, shellfish, potatoes, tomatoes, onions, and olive oil. The other popular fish plate is *bife de atum,* a hearty tuna steak. Those with more adventurous tastes should search out *polvo com vinagre*—a tangy octopus salad.

Another specialty is *carne de vinhos e alhos* (pork marinated in wine, oil, garlic, and spices, then gently boiled and quickly browned over a high flame). *Espetada,* a beef shish kebab seasoned with bay leaves and butter, was traditionally a party dish prepared in the country over open fires. The meat was once skewered on bay twigs, but nowadays it's served on iron skewers hung vertically from special stands placed in the center of a table so that all diners can share. Espetada is usually accompanied by *milho frito* (fried cubes of savory corn pudding), a side dish native to Madeira. Also on the table of many Madeiran restaurants is *bolo de caco,* a round, flat bread smeared with garlic butter.

Typical desserts are bananas (small, sweet, silvery ones that aren't exported), mango, *paw paw* (papaya), *anonas* (custard apples), and *maracujá* (passion fruit). Don't leave without trying the *bolo de mel,* a spicy honey cake made with molasses and traditionally served with a glass of Madeira, the unique wine that has become synonymous with the island. Most restaurants serve Madeira (indeed, many offer diners a complimentary glass). Look also for *vinho da casa,* a local table wine. It's much cheaper than imported ones and generally of high quality. Coral, a light lager, is the local *cerveja* (beer). For a tasty nonalcoholic drink, try *brisa* maracujá, a sparkling passion-fruit soda.

CATEGORY	COST*
$$$$	over €21
$$$	€14–€21
$$	€7–€14
$	under €7

per person for a main course at dinner

Fishing

Madeira and Porto Santo are meccas for those hoping to reel in huge blue marlin, yellowfin tuna, albacore, swordfish, and dorado. The list of gilled gentry inhabiting the surrounding waters also includes big-eye tuna, barracuda, dolphinfish, wahoo, and shark.

Folkloric Traditions

Although many islanders prefer more sophisticated leisure pastimes, Madeira proudly makes the most of its folkloric traditions for visitors. No matter when you visit, there's a good chance you'll see folk dances performed at a restaurant or hotel. Costumed dancers whirl to the music of a small guitarlike instrument called a *machête*. Musicians also shake a colorful pole decorated with tiny folk-dancer dolls that jangle like a tambourine.

Hiking

The island is covered with footpaths that run among peaks and alongside levadas. These canals crisscross the island and often flow through tunnels, bringing valuable water from the mountains to the tiny terraced farms. You can follow the thin cement or dirt paths that run alongside the levadas for hundreds of miles. The footpaths were made so the *levadeiro,* the person tending the levadas, could clear anything that blocked the flow of water. Some date from as far back as the 15th century.

The island has many microclimates and a varied topography. You'll encounter powerful jagged mountains, desertlike valleys, waterfalls, dense forest, and luxuriant hillsides. Every view seems better than the last. One of the most breathtaking is from Madeira's highest peak, 6,106-ft Pico Ruivo. On a clear day you can nearly see from one end of the island to the other. The tourist office has several publications listing hikes of varying length and difficulty.

Lodging

In Funchal your options range from majestic old hotels to quiet *pensões* (pensions). Elsewhere on the island, consider staying in a *pousada* (which literally means "resting place," but which shouldn't be confused with mainland Portugal's government-owned *pousadas,* which are truly inns). At the Pousada do Pico do Arieiro at 6,107 ft, you'll feel as if you're walking on air because sometimes you actually are above the clouds. Several low-key inns and bed-and-breakfasts also dot the island.

Some of the larger Madeiran hotels cater to package-tour operators, who offer relatively low prices and reserve huge blocks of rooms during peak holiday-travel periods. This may be one place where do-it-yourself travelers are better off going through an agency.

CATEGORY	COST*
$$$$	over €275
$$$	€175–€275
$$	€75–€175
$	under €75

For a standard double room, including tax, in high season (off-season rates may be lower).

Wine Tasting

Madeira's wine has been enjoyed for more than 500 years. It has graced the tables of Napoléon, the Russian czars, and even George Washington. In fact, the glasses raised to toast the signing of America's Declaration of Independence were filled with it. And Shakespeare wrote of Falstaff's willingness to trade his soul for "a cup of Madeira and a cold capon."

The fortified wine is served as an aperitif or with dessert, depending on its sweetness. Unlike other wines, Madeira is heated to produce its distinctive mellow flavor—a process that supposedly developed after thirsty sailors sampled the Madeira that had been shipped through equatorial heat and discovered its improved taste. The four varieties, from driest to sweetest, are Sercial, Verdelho, Boal, and Malmsey.

The many famous brands of Madeira include Blandy's, Leacock's, and Cossart Gordon, to name a few. Although all are now produced by the Madeira Wine Company, each brand is blended to maintain its individual characteristics. To learn the history of these wines, see how they're made, and sample a few, you can visit the São Francisco Wine Lodge in Funchal or the Henriques & Henriques Vinhos (Winery) in Câmara de Lobos.

Exploring Madeira

For ease of planning you can split Madeira into five regions: Funchal, the capital; its environs; the eastern side of Madeira; the peaks, gorges, and plateaus of the interior; and the powerful cliffs of the rocky northwest coast. Additionally, there are the neighboring islands of Porto Santo and Ilhas Desertas, although if time is limited, Madeira's pleasures are more than enough.

Great Itineraries

To tour Madeira, begin in Funchal. It's small, and its charm is contagious. Although it can be thronged with tour groups—especially when a large cruise ship arrives for a day, it's not hard to avoid them. To fully appreciate the island, get out—by rental car, taxi, even tour bus if that's the only option—and explore Madeira's greatest asset: nature. The rocky mountains and green hillsides, moors, and valleys can hold their own with those in New Zealand or Scotland. And don't wait until the last day to head inland: plan things so that this floating garden has a few days to invade your psyche with its lushness and drama.

Three days are the minimum for exploring Funchal and its environs, along with some of the interior or the western coast; five days allows for a less hurried and more complete exploration of the island including the northeast; a full week lets you circumnavigate the "big" island and perhaps spend a day on nearby Porto Santo. You should use the old scenic roads as much as possible, and allow plenty of time for driving around. If, however, you're on a tight schedule or must travel at night, take advantage of the fast new roads.

Numbers in the text correspond to numbers in the margin and on the Madeira and Funchal maps.

IF YOU HAVE 3 DAYS

Devote your first day to the flower-bedecked capital city of ▦ **Funchal** ①–⑭. Start day two early, heading for the hills just outside the city. In the morning, visit the nearby Jardim Botânico, on the grounds of an aristocratic plantation, and the village of **Monte** ⑮, home of the unusual snowless sled ride. Next, go west from Funchal toward Pico dos Barcelos, whose view of the city can easily use up a roll of film. Then move on to the coast and a late lunch in or near the fishing village of **Câmara de Lobos** ⑲. Continue to **Cabo Girão** ⑳, with its spectacular views across the island. The terrain changes to forests as you continue along the coast to **Ribeira Brava** ㉑, another lovely seaside town. Turn inland through a rugged canyon and into a vivid green forest. You'll soon come to the mystical, cloud-shrouded peaks of the ▦ **Serra de Água** ㉒. Plan well ahead to overnight at the charming pousada here. On your last day, wake up very early and walk in the mountains. Drive back to Funchal, where you can spend another night or catch a flight to Lisbon or home.

Madeira

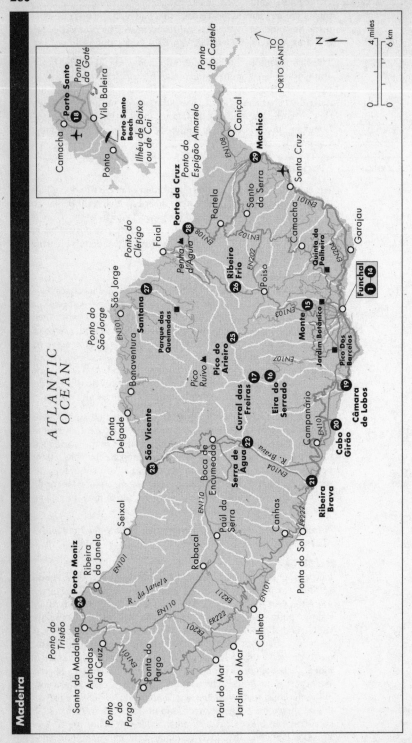

ATLANTIC OCEAN

4 miles
6 km

TO
PORTO SANTO

Porto Santo
Ponta da Gaté
Vila Baleira
Camacha 18
Porto Santo Beach
Ilhéu de Baixo ou de Cai
Ponta

Ponta do Castela

Ponta do Espigão Amarelo
Ponto do Espigão Amarelo

Caniçal
EN108
Machico 29
Santa Cruz

Ponto do Clérigo
Faial
Portela
Porto da Cruz 28
Penha d'Aguia
EN108
Santo da Serra
EN102
Camacha
EN101
Garajau

Ribeiro Frio 26
EN202
Poiso
Quinta da Palheiro
ER204
Funchal 1 14

Ponto do São Jorge
Santana 27
São Jorge
EN101
Parque das Queimadas
Pico do Arieiro 25
Monte 15
EN103
Jardim Botânico
Pico Dos Barcelos

Ponto do São Jorge
Bonaventura
Pico Ruivo
EN107

Ponta Delgada
São Vicente
Curral das Freiras
Eira do Serrado 17 16
Campanário
EN101
Câmara de Lobos 19
Cabo Girão 20

Boca de Encumeada
Serra de Água 22
R. Brava
EN104

São Vicente 23
Rabaçal
Paúl da Serra
EN110
EN210
Canhas
Ribeira Brava 21

Porto Moniz
Ribeira da Janela
Seixal
EN101

Ponto do Tristão
Santa da Madalena
Archadas da Cruz
Porto Moniz 24
R. da Janela
EN110
ER211
Ponta do Sol
Calheta
EN101
ER222

Ponta do Pargo
EN101
Ponta do Pargo
Paúl do Mar
Jardim do Mar

IF YOU HAVE 5 DAYS

Spend your first day getting into the island rhythm by touring ⊡ **Funchal** ①–⑭. In the morning of your second day, explore its environs, and visit the Jardim Botânico and the Quinta do Palheiro (Blandy Gardens). Next, head toward the village of **Monte** ⑮ for a quick look around. Afterward, using a good road map, follow the road to Poiso. Here, turn left and follow the signs to ⊡ **Pico do Arieiro** ㉕. Plan well ahead to overnight in the memorable pousada here, and the next day, head out for an exhilarating hike. If you're up to the challenge, try to reach Pico Ruivo. Later, backtrack to Poiso and head north to **Ribeiro Frio** ㉖. Walk along a levada and take a break at Victor's Bar, near the town's trout hatchery. Next head for **Santana** ㉗ to see the thatch-roof houses for which the village is famous, then west along the stunning coastal road toward ⊡ **São Vicente** ㉓. You can either overnight in São Vicente or push on to ⊡ **Porto Moniz** ㉔.

In Porto Moniz pick up picnic fare, then turn inland—past Santa Madalena—toward Rabaçal, full of waterfalls and quiet pools. Follow the road to Paúl da Serra, where you'll see sheep grazing across the moors. Next, follow the signs to the flower-filled town of Canhas and on to the coastal road back into Funchal. Spend your fourth night and the next day enjoying the capital; then bid the island a fond *até a prossima* (until next time).

IF YOU HAVE 7 DAYS

If you're lucky enough to have a week's time, you might combine the five-day itinerary described above with one of two options: ⊡ **Porto Santo** ⑱, the tiny, fast-developing resort island 50 km (31 mi) northeast of Madeira still provides sun-lovers with a 10-km (6-mi) stretch of golden sand and some scenic walks or drives. The only "don't-miss" sight is the modest Casa de Cristóvão Colombo (Columbus Museum and Home), actually the house of the first governor, who also happened to be the explorer's father-in-law. Alternatively, you could follow the five-day itinerary and spend at least two more days in ⊡ **Funchal** ①–⑭.

When to Tour Madeira

The island's lower elevations are blessed by constant soft, warm breezes, and subtropical vegetation that perfumes the air year-round. Every day seems like spring. The Christmas and New Year's period is the busiest; book far in advance. Summer can also be crowded, especially during August, when the Portuguese take vacations.

FUNCHAL

When colonists arrived in Madeira in July 1419, the valley they settled was a mass of bright yellow fennel, or *funchal* in Portuguese. Today the bucolic fields are gone, and the community that replaced them is the self-governing island's bustling business and political center.

Exploring Funchal

To get to know Funchal best, spend time at the waterfront, market, and city squares—daily haunts of the islanders.

A Good Walk

A good place to start is the **Parque Santa Catarina** ①, which is between the harbor and Avenida do Infante. In spring, the jacaranda trees that line this main road are vivid purple. You can walk into the center of Funchal from any of the big seafront hotels—either on the Avenida do Infante or, edging the ocean, the Avenida Sá Carneiro, which passes

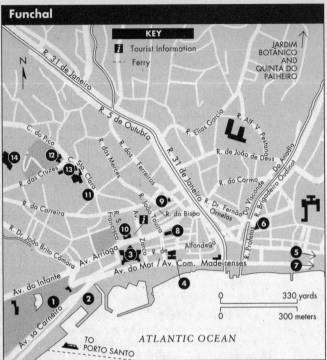

the **Porto do Funchal** ② and brings you to the **Palácio de São Lourenço** ③. One block east of the palace is *parlamento* (parliament), housed in the restored 16th-century **Antiga Alfândega** ④. Continue west along the waterfront to the **Fortaleza de São Tiago** ⑤ and its small museum of contemporary art. Head back the way you came, but at the traffic circle wander up Rua Profetas to the **Mercado dos Lavradores** ⑥, with its pyramids of fruits, flowers, and fish.

If mist and cloud aren't rolling in, take the **Teleférico da Madeira** ⑦ up to Monte. The lower terminal is just a few yards from the Mercado dos Lavradores, on the seafront and near the fort; just follow the flight of the cable cars. Allow for at least a couple of hours at the top to visit the Monte Tropical Gardens or take a toboggan ride—or both. Return to Rua Dr. Fernão Ornelas, which changes into Rua do Aljube before becoming Avenida Arriaga at the 15th-century **Sé** ⑧. From the square in front of the cathedral, walk north on Rua João Tavira and turn right at Rua do Bispo to the **Museu de Arte Sacra** ⑨. When strolling on Avenida Arriaga, stop at the **Adegas de São Francisco** ⑩, if not for a tour then at least to try some Madeira.

From the Adegas de São Francisco head uphill and north three blocks on Rua São Francisco and Calçada Santa Clara to the **Museu Municipal** ⑪. Afterward, climb Calçada Santa Clara to **Museu da Quinta das Cruzes** ⑫, housed in a gracious mansion. The big pink building near the top of Calçada Santa Clara is **Convento de Santa Clara** ⑬. Near the convent, you can't miss the old walls of the **Fortaleza do Pico** ⑭, which dominates the upper part of the city.

On another day, you may want to head just outside the city to the **Quinta do Palheiro** or the **Jardim Botânico,** where the heady scent of the blooms will relax you.

Sights to See

★ ⑩ **Adegas de São Francisco.** The St. Francis Wine Lodge takes its original name from the convent that once stood on this site. Today the operation is owned by the island's famous wine-making Blandy family and is also known as the Old Blandy Wine Lodge. Here you can see how wine barrels are made, visit cellars where the wine is stored, and hear tales about Madeira wine. One legend has it that when the Duke of Clarence was sentenced to death in 1478 for plotting against his brother, King Edward IV, he was given his choice of execution methods. He decided to be drowned in a "vat of Malmsey," a barrel of the drink. There's plenty of time for tasting at the end of the visit. (Note that the production-line wineries are outside town and are closed to visitors.) ⊠ *Av. Arriaga 28,* ☎ *291/740110,* WEB *www.madeirawinecompany.com.* 🎫 *€2.99.* ◎ *Tours: weekdays at 10:30 and 3:30, Sat. at 11. Wine shop: weekdays 9:30–6:30.*

❹ **Antiga Alfândega.** The stately Old Customs House is home to Madeira's parliament (closed to the public). From here deputies govern the island, which is part of Portugal but enjoys greater autonomy than the mainland provinces. The building's original 16th-century Manueline style was given baroque touches during renovations that followed the devastating 18th-century earthquake that almost leveled faraway Lisbon. ⊠ *Av. do Mar and Av. das Comunidades Madeirenses,* ☎ *no phone.*

⑬ **Convento de Santa Clara.** Inside the Santa Clara Convent, the painted wood walls and the ceiling are lined with ceramic tiles, giving the sanctuary an Arabic look. ⊠ *Calçada de Santa Clara,* ☎ *291/742602.* ◎ *Daily 10–noon and 3–5.*

⑭ **Fortaleza do Pico.** The Fort of the Peak was built in the late 1500s to protect the settlement against pirate attacks. One of the worst raids on Funchal was in the 16th century by the pirating nobleman Bertrand de Montluc, who sacked the churches and stole barrels of Madeira. He resold the wine to his noble friends and unwittingly helped spread the reputation of the island's drink. The fortress has been in the possession of the navy since 1933 but you can view parts of it, including a balcony with a fine panorama of the city. ⊠ *Calçada do Pico,* ☎ *no phone.* 🎫 *Free.* ◎ *Daily 9–6.*

❺ **Fortaleza de São Tiago.** The construction of the Fort of St. James was started by 1614, if not earlier, when French corsairs began to threaten Funchal's coveted deep-water harbor. Thanks to continuous use—by British troops when their nation was allied with Portugal against Napoléon, and during the visit of the Portuguese king Dom Carlos in 1901—much of the fort has been preserved. A former governor's house inside it is now the **Museu de Arte Contemporânea**, with changing exhibitions of works from the 1960s and later, most by local artists. ⊠ *Rua do Portão de São Tiago,* ☎ *291/226456.* 🎫 *€2 for exhibitions, free at other times.* ◎ *Mon.–Sat. 10–12:30 and 2:30–5:45.*

OFF THE
BEATEN PATH

JARDIM BOTÂNICO – The Botanical Garden is on the grounds of an old plantation 3 km (2 mi) northeast of Funchal. Its well-labeled plants—including anthuriums, bird-of-paradise flowers, and a large cactus collection—come from four continents. Savor wonderful views of Funchal, and check out the petrified trunk of a 10-million-year-old heather tree. There's also a natural-history museum, an orchid garden with year-round flowers, and a small exotic-birds garden. You can get here on Bus 30, which stops across the street from the market in front of Madeira's Electric Company. To hike up, turn uphill on Rua da Rochina, from Avenida Arriaga, to Caminho do Meio and follow

it for at least 45 minutes. ⌂ *Caminho do Meio,* ☎ *291/211200.*
🎟 *€1.50.* ☉ *Gardens: daily 9–6. Museum: daily 9–1:30.*

★ ⑥ **Mercado dos Lavradores.** In the center patio of the Workers' Market,
women—sometimes in Madeira's native costume of a full, homespun
skirt with yellow, red, and black vertical stripes and an embroidered
white blouse—sell orchids, bird-of-paradise flowers, anthuriums, and
other blooms. The lower-level seafood market displays the day's catch.
Note the rows of fierce-looking espada. Their huge, bulging eyes are
caused by the fatal change in pressure between their deep-water habitat and sea level. ⌂ *Rua Brigadeiro Oudinot.* ☉ *Weekdays 7 AM–8 PM,
Sat. 7 AM–2 PM.*

⑨ **Museu de Arte Sacra.** Funchal's Museum of Sacred Art has Flemish
paintings, polychrome wood statues, and other treasures gathered
from the island's churches. Most of the paintings were commissioned
by the first merchants of Madeira, many of whom came from Brugge,
Belgium. The *Adoration of the Magi* was painted in 1518 for a wealthy
trader from Machico and paid for not in gold, but in sugar. You can
tell how important this commodity was to the island by examining Funchal's coat of arms: it depicts five loaves of sugar in the shape of a cross.
⌂ *Rua do Bispo 21,* ☎ *291/228900.* 🎟 *€2.25.* ☉ *Tues.–Sat. 10–12:30
and 2:30–6. Also open for temporary exhibitions Sun. 10–1 and 2–6.*

NEED A   A good place to stop for a light lunch or afternoon tea is **O Patio** (⌂
BREAK?   Rua da Carreira 43, ☎ 291/227376), which entirely lives up to its
           name—it's a tiled open-air patio. At the same address, Livraria Inglesa,
           Funchal's only English-language bookstore, sells magazines, novels, and
           books about Portugal.

🔆 ⑪ **Museu Municipal.** Animals found on Madeira and in its seas—including a ferocious-looking collection of stuffed sharks—are on display in
the City Museum. Attached is a small aquarium, where you can watch
the graceful movements of an octopus and view a family of sea tur-
tles. ⌂ *Rua Mouraria 31,* ☎ *291/229761.* 🎟 *€1.50.* ☉ *Tues.–Fri. 10–
6, weekends noon–6.*

⑫ **Museu da Quinta das Cruzes.** The building and grounds of this museum are as impressive as its collection of antique furniture. Of special interest are the palanquins—lounge chairs once used to carry the
grand ladies of colonial Madeira around town. Don't miss the small
garden filled with ancient stone columns, window frames, arches, and
tombstone fragments. ⌂ *Calçada do Pico 1,* ☎ *291/740670.* 🎟 *€2.*
☉ *Tues.–Sat. 10–12:30 and 2–5:30, Sun. 10–1.*

❸ **Palácio de São Lourenço.** Built in the 17th century as Madeira's first
fortress, the St. Lawrence Palace is still used as a military headquarters. On occasion its grand rooms are open to visitors (call the palace
or ask at the tourist office for details); at other times its small Museu
Militar (Military Museum) offers a glimpse inside the building. ⌂ *Entrance to Museu Militar on Av. Arriaga.* ☎ *291/202530.* 🎟 *Free.* ☉
Weekdays 9:30–noon and 2–5:30, Sat. 9:30–noon.

❶ **Parque Santa Catarina.** At the top of this park, where flowers bloom
year-round, is a pink mansion called Quinta Vigia, the residence of the
president of Madeira (closed to the public). In the center of the park
rests the tiny Capela de Santa Catarina (St. Catherine's Chapel), built
by Madeira's discoverer, João Gonçalves Zarco, in 1425 and one of
the island's oldest buildings. ⌂ *Between Av. do Infante and Av. Sá
Carneiro, overlooking the harbor.*

NEED A BREAK?	A classic spot to sit back and relax is the **Casa Minas Gerais** (✉ Av. do Infante 2, at Rua João Brito Câmara, ☎ 291/223381). Pick out your pastry from the central bar, and a waiter will bring it to your table with a pot of tea or coffee. The café retains many of its original 1920s fittings and has music to match: in the evening, from Wednesday through Sunday, a jazz band plays.

❷ **Porto do Funchal.** This is where growing numbers of cruise ships moor for one- or two-day visits to the island, and where big container ships— mostly from northern Europe—unload. Walk east on Avenida das Comunidades Madeirenses (known as Avenida do Mar), the seafront boulevard, and enjoy the view.

OFF THE BEATEN PATH	**QUINTA DO PALHEIRO –** Also known as the Blandy Gardens, this 30-acre estate 5 km (3 mi) northeast of Funchal is owned by the Blandy wine family. The formal gardens have flowering perennials. You can stroll the gardens and the grounds, where camellia trees bloom between December and April, but you can't tour the family's house. To get here, head out of town on N101, the road to the airport. At the fork make a left onto N102 and follow the signs toward Camacha. Also, Bus 36 departs weekday mornings at 9:45 from the intersection of Avenida do Mar and Avenida das Comunidades Madeirenses (next to the marina, in front of the Palácio de São Lourenço). It returns at 12:30. ☎ 291/793044. ⊡ €7. ⊙ Weekdays 9:30–noon.

❽ **Sé.** Renowned for its ceiling with intricate geometric designs of inlaid ivory, Funchal's cathedral reveals an Arabic influence throughout. Don't miss the carved choir stalls in the side entrance and in the chancel (they depict the prophets and the apostles), or the tile work at the side entrance and in the belfry. ✉ Av. Arriaga, ☎ no phone. ⊙ Mon.– Sat. 8–11:30 and 5–6:30.

❼ **Teleférico da Madeira.** The sleek, Austrian-engineered, cable-car service has more than 40 cars that travel from Funchal's waterfront up to Monte at 1,804 ft above sea level. The trip takes 15 minutes one way, and there are great views to enjoy as you float silently up and over the city. ✉ Campo Almirante Reis, ☎ 291/780280, WEB www. madeiracablecar.com. ⊡ €8 1-way, €13 round-trip. ⊙ Daily 10–6 (last round-trip 5:30, last uphill trip 5:45).

Dining

$$$$ ★	✕ **Les Faunes.** Named for the series of Picasso lithographs that adorns its walls, Les Faunes is done in a sophisticated blue-gray, with tables on two tiers—guaranteeing stunning views of Funchal. A pianist plays romantic music during your meal. The nouvelle menu changes daily, but expect to find such dishes as artichoke custard with sweet red-pepper sauce, carpaccio of sea bass with caviar, duck breast baked with peaches, and hot passion-fruit soufflé. ✉ Reid's Palace hotel, Estrada Monumental 139, ☎ 291/763001. Reservations essential. Jacket and tie. AE, DC, MC, V. Closed June–Sept. No lunch.
$$–$$$$	✕ **Casa Madeirense.** This restaurant—wedged into a restored house next to Reid's Palace hotel—has lavish tile work, hand-painted murals, and a bar that resembles one of Santana's thatch-roof dwellings. The menu is heavy on fresh seafood and regional dishes (including espada), which the chef likes to dress up with tropical fruits and flambé presentations. ✉ Estrada Monumental 153, ☎ 291/766700. AE, DC, MC, V. Closed Sun.

\$\$–\$\$\$\$ ✕ **Casa Velha.** In the tiled dining room, exuberant floral arrangements, white-lace curtains, and green tablecloths rustle gently in the breeze of ceiling fans. The food is prepared with great care. Start with the cream of seafood soup or the salmon rillettes with shrimp, then move on to the seafood fricassee or lobster Thermidor. Dessert might be apple with kirsch flambé. ⊠ *Rua Imperatriz Dona Amelia 69,* ☎ *291/225749. AE, MC, V.*

\$\$–\$\$\$\$ ✕ **Quinta Palmeira.** Go down the steps beside this 1735 estate to reach the elegant, beautifully lit restaurant (rather than the funky bar and diner at the front). You can sit in the airy, pastel dining room or out on the large terrace. Island specialties and international dishes are served with creative flair. Try espada *com bananas e molho de maracujá* (with a rich banana and passion-fruit sauce) or *filete de carneiro com molho de menta* (grilled lamb fillet with a fresh mint sauce). For dessert, the *cassata de abacate* (homemade avocado ice cream) is a good bet. ⊠ *Av. do Infante 5,* ☎ *291/221814. AE, DC, MC, V.*

\$\$–\$\$\$ ✕ **O Celeiro.** The traditional Portuguese cooking seems right at home
★ in the farmhouse decor. The dining room fills up with businesspeople at lunch and a mix of visitors and locals at dinner. Among the most popular items are the Algarve-style *cataplanas,* seafood stews served in special copper-lidded pots. *Pudim,* a flanlike pudding, makes a soothing dessert. ⊠ *Rua das Aranhas 22,* ☎ *291/230622. AE, DC, MC, V.*

\$\$–\$\$\$ ✕ **A Seta.** It's not fancy, and the parking area is crammed with tour
★ buses, but this restaurant on a hill above Funchal serves some of the island's best espetada. You'll share long narrow tables with other diners while waiters dodge in and out among folk dancers and fado singers. The meat is cooked over a charcoal fire; then the skewers are suspended from wrought-iron hooks at each table. ⊠ *Estrada do Livramento 80,* ☎ *291/743643. AE, DC, MC, V. Closed Wed.*

\$\$ ✕ **Golden Gate Grand Café.** Just steps from the tourist office in the heart of Funchal, this restaurant-café has been open for business on and off since 1814. Sit in the airy interior, capture one of the tables that flank the sidewalk, or—even better—bag a seat on the balcony. You can pop in for coffee, light local dishes, or British-style afternoon tea, or you can settle in for a feast of creative Portuguese and international dishes. Don't miss the delicious desserts such as *sorvete de banana e maracujá* (banana and passion-fruit sorbet). ⊠ *Av. Arriaga 29,* ☎ *291/234383. AE, DC, MC, V.*

\$–\$\$ ✕ **Carochinha.** This deliberately old-fashioned restaurant beside the municipal gardens is an enduring, and to many, an endearing Funchal culinary oddity. Expect such English standards as steaks, liver and onions, as well as such Continental classics as duck à l'orange, beef Stroganoff, and coq au vin. ⊠ *Rua São Francisco 2A,* ☎ *291/223695. AE, DC, MC, V. Closed Sun.*

\$–\$\$ ✕ **Combatentes.** The inexpensive lunch specials at this large, streamlined dining room behind the municipal gardens are popular with Funchal's businesspeople. Big portions of simple Madeiran cooking, such as espada, tuna, and grilled pork chops, are served with milho frito. If you want something lighter, try the *sopa de tomate e cebola com ovo* (tomato and onion soup, garnished with a poached egg). ⊠ *Rua Ivens 1,* ☎ *291/221388. MC, V. Closed Sun.*

\$–\$\$ ✕ **Pizzaria Xaramba.** When young Madeirans want a break from seafood, they head to this tiny restaurant behind a church in the old section of town. The ovens stay hot until 3 AM, and the place is often packed late at night. Individual-size pizzas are prepared behind a long bar while you watch. (Be careful not to confuse this restaurant with Pizzaria Xarambinha—no relation—a few doors away, next to the church). ⊠ *Rua Portão São Tiago 11,* ☎ *291/229785. Reservations not accepted. No credit cards. No lunch.*

Lodging

$$$$ 🏨 **Savoy Hotel.** It may be hard to leave the grounds of the Savoy: everywhere you look there are fresh flowers, and every time you turn around there's yet another concert or cocktail party to attend. Do make the effort to get out and about, though, as this hotel is an easy 10-minute walk from downtown and is a hospitable base for explorations farther afield as well. Beyond lovely gardens is the Royal Savoy Resort, a sister establishment with time-share and hotel accommodations. The two properties share pool, spa, and other facilities. ⊠ *Rua Imperatriz D. Amelia 108/112, 9000-542,* ☎ *291/213000,* 𝖥𝖠𝖷 *291/223103,* 𝖶𝖤𝖡 *www.hotelsavoy.co.pt. 325 rooms, 12 suites. 4 restaurants, 4 bars, 3 cafés, in-room safes, cable TV, minibars, room service, 5 pools (2 indoor), hair salon, hot tub, 2 spas, driving range, miniature golf, putting green, 2 tennis courts, library, shops, business services, meeting rooms, convention center. AE, MC, V. BP, MAP, FAP.*

$$$ 🏨 **Cliff Bay Resort.** This elegant hotel is on a spectacular promontory at the outskirts of town. Its cheerful guest quarters have marble baths with twin sinks. Rooms also take in sweeping views of the Atlantic, the Bay of Funchal, or the property's inviting gardens. ⊠ *Estrada Monumental 147, 9000-100,* ☎ *291/707700,* 𝖥𝖠𝖷 *291/762524,* 𝖶𝖤𝖡 *www. portobay.com. 201 rooms. 3 restaurants, 4 bars, in-room safes, cable TV with movies, room service, 2 pools (1 saltwater pool), hot tub, massage, sauna, spa, golf privileges, tennis court, aerobics, gym, Ping-Pong, squash, children's programs. AE, DC, MC, V. BP, MAP, FAP.*

$$$ 🏨 **Crowne Plaza Resort Madeira.** All of the light, cheerful rooms and suites here have ocean views; suites also have hot tubs. A multitude of perks and amenities ensure that you'll be entertained during your stay. Panoramic elevators take you down to the sea, where can you can sail, splash about in a pedal boat, or arrange to go diving at the PADI dive center. ⊠ *Estrada Monumental 176–177, 9000-100,* ☎ *291/717700,* 𝖥𝖠𝖷 *291/717701,* 𝖶𝖤𝖡 *www.crowneplaza.madeira.com. 276 rooms, 24 suites. 4 restaurants, 3 bars, pub, in-room data ports, in-room safes, cable TV, minibars, no-smoking rooms, room service, 4 pools (2 indoor), hair salon, massage, sauna, spa, steam room, driving range, golf privileges, putting green, 2 tennis courts, aerobics, gym, badminton, basketball, billiards, Ping-Pong, squash, volleyball, beach, dive shop, snorkeling, windsurfing, boating, fishing, recreation room, Internet, children's programs, playground, laundry service, business services, convention center, meeting rooms. AE, MC, V. BP, MAP.*

$$$
★ 🏨 **Reid's Palace.** Since 1891, a mix of royalty and film stars, tycoons and statesmen have frequented Reid's. It's the kind of gracious place where the corridors smell of furniture wax and a jacket and tie are de rigueur for the evening meal—announced by a bellhop who plays a chime—in the Dining Room restaurant. The hotel is on rocky point surrounded by 10 acres of gardens that are full of hibiscus, salvia, and jasmine. The large rooms are extremely comfortable, with pastel bedspreads, fresh linens daily, and wide balconies with sea views. Baths have big showerheads, towel warmers, and Molton Brown toiletries. ⊠ *Estrada Monumental 139, 9000-098,* ☎ *291/717030,* 𝖥𝖠𝖷 *291/717033,* 𝖶𝖤𝖡 *www.reidspalace.com. 130 rooms, 32 suites. 5 restaurants, 3 bars, in-room safes, cable TV, in-room VCRs, minibars, room service, 3 saltwater pools, hair salon, massage, sauna, spa, golf privileges, 2 tennis courts, gym, billiards, dive shop, windsurfing, waterskiing, fishing, recreation room, library, shops, baby-sitting, children's programs. AE, MC, V. BP, MAP, FAP.*

$$–$$$ 🏨 **Pestana Carlton Madeira.** Many guests at this 18-story, beachfront high-rise, 10 minutes on foot from central Funchal, have come every season since the hotel opened in 1971. They're no doubt attracted by the friendly service, the range of sports and health facilities, and the large guest rooms with pastel fabrics and tile baths as well as terraces overlooking ocean or mountains. ⊠ *Largo António Nobre 9004–531,* ☏ *291/239500,* FAX *291/223377,* WEB *www.pestana.com. 373 rooms. 3 restaurants, 3 bars, pub, in-room safes, cable TV, room service, 2 saltwater pools, indoor pool, hot tub, sauna, spa, steam room, golf privileges, miniature golf, tennis court, gym, health club, dive shop, windsurfing, dance club, nightclub, meeting rooms. AE, DC, MC, V. BP, MAP, FAP.*

$$-$$$ ⊞ **Pestana Carlton Park Hotel.** Part of a complex designed by Oscar Niemeyer, the architect of Brasília (capital of Brazil), this drab concrete hotel sits next to what looks like a nuclear reactor but is actually the Casino da Madeira. Inside, though, the hotel is pleasant: public rooms have lots of glass and mirrors and are flooded with light from floor-to-ceiling windows that overlook gardens and the sea. Guest rooms are bright and airy, and the restaurant is popular for its buffet dinner and folklore performances. ⊠ *Quinta da Vigia 67, 9000-513,* ☏ *291/ 209100,* FAX *291/232076,* WEB *www.pestana.com. 373 rooms. 2 restaurants, 3 bars, coffee shop, cable TV, room service, saltwater pool, hot tub, sauna, tennis court, gym, health club, billiards, casino, nightclub, convention center, meeting rooms. AE, DC, MC, V. BP, MAP, FAP.*

$$ ⊞ **Eden Mar.** This seven-story block won't win any exterior beauty contests, nor is it overloaded with sports and leisure facilities, but it is one of several hotels in Funchal that offer good-value packages. It's a favorite with families, who settle in for long stays and appreciate the kitchenettes in each unit. The lobby is full of stark, white marble, but rooms have homey floral-print fabrics, cheerful tiled bathrooms, and sea views. ⊠ *Rua do Gorgulho 2, 9004-537,* ☏ *291/709700,* FAX *291/761966,* WEB *www.edenmar.com. 70 suites, 37 studios. Restaurant, bar, coffee shop, in-room data ports, in-room safes, cable TV, kitchenettes, 2 pools (1 indoor), saltwater pool, hot tub, massage, sauna, gym, squash, Internet, meeting room. AE, DC, MC, V. BP, MAP.*

$$ ⊞ **Estrelicia.** Named for Madeira's bird-of-paradise flower, this Best Western accommodation is the topmost of three high-rise towers built uphill from the hotel strip. Perhaps because of its somewhat inconvenient location, the hotel is an especially good value. Large, carpeted guest rooms have gold bedspreads and brown leather chairs. ⊠ *Caminho Velho da Ajuda, 9000–113,* ☏ *291/706600,* FAX *291/764859,* WEB *www.dorisol.pt. 145 rooms. Restaurant, bar, piano bar, in-room safes, cable TV, minibars, saltwater pool, tennis court, dance club. AE, MC, V. BP, MAP, FAP.*

$$ ⊞ **Ocean Park Resort Hotel.** At the end of Funchal's seafront promenade, this sleek hotel is about a 25-minute walk from town. All the well-equipped rooms have sea-view balconies; suites have hot tubs. The heated indoor pool is excellent. Lovers of Asian food might like to note the resort has the island's only Japanese restaurant. ⊠ *Estrada Monumental, 9000-100,* ☏ *291/702000,* FAX *291/702020,* WEB *www.dorisol. pt. 260 rooms, 57 suites. 3 restaurants, 3 bars, tea shop, in-room safes, cable TV, no-smoking floor, room service, 2 pools (1 indoor), spa, health club, squash, nightclub, recreation room, children's programs, convention center. AE, MC, V. BP, MAP, FAP.*

$$ ⊞ **Quinta da Bela Vista.** The hospitable staff at this hotel, in the hills
★ above Funchal and formerly the estate of Dr. Roberto Monteiro, makes you feel you're visiting a well-to-do friend. The original house contains a sophisticated restaurant and four guest rooms. Other rooms are in two buildings, constructed in the same gracious style as the main house. Guest quarters have French doors that open onto gardens and are filled with mahogany furniture—including four-poster beds—and

beautifully framed pastoral prints. ⊠ *Caminho do Avista Navios 4, 9000-129,* ☎ *291/706400,* FAX *291/706411,* WEB *www.qbvista.pt. 72 rooms. 2 restaurants, bar, in-room data ports, in-room safes, cable TV, room service, pool, hot tub, sauna, golf privileges, tennis court, gym, billiards, library. AE, DC, MC, V. BP, MAP, FAP.*

$$ 🏨 **Quinta da Penha de França.** In an unbeatable location—just above Funchal Harbor—this place pleases those who prefer their resorts casual rather than glitzy. The white, four-story Portuguese manor house with green shutters is surrounded by gardens and a sun-drenched pool. Every room is slightly different, and furnishings border on the antique. There's a more modern seaside wing, about a five-minute walk from the main house, with large terraces overlooking the sea, but its rooms aren't as charming. ⊠ *Rua Imperatriz Dona Amélia 85, 9000-014,* ☎ *291/204650,* FAX *291/229261,* WEB *www.hotelquintapenhafranca.com. 76 rooms. Restaurant, bar, in-room safes, cable TV, minibars, saltwater pool, billiards; no air-conditioning in some rooms. AE, MC, V. BP, MAP.*

$ 🏨 **Hotel Madeira.** This hotel on a quiet street in central Funchal has a marble lobby and tiny rooftop pool. Rooms are basic, but each is carpeted and has a comfortable bed as well as a balcony with, in some instances, a view of the municipal gardens. ⊠ *Rua Ivens 21, 9000-046,* ☎ *291/230071,* FAX *291/229071. 53 rooms. Restaurant, bar, coffee shop, lounge, cable TV, pool, billiards, meeting rooms. AE, MC, V. BP, MAP.*

Nightlife and the Arts

Nightlife

BARS

If you prefer to while away the night in the company of trendsetters, try **Amarras Café** (⊠ Rua das Murças, ☎ 291/241930), a funky, kitsch-filled space. Curl up on one of the cushy couches with a Coral (lager) or two. At **Dó Fá Sol** (⊠ Galerias São Lourenço, next to Palácio de São Lourenço, ☎ 291/241464), live bands (jazz, rock, blues) play regularly, and the crowds often spill out onto the terrace. Nothing much happens here until quite late—it's best to arrive at around 11 PM. Wednesday through Saturday jazz bands play at **Jam** (⊠ Av. Sá Carneiro 9, ☎ 291/234800), a classy lounge. Shows start at 11 PM.

CABARET

The somewhat informal **O Fugitivo Pub** (⊠ Rua Imperatriz D Amélia 68, ☎ 291/222003) has Brazilian-style cabaret. The glitziest of all the hotel floor shows takes place every weekend at the **Pestana Carlton Park Hotel** (⊠ Quinta da Vigia 67, ☎ 291/233111), where the theme is usually Brazilian.

CASINO

Gamblers can try their luck in the **Casino da Madeira** (⊠ Av. do Infante, ☎ 291/209100), which is open Sunday–Thursday 3 PM–3 AM, Friday–Saturday 4 PM–4 AM. Its unusual building was designed by architect Oscar Niemeyer. The entrance fee is at €5, and you must be at least 18 years old; dress is smart casual (no sports shoes allowed).

DANCE CLUBS

At **Copacabana** (⊠ Av. do Infante, ☎ 291/233111), beneath the Casino da Madeira, there's often live Brazilian music. A lively, over-30 crowd dances to hits from the '70s and '80s—as well as some contemporary tunes—at **O Farol** (⊠ Largo António Nobre, ☎ 291/231031) in the Pestana Carlton Madeira hotel. Drum, bass, hip-hop, trance—or whichever type of music is currently in vogue—is on tap at **Vespas** (⊠ Av. Sá Carneiro 60, ☎ 291/231202), a warehouse club next to the docks.

FADO

You'll find good food as well as tear-jerking fado and vibrant Brazilian at **Arsénios** (⊠ Rua de Santa Maria 169, ☎ 291/224007). Reservations are a good idea. **Marcelino Pão y Vinho** (⊠ Travessa da Torre 22-A, ☎ 291/230834) attracts fado aficionados as well as the just plain curious, who come to hear Portugal's soulful national music played each night from 9:30 until about 2 AM.

The Arts

The **Teatro Municipal Baltazar Diaz** (⊠ Av. Arriaga, ☎ 291/220416) offers occasional concerts and plays. The local newspaper carries listings, but the easiest way to find out the schedule is to check posters outside the theater. You can buy tickets at the box office.

Outdoor Activities and Sports

Fishing

You can arrange fishing excursions at the Funchal Harbor through **Turipesca** (☎ 291/231063).

Golf

The 18-hole course at **Palheiro Golf** (⊠ São Gonçalo, ☎ 291/792116) is in a pine forest at the edge of Blandy Gardens. Greens fees are €58. The clubhouse restaurant has fine town views. The area's oldest course is the 27-hole, Robert Trent Jones, Jr.–designed **Santo da Serra Golfe** (⊠ Hwy. N102, ☎ 291/552345), near the airport in Santo da Serra. Greens fees are €28–€42.

Scuba Diving

Madeira is too far north for colorful tropical fish, but divers enjoy the clear, still seas of summer and report lots of interesting marine life and coral formations. The diving center at the **Pestana Carlton Madeira** (⊠ Largo António Nobre, ☎ 291/239500) hotel rents scuba gear to nonguests.

Shopping

In addition to wine, look for baskets, wicker items, embroidered linens, and tropical flowers. In the village of Camacha, about 10 km (6 mi) northeast of Funchal, there's a large cooperative shop on the main square that sells every imaginable type of basket as well as some wicker furniture. Most of the work is done at home; on rural roads it's common to see men carrying large bundles of willow branches to be used for basketry.

Thousands of local women spend their days stitching intricate floral patterns on organdy, Irish linen, cambric, and French silks. Their handiwork decorates tablecloths, place mats, and napkins, all of which are expensive (and almost all need ironing). When buying embroidery, make sure it has a lead seal attached, certifying it was made on the island and not imported.

Tropical flowers are available boxed from any florist for shipping home. (It's legal to bring flowers into the United States from Madeira as long as they're inspected at the U.S. airport upon arrival.) Flower stands in the market and behind the church in Funchal are good value and, like most island shops that deal with visitors, pack their bouquets in special boxes to withstand trips in luggage holds.

Despite its unpromising name, the **Casa do Turista** (⊠ José S. Ribeiro 2, on the corner with the seafront, ☎ 291/224907) sells museum-quality Madeiran crafts of all types. Prices are reasonable, if not the cheapest in town.

Baskets

Although you'll find baskets and other wicker items all over Funchal, **Sousa & Gonçalves** (⊠ Rua do Castanheiro, ☎ 291/223626) is one of the largest manufacturers and exporters.

Clothing

Globe Line (⊠ Av. Arriaga 43, ☎ 291/229551) has dressy women's clothes at moderate prices. **Rodier** (⊠ Rua das Pretas 23, ☎ 291/228601), the upscale French chain, is a good place to go if you've forgotten your designer jeans or need a casual-chic outfit.

Flowers

The **Quinta da Boa Visita** (⊠ Rua Lombo da Boa Vista, ☎ 291/220468), on the outskirts of town, sells orchid seedlings, orchids, and other exotic flowers.

Needlework

Needlepoint and tapestry making were introduced to Madeira in the early part of this century by a German family, and you can visit their factory, **Kiekeben Tapestries** (⊠ Rua da Carreira 194, ☎ 291/222073). To buy pieces, stop by the shop, **Bazar Maria Kiekeben** (⊠ Av. do Infante 2, ☎ 291/227857), which also has a branch in Tampa, Florida.

One of the most popular embroidery shops is **Patricio & Gouveia** (⊠ Rua do Visconde de Anadia 33, ☎ 291/220801), where you can visit the upstairs workshop and see the white-uniformed employees stencil patterns and check production; the actual embroidery is done by an army of women in their homes.

SIDE TRIPS FROM FUNCHAL

Monte

★ ☕ ⑮ *6 km (4 mi) northeast of Funchal.*

The village of Monte is home of one of Madeira's oddest attractions: the snowless sled ride. The sleds were first created to carry supplies from Monte to Funchal; later, passenger sleighs hauled as many as 10 people at a time and required six drivers. Nowadays the rides are just for fun.

Drivers dressed in white and wearing goatskin boots with soles made of rubber tires line up on the street by the Nossa Senhora do Monte church. The sleds, which have cushioned seats, look like big wicker baskets; their wooden runners are greased with lard. Two drivers run alongside the sled, controlling it with ropes as it races downhill on a 20-minute trip back to Funchal. If the sled starts going too fast, the drivers jump on the back to slow it down. (At one time, slippery cobblestones lined the hill, making the trip even faster than it is today.) A ride costs €9 per person with a minimum of two riders.

To drive up to Monte from Funchal, take Rua 31 de Janeiro. You can also hop a taxi or take Bus 20 or 21. But a ride up in a cable car on the Teleférico da Madeira seems the best complement to the singular trip back down by sled.

The **Monte Palace Tropical Gardens** has indigenous flora as well as plants from all over the world. The Monte Palace was a grand hotel from 1897 until 1943, but, with the death of the last owner, it went out of business and the building and grounds were neglected for more than 40 years. In 1987 millionaire entrepreneur José Manuel Rodrigues Berardo bought the property and transformed it into this garden. Antique statues, windows, niches, and other architectural artifacts dot the grounds, tiled panels recall the adventures of the Portuguese explorers, Asian pagodas and gateways lend touches of the exotic, and cannons pour their salvos of water from a stone galleon in a lake. All this and wonderful views down to Funchal, too. ⊠ *Caminho do Monte 174,* ☎ *291/ 782339.* ▨ *€7.50.* ⊘ *Mon.–Sat. 9–6.*

Standing tall at the highest point in Monte is the white-stucco church of **Nossa Senhora do Monte** (Our Lady of the Mountain). The tiny statue above the altar was found by a shepherdess in the nearby town of Terreira da Luta in the 15th century and has become the patron saint of Madeira. The church also contains the tomb of Emperor Charles I of Austria, the last Hapsburg monarch. He came to Madeira hoping that its more temperate climate would help him recover from tuberculosis, but he succumbed to the disease and died on the island in 1922. The church is open daily 8–6.

NEED A BREAK?	If you need refreshment before sledding back to Funchal, stop at the **Bar Alecrim,** just up the hill to the right of Nossa Senhora do Monte. The friendly owner makes a mean *poncha,* the island specialty drink of cane spirits, honey, and lemon juice. The food is also very good here. Notice the old photos of sleds and drivers. Not much has changed over the years.

Eira do Serrado

🔞 *16 km (10 mi) northwest of Funchal.*

The *miradouro* (viewpoint) at Eira do Serrado overlooks the Grande Curral—the crater of a long-extinct volcano in the center of the island, sometimes referred to as Madeira's belly button. From here, Pico Ruivo and the craggy central summits look like a granite city. Island legend says the peaks are the castle fortress of a virgin princess, who can be seen sleeping peacefully in the *rocha da cara* (rock face). It's said that she wanted to live in the sky like the clouds and the moon, and was so unhappy at being earthbound that her father—the volcano god—caused an earthquake that pushed the rocky cliffs high into the sky so she could live near the heavens. To get here from Funchal head west on Rua Dr. João Brito Câmara, which turns into N101, and head for the miradouro at Pico dos Barcelos.

Curral das Freiras

🔞 *6 km (4 mi) north of Eira do Serrado.*

Along the N107 north from Eira do Serrado, you'll pass through a series of switchbacks and two tunnels that lead down to the village of Curral das Freiras (Nuns' Shelter). The sisters of the Convent of Santa Clara took refuge here from bands of lonely, marauding pirates. Nearly the geographic center of Madeira, the valley sits in the middle of a circle of extinct volcanoes that long ago pushed the island up from the bottom of the sea.

Porto Santo

🔞 *50 km (31 mi) northeast of Madeira.*

Beachcombers have long loved the tiny, dry island of Porto Santo, as its golden beach runs along the entire south coast. The islet is still a getaway destination, though development projects are underway that will likely change that.

If you decide to come by boat, the 2½-hour ferry ride from Funchal ends in **Vila Baleira.** You'll find cobblestone streets, whitewashed buildings, and a park containing an idealized statue of Christopher Columbus. Before gaining fame and his place in history, he married Isabela Moniz, daughter of Bartolomeu Perestrelo, the first governor of the island, in 1479. She died not long after, at the time of the birth of their son.

The **Casa de Cristóvão Colombo** (Columbus Museum and Home) is in the old governor's house. Inside, lithographs illustrate the life of Columbus, and there are copies of 15 portraits of the discoverer, which prove nobody really knows what he looked like. Ask to see the restored kitchen and bedroom in the upper part of the house. ⊠ *Rua Cristóvão Colombo 12,* ☎ *291/983405.* 🎟 *Free.* ☉ *Tues.–Fri. 10–6, weekends 10–1.*

One of your first stops on Porto Santo should be at the **Portela** viewpoint, which overlooks the harbor, the town, and the long ribbon of beach. Move on to Serra de Foca, where a track passes old salt flats before winding down to a rocky beach popular with divers. As you continue around the island, you may have to dodge goats grazing along the edges of the road.

Pico do Castelo is a favorite picnic spot, named for the castle that once stood here to protect the town from pirates. Only four cannons remain. The young pine trees planted on the slopes will never grow taller than 9 ft so the view won't be obstructed. From here it's an easy walk to Pico do Facho (1,552 ft), the island's highest point.

The **Fonte da Areia** (Spring in the Sand) flows out of a sandstone cliff. Women came here to do their washing before water began to be piped into town. As you head to the southern tip of the island, you'll pass several windmills in disrepair that were once used for grinding wheat.

Pico das Flores—a lookout at the end of a bumpy ride—offers fine views of Madeira and the rocky, uninhabited islet called Ilhéu de Baixo. On the road that runs along the beach, encroaching development becomes apparent: you'll see a handful of high-rise apartment blocks—if not more by the time you arrive.

Dining and Lodging

$$ ✕ **Arsénios.** Red-and-white-check tablecloths are your clue that this is the place for pizza, spaghetti, and lasagna. Portuguese specialties are also served in the rustic dining room. ⊠ *Av. Dr. Manuel Pestana Jr., Vila Baleira,* ☎ *291/984348. AE, DC, MC, V.*

$$ ✕ **Baiana.** A covered patio serves as a combination sidewalk café and town meeting place, as just about everybody wanders by in the morning for coffee. Baiana also serves sandwiches, *feijoada* (bean stew), and carne de vinhos e alhos. ⊠ *Rua Dr. Nuno S. Teixeira, Vila Baleira,* ☎ *291/984649. AE, MC, V.*

$$ ✕ **Gazela.** Not far from the Campo de Cima Airport, this large, modern house is where islanders go for Sunday lunch or to celebrate special occasions. The menu is basic Madeiran—espada, espetada, and a seafood soup. ⊠ *Campo de Cima,* ☎ *291/984425. MC, V.*

$$ ✕ **Pôr do Sol.** This fish restaurant is at the far end of the beach, near Ponta da Calheta. Just 24 tables fill the simple dining room slung with fishing nets. You can also dine on a sun terrace. There's a free shuttle to and from town. ⊠ *Ponta da Calheta,* ☎ *291/984380. Reservations not accepted. AE, DC, MC, V.*

$$ ✕ **Teodorico.** In this farmhouse restaurant, authentic espetada is *the* dish (it is, in fact, the *only* dish), best accompanied by carafes of local dry red wine and *pão de caco,* the local bread. You can sit at outdoor tables made from tree stumps or in a tiny tiled dining room with a wood-

burning oven. ⊠ *Sera de Fora*, ☎ *291/982257. No credit cards. No lunch.*

$$ 🏨 **Hotel Porto Santo.** On the beach about a 15-minute walk from town,
★ this hotel is a beachcomber's dream—at least until more development comes. It's like a country club, with sports activities, a library-lounge, and rooms overlooking the interior instead of the shore. The hotel is often heavily booked throughout August, but in spring and fall you may have the place to yourself. ⊠ *Campo de Baixo, 9400–015,* ☎ *291/ 980140,* 🖷 *291/980149,* 🌐 *www.qbvista.pt. 100 rooms. Restaurant, 2 bars, in-room safes, saltwater pool, miniature golf, tennis court, gym, Ping-Pong, beach, bicycles, library. AE, DC, MC, V. BP, MAP, FAP.*

$$ 🏨 **Praia Dourada.** This comfortable, modern hotel in the middle of the village is a five-minute walk from the beach and is popular with bud-get-minded German and Portuguese travelers. The corridors are dark, but the carpeted rooms are bright, and there's a small pool with a sun-deck. ⊠ *Rua D. Estevão D'Alencastre, Vila Baleira 9400–161,* ☎ *291/ 982315,* 🖷 *291/982489. 108 rooms. Bar, cable TV, saltwater pool, meeting room; no air-conditioning. AE, DC, MC, V. BP, MAP, FAP.*

$$ 🏨 **Torre Praia Suite Hotel.** Right on the beach, a five-minute walk from the center of town, this simple two-story hotel was built around an old watchtower that's now the restaurant. All rooms have kitchenettes, and the hotel has all the amenities you need for a relaxing vacation in the sun. ⊠ *Rua Goulart Medeiros, Vila Baleira 9400–164,* ☎ *291/ 985292,* 🖷 *291/982487. 67 suites. Restaurant, bar, coffee shop, in-room safes, cable TV, kitchenettes, minibars, pool, hot tub, sauna, aer-obics, gym, squash, beach, Internet. BP, MAP, FAP.*

Outdoor Activities and Sports

Camping

On Madeira there are really no organized campgrounds, but on Porto Santo **Parque Porto** (☎ 291/982361 to Porto Santo Tourist Office) is a stretch of beach just waiting—thus far—for you to unroll your sleep-ing bag and pitch a tent.

Scuba Diving

For diving excursions off Porto Santo contact **The Dive Center** (⊠ Naval Clube de Porto Santo, Vila Baleira, ☎ 291/983259).

WESTERN MADEIRA

The western region is the greenest and lushest part of Madeira: in some places you can see a dozen waterfalls spilling into a cool pine forest. On the dramatic north coast, a narrow highway clings to the cliff face.

Câmara de Lobos

⑲ *20 km (12 mi) west of Funchal.*

On coastal route N101, you'll pass many banana plantations on the way to Câmara de Lobos—a fishing village made famous by Winston Churchill, who came here (in a borrowed Rolls-Royce equipped with a bar) to paint pictures of the multicolored boats and the fishermen's tiny homes during a stay at Reid's Hotel in 1950. A plaque marks the spot where he set up his easel. Although the coast here is changing as more and more people commute to jobs in Funchal, the boats are still pulled up onto the rocky beach during the day. Women still occasion-ally wash clothes in public fountains, while children run and play in the narrow streets and grizzled old fishermen stand around chatting. The promenade that protrudes from the main plaza offers magnificent views west to Cabo Girão.

If you're interested in sampling Madeira wine, visit the **Henriques & Henriques Vinhos,** a winery very close to Câmara de Lobos's promenade. You'll be made to feel right at home during a tour of a facility that combines state-of-the-art technology with down-home hospitality. And, yes, the bottles are for sale. ✉ *Sitio de Belém,* ☎ *291/941551.* 🎫 *Free.* ☉ *Weekdays 9–1 and 2:30–5:30.*

Dining and Lodging

$–$$$ ✕ **Coral Bar.** Just behind the cathedral and up the hill from the port, this welcoming restaurant has pleasant tables on the plaza and a simple rooftop terrace, with a great view of Cabo Girão and its dramatic cliffs. The day's catch is unloaded about a block away and served in big earthenware bowls. Try the delicious *peixe mista* (a combination of grilled fish, squid, and prawns) or the espada with fried bananas. ✉ *Largo República 2,* ☎ *291/942469. AE, DC, MC, V.*

$$ ✕⊞ **Estalagem Quinta do Estreito.** This onetime estate house is the perfect base from which to explore the Levada do Norte, one of Madeira's most popular walking trails. The views from here—across fields and down to the sea—are superb. Oak is lavishly used throughout the inn. Rooms have balconies and marble baths as well as such thoughtful touches as heated towel racks and a welcoming bottle of wine and a Madeira cake. Stairs lead up to a tower library that invites you to linger. The Bacchus Restaurant ($$–$$$), which serves nouvelle Madeira cuisine, may be reason enough for a visit. ✉ *Rua José Joaquim da Costa, 9325-034,* ☎ *291/910530,* 𝔽𝔸𝕏 *291/910549,* 𝕎𝔼𝔹 *www.charminghotelsmadeira. com. 48 rooms. 2 restaurants, 2 bars, in-room safes, cable TV with movies, no-smoking rooms, room service, pool, hot tub, sauna, Turkish bath, exercise equipment, library, Internet, dry cleaning, laundry service, meeting room. MC, V. BP, MAP.*

Cabo Girão

⓴ *16 km (10 mi) west of Câmara de Lobos.*

At 1,900 ft, Cabo Girão is on one of the highest sea cliffs in the world. From here you can see ribbons of terraces carved out of even the steepest slopes and farmers daringly cultivating grapes or garden vegetables. Neither machines nor animals are used on Madeiran farms because the plots are so small and difficult to reach. Not long ago, farmers blew into conch shells as a means of communication with neighbors across the deep ravines.

Ribeira Brava

㉑ *14 km (9 mi) west of Cabo Girão.*

This pleasant village, with a pebbly beach and bustling seafront fruit market, was founded in 1440 at the mouth of the Ribeira Brava (meaning "wide river"); hence the name. It's one of the island's sunniest spots. Only a single tower remains of the 17th-century **Forte de São Bento,** built to protect the Ribeira Brava's citizens from pirates. It now houses the local tourist office.

Serra de Água

㉒ *7 km (4 mi) north of Ribeira Brava.*

North from Ribeira Brava the N104 snakes through a sheer-sided canyon. In every direction you can see high waterfalls tumbling down canyon walls and into a pine forest. Eventually you'll come to Serra de Água, an ideal starting point for a trek into Madeira's interior. Even if you don't plan to hike, consider spending the night here at the stone pousada, surrounded by moss-green rocks, ferns, and more waterfalls.

Dining and Lodging

$$ ✕🏨 **Pousada dos Vinháticos.** Guests rooms at this tiny stone lodge on the edge of a pine forest are inviting in shades of blue, green, and orange; some quarters are in log cabins. Do bring a good book in case fog weaves its otherworldly spell, forcing you to forego your hike. Madeira specialties are featured in the restaurant ($–$$), which has an outdoor terrace where you might feel truly part of the mountain scenery. ✉ *Hwy. N104, 9350,* ☎ *291/952344 or 291/765658,* ℻ *291/952140,* 🌐 *www.dorisol.pt. 21 rooms. Restaurant, cable TV, bar; no air-conditioning. AE, MC, V. BP.*

En Route   From Serra de Água the road climbs north for 6 km (4 mi) to **Boca de Encumeada** (Mouth of the Heights). There are several trailheads here as well as good views of both the north and south coasts.

São Vicente

㉓   *16 km (10 mi) northwest of Serra de Água.*

At the town of São Vicente, the road joins the one-lane north-coast highway that's chiseled out of the cliff face and is said to be one of the most expensive road projects, per mile, ever undertaken. In the early 19th century, workers in baskets were suspended by rope so they could carve out ledges and tunnels along the planned route. Proceed with caution and make sure to sound your horn when going around blind curves. Large tour buses constantly use this narrow road; if you happen to meet one, you may be forced to back up to a turnout.

Lodging

$ 🏨 **Estalagem do Mar.** All the rooms in this basic inn are done in sea green and white, a color scheme that complements the ocean views. The sparkling white-tile bathrooms are a comfortable place to freshen up after a day of exploring the area. ✉ *Fajã da Areia, 9240–2210,* ☎ *291/840010,* ℻ *291/840019. 91 rooms, 8 suites. Restaurant, 2 bars, cable TV, 2 pools (1 indoor), hot tub, sauna, tennis court, gym, billiards. AE, DC, MC, V. BP, MAP.*

En Route   As you wind west along the coast, there are a number of waterfalls ahead: at one point the road passes behind a falls, and there's another delightful cascade right onto the road, so you have to drive through it. Stop at one of the viewpoints and notice the windbreaks—made of thick mats of purple heather—that protect the terraced vineyards such as the one in the pretty village of Seixal.

Porto Moniz

㉔   *16 km (10 mi) west of São Vicente.*

Porto Moniz, with its natural pools formed by ancient lava, is the destination of nearly all visitors taking full-day trips in Madeira. That said, there's not much to do here except splash around the pools (there are changing facilities), eat, and sunbathe: it's getting here that's the fun. The island's northernmost village was a whaling station in the 19th-century. Thanks to modern development, however, little remains of its old houses and twisting cobblestone streets.

Dining and Lodging

$ ✕🏨 **Residencial Orca.** Guest rooms here are tidy and pleasant though unremarkable unless you get one by the sea; if so, your large, tiled terrace will overlook the lava-walled pool and the blue-green ocean beyond. The Orca Restaurant ($–$$$), with equally good views, serves espada prepared in every way imaginable. Try it fried with orange, banana, kiwi, or passion fruit. ⊠ *Sitio das Poças, 9270–095,* ☎ *291/ 850000,* ℻ *291/850019. 12 rooms. Restaurant, cable TV, bar; no airconditioning. AE, MC, V. BP, MAP.*

En Route As you drive along the winding uphill road out of Porto Moniz to the viewpoint near Santa Madalena, look back and see the patterns made by the scrub windbreaks. At the fork, turn left on N110, a road that crosses through Madeira's wildest area, providing a unique perspective of both sides of the island. If you have time, take the hair-raising lane to **Rabaçal,** a remote trailhead 22 km (14 mi) southeast of Porto Moniz. From here trails fans out in all directions. Madeirans love to come here to picnic alongside the cascades (bring food with you) or walk along a levada.

Past Rabaçal, the road heads into a moorland called **Paúl da Serra** (Desert Plain), where sheep and cattle graze and seagulls spiral overhead. This is the closest thing to flatland in Madeira, and its scrubby landscape looks out of place. From Paúl da Serra, you can turn right on N209 and follow signs south to the village of **Canhas.** The twisting road passes more terraced farms and, in 20 km (12 mi), joins the southern coastal road N101, which runs to Funchal. Or you can take the route to Boca de Encumeada and rejoin the main road (the N104).

CENTRAL PEAKS AND THE VILLAGE OF SANTANA

The barren peaks of central Madeira offer spectacular views and great hikes. This part of the island includes the much-photographed village of Santana, with its thatch-roof A-frame houses.

Pico do Arieiro

★ ㉕ *7 km (4½ mi) northwest of Poiso, 30 km (19 mi) northeast of Funchal.*

Pico do Arieiro, at 5,963 ft, is Madeira's second-highest mountain. On your way here, you'll travel over a barren plain above the tree line: watch for errant sheep and goats wandering across the pavement on their way to graze stubbly gorse and bilberry. Stop in the parking lot of the pousada and make the short climb to the lookout, where you can scan the rocky central peaks. There are often views of the clouds (below unless you're in them), and to the southeast is the Curral das Freiras valley—literally, Corral of the Sisters, so-named after the Nuns of the Santa Clara convent who fled Funchal in 1565 to escape pirate raids. It's also known as the Grande Curral (Great Corral). Look in the other direction and try to spot the huge Penha de Aguia (Eagle Rock), a giant monolith on the north coast. The trail from the lookout that crosses the narrow ridge leads to Pico Ruivo (6,104 ft), the island's highest point. You don't need to be an expert to make this three-hour trek, but you will need good boots, warm clothing, plenty of water, and a good head for heights. And don't forget to arrange a lift back when you reach the other end—unless you want another three-hour walk, that is.

Dining and Lodging

$$ ✕▦ **Pousada do Pico do Arieiro.** The air can be chilly high above the
★   tree line, so there's often an inviting fire blazing in the bar of this pousada. The exterior may be unprepossessing, but inside you'll find cozy, chintz-adorned rooms with balconies. Hiking, playing chess, reading, and gazing out at the mountains are the main activities here. On clear

days, the views from the large picture windows in the dining room ($$–
$$$) are spectacular. The traditional island menu often includes deli-
cious (and warming) soups. ⊠ *Pico do Arieiro (Funchal 9000),* ☏ *291/
230110 or 291/702030,* FAX *291/228611,* WEB *www.dorisol.pt. 21 rooms.
Restaurant, bar, coffee shop, cable TV. AE, MC, V. BP, MAP, FAP.*

Ribeiro Frio

★ ㉖ *11 km (7 mi) north of Poiso.*

The landscape grows more lush on the northern side of the island, and
the road is full of waterfalls. At the village of Ribeiro Frio, there's a
trout hatchery and, next to Victor's Bar, a garden that shows off the
variety of the indigenous flora. Ribeira Brava is also the starting point
for two popular levada walks. The first is one of the island's easiest
and prettiest, taking around 40 minutes round-trip. At the lookout of
Balcões (meaning "balconies") jagged peaks tower behind you, and there
are views of a sleepy valley dotted with minuscule houses. A longer,
12-km (7-mi) hike leads along a levada to Portela. If you attempt this
it should take three to four hours. Arrange for a taxi back.

Dining

$$ ✕ **Victor's Bar.** After your hike, stop at this family-owned mountain
restaurant for afternoon tea and, some would say, the island's best bolo
de mel. Full meals, including trout prepared many ways, are served here,
too. Inside the rustic wood-and-glass building are a couple of welcoming
fireplaces. The friendly owner, Victor Reinecke, is a font of island
knowledge and can advise you on how to find Madeira's most remote
and beautiful corners. ⊠ *N103,* ☏ *291/575898. AE, DC, MC, V.*

En Route Continue north from Ribeiro Frio on N101 and follow signs to **Faial,**
with the road descending in a series of steep curves into a deep ravine.
The tiny A-frame huts that dot the terraces along the steep sides are
barns for cows, which are prohibited from grazing. There's no hori-
zontal pastureland, and they could easily fall off a ledge.

Santana

★ ㉗ *18 km (11 mi) northwest of Ribeiro Frio, 39 km (24 mi) north of Fun-
chal.*

Santana is a village famous for its A-frame, thatch-roof *palheiros* (cot-
tages), which are painted in bright colors and look as if they've come
straight from the pages of a fairy tale. Some are reproductions of more
traditional versions; only a handful of islanders still live in earlier in-
carnations of these dwellings.

OFF THE   **PARQUE DAS QUEIMADAS** – From Santana, you can follow a road that
BEATEN PATH   leads southwest to this spot, where you can stop to picnic or pick up a
               hiking trail that goes to Pico Ruivo.

Dining and Lodging

$$ ✕🏠 **Quinta do Furão.** In a peaceful setting, amid a vineyard high on
the cliffs, this hotel and restaurant ($$) have sweeping views of the sea.
The place is such a north-coast draw that Funchal residents arrange
to be flown here by helicopter for Sunday lunch. The food is a cut above
the typical island fare, featuring such dishes as steak in pastry with Roque-
fort sauce, and prawns on a spit with avocado sauce. Regional wines
are served. ⊠ *Achado do Gramacho, 9230–082,* ☏ *291/570100,* FAX
291/573560, WEB *www.quintadofurao.com. 43 rooms. Restaurant, bar,
wine bar, cable TV, room service, indoor-outdoor pool, sauna, gym,
recreation room. AE, DC, MC, V, BP, MAP, FAP.*

Porto da Cruz

㉘ *20 km (12 mi) southeast of Santana.*

The road from Santana to Porto da Cruz skirts the back of the landmark **Penha de Aguia** (Eagle Rock), whose sheer cliffs tower over the village of São Roque do Faial. The fertile valley setting is filled with tiny farms and gardens. It's also where you can find the island's last working sugar mill, used during March and April to make *aguardente*. This firewater, a sugarcane brandy, can be tasted at the small no-name bar opposite the church. It's far more palatable when tasted as part of the island's famous cocktail, poncha, mixed with honey and lemon juice.

En Route   Start your climb again on N101 and continue to **Portela,** where the view looks south over the gentler valley of Machico. From here it's an easy drive through pine woods and sugarcane fields and into the town of Machico.

Machico

㉙ *15 km (9 mi) southeast of Porto da Cruz, 26 km (16 mi) northeast of Funchal.*

Local folklore says the bay of Machico was discovered in 1346 by two English lovers, Robert Machin and Anne d'Arfet, who set sail from Bristol to escape Anne's disapproving parents. The couple's ship was thrown off course by a storm and wrecked in this bay. Anne died a few days after becoming ill, and Robert then died of a broken heart. But their crew, according to legend, escaped on a raft, and news of the island made its way back to Portugal. (Legend also has it that Shakespeare heard the tale before he wrote *The Tempest*.) When the explorer Zarco arrived in 1420, he found a wooden cross with the lovers' story and the church—the island's first—where they were buried. He named the place in memory of Machin. You can visit the replacement church and wander through the old quarter. Among the handful of atmospheric restaurants is the Mercado de Velho, a café with a terrace in a former market.

OFF THE BEATEN PATH   **CANIÇAL –** Multicolored boats bob in water that has been witness to this village's long history as a whaling station, which it remained until the not-so-distant year of 1981. A whaling museum (closed Monday) tells the story. In 1985, 5 acres of the sea surrounding the town were designated a national marine park. On the way to Caniçal, 10 km (6 mi) northeast of Machico, stop for a coffee at Bar Crespo.

MADEIRA A TO Z

To research prices, get advice from other travelers, and book travel arrangements, visit www.fodors.com.

AIR TRAVEL

Madeira is served by TAP Air Portugal, which has frequent flights daily from Lisbon (1¾ hrs) and London (4 hrs). British Airways has nonstops between London and Funchal several times a week. Numerous flights link Funchal with other European capitals.

The 15-minute interisland flight to Porto Santo from Madeira provides spectacular low-altitude views of Machico and São Lourenço Peninsula. TAP Air Portugal runs a shuttle between the islands several times a day. One-way fares start at €41.75. Reservations should be made in advance, especially for July and August.

➤ AIRLINES AND CONTACTS: **British Airways** (✉ Aeroporto da Madeira, ☎ 291/520870). **TAP Air Portugal** (✉ Av. das Comunidades Madeirenses 8–10, Funchal, ☎ 291/239290; 808/321–3141 flight information; ✉ Aeroporto da Madeira, ☎ 291/520821).

AIRPORTS AND TRANSFERS

The Aeroporto da Madeira is a 35-minute drive east of Funchal, near Santa Cruz. On Porto Santo, the tiny Aeroporto Campo de Cima is a 10-minute drive north of Vila Baleira. There are no buses. A taxi transfer costs around €5.

➤ AIRPORT INFORMATION: **Aeroporto Campo de Cima** (☎ 291/980120). **Aeroporto da Madeira** (☎ 291/520700).

BOAT TRAVEL

The *Lobo Marinho* ferry sails from Madeira to Porto Santo every day except Tuesday. Boats leave Funchal Harbor at 8 AM and return at 6 PM. The sometimes choppy one-way passage takes 2½ hours. Tickets cost €35.10–€44.50 round-trip, and you can buy them on board or through the Porto Santo Line office, which is open weekdays 9–12:30 and 2:30–6. For sailings on summer weekends, buy tickets in advance.

➤ BOAT INFORMATION: **Porto Santo Line** (✉ Rua da Praia 6, Funchal, ☎ 291/210300).

BUS TRAVEL

Madeira has two extensive bus systems. Yellow buses serve Funchal and its surrounding neighborhoods: Buses 1 and 3 run west from the city and make stops along the Estrada Monumental, where most of the hotels are; beige-and-red buses fan out to other points on the island. Both systems leave from an outdoor terminal at the end of Avenida do Mar. Generally several buses a day travel to each village on the island, but schedules change constantly, so inquire at your hotel or the tourist office for departure times.

➤ SCHEDULES: **Bus Information** (291/705500).

CAR RENTAL

Most major car-rental companies have offices at the airport and in Funchal, including Atlas, Avis, Europcar, and Hertz. On Porto Santo call Moinho.

➤ AGENCIES: **Atlas** (✉ Av. do Infante 29, Funchal, ☎ 291/223100). **Avis** (✉ Largo António Nobre 164, Funchal, ☎ 291/764546). **Europcar** (✉ Aeroporto da Madeira, ☎ 291/524633). **Hertz** (✉ Aeroporto da Madeira, ☎ 291/9523040). **Moinho** (✉ Rua Levada Canha 2, Porto Santo, Vila Baleira, ☎ 291/982780).

CAR TRAVEL

Although the best way to explore Madeira is by car, the terrain is steep, and driving can be tortuous and slow. For example, the twisting, turning drive from Funchal to Porto Moniz on the western end is only 156 km (97 mi) round-trip, but takes all day if you go the scenic route. Road signs are generally adequate, but get an up-to-date map, particularly if you want to take advantage of Madeira's fast new highways.

BY TAXI

Taxis that are licensed to carry passengers within Funchal have a light on top, which is turned on if they are for hire. Taxis from outside Funchal won't pick up in the city limits. They're all metered, but, if for any reason, the meter is off or "not working," be sure to agree on a price before starting the journey. Rates are relatively low; a ride across town shouldn't cost much more than €4–€5, depending upon traffic. Porto Santo roads are easy to handle by car, but most visitors cover

the 10-km-long (6-mi-long) island on foot or by taxi. It's fairly easy to hail cabs as they cruise around, and you can also phone for one.
➤ CONTACT: **Porto Santo Taxis** (☎ 291/982334).

EMERGENCIES

A 24-hour emergency service is provided by Clínica de Santa Luzia and Clínica de Santa Catarina. Pharmacies are open at night and on Sunday according to a rotating schedule. Dial 166 for information.
➤ EMERGENCY SERVICES: **Funchal fire department** (☎ 291/223056). **Funchal police** (☎ 291/208400). **General emergencies** (☎ 112).
➤ HOSPITALS: **Clínica de Santa Catarina** (✉ Rua 5 de Outubro 115, Funchal, ☎ 291/741127). **Clínica de Santa Luzia** (✉ Rua da Torrinha 5, Funchal, ☎ 291/233434).

MAIL

The post office branch in Funchal has hours weekdays 9–1 and 3–7 and on Saturday 9–1. Elsewhere on the island, post offices are generally open weekdays 9–12:30 and 2:30–5:30 and Saturday 9–12:30.
➤ POST OFFICE: **CTT Funchal** (✉ Av. Zarco, Funchal).

TELEPHONES

Phone numbers in Madeira and Porto Santo are all preceded by 291. Public phones from which you can make direct-dial international (using prepaid phone cards available from newsagents and other shops) are easy to find in Funchal, not so easy elsewhere on Madeira. On Porto Santo try the main post office in Vila Baleira which has a number of phone booths.

DIRECTORY AND OPERATOR ASSISTANCE

The general information number on Madeira is 118. For the local operator dial 090; for the international operator dial 171.

TOURS AND PACKAGES

BOAT TOURS

Boat excursions around Funchal's coast take place year-round. Choose from a range of 2- to 2½-hour charters to Cabo Girão, Ponta do Sol, Machico, Ribeira Brava, or a shorter 1½-hour trip to Caniçal. Costs range from €15 to €20 per person.
➤ CONTACT: **Costa do Sol, Lda.** (✉ Marina do Funchal, Funchal, ☎ 291/238538 or 291/224390).

HIKING TOURS

Viva Travel offers a different hiking tour through the mountains every day. Levels of difficulty vary, and each excursion includes something extra, such as a peek at local weavers or a wine tasting in a hidden cave. Other companies that organize walking tours are Turismo Verde e Ecologico da Madeira (TURIVEMA) and Terras de Aventura & Turismo.
➤ CONTACTS: **Terras de Aventura & Turismo** (✉ Caminho do Amparo 25, Funchal, ☎ 291/776818). **TURIVEMA** (✉ Estrada Monumental 187, Funchal, ☎ 291/766109). **Viva Travel** (✉ Largo António Nobre, Funchal, ☎ 291/230724).

ISLAND TOURS

Travel agencies specializing in island tours abound in Funchal. Visits in buses or minivans usually include lunch and multilingual guides. Trips generally take in Cabo Girão, the inland peaks, Porto Moniz, and the village of Santana. Among the best operators are Blandy's and Orion.
➤ CONTACTS: **Blandy's** (✉ Rua de São Francisco 20, Arcadas de São Francisco [behind winery], Funchal, ☎ 291/200620). **Orion** (✉ Rua de João Gago 2-A, Funchal, ☎ 291/228222).

WINE-TASTING TOURS

Blandy's runs full-day (Thursday) excursions for wine lovers to vine-yards on the east side of the island. Trips include a stop for lunch in the village of Santana.

➤ CONTACT: **Blandy's** (✉ Rua de São Francisco 20, Arcadas de São Francisco [behind winery], Funchal, ☎ 291/200620).

VISITOR INFORMATION

In Funchal, Madeira's busy tourist office is open weekdays 9–8 and weekends 9–6. It dispenses maps, brochures, and up-to-date information on the constantly changing bus schedules. There are also tourist offices in other towns as well as on Porto Santo; their hours are generally weekdays from 9 or 10 to noon or 12:30 and from 2 to 5 or 5:30, as well as Saturday from 9 to noon or 12:30.

➤ TOURIST OFFICES: **Funchal** (✉ Av. Arriaga 18, ☎ 291/211902). **Machico** (✉ Forte do Amparo, Praça José António Almada, ☎ 291/962289). **Porto Santo tourist office** (✉ Av. Henrique Vieira de Castro, Vila Baleira, ☎ 291/982361). **Ribeira Brava** (✉ Forte de São Bento, Vila de Ribeira Brava, ☎ 291/951675).

10 BACKGROUND AND ESSENTIALS

Portraits of Portugal

Portuguese Vocabulary

ART, ARCHITECTURE, AND AZULEJOS

PORTUGUESE SCULPTING and painting styles were inspired first by the excitement of the newly emerging nation and then by the baroque experimentation that the wealth from the colonies made possible. Sculpture found its first outlet in grand royal and noble funerary monuments, as witnessed by the realism of the Gothic tombs in the cathedrals of Lisbon, Guarda, and Braga. These were precursors of the masterpiece of their kind, including the 14th-century tombs of Pedro and Inês at Alcobaça and the eloquent hand-clasped figures of Dom João I and his queen, Philippa, in the chapel at Batalha.

Painting came into its own in the 15th century with the completion of Nuno Gonçalves's Flemish-inspired polyptych of São Vicente (St. Vincent), which portrayed the princes and knights, monks and fishermen, court figures and ordinary people of imperial Portugal in six panels. It's on display in Lisbon's Museu de Arte Antiga. The work of the next great Portuguese painter, the 16th-century Vasco Fernandes (known as Grão Vasco, or the Great Vasco), has an expressive, realistic vigor. His masterpieces are on display in Viseu. The later baroque styles in art and sculpture said less about the country and more about its wealth. There were flamboyant creations, to be sure—including the unsurpassed granite-and-plaster staircases, pilgrimage shrines, and sculptures at Bom Jesus and Lamego, in the Minho—but these were built at a time when the monarchy had lost the vision and morals of earlier, greater periods. Nevertheless, there were always artists ready to work in styles that drew on the strengths of the Portuguese character and not the weaknesses.

The elaborate decoration that is the hallmark of Manueline architecture is inspiring in its sheer novelty. Buildings and monuments are supported by twisted stone columns and covered with sculpted emblems of Portugal's conquests on the high seas and in distant lands—particularly under Dom Manuel I (1495–1521). Representations of anchors, seaweed, and rigging mingle with exotic animals and strange, occasionally pagan, symbols—a fusion of diverse cultures and civilizations brought together under the umbrella of a Christian Portuguese empire.

Following the discovery of gold in Brazil at the end of the 17th century, buildings—churches, in particular—began to be embellished in an extraordinary rococo style, which employed *talha dourada* (polychrome and gilded carved wood) to stupendous pictorial effect. There are superb examples at the churches of São Francisco in Oporto and Santo António in Lagos, and at the Convento de Jesus at Aveiro. In contrast, to see rococo at its most restrained, you must visit the royal palace at Queluz, near Lisbon.

The 18th century saw the emergence of the sculptor Machado de Castro, who produced perhaps the greatest equestrian statue of his time, that of Dom José I in Lisbon's Praça do Comércio. Domingos António Sequeira (1768–1837) painted historic and religious subjects of international renown. Portrait and landscape painting became popular in the 19th century; the works of José Malhoã and Miguel Angelo Lupi can be seen in the Museu de José Malhoã in Caldas da Rainha. Museums throughout the country display the works of talented contemporaries. The Museu Soares dos Reis in Oporto—named after the 19th-century sculptor António Soares dos Reis (1847–89)—was the country's first national museum. His pupil was António Teixeira Lopes (1866–1942), who achieved great popular success, and who also has a museum named after him in the Oporto suburb of Vila Nova de Gaia.

Of all the country's artistic images, its *azulejos* (painted ceramic tiles) may well be the most enduring. The Moors introduced these tiles to Portugal, and although many of them are blue, the term they are known by doesn't come from *azul*, the Portuguese word for that color, but rather from the Arabic word *az-zulayj*, which means "little stones." By the 17th century the early styles were replaced by whole panels depicting religious or secular motifs. There are fine examples throughout the country, especially at the Fronteira palace on the outskirts of Lisbon.

The tiles, which feature geometric designs and come in a wide variety of colors, adorn many fountains, churches, and palaces. The Paço Real (Royal Palace) in Sintra is one of the most remarkable examples of their decorative effect. Look for delightful combinations on the nation's *quintas* or *solares* (country residences): for instance, an elegant pastel-color house whose outside walls and landscaped gardens are lavishly adorned with grandiose panels. The most interesting examples are found in the Minho region in the north. There are also well-preserved tile works on display in several museums including Lisbon's Museu Nacional do Azulejo and Museu de Arte Antiga and Coimbra's Museu Machado de Castro.

THE PLEASURES OF PORTUGUESE WINE

With the exception of those classic kings of wines, port and Madeira, the wines that Portugal produces are mainly honest and straightforward. This is a country where you can enjoy an endless procession of delicious experiments for little more than the cost of a good beer. You can also buy wines of some age at a very moderate cost.

Portuguese wine making stretches back beyond the Romans to the Phoenicians; it flourished under the teetotaling Muslims, and went through a checkered time after the Moors were expelled. A firm link with Britain enabled the wine trade to remain prosperous, especially where port was concerned. Trade between the two countries predates the 1386 Treaty of Windsor possibly by two centuries. After a long period of spasmodic development, with some regions flourishing and others, such as the Algarve, almost ceasing production, the situation was taken in hand by the Marquês de Pombal. In 1756 he demarcated the regions, geographically delineating growing areas and controlling their output and marketing; the port-making region was the first to be demarcated.

Demarcation, and the attendant quality control, took off in the first years of this century. Today there are 10 regions officially demarcated—the Algarve, Moscatel de Setúbal, Bucelas, Carcavelos, Colares, Bairrada, Dão, Douro, Vinho Verde, and the island of Madeira. Several areas that are still undemarcated also produce excellent wines. The official body that regulates wine production is the Instituto do Vinho do Porto, based in Lisbon. It controls all the facets of viniculture and of marketing, runs competitions, promotes cooperatives, and empowers growers to use a *selo de origem* (seal of origin). Rather like the French *appellation d'origine contrôlée,* the seal acts as a guarantee of a wine's pedigree.

The Algarve and the Alentejo
In the Algarve wine is produced on a narrow strip of land between the mountains and the sea. Algarve wine is largely red and is usually no better than an undistinguished

table wine. Among the better makes are Lagoa and Tavira.

Alentejo vineyards are almost all in the top part of the province, around Évora and over toward the Spanish border. The wines they produce are now among the best in Portugal—Redondo, Borba (with its lovely dark color and slightly metallic flavor), Reguengos, and Vidigueira. The reds are rich in color, the whites pale and fruity.

Moscatel de Setúbal
Wines produced on the Setúbal Peninsula are well known abroad, mainly through the 150-year efforts of the House of Fonseca, based in Azeitão. The Moscatel that Fonseca—together with the small vine growers who make up the local cooperative a few miles east of Azeitão in Palmela—produces is best known as a fortified dessert wine, aged and with a mouthwatering taste of honey. If you find some that is, say, 25 years old, you'll see that it has developed a licorice color; enjoy its sweet scent and taste. Fonseca and the cooperative produce many other wines besides the Moscatel—fine reds (notably one called Periquita, or "little parrot"); rosés, of which Lancers and Faisca are often exported; and a few regular whites.

Bucelas
The Bucelas region is about 30 km (19 mi) north of Lisbon, in the valley of the Rio Trancão (Trancão River). Although wine from here has a considerable history and was very popular with the British soldiers under Wellington in the Peninsular War, this is quite a small demarcated region, and all the wine it produces appears under the Caves Velhas label. Bucelas wine is usually straw color, with a distinctively full nose and a fruity taste that can sometimes verge on the citrusy. It goes extremely well with veal, poultry, and fish.

Carcavelos
Carcavelos consists of just one small vineyard, the Quinta do Barão, between Lisbon and Estoril along a stretch of coast. This isn't an easy wine to find—the yearly output is small—but if you like wines with a history, it's worth looking for. Carcavelos is another fortified dessert wine, topaz color, with a nutty aroma and a

slightly almond taste, mostly drunk as an aperitif.

Colares

The Colares region is at Portugal's westernmost tip, beyond Sintra. It's a fairly hostile place for vine growing, with sandy soil and exposure to the Atlantic winds. But it has a long and distinguished history of wine production, and it yields some very individual vintages. The red improves with age (it can be a little astringent when young) and has a full ruby color, an aromatic nose, and an aftertaste likened to black currants. One label to seek out is Colares Chita. The Colares whites are straw color, slightly nutty in taste, and—like the reds—improve with age. They should be drunk well chilled.

Bairrada and Dão

Not far south of Oporto is the coastal region of Bairrada. Although it wasn't that long ago—1979—that Bairrada was demarcated, the quality of its output suggests that it probably should have received that status long before. The region is made up mainly of small holdings, gathered into six cooperatives. Taken all together, they turn out a fairly large quantity of wine. The reds are of an intense color, with a delicious nose and a fruity, rich, and lasting taste. They mellow with age and go very well with stronger dishes such as game, roasts, and pungent cheeses. There aren't too many whites in this region, and most of them are slightly sparkling (*espumantes*). The whites have a slightly darkish straw color, with a heavy, rather spicy nose. They go well with fish, pasta, and pâtés. One of the biggest names in the region is Aliança, although several others such as São Domingos and Frei João are worth tracking down. The hotel at Buçaco has its own wines in an extensive cellar.

The Dão region is just south of the Douro, in the mountainous heart of the north, and is crossed by the valleys of the Dão, Mondego, and Alva rivers. The climate is capricious—cold, wet winters, scorchingly hot summers. Unlike the sandy or clay soils to the south, the terrain is made up of granite and schist, a rock that shatters easily. Much of the wine here is red and is matured in oak casks for at least 18 months before being bottled. When mature, Dão wines have a dark reddish-brown color—almost the hue of garnets—a "complex" nose, and a lasting velvety taste. They're best drunk at room temperature after being allowed to breathe well, and they go with roast lamb and pork. Look for São Domingos, Terras Altas, and Porta dos Cavaleiros, or any of the labels where "Dão" precedes the name of the supplier—Dão Aliança, Dão Caves Velhas, Dão Serra, or Dão Fundação. Dão whites are less common. They spend shorter times (10 months or so) maturing in casks and have the color of light straw, a full nose, and a dry, earthy flavor. The white Grão Vasco or the Meia Encosta is worth trying.

Douro and Port

The secret of port is found first of all in the nature of the arid, volcanic soil and the hothouse temperature of the Douro Valley. Some 800 years ago, when the father of Afonso Henriques took possession of his domain between Douro and Minho, he planted a stock brought from Burgundy. "Eating lava and drinking sunshine," the Burgundy vines stretched, little by little, to the river's edge. They fought a bitter fight, strangling in ravines, wandering in fits and starts, to force their roots through schistose soil. Nothing but the vine could survive in this torrid pass. With tireless obstinacy, the men of the Douro broke up slate, built terraces with stone retaining walls, struggled against drought and phylloxera, and made the lost valley the most prosperous in Portugal.

The region comes alive during the grape gathering, which lasts for several weeks. (In lower-level vineyards, the gathering is often finished long before the higher plantations are ripe.) From dawn until dusk women fill the baskets that the men carry on their backs, supporting as much as 150 pounds with the aid of a leather band looped over their foreheads. They descend in long files toward the *lagares* at the foot of the slopes and pile the fruit in these enormous vessels, ready for treading. More than 40 varieties of grape go into making port, creating a wide diversity of taste. The harvesters gather about the vats before the must has begun to ferment; the atmosphere is steamy, the feverish excitement of new wine induces singing and dancing. In the spring the young wine goes down by road to the lodges in Vilã Nova de Gaia. Since the building of a dam across the river the transporting of wine in traditional *rabelos*, boats that look somewhat like ancient Phoenician craft, has ceased.

Port, born as it is of a soil rich in lava, is divided into two great families—vintage and blended. When a year is outstanding—as in 1945, '47, '48, '55, '58, '63, '70, '75, '77, '80, '83, '85, '94, '95, and '98—the wine is unblended and, after reinforcement and bottling, left to mature. These are the vintage wines, which will take upwards of 20 years to mature; the old bottles, dusty with cobwebs, are brought up from the cellar for weddings and christenings and must be decanted before drinking. Most port, however, is a carefully studied blend of new wine with old vintages. For a long time, when England was the biggest market for port, the first choice was given to full-bodied tawnies; these were served at the end of dinner, with cheese or an apple and walnuts. However, there's a lot to be said for the white ports, either sweet, as an after-dinner drink, or dry, as an aperitif with ice and a twist of lemon.

In Oporto you can visit a lodge to learn more about port, taste it, and maybe buy a bottle. Seeing these huge old cellars and finding out about the long, fascinating history of port is a memorable experience. Language won't be a problem, as there has been an alliance for more than 200 years between the English and Portuguese in the port trade, and many of the families are bilingual.

Not all the wine produced in the Douro region is port. The reds here are of a deep ruby color, extremely fruity, and with a rounded taste. They go well with richer foods, a variety of meats, casseroles, and stews—anything that tends to be well flavored with herbs. The whites are dry, by and large, and have a pleasant pale-yellow color with a full nose. They go well with salads, hors d'oeuvres, and chicken dishes. Look for Mesão Frio, San Marco, Quinta da Cotto, and Santa Marta.

Vinho Verde

Portugal's largest demarcated region is divided into six subregions: Monção, Lima, Amarante, Basto, Braga, and Penafiel. Inland from the coast and threaded by a sequence of westward-flowing rivers, the region has a fairly mild climate and the country's highest rainfall. The vineyards here are often terraced, climbing hillsides away from the rivers like agricultural fortifica-

tions. In places they march alongside and arch over roads, the vines held up on colonnaded rows of pillars. The grapes hang so high they ripen in direct sunlight without any rising heat from the ground.

The name vinho verde, which translates as "green wine," refers not to the wine's color but to the fact that it's not aged. If you enjoy wine purely as a refreshing, mildly intoxicating beverage—a kind of celestial 7-Up—vinho verde is *the* drink—gently sparkling (what the experts call *pétillant*), with a delicate fruity flavor, it embodies the coolness and fragrance of summer gardens. Vinho verde goes well with any kind of seafood. The reds are important to the region, but will mostly be found on their home ground; they don't travel much. They're also refreshingly thirst quenching, sharp rather than heavy, with a vermilion-to-purple color. They go ideally with any meat dish. Look for Alvarinho and Quinta de São Claudio.

Madeira

Like port, Madeira—the wine and its preparation—is a way of life, and a way of life in which Portuguese and British families are bound together. When Charles II married Catherine of Bragança in 1662 he, perhaps foolishly, declined to accept the island, which was offered as part of her dowry. Madeiran soil is volcanic, and its beaches, such as they are, are black. The temperate climate here, which can be humid in summer, provides exactly the conditions in which vines can thrive—although they seldom grow below 300 ft above sea level; that warmer zone is taken up by bananas and sugarcane.

Madeira is a fortified wine, and most often blended. Boal and Malmsey or Malvasia styles are sweet and heavy, and make excellent dessert wines; Verdelho, not so sweet, is a nice alternative to sherry; and Sercial, dry and light, makes an excellent aperitif. All are attractive—particularly when they're really aged—occasional wines. The labels to look for—and they date back in some cases for a couple of centuries—include Blandy, Cossart Gordon, Rutherford and Miles, Leacock, and Miles and Luís Gomes. A visit to a wine lodge in Funchal is an educational and delectable way to spend a couple of hours.

Portuguese Wine Terms

Adamado	Medium sweet
Adega	Wine vault
Adega cooperativa	Wine cooperative
Aguardente	Brandy
Branco	White
Bruto	Extra dry (for sparkling wines)
Caves	Wine cellars
Colheita	Grape harvest (thus a vintage, e.g., Colh. 1980)
Doce	Sweet
Espumante	Sparkling wine
Garrafeira or *reserva*	Fine, mature wine, or a special vintage
Generoso	A sweet dessert wine, highly alcoholic
Meio seco	Medium dry
Região demarcada	Demarcated region
Rosado	Rosé
Seco	Dry
Tinto	Red
Velho	Old
Vinho da mesa	Table wine
Vinho da casa	House wine
Vinho do porto	Port

PORTUGUESE VOCABULARY

If you have reading knowledge of Spanish and/or French, you will find Portuguese easy to read. Portuguese pronunciation, however, can be somewhat tricky. Despite obvious similarities in Spanish and Portuguese spelling and syntax, the Portuguese sounds are a far cry—almost literally so—from their ostensible Spanish equivalents. Some of the main peculiarities of Portuguese phonetics are the following.

Nasalized vowels: If you have some idea of French pronunciation, these shouldn't give you too much trouble. The closest approach is that of the French *accent du Midi,* as spoken by people in Marseille and Provence, or perhaps an American Midwest twang will help. Try pronouncing *an, am, en, em, in, om, un,* etc., with a sustained *ng* sound (e.g., *bom = bong,* etc.).

Another aspect of Portuguese phonetics is the vowels and diphthongs written with the tilde: *ã, ão, ães.* The Portuguese word for wool, *lã,* sounds roughly like the French word *lin,* with the *-in* resembling the *an* in the English word "any," but nasalized. The suffix "-tion" on such English words as "information" becomes in Portuguese spelling *-ção,* pronounced *-sa-on,* with the *-on* nasalized: *Informação,* for example. These words form their plurals by changing the suffix to *-ções,* which sounds like "*-son-ech*" (the *ch* here resembling a cross between the English *sh* and the German *ch:* hence *informações*).

The cedilla occurring under the "c" serves exactly the same purpose as in French: It transforms the "c" into a *ss* sound in front of the three so-called "hard" vowels ("a," "o," and "u"): e.g., *graça, Açores, açúcar.* The letter "c" occurring without a cedilla in front of these three vowels automatically has the sound of "k": *pico, mercado, curto.* The letter "c" followed by "e" or "i" is always *ss,* and hence needs no cedilla: *nacional, Graciosa, Terceira.*

The letter "j" sounds like the "s" in the English word "pleasure." So does "g" except when the latter is followed by one of the "hard" vowels: hence, *generoso, gigantesco, Jerónimo, azulejos, Jorge,* etc.

The spelling *nh* is rendered like the *ny* in "canyon": e.g., *senhora.*

The spelling *lh* is somewhere in between the *l* and the *y* sounds in "million": e.g., *Batalha.*

In the matter of syllabic stress, Portuguese obeys the two basic Spanish principles: (1) in words ending in a vowel, or in "n" or "s," the tonic accent falls on the next-to-the-last syllable: *fado, mercado, azulejos;* (2) in words ending in consonants other than "n" or "s," the stress falls on the last syllable: *favor, nacional.* Words in which the syllabic stress does not conform to the two above rules must be written with an acute accent to indicate the proper pronunciation: *sábado, república, politécnico.*

Numbers

1	um, uma
2	dois, duas
3	três
4	quatro
5	cinco
6	seis
7	sete
8	oito
9	nove
10	dez
11	onze
12	doze
13	treze
14	catorze
15	quinze
16	dezaseis
17	dezasete
18	dezoito
19	dezanove
20	vinte
21	vinte e um
22	vinte e dois
30	trinta
40	quarenta
50	cinquenta
60	sessenta
70	setenta
80	oitenta
90	noventa
100	cem
110	cento e dez
200	duzentos
1,000	mil
1,500	mil e quinhentos

Days of the Week

Monday	Segunda-feira
Tuesday	Terça-feira
Wednesday	Quarta-feira
Thursday	Quinta-feira
Friday	Sexta-feira
Saturday	Sábado
Sunday	Domingo

Months

January	Janeiro
February	Fevereiro
March	Março
April	Abril
May	Maio
June	Junho
July	Julho
August	Agosto

September	Setembro
October	Outubro
November	Novembro
December	Dezembro

Useful Phrases

Do you speak English?	Fala Inglês?
Yes	Sim
No	Não
Please	Por favor
Thank you	Obrigado/a
Thank you very much	Muito obrigado/a
Excuse me, sorry	Desculpe, Com licença
I'm sorry	Desculpe-me
Good morning or good day	Bom dia
Good afternoon	Boa tarde
Good evening or good night	Boa noite
Goodbye	Adeus
How are you?	Como está?
How do you say in Portuguese?	Como se diz em Português?
Tourist Office	Turismo
Fine	Optimo
Very good	Muito bem (muito bom)
It's all right	Está bem
Good luck	Felicidades (boa sorte)
Hello	Olá
Come back soon	Até breve
Where is the hotel?	Onde é o hotel?
How much does this cost?	Quanto custa?
How do you feel?	Como se sente?
How goes it?	Que tal?
Pleased to meet you	Muito prazer em o (a) conhecer
The pleasure is mine	O prazer é meu
I have the pleasure of introducing Mr., Miss, Mrs., or Ms. . . .	Tenho o prazer de lhe apresentar o senhor, a senhora . . .
I like it very much	Gosto muito
I don't like it	Não gosto
Don't mention it	De nada
Pardon me	Perdão
Are you ready?	Está pronto?
I am ready	Estou pronto
Welcome	Seja benvindo
What time is it?	Que horas são?
I am glad to see you	Muito prazer em o (a) ver
I don't understand	Não entendo
Please speak slowly	Fale lentamente por favor
I understand (or) It is clear	Compreendo (or) Está claro
Whenever you please	Quando quizer
Please wait	Faça favor de esperar
Toilet	Casa de banho
I will be a little late	Chegarei um pouco atrasado
I don't know	Não sei
Is this seat free?	Está vago este lugar?

Would you please direct me to . . . ?	Por favor indique-me . . . ?
Where is the station, museum . . . ?	Onde fica a estação, museu . . . ?
I am American, British	Eu sou Americano, Inglês
It's very kind of you	É muito amavel
Please sit down	Por favor sente-se

Sundries

cigar, cigarette	charuto, cigarro
matches	fosforos
dictionary	dicionário
key	chave
razor blades	laminas de barbear
shaving cream	creme de barbear
soap	sobonete
map	mapa
tampons	tampões
sanitary pads	pensos higiénicos
newspaper	jornal
magazine	revista
telephone	telefone
envelopes	envelopes
writing paper	papel de carta
airmail writing paper	papel de carta de avião
postcard	postal
stamps	selos

Merchants

bakery	padaria
bookshop	livraria
butcher's	talho
delicatessen	charutaria
dry cleaner's	limpeza a seco
grocery	mercearia
hairdresser, barber	cabeleireiro, barbeiro
laundry	lavandaria
shoemaker	sapateiro
supermarket	supermercado

Emergencies/Medical

ill, sick	doente
I am ill	Estou doente
I have a fever	Tenho febre
My wife/husband/ child is ill	Minha mulher/marido/ criança está doente
doctor	doutor/médico
nurse	enfermeira/o
prescription	receita
pharmacist/chemist	farmacia
Please fetch/call a doctor	Por favor, chame o doutor/medico
accident	acidente
road accident	acidente na estrada
Where is the nearest hospital?	Onde é o hospital mais proximo?

Where is the American/ British Hospital?	Onde é o hospital Americano/ Britanico?
dentist	dentista
X-ray	Raios-X
aspirin	aspirina
painkiller	analgésico
bandage	ligadura
ointment for bites/stings	pomada para picadas
cough mixture	xarope para a tosse
laxative	laxativo
thermometer	termómetro

On the Move

plane	avião
train	comboio
boat	barco
taxi	taxi
car	carro/automovel
bus	autocarro
seat	assento/lugar
reservation	reserva
smoking/no-smoking compartment	compartimento para fumadores/ não fumadores
rail station	estação caminho de ferro
subway station	estação do Metropolitano
airport	aeroporto
harbor	estação mártima
town terminal	estação/terminal
shuttle bus/train	autocarro/comboio com ligação constante
sleeper	cama
couchette	beliche
porter	bagageiro
baggage/luggage	bagagem
baggage trolley	carrinho de bagagem
single ticket	bilhete de ida
return ticket	bilhete de ida e volta
first class	primeira classe
second class	segunda classe
When does the train leave?	A que horas sai o comboio?
What time does the train arrive at . . . ?	A que horas chega o comboio a . . . ?

INDEX

NOTES

NOTES

NOTES

NOTES

NOTES

NOTES

Fodor's Key to the Guides

America's guidebook leader publishes guides for every kind of traveler. Check out our many series and find your perfect match.

Fodor's Gold Guides
America's favorite travel-guide series offers the most detailed insider reviews of hotels, restaurants, and attractions in all price ranges, plus great background information, smart tips, and useful maps.

Fodor's Road Guide USA
Big guides for a big country—the most comprehensive guides to America's roads, packed with places to stay, eat, and play across the U.S.A. Just right for road warriors, family vacationers, and cross-country trekkers.

COMPASS AMERICAN GUIDES
Stunning guides from top local writers and photographers, with gorgeous photos, literary excerpts, and colorful anecdotes. A must-have for culture mavens, history buffs, and new residents.

Fodor's CITYPACKS
Concise city coverage with a foldout map. The right choice for urban travelers who want everything under one cover.

Fodor's EXPLORING GUIDES
Hundreds of color photos bring your destination to life. Lively stories lend insight into the culture, history, and people.

Fodor's POCKET GUIDES
For travelers who need only the essentials. The best of Fodor's in pocket-size packages for just $9.95.

Fodor's To Go
Credit-card–size, magnetized color microguides that fit in the palm of your hand—perfect for "stealth" travelers or as gifts.

Fodor's FLASHMAPS
Every resident's map guide. 60 easy-to-follow maps of public transit, parks, museums, zip codes, and more.

Fodor's CITYGUIDES
Sourcebooks for living in the city: Thousands of in-the-know listings for restaurants, shops, sports, nightlife, and other city resources.

Fodor's AROUND THE CITY WITH KIDS
68 great ideas for family days, recommended by resident parents. Perfect for exploring in your own backyard or on the road.

Fodor's ESCAPES
Fill your trip with once-in-a-lifetime experiences, from ballooning in Chianti to overnighting in the Moroccan desert. These full-color dream books point the way.

Fodor's FYI
Get tips from the pros on planning the perfect trip. Learn how to pack, fly hassle-free, plan a honeymoon or cruise, stay healthy on the road, and travel with your baby.

Fodor's Languages for Travelers
Practice the local language before hitting the road. Available in phrase books, cassette sets, and CD sets.

Karen Brown's Guides
Engaging guides to the most charming inns and B&Bs in the U.S.A. and Europe, with easy-to-follow inn-to-inn itineraries.

Baedeker's Guides
Comprehensive guides, trusted since 1829, packed with A–Z reviews and star ratings.

At bookstores everywhere.   www.fodors.com/books